# Lecture Notes in Artificial Intelligence 13406

Subseries of Lecture Notes in Computer Science

## Series Editors

Randy Goebel
*University of Alberta, Edmonton, Canada*

Wolfgang Wahlster
*DFKI, Berlin, Germany*

Zhi-Hua Zhou
*Nanjing University, Nanjing, China*

## Founding Editor

Jörg Siekmann
*DFKI and Saarland University, Saarbrücken, Germany*

Mufti Mahmud · Jing He · Stefano Vassanelli ·
André van Zundert · Ning Zhong (Eds.)

# Brain Informatics

15th International Conference, BI 2022
Padua, Italy, July 15–17, 2022
Proceedings

 Springer

*Editors*
Mufti Mahmud
Nottingham Trent University
Nottingham, UK

Jing He
University of Oxford
Oxford, UK

Stefano Vassanelli
University of Padua
Padua, Italy

André van Zundert
University of Queensland
Brisbane, QLD, Australia

Ning Zhong
Maebashi Institute of Technology
Maebashi, Japan

ISSN 0302-9743          ISSN 1611-3349 (electronic)
Lecture Notes in Artificial Intelligence
ISBN 978-3-031-15036-4          ISBN 978-3-031-15037-1 (eBook)
https://doi.org/10.1007/978-3-031-15037-1

LNCS Sublibrary: SL7 – Artificial Intelligence

This Springer imprint is published by the registered company Springer Nature Switzerland AG
The registered company address is: Gewerbestrasse 11, 6330 Cham, Switzerland

# Preface

The International Conference on Brain Informatics (BI) series has established itself as the world's premier research conference on brain informatics, which is an emerging interdisciplinary and multidisciplinary research field that combines the efforts of cognitive science, neuroscience, medical science, data science, machine learning, artificial intelligence (AI), and information and communication technology (ICT) to explore the main problems that lie in the interplay between human brain studies and informatics research. The 15th International Conference on Brain Informatics (BI 2022) provided an international forum to bring together researchers and practitioners from diverse fields for the presentation of original research results, as well as the exchange and dissemination of innovative and practical development experiences on brain informatics. The main theme of BI 2022 was "Brain Science Meets Artificial Intelligence" with respect to the five tracks: Cognitive and Computational Foundations of Brain Science; Human Information Processing Systems; Brain Big Data Analytics, Curation and Management; Informatics Paradigms for Brain and Mental Health Research; and Brain-Machine Intelligence and Brain Inspired Computing.

The WICI International Workshop on Web Intelligence Meets Brain Informatics, held in Beijing, China, in 2006, kicked off the Brain Informatics conference series. It was one of the first conferences to focus on the application of informatics to brain sciences. The 2nd, 3rd, 4th, and 5th BI conferences were held in Beijing, China (2009), Toronto, Canada (2010), Lanzhou, China (2011), and Macau, China (2012), respectively. In 2013, health was added to the conference title, with Brain Informatics and Health (BIH) events placing an emphasis on real-world applications of brain research in human health and well-being. BIH 2013, BIH 2014, BIH 2015, and BIH 2016 were held in Maebashi, Japan, Warsaw, Poland, London, UK, and Omaha, USA, respectively. In 2017, the conference returned to its original design and vision to investigate the brain from an informatics perspective and to promote a brain-inspired information technology revolution. Thus, the conference name was changed back to Brain Informatics at Beijing, China, in 2017. The editions in 2018 and 2019 were held in Arlington, Texas, USA, and Haikou, China, respectively.

The COVID-19 pandemic had the most significant impact on BI 2020, with the conference originally scheduled for Padua, Italy, being hosted virtually and shortened to one day. In 2021, the conference was still held online due to the impact of the pandemic; however, to increase participation, we decided to go back to the usual three-day event, with one day dedicated to workshops and special sessions, one day to the excellent keynote sessions, and one day to the technical sessions.

Drawing from our years of offline and two years of online experience designing and facilitating the BI conference, we organized a three-day hybrid conference in 2022. The hybrid format of this conference was unique in that it was co-hosted in Padua, Italy (in person) and Queensland, Australia (online). The most exciting thing is that the University of Padua celebrated its 800th anniversary in 2022, and we took the opportunity to celebrate by hosting the 15th International Conference on Brain Informatics in Padua.

During the conference, we took measures to safeguard the health of all attendees and employees due to the ongoing pandemic.

The BI 2022 hybrid conference was supported by the Web Intelligence Consortium (WIC), the University of Padua, the Padova Neuroscience Centre, the University of Oxford, the University of Queensland, the Chinese Association for Artificial Intelligence, Peking Union Medical College, the IEEE Computational Intelligence Society, the International Neural Network Society, and Springer.

BI 2022 solicited high-quality papers and featured keynote talks from world-class speakers, panel discussions, workshops, and special sessions. The conference involved several world leaders in brain research and informatic technologies, including Silvestro Micera, Robert Legenstein, Gustavo Deco, Themis Prodromakis, and Christian Georg Mayr. This proceedings contains 30 high-quality papers accepted and presented at BI 2022, which provide a good sample of state-of-the-art research advances on BI from methodologies, frameworks, and techniques to case studies and applications.

We would like to express our gratitude to all BI 2022 committee members for their instrumental and unwavering support. BI 2022 had a very exciting program which would not have been possible without the dedication of the Program Committee members in reviewing the conference papers and abstracts. BI 2022 could not have taken place without the great team effort and the generous support from our sponsors. Our gratitude goes to Springer for sponsoring student first-author registrations, which were selected based on the quality of the submitted papers and their need for financial support. We are grateful to the LNCS/LNAI team at Springer for their continuous support in coordinating the publication of this volume. Also, special thanks to Yang Yang, Hongzhi Kuai, Yu Cao and for their great assistance and support. Last but not least, we thank all our contributors and volunteers for their support during this challenging time to make BI 2022 a success.

July 2022

Mufti Mahmud
Jing He
Stefano Vassanelli
André van Zundert
Ning Zhong

# Organization

## Advisory Board

| | |
|---|---|
| Ning Zhong (Chair) | Maebashi Institute of Technology, Japan |
| Maurizio Corbetta | Padova Neuroscience Center and University of Padua, Italy |
| Tianzi Jiang | Institute of Automation, CAS, China |
| Nikola Kasabov | Auckland University of Technology, New Zealand |
| Peipeng Liang | School of Psychology of GNU, China |
| Hesheng Liu | Harvard Medical School and Massachusetts General Hospital, USA |
| Guoming Luan | Sanbo Brain Hospital, China |
| Stefano Panzeri | University Medical Center Hamburg-Eppendorf, Germany |
| Hanchuan Peng | SEU-Allen Institute for Brain and Intelligence, China |
| Shinsuke Shimojo | California Institute of Technology, USA |

## General Chairs

| | |
|---|---|
| Mufti Mahmud | Nottingham Trent University, UK |
| Stefano Vassanelli | University of Padua, Italy |
| André van Zundert | The University of Queensland, Brisbane, QLD, Australia |

## Program Chairs

| | |
|---|---|
| Alessandra Bertoldo | University of Padua, Italy |
| Gopikrishna Deshpande | Auburn University, USA |
| Jing He | University of Queensland, Australia |

## Publication Chair

| | |
|---|---|
| Can Wang | Griffith University, Australia |

## Workshop/Special Session/Tutorial Chairs

| | |
|---|---|
| Alessia Sarica | Magna Græcia University, Italy |
| Xiaohui Tao | University of Southern Queensland, Australia |

| Alberto Testolin | University of Padua, Italy |
| Vassiliy Tsytsarev | University of Maryland, USA |
| Juan Velasquez | University of Chile, Chile |
| Vicky Yamamoto | Keck School of Medicine of USC, USA |
| Yang Yang | Department of Psychology of BFU, China |

## Local Organization Chairs

| Michele Allegra | University of Padua, Italy |
| Claudia Cecchetto | University of Padua, Italy |
| Daniela Pietrobon | University of Padua, Italy |
| Samir Suweis | University of Padua, Italy |
| Mattia Tambaro | University of Padua, Italy |

## Publicity Chairs

| Abzetdin Adamov | ADA University, Azerbaijan |
| M. Shamim Kaiser | Jahangirnagar University, Bangladesh |
| Hongzhi Kuai | Maebashi Institute of Technology, Japan |
| Francesco Morabito | Mediterranean University of Reggio Calabria, Italy |
| Yanqing Zhang | Georgia State University, USA |

## Web Master

| Hongzhi Kuai | Maebashi Institute of Technology, Japan |

# Contents

## Brain Big Data Analytics, Curation and Management

## Informatics Paradigms for Brain and Mental Health Research

## Brain-Machine Intelligence and Brain-Inspired Computing

# Cognitive and Computational Foundations of Brain Science

# Estimating the Temporal Evolution of Synaptic Weights from Dynamic Functional Connectivity

Marco Celotto[1,2,3]([✉]) [iD], Stefan Lemke[1,4] [iD], and Stefano Panzeri[1,3] [iD]

[1] Neural Computation Laboratory, Center for Neuroscience and Cognitive Systems, Istituto Italiano di Tecnologia, Rovereto, Italy
marco.celotto@iit.it
[2] Department of Pharmacy and Biotechnology, University of Bologna, Bologna, Italy
[3] Department of Excellence for Neural Information Processing, Center for Molecular Neurobiology (ZMNH), University Medical Center Hamburg-Eppendorf (UKE), Hamburg, Germany
s.panzeri@uke.de
[4] Department of Cell Biology and Physiology, University of North Carolina, Chapel Hill, USA
stefan.lemke@unc.edu

**Abstract.** How to capture the temporal evolution of synaptic weights from measures of dynamic functional connectivity (DFC) between the activity of different simultaneously recorded neurons is an important and open problem in systems neuroscience. To address this issue, we first simulated models of recurrent neural networks of spiking neurons that had a spike-timing-dependent plasticity mechanism generating time-varying synaptic and functional coupling. We then used these simulations to test analytical approaches that relate dynamic functional connectivity to time-varying synaptic connectivity. We investigated how to use different measures of directed DFC, such as cross-covariance and transfer entropy, to build algorithms that infer how synaptic weights evolve over time. We found that, while both cross-covariance and transfer entropy provide robust estimates of structural connectivity and communication delays, cross-covariance better captures the evolution of synaptic weights over time. We also established how leveraging estimates of connectivity derived from entire simulated recordings could further boost the estimation of time-varying synaptic weights from the DFC. These results provide useful information to estimate accurately time variations of synaptic strength from spiking activity measures.

**Keywords:** Dynamic functional connectivity · Spiking neural network · Communication delay · Transfer entropy · Cross-covariance

## 1 Introduction

Neurons in biological networks are connected by directed, plastic synapses. Neurons are sparsely connected and the identity, the strength, and the

© Springer Nature Switzerland AG 2022
M. Mahmud et al. (Eds.): BI 2022, LNAI 13406, pp. 3–14, 2022
https://doi.org/10.1007/978-3-031-15037-1_1

communication delay of the connections between cells-pairs determine the network dynamics [6,15,16]. Importantly, the strength of each synapse can change over different time scales - ranging from tenths of milliseconds to days - due to processes including synaptic potentiation and depression [2]. Such changes in synaptic weights are thought to be neural-activity dependent and driven by Hebbian mechanisms of plasticity such as spike-timing dependent-plasticity (STDP).

Many electrophysiological *in vivo* experiments record simultaneously the spiking activity of several neurons within a network, but without the ability to measure directly synaptic activity. Robust methods to estimate synaptic weights and how they evolve over time from functional measurements of neural activity are thus critical to investigate several neuroscientific questions. For example, sleep is thought to play an essential role in synaptic homeostasis and memory formation. Several theories and experimental findings support the idea that specific features of non-REM sleep might contribute to the up- and down-scaling of synaptic weights [23]. Experimentally, it has been shown that the nesting between spindles and slow oscillations can increase the dynamic functional connectivity (DFC), measured as peaks of cross-correlation between pairs of putatively connected cells, over the temporal range of minutes [14]. However, the corresponding synaptic changes over the same time span are difficult to characterize. In general, it remains unclear how changes in DFC measures relate to the temporal dynamics of synaptic weights in spiking neural networks.

Previous works investigating the relationship between functional connectivity measures and ground truth synaptic connectivity have often utilized the Izhikevich network [11] as a reasonably realistic model of a cortical spiking neural network [9,18]. These studies highlighted that bivariate connectivity measures, such as cross-covariance and transfer entropy, can provide robust estimates of the underlying directed connectivity in simulated networks. However, they did not examine the temporal evolution of functional and structural connectivity within spiking networks incorporating STDP. Here, we examined the performance of several different DFC methods in estimating the temporal dynamics of synaptic weights (termed dynamic structural connectivity or DSC) from up to 90 min of spiking activity in simulated spiking networks with STDP. We first determined the performance of DFC measures in inferring static properties of the simulated networks (such as pairwise synaptic connectivity and the associated communication delays). We then applied these measures with a sliding window approach to compute DFC and quantify its relationship with DSC. We found, that, among all tested DFC measures, the cross-covariance better captured the evolution of synaptic weights over time. Importantly, we also established how to use the information obtained from the static, time-averaged analysis of the network, to enhance the estimate of DSC from DFC.

## 2    Simulated Spiking Network and Inference Pipeline

To investigate the relationship between DSC and DFC, we simulated a spiking neural network in which the strength of synaptic weights changed over time according to an STDP rule. We then compared the performance of different functional connectivity measures in estimating both the ground truth structure of the network (i.e. which pairs of neurons were connected, their communication lag, and the type of synapse), and how the strengths of the synaptic weights changed over time (Fig. 1). We simulated a spiking network of N = 100 neurons in which the dynamics of each neuron was described using the Izhikevich neuron model [10]. This model has a good tradeoff between biological plausibility and computational efficiency. The structure of the network was set by Izhikevich [11] to mimic the connectivity of a real population of cortical neurons (Fig. 1A). 80% of neurons in the network were excitatory and 20% were inhibitory. Excitatory neurons were randomly connected to 10 postsynaptic neurons which could be either excitatory or inhibitory (800 excitatory synapses in total). Each excitatory synapse had a random communication delay ($\delta$) whose value was uniformly distributed between 1 and 20 ms and was constant over time. Inhibitory neurons were randomly connected to 10 postsynaptic excitatory neurons (200 inhibitory synapses), therefore no inhibitory-to-inhibitory (I-I) connections were present in the network. The lack of I-I synapses caused the average firing rate of excitatory neurons ($5.11 \pm 0.03$ Hz) to be lower than the one of inhibitory neurons ($8.23 \pm 0.04$ Hz). Inhibitory connections had a communication delay of 1 ms. The simulation ran with 1 ms temporal precision for a duration decided by the user. During the simulation, the strength of excitatory synapses - which were all initialized to the same, positive, value - changed dynamically due to an STDP rule: when a presynaptic neuron $i$ fired before a postsynaptic neuron $j$ the strength of the synapse from $i$ to $j$ ($w_{ij}$) was strengthened, on the other hand when $j$ fired before $i$ $w_{ij}$ got weaker (Fig. 1B). The decay time of the STDP rule was $\tau = 20$ ms and synaptic weights were updated every 1 s with a memory factor which made the weights change, on average, over the timescale of 1–2 min (obtained measuring the synaptic weights autocorrelation, not shown).

We used different measures to compute the static and dynamic functional connectivity of the network from the spiking activity (Fig. 1C). Such measures were all directed (meaning that, for each pair of neurons, they could take different values in the two directions) and allowed computing the strength of communication for different delays ($\delta$). When computing static functional connectivity, we used data from the whole simulated recording to compute a single connectivity value for each pair of neurons $(i, j)$. We computed all connectivity measures with $\delta$ ranging from 1 to 50 ms then, for each pair, we determined the static functional connectivity ($w_{ij}$) as the maximum connectivity value across delays. We selected the communication delay ($\delta_{ij}$) as the lag that maximized the functional connectivity. Calling $f_{ij}(\delta)$ the generic measure of functional connectivity, then: $w_{ij} = max_{\delta}(f_{ij}(\delta))$ and $\delta_{ij} = argmax_{\delta}(f_{ij}(\delta))$. By taking the top percentile of connectivity values for each measure we obtained sparse static networks (Fig. 1D). If the measure $f$ was signed we could also infer whether a synapse was excitatory or inhibitory. Then, we used a sliding window approach to compute, for each measure, the DFC of all the synapses that were inferred as present (Fig. 1E). We exploited the static measures of communication delay between pairs to compute delay-consistent DFC and then evaluated the performance of the different measures in recovering the ground-truth dynamics of synaptic weights.

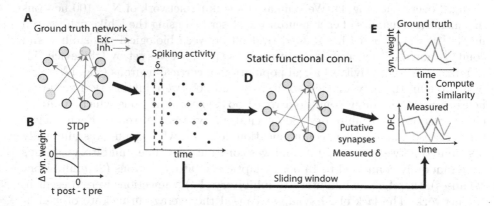

**Fig. 1.** Graphical depiction of the method. A) Structural connectivity of the simulated network for N = 10 neurons. Synaptic weights could be either excitatory (green) or inhibitory (purple). Excitatory connections had randomly distributed communication delays. B) The strength of the synaptic weights changed over time due to STDP. C) Structural and biophysical properties of the network determined the spiking activity of the neural population. D) Static functional connectivity was measured from spiking activity. E) Dynamic functional connectivity was measured from activity, also leveraging on the inferred static connectivity of the network. (Color figure online)

## 3   Inferring the Presence of Synapses

We tested the performance of different measures of functional connectivity in estimating the presence of synapses from spiking activity. Two of these measures were based on Pearson correlation, which is commonly used to estimate the connectivity between pairs of neurons [3,9,14]. The first method was normalized cross-correlation ($XCorr$):

$$XCorr_{ij}(\delta) = \frac{E[i_{t-\delta}j_t]}{\sigma_i\sigma_j} \tag{1}$$

where $i_t$ and $j_{t'}$ are the binary values of the spike trains from neurons $i$ and $j$ at times $t$ and $t'$, and the expected value was computed across time. $\sigma_i$ and $\sigma_j$ are standard deviations of the spike trains of neurons $i$ and $j$, respectively.

The second method was the normalized cross-covariance ($XCov$), which is insensitive to correlations in the average firing rate due to subtraction of the average activity value from the spike trains before computing the correlation:

$$XCov_{ij}(\delta) = \frac{E[(i_{t-\delta} - \bar{i})(j_t - \bar{j})]}{\sigma_i\sigma_j} \tag{2}$$

Here $\bar{i}$ and $\bar{j}$ are the average firing rates of neurons $i$ and $j$, respectively.

Additionally, we computed the functional connectivity using two variants of the information-theoretic measure of information transfer known as transfer entropy [8,21], a measure that has been successfully used to characterize time-dependent changes in recurrent connectivity between mass signals [1]. Transfer entropy has the theoretical advantage - with respect to correlation measures - of being assumption-free in terms of the joint probability distribution of the lagged activity of neuron $i$ and $j$. This also means that transfer entropy does not assume that the interactions between neurons are linear. Additionally, this measure respects the Wiener-Granger causality principle of causal communication by conditioning the information between the past of the emitter and the present of the receiver neuron on the past activity of the receiver neuron. Our first implementation of transfer entropy uses single time-points statistics to build the probability distribution of lagged neural activity. We refer to this implementation as $TE$:

$$TE_{ij}(\delta) = I(i_{t-\delta}; j_t | j_{t-1}) = \sum p(i_{t-\delta}, j_t, j_{t-1}) \log_2 \frac{p(j_t | i_{t-\delta}, j_{t-1})}{p(j_t | j_{t-1})} \quad (3)$$

where $p(i_{t-\delta}, j_t, j_{t-1})$ is the joint probability distribution of the present state of the receiver neuron $j_t$, its past lagged by one time step $j_{t-1}$ and the past state of the emitter neuron lagged by $\delta$ time steps $i_{t-\delta}$. The sum occurs over all the $(i_{t-\delta}, j_t, j_{t-1})$ triplets of events in the probability space. The probability distribution is sampled across time. The lag of the receiver past is set to $-1$ since it has been proven to be theoretically optimal for determining real communication delays [24].

The second implementation of transfer entropy uses multidimensional pasts of the emitter and the receiver neuron to consider the possible relevance of time windows longer than 1 ms when transmitting information. Using the terminology of [9] we refer to this measure as Higher Order Transfer Entropy ($HOTE$):

$$HOTE_{ij}(\delta) = I(i^{(k)}_{t-\delta}; j_t | j^{(l)}_{t-1}) = \sum p(i^{(k)}_{t-\delta}, j_t, j^{(l)}_{t-1}) \log_2 \frac{p(j_t | i^{(k)}_{t-\delta}, j^{(l)}_{t-1})}{p(j_t | j^{(l)}_{t-1})} \quad (4)$$

where $k$ and $l$ are the dimensions of the past activity of the emitter and the receiver neuron $i$ and $j$, respectively. For the analysis reported in this paper we set $k = l = 5$ ms.

We computed these four functional connectivity measures between all pairs of neurons in the network and estimated the communication strength and delay for each pair as described in the previous section. We then evaluated the performance of the different metrics in determining the presence or absence of synapses between pairs of neurons, varying the threshold probability of connectivity strength incrementally from 0 to 1 in steps of 0.01. Since the two classes of present and absent synapses were unbalanced (only 10% of all the possible synapses were present in the network) we used precision-recall (PR) curves to study the performance in this classification task [4] (Fig. 2A). Calling $TP$, $FP$

and $FN$ the number of true positive, false positive and false negative inferred synapses, respectively, we have that $precision = \frac{TP}{TP+FP}$ and $recall = \frac{TP}{TP+FN}$. Therefore, if for a given measure the two distributions of present and absent links were perfectly separable, we would get that for $recall = 1$ also $precision = 1$. On the other hand, a random classifier would always have a precision equal to the ratio of synapses present in the model (10%, dashed line in Fig. 2A) for each recall value.

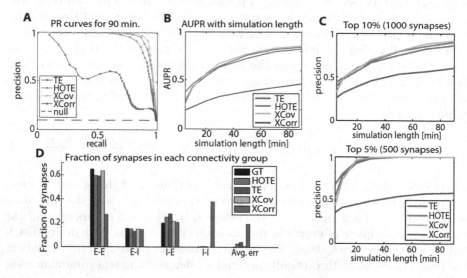

**Fig. 2.** Performance of functional connectivity measures in estimating structural connectivity. A) Precision-recall (PR) curves computed from 90 min of simulated activity for TE, HOTE, XCov and XCorr. Each point is one percentile of the distribution of functional connectivity values across pairs. B) AUPR trend with simulation length (length ranges from 5 to 90 min). C) Comparison of precision in identifying connected pairs with simulation lengths, for top 10th (1000 pairs) and top 5th (500 pairs) percentiles of each measure's distribution. D) Fraction of pairs belonging to each group of synapses, from 90 min simulation and using the top 10th percentile of connections. GT = ground truth. (Color figure online)

After 90 min of simulation, XCov, TE and HOTE all performed well in the classification task, having a PR curve whose shape approached the optimal one. Among these three measures, XCov showed the best PR curve and TE the worst one. XCorr, on the other hand, performed poorly, with a PR curve far from optimal. The area under the precision-recall curve (AUPR) is a useful metric to summarize the goodness of a PR curve; a perfect classifier has an AUPR equal to one. We computed how AUPR scales with simulation length for different measures. This analysis confirmed that XCov and HOTE were the best metrics in evaluating which links were present for long recordings, while HOTE worked better than XCov and TE for recording shorter than 10 min (Fig. 2B). We measured how the precision of the different measures scaled with the simulation time for the top 10th and top 5th percentile of inferred synapses. For the top 10th percentile (i.e. 1000 inferred synapses, which equals the ground truth number of connections) we found that the maximum precision in the classification was obtained with XCov, which topped at 92% for 90 min of simulated recording (Fig. 2C top). With a more conservative threshold of the top 5th percentile of connections (i.e. half of the true total number), we captured the top 500 real connections after 30 min of simulation (Fig. 2C bottom) for all measures but XCorr. To investigate why XCorr performance was so poor when compared to the other measures, we computed the fraction of links inferred by each measure as the top 10th percentile of synapses in the four subgroups of excitatory-to-excitatory (E-E), excitatory-to-inhibitory (E-I), inhibitory-to-excitatory (I-E) and inhibitory-to-inhibitory (I-I) synapses (Fig. 2D). XCov performed best in determining the correct fraction of synapses belonging to each group, while XCorr overestimated the number of I-I connections and underestimated the number of E-E connections. This behavior of XCorr is due to the aforementioned differences in average firing rate between inhibitory and excitatory neurons, with a higher firing rate for inhibitory neurons, as XCorr is sensitive to the correlation between average firing rates. Given the poor performance of XCorr in estimating the presence of synapses, we discarded it in the following analyses.

## 4 Inferring Synapse Type and Communication Delay

We studied how, for each ground truth synapse, different functional connectivity measures performed in inferring whether the synapse was excitatory or inhibitory, and the value of the communication delay of that pair of neurons.

We could not use information-theoretic measures to infer whether synapses were excitatory or inhibitory as these measures are only positively defined. Therefore, we only examined the XCov performance on this excitatory/inhibitory classification task. We classified a connection as excitatory and inhibitory based on XCov value, with positive correlation values assigned as excitatory connections and negative correlation values as inhibitory connections. After 90 min of recording XCov could reliably separate excitatory and inhibitory synapses (Fig. 3A). We found that the performance of the classifier increased with recording time for both the excitatory and the inhibitory class (Fig. 3B).

We also compared how functional connectivity measures performed in inferring ground truth communication delays. After 90 min of simulation, all measures estimated delays with a correlation across synapses that was above 0.85 (see Fig. 3C for the relationship between the ground truth delays and those estimated using XCov - on the top - and using HOTE - on the bottom). The trend of the correlation between ground truth and estimated delays with simulation lengths was approximately linear in the explored range (Fig. 3D). Nonetheless, HOTE estimated the delays more precisely than XCov and TE. After 90 min of simulation, HOTE had an average delay error, measured as the absolute value of the difference between ground truth and inferred delay, below 1 ms. On the other hand, XCov and TE showed a systematic error in the delay estimation of approximately 2 ms (see Fig. 3C and Fig. 3E).

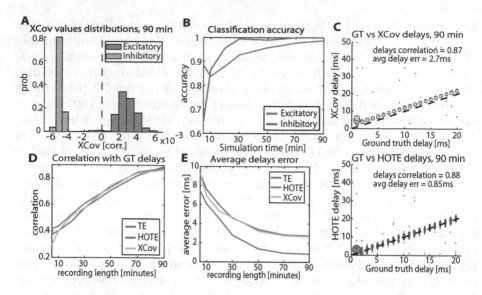

**Fig. 3.** Performance of the measures in estimating connection type and delays. A) Distributions of functional connectivity values measured using XCov for excitatory (green) and inhibitory (purple) cells. B) Performance of a classifier in identifying excitatory and inhibitory synapses with simulation length. The decision boundary of the classifier was set to $XCov = 0$. C) Scatter plots of real and estimated delays across cell pairs using XCov (top) and HOTE (bottom). The size of the markers is proportional to the number of pairs having that specific combination of ground truth and estimated delay. The dashed line is the identity line $x = y$. Black dots far from the identity line correspond to pairs of measured and real delays that occurred only once. D) Correlation between ground truth and estimated delays with simulation length. E) Average error in delay estimation with simulation length. (Color figure online)

## 5  Relationship Between Dynamic Functional Connectivity and the Temporal Evolution of Synaptic Weights

Finally, we investigated how the ground truth evolution of the synaptic weights, that is the DSC, related to the measured DFC. We computed DFC using a sliding window approach. We first selected a size for the sliding window $T$ and then shifted it through the simulated recording in steps of length $T$. We computed DFC only for pairs of neurons that were putatively connected, which we selected as the top 5th percentile of links for each measure after 90 min of simulation (Fig. 1C), and only at the communication delay that we measured for each pair (Fig. 3C). Moreover, we computed DFC only for excitatory synapses since the inhibitory ones had a constant synaptic weight in the simulated network. We calculated the across-time correlation between DFC and DSC for all synapses to quantify the performance of each functional connectivity measure in estimating the DSC. To do this, we averaged the DSC over windows of width $T$, so that the number of DSC and DFC samples over time were matched.

In Fig. 4A we show the DSC (top left), the DFC computed using TE (top right), HOTE (bottom left) and XCov (bottom right) for three example synapses and $T = 10$ min. It is visible that, while all measures work reasonably well in tracking how the strength of the gray and the green synapses change over time, TE and HOTE fail in quantifying the temporal evolution of the brown synapse. We found that, on average, DFC computed via XCov correlates with DSC better than the DFC computed via TE or HOTE (Fig. 4B). In particular, while DFC computed via TE and HOTE had a high temporal correlation with DSC (above 0.7) for the majority of synapses, their distributions showed a large tail of synapses whose correlation between DSC and DFC was distributed around zero (such as the brown one in Fig. 4A). For XCov, the number of synapses whose DSC was poorly estimated decreased rapidly with the correlation strength, and the average correlation was 0.82 (Fig. 4B, right). Therefore, the DFC computed using XCov outperformed the one obtained from TE and HOTE in inferring the simulated changes of the synaptic weights over time.

We then studied how the across-time correlation between DSC and DFC depends on the width of the sliding window $T$. The correlation between DFC and DSC increased with the window size, reaching a plateau around $T = 5$ min (Fig. 4C, left). Below $T = 5$ min the correlation dropped due to the limited sample size used to compute DFC, manifesting a tradeoff between the temporal precision of the DFC measures ($T$) and their performance in estimating DSC. We repeated the same analysis without keeping the delay consistent when computing DFC but simply taking the maximum connectivity value across delays (between 1 and 50 ms) for each window (Fig. 4C, middle). When not keeping the delay consistent with the previously measured one, the correlation between DSC and DFC dropped substantially. For sizes of the sliding window lower than $T = 5$ min, the advantage of keeping a consistent delay was particularly evident, with a boost in the correlation between DSC and DFC larger than 0.2 (Fig. 4C, right). This result showed a clear benefit in leveraging estimates of delay derived from entire simulated recordings when inferring DSC from DFC.

## 6   Discussion

We studied how different measures of functional connectivity can be used to infer the static and dynamic properties of synapses from spiking activity in a simulated neural network. This problem is of relevance because in many *in vivo* experiments only spiking activity is measured, but it is important to also infer the changes in synaptic connectivity to understand the evolution of the neural network under study. We addressed the problem at the level of simulated recordings with single-neuron cellular resolution. As such, our approach differs from and complements other studies of DFC at the level of mass neural activity [7], which lack the ability to resolve interactions between pairs of individual neurons.

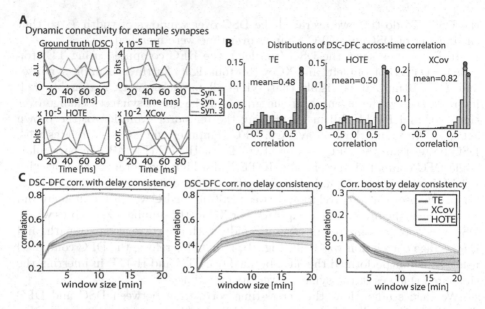

**Fig. 4.** Relationship between dynamic structural and functional connectivity. A) Dynamic connectivity for 3 example synapses, $T = 10$ min. Top left: ground truth dynamics of synaptic weights (DSC). Top right: Transfer entropy DFC. Bottom left: HOTE DFC. Bottom right: Cross-covariance DFC. B) Distribution of the across-time correlation coefficients between DSC and DFC, $T = 10$ min. Left: Transfer entropy. Middle: HOTE. Right: Cross-covariance. Colored dots show where the synapses in panel A are in the correlation distributions. C) Average correlation between DSC and DFC over time for different sizes of the moving window. Shaded areas are SEM across synapses. Left: DFC keeping delay consistency (i.e. measures computed only at previously estimated delay); Middle: DFC without delay consistency; Right: Boost in correlation between DFC and DSC when keeping delay consistency (difference between left and middle panels). (Color figure online)

Consistent with previous studies, we found that among the considered functional connectivity measures, XCov and HOTE performed best in identifying which pairs of neurons were connected [9]. Cross-covariance could also reliably classify excitatory and inhibitory synapses, while HOTE was the best measure in recovering the ground-truth communication delay between neurons. Cross-covariance performed best in inferring DSC, with an across-time correlation above 0.8 between DFC and DSC for sliding window sizes larger than 5 min. We also found that, when computing DFC, keeping the communication delay consistent with the one obtained from the static network analysis boosted the relationship between DFC and DSC, especially for moving windows shorter than 5 min. It is possible that this correlation boost by keeping the delay constant is because considering delays that differ from the ground truth one enhances the detection of spurious correlations. This specifically holds under the assumption that communication delays are constant in the recording period as is the case of our spiking network. Such spurious correlations might possibly be induced by other neurons in the population connected with a lag to both neurons in a putatively connected pair.

The present study has limitations that we plan to address in future works. First of all, it will be important to validate the DFC measures on more biologically realistic simulated neural networks presenting global oscillations, correlated inputs to neurons (mimicking sensory perception and motion), and more heterogeneity in the firing rates and in the average synaptic weights over time. Indeed, such effects could act as confounders of the relationship between DFC and DSC [19] or could require refined null hypotheses based on permutation tests to assess the presence of links. In the model we also assumed that (i) the communication delays are constant and (ii) no synapses are formed or eliminated over time. (i) assumes that the main parameters determining the conductance velocity of action potentials (e.g. axons diameters and myelin levels) are approximately constant over time scales of tens of minutes. Experimental finding suggest that this assumption is reasonable, especially in adult mice where the formation of new myelin occurs in the range of weeks [17]. Assumption (ii) is more delicate since in mice it has been shown that, especially during sleep, dendritic spines can be formed and eliminated within hours [25]. It will be important to investigate how much we can relax these hypotheses while still exploiting the knowledge obtained from the static network inference. Moreover, we plan to test the performance of other bivariate (e.g. Granger causality) and, especially, other multivariate measures for estimating DSC. These measures might include using Granger Causality estimates based on Generalized Linear Models (GLMs) [5,13,22] and maximum entropy models [12,20]. Such multivariate measures could be useful e.g. to alleviate the effect of confounders such as common inputs.

To conclude, here we lay down foundations for relating dynamic functional connectivity to the temporal evolution of synaptic weights in spiking neural networks. The results obtained here provide a benchmark for further improving methodologies that infer DSC from DFC.

# References

1. Besserve, M., Lowe, S.C., Logothetis, N.K., Schölkopf, B., Panzeri, S.: Shifts of gamma phase across primary visual cortical sites reflect dynamic stimulus-modulated information transfer. PLoS Biol. 13(9), e1002257 (2015)
2. Citri, A., Malenka, R.C.: Synaptic plasticity: multiple forms, functions, and mechanisms. Neuropsychopharmacology 33(1), 18–41 (2007)
3. Cutts, C.S., Eglen, S.J.: Detecting pairwise correlations in spike trains: an objective comparison of methods and application to the study of retinal waves. J. Neurosci. 34(43), 14288–14303 (2014)
4. Davis, J., Goadrich, M.: The relationship between Precision-Recall and ROC curves. In: Proceedings of the 23rd International Conference on Machine Learning - ICML 2006, pp. 233–240 (2006)
5. Francis, N.A., Mukherjee, S., Koçillari, L., Panzeri, S., Babadi, B., Kanold, P.O.: Sequential transmission of task-relevant information in cortical neuronal networks. Cell Rep. 39(9), 110878 (2022)

6. Ganguli, S., Sompolinsky, H.: Compressed sensing, sparsity, and dimensionality in neuronal information processing and data analysis. Ann. Rev. Neurosci. **35**(1), 485–508 (2012)
7. Hindriks, R., et al.: Can sliding-window correlations reveal dynamic functional connectivity in resting-state fMRI? Neuroimage **127**, 242–256 (2016)
8. Hlavackovaschindler, K., Palus, M., Vejmelka, M., Bhattacharya, J.: Causality detection based on information-theoretic approaches in time series analysis. Phys. Rep. **441**(1), 1–46 (2007)
9. Ito, S., Hansen, M.E., Heiland, R., Lumsdaine, A., Litke, A.M., Beggs, J.M.: Extending transfer entropy improves identification of effective connectivity in a spiking cortical network model. PLoS ONE **6**(11), e27431 (2011)
10. Izhikevich, E.: Simple model of spiking neurons. IEEE Trans. Neural Netw. **14**(6), 1569–1572 (2003)
11. Izhikevich, E.: Polychronization: computation with spikes. Neural Comput. **18**(2), 245–282 (2006)
12. Jaynes, E.T.: Information theory and statistical mechanics. Phys. Rev. **106**(4), 620–630 (1957)
13. Kobayashi, R., et al.: Reconstructing neuronal circuitry from parallel spike trains. Nat. Commun. **10**(1), 4468 (2019)
14. Lemke, S.M., Ramanathan, D.S., Darevksy, D., Egert, D., Berke, J.D., Ganguly, K.: Coupling between motor cortex and striatum during sleep over long-term skill learning. eLife **10**, e64303 (2021)
15. Mastrogiuseppe, F., Ostojic, S.: Linking connectivity, dynamics, and computations in low-rank recurrent neural networks. Neuron **99**(3), 609–623 (2018)
16. Ostojic, S., Brunel, N., Hakim, V.: How connectivity, background activity, and synaptic properties shape the cross-correlation between spike trains. J. Neurosci. **29**(33), 10234–10253 (2009)
17. Pan, S., Mayoral, S.R., Choi, H.S., Chan, J.R., Kheirbek, M.A.: Preservation of a remote fear memory requires new myelin formation. Nat. Neurosci. **23**(4), 487–499 (2020)
18. Pastore, V.P., Massobrio, P., Godjoski, A., Martinoia, S.: Identification of excitatory-inhibitory links and network topology in large-scale neuronal assemblies from multi-electrode recordings. PLoS Comput. Biol. **14**(8), e1006381 (2018)
19. Satterthwaite, T.D., et al.: An improved framework for confound regression and filtering for control of motion artifact in the preprocessing of resting-state functional connectivity data. Neuroimage **64**, 240–256 (2013)
20. Schneidman, E., Berry, M.J., Segev, R., Bialek, W.: Weak pairwise correlations imply strongly correlated network states in a neural population. Nature **440**(7087), 1007–1012 (2006)
21. Schreiber, T.: Measuring information transfer. Phys. Rev. Lett. **85**(2), 461–464 (2000)
22. Sheikhattar, A., et al.: Extracting neuronal functional network dynamics via adaptive Granger causality analysis. Proc. Natl. Acad. Sci. U.S.A. **115**(17), E3869–E3878 (2018)
23. Tononi, G., Cirelli, C.: Sleep and the price of plasticity: from synaptic and cellular homeostasis to memory consolidation and integration. Neuron **81**(1), 12–34 (2014)
24. Wibral, M., et al.: Measuring information-transfer delays. PLoS ONE **8**(2), e55809 (2013)
25. Yang, G., Lai, C.S.W., Cichon, J., Ma, L., Li, W., Gan, W.B.: Sleep promotes branch-specific formation of dendritic spines after learning. Science **344**(6188), 1173–1178 (2014)

# From Concrete to Abstract Rules:
# A Computational Sketch

Snigdha Dagar[(✉)], Frederic Alexandre, and Nicolas Rougier

Inria Bordeaux Sud Ouest, University of Bordeaux, CNRS, Bordeaux, France
snigdha.dagar@inria.fr

**Abstract.** A multi-dimensional stimulus can elicit a range of responses depending on which dimension or combination of dimensions is considered. Such selection can be implicit, providing a fast and automatic selection, or explicit, providing a slower but contextualized selection. Both forms are important but do not derive from the same processes. Implicit selection results generally from a slow and progressive learning that leads to a simple response (concrete/first-order) while explicit selection derives from a deliberative process that allows to have more complex and structured response (abstract/second-order). The prefrontal cortex (PFC) is believed to provide the ability to contextualize concrete rules that leads to the acquisition of abstract rules even though the exact mechanisms are still largely unknown. The question we address in this paper is precisely about the acquisition, the representation and the selection of such abstract rules. Using two models from the literature (PBWM and HER), we explain that they both provide a partial but differentiated answer such that their unification offers a complete picture.

**Keywords:** Cognitive control · Prefrontal cortex · Computational model · Abstract rules

## 1  Introduction

Two main strategies are generally reported for the selection of behavior [5,6]. On the one hand, implicit memory elaborated by slow learning processes can generate a rigid behavior (also called default behavior), robust in stable worlds, easy to generate but difficult to quickly adapt to changes. On the other hand, explicit memory manipulating models of the world can be used for the prospective and explicit exploration of possible behaviors, yielding a flexible and rapidly changing strategy, where behavioral rules can be associated to contexts and selected quickly as the environment changes. In the simplest case, this means learning rules defined as associations between an object's properties and a direct response. Such rules can be called concrete, while more complex or abstract rules may involve the learning of second order relations on top of the first-order rules. The prefrontal cortex (PFC) is believed to provide the ability to contextualize concrete rules that leads to the acquisition of abstract rules [6]. Considering the

© Springer Nature Switzerland AG 2022
M. Mahmud et al. (Eds.): BI 2022, LNAI 13406, pp. 15–26, 2022
https://doi.org/10.1007/978-3-031-15037-1_2

number of contexts we encounter every day and the ease with which we select appropriate strategies for each, some relevant questions arise: How do we represent these strategies or rules and how do we determine which one is appropriate? An important way of understanding how the PFC supports contextual learning and implements cognitive control is thus to understand how its representations are organized and manipulated.

There is sufficient evidence to suggest that the PFC is organized hierarchically [3] with more caudal areas learning first-order associations and more rostral areas putting them in context to facilitate learning of abstract rules. This can be done by top-down modulation in the PFC, which underlies the ability to focus attention on task-relevant stimuli and ignore irrelevant distractors, in two ways: either as a result of weight changes in modulated pathways and predictions, or through activation-based biasing provided by a working memory system. These mechanisms have been explored in two prominent models of the PFC. One well established model for cognitive control function through the working memory system is the Prefrontal cortex and Basal ganglia Working Memory model (PBWM) [10] in which a flexible working memory system with an adaptive gating mechanism is implemented. At the biological level, the model proposes that the PFC facilitates active maintenance for sustaining task-relevant information, while the Basal Ganglia (BG) provides the selective gating mechanism. A hierarchical extension of this model [7] proposes that hierarchical control can arise from multiple such nested frontostriatal loops (loops between the PFC and the BG). The system adaptively learns to represent and maintain higher order information in rostral regions which conditionalize attentional selection in more caudal regions.

A second hierarchical model, Hierarchical Error Representation (HER) [1], explains cognitive control in terms of the interaction between the dlPFC (dorsolateral prefrontal cortex) and the mPFC (medial part of the PFC). The dlPFC learns to maintain representations of stimuli that reliably co-occur with outcome prediction error and these error representations are used by the mPFC to refine predictions about the likely outcomes of actions. The error is broadcasted through the PFC in a bottom-up manner, and modulated predictions from top-down facilitate selection of an appropriate response. Thanks to its recursive architecture, this model, presented in more details below, can elaborate hierarchical rules on the basis of learning by weight updating, both to select pertinent stimuli and to map a representation inspired with principles of predictive coding [2]. In addition to its elegant recursive mechanism, proposing an original computational mechanism to account for the hierarchical structure of the PFC, the HER model is also very interesting because its proposes to decompose the functioning of the PFC between, on the one hand, the prediction of the outcome and the monitoring of the error of prediction and, on the other hand, the elaboration of contextual (and possibly hierarchical) rules to compensate errors. This distribution of functions has also been reported between respectively the medial and lateral parts of the PFC [6], yielding more importance to the biological plausibility of the HER model. For these reasons, the HER model could be presented as a more elaborated and accurate model of the PFC, except for one point of discussion that we put forward here. All the adaptations of the HER model are made through learning by weight modifications, whereas the property of working memory of the PFC, as it is for example exploited in the PBWM model, is often presented as a key mechanisms for its adaptive capabilities. An important question is consequently to determine up to which point working memory and attentional modulations are necessary for the learning of hierarchical rules in cognitive control.

In the work presented here, we seek to answer specific questions about the nature of top-down modulation and selective attention, through the lens of hierarchical learning and representations. We start from the implementation of the hierarchical HER model and its study for a task in which individual first-order rules can be learned alone or associated within specific contexts to form second-order rules. We can evaluate the performances of the HER model in these different cases and compare them with a case where an attentional mechanism should be deployed to facilitate and orient its learning. As discussed in the concluding part, we observe that the attentional mechanism should be considered not only for the processing of information but also for the learning of rules, particularly in the hierarchical and contextual case.

## 2   Methods

This section first summarizes the HER model algorithm and equations, as described in the original paper [1] and subsequently presents the task that we have chosen for our study.

### 2.1   Model Details: HER

**Working Memory Gating.** At each level of the hierarchy, external stimuli presented to the model may be stored in WM based on the learned value of storing that stimulus versus maintaining currently active WM representations.

External stimuli are represented as a vector $\mathbf{s}$, while internal representations of stimuli are denoted by $\mathbf{r}$. The value of storing the stimulus represented by $\mathbf{s}$ in WM versus maintaining current WM representation $\mathbf{r}$ is determined as:

$$\mathbf{v} = \mathbf{X}^\mathbf{T}\mathbf{s} \tag{1}$$

where $\mathbf{X}$ is a matrix of weights associating the external stimuli ($\mathbf{s}$) with corresponding WM representations ($\mathbf{r}$).

The value of storing stimulus $s_i(v_i)$ is compared to the value of maintaining the current contents $r_j$ of WM ($v_j$) using a softmax function:

$$\text{probability of storing} s_i = \frac{(exp^{\beta v_i} + bias)}{(exp^{\beta v_i} + bias) + exp^{\beta v_j}} \tag{2}$$

**Outcome Prediction.** Following the update of WM, predictions regarding possible responses and outcomes are computed at each hierarchical layer, using a simple feedforward network:

$$\mathbf{p} = \mathbf{W}^{\mathbf{T}}\mathbf{r} \tag{3}$$

where $\mathbf{p}$ is a vector of predictions of outcomes and $\mathbf{W}$ is a weight matrix associating $\mathbf{r}$ and $\mathbf{p}$.

**Top-Down Modulation.** Beginning at the top of the hierarchy, predictions are used to modulate weights at inferior layers and modulated predictions are computed, as shown with the red arrows in Fig. 1.

For a given layer, the prediction signal $\mathbf{p'}$ additively modulates stimulus-specific predictions $\mathbf{p}$ generated by the lower layer. In order to modulate predictive activity, $\mathbf{p'}$ is reshaped into a matrix $\mathbf{P'}$ and added to $\mathbf{W}$ in order to generate a modulated prediction of outcomes:

$$\mathbf{m} = (\mathbf{W} + \mathbf{P'})^{\mathbf{T}}\mathbf{r} \tag{4}$$

These modulated predictions are then used to modulate predictions of additional inferior layers (if any exist)

$$\mathbf{m} = (\mathbf{W} + \mathbf{M'})^{\mathbf{T}}\mathbf{r} \tag{5}$$

**Response Selection.** Actions are learned as response-outcome conjunctions at the lowest layer of the hierarchy. To select a response, the model compares the modulated prediction of correct feedback to the prediction of error feedback, for each candidate response:

$$u_{response} = m_{response/correct} - m_{response/error} \tag{6}$$

This is then used in a softmax function to determine a response:

$$Prob(u_i) = \frac{\exp^{\gamma u_i}}{\sum \exp^{\gamma u}} \tag{7}$$

**Bottom-Up Process.** Following the model's response, it is given feedback regarding its performance and two error signals are computed at the bottom most hierarchical layer, one comparing the unmodulated predictions to the outcome:

$$\mathbf{e} = \mathbf{a}(\mathbf{o} - \mathbf{p}) \tag{8}$$

and another comparing the modulated predictions to the outcome:

$$\mathbf{e} = \mathbf{a}(\mathbf{o} - \mathbf{m}) \tag{9}$$

where $\mathbf{o}$ is the vector of observed outcomes and $\mathbf{a}$ is a filter that is 0 for outcomes corresponding to unselected actions and 1 everywhere else.

The outer product of the first error signal and the current contents of the WM at the bottom level is used as the feedback signal for the immediately superior layer where this process is repeated (Fig. 1).

$$O' = re^T \tag{10}$$

Effectively, at the second layer, the outcome matrix is a conjunction of stimuli, actions and outcomes. This matrix is reshaped into a vector $o'$ and used to compute the prediction error at the superior layers:

$$e' = a'(o' - p') \tag{11}$$

**Weights Updating.** The second error signal is used to update weights within the bottom-most hierarchical layer, it updates the weights connecting the WM representation to prediction units ($W$), as well as weights in the WM gating mechanism ($X$):

$$X_{t+1} = X_t + (e_t^T W_t \cdot r_t)d_t^T \tag{12}$$

An eligibility vector $d$ is used instead of the stimulus vector $s$. When a stimulus $i$ is presented, the value of $d_i$ is set to 1, indicating a currently observed stimulus and at each iteration of the model, $d$ is multiplied by a constant decay parameter indicating gradually decaying eligibility traces.

$$W_{t+1} = W_t + \alpha(e_t r_t^T) \tag{13}$$

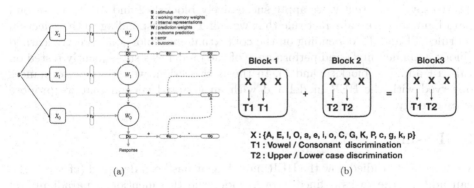

(a)                                                    (b)

**Fig. 1. (a)** Model schematics: Figure adapted from [1] **(b)** Task schematics: Figure adapted from [8] (Color figure online)

## 2.2   Task

To design our task, we consider the framework introduced by [8] which is composed of three subtasks where the stimuli are letters having three dimensions: color (red, green or black), case (upper or lower) and sound (vowel or consonant).

In the first subtask (Block 1 in Fig. 1(b)), black color indicates to ignore the stimulus and green color indicates to discriminate the case (rule T1: left button for upper, right button for lower). In the second one (Block 2 in Fig. 1(b)), black color indicates to ignore the stimulus and red color indicates to discriminate the sound (rule T2: left button for vowel, right button for consonant). The third one (Block 3 in Fig. 1(b)) is a random mix of trials from the other two blocks. This framework is interesting because, whereas rules T1 and T2 in blocks 1 and 2 require the subject to attend to a single dimension of the stimulus, block 3 requires to pay attention to both and to decide which rule to apply based on the third (contextual) dimension. Let us also mention here that, while there is no apparent difficulty with such tasks, it is actually harder than it appears depending on the way a task is learnt. During block 1, one can either learn the rule: "green means case and black ignore" or the rule: "black ignore, else case". The same is true for block 2 with sound. If we now consider block 3 and depending on how a subject learnt the first two blocks, she may succeed or fail immediately. In this latter case, this means block 3 cannot exploit previous learning and has to be (re)learnt.

The original task was cued by instruction and corresponding performances were reported in the paper [8]. Here, we wish to explore the inherent capability of a model to learn an abstract and hierarchical rule task without instructional cues, as in the paradigm reported by [4] and also to consider how the hierarchy can be learnt, depending on how information is represented in the model. We used two types of learning paradigms for the simulations: the first paradigm in which rules T1 and T2 were learned one after the other, and the performance of the model was then tested on random trials interleaved from rule T1 and T2 (to say it differently, we apply successively block 1, 2 and 3). In the second paradigm, an entire abstract rule that we call T3, corresponding to the selection on rules T1 and T2 depending on the contextual cue 'color' was directly learned (block 3 applied first) and performance of the model was subsequently tested on rule T1 and T2 (blocks 1 and 2). In the next section, we report performances observed with the HER model and with an adapted version that we propose subsequently.

## 3   Results

We have first studied how the HER model, as it has been designed (cf Sect. 2.1), can address the tasks defined above, under the two mentioned paradigms (cf Sect. 2.2). Due to the design of the HER model, each layer can only map or process one stimulus value, thus requiring as many layers as there are stimulus dimensions. The mapping in the model is also highly sensitive to the stimulus dimensions relative to one another, particularly higher-dimensional stimulus are preferentially mapped onto the lowest hierarchical layer. This rests on the assumption that stimulus dimensions better able to predict and reduce uncertainty about the response are mapped to lower layers.

This may not always be the case in real life situations though. We often have to adapt and generalize the same rules over several different contexts. In the task we consider as well, the context is determined by the color, which has 3 possible values - one of which always maps to the same response (to ignore) and the other 2 determine the response based on other stimulus dimensions.

## 3.1  Learning Curves

Performance observed for the first and second learning paradigms are reported in Figs. 2(a) and (b) respectively. We see in the Fig. 2(b) that due to its hierarchical structure, when there is an underlying abstract rule to learn (rule T3), the model is able to use the hierarchical information to acquire the rule while retaining performance in each of the sub-rules (Rule T1 and T2). It does so by monitoring an "error of errors" at each hierarchical layer, broadcasting this error to superior layers (bottom-up processing) that put it in context with the stimulus feature being attended to and finally sends this prediction information to the lower layers (top-down modulation) which are able to then select the appropriate response. In the Fig. 2(a), we show that when the composite rules are first learnt sequentially, the model is not able to compose them into a single rule, but instead has to relearn its representations to reach optimal performance.

Next we show that due to the design of the model, a task which has only one level of hierarchy, such as the one considered here, can not be learnt with a model with 2 layers. In Fig. 2(c) we see that with 2 layers, the model is able to learn the subparts of the rule (rules T1 and T2), but performance on the composite rule T3 saturates at 80%. By exploiting the gating mechanism, each sub-rule can be learnt individually by gating the 2 relevant feature dimensions at the 2 layers (color, vowel/consonant for rule T1 and color, lower/upper case for rule T2). However, in the third rule T3 when the 2 relevant features change from trial to trial to determine the correct response, the model fails to learn, since the contextual stimulus features don't provide top-down information about "which" other stimulus feature to attend to at the lower layer.

## 3.2  Gating Weights

In the model, the gating weights determine both, when to update or maintain a stimulus feature, and also which of the stimulus features is to be gated. We observed the adjusted weights after each rule that is learned. In the first block, vowel, consonant and black have high values of getting updated at the lowest layer, while in rule T3 all the "lower level" cues have high values of getting updated. In such a case, there is again competition between which one of them to gate, and both can win with close probabilities, in the absence of any information from the superior layers. Depending on what is gated into the top two layers, any of those mappings could emerge.

## 3.3  Prediction Weights

The prediction weights at layer 0 are Stimulus-Action-Outcome conjugations and the gating mechanism determines which stimulus and in turn which

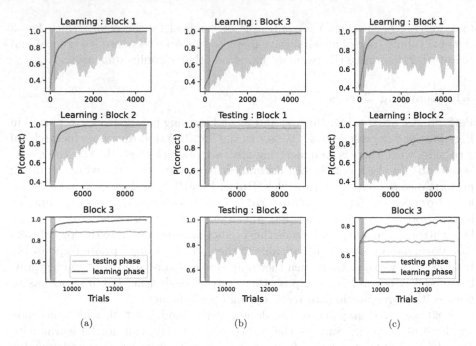

**Fig. 2.** Performance of the model with 3 layers for the two paradigms **(a, b)**, plotted as an average over 100 runs, only for the runs that reached convergence criteria. The convergence criteria was defined as having a performance greater than 85% in the last 200 trials. **(c)** Performance for the model with 2 layers on the first learning paradigm.

action-outcome association is to be selected. The selected associations are then modulated by superior layers and used the determine the response. At layer 1, the prediction errors of layer 0 are contextualized to make SxSxAxO conjugations and so on.

In the task considered for all our simulations, there are 5 concrete rules or S-A-O predictions to learn: Black - Action3, Vowel, Lower case - Action1 and Consonant, Upper case - Action2 (Fig. 1(b)). In Fig. 3, we present examples of how a model with 3 layers selects a response by additive prediction modulation. We observed that elaborating a mapping between the stimulus and what is gated into the internal representation (**r**) at different layers could be done in different ways, including randomly, as long as these mappings led to orthogonal and mutually exclusive activations of predictions (in **W**). For example, in Fig. 3(e), in Block 2, the color red was not gated into the internal representation, but the random gating of the other 2 dimensions still led to an appropriate modulated prediction that could initiate the correct response.

### 3.4    New Model

To explain the deficit of attentional mechanism in the HER model, and illustrate the advantage of our proposal, we performed some simple simulations. The model

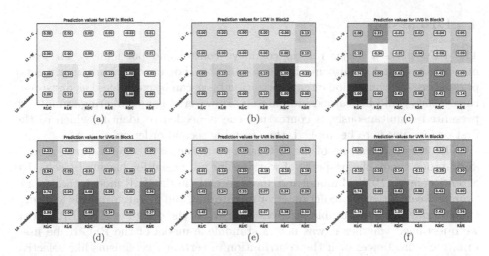

**Fig. 3.** Examples of how the model solves different cases of stimuli. The matrix shows the prediction values at different layers (first 3 rows), given the internal representation of the stimulus, and how they are modulated additively (row 4) to give the final Action-Outcome predictions that are used for response selection. **a, b** show the case when the stimulus is black, in rules 1 and 2 respectively. **d, e** show the case when the stimulus is Green, Vowel (rule T1) and Red, Upper case (rule T2). **c, f** show the case for Green, Vowel and Red, Upper case in rule T3 (Color figure online)

was trained individually on the two discrimination tasks ie, on the two concrete rules (T1 - vowel/consonant and T2 - lower/upper case), to obtain prediction weights or Stimulus-Action-Outcome associations as in Fig. 4(b). We tested the ability of the HER model with 2 layers, to use this information and contextualize it to learn the abstract rule. The bottom layer of the model was initialized to the predictions previously learned and moreover, it was "frozen" such that no learning happened at this level, implying that these behaviors were rigid. At the upper layer, the gating weights were biased to update the internal representation with the context, which was the color in this case, implying saliency to previously unattended cues. As expected, the model failed to learn the abstract rule with these modifications. With the modified model, we used the same protocol i.e. the bottom layer was kept frozen, and there was a bias added to the upper layer to encourage gating of the color. However, instead of an independent gating at the bottom layer, we included an output gating from the upper layer, which used the prediction errors at the upper layer to select which stimulus dimension was going to be gated into the bottom layer (Fig. 4(a)). To put it more generally, the bottom layer was responsible for response selection while the upper layer was responsible for action-set selection through targeted attention (cf [6] for more details about the structuring concept of action-set and its role in PFC information processing). Our modified model achieved optimal performance fairly quickly, as shown in Fig. 4(c).

## 4   Discussion

The PFC plays a major role in cognitive control and particularly for learning, selecting and monitoring hierarchical rules. For example, in experimental paradigms, discrimination or categorization tasks can be considered as first-order rules which could be learned individually. However, when conflicting stimuli are presented simultaneously, a contextual cue is needed to identify which of the first order rules is to be applied, thus forming second-order rules.

The inner mechanisms of the PFC have been studied in computational models and among them, the property of working memory used for biasing by selective attention in the PBWM model and, more recently in the HER model, the separation between outcome prediction error monitoring, and hierarchical rule learning. Considering the indisputable progress brought by the design of the HER model, we questioned whether it was now a standalone model of the PFC to be used in any circumstances or if the contribution of certain mechanisms like selective attention was still to be considered in some cases and possibly added to the

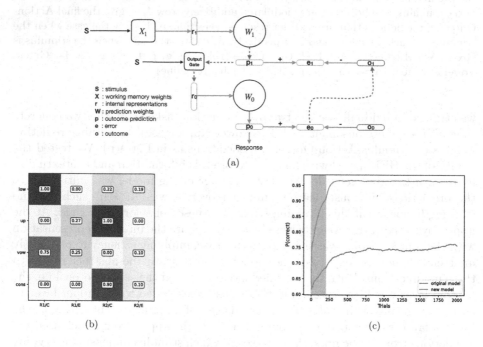

**Fig. 4. (a)** The modified model with output gating from layer 1. The gating weights in layer 1 ($X_1$) learn over time to gate the context into $r_1$. The selected prediction units from layer 1 ($p_1$) are then used to make a decision on which value of the stimulus $s$ is gated into $r_0$ (the output gate). **(b)** Prediction weights ($W_0$) for the concrete rules at layer 0. These weights are pre-learned by training the model with rules T1 and T2, independently. **(c)** Performance of the original model compared to the modified model over a 100 runs, when layer 0 is fixed to the weights in figure (b) and only layer 1 prediction weights ($W_1$) and gating weights ($X_1$) are learned.

general framework of PFC modeling. More specifically, considering the deployment of cognitive control in realistic behavioral tasks and considering that most hierarchical representations arise from the intersection between agents and the problems they face, and are created over time in a learning process, in a rapid and flexible way, our question was to know if the HER model could account for this kind of process.

Using a task elaborated along two paradigms, we show that, when concrete rules are already learnt and need to be contextualized, the use of a biasing selective attention mechanism is more effective than modulated weights changes in displaying effective cognitive control. When concrete rules are acquired first, superior layers must learn to select the appropriate concrete rule by targeted attention, rather than by relearning representations. We observe that a subject can perform optimally on a given task even though she uses a different rule representation compared to the *official* one. On a single task, this has no consequence and there is actually no way to know which exact rule is used internally. However, when this rule needs to be composed with another rule such as to form a new rule, this may pose problem and lead to bad performance. This has been illustrated on the task: if a subject uses any of the alternative rules for tasks T1 or T2, she'll be unable to solve task T3 even though this task is merely made of a mix of T1 or T2 trials. The reason for the failure of the HER model in this case is to be found in the failure to attend the relevant dimension of the task, here, color, thus claiming for considering and incorporating this mechanism to a versatile PFC model. Analyzing these results in a more general view, we can remark that most experimental paradigms that study hierarchy break down the complexity of a task by providing instructional cues to the participant. Even in studies with rodents and non-human primates, shaping is used in learning paradigms to enable the learning of complex or abstract rules. In developmental learning, this kind of shaping is called curriculum learning. It is evident that such breaking down of complexity must facilitate the acquisition of abstract rules, and hence modeling approaches must demonstrate these behavioral results.

From a more conceptual point of view, the term *hierarchy* can be used in many different ways, two common ones being *processing hierarchies* and *representational hierarchies*. In the first, higher levels exert control over lower levels, for example by controlling the flow of information or by setting the agenda for lower levels [9]. In the second one, higher levels form abstractions over lower levels, such that lower levels contain concrete, sensory and fine-grained information, whereas higher levels contain general, conceptual and integrated information [3, 11]. It is thus important that a model of the PFC to exploit both views, suggesting to incorporate an attentional mechanism for the flexible and controlled design of hierarchical rules from previously learned concrete rules, as we proposed in the new model sketched here.

# References

1. Alexander, W.H., Brown, J.W.: Hierarchical error representation: a computational model of anterior cingulate and dorsolateral prefrontal cortex. Neural Comput. **27**(11), 2354–2410 (2015)
2. Alexander, W.H., Brown, J.W.: Frontal cortex function as derived from hierarchical predictive coding. Sci. Rep. **8**(1), 3843 (2018). https://doi.org/10.1038/s41598-018-21407-9
3. Badre, D.: Cognitive control, hierarchy, and the rostro-caudal organization of the frontal lobes. Trends Cogn. Sci. **12**(5), 193–200 (2008)
4. Badre, D., Kayser, A.S., D'Esposito, M.: Frontal cortex and the discovery of abstract action rules. Neuron **66**(2), 315–326 (2010)
5. Daw, N.D., Niv, Y., Dayan, P.: Uncertainty-based competition between prefrontal and dorsolateral striatal systems for behavioral control. Nat. Neurosci. **8**(12), 1704–1711 (2005). https://doi.org/10.1038/nn1560
6. Domenech, P., Koechlin, E.: Executive control and decision-making in the prefrontal cortex. Curr. Opin. Behav. Sci. **1**, 101–106 (2015). https://doi.org/10.1016/j.cobeha.2014.10.007
7. Frank, M.J., Badre, D.: Mechanisms of hierarchical reinforcement learning in corticostriatal circuits 1: computational analysis. Cereb. Cortex **22**(3), 509–526 (2012)
8. Koechlin, E., Ody, C., Kouneiher, F.: The architecture of cognitive control in the human prefrontal cortex. Science **302**(5648), 1181–1185 (2003)
9. Miller, E.K., Cohen, J.D.: An integrative theory of prefrontal cortex function. Annu. Rev. Neurosci. **24**(1), 167–202 (2001)
10. O'Reilly, R.C., Frank, M.J.: Making working memory work: a computational model of learning in the prefrontal cortex and basal ganglia. Neural Comput. **18**(2), 283–328 (2006)
11. Tenenbaum, J.B., Kemp, C., Griffiths, T.L., Goodman, N.D.: How to grow a mind: statistics, structure, and abstraction. Science **331**(6022), 1279–1285 (2011)

# Detection of Healthy and Unhealthy Brain States from Local Field Potentials Using Machine Learning

Marcos I. Fabietti[1(✉)], Mufti Mahmud[1,4,5], Ahmad Lotfi[1],
Alessandro Leparulo[2], Roberto Fontana[3], Stefano Vassanelli[2],
and Cristina Fassolato[2]

[1] Department of Computer Science, Nottingham Trent University, Clifton,
Nottingham NG11 8NS, UK
ignaf93@gmail.com, mufti.mahmud@ntu.ac.uk
[2] Department of Biomedical Sciences, University of Padua,
Via U. Bassi 58/B, 35131 Padua, Italy
[3] Sapienza Università di Roma, Rome, Italy
[4] Computing and Informatics Research Centre, Nottingham Trent University,
Clifton, Nottingham NG11 8NS, UK
[5] Medical Technologies Innovation Facility, Nottingham Trent University,
Clifton, Nottingham NG11 8NS, UK

**Abstract.** Neural signals are the recordings of the electrical activity individual or groups of neurons, and they are used for disease staging, brain-computer interface control and understanding the neural processes. When carrying out a functional connectivity study in rodents, processing must be done to eliminate disturbance in the data in order to have the most faithful representation of the neural activity. This step mainly includes filtering and artefact removal, where the latter can be approached by diverse methods. Furthermore, it is important to identify when the rodent is stressed, as the local field potentials can be coupled to theta oscillations. To this end, we set out to develop a machine learning-based model for the detection of stress in rodents with multi-modal recordings, namely local field potentials, respiration and electrocardiography. We explore subject-specific and cross-subject models, as well as employing an artefact detection model as a generic anomaly detector. Results show that subject-specific models can achieve a good performance, but the variability is significant across all three signals among rodents of the same age, gender and species.

**Keywords:** Computational neuroscience · Machine learning · Physiological signals

## 1 Introduction

Neural signals are used in many applications, such as the detection of Alzheimer's disease, attention deficit hyperactivity disorder, Parkinson's disease, seizures,

M. Mahmud et al. (Eds.): BI 2022, LNAI 13406, pp. 27–39, 2022
https://doi.org/10.1007/978-3-031-15037-1_3

etc. [1, 2]. When studying specific structures within the brain, animal models allow the recording of neural activity via invasive methods carried out without the limitations of human experimentation, both technical and ethical. Benefits of the invasive signals include less susceptibility to noise and a higher spatial resolution, allowing specific structures within the brain to be studied.

To achieve a successful analysis of neuronal signals, they must have a minimal amount of disturbance. To this end, processing is applied to the signals to standardise the data by removing phenomenons that may interfere with the study [3]. This includes filtering, baseline drift removal, artefact removal and stress removal. The first one is used to capture the band-with of interest, e.g. less than 300 Hz for LFP, and to remove power-line noise, as it has a specific band of 50 or 60 Hz. Baseline drift can be generated from a diverse range of sources, including perspiration, respiration, body movements, and poor electrode contact, and is detrimental to power spectral analysis. Similarly, artefacts detection and removal techniques have been developed to counter the diverse range of disturbances, from stimulation to spike bleeding [4, 5]. However, no research has been done which focuses on automatic systems which detect anaesthesia-related stress in a rodent, as mostly it is done by a manual review of the data, via supporting channels of other modalities, or video recordings [6]. The detection and removal of these segments are crucial, as they can distort the neural recordings, biasing results. We define stress as a period where alterations in the respiration frequency or heart rate are measured compared to the baseline.

The process of manual review of neural recording requires a significant amount of time, which could be used instead for posterior analysis. In this scenario, developing automatic techniques to identify stress can be of great benefit to researchers. Machine Learning (ML) techniques are algorithms that learn from patterns in data and are able to make predictions of new data based on it. Within neuroscience, the application of these models to process large datasets to diagnose, classify patterns, control brain-machine interfaces and gain insight into the brain has risen [7].

In this article, we present our research into ML-based stress detection in LFP obtained from rodents. The remainder of the paper is organised as follows: in Sect. 2 we explain the methodology, including data acquisition, processing and the employed ML models. Afterwards Sect. 3 we show the results, followed by a discussion in Sect. 4 and lastly Sect. 5 finished with the conclusion.

## 2 Methodology

The methodology is composed of three sections, where we describe first the data acquisition, second the signal processing and lastly the ML models used.

### 2.1 Data Acquisition

For the analysis, five three-month-old female C57BL/6J (WT) mice were used. The mice were anaesthetised for the recording process with a initial dose of urethane followed by a mixture of xylazine/tiletamine-zolazepam after 30 min. A

32-electrode-silicon probe (ATLAS Neuro Probe: E32-100-S1-L6-NT; pointy tip feature; 100 $\mu$m spaced electrodes; mean impedance 0.28 M$\Omega$ in Krebs' solution) was utilised to record the LFP from the dentate gyrus up to the cortical layers. The LFP, along with the supporting electrocardiogram (ECG) and respiration signals were recorded at 10 kHz for further processing. All of the animals were kept in an SPF animal facility with a 12-hour duration of light and dark cycles and unrestricted access to food and water. The experimental procedures were performed according to the European Committee guidelines (decree 2010/63/CEE) and the Animal Welfare Act (7 USC 2131), in compliance with the ARRIVE guidelines. They were approved by the Animal Care Committee of the University of Padua and the Italian Ministry of Health (authorisation decree 522/2018-PR). For more details, we refer the reader to the published experimental analysis [1,8].

## 2.2   Signal Processing

Offline data processing of electrophysiological signals was carried out in Matlab utilising custom-written scripts. To begin, the Open-Ephys format files with the recorded signals from the different channels were converted to Matlab file format. Subsequently, the raw signals had the 50 Hz noise and its harmonics removed via the application of a gaussian filter. The first 24 channels' signals were filtered using the built-in non-causal zero-phase distortion filtering algorithm, which in order to avoid phase distortion, the data is processed in both forward and reverse directions using coefficients from the built-in Butterworth transfer function. Using a median estimation approach, baseline drift was eliminated from the ECG and respiration signals. Afterwards, the recordings were low-pass filtered (filter order: 5; cut-off frequency: 190 Hz for LFP, 25 Hz for ECG, and 10 Hz for respiration) and down-sampled to 500 Hz, 50 Hz and 20 Hz, respectively.

A three-step method was used to automatically identify stable LFP windows using respiratory and ECG data. In the first step, a script calculates the respiration and heartbeat rates and using specific upper and lower bounds, anomalous patterns were identified. By taking the median of the individual rates and adding/subtracting a tolerance margin of 20%, the boundary values were obtained. As a result, we have a labelled LFP as normal where both signals were steady and stressed when either one was not stable. Figure 1 showcases the behaviour of the three signals under normal (A) and stress (B) cases, where in the latter, there are some fast oscillations in the LFP, irregular heartbeats in the electrocardiogram, and abnormal cycles in the respiration recording.

The LFP of the five rodents were labelled with −1 for stress and 1 for normal. The statistical model of the duration of stress segments was 10 s, the shortest lasting 4 s and the longest 48 s. Out of each stress segment, non-overlapping windows of 1 s were extracted to create the examples which would be shown to the model, and the same amount was randomly sampled from normal segments. A total of 47808 stress examples and 47808 normal examples constituted the final dataset.

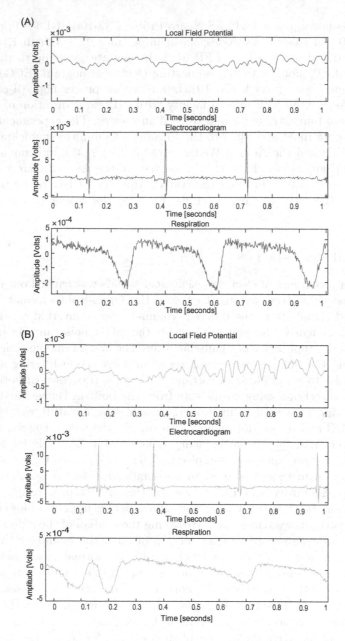

**Fig. 1.** One second segments of local field potential, electrocardiogram and respiration signals in (A) normal state (B) stressed state.

We then created models trained with different characteristics or features of the examples, including the following set of features:

– The raw signal.

- From the Pawfe Toolbox [9]: integrated absolute value, mean absolute value, slope sign change, zero crossing, mean absolute value slope, root mean square, RMS, waveform length, time domain, histogram, the marginal discrete wavelet transform.
- From the EEG-FET Toolbox [10]: ratio of band power alpha to beta, band power gamma, band power beta, band power alpha, band power theta, band power delta, hjorth activity, hjorth mobility, hjorth complexity, skewness, kurtosis, first difference, normalised first difference, second difference, normalised second difference, mean curve length, mean energy, mean teager energy, log root sum of sequential variation, tsallis entropy, shannon entropy, log energy entropy, renyi entropy, arithmetic mean, standard deviation, variance, median value, auto-regressive model, maximum value, minimum value.
- The Fourier transform of the signal.
- Spectral features: power per band, ratios among bands and relative power, where the bands are defined as: 0.1–1.7 Hz slow oscillations, 1.7–4.7 Hz delta, 4.7–10 Hz theta, 10–25 Hz beta, 25–45 Hz low gamma, 45–90 Hz high gamma and 90–125 Hz fast oscillations.

For the subject-specific models, data from each rodent was split into training (80%) and validation (20%), and tested with the full data of the other rodents. Similarly, for the cross-subject models, we combined the samples of all the rodents and split them into training (80%) and testing (20%). In both cases, no normalisation of features was used.

## 2.3  Machine Learning Classification Models

ML techniques are a series of algorithms that can learn patterns in data in order to make accurate predictions in unseen examples. While there are a substantial amount of techniques and models, including the sub-topic of deep learning, we explored five different models which can be used to deal with non-linear data such as neural signals. These techniques are the following:

*Decision Trees:* Decision Tree (DT) algorithms can be used to build both classifications and regression trees, where each internal node has exactly two outgoing edges, namely binary trees. The splits are selected using Gini index as a splitting criterion and the obtained tree is pruned by cost-complexity pruning.

*Ensemble of Decision Trees:* Ensemble Techniques (ET) combines many decision tree classifiers to create more accurate predictions than a single decision tree classifier. The basic idea underlying the ensemble model is that a number of weak learners cooperate to produce a strong learner, enhancing the model's accuracy.

*Multi Layered Perceptron:* A Multi-Layered Perceptron (MLP) is an ML algorithm for the analysis of patterns and classification. It consists of no less than three parts: an input layer, a hidden layer and an output layer. When it contains multiple numbers of hidden layers, it helps in modelling complex non-linear relations better than the shallow architecture.

*Support Vector Machines:* Support vector machines (SVM) are learning machines premised on the statistical learning theory, where the model optimally separates the classes by determining the maximal margin hyperplane. This optimal hyperplane should maximise the margin between the data from the positive class and the negative class.

*k-Nearest Neighbours:* The k-Nearest Neighbours (kNN) classifier employs metrics of distance to labeled examples as to categorise new ones. The parameter k indicates the number of neighbours that will be chosen to compare, which has a major influence on the accuracy of kNN algorithm.

Having described the different classification models used, we proceed to report on the results obtained by the various approaches to the stress detection task.

## 3   Results

In this section, we will first report the results obtained by the subject-specific model with ECG and respiration, followed by the cross-subject model with LFP and lastly, a generic LFP anomaly detector.

### 3.1   Subject-Specific Model with ECG and Respiration

In Fig. 2, the box plot of the heartbeat per second and respiration rate are shown, for both normal and stress states of each rodent. Each rodent behaves differently, more so than the difference among the states. This means that a cross-subject model is unlikely to achieve good results. In order to test this, we build first several classifiers with the heartbeat per second and respiration rate of a single rodent, where the best performance was obtained by the kNN. Afterwards, we built a model for each rodent and classified the recording of the other rodents, where the results are compiled in Table 1. The row in the table indicates the rodent used to train the model, and the column the rodent whose data is being predicted. The inability of a model trained with the data of a single rodent to have a stress detection accuracy perform well with another rodent confirms that there is a bigger difference between the animal's respiration and ECG than between the individual "stress" and "normal" states. With the results of these modalities in mind, we proceed to train the models with LFPs in cross-subject and inter-subject manners in order to evaluate their feasibility.

### 3.2   Cross Subject Model with LFP

We trained several classifiers for a cross-subject model, that are compiled in Table 2. The features with the best performances are achieved by the raw signal followed by the Fourier transform of the signal. In regards to the methods, DT achieves the lowest accuracies, with the best performing features being the Fourier transform. The use of ET boost the performance significantly, however

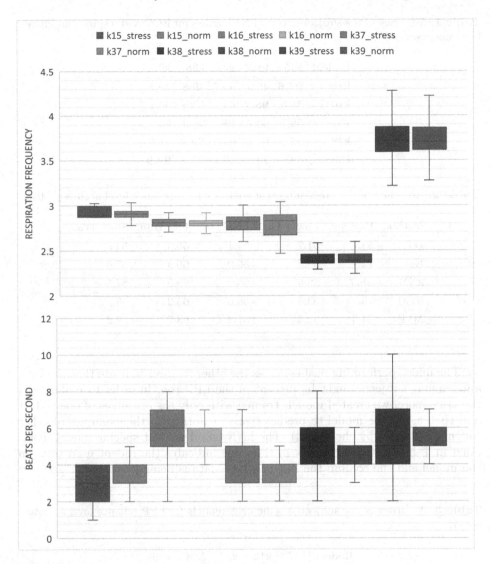

**Fig. 2.** Respiration frequency and beats per second of normal and stress segments per rodent.

the best model is the one trained with the raw signal. Both SVM and MLP perform similarly, where the best models are those trained with the raw signal.

Lastly, the model with the best performance is the kNN with raw signal, where the model has been able to accurately classify 95.2% of the stress segments and 84.2% of the normal segments. This means that the euclidean distance among stress segments is smaller than in the normal segments. As it has yielded the best results, for the remainder of the article, we will be using the combination of kNN with the raw signal.

**Table 1.** Accuracy of the subject-specific kNN models for ECG and respiration (chance level accuracy 50%).

| Rodent | k15 | k16 | k37 | k38 | k39 |
|--------|------|------|------|------|------|
| k15 | **97.6** | 49.9 | 49.7 | 49.8 | 50.1 |
| k16 | 54.6 | **98.7** | 54.1 | 53.6 | 50.1 |
| k37 | 58.7 | 63.7 | **98** | 98.9 | 53.2 |
| k38 | 59 | 64.2 | 51.3 | **99.2** | 51.5 |
| k39 | 42.3 | 50 | 50.1 | 50 | **99.9** |

**Table 2.** Accuracy of the cross-subject models for LFP (chance level accuracy 50%).

| Method | Raw sig. | Pawfe Tbx. | EEGTbx. | Fou.Tran. | Spec. Fea. |
|--------|----------|------------|---------|-----------|------------|
| DT | 53.7 | 51.7 | 54.1 | 55.3 | 54.5 |
| ET | 72.7 | 53.3 | 56.9 | 60.3 | 57.6 |
| kNN | **89.7** | 53.5 | 55.2 | 69.5 | 57.5 |
| SVM | 76.7 | 53.5 | 56.6 | 65.2 | 56 |
| MLP | 74.3 | 52.3 | 57.3 | 63.7 | 57.2 |

The under-performing results across the other features indicate that the variance among subjects might be present in the LFP too. In order to understand the issue more, we created models trained with only the examples of one rodent and then asked the model to predict stress or normal in the examples of other rodents (not seen by the model). The kNN-based subject specific models compiled in Table 3, where the row in the table indicates the rodent used to train the model and the column the rodent whose data is being predicted.

**Table 3.** Accuracy of the subject-specific kNN models for LFP (chance level accuracy 50%).

| Rodent | k15 | k16 | k37 | k38 | k39 |
|--------|------|------|------|------|------|
| k15 | **96.6** | 53.4 | 49.1 | 48.4 | 49.9 |
| k16 | 47.0 | **99.8** | 46.8 | 51.0 | 49.7 |
| k37 | 45.1 | 49.7 | **94.3** | 49.6 | 49.3 |
| k38 | 49.6 | 53.2 | 47.1 | **99.1** | 50.6 |
| k39 | 49.3 | 54.7 | 47.4 | 52.6 | **85.0** |

Overall there is a poor cross-subject generalisation; therefore, instead of identifying the stress in a signal, we changed the example's labels instead to which animal they had come from (regardless of stressed or normal). This was done in order to evaluate that if the computational methods are able to correctly identify from which animal the example came from, the differences among animals is significant and bigger than the difference among stress and normal states. The results are compiled in Table 4, where several methods achieve good performance. The best results across all models are obtained with the Fourier transform of the signal, indicating that the differences among rodents are strongly represented in the spectral properties of the signals. This is why the extracted spectral features and the features from the EEG toolbox perform noticeably better than the Pawfe toolbox and the raw signal. It is worth noting that even those sets of features that were poorly discriminant for stress and normal classes produce a great result for identifying the animal.

**Table 4.** Accuracy of the subject identifier models of LFP (chance level accuracy 50%).

| Method | Raw Sig. | Pawfe Tbx. | EEGTbx. | Fou.Tran. | Spec. Fea. |
|--------|----------|------------|---------|-----------|------------|
| DT  | 67.9 | 77.4 | 90.2 | 95.2 | 90.9 |
| ET  | 87.2 | 81.1 | 91.9 | 96.5 | 93.0 |
| kNN | 96.3 | 78.4 | 89.1 | 95.6 | 91.3 |
| SVM | 87.4 | 80.3 | 91.5 | 97.3 | 93.0 |
| MLP | 97.3 | 83.5 | 92.4 | 97.5 | 93.4 |

### 3.3   LFP Anomality Detector

Alternatively, we also explored the possibility of using a classifier trained for artefact detection as a generic anomaly detector. We propose three approaches: (1) using the trained classifier in this new task, (2) applying transfer learning and lastly (3) using it for feature extraction in conjunction with a classifier. We used a private dataset of LFP acquired in freely moving rodents, where specialists have labelled segments of the signal as artefactual or not based on the power of an artefact-free portion [11]. In order to not introduce a new bias of the model, signal processing was done to match the characteristics between the datasets, including down-sampling from 1 kHz to 500 Hz and up-scaling from microvolts to millivolts.

Afterwards, we extracted 1-second non-overlapping normal and artefacts and used it to train a 1D-CNN, a model which has achieved the best performance for the task [12]. The network is an adaptation of AlexNet [13], which was done by flattening one dimension of the filters and pooling layers, and the components of the 12-layer architecture are listed in Table 5. The convolutional layer filter sizes are expressed inside brackets, multiplied by the quantity and succeeded by the stride (s) and the same notation is used for the pooling window's sizes and stride. The input size, number rectified linear unit in the fully connected layers and soft max units in the classification layer are within brackets as well. The number of filters was decreased to multiples of 16 due to the lower dimensionality of the input. The optimisation algorithm used to train it was Adam, with an initial learning rate of 0.001, the momentum of 0.9 and a batch size of 256. A balanced dataset of 43840 examples was split into training (70%), validation (15%) and testing (15%), where the performance accuracy on the different sets was 98.44% for training, 98.21% for validation and 96.8% for testing.

**Table 5.** Architecture of the 1D-CNN model.

| Architecture | Component |
|---|---|
| Layer 1 | Input [500] |
| Layer 2 | Convolution 1 [1,11] x 32, s = 1 |
| Layer 3 | Max Pooling 1 [1,3], s = 2 |
| Layer 4 | Convolution 2 [1,5] x 64, s = 1 |
| Layer 5 | Max Pooling2 [1,3], s = 2 |
| Layer 6 | Convolution 3 [1,3] x 128, s = 1 |
| Layer 7 | Convolution 4 [1,3] x 128, s=1 |
| Layer 8 | Convolution 5 [1,3] x 128, s = 1 |
| Layer 9 | Max Pooling 3 [1,3], s =2 |
| Layer 10 | Fully Connected [1024] |
| Layer 11 | Fully Connected [512] |
| Layer 12 | Classification [2] |

The results of the three approaches are compiled in Table 6. Employing the classifier directly shows poorer results, as most of the stress segments are classified as normal. This can be attributed to the fact that artefacts have a higher amplitude and the waveform has no resemblance to physiological activity. Fine-tuning leads to slightly better results, but the model struggles with this new task. Lastly, feature extraction and a KNN classifier yield worse results than the previous subject-specific models in Table 3 as the waveform information is lost, in addition to the same lack of generalisation when used in other rodents.

**Table 6.** Results of the generic anomaly detector (chance level accuracy 50%).

| Method | Metric | k15 | k16 | k37 | k38 | k39 |
|---|---|---|---|---|---|---|
| Classification | Accuracy | 43.6% | 50.9% | 49.8% | 49.7% | 50.0% |
| | Specificity | 78.0% | 87.8% | 92.0% | 94.0% | 95.5% |
| | Sensitivity | 18.3% | 12.5% | 7.9% | 6.0% | 4.5% |
| Fine-tuning | Val. Accuracy | 55.9% | 55.9% | 53.7% | 52.6% | 52.7% |
| Feature extraction + kNN | Acc | 89.5% | 88.0% | 75.3% | 70.7% | 65.9% |
| | Specificity | 84.7% | 85.5% | 75.2% | 69.6% | 65.0% |
| | Sensitivity | 96.2% | 90.4% | 75.5% | 71.9% | 66.8% |

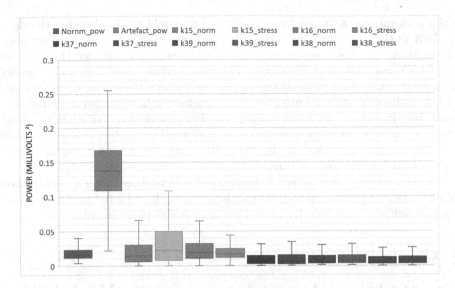

**Fig. 3.** From left to wright, box-plots of the power of normal and artefact examples from external dataset and power of normal and stress segments per rodent.

In order to understand the difference among the tasks and transfer-learning limitations, boxplots of the power of each segment for normal and artefact examples from external dataset and power of normal and stress segments per rodent is presented in Fig. 3. The power of a signal is the main characteristic used to label artefacts, and as it is shown in the figure it is significantly bigger compared to normal signals. While stressed states have slightly higher power than normal ones, the difference is smaller, explaining why the network struggles in this new task.

## 4 Discussion

Researchers in the field of neuroscience are familiar with the struggles of variability. Comparing the brain and neural activity, the most complex organ, among subjects is no simple task. The variability can be inter-subject (when comparing different subjects), intra-subject (the same subject, over time) and inter trials (the same subject across trials). The impact of this uncontrollable variable limits the performance of ML classifiers, and is one of the main challenges of several applications. For example, in emotion recognition with EEG, we find reported cross-subject accuracies from 38.7% to 53.8% [14]. The impact of variability have also been explored for brain computer interface decoding [15], inhibition brain function [16], drowsiness detection [17] and others.

For newcomers to the field or those from other areas such as computer science, a cross-subject performance nearing 50% is arguably a positive result, especially when compared to other fields such as image recognition. In such fields, the models are expected to out-perform the chance level accuracy, that is referred to as the performance achieved by a classifier that would randomly label the data (i.e. 50% in the balanced binary classification scenario). However, we have been able to achieve subject-specific models with excellent performance through the use of kNN and the raw LFP signal. This means that a portable online model could be developed for stress detection in cases where these supporting signals are not available due to the presence of an artefact or have gotten disconnected. To our best knowledge, no other studies have been conducted on automatic stress detection on animal models, which can be attributed to the fact that researchers still rely on manual review of the data. We hope this research can aid those looking to reduce the review time.

Future work includes the use of transfer learning to show that a model trained with the data of a group of rodents can be successfully adapted to detect stress in a new subject with little training data sample size requirements.

## 5   Conclusion

We set out to build a model to identify stressed segments in LFP obtained from rodents. First, we developed models with features of the supplementary signals, respiratory frequency and beats per second. Wewe found that while a subject-specific model could be achieved (>98% accuracy on average), these models couldn't be used to predict stress in other rodents with good results. Thus, we focused on analysing the LFP signal in itself, where we extracted different features for a cross-subject model and achieved good performance with a kNN and the raw signal. Commonly extracted features of local field potential such as power bands, relative power and ratios to the theta band were not class-discriminative, suggesting that the LFP activity during stress presents subtle differences compared to normal activity.

When looking at subject-specific models, we found the same lack of generalisation present in the models built with the supporting signals. This means that the difference among subjects is bigger than the states of "normal" and "stressed" across all the modalities. While this may be attributed to biological differences, the effect of anaesthesia may also have a role in it. To sum up, achieving good generalisation is not possible due to these differences; however, the results are acceptable compared to other brain signal cross-subject ML applications.

## References

1. Leparulo, A., Mahmud, M., Scremin, E., Pozzan, T., Vassanelli, S., Fasolato, C.: Dampened slow oscillation connectivity anticipates amyloid deposition in the ps2a pp mouse model of Alzheimer's disease. Cells **9**(1), 54 (2020)
2. Lenartowicz, A., Loo, S.K.: Use of EEG to diagnose ADHD. Curr. Psychiatry Rep. **16**(11), 1–11 (2014)
3. Mahmud, M., Vassanelli, S.: Processing and analysis of multichannel extracellular neuronal signals: state-of-the-art and challenges. Front. Neurosci. **10**, 248 (2016)

4. Hashimoto, T., Elder, C.M., Vitek, J.L.: A template subtraction method for stimulus artifact removal in high-frequency deep brain stimulation. J. Neurosci. Methods **113**(2), 181–186 (2002)
5. Boroujeni, K.B., Tiesinga, P., Womelsdorf, T.: Adaptive spike-artifact removal from local field potentials uncovers prominent beta and gamma band neuronal synchronization. J. Neurosci. Methods **330** (2020)
6. Fabietti, M., Mahmud, M., Lotfi, A.: Channel-independent recreation of artefactual signals in chronically recorded local field potentials using machine learning. Brain Inform. **9**(1), 1–17 (2022). https://doi.org/10.1186/s40708-021-00149-x
7. Fellous, J.-M., Sapiro, G., Rossi, A., Mayberg, H., Ferrante, M.: Explainable artificial intelligence for neuroscience: behavioral neurostimulation. Front. Neurosci. **13**, 1346 (2019)
8. Leparulo, A., Bisio, M., Redolfi, N., Pozzan, T., Vassanelli, S., Fasolato, C.: Accelerated Aging Characterizes the Early Stage of Alzheimer's Disease. Cells **11**(2), 239 (2021)
9. Atzori, M., Müller, H.: PaWFE: fast signal feature extraction using parallel time windows. Front. Neurorobot. **13**, 74 (2019)
10. Too, J.: EEG feature extraction toolbox. [Online]. https://github.com/JingweiToo/EEG-Feature-Extraction-Toolbox
11. Averna, A., et al.: Differential effects of open-and closed-loop intracortical microstimulation on firing patterns of neurons in distant cortical areas. Cerebral Cortex **30**(5), 2879–2896 (2020)
12. NeuroImage Fabietti, M., et al.: Adaptation of convolutional neural networks for multi-channel artifact detection in chronically recorded local field potentials. In: 2020 IEEE Symposium Series on Computational Intelligence (SSCI), pp. 1607–1613. IEEE (2020)
13. Krizhevsky, A., Sutskever, I., Hinton, G.E. ImageNet classification with deep convolutional neural networks. In: Advances in Neural Information Processing Systems, pp. 1097–1105 (2012)
14. Cimtay, Y., Ekmekcioglu, E., Caglar-Ozhan, S.: Cross-subject multimodal emotion recognition based on hybrid fusion. IEEE Access **8**, 168 865–168 878 (2020)
15. Saha, S., Baumert, M.: Intra-and inter-subject variability in EEG-based sensorimotor brain computer interface: a review. Front. Comput. Neurosci. **13**, 87 (2020)
16. Chikara, R.K., Ko, L.-W.: Prediction of human inhibition brain function with inter-subject and intra-subject variability. Brain Sci. **10**(10), 726 (2020)
17. Wei, C.-S., Lin, Y.-P., Wang, Y.-T., Lin, C.-T., Jung, T.-P.: A subject-transfer framework for obviating inter-and intra-subject variability in EEG-based drowsiness detection. NeuroImage **174**, 407–419 (2018)

# COSLETS: Recognition of Emotions Based on EEG Signals

R. Narendra[1]([⊠])(ID), M. Suresha[1](ID), and V. N. Manjunatha Aradhya[2](ID)

[1] Department of Computer Science, Kuvempu University, Shivamogga 577451, India
naren44.mys@gmail.com, suresham@kuvempu.ac.in
[2] Department of Computer Applications, JSS Science & Technology University, Mysuru 570006, India
aradhya@sjce.ac.in

**Abstract.** In the recent years, one of the leading technology which is earning greater mode of interest in the growing various fields of artificial intelligence is Brain computer interfaces (BCI). Recognizing emotions based on physiological signals specifically, Electroencephalography (EEG) signals with advancement of BCI applications, has turn into a very popular research topic. In this paper for effective representation of features the proposed model adopts COSLETS transformation approach, a combination DCT (Discrete Cosine Transform) and wavelets Transform. The obtained set of features is mapped on to the low dimensional subspace to employ principal components using PCA and finally GRNN (General Regression Neural Network) is presented for effective classification of four different emotional states from publicly available EEG based GAMEEMO dataset. The experimental results are promising and performed well, compared to other state of methods.

**Keywords:** BCI-Brain computer interfaces · EEG signals · Emotion recognition · COSLETS · GRNN

## 1 Introduction

Interaction of every individual along various external environment in their day-to-day activities relies on emotions. Emotion plays a essential role in the life of human beings as they produce different aspects, which is indicial of human behaviour and described in assorted ways depending upon the particular situations, perceiving and understanding emotional states is part of human interaction. It is defined as the mental condition of a person which includes thoughts, feelings, behaviour, and psycho-physiological responses to external or internal stimuli. Reciprocal action between humans and machines exists in many environs, by the means of BCI technology [9]. More and more researchers across the globe have evaluated the nature of emotions significantly by the means of facial expressions, speech, body gesture in various areas such as e-learning, recommend system, smart home, smart city and intelligent conversational systems.

M. Mahmud et al. (Eds.): BI 2022, LNAI 13406, pp. 40–49, 2022
https://doi.org/10.1007/978-3-031-15037-1_4

According to the experience of researchers from previous studies, resolving with lack of compatibility in traditional emotion recognition based on facial expression, speech, and other characteristics was not more accurate with recognizing emotions based on physiological electrical signals, which is more arduous to be counterfeit thereby reflecting the individual's true emotions. With the advancement of cost-effective sensor technologies, an investigation into emotion recognition has grown progressively popular among EEG [7,8] signals which are depicted by the fact that EEG signals are tough to cover up and have a real-time discrepancy. It is leading non-invasive type of BCI involved in measuring brain's electrical activity. Established the antecedent methods of EEG-based emotions recognition from it's enlighten characteristics are reported in brief. In the past, recent for intently recognizing emotions of different classes upon different applications, researchers focused on the following benchmark data sets: SEED [1], DEAP [3], MANHOBHCI [2], DREAMER [9], ASCERTAIN [4], AMIGOS [6] and GAMEEMO [5] and in-depth knowledge and extensive works on these familiar datasets can found in [10–13]. Recognition of emotions based on EEG signals are split into the sequence of steps: (1) inducing emotions, (2) recording EEG signals, (3) prepossessing of signals, (4) feature extraction, (5) EEG feature dimensional reduction from feature selection or feature transformation techniques, (6) Study of emotional patterns and classifications. In above all mentioned phases, each one is bottom-line factors in analysing emotional states. Good deal of efforts from researchers for all phases have been accomplished in adaptive EEG based BCI systems. In this paper proposed study targeted interest on mapping Large/High dimension data into new decreased low dimension one for making classification stage easier in predicting different emotional states.

## 2   Related Work

In the area of machine learning there are often many factors arise resulting in different problems on the basis of which final classification is done, one of the most essential factor is number of input features. When there is a higher number of input feature, it gets tough to visualize the training set and then working on it, generally most of these features are correlated, and leads to redundancy. At this situation, dimension reduction (DR) algorithms come into play [14]. It is the processes of reducing enormous amount of random variables under consideration, by gathering a set of principal variables. It is increasingly becoming very popular in growing research fields of various applications such as Signal processing [17], Speech processing, Neuroinformatic [15], Bioinformatic [16]. Necessary benefits can be obtained by processing dimension reduction techniques some of them are: data storage reduction, minimum computation time, redundant data can be eliminated, minimization of noise can be achieved to have good quality of data. It simplifies classification process, resulting best accuracy rates and visualization of data can be boosted. Basically DR can be divided into feature selection and feature extraction. In the past, recent literature, researchers focused on various DR algorithms such as PCA (Principal Component Analysis), ICA (Independent Component Analysis),

GA (Genetic Algorithm), LDA (Linear Discriminant Analysis) etc., for different applications of EEG signals. In the year 2020 Gao et al. [18], PCA algorithm was applied on EEG signal for classifying emotion along with fusion of power Spectrum and wavelet energy entropy features resulting in good classification accuracy. In the study of Granados et al. [19] used EEG signals, electrocardiogram and galvanic skin response for developing emotion classification model based on advanced classical machine learning approaches. According to the 2-dimensional emotion model (valence/arousal). Li et al. [24] proposed emotion recognition model from extraction of frequency related features using RASM (rational asymmetry) and LSTM (Long-short-term-memory network) for temporal related EEG signals. Alhagry et al. [20] presented a model for classifying emotions into low/high arousal valence and liking states from raw EEG signals of DEAP dataset by applying LSTM to extract relevant features. In this study productive emotion classification method for EEG signals from various types of video games is presented using GAMEEMO database. This particular dataset was focused by researchers in emotion recognition using different methods in recent years some of them are Turcer et al. [21], developed LEDPatNet19 model by achieving 92% of classification accuracy. GoogleNet model based deep learning approach was proposed by Muzaffer Aslan [22] by converting EEG signals into EEG images using continuous wavelet transform with classification accuracy of 98.53 for SVM and 98.78 for K-NN. Sengul Dogan [23] achieved 99% of results in developing accurate emotion classification system in bringing about novel feature generation tetromino pattern.

Being motivated from the above mentioned literature, any machine learning algorithm primary desire is to have small number of features as input for appropriately producing outstanding results for all type of data domains. In this backdrop we begin our proposed study in conducting experiments for enhanced classification rates in recognizing emotions from EEG signals followed by designing feature generation algorithm using transformation technique called COSLETS. The proposed algorithm has been tested on GAMEEMO EEG dataset. The presented work performed well in achieving promising results when compared to other state of art techniques. This paper has followed by different sections. Section 3 explains proposed methodology and related theory to the proposed work. Section 4 explains about the classifications. Section 5 tells about the dataset, experimental results, discussion and conclusion of proposed study.

## 3    Proposed Method

The proposed research study is carried out for developing the classification model in recognizing four different emotional states. The proposed method adopts Coslets transformation technique which is inspired by the work [25]. Coslet transformation technique is a combination of two different approaches, DCT and Wavelet Transform. The main objective of this research work is to design feature generation algorithm in reducing dimension of data for recognizing emotions. In accomplishing this task we concentrated on DCT approach which is very popular on compressing the data size. In this work it has been examined to represent EEG data by preserving information with low frequency. Wavelet transforms [33] is used for measuring signal properties which is changing overtime. In this study proposed model extracts features by implementing coslets transformation approach on pre-processed EEG signals, the obtained features vector after transformation are projected onto the lower dimensional feature space employing PCA and finally the data will be given to GRNN for classifying four different emotions classes such as happy, funny, boring and clam.

## 3.1   Discrete Cosine Transform (DCT)

It is one of the popular and suitable transformation technique which plays prominent role in compression schemes [26] and its enlightened properties helps in converting signals which is time series into fundamental frequency components, considerably co-efficients with low frequency are fixed initially and high frequency are followed in the next. DCT is linear Invertible function, defined $f : R^N \rightarrow R^N$ where R is set of Real Numbers and N is the length of the sequence.

Let $f(x)$, $x = 0, 1, 2, 3 \ldots N-1$ be a sequence of length $N$. Then the Notation for 1D DCT consisting $N$ real number is expressed by the following equation

$$\text{F(u)} = \left(\frac{2}{N}\right)^{\frac{1}{2}} + \sum_{x=0}^{N-1} \Delta(x) \left[\cos \frac{(2x+1)u}{2N}\right] f(x) \qquad (1)$$

where $\forall u = 1, 2 \ldots .. m$  are scaling factors

For highly correlated signals DCT is capable of exploring good energy compaction [26]. Employing DCT for EEG Signals let on compressing the useful data to the few primary co-efficient as a consequence only these co-efficient can be used in machine learning algorithm at the stage of classification.

## 3.2   Wavelets

The majority of existent signals are non-stationary in nature, which means signal properties may change over time. To meet the interest of events in this area, analysis of time-frequency approaches are widely used. Short-Time Fourier Transform (STFT) is convention way of Time-frequency analysis, which results in Spectrogram plot. In STFT, Fourier transform of the signal is considered over Short-time-window, although STFT is mostly used time frequency approach it also has limitation, on improvement in time resolution impacting poor frequency resolution (due to Heisenberg's uncertainty principle) to overcome this issue, the substitute to STFT is wavelet transform. Its properties accomplish the task of signals with low frequency being spread over time and high frequency burst appearing on Short intervals. Wavelet transform use wavelet function along with variable size of windows [28]. From the previous sections the obtained DCT co-efficient are analysed using wavelets and proved that it is very effective way for describing information content of signals. Most importantly selection as wavelets bases are highly subjective in nature since it depends on the data being used. We choose 'Haar' as the wavelet basis for representation of data. The difference in information between approximation of signals at $2^{j+1}$ and $2^j$ can be gathered by decomposing the signal on orthogonal basis. In the case where $\varphi(t)$ is orthogonal wavelet, an orthogonal basis of $H_{2j}$ is calculated by scaling the wavelet with co-efficient $2j$ and transforming it on a lattice with an interval $2^{-j}$.

The Haar wavelet's mother wavelet function $\varphi(t)$ can be described as

$$\varphi(t) = \begin{cases} 1, & \& \ 0 \leq t < 1/2, \\ -1, & \frac{1}{2} \leq t < 1, \\ 0, & \& \ otherwise \end{cases}$$

Its scaling function $\varphi(t)$ can be described as

$$\varphi(t) = \begin{cases} 1, & \& \ 0 \leq t < 1, \\ 0, & \& \ otherwise \end{cases}$$

It is perceived that selection of basis, scaling function and wavelets, which leads to achieve good localization in each spatial and Fourier domains. Assuming 'x' as given 1D signal, wavelet composed of stages at the most. Initially we attained two set of co-efficient namely: Approximation co-efficient CA1 and detailed co-efficient CD1. These co-efficient are acquired through convolving signal 'x' with low pass filter for approximation and detail with high pass filter: observed by dyadic decimation.

### 3.3 Principal Component Analysis (PCA)

It is most powerful and premise approach of dimension reduction and it plays vital role for extracting features based on Statistical Analysis [31]. The feature obtained after COSLETS transformation end up with high dimension which result in complex computation and time consuming. PCA discover principal patterns of data with high dimension displaying their similarity and differences. In order to find the dominant correlations in the data, large dimension data point are mapped onto the smaller dimensional feature space verifying orthogonality with maximum Covariance of the data which is aligned in the direction of principal axis. The most relevant features attained after applying PCA is ten EEG features, which will be given as input to GRNN (General Regression Neural Network) classifier. The proposed model architecture is represented in the below Fig. 1.

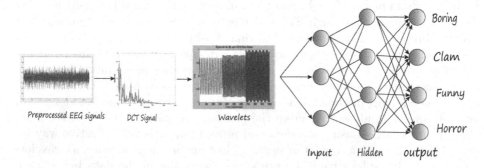

**Fig. 1.** Architecture of proposed coslets transformation for emotion recognition.

# 4   Classification

Due to the major advantage of considering first few transform co-efficients as discriminating features for exhibiting the actual information in a signal by nearly neglecting other co-efficient information. We gained large number of observed EEG data to be processed at the phase of classification of EEG signals. In this regard, PCA (Principal component Analysis) is applied to observed data and transformed on to the reduced orthogonal feature space [27]. The EEG features obtained after PCA is 10 in number which will be given as input to GRNN which is supervised learning model associated with inherent abilities also good at time series classification and prediction tasks when compared with other classifiers [32]. It is variants of radial basis function, where systematically the weights of these network are evaluated and in the hidden layers it uses Gaussian activation function. Some of the prime advantage of GRNN: It is a single pass and fast learning network as there is no requirement for iterative training as other Neural Network follow, even it performs well for data contaminated with noisy environment. The Topology of GRNN consists of three layers namely: Input layer, Hidden layer and Output layer. The general Notation for calculating weights vector of this network is given below.

$$F(I) = \frac{\sum_{i=1}^{n} T_i W_i}{\sum_{i=1}^{n} W_i}, \quad W_i = e[\frac{||I - I_t||^2}{2h^2}] \tag{2}$$

where the output $F$ (I) is weighted average of the target values $T_i$ of training cases $I_i$ close to a given input case $I$.

# 5   Experiments and Results

This section describes the experimental design, results and about the dataset we have chosen for evaluation of the proposed work.

## 5.1   Dataset

GAMEEMO [5] is challenging benchmark dataset for EEG based emotion recognition application. The dataset consists of EEG signals recorded using 14 (AF4, AF3, F7, F8, P7, P8, T7, T8, FC5, FC6, O1, O2, F4, F3) channel Emotiv Epoc+ EEG sensor, sampling rate of EEG device is 2048 Hz, from 28 participants aged between 20–27 while they were playing four different types of computer games for 20 min duration (5 min for each game). After playing each game, participant exhibited four different types of emotions such as Horror, Funny, Calm and Boring. The dataset contains both raw EEG signals and pre-processed EEG signals, specifically all the subjects contain 38252 samples for each class of emotion. We have opted pre-processed EEG signals for implementation, the recorded signals were down sampled at 128 hz, and are prepossessed using 5th order sinc filter (built in filter of EEG device) which eliminates movements of hands, head and arms which are considered as artifacts.

## 5.2 Experimental Results and Performance Analysis

This section presents the results based on bench-mark publicly available video game based EEG dataset. As we mentioned in the earlier section the dataset consists of 14 channel EEG signals recorded from 28 healthy subjects while they were playing four different video games. Previous sections detailed about how DCT is used for data compression resulting from higher dimension to lower dimension. To start with the implementation phase, the pre-processed EEG features which is in time domain of all subjects in each class of emotion with the length of 38000 were divided into training and testing phase in the ratio of 80:20 for classification purpose, the same procedure was followed for all 14 channels EEG signals collected from 28 subjects in all four class of emotion. Initially all the prepossessed EEG features were used for DCT transformation (compressing higher dimension data to lower dimension), this approach convert time domain EEG features into fundamental frequency components, EEG feature with low frequency co-efficients are mainly concentrated for further process and co-efficient with high frequency are neglected, because most of the transformed co-efficient produced by DCT consists of zero or small in number and only few of them are with large in numbers, after applying DCT to prepossessed EEG features (38000 for each person from each emotion), the dimension of the features were reduced from 38000 to 9000 features and to obtain highly discriminating features, 1D wavelet is applied to DCT transformed features space. In order to reduce the orthogonal feature space of EEG data PCA is applied to reduce the dimension of the data which finally gave us 10 most relevant features for further classification of different emotions. GRNN was preferred due to its good performance in wide range of applications and it also good at prediction task. In the proposed method the results obtained for all channel of EEG signal is given below the Table 1 (Comparison Table of Different Dimensional Reduction Methods) and Table 2 (Comparison Table of Different Classifiers for GAMEEMO Dataset). It is observed that tabulated results comparing existing methods with our proposed study outperforms well with combination of DR and GRNN as classifiers.

**Table 1.** Comparison table of different dimensional reduction methods.

| Study | Methods | Dataset | Accuracy |
|---|---|---|---|
| Yu Chen [30] | LDA + Ada-boost | DEAP | 88.70 |
| Qiang GAO [18] | PCA + SVM | Own data-set | 89.17 |
| DongKoo [29] | Genetic algorithm | DEAP | 71.76 |
| **Proposed method** | **Coslets approach** | **GAMEEMO** | 100 |

Table 2. Comparison table of different classifiers for GAMEEMO dataset.

| Method | AF3 | AF4 | F3 | F4 | F7 | F8 | FC5 | FC6 | O1 | O2 | P7 | P8 | T7 | T8 |
|---|---|---|---|---|---|---|---|---|---|---|---|---|---|---|
| Alakus et al. method+KNN | 61 | 75 | 59 | 67 | 67 | 75 | 64 | 68 | 65 | 65 | 61 | 73 | 61 | 64 |
| Alakus et al. method+SVM | 81 | 88 | 63 | 72 | 84 | 80 | 66 | 68 | 57 | 70 | 59 | 81 | 65 | 81 |
| Alakus et al. method+MLPN | 86 | 87 | 79 | 83 | 84 | 84 | 79 | 85 | 79 | 83 | 79 | 77 | 75 | 79 |
| Tuncer et al. method+SVM | 98.75 | 98.57 | 99.11 | 98.39 | 98.21 | 98.75 | 98.57 | 99.29 | 99.11 | 98.39 | 98.57 | 98.57 | 98.04 | 98.57 |
| **Our Proposed method+GRNN** | 100 | 100 | 100 | 100 | 100 | 100 | 100 | 100 | 100 | 100 | 100 | 100 | 100 | 100 |

## 5.3 Discussion and Conclusion

Analysis of this research work is to present a new emotion classification model based on EEG Signals. The main purpose in this study was to reduce the higher dimensional data into smaller one without information loss for better classification. The presented model is defined as COSLETS transformation. Which is combination of DCT and Wavelet transform. Our main concern with data in hand was to reduce the size/dimension, where DCT is widely used for data compression. Importantly its properties is capable of working with correlated input data and examine energy of first few transform co-efficients, the other followed co-efficients are simply neglected. Wavelet transforms was primarily designed for extracting features with non-stationary signals we applied 1D wavelet transform for DCT co-efficients and to enhance the numerical strength of the model PCA is used for better representation of data. Conventional networks such as GRNN have generalization and convergence properties, in this direction we used GRNN as for classifying four different emotions. Experimental results revealed that COSLET transformation is the first of this kind in the literature for EEG based emotion recognition and it has superiorly performed well for all 14 channel of EEG Signals in the particular dataset. In future we wish to work with several new dimension reduction approaches which is necessary for recognizing more classes of emotions with different applications in the field of machine learning.

## References

1. Zheng, W.-L., Lu, B.-L.: Investigating critical frequency bands and channels for EEG-based emotion recognition with deep neural networks. IEEE Trans. Autonom. Mental Dev. (IEEE TAMD) 7(3), 162–175 (2015)
2. Faria, G., Margarida, H.: Towards the Identification of Psychophysiological States in EEG (2018)
3. Koelstra, S., Muhl, C., Soleymani, M., Lee, J.-S.: DEAP: a database for emotion analysis using physiological signals. IEEE Trans. Affect. Comput. 3(1), 18–31 (2012). https://doi.org/10.1109/T-AFFC.2011.15
4. Subramanian, J., Wache, M.K., Abadi, R.L., Vieriu, S.W., Sebe, N.: ASCERTAIN: emotion and personality recognition using commercial sensors. IEEE Trans. Affect. Comput. 9(2), 147–160 (2018). https://doi.org/10.1109/TAFFC.2016.2625250

5. Alakuş, T., Gonen, M., Turkoglu, I.: Database for an emotion recognition system based on EEG signals and various computer games - GAMEEMO. Biomed. Signal Process. Control **60**, 101951 (2020). https://doi.org/10.1016/j.bspc.2020.101951
6. Miranda-Correa, J.A., Abadi, M.K., Patras, S.N.: Amigos: a dataset for affect, personality and mood research on individuals and groups. IEEE Trans. Affect. Comput. **12**(2), 479–493 (2018)
7. Sanei, S., Chambers, J.A.: EEG Signal Processing. John Wiley & Sons, Hoboken (2013)
8. Wirawan, I.M.A., Wardoyo, R., Lelono, D.: The challenges of emotion recognition methods based on electroencephalogram signals: a literature review. Int. J. Elect. Comput. Eng. **12**(2), 1508 (2022)
9. Katsigiannis, S., Ramzan, N.: DREAMER: a database for emotion recognition through EEG and ECG signals from wireless low-cost off-the-shelf devices. IEEE J. Biomed. Health Inform. **22**, 98–107 (2018). https://doi.org/10.1109/JBHI.2017. 2688239
10. Bhattacharyya, T., Garg, L., Pachori, R.B.: A novel multivariate-multiscale approach for computing EEG spectral and temporal complexity for human emotion recognition. IEEE Sens. J. **21**(3), 3579–3591 (2020)
11. Zhang, J., Chen, M., Hu, S., Cao, Y., Kozma, R.: PNN for EEG-based emotion recognition. In: 2016 IEEE International Conference on Systems, Man, and Cybernetics (SMC). IEEE (2016)
12. Li, P., et al.: EEG based emotion recognition by combining functional connectivity network and local activations. IEEE Trans. Biomed. Eng. **66**(10), 2869–2881 (2019)
13. Jingzhao, H., Wang, C., Jia, Q., Qirong, B., Sutcliffe, R., Feng, J.: ScalingNet: extracting features from raw EEG data for emotion recognition. Neurocomputing **463**, 177–184 (2021)
14. Sorzano, C.O.S., Vargas, J., Pascual Montano, A.: A survey of dimensionality reduction techniques. arXiv preprint arXiv:1403.2877 (2014)
15. Cao, X., Chen, C., Tian, L.: Supervised multidimensional scaling and its application in MRI-based individual age predictions. Neuroinformatics **19**(2), 219–231 (2020). https://doi.org/10.1007/s12021-020-09476-6
16. Ali, U., Ahmed, S., Ferzund, J., Mehmood, A., Rehman, A.: Using PCA and factor analysis for dimensionality reduction of bio-informatics data. arXiv preprint arXiv:1707.07189 (2017)
17. Rui, L., Nejati, H., Cheung, N.-M.: Dimensionality reduction of brain imaging data using graph signal processing. In: 2016 IEEE International Conference on Image Processing (ICIP). IEEE (2016)
18. Gao, Q., Wang, C., Wang, Z., Song, X., Dong, E., Song, Y.: EEG based emotion recognition using fusion feature extraction method. Multimed. Tools. App. **79**(37), 27057–27074 (2020)
19. Sarasa, G., Granados, A., Rodriguez, F.B.: Algorithmic clustering based on string compression to extract P300 structure in EEG signals. Comput. Methods Progr. Biomed. **176**, 225–235 (2019)
20. Alhagry, S., Fahmy, A.A., El-Khoribi, R.A.: Emotion recognition based on EEG using LSTM recurrent neural network. Emotion **8**(10), 355–358 (2017)
21. Tuncer, T., Dogan, S., Subasi, A.: LEDPatNet19: automated emotion recognition model based on nonlinear LED pattern feature extraction function using EEG signals. Cogn. Neurodyn. **16**, 1–12 (2021). https://doi.org/10.1007/s11571-021-09748-0
22. Aslan, M.: CNN based efficient approach for emotion recognition. J. King Saud Univ. Comput. Inf. Sci. (2021)

23. Tuncer, T., Dogan, S., Baygin, M., Rajendra Acharya, U.: Tetromino pattern based accurate EEG emotion classification model. Artif. Intell. Med. **123**, 102210 (2022)
24. Li, Z., Tian, X., Shu, L., Xu, X., Hu, B.: Emotion recognition from EEG using RASM and LSTM. In: Huet, B., Nie, L., Hong, R. (eds.) ICIMCS 2017. CCIS, vol. 819, pp. 310–318. Springer, Singapore (2018). https://doi.org/10.1007/978-981-10-8530-7_30
25. Mahantesh, K., Aradhya, V.N.M., Niranjan, S.K.: Coslets: a novel approach to explore object taxonomy in compressed DCT domain for large image datasets. In: El-Alfy, E.-S.M., Thampi, S.M., Takagi, H., Piramuthu, S., Hanne, T. (eds.) Advances in Intelligent Informatics. AISC, vol. 320, pp. 39–48. Springer, Cham (2015). https://doi.org/10.1007/978-3-319-11218-3_5
26. Birvinskas, V., Jusas, I.M., Damasevicius, R.: EEG dataset reduction and feature extraction using discrete cosine transform. In: 2012 Sixth UKSim/AMSS European Symposium on Computer Modeling and Simulation. IEEE (2012)
27. Prakash, B.V., Ajay, D.V.A., Manjunath Aradhya, V.N.: An Exploration of PNN and GRNN Models For Efficient Software Development Effort Estimation (2015)
28. Kiymik, M.K., Güler, I., Dizibüyük, A., Akin, M.: Comparison of STFT and wavelet transform methods in determining epileptic seizure activity in EEG signals for real-time application. Comput. Biol. Med. **35**(7), 603–616 (2005)
29. Shon, D., Im, K., Park, J.H., Lim, D.S., Jang, B., Kim, J.M.: Emotional stress state detection using genetic algorithm-based feature selection on EEG signals. Int. J. Environ. Res. Publ. Health. **15**(11), 2461 (2018)
30. Chen, Y., Chang, R., Guo, J.: Emotion recognition of EEG signals based on the ensemble learning method: AdaBoost. Math. Probl. Eng. **2021**, 1–12 (2021)
31. Hemantha, K.: Principal component analysis and generalized regression neural networks for efficient character recognition. In: 2008 First International Conference on Emerging Trends in Engineering and Technology. IEEE (2008)
32. Aradhya, V.M., Niranjan, S.K., Kumar, G.H.: Probabilistic neural network based approach for handwritten character recognition. Spec. Issue IJCCT **1**(2), 3 (2010)
33. Aradhya, V.M., Pavithra, M.S., Naveena, C.: A robust multilingual text detection approach based on transforms and wavelet entropy. Proc. Technol. **4**, 232–237 (2012)

# Influences of Social Learning in Individual Perception and Decision Making in People with Autism: A Computational Approach

Tanu Wadhera[1] and Mufti Mahmud[2,3,4]

[1] School of Electronics, Indian Institute of Information Technology Una, Una, Himachal Pradesh 177209, India
tanu.wadhera@iiitu.ac.in
[2] Department of Computer Science, Nottingham Trent University, Clifton Lane, NG118NS Nottingham, UK
[3] Medical Technologies Innovation Facility, Nottingham Trent University, Clifton Lane, NG118NS Nottingham, UK
[4] Computing and Informatics Research Centre, Nottingham Trent University, Clifton Lane, NG118NS Nottingham, UK
muftimahmud@gmail.com, mufti.mahmud@ntu.ac.uk

**Abstract.** The present paper proposes a computational approach to explore the influences of social learning on social cognition among individuals with Autism Spectrum Disorder (ASD) compared to the Typically Developing (TD) group. An experimental paradigm is designed to perceive and differentiate social cues related to real-time road and traffic light situations. The computational metrics such as sensitivity index ($d'$), response bias ($c$) and detection accuracy ($DA$) are recorded and analysed using machine learning classifiers. The results revealed that cognitive level is attenuated in ASD ($d' = 0.427$, $c = -0.0076$ and $DA = 51.67\%$) compared to TD ($d' = 1.42$, $c = -0.0027$ and $DA = 80.33\%$) with an improvement considering social influence as key factor ($S_f$) with best-fit quantitative value for ASD ($S_f = 0.3197$) when compared to TD ($S_f = 0.3937$). The automated classification with an accuracy of 96.2% supported the significance of the metrics in distinguishing ASD from TDs. The present findings revealed that social conformity and social influence imparted growth in ASD cognition.

**Keywords:** Support Vector Machine (SVM) · Machine learning · Correlation coefficient · Social learning

## 1 Introduction

Autism Spectrum Disorder (ASD) refers to a group of neurodevelopmental conditions that involve social atypicality and repetitive/stereotyped behaviour [26]. These conditions cannot be cured through conventional medication and often lead to reduced quality of life [7]. Therefore, ASD should be identified as early

© Springer Nature Switzerland AG 2022
M. Mahmud et al. (Eds.): BI 2022, LNAI 13406, pp. 50–61, 2022
https://doi.org/10.1007/978-3-031-15037-1_5

as possible to allow the selection and administration of therapies to mitigate this reduction and support these people effectively [5,22]. However, the spectrum of impairments in the behavioural and neural domain increases disorder heterogeneity making the identification and diagnosis of ASD extremely difficult [16]. ASD normally can be detected at an early age (about two years ) but may also be detected later, depending on the severity of symptoms [4]. Although several tools have been developed to detect and identify subtypes of ASD, the procedures are onerous and normally are not used unless there is a strong doubt or a high risk of ASD [1,2].

Several studies theoretically reported the ability to visually search and perceive information that is intact in ASD. In a theoretical framework, a study demonstrated cognition using different vital parameters such as visual inference drawn from present information, reliable prior experiences, and statistical learning [13]. The social learning parameter significantly aids in evoking cognition, working memory and prediction ability among individuals [8,20,24]. Social learning is a process where one learns by observing, following, and reproducing other person's experiences [19]. For example, when Typically Developing (TD) children were provided with others' responses related to systematic risks (playing with fire), they changed their perspective and conformity style very quickly [10,17]. Quantitatively, on average, the influence factor in a social learning process lies in the range between 0.3 and 0.5 for healthy individuals [18,23]. The models which make use of others' experiences such as observational (Haaker et al., 2017), instruction-based learning [17], and social learning and influence [11,21], suggesting that perception can also be learned without directly experiencing the stimulus. Their simplicity allows individuals to take advantage of others' experiences and enhance their social interaction. With this fact in mind, the present paper has utilised social learning as one of the factors in building cognition in neuro-affected individuals. However, to our information, there is no study examining the social influence and its impact with a motive to provide objective markers for ASD diagnosis.

The present paper has mathematically modelled independent response-making and social learning-based responses to provide cognition levels in ASD. The paper has evaluated cognition level and influential level by answering the hypothesis of whether social influence can alter cognition level.

The rest of the paper is organised as follows: Sect. 2 introduces the cognitive model, Sect. 3 discusses the methodology of this work, Sect. 4 contains the results and discussion, and Sect. 5 concludes the paper with future recommendations.

## 2   Cognitive Model

A Two-Alternative Forced-Choice (TAFC) task is designed to practically acquire and assess the independent social response and social-influence impact on response patterns. An experimental paradigm is designed in which the participants perceive, discriminate, and decide independently which stimuli are risk-involving and which one is safe [25]. The non-trivial behavioural task involves two stimuli - risky and safe condition images (related to road incidences), randomly presented to participants in $N = 120$ trials. They were instructed to perceive and distinguish the stimuli into their correct category and respond accordingly. The computational parameter is modelled mathematically as the sum of independent learning ($P_n^{IL}$) and social learning ($P_n^{SL}$), which is given as in Eq. 1:

$$P_n = P_n^{IL} + P_n^{SL}; 0 < P_n < 1 \tag{1}$$

The term $P_n^{IL}$ is determined by computing whether the provided risk/safe stimuli are correctly identified and responded to by participants for any trial. It is given by Eq. 2:

$$P_n^{IL} = \begin{cases} 1, & \text{if response is correct, and} \\ 0, & \text{if response is incorrect} \end{cases} \tag{2}$$

for $n$ varying from 1 to $N$, where $n$ is current trial number, and $N$ represents the total number of trials. The value $\{P_n^{IL} = 1\}$ indicates that the individual has categorised the trial correctly, whereas $\{P_n^{IL} = 0\}$ suggests that the individual has not perceived stimuli. The term $P_n^{SL}$ represents social learning with a value = 1 to indicate improvement in response with the observation of others' responses. It is given by the Eq. 3:

$$P_n^{SL} = S_f(\beta_n - P_n^{IL}), \tag{3}$$

where $S_f$ is the influential factor, which quantitatively represents the influence of others on an individual. Its value lies between 0 (no influence) and 1 (full influence). In the present work, numerous computer simulations are performed on the experimental data acquired from all the participants to investigate $S_f$ in ASD and TD. The constant ($\beta_n$) represents the standard responses shown to the individuals. The term ($\beta_n - P_n^{IL}$) measures the difference in response provided for observation ($\beta_n$) and the individual's own response ($P_n^{IL}$). In case the response of individual and standard responses match (i.e., $\beta_n = P_n^{IL}$), then $P_n = P_n^{IL}$, which reflects that the individual need not rethink their decision.

## 3   Methodology

### 3.1   Participant's Demographic Data

A total of Fifty children with ASD (6–21 years) were selected from local Non-Governmental Organisations (NGOs) after assuring those who already followed the conventional Diagnostic and Statistical Manual of Mental Disorders, Fifth Edition [3] diagnostic criteria to maintain homogeneity among ASD participants. The TD individuals (5–20 years) were recruited via word-of-mouth, considering their medical and neurological (ASD, epilepsy) status. The parents of both groups were also interviewed to follow the further exclusion criteria: any psychiatric problem such as anxiety or any other disorder (dyslexia, cerebral palsy, schizophrenia) or impairment (specific language impairment) (Table 1).

**Table 1.** Summary of demographic statistics and psychological evaluations

| Participants/ Characteristics | | ASD | | | | TD | | | |
|---|---|---|---|---|---|---|---|---|---|
| | | Data | Normality | | | Data | Normality | | |
| | | | p | k | s | | p | k | s |
| Number | | 50 | – | | | 50 | – | | |
| Male: Female ratio | | 9:1 | – | | | 3:2 | – | | |
| Age years | | 13.9 ± 3.1 (8–21) | 0.30 | −1.22 | 0.38 | 11.8 ± 2.9 (8–18) | 0.15 | −1.14 | 0.64 |
| Non-verbal IQ | | 112.8 ± 11.2 (90–130) | 0.57 | −1.0 | −0.29 | 111.1 ± 10.4 (88–128) | 0.23 | −0.20 | -1.38 |
| ADOS CSS | | 8.52 ± 4.73 | 0.54 | 0.008 | 0.29 | – | – | – | – |
| Verbal IQ | MISIC | 109.1 ± 11.12 (79–120) | 0.23 | −1.51 | 1.3 | 113.1 ± 12.3 (85–128) | 0.09 | −0.01 | −1.49 |
| Performance IQ | | 110.3 ± 12.8 (84–128) | 0.34 | −1.51 | −0.33 | 111.2±11.8 (85–132) | 0.21 | −0.73 | −0.48 |
| Full-scale IQ | | 107.5 ± 11.09 (80–126) | 0.48 | −1.0 | 0.89 | 112.6 ± 11.5 (87–130) | 0.15 | −1.12 | 0.93 |
| BRP | | 2.97 ± 0.12 (2.72–3.24) | 0.23 | −0.12 | −0.29 | 3.94 ± 0.15 (3.67–4.36) | 0.70 | −0.13 | 0.34 |

(k: Kurtosis; p: Significance probability; s: Standard deviation)

## 3.2 Experimental Paradigm

The stimuli were in the animated images (1396 × 561), representing risk involving and safe situations, as shown in Fig. 1. The stimuli were designed in the PsychToolbox software [6] of the MATLAB toolbox and presented on a Dell Inspiron laptop (1366 × 768 pixels, 40 pHz refresh rate). The experiment is a visual-perception based TAFC task in which the participants have to choose one of the choices to proceed further. The inter-stimulus interval was of 800 ms duration and distance between the participants, and the laptop screen was kept at 51 cm. It was made sure that selected images provided sufficient information to participants without any requirement for contextual details. The response levels were binary, either yes or no and without any intermediate level. Participants were instructed to respond only after the stimulus was shown by pressing the corresponding key ('R' for risky and 'S' for safe). The experimental design was such that pressing any other key would not affect the experiment or response. Each participant was instructed to complete 120 trials ($N = 120$) without any time restriction.

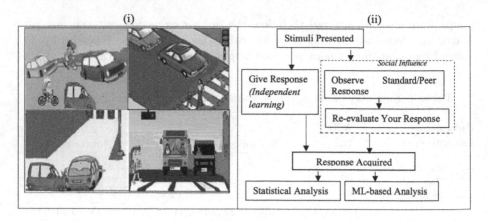

**Fig. 1.** (i) Stimulus provided to participants (ii) Layout of experimental task.

### 3.3  Theoretical Foundations and Experimental Phases

Theoretically cognitive metrics such as independent and social learning are found implicitly contributing to perception and decision-making. Following which, in the present paper, the experiment was conducted in two phases with a motive to evaluate the cognitive performances of the ASD and TD participants computationally. In the first phase, the independent learning (i.e., $P_n^{SL} = 0$, $P_n = P_n^{IL}$) responses are acquired from the participants. In the second phase, the impact of social learning is considered along with independent knowledge $(\widetilde{P_n} = P_n^{IL} + P_n^{SL})$ in evaluating the response of the participants. The standard responses and peer responses were provided to ASD and TD individuals for social learning. After observing provided responses, the ASD and TD participants were asked to re-evaluate their responses, and their experimental data were recorded again. The main goal is to quantitatively compute $S_f$.

### 3.4  Data Analysis

**Statistical Analysis of Experimental Data.** The behavioural (signal detection) statistics are evaluated to ensure the unbiased task performance of participants. The two behavioural parameters-sensitivity index ($d'$) and response bias ($c$) have been assessed by computing the participant's Hit Rate ($HR$) and False Alarm Rate ($FAR$) using Eqs. 4 and 5, respectively, adopted from [12]. The $HR$ gives the probability of correctly discriminated responses for change in the trials while $FAR$ providing the likelihood of incorrectly discriminated response (mistake) corresponding to no-change in trials.

$$HR = \frac{X}{X + (Y\,for\,X)} \tag{4}$$

$$FAR = \frac{(X\,for\,Y)}{(X\,for\,Y) + Y} \tag{5}$$

The equation used to compute $d'$ is given in Eq. 6 as adopted from [15]:

$$d' = z(HR) - z(FAR) \qquad (6)$$

in which $z$ represents the $z$-transform of the $(HR)$ and $(FAR)$. The values can measure how discriminable participants' intentions are within the experimental task. The higher values indicate that participants have learned to perform better on the given task. It lies in the range of 0 to 4.0, and relatively, the proportion of correct responses $(A)$ (Macmillan & Creelman, 2004) lies within a range of 0.5 to 0.98 [14]. The parameter $(A)$ can be computed using Eq. 7.

$$A = 0.5 + \left( \frac{HR + FAR}{2} \right) \qquad (7)$$

The parameter $c$ measures the bias and reflects observers' valuation, i.e., care about correct responses $(HR,$ and $correct rejections(1 - FAR))$ and mistakes $(misses(1 - HR),$ and $FAR)$. It can be computed using Eq. 8 adopted from [9].

$$c = 0.5(z(HR) + z(FAR)) \qquad (8)$$

The value of $c$ can be positive, negative, or equal to zero [15]. The case indicates a neutral/unbiased decision such that both stimuli (risky & safe) are of equal importance to participants. The best-fit value of factor $S_f$ is deduced by comparing the performance of ASD participants with standard responses and peer-group responses.

**Machine Learning Based Analysis of Experimental Data.** Two state-of-the-art models, namely Support Vector Machine (SVM) and K-Nearest Neighbour (KNN) classifiers, are utilised to classify ASD and TDs. 10-fold cross-validation is utilised in dividing data into training and testing sets prior to providing to SVM and KNN classifiers. The training dataset is further divided into 80% for training and 20% for validation purposes. The efficacy of the SVM classifier is validated using different performance metrics such as sensitivity, specificity, and area under the curve (AUC).

## 4 Results and Discussion

### 4.1 Statistical Results from First and Second Phase

The range of $d'$ indexes and $c$ values for both the groups in both phases has been reflected through a histogram (Fig. 2 (i, ii)). The distribution obtained for $d'$ values shows diversity in participants' policies to increase classification accuracy. On average, the $c$ values reflect that participants have followed a neutral decision criterion (approximately) while interpreting the given risk-involving stimulus category (risky or safe). The scatter plot (Fig. 2(iii)) shows that $d'$ and $c$ are negatively correlated for both the groups $(r(ASD) = -0.112; r(TD) = -0.167)$, suggesting more discriminable and less biased decision criteria in both groups.

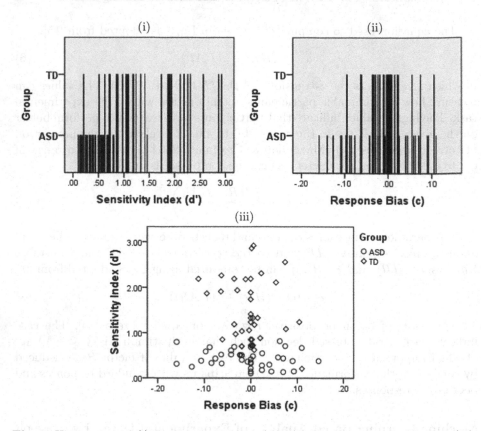

**Fig. 2.** Histograms of (i) Sensitivity indexes (d'), (ii) Response biases (c), and (iii) Scatter plot of d' versus c in ASD and TD participants.

A paired samples t-test on values revealed that TDs' performance is significantly higher than ASD (Mean $\pm$ $\sigma$ = 0.99 $\pm$ 0.72, t(49) = 8.625, p = 0.001) in first and second phase (Mean $\pm$ $\sigma$ = 0.87 $\pm$ 0.53, t(49) = 6.302, p = 0.01). The results from the two-sampled t-test on (c) values yielded an insignificant difference in the performance of TD and ASD participants (First Phase: Mean $\pm$ $\sigma$= 0.0058 $\pm$ 0.005, t(49) = 0.413, p = 0.68) and (Second Phase: Mean $\pm$ $\sigma$ = 0.0032 $\pm$ 0.002, t(49) = 0.355, p = 0.45). It reflects the tendency of participants of both groups to provide a neutral decision.

The bar graphs plotted in Fig. 3 (i, ii) show $d'$ and $c$ mean values (with a 95% confidence interval) of ASD and TD participants for the experimental task. In ASD, the $d'$ mean is 0.427, indicating their moderate performance with classification accuracy (computed using equation (14)) of about 51.67%. And comparatively, the $d'$ index is higher for TD participants with a mean value of 1.42 and classification accuracy of 80.33%. The $c$ value (Fig. 3 (ii)) in ASD (Mean = $-0.0076$) and in TD (Mean = $-0.0027$) is approximately equal to zero reflecting no biasing in their approach.

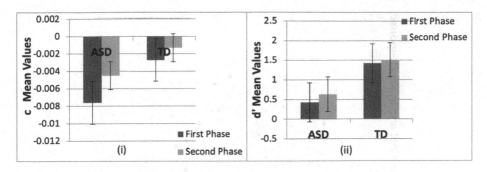

**Fig. 3.** Mean values of (i) Sensitivity index ($d'$) and, (ii) Response bias ($c$) in ASD and TD participants for first and second phase with standard error (95% confidence interval).

To reflect the impact of social learning, the relationship between $\Delta_P(\widetilde{P_n} - P_n)$ and $(\beta_n - P_n^{IL})$ (i.e., deviation in the provided and initial response) has been computed. In case, the participants' initial response is already similar to the response of an influential person ($\beta_n = P_n^{IL}$) then ($\Delta_P = 0$), otherwise $\Delta_P$ will change corresponding to $(\beta_n - P_n^{IL})$. After analysing the responses ($\widetilde{P_n}$ and $P_n$), it is observed that ASDs have changed their response on an average by ($\Delta_P = \widetilde{P_n} - P_n = 0.13$) and TDs by ($\Delta_P = \widetilde{P_n} - P_n = 0.09$, where $\widetilde{P_n}$ is the response of participant after social learning and $P_n$ is the initial response of the same participant before social learning (independent learning) and $\Delta_P$ is the change in final and initial response. The scatter plots, as shown in Fig. 4 (i, ii), represent the variation in $\Delta_P$ concerning $(\beta_n - P_n^{IL})$ for participants with ASD and TD. The equation of the fit line has been used to attain the value of the influence factor $S_f$ in ASD. The participants with ASD get more influenced ($S_f = 0.3937$) than TDs ($S_f = 0.3197$).

**Machine Learning Based Classification.** The $d'$, $c$, and detection accuracy ($DA$) values of ASD and TD individuals are fed to the SVM and KNN classifier for classifying ASD and TD individuals. A 10-fold cross-validation methodology is trailed in structuring balanced training and testing sets beforehand provide for SVM and KNN classifiers. The dataset comprises of 80% training data including 20% data for validation purposes and rest 20% was testing data. We have checked for any incomplete data information, or outliers and noise in the data. The not available values and near zero variance values were removed from the dataset at priority basis. The effectiveness of classifiers is computed via sensitivity, specificity, accuracy and area under the curve (AUC).

The performance of the classifiers is summarised in a tabular form in Table 2. The tabular comparison shows that SVM classifier performs better in classifying ASD and TD individuals in comparison to KNN classifier. Among different combination of the features, the SVM classifier has shown high sensitivity, specificity, accuracy and AUC for combined set of all the four features.

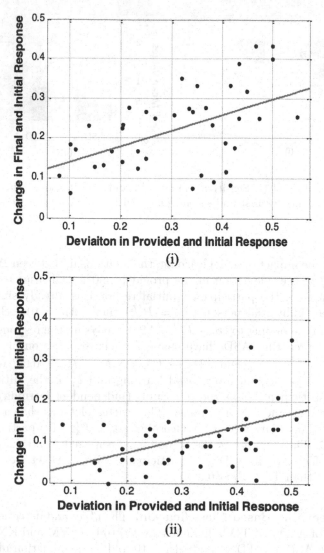

**Fig. 4.** Scatter plots representing social influence in (i) ASD, and (ii) TD participants. The equation of Fit line is (i) $y = 0.3937x + 0.1001$ and (ii) $y = 0.3197x + 0.0099$.

## 4.2   Discussion

The main objective of the paper is to quantitatively address cognition in ASD which involves individual knowledge (based on independent learning) and social influence. The individuals with ASD were given a risk-based decision-making task in two phases. In the first phase, the individuals have to complete the task on their intellect (without social influence). In the second phase, the social learning is included and the participants have to re-evaluate their prior decision after observing standard responses. On analysing the performance of individuals with ASD in

**Table 2.** Summary of SVM performance metrics in ASD and TD classification

| Feature input | Sensitivity (%) | | Specificity (%) | | Accuracy (%) | | AUC | |
|---|---|---|---|---|---|---|---|---|
| | SVM | KNN | SVM | KNN | SVM | KNN | SVM | KNN |
| $d' + c$ | 80.2 | 77.5 | 75.5 | 71.2 | 78.1 | 74.6 | 0.801 | 0.788 |
| $d' + DA$ | 87.3 | 84.7 | 84.4 | 79.9 | 85.2 | 82.4 | 0.862 | 0.834 |
| $c + DA$ | 80.3 | 76.5 | 74.6 | 73.4 | 76.3 | 75.4 | 0.786 | 0.784 |
| $d' + c + DA$ | 97.8 | 93.2 | 95.3 | 88.9 | 96.2 | 89.4 | 0.988 | 0.903 |

the first phase, it has been found that cognition is intact but attenuated in comparison to TD. The second phase results depicted that social learning has an amplified the cognition level in ASD. Thus, suggesting that cognition can be induced in ASD, through repetitive observational learning. Finally, the computational parameters were fed to SVM and KNN classifiers to find the performance of the proposed parameters in classifying ASD and TD groups. The SVM classifier outperforms KNN classifier and provides an accuracy of 95.3% for a combined set of all the input features $(d', c, DA)$ while classifying ASD and TD groups. The present study is significantly important as through quantitative values the cognitive deficits and other behavioural signs can be targeted mathematically and objectively, which will pace the ASD diagnostic procedure.

The statistical analysis suggested that participants with ASD have a specific ability to distinguish between risky and safe stimuli with $d' = 0.42$ (mean value) though poor in comparison to TD $(d' = 1.42)$. The finding 'no bias' (neutral decision criterion; $c = -0.0076$) means that individuals with ASD did not tend to prefer safe stimuli more than risky or vice versa. The negative correlation between $d'$ and $c$ for both ASD and TD group showed that their decision criteria became more discriminable and less biased with the practice. The comparison of the performance of ASD individuals with standard results revealed the best-fit value for social influence factor as $S_f = 0.3937$ in ASD and $S_f = 0.3197$ with TD individuals. In this manner, the present work has experimentally analysed impact of social learning on ASD individuals at the individual and group levels. Thus, it can be said that individuals with ASD have influential factor value (0.3937 average) which is consistent with the previous studies suggesting that, on average, the influence factor lies in the range between 0.3 and 0.5 (Soll & Larrick, 2009). The positive impact of social learning in individuals with ASD also reflects that their working-memory is adaptive enough to revise the opinion by observing others' responses. Thus, the positive impact of social learning has generated a possibility of enhancing the cognition of ASD through social interaction.

## 5  Conclusion

The present work provides quantitative insights into the contribution of social learning as a knowledge amplifying process for building perception and enhancing independent knowledge in ASD individuals. Social learning positively contributes to enhancing cognition and decision-making and amplifying independent learning in individuals with ASD. It can shape the knowledge and develop a predictive and a judging eye in ASD individuals. The SVM classifier provides an accuracy of 96.2% for a combination of features $(d', c, DA)$ in classifying ASD and TD groups. Thus, it can be said that ASD individuals may have risk knowledge, but atypical visual judgement and prediction might be responsible for not utilising or regulating this knowledge properly. In future, it is important to investigate the extent to which ASD individuals show long-lasting effects in their performance under the influence of untrained peers. The direction of influence and impact of gender and age on risk-perception and risk-taking behaviour is an important factor that needs to be studied. Further research coupling individual decision-making with low-probability or high-impact risk could provide precise levels of risk perception in ASD. For that purpose, the present study, which considers the basic perceptual features, can provide significant pieces of evidence.

# References

1. Ahmed, S., et al.: Toward machine learning-based psychological assessment of autism spectrum disorders in school and community. In: Proceedings of TEHI, pp. 139–149 (2022)
2. Akter, T., et al.: Towards autism subtype detection through identification of discriminatory factors using machine learning. In: Proceedings Brain Informatics, pp. 401–410 (2021)
3. American Psychiatric Association, D., et al.: Diagnostic and statistical manual of mental disorders: DSM-5, vol. 5. American psychiatric association Washington, DC (2013)
4. Biswas, M., et al.: An XAI based autism detection: the context behind the detection. In: Mahmud, M., Kaiser, M.S., Vassanelli, S., Dai, Q., Zhong, N. (eds.) BI 2021. LNCS (LNAI), vol. 12960, pp. 448–459. Springer, Cham (2021). https://doi.org/10.1007/978-3-030-86993-9_40
5. Biswas, S., et al.: Cloud based healthcare application architecture and electronic medical record mining: an integrated approach to improve healthcare system. In: Proceedings of ICCIT, pp. 286–291 (2014)
6. Brainard, D.H., Vision, S.: The psychophysics toolbox. Spat. Vis. **10**(4), 433–436 (1997)
7. Ghosh, T., et al.: Artificial intelligence and internet of things in screening and management of autism spectrum disorder. Sustain. Cities Soc. 103189 (2021), [ePub ahead of print]. https://doi.org/10.1016/j.scs.2021.103189
8. Haaker, J., Golkar, A., Selbing, I., Olsson, A.: Assessment of social transmission of threats in humans using observational fear conditioning. Nat. Protoc. **12**(7), 1378–1386 (2017)
9. Harvey Jr, L.O.: Detection sensitivity and response bias. Psychol. Percept. Psychol. **4165**, 1–15 (2003)
10. Knoll, L.J., Leung, J.T., Foulkes, L., Blakemore, S.J.: Age-related differences in social influence on risk perception depend on the direction of influence. J. Adolesc. **60**, 53–63 (2017)

11. Knoll, L.J., Magis-Weinberg, L., Speekenbrink, M., Blakemore, S.J.: Social influence on risk perception during adolescence. Psychol. Sci. **26**(5), 583–592 (2015)
12. Lerman, D.C., et al.: Applying signal-detection theory to the study of observer accuracy and bias in behavioral assessment. J. Appl. Behav. Anal. **43**(2), 195–213 (2010)
13. Ludvig, E.A., Madan, C.R., Spetch, M.L.: Priming memories of past wins induces risk seeking. J. Exp. Psychol. Gener. **144**(1), 24 (2015)
14. Lynn, S.K., Barrett, L.F.: "utilizing" signal detection theory. Psychol. Sci. **25**(9), 1663–1673 (2014)
15. Macmillan, N., Creelman, C.: Detection Theory: A User's Guide [internet] (2004)
16. Mahmud, M., et al.: Towards explainable and privacy-preserving artificial intelligence for personalisation in autism spectrum disorder. In: Antona, M., Stephanidis, C. (eds.) Universal Access in Human-Computer Interaction. User and Context Diversity. HCII 2022. LNCS, vol. 13309, pp. pp. 1–14. Springer, Cham (2022). https://doi.org/10.1007/978-3-031-05039-8_26
17. Mechias, M.L., Etkin, A., Kalisch, R.: A meta-analysis of instructed fear studies: implications for conscious appraisal of threat. Neuroimage **49**(2), 1760–1768 (2010)
18. Moussaïd, M.: Opinion formation and the collective dynamics of risk perception. PLoS One **8**(12), e84592 (2013)
19. Moussaïd, M., Brighton, H., Gaissmaier, W.: The amplification of risk in experimental diffusion chains. Proc. Natl. Acad. Sci. **112**(18), 5631–5636 (2015)
20. Ochsner, K.: Learning to fear what others have feared before. Soc. Cogn. Affect. Neurosci. **2**(1), 1–2 (2007)
21. Olsson, A., Nearing, K.I., Phelps, E.A.: Learning fears by observing others: the neural systems of social fear transmission. Soc. Cogn. Affect. Neurosci. **2**(1), 3–11 (2007)
22. Paul, M.C., Sarkar, S., Rahman, M.M., Reza, S.M., Kaiser, M.S.: Low cost and portable patient monitoring system for e-health services in Bangladesh. In: Proceedings of ICCCI, pp. 1–4 (2016)
23. Soll, J.B., Larrick, R.P.: Strategies for revising judgment: how (and how well) people use others' opinions. J. Exp. Psychol. Learn. Mem. Cogn. **35**(3), 780 (2009)
24. Vivanti, G., Rogers, S.J.: Action understanding and social learning in autism: a developmental perspective. Life Span Disabil. **14**, 7–29 (2011)
25. Wadhera, T., Kakkar, D.: Multiplex temporal measures reflecting neural underpinnings of brain functional connectivity under cognitive load in autism spectrum disorder. Neurol. Res. **42**(4), 327–337 (2020)
26. WHO: Autism spectrum disorders. online (2022). https://www.who.int/newsroom/fact-sheets/detail/autism-spectrum-disorders. Accessed 15 Feb 2022

# Investigations of Human Information Processing Systems

# Analysis of Alpha Band Decomposition in Different Level-k Scenarios with Semantic Processing

Dor Mizrahi[✉] [ID], Inon Zuckerman[ID], and Ilan Laufer[ID]

Department of Industrial Engineering and Management, Ariel University, Ariel, Israel
Dor.mizrahi1@msmail.ariel.ac.il, {inonzu,ilanl}@ariel.ac.il

**Abstract.** A coordination game is one in which two players are rewarded for making the same choice from the same set of alternatives. The ability of humans to tacitly coordinate effectively is based on the identification of pronounced solutions associated with salient features attracting the player's attention. These prominent solutions are referred to as focal points. Game theory fails to account for how people make decisions in tacit coordination games, and human behavior in these games cannot be explained by a single theory. One of the accepted theories for explaining human behavior is level-k theory. This theory assumes that each player has a different level of reasoning by which she assesses the behavior of other players in the game and makes strategic decisions based on that assessment. In Previous studies, we have found an association between the players' cognitive load as reflected by EEG power and the level-k during the coordination game. The goal of the current study was to examine the relationship between alpha frequency and its sub-bands and level-k during a tacit coordination game in the context of semantic processing.

**Keywords:** EEG · Tacit coordination games · Focal points · Alpha band

## 1 Introduction

A coordination game is one in which two players are rewarded for making the same choice from the same set of alternatives [1]. Research has shown that humans have the ability to successfully play coordination games even when communication is not possible (e.g. [1–4]). The ability of humans to tacitly coordinate effectively is based on the identification of pronounced solutions associated with salient features attracting the player's attention [1]. At present, no single consensus exists about how humans converge on the same focal point solution [5].One of the accepted theories of human behavior is level-k theory. This theory [6–8] assumes that humans make predictions about other players' actions based on their level k value, which reflects their depth of reasoning ability. That is, the level-k theory implies that each player believes that she is the most sophisticated person in the game and bases her actions on the assumption that everyone else is at one level below her. Previous studies that have examined the relationship between electrophysiological metrics in the framework of level-k theory have found that a linear relationship exists

© Springer Nature Switzerland AG 2022
M. Mahmud et al. (Eds.): BI 2022, LNAI 13406, pp. 65–73, 2022
https://doi.org/10.1007/978-3-031-15037-1_6

between the player's coordination ability and game difficulty with the that-beta ration (TBR) which reflects the cognitive load of the player [9, 10]. In addition the researches in [11] showed that the level-k of the player can be predicted based on the EEG signal using deep learning methods. In the current study we aimed to examine the power distribution of alpha frequency and its various components when performing tasks at different levels of reasoning based on level-k theory. To that end, an electrophysiological-behavioral experimental design was constructed. In this experiment, players were presented twice with the same set of 12 tasks. In the first presentation, the players performed a picking task in which each player had to freely select a word from a string of four words displayed on the screen. In the second presentation, the same 12 tasks were displayed again, but this time each player had to coordinate the choice of the specific word with an unknown player. According to level-k theory, it could be assumed that the picking task is level-k = 0 whereas the coordination task is level-k > 0. EEG was recorded from the scalp of each of the players while performing each of the tasks. Based on the electrophysiological results we examined the individual alpha frequency power distribution as a function of the level-k.

## 2    Materials and Methods

### 2.1    Measures

Level-K Theory. One main cognitive theory that tries to analyze and explain human behaviors in case of tacit coordination scenarios is the level-k theory which is derived from the cognitive hierarchy theory [13, 16, 17]. The level-k theory holds that players' reasoning depth relies on their subjective level of reasoning k. For example, players in which k = 0 (sometimes referred to as $L_0$ players) will act and choose randomly in their given space of solutions, while $L_1$ players assume that all other players are $L_0$ reasoners and will act according to this assumption, i.e., their strategy will assume all other players select a random solution. That is, $L_0$ players might utilize rules but will apply them randomly (picking), whereas $L_{k \geq 1}$ players will apply their strategy based on their beliefs regarding the actions the other players (coordination).

### 2.2    Experimental Design

Procedure. The study comprised the following stages. First, participants received an explanation regarding the overarching aim of the study and were given instructions about the experimental procedure and the interface of the application. Participants were offered a reward based on the total number of points they earned in both tasks (picking and coordination). The experiment consisted of two sets of 12 different trials each with a different set of words. For example, game board #1 displays a trial containing the set {"Water", "Beer", "Wine", "Whisky"} appearing in Hebrew, respectively. Each set of words was displayed between two short vertical lines following a slide containing only the lines without the word set so that participants will focus their gaze at the center of the screen (Fig. 1, A and B).

In the first experimental condition, the task presented to the players was a picking task, i.e., participants were only required to freely pick a word out of each set of four words presented to them in each of the 12 trials. Subsequently, participants were presented with the coordination task, comprising the same set of 12 different trials. However, in the coordination condition participants were instructed to coordinate their choice of a word with an unknown partner so that they would end up choosing the same word from the set. Each participant sat alone in front of the computer screen during the entire experimental session. It is important to note that no feedback was given between the games. That is, the participants were not informed whether they have coordinated successfully or not with their unknown co-player.

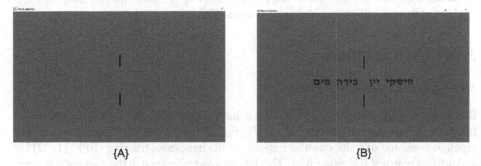

**Fig. 1.** (A) Stand by screen (B) Game #1 {"Water", "Beer", "Wine", "Whisky"}

Figure 2 portrays the outline of the experiment. Each slide containing the set of words (task trials) was preceded by a slide containing only the vertical lines without the word set (stand-by slides) to keep the gaze of participants in the middle of the screen throughout the experiment. Each of the stand-by slides was presented for $U(2,2.5)$ sec., while each slide containing the set of words was presented for a maximal duration of 8 s. Following a task trial, participants could move to the next slide with a button press. The sequence of the task trials was randomized in each session.

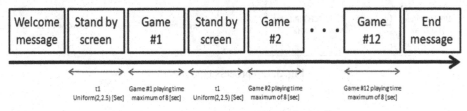

**Fig. 2.** Experimental paradigm with timeline

**Participants.** The experiment involved 10 university students that were enrolled in one of the courses on campus (right-handed, mean age = ~26 [years], SD = 4). The study was approved by the IRB committee of the University. All participants provided written informed consent for the experiment.

**EEG Recordings.** EEG was recorded from participants while they were performing the tasks. The EEG was recorded by a 16-channel g.USBAMP biosignal amplifier (g.tec, Austria) at a sampling frequency of 512 Hz. 16 active electrodes were used for collecting EEG signals from the scalp based on the international 10–20 system. The recording was done by the OpenVibe [12] recording software. The impedance of all electrodes was kept below the threshold of 5K [ohm] during all recording sessions. Before performing the actual experiment, participants underwent a training session while wearing the EEG cap, to get them familiar with the application and task.

## 3   Results and Discussion

### 3.1   EEG Preprocessing Scheme

Based on the literature (e.g. [13–17]), we have focused on the following cluster of frontal and prefrontal electrodes (Fp1, F7, Fp2, F8, F3, and F4). The preprocessing pipeline consisted of finite impulse response (FIR) band-pass filtering (BPF) [1, 32] Hz and artifact removal following ICA. The data was re-referenced to the average reference and down sampled from 512 Hz to 64 Hz following baseline correction (see Fig. 3). Data was analyzed on 1-s epoch windows from game onset which resulted in a total of 12 decision points (i.e., EEG epochs) per participant.

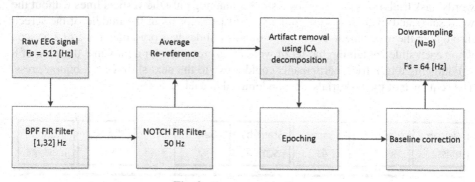

**Fig. 3.** Preprocess pipeline

### 3.2   Alpha Band Decomposing Analysis in Coordination Process

The oscillations in the alpha band can be divided into two main sub-bands, lower-alpha (8–10 [Hz]) and upper-alpha (10–13 [Hz]) [18–20]. Previous research has already shown that coordination necessitates the exertion of additional resources compared to picking as reflected by the modulation of the alpha frequency band (see for example [9–11, 17]). Here, based on previous findings, we assumed that as the complexity of the task increases, i.e., the progression form picking (level-k = 0) to coordination (level-k > 0), alpha frequency should decrease more in the upper-alpha than in the lower-alpha, especially in the context of semantic processing [18–22].

The statistical comparison was performed as follows. For each EEG epoch which was recorded during the picking and coordination tasks we calculated the relative energy of the lower-alpha and upper-alpha frequency bands (see Fig. A.1 in Appendix A). Then, we divided the relative energy values between the corresponding picking and coordination games in order to estimate the change in energy that occurred in the different alpha bands. That is, for each two corresponding epochs we estimated the energy changes within the alpha band according to the ratio $\frac{E_{lower-Alpha}|coordination}{E_{lower-Alpha}|picking}$ and $\frac{E_{upper-Alpha}|coordination}{E_{upper-Alpha}|picking}$, for the lower- and upper-alpha band, respectively.

Analysis of the results of all 12 games showed that the decrease in upper-alpha between coordination and picking was significantly more pronounced compared to the decrease in lower-alpha ($t(1438) = 3.9937$, $p < 0.001$). In order to estimate the dynamic changes in the power distribution of the alpha frequency band throughout the course of the experiment, we split the set of 12 games into thirds. The first third included games 1 through 4, the middle third, games 5 through 8, and the final third, games 9 through 12. Table 1 displays the average values of the relative changes in upper- and lower-alpha together with the p-value associated with each of the paired t-tests.

It is evident form Table 1 that the same trend appeared at the first (games 1–4) and middle (games 5–8) thirds of the experiment ($t(478) = 5.7788$, $p < 0.001$; $t(478) = 3.5248$, $p < 0.001$, respectively). Regarding the final third (games 91–2), it can be seen that the average change in upper-alpha was lower than in lower-alpha, but the difference was not significant. Figure 4 resents graphically the distribution of the data by box plots. The three upper panels present the boxplots for upper- and lower-alpha according to the split of the data by thirds. The lower panel displays the boxplot corresponding to each sub-band for the entire dataset of 12 games.

**Table 1.** Relative power change between coordination and picking in alpha sub-band (lower and upper) – t-test results.

| | All games | Games 1- 4 | Games 5- 8 | Games 9- 12 |
|---|---|---|---|---|
| Mean ($\frac{E_{lower-Alpha}|coordination}{E_{lower-Alpha}|picking}$) | 0.9084 | 0.8812 | 0.9052 | 0.9389 |
| Mean ($\frac{E_{upper-Alpha}|coordination}{E_{upper-Alpha}|picking}$) | 0.8740 | 0.8284 | 0.8550 | 0.9385 |
| t-test p-value | p < 0.001 | p < 0.001 | p < 0.001 | p > 0.05 |

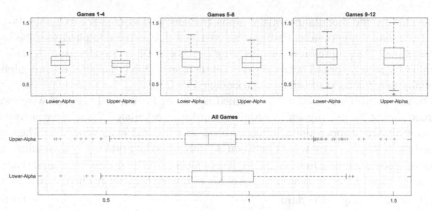

**Fig. 4.** Relative power change between coordination and picking in alpha sub-band (lower and upper) – boxplot scheme

## 4   Conclusions and Future Work

The alpha frequency band has been previously shown to be modulated by mental workload [23, 24], and alertness [25]. The overarching goal of the current study was to examine the susceptibility of the lower- and higher-alpha frequency bands to varying levels of mental effort corresponding to different level-k. In this study we employed two cognitive tasks, i.e., picking and coordination, each associated with a different level-k (level-k = 0 and level-k > 0, respectively).

Our results indicate that the differential effect of level-k on the alpha sub-bands was modulated as a function of task progression. Specifically, in the first and middle thirds of the dataset (games 1–4 and games 5–8, respectively) the difference in relative energy in the alpha band was significant, whereas, in the case of the last third of the dataset (games 9–12) there was no difference in the relative energy in the alpha band indicating that the alpha sub-bands were less sensitive to the differential effect of level-k in the final section of the experiment. The decrease in the upper alpha frequency band in the coordination task (level-k > 0) was more pronounced compared to the lower-alpha subband (see Table 1). The more pronounced decrease in upper alpha is further confirmation of the effect of performing the semantic task which known as alpha desynchronization [26]. These results are consistent with previous studies [26–28] that showed that there is connection between intensity and fluctuations in alpha frequency band to abilities such as language, imagination, perception, and planning abilities that can be termed brain cognition.

There are a number of possible directions for future research. Behavioral experiments have shown that players in coordination games are influenced by a variety of factors such as loss-aversion [29], social value orientation [30–32] revenue distribution [30] and culture [31, 33]. The effect of these factors and the possible interaction effects should be examined in the context of level-k and since they may contribute to the variability in the individual coordination ability of players [34, 35] and therefore modulate the associated electrophysiological patterns. Moreover, extracting the brain sources associated with different level-k may improve models that aim to simulate the behavior of autonomous agents [36–39] as well as brain-computer interfaces.

## Appendix A: Alpha Band Decomposition and Relative Power Estimation

Following the pre-processing step, we have estimated the relative power in the alpha sub-bands (lower and upper alpha) for each picking and coordination epoch. The full process of alpha band power estimation is presented in Fig. A.1. we have used the Discrete Wavelet Transform (DWT) [40, 41] (black rectangles). The DWT is based on a multiscale feature representation. Every scale represents a unique thickness of the EEG signal [42]. Each filtering step contains two digital filters, a high pass filter, $g(n)$, and a low pass filter $h(n)$. After applying each filter, a down sampler with factor 2 is used in order to adjust time resolution. In our case, we used a 3-level DWT, with the input signal having a sampling rate of 64 Hz (left red rectangle). As can be seen in Fig. A.1, this specific DWT scheme resulted in the coefficients of the four EEG main frequency bands (green rectangles). Next, we use two band pass filters to split the alpha band into the upper-alpha ([8–10] Hz) and lower-alpha (10–13 [Hz]) sub bands. Finally, to calculate the relative energy (right red rectangle), we divided the energy of each band by the sum of all the different bands (delta, theta, alpha, beta).

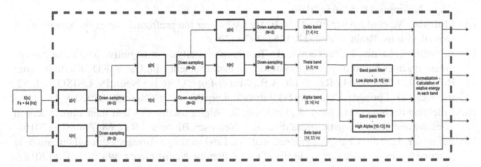

**Figure A.1.** EEG Alpha band power estimation and decomposition to lower and upper sub bands using 3 level DWT scheme

## References

1. Schelling, T.C.: The Strategy of Conflict. Harvard University Press, Cambridge (1960)
2. Mehta, J., Starmer, C., Sugden, R.: The nature of salience: an experimental investigation of pure coordination games. Am. Econ. Rev. **84**, 658–673 (1994)
3. Dong, L., Montero, M., Possajennikov, A.: Communication, leadership and coordination failure. Theor. Decis. **84**(4), 557–584 (2017). https://doi.org/10.1007/s11238-017-9617-9
4. Mizrahi, D., Laufer, I., Zuckerman, I.: Individual strategic profiles in tacit coordination games. J. Exp. Theor. Artif. Intell. **33**, 1–16 (2020)

5. Bardsley, N., Mehta, J., Starmer, C., Sugden, R.: Explaining focal points: cognitive hierarchy theory versus team reasoning. Econ. J. **120**, 40–79 (2009)
6. Jin, Y.: Does level-k behavior imply level-k thinking? Exp. Econ. **24**, 330–353 (2021)
7. Strzalecki, T.: Depth of reasoning and higher order beliefs. J. Econ. Behav. Organ. **108**, 108–122 (2014)
8. Faillo, M., Smerilli, A., Sugden, R.: The roles of level-k and team reasoning in solving coordination games (2013)
9. Mizrahi, D., Laufer, I., Zuckerman, I.: The effect of individual coordination ability on cognitive-load in tacit coordination games. In: Davis, F.D., Riedl, R., vom Brocke, J., Léger, P.-M., Randolph, A.B., Fischer, T. (eds.) NeuroIS. LNISO, vol. 43, pp. 244–252. Springer, Cham (2020). https://doi.org/10.1007/978-3-030-60073-0_28
10. Laufer, I., Mizrahi, D., Zuckerman, I.: An electrophysiological model for assessing cognitive load in tacit coordination games. Sensors. **22**, 477 (2022)
11. Mizrahi, D., Laufer, I., Zuckerman, I.: Level-K classification from EEG signals using transfer learning. Sensors. **21**, 7908 (2021)
12. Renard, Y., et al.: OpenViBE: an open-source software platform to design, test, and use brain–computer interfaces in real and virtual environments. Presence Teleoperators Virtual Environ. **19**, 35–53 (2010)
13. Gartner, M., Grimm, S., Bajbouj, M.: Frontal midline theta oscillations during mental arithmetic: effects of stress. Front. Behav. Neurosci. **9**, 1–8 (2015)
14. De Vico Fallani, F., et al.: Defecting or not defecting: How to "read" human behavior during cooperative games by EEG measurements. PLoS One **5**, e14187 (2010)
15. Boudewyn, M., Roberts, B.M., Mizrak, E., Ranganath, C., Carter, C.S.: Prefrontal transcranial direct current stimulation (tDCS) enhances behavioral and EEG markers of proactive control. Cogn. Neurosci. **10**, 57–65 (2019)
16. Moliadze, V., et al.: After-effects of 10 Hz tACS over the prefrontal cortex on phonological word decisions. Brain Stimul. **12**, 1464–1474 (2019)
17. Mizrahi, D., Laufer, I., Zuckerman, I.: Topographic analysis of cognitive load in tacit coordination games based on electrophysiological measurements. In: Davis, F.D., Riedl, R., vom Brocke, J., Léger, P.-M., Randolph, A.B., Müller-Putz, G. (eds.) NeuroIS. LNISO, vol. 52, pp. 162–171. Springer, Cham (2021). https://doi.org/10.1007/978-3-030-88900-5_18
18. Eidelman-Rothman, M., Levy, J., Feldman, R.: Alpha oscillations and their impairment in affective and post-traumatic stress disorders. Neurosci. Biobehav. Rev. **68**, 794–815 (2016)
19. Jaquess, K.J., et al.: Changes in mental workload and motor performance throughout multiple practice sessions under various levels of task difficulty. Neuroscience **393**, 305–318 (2018)
20. Shaw, E.P., et al.: Cerebral cortical networking for mental workload assessment under various demands during dual-task walking. Exp. Brain Res. **237**(9), 2279–2295 (2019). https://doi.org/10.1007/s00221-019-05550-x
21. Micheloyannis, S., Vourkas, M., Bizas, M., Simos, P., Stam, C.J.: Changes in linear and nonlinear EEG measures as a function of task complexity: evidence for local and distant signal synchronization. Brain Topogr. **15**, 239–247 (2003). https://doi.org/10.1023/A:1023962125598
22. Neubauer, A.C., Fink, A.: Fluid intelligence and neural efficiency: effects of task complexity and sex. Pers. Individ. Dif. **35**, 811–827 (2003)
23. Sterman, M.B., Mann, C.A.: Concepts and applications of EEG analysis in aviation performance evaluation. Biol. Psychol. **40**, 115–130 (1995)
24. So, W.K.Y., Wong, S.W.H., Mak, J.N., Chan, R.H.M.: An evaluation of mental workload with frontal EEG. PLoS ONE **12**, e0174949 (2017)
25. Kamzanova, A.T., Kustubayeva, A.M., Matthews, G.: Use of EEG workload indices for diagnostic monitoring of vigilance decrement. Hum. Factors **56**, 1136–1149 (2014)

26. Klimesch, W.: EEG alpha and theta oscillations reflect cognitive and memory performance: a review and analysis. Brain Res. Rev. **29**, 169–195 (1999)
27. Dahal, N., Nandagopal, N., Nafalski, A., Nedic, Z.: Modeling of cognition using EEG: a review and a new approach. In: TENCON 2011–2011 IEEE Region 10 Conference, pp. 1045–1049 (2011)
28. Antonenko, P., Paas, F., Grabner, R., van Gog, T.: Using electroencephalography to measure cognitive load. Educ. Psychol. Rev. **22**, 425–438 (2010). https://doi.org/10.1007/s10648-010-9130-y
29. Mizrahi, D., Laufer, I., Zuckerman, I.: The effect of loss-aversion on strategic behaviour of players in divergent interest tacit coordination games. In: Mahmud, M., Vassanelli, S., Kaiser, M.S., Zhong, N. (eds.) BI 2020. LNCS (LNAI), vol. 12241, pp. 41–49. Springer, Cham (2020). https://doi.org/10.1007/978-3-030-59277-6_4
30. Mizrahi, D., Laufer, I., Zuckerman, I.: The effect of expected revenue proportion and social value orientation index on players' behavior in divergent interest tacit coordination games. In: Mahmud, M., Kaiser, M.S., Vassanelli, S., Dai, Q., Zhong, N. (eds.) BI 2021. LNCS (LNAI), vol. 12960, pp. 25–34. Springer, Cham (2021). https://doi.org/10.1007/978-3-030-86993-9_3
31. Mizrahi, D., Laufer, I., Zuckerman, I., Zhang, T.: The effect of culture and social orientation on Player's performances in tacit coordination games. In: Wang, S., Yamamoto, V., Su, J., Yang, Y., Jones, E., Iasemidis, L., Mitchell, T. (eds.) BI 2018. LNCS (LNAI), vol. 11309, pp. 437–447. Springer, Cham (2018). https://doi.org/10.1007/978-3-030-05587-5_41
32. Mizrahi, D., Laufer, I., Zuckerman, I.: Predicting focal point solution in divergent interest tacit coordination games. J. Exp. Theor. Artif. Intell. 1–21 (2021)
33. Mizrahi, D., Laufer, I., Zuckerman, I.: Collectivism-individualism: strategic behavior in tacit coordination games. PLoS One **15**, e0226929 (2020)
34. Mizrahi, D., Laufer, I., Zuckerman, I.: Modeling individual tacit coordination abilities. In: Liang, P., Goel, V., Shan, C. (eds.) BI 2019. LNCS, vol. 11976, pp. 29–38. Springer, Cham (2019). https://doi.org/10.1007/978-3-030-37078-7_4
35. Mizrahi, D., Laufer, I., Zuckerman, I.: Modeling and predicting individual tacit coordination ability. Brain Inf. **9**, 4 (2022). https://doi.org/10.1186/s40708-022-00152-w
36. Mizrahi, D., Laufer, I., Zuckerman, I.: Optimizing performance in diverge interest tacit coordination games using an autonomous agent. In: The 21st Israeli Industrial Engineering and Management Conference (2019)
37. Mizrahi, D., Zuckerman, I., Laufer, I.: Using a stochastic agent model to optimize performance in divergent interest tacit coordination games. Sensors **20**, 7026 (2020)
38. Cheng, K.L., Zuckerman, I., Nau, D., Golbeck, J.: The life game: cognitive strategies for repeated stochastic games. In: 2011 IEEE Third International Conference on Privacy, Security, Risk and Trust and 2011 IEEE Third International Conference on Social Computing, pp. 95–102 (2011)
39. Kraus, S.: Predicting human decision-making: from prediction to action. In: Proceedings of the 6th International Conference on Human-Agent Interaction, p. 1 (2018)
40. Shensa, M.J.: The discrete wavelet transform: wedding the a Trous and Mallat algorithms. IEEE Trans signal Process **40**, 2464–2482 (1992)
41. Jensen, A., la Cour-Harbo, A.: Ripples in Mathematics: The Discrete Wavelet Transform. Springer, Heidelberg (2001). https://doi.org/10.1007/978-3-642-56702-5
42. Hazarika, N., Chen, J.Z., Tsoi, A.C., Sergejew, A.: Classification of EEG signals using the wavelet transform. Signal Process. **59**, 61–72 (1997)

# Toward the Study of the Neural-Underpinnings of Dyslexia During Final-Phoneme Elision: A Machine Learning Approach

Christoforos Christoforou[1]([⊠]), Timothy C. Papadopoulos[2], and Maria Theodorou[1]

[1] Division of Computer Science, Mathematics and Science, St. John's University, New York, USA
christoc@stjohns.edu
[2] Department of Psychology and Center for Applied Neuroscience, University of Cyprus, Nicosia, Cyprus

**Abstract.** Identifying the neural basis of dyslexia is a fundamental goal of developmental neuroscience. Final-phoneme elision (PE) test is a paradigm used for assessing phonological deficit (PD), which is widely considered a causal risk factor for dyslexia. However, the causal relationship between PD to dyslexia has been examined primarily based on behavioral observations. Towards facilitating the exploration of the neurophysiological origins of the theorized link between PD and dyslexia, we set out to isolate differential neural activation patterns in children with dyslexia during PE. Accordingly, we present a machine-learning-based approach to identifying differential brain activity in children with dyslexia and controls during the PE. Our method formulates an optimization problem to extract informative EEG components based on the 'Neural-congruency hypothesis', termed Phoneme-related Neural-congruency components. It then uses a machine-learning algorithm to optimally combine the resulting components to differentiate between the neural activity of children with dyslexia and controls. We apply our approach to a real EEG dataset involving children with dyslexia and controls. Our findings demonstrate that our method generates novel insights into the neural underpinnings of dyslexia and the potential neural origins of phonological deficits as a causal factor of dyslexia. Notably, our approach overcomes several methodological challenges in conventional EEG analysis methods; therefore, it could be utilized in studying the neural origins of other behaviorally defined developmental disorders previously overlooked because of such methodological constraints.

**Keywords:** Electroencephalography · EEG · Neural-congruency · Dyslexia · Final-phoneme Elision · Neural-based models

## 1 Introduction

Developmental dyslexia is a neuro-developmental disorder characterized by the difficulty of children learning to read, affecting 5%–20% of children [15, 15]. Current research suggests that dyslexia originates from a weakness in phonological awareness -

M. Mahmud et al. (Eds.): BI 2022, LNAI 13406, pp. 74–85, 2022
https://doi.org/10.1007/978-3-031-15037-1_7

one's ability to make judgments of and perform conscious manipulations on the sound structure of spoken words [13]. Indeed, the Phonological Deficits Hypothesis (PDH) postulates that Phonological Deficits (PD) are causally linked to dyslexia [16]. However, the relationship between PD to dyslexia has been primarily considered for behavioral observations [12]. Hence, studies need to explore the neurophysiological origins of the link between PD and dyslexia.

One paradigm for capturing behavioral measures of PD is the Final-phoneme Elision Test (PE) which is used as part of dyslexia screening protocols for children. PE measures phonological awareness at the phonemic sensitivity level [14]. As part of the PE test, participants are asked to identify which word is produced after eliminating the final phoneme from a given target word. Behavioral measures of accuracy (i.e., number of correct responses) and response time quantify performance. These measures are robust, concurrent and longitudinal predictors of children's reading ability [13] across languages (e.g., [2]). However, to our knowledge, few studies explore the neurophysiological basis of these differences observed during PE [11]. We argue that this lack of studies is due to methodological challenges in isolating informative neural components in neurophysiological measures during PE.

Electroencephalography (EEG) signals are often used as a neuro-imaging modality to study the underlying neural basis of neurocognitive processes and explore their connection to behavioral observations of cognitive deficits. Such studies typically involve participants performing an experimental paradigm pertinent to the neurocognitive function being researched while their EEG signals are recorded. Typically, such experiments elicit time-locked Event-related Potentials (ERP) - stereotypical neural waveforms evoked in the brain in response to an event, such as the presentation of the brief stimulus or event. ERPs are known to be modulated by the underlying cognitive processes involved in the experimental task performance. EEG analysis methods can then be employed to extract informative components from the ERP waveforms and gain insights into the underlying neural basis of the cognitive process. However, isolating such information from the EEG responses can be a challenging methodological task in general because of the feeble signal strength of ERP and the low signal-to-noise ratio (often less than $-20$ dB) in the EEG data. Therefore, analysis methods need to consider prior domain knowledge about the nature of the ERP waveforms (i.e., spatial distribution) that can be experimental paradigm specific.

Traditional ERP analysis methods attempt to extract ERP components from the EEG signals by averaging participants' neural responses across multiple trials and obtaining a grant-average ERP waveform for each participant or group. The resulting grant-average ERP waveform exhibit visually recognizable features (i.e., peaks or valleys in the waveform at specific timestamps after the event's onset) referred to as ERP components. The latency and amplitude of these ERP components are used as dependent variables to establish differences between groups and conditions and to gain insights into the neural underpinning of the cognitive process [1]. However, a limitation of ERP analysis is that it only explores neural-activity time-locked to the event's onset and only for a short time window after the onset (typically < 500 ms). Thus, it cannot efficiently capture differential neural activity occurring beyond this time window. Moreover, EPR analysis only explores neural activity differences at predefined timestamps where the peaks and valleys of the ERP waveform appear, ignoring the rest of the signal. As we argue below, these assumptions do not hold during the PE task, which limits the applicability of ERP analysis in our study.

Despite its limitations, ERP analysis has been successfully employed in studying the neural basis of several psychological processes, including attention, memory and conditions, decision making, personality traits, perception, and intelligence [3]. In addition, ERP analysis has been used for studying auditory speech-processing deficits and their relation to dyslexia (see [9, 10, 18] and references therein). However, this was done through surrogate experimental paradigms, such as the oddball experiment and the mismatch negativity, and not directly on the phoneme elision task.

Machine Learning (ML) methods have also been employed to analyze EEG signals for studying neurocognitive processes. Typically, these ML methods attempt to extract neural components by identifying spatial projections (i.e., a weighted average across channels) of the single-trial ERP components that are informative of differences across conditions and groups. For example, Single-trial Discimiminant Analysis [17] was proposed to characterize the neural correlates of perceptual decision-making by employing a moving-window classifier trained locally over the time of the ERP. In the context of spatial cognition, a Commons Spatial Pattern (CSP)-based single-trial analysis [6] was proposed for the neural basis disambiguation of the spatial-cognition processes- namely, Perspective Taking and Mental Rotation. Single-trial Correlation Analysis [3] was proposed for studying the neural underpinnings for the Stimulus Presentation Modality Effects in Traumatic-Brain-Injury treatment protocols. In general, ML methods isolate more informative neural components when compared to traditional ERP analysis methods by increasing the signal-to-noise ratio. However, they still rely on local features that are time-locked to the event onset and are typically limited to within-participant comparisons because of the large inter-subject variability in the EEG signals [5]. Therefore, current ML approaches do not consider differences in neural activity beyond the limited time window of the ERP waveform and are often localized at predefined timestamps.

Some characteristics of the PE paradigm are incongruous with the methodological assumptions of current EEG analysis approaches (both ML-based and traditional ERP analysis), making their direct application to the paradigm ineffective. First, PE generates varying-duration neural responses beyond traditional ERP time windows. Specifically, the stimuli employed in the paradigms are auditory and vary in duration from 500 ms-1500 ms across trials. As such, information of recognizing the phoneme elision span beyond the time window of traditional ERP components (typically less than 600 ms, i.e., N100, N200, P300, N400 component sets), which traditional approaches primarily exploit. Moreover, the variability in the stimulus duration suggests that neural differences likely spread throughout the signal and are not localized in a narrow time window following the stimulus onset as assumed by many ML-based methods. These PE paradigm characteristics limit the application of traditional EEG analysis methods that expect fixed-duration neural responses and localized and time-locked activations and focus primarily on exploiting differences in traditional ERP components.

This paper presents a novel machine-learning-based approach to identifying differential brain activity in children with dyslexia during the PE test. This approach overcomes many of the methodological limits of existing methods. Our method formulates an optimization problem to extract informative EEG components based on the "Neural-congruency hypothesis". This relates to the premise that neural activity elicited during a cognitive task is similar (i.e., congruent) among participants that have mastered the task but less congruent otherwise [7, 8]. In doing so, our approach overcomes the need for having fixed-duration stimuli and localized time-locked activations. It can exploit neural activations beyond the traditional ERP components and spread throughout the stimulus-response. It then uses a machine-learning algorithm to optimally combine the resulting components to differentiate between children with dyslexia and controls. We evaluate the utility of our approach to identify novel neural components informative of the neural underpinnings of dyslexia for PD using a real EEG dataset involving children with dyslexia and controls.

## 2  Materials and Methods

### 2.1  Experimental Paradigm and Data Collection

The data for this study were collected as part of a broader project aiming to study the neural underpinnings of dyslexia in children [4] and its relation to core cognitive deficits. This section introduces a specific task's design and data collection apparatus: final phoneme elision.

**Final Phoneme Elision Paradigm.** The Final-phoneme Elision test comprises a set of 100 trials where in each trial, participants listen to a target word followed by a 1500 ms pause and then listen to a second word. In 50% of the items, the second word is formed by removing the final phoneme from the target word. A participant's task was then to respond (by pressing an appropriate key on the keyboard after each trial) to whether the second word was formed by the omission of the final phoneme from the target word or not. The participants had up to 2500 ms to respond. A training session demonstrated the task to the participants before completing the main trial sequence.

**Participants and EEG Data Collection.** Participants for the experiment were recruited from inner-city public elementary schools in Cyprus. A total of 90 children were recruited, half of which (i.e., 45 children) were identified as children with Dyslexia (DYS) and the other half as a group of chronological-age control (CAC). All participants were native Greek speakers in Grades 3 and 6 (refer to [4] for details on the recruiting and screening procedures). As part of the study, participants had to complete the Final-phoneme Elision test while EEG signals were measured. As part of the experiment session, participants were fitted with a standard 64-channel EEG cap. Electrodes were placed following the 10/20 layout. DC offsets of all sensors were kept below 20 mV using electro-gel. A trigger channel was used to record time markers denoting the onset of all events in interest (i.e., presentation of the first and second word and participants' response). A Biosemi Active-two system (BioSemi, Amsterdam, Netherlands) was used to collect the EEG data. The study was carried out per the Cyprus National Bioethics Committee recommendations and received approval from the Ministry of Education and Culture, Cyprus (#7.15.01.27/17).

**EEG Pre-processing.** All EEG data preprocessing was implemented using custom python code and the MNE library. Preprocessing was done separately on the recordings of each individual. First, all EEG channels were re-referenced to the average channel. Then, a 0.5 Hz high pass filter was applied to the continuous EEG data to remove DC drifts, followed by the application of notch filters at 50 Hz and 100 Hz to reduce the power-line noise interference. As the study focused on exploring neural activity relevant to PD and the recognition of the final-phoneme elision, continuous EEG data were epoched based on the onset of the second word (i.e., the elision word). Specifically, continuous EEG was epoched starting $-200$ ms before the second word's onset until the second word's articulation. Each epoch was then normalized by dividing each channel by the standard deviation across time.

After all preprocessing steps, the observations of each participant $i$, comprise a set of EEG trials $\{X_i^1, X_i^2, \ldots X_i^N\}$, where each, $X_i^k \in \mathbb{R}^{D \times T_k}$ corresponds to the neural activity following the onset of the elision word of the k-th trial; $T_k$ is the trial duration; $D = 64$ denotes the number of channels, and $N = 100$ is the number of trials.

## 2.2 Phoneme-Related Neural-Congruency Components

Our goal in this analysis was to isolate those components in the EEG signal modulated by the final phoneme-elision processing and are predictive of differences between DYS and CAC groups. Our approach is motivated by the hypothesis that a group of individuals with developed phonological skills (i.e., the CAC group) would exhibit congruent neural activation patterns when engaged in phoneme-elision. On the contrary, the corresponding neural activation patterns of individuals with phonological deficits (i.e., DYS) will deviate from such consonance. Grounded on this hypothesis, we formulated an optimization procedure to isolate neural components congruent among participants in the CAC group and explore those components as potential differentiating metrics between CAC and DYS. This section introduces our approach for isolating such phoneme-related neural-congruency components. The following section discusses how we employ machine learning to differentiate between DYS and CAC using the extracted neural components.

Consider the group of participants in the CAC group as $S = \{s_1, s_2, .., s_S\}$ where $s_i \in \mathbb{Z}^+$ denotes the participants' index. We define the *between-subject*, $R_b \in \mathbb{R}^{D \times D}$ and *within-subject* $R_w \in \mathbb{R}^{D \times D}$ cross-covariance matrix as follows:

$$R_b = \frac{1}{S(S-1)} \sum_{i \in S} \sum_{j \in S} (1 - \delta_{ij}) R_{ij}$$

$$R_w = \frac{1}{S} \sum_{i \in S} R_{ii}$$

where

$$R_{ij} = \frac{1}{K} X_i X_j^T$$

K is a normalizing constant, and $X_i \in \mathbb{R}^{D \times T}$ is the matrix comprised of all single-trial EEG of participant $i$, concatenated across columns, defined as:

$$X_i = [X_i^1, X_i^2, \ldots X_i^N]$$

For a given projection vector $w \in \mathbb{R}^D$, the average Pearson Product Moment Correlation Coefficient between the concatenated single-trial responses, projected onto vector $w$, across every pair of participants in group $S$ is defined as:

$$\rho = \frac{w^T R_b w}{(w^T R_w w)}$$

The correlation coefficient $\rho$ can be considered as a measure of the degree of congruency in neural activity of the component $w$, among participants with intact phonological awareness. Therefore, we aim to identify those components $w$ that maximize $\rho$. That is

$$\hat{w} = \arg_w \max \frac{w^T R_b w}{(w^T R_w w)} \tag{1}$$

The solution of the optimization in (1) are the eigenvectors of the generalized eigenvalue problem:

$$(R_w^{(-1)} R_b) w_k = \lambda_k w_k$$

where $w_k$ is the k-th eigenvector of the matrix $(R_w^{-1} R_b)$ and corresponds to the components that capture the k-th most considerable correlation in neural activity, while $\lambda_k$ is the corresponding eigenvalue that captures the strength of the correlation. We note that Eq. (1) has $D$ solutions (i.e., $\{\hat{w}_1, \hat{w}_2, \ldots, \hat{w}_D,\}$) corresponding to the D eigenvectors of the matrix $(R_w^{-1} R_b)$, and the solutions are ordered from the highest to the lowest eigenvalue.

Given the set of solution vectors $\{\hat{w}_1, \hat{w}_2, \ldots, \hat{w}_D,\}$, we define the *phoneme-related neural congruency* (PRNC) of an individual $s \notin S$ with respect to the k-th component $\hat{w}_k$, as:

$$PRNC_{s,k} = \frac{\hat{w}_k^T R_s^b \hat{w}_k}{\hat{w}_k^T R_s^b \hat{w}_k}$$

where

$$R_s^b = \frac{1}{S} \sum_{i \in S} R_{si} + R_{is}, \quad R_s^w = \frac{1}{S} \sum_{i \in S} R_{ss} + R_{ii},$$

In our analysis, we calculated the *Phoneme-related neural congruency* scores (i.e. PRNC) separately for each participant. The participants' data for which the PRNC score was to be calculated was excluded from the component extraction step to avoid training bias during the optimal component extraction. The PRNC measures the strength of the congruency of the neural activity between a given individual and the CAC group for each component. Therefore, the congruent activity of each participant for the first $\dot{D} = 10$

components (i.e., those with the highest eigenvalues) is captured by a vector $\boldsymbol{u}(s)$ defined as:

$$\boldsymbol{u}(s) = \left[PRNC_{s,1}, PRNC_{s,2}, \ldots PRNC_{s,D}, \right]^T$$

The vector $\boldsymbol{u}(s)$ is a feature vector that captures the strength of congruency in neural activity of participant $s$ in the CAC group for the first $\dot{D}$ components.

### 2.3 Classification of Phoneme-Related Neural-Congruency Components

Our goal was to explore the use of the feature vector of neural-congruency components $\boldsymbol{u}(s)$ as a predictor of a participant's group assignment (i.e., DYS or CAC). Moreover, we aimed to investigate which neural-congruency components carry predictive information. Towards this goal, we formulated a classification model. Specifically, we considered the dataset.

$$\left\{\boldsymbol{u}(s) \in \mathbb{R}^{\dot{D}}, y_s \in \{DYS, CAC\}\right\}_{\forall s \in S}$$

and employed a sparse logistic regression classifier using the vector $\boldsymbol{u}(s)$ as independent variables, and an individual's group $y_s$ as the dependent variable. The classifier is trained using a leave-one-participant-out cross-validation procedure to avoid training bias. The generalization performance of the classifier was calculated as the area under the Receivers Operator Characteristic curve (AUC). The statistical significance of AUC scores was established using a permutation test (10,000 repetitions). Finally, the coefficients of the lasso classifier were inspected to identify components that likely carry predictive information between the groups.

### 2.4 Spatiotemporal Profiles of Phoneme-Related Neural-Congruency Components

Given the solutions to the generalized eigenvalue problem, the temporal profile of each component was calculated as the product of each component $\widehat{w}_k$, with each of the single-trial responses and taking the grant-average response of the projected components. Moreover, the topographical profile (i.e. the forward model) of each component was calculated as:

$$a_k = \frac{R_w \widehat{w}_k}{\widehat{w}_k^T R_w \widehat{w}_k}$$

The forward model captures the covariance between each component's activity as measured by each electrode.

## 3  Results

We aimed to explore whether neural activity measured by the extracted phoneme-related neural congruency components is informative in differentiating between children with dyslexia and CAC; therefore, to gain insights into the neural basis of the causal link between PD, as captured in the PE task, and dyslexia. To assess this, we trained a sparse lasso classifier using the PRNC scores as features and evaluated the ability of the classifier to differentiate between groups. A leave-one-participant-out cross-validation assessment indicates that the classifiers achieved an area-under-the-curve (AUC) score of 0.79. The Receiver Operating Characteristic (ROC) curve that illustrates the classifier's performance is shown in Fig. 1. The permutation test confirms that the classifier's AUC score is statistically significantly higher than random performance $p < .001$, thus rejecting the null hypothesis. The strong classifier performance indicates that the neural activity carried within the phoneme-related neural congruency components encapsulates the neural underpinnings of PD and dyslexia.

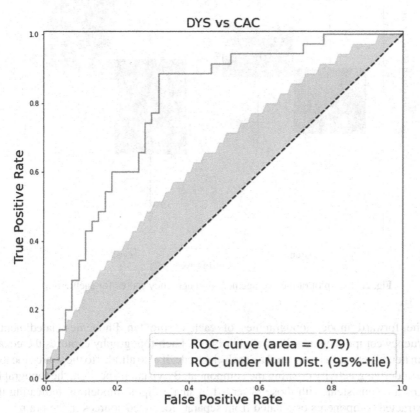

**Fig. 1.** Receiver Operating Characteristic (ROC) curve showing the cross-validation classification performance. Light-gray indicates the expected performance under the null-hypothesis

Further, a two-way ANOVA comparing the effect of participants' grade (i.e., Grade 3 vs Grade 6) and Group (DYS vs CAC) showed a significant main effect ($F(2,86) = 12.15, p < .0001$), and also significant group differences ($T(2,86) = 4.94, p < .0001$), and intercept ($T(2,96) = 12.16, p < .0001$) were revealed. The ANOVA model did not yield significant age group differences ($T(2,86) = 0.24$, *ns*). The box plots for the two-way ANOVA (Fig. 2) show that the lasso-weighted PRNC scores are higher in the CAC group than in the DYS group.

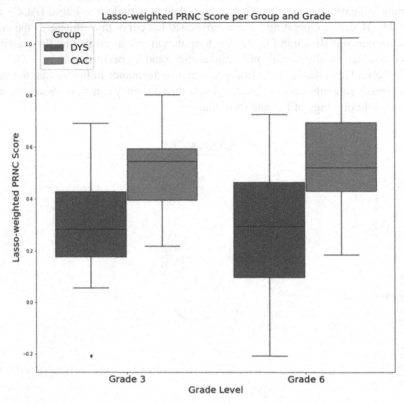

**Fig. 2.** Box-plot of the average neural-congruency scores for each group.

The forward model topographies of each of the ten Phoneme-related neural-congruency components are illustrated in Fig. 3. Each topography captures the covariance in neural activity as measured by each electrode. It also alludes to the source location of the underlying activity eliciting the component. By visual inspection, the topographic patterns are consistent with those observed in single-dipole modeling, indicating that the extracted components originated from separate localized sources in the brain.

## 4   Discussion and Conclusion

In this study, we explore whether neural activity captured by the proposed phoneme-related neural-congruency components was informative of differences between children with dyslexia (DYS) and without (i.e., CAC) to facilitate the exploration of the neurophysiological origins of the theorized link between PD and dyslexia. Towards this investigation, we propose a novel machine-learning-based approach to identify differential neural activity between children with dyslexia and a chronological-age control group during the final-phoneme elision test. Our method overcomes several methodological challenges in existing EEG analysis methods that have hindered exploring such neural components during PE. Specifically, our approach overcomes traditional methods requiring experiments with fixed-duration neural responses that assume localized time-locked activations. Therefore, our approach can isolate neural components during PE characterized by varying stimulus-response durations and whose activations are not localized in a narrow time window. Moreover, our method does not explicitly target traditional ERP components. Instead, it captures regularities spread throughout the stimulus-response and beyond the conventional ERP components window, which allows it to capture the differences in PE responses traditional methods cannot. The utility of our approach is demonstrated on a real-life EEG dataset.

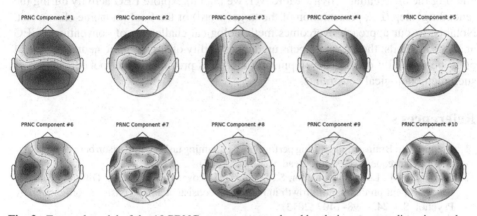

**Fig. 3.** Forward model of the 10 PRNC components, ordered by their corresponding eigenvalue

The primary result of this study is evidence suggesting that congruency among neural activations captures information about the underlying neural basis of the causal link between phonological deficits and dyslexia in children. Particularly, the proposed phoneme-related neural-congruency components carry information that differentiates between DYS and CAC (AUC 0.79, $p < .0001$), suggesting that the neural activation patterns of the two groups differ. Specifically, results show that children without phonological deficits (i.e., CAC) exhibit similar neural activation patterns with respect to the phoneme-related neural congruency components, which suggest a set of common underlying neural basis that are activated synchronously to identify and recognize phone elision. In contrast, the neural activation patterns in children with dyslexia deviate from this congruency pattern, which points to the potential underlying neural causes of phonological deficits. We interpret these findings as indicating that children with phonological deficits have not yet optimized the neural pathways for recognizing phoneme elision.

Further examination of the results provides additional insights into interpreting the neural-congruency components. In particular, the two-way ANOVA revealed a main effect on the group (DYS vs CAC) factor but no effect on the participant's age factor, suggesting that neural-congruency components capture neural activity relevant to a core phonological deficit independent of age. Moreover, an inspection of the neural-congruency components' forward model exhibit topographies consistent with the single-dipole model, suggesting that the source of their neural activity in the brain is localized. Moreover, differences between DYS and CAC groups are observed in the combined neural activity of a small set of neural-congruency components. Hence, we infer the differences in the final-phoneme elision occur by contributions from multiple brain regions and spread over the entire time window processing the elision stimulus.

In conclusion, we proposed a novel approach to extracting informative components from EEG activity during the final-phoneme elision test. Our findings demonstrate that our method generates novel insights into the neural underpinnings of dyslexia and the potential neural origins of phonological deficits as a causal factor of dyslexia. In future studies, we plan to explore the spatial sources of the identified neural-congruency components by using source localization techniques to identify the corresponding brain areas eliciting the differential activity. Moreover, we plan to explore EEG activity during the 'encoding' step (i.e., presentation of the target word) of the final-phoneme elision test. Notably, as our approach overcomes methodological challenges of conventional EEG analysis methods; therefore, it opens up the possibility of studying the neural origins of other behaviorally defined developmental disorders previously overlooked because of such methodological constraints.

## References s

1. Breznitz, Z.: Brain activity during performance of naming tasks: comparison between dyslexic and regular readers. Sci. Stud. Read. **9**, 17–42 (2005)
2. Caravolas, M., Lervåg, A., Defior, S., Seidlová Málková, G., Hulme, C.: Different patterns, but equivalent predictors, of growth in reading in consistent and inconsistent orthographies. Psychol. Sci. **24**, 1398–1407 (2013)
3. Christoforou, C., Constantinidou, F., Shoshilou, P., Simos, P.: Single-trial linear correlation analysis: application to characterization of stimulus modality effects. Front. Comput. Neurosci. **7**, 15 (2013)
4. Christoforou, C., Fella, A., Leppänen, P.H.T., Georgiou, G.K., Papadopoulos, T.C.: Fixation-related potentials in naming speed: a combined EEG and eye-tracking study on children with dyslexia. Clin. Neurophysiol. **132**, 2798–2807 (2021)
5. Christoforou, C., Haralick, R.M., Sajda, P., Parra, L.C.: The bilinear brain: towards subject-invariant analysis. In: 2010 4th International Symposium on Communications, Control and Signal Processing (ISCCSP), pp. 1–6. IEEE (2010)
6. Christoforou, C., Hatzipanayioti, A., Avraamides, M.: Perspective taking vs mental rotation: CSP-based single-trial analysis for cognitive process disambiguation. In: Wang, S., et al. (eds.) BI 2018. LNCS (LNAI), vol. 11309, pp. 109–118. Springer, Cham (2018). https://doi.org/10.1007/978-3-030-05587-5_11
7. Christoforou, C., Papadopoulos, T.C., Theodorou, M.: Single-trial FRPs: a machine learning approach towards the study of the neural underpinnings of reading disorders. In: The International FLAIRS Conference Proceedings, vol. 34 (2021)
8. Christoforou, C., Theodorou, M.: Towards EEG-based emotion recognition during video viewing: neural-congruency explains user's emotion experienced in music video. In: The International FLAIRS Conference Proceedings, vol. 34 (2021)
9. Desroches, A.S., Newman, R.L., Robertson, E.K., Joanisse, M.: Electrophysiological indices of phonological impairments in dyslexia. J. Speech Lang. Hear. Res. **56**, 250–264 (2013)

10. Hämäläinen, J.A., Landi, N., Loberg, O., Lohvansuu, K., Pugh, K., Leppänen, P.H.T.: Brain event-related potentials to phoneme contrasts and their correlation to reading skills in school-age children. Int. J. Behav. Dev. **2**, 357–372 (2018)
11. Kovelman, I., et al.: Brain basis of phonological awareness for spoken language in children and its disruption in dyslexia. Cereb. Cortex **22**, 754–764 (2012)
12. O'Brien, B.A., Wolf, M., Lovett, M.W.: A taxometric investigation of developmental dyslexia subtypes. Dyslexia **18**, 16–39 (2012)
13. Papadopoulos, T.C., Spanoudis, G., Kendeou, P.: The dimensionality of phonological abilities in Greek. Read. Res. Q. **44**, 127–143 (2009)
14. Papadopoulos, T.C., Georgiou, G.K., Parrila, R.K.: Low-level deficits in beat perception: neither necessary nor sufficient for explaining developmental dyslexia in a consistent orthography. Res. Dev. Disabil. **33**, 1841–1856 (2012)
15. Parrila, R.K., Georgiou, G.K., Papadopoulos, T.C.: Dyslexia in a consistent orthography: evidence from reading-level match design. Dyslexia **26**, 343–358 (2020)
16. Parrila, R.K., Protopapas, A.: Dyslexia and word reading problems. In: Cain, K., Compton, D., Parrila, R. (eds.) Theories of Reading Development, pp. 333–358. John Benjamins, Amsterdam (2017)
17. Philiastides, M.G., Sajda, P.: Temporal characterization of the neural correlates of perceptual decision-making in the human brain. Cereb. Cortex **16**, 509–518 (2005)
18. Schulte-Körne, G., Bruder, J.: Clinical neurophysiology of visual and auditory processing in dyslexia: a review. Clin. Neurophysiol. **121**, 1794–1809 (2010)
19. Wagner, R.K., et al.: The prevalence of dyslexia: a new approach to its estimation. J. Learn. Disabil. **53**, 354–365 (2020)

# Root-Cause Analysis of Activation Cascade Differences in Brain Networks

Qihang Yao[1], Manoj Chandrasekaran[1], and Constantine Dovrolis[1,2(✉)]

[1] Georgia Institute of Technology, Atlanta, GA 30332, USA
{qihang,manojc,constantine}@gatech.edu
[2] KIOS Research and Innovation Center of Excellence, Aglandjia, Cyprus

**Abstract.** Diffusion MRI imaging and tractography algorithms have enabled the mapping of the macro-scale connectome of the entire brain. At the functional level, probably the simplest way to study the dynamics of macro-scale brain activity is to compute the "activation cascade" that follows the artificial stimulation of a source region. Such cascades can be computed using the Linear Threshold model on a weighted graph representation of the connectome. The question we focus on is: *if we are given such activation cascades for two groups, say A and B (e.g., controls versus a mental disorder), what is the smallest set of brain connectivity (graph edge weight) changes that are sufficient to explain the observed differences in the activation cascades between the two groups?* We have developed and computationally validated an efficient algorithm, TRACED, to solve the previous problem. We argue that this approach to compare the connectomes of two groups, based on activation cascades, is more insightful than simply identifying "static" network differences (such as edges with large weight or centrality differences). We have also applied the proposed method in the comparison between a Major Depressive Disorder (MDD) group versus healthy controls and briefly report the resulting set of connections that cause most of the observed cascade differences.

**Keywords:** Connectome · Structural brain networks · Activation cascade · Root-cause analysis

## 1 Introduction

Diffusion MRI imaging and tractography algorithms have enabled the mapping of the macro-scale connectome of the entire brain [23]. This network representation enables the application of powerful tools from graph theory and graph algorithms in the study of the brain's structure and function. Earlier work has focused on various important network properties of the brain such as small worldness [1], presence of hubs [12], modularity [22], etc. These studies have revealed that seemingly local pathologies in specific regions can have far-reaching global effects on other parts of the brain [19, 24].

© Springer Nature Switzerland AG 2022
M. Mahmud et al. (Eds.): BI 2022, LNAI 13406, pp. 86–98, 2022
https://doi.org/10.1007/978-3-031-15037-1_8

Probably the simplest way to study the dynamics of brain activity at the macro-scale is to compute the "activation cascade" that is generated by the artificial stimulation of a source region. Activation cascades, represented in the form of directed acyclic graphs (DAGs), describe how an activation starting from one region (i.e., source node) propagates to the rest of the brain, activating other brain regions along the way. Previous work has applied the Asynchronous Linear Threshold (ALT) model on the mouse meso-scale connectome to simulate the propagation and integration of sensory signals through activation cascades [21]. Those modeling results were validated with functional data from cortical voltage-sensitive dye imaging, showing that the order of node activations in the model matches quite well with the empirical activation order observed experimentally [21].

The question that we focus on in this study is: suppose we are given two groups with significant differences in the activation cascades generated in their brain networks, what is the smallest set of brain connectivity (i.e., graph edge weight) changes that are sufficient to explain the observed differences in the activation cascades between the two groups? Answering this question can be valuable in many studies when two groups should be compared, not only in terms of structural connectome differences, but also in terms of functional dynamics. For example, we can identify a (generally small) set of brain connectivity changes that appear to cause the functional activation differences in a given disorder, by comparing the corresponding activation cascades with healthy controls. Further, the corresponding connections can be used as possible targets in interventions and treatments such as deep brain stimulation [20, 26].

We have developed an algorithm named TRACED (The Root-cause of Activation Cascade Differences) to solve the previous problem, as illustrated in Fig. 2. TRACED starts by identifying node membership differences between the two groups (say A and B) within the activation cascade of each source. Then, for each source, we identify the smallest set of edges that, if their weights in group A are modified to be equal to the weights in group B, the corresponding activation cascades will be the same in both groups. We have computationally validated TRACED across many test cases. Additionally, we have applied TRACED in the comparison between a group of patients with major depressive disorder (MDD) and a group of controls. This paper focuses on the proposed computational method – a more comprehensive MDD-focused study of the two groups will be presented in a different article.

Previous work detected significant topological differences in terms of network metrics such as edge weights and centrality measures for various neurological disorders, including multiple sclerosis [7, 15], Alzheimer's disease [6], Parkinson's disease [27], and schizophrenia [8]. We argue that the activation cascade approach to comparing the connectomes of two groups is more insightful than simply identifying such "static" network differences. The former makes some clear and simple assumptions about the processing and propagation of information in the brain, and it creates a causal connection between structural changes and functional effects. Therefore, the identified abnormalities are more interpretable and robust to subject variability.

## 2   Linear Threshold Model and Activation Cascades

Our starting point is a structural macro-scale brain network. In this network representation, the graph is denoted by $G = (V, E)$, each node in $V$ corresponds to a brain region, and $E$ contains edges that correspond to connectivity between brain regions. For structural networks constructed with diffusion tensor imaging (DTI), the edges are undirected. Each edge $(x, y)$ in $E$ is associated with a weight $w(x, y)$ that represents the strength of the corresponding connection.

In the linear threshold model, each node can be either active or inactive. Initially, all nodes are inactive, except a single source node. If a neighbor $y$ of a node $x$ is active, then we say that $x$ "receives an activation" from $y$ with strength $w(y, x)$. Node $x$ becomes active if it receives a cumulative activation from all its active neighbors that is more than a threshold $\theta$.

More formally, a node $x$ at time $t$ is associated with a binary state variable $A(x, t)$ indicating whether $x$ is active (1) or not (0). For the source node $s$, we have that $A(s, t = 0) = 1$ and for all other nodes:

$$A(x, t + 1) = 1 \text{ if } \sum_{y|(y,x)\in E} w(y, x)A(y, t) \geq \theta \tag{1}$$

for $t \geq 0$. If $x$ becomes active in the cascade of source $s$, $t_s(x)$ is the time of its activation. By convention, $t_s(x) = \infty$ if node $x$ never gets active.

An activation cascade, in the form of a directed acyclic graph (DAG), shows whether as well as how each node becomes active. The nodes in the activation cascade of source $s$ form the following set:

$$U(s) = \{x \in V \mid t_s(x) < \infty\} \tag{2}$$

The edges in the activation cascade include $(x, y) \in E$ if node $x$ becomes active before $y$. So, the presence of this edge in the cascade DAG means that $x$ participates in the activation of $y$. Mathematically,

$$F(s) = \{(x, y) \in E \mid t_s(y) < t_s(x)\} \tag{3}$$

We denote the activation cascade as $H(s) = \{U(s), F(s)\}$. In Fig. 1 we show a simple example illustrating an activation cascade generated in a toy network using the linear threshold model.

For a given $\theta$, different source nodes may give different cascade sizes. Some source nodes do not activate any other node giving rise to *empty cascades*, while other source nodes may activate every node in the network causing a *full cascade*. The third case is that of a *partial cascade*, which is more likely in practice. It would be unrealistic to set the threshold $\theta$ so high that we get many empty cascades – that would correspond to a comatose brain! However, it would also

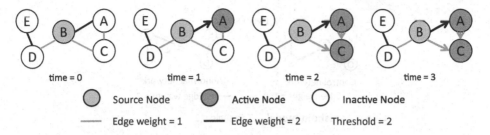

**Fig. 1.** An illustrative example of an activation cascade obtained using the linear threshold model. Node B is the source of the cascade. The threshold $\theta = 2$. Node A gets active through the edge (A, B), and node C becomes active after both A and B are active. The rest of the nodes stay inactive in this cascade.

be unrealistic to set $\theta$ so low that we get many full cascades. The previous observations guide us to choose a range of $\theta$ values that result in more partial cascades, across different source nodes.

When comparing the structural brain networks of two subjects, or two groups, we rely on the membership of each source's cascade: If a node $x$ is active in the cascade of source $s$ in one network, is $x$ also active in the corresponding cascade of the other network? The similarity between the node membership of two cascades is quantified using the Jaccard similarity metric, applied on the set of active nodes in the two cascades. A small Jaccard similarity represents a large difference between the two cascades. If $U(s)$ and $U'(s)$ denote the set of nodes activated from source $s$ in networks $G$ and $G'$, respectively, the difference between the two cascades is quantified by:

$$d\{U(s), U'(s)\} = 1 - J\{U(s), U'(s)\} = 1 - \frac{|U(s) \cap U'(s)|}{|U(s) \cup U'(s)|} \tag{4}$$

where $J\{U(s), U'(s)\}$ is the Jaccard similarity of the two cascades.

## 3   TRACED Algorithm

We expect that a mental disorder (or any other genuine distinction in the structural brain networks of a group) would cause cascade membership differences for several different sources [25, 28]. Additionally, it is reasonable to expect that these cascade membership differences will be caused by a rather small set of brain connectivity abnormalities (a larger set of abnormalities would probably be lethal). Under these assumptions, we aim to detect the smallest set of edge weight changes that can explain the observed cascade membership differences between the two groups.

**The Case of a Single Source Node:** The problem of finding the root-cause for the activation cascade differences of a single source $s$ can be formulated as follows: We are given the cascade of $s$ in the control and the abnormal networks.

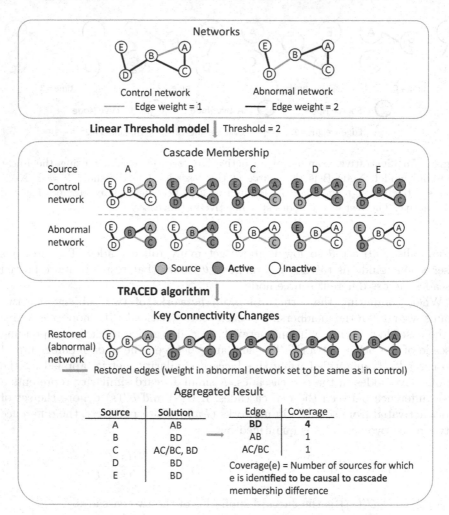

**Fig. 2.** Method overview: the abnormal and control networks may have several edges with different weights. We generate the activation cascade for each source using the linear threshold model, and identify the cascade membership differences across the two networks. We identify a subset of edges (containing only edge BD in this example) whose weight change can explain the majority of the observed cascade differences. In other words, if we restore the weights of this subset of edges in the abnormal network to be equal to the corresponding weights in the control network, the majority of the cascade differences between two networks no longer exist.

*Compute the minimum set of edges C in the abnormal network so that, if we restore the weights of those edges to be equal to the corresponding weights in the control network, the activation cascade of s will be identical in the two networks. We create C-restored network by replacing the weight of edge e (e ∈ C), in the abnormal network with the weight of e in the control network.*

The mathematical formulation of the previous problem is:

$$\hat{C} = \underset{C \in \{E \cup E'\}}{\arg\min} |C| \text{ s.t. } U'_C(s) = U(s) \tag{5}$$

where the set of active nodes in the control cascade of $s$ is denoted by $U(s)$, the set of active nodes in the abnormal cascade of $s$ is $U'(s)$, and the set of active nodes in the $C$-restored network of $s$ is $U'_C(s)$. By convention, we take the weight of any edges that are not present as 0.

A naive algorithm would be to search among all $2^m$ solutions ($m = |E \cup E'|$) but that would be computationally infeasible for the scale of structural brain networks.

Instead, the TRACED algorithm starts from an empty set $C$ and gradually "grows" the solution by adding one edge at a time. The original empty set $C$ can grow into $m$ different sets, each with a distinct edge. In the next step, each of these $m$ sets can include one of the remaining $m - 1$ edges, creating a total of $m(m - 1)$ sets with two edges each. This way, when $\hat{C}$ is found, the number of candidate solutions is $m^k$, where $k = |\hat{C}|$. Since we are adding edges step by step following an approach similar to breadth-first-search, the solution is guaranteed to be optimal. Note that even though the run-time of this approach grows exponentially with the solution size $k$, we expect (as previously mentioned) that $k$ will be small in practice.

The run-time of the algorithm can be improved however based on the following observation. Let us define as "candidate edges" the edges that point from $U(s) \cap U'_C(s)$ (nodes active in both cascades) to $U(s) \triangle U'_C(s)$ (nodes active in one cascade but not the other). We know that at each "growth" step at least one of the candidate edges should be added to the solution. Otherwise, it is impossible to change the activation status of the nodes in $U(s) \triangle U'_C(s)$. Therefore, in each step we only consider candidate edges, and thus limit the number of new possible solutions created. If $b$ is an upper bound on the number of candidate edges, the number of total solutions generated during the search is at most $b^k$.

Figure 3 illustrates the execution of the TRACED algorithm with a small example. We start with an empty solution $C$ and with the two activation cascades (control and abnormal) for a single source $s$. Then, we identify the candidate edges between the two cascades. For each candidate edge we "grow" a new branch of the solution tree. We repeat these steps until $U(s) = U'_C(s)$.

TRACED has a time complexity of $O(b^k(|V| + |E'|))$ because it iterates through $b^k$ candidate solutions and executes the linear threshold model once for each possible solution.

In Sect. A.1 we introduce an improvement that further reduces the average run-time and allows multiple optimal solutions to be found, by adding more than one edge into a candidate solution at each step. That improvement does not change the algorithm's main idea or its worst-case run time.

To computationally validate the correctness of the algorithm, we created pairs of small-scale graphs for which we know the edges that cause activation cascade differences between the two networks. These examples are designed so that they vary in several factors: they can have one or multiple optimal solutions,

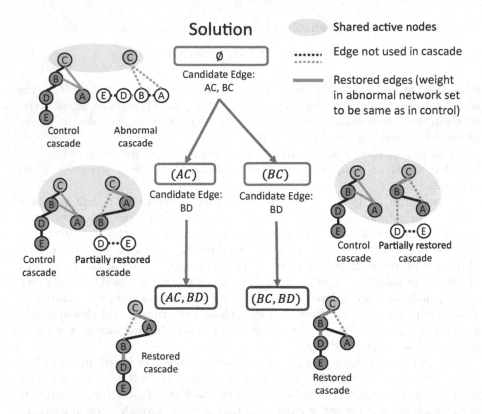

**Fig. 3.** Illustration of TRACED: the tree structure shows how the solution is gradually computed one edge at a time – different branches of the tree can lead to different solutions. The final solutions are marked in red. Along with each candidate solution $C$, we present the corresponding cascade $H'_C(s)$. In this example, two solutions can explain equally well the observed differences between the two cascades that originate from source $C$. (Color figure online)

only one edge or multiple edges in one solution, and edges in a solution that are dependent on each other (i.e., an edge included in the cascades only when the weight of another edge is restored). TRACED results in the correct results in all cases, identifying one or multiple optimal solutions correctly.

**Aggregation Across Different Source Nodes:** The previous algorithm may produce different sets of edges for different source nodes. Some of these edges may be the result of noise in the data or other artifacts. We select a subset of these edges based on the following argument: if TRACED identifies a certain edge as causal, not only for one source but for multiple, it is likely that edge represents a genuine and important difference between the control and abnormal networks.

We use the *coverage* metric to measure the number of sources for which an edge $e$ has been identified as causal for the cascade membership differences.

Edges with higher *coverage* play a more central role in the observed differences between the two networks.

To test if the *coverage* of an edge is significant or not, we construct a null hypothesis that all edges in the network have the same probability ($\frac{|\hat{C}(s)|}{|E|}$, where $\hat{C}(s)$ refers to the set of edges identified to be causal to cascade membership differences with source node $s$) to be reported as causal for source $s$. Under that assumption, the *coverage* metric follows a binomial distribution:

$$coverage'(e) \sim B\left(\sum_s |\hat{C}(s)|, \frac{1}{|E|}\right) \quad (6)$$

So, the final output of TRACED is the set of edges for which the *coverage* value is much higher than expected based on chance ($p < 0.05$ in the binomial distribution).

This final step makes the TRACED algorithm heuristic - the set of edges that we finally report is no longer guaranteed to explain all differences in the activation cascades of all sources. Nevertheless, the result captures edges that have influenced the activation cascades across many source nodes, and is therefore more reliable.

## 4    A Case Study on Major Depressive Disorder

The focus of this paper is on the analysis method presented in the previous section, rather than a specific application. To illustrate one potential application of this method, however, we summarize here the results of a comparison between a group of severe MDD patients and a group of healthy controls. The DTI data for this comparison was provided to us by Dr. Helen Mayberg's group and they were originally used in the PReDICT study [3,4]. The PReDICT study was approved by Emory's Institutional Review Board and the Grady Hospital Research Oversight Committee. We constructed structural brain networks applying probabilistic tractography on diffusion MRI scans of 90 MDD patients and 18 control subjects. The brain was parcellated into 396 regions (198 regions for each hemisphere) using the multi-modal cortical parcellation of Glasser et al. [9], and the Brainnetome Atlas [5] for sub-cortical regions. We applied the linear threshold model and generated an activation cascade for each source node, and measured the cascade membership differences between the two groups. The threshold that we used ranges from 0.1 to 0.3 among different source nodes, and is determined for each source node as the one associated with most significant cascade membership differences. We then applied TRACED to identify the minimal set of connections that can explain the observed cascade differences.

Table 1 lists the connections that we identified as causal for the cascade membership differences between the two groups. These connections have a significant overlap with findings of earlier studies reporting MDD-related structural/functional changes. The connections identified as causal are adjacent to parts of Brodmann area 24 [14], area 32 [10], area 9 [13], area 10 [16], and the orbitofrontal region [18]. All of these regions have been reported to be patholog-ically relevant for MDD in earlier studies. Some of the reported connections are also in the default mode network (DMN), which has been shown to be heavily affected by MDD [14], with increased functional connectivity [11]. We are going to further analyze this dataset and also compare our findings with those of other network analysis methods in a follow-up MDD-specific article.

**Table 1.** The connections that can explain the cascade differences between a group of MDD patients and a group of controls. The name of each node is based on the parcellation of Glasser et al. [9], followed with a brief description of the location of that region (L: left hemisphere, R: right hemisphere).

| Node 1 | Description | – | Node 2 | Description |
|--------|-------------|---|--------|-------------|
| p24 (L) | area-24 posterior | – | a24 (L) | area-24 anterior |
| 10v (L) | area-10 ventral | – | 10pp (L) | medial polar area-10 |
| a24 (L) | area-24 anterior | – | 9m (L) | area-9 medial |
| Pir (L) | piriform olfactory cortex | – | pOFC (L) | posterior OFC |
| 13l (L) | area-13 lateral | – | OFC (L) | orbital frontal complex |
| p32 (L) | area-32 posterior | – | 10d (L) | area-10 dorsal |
| p32 (L) | area-32 posterior | – | 9m (L) | area-9 medial |
| 10v (R) | area-10 ventral | – | 10pp (R) | polar 10p |
| pOFC (L) | posterior OFC | – | 13l (L) | area-13 lateral |
| 10pp (L) | medial polar area-10 | – | OFC (L) | orbital frontal complex |
| p32 (L) | area-32 posterior | – | 10pp (L) | medial polar area-10 |

## 5   Discussion

Various network analysis metrics and methods have been proposed in the past to compare structural brain networks. For instance, earlier work has investi-gated the differences between brain networks in terms of small-worldness [1], effi-ciency [2], and modularity [22]. At the node level, the clustering coefficient, par-ticipant coefficient, and different node centrality metrics (especially the between-ness centrality) have been widely adopted [17, 29]. At the edge level, researchers have investigated the edges with significant weight differences and the subnet-work they form [14].

TRACED falls in the spectrum of the edge-level analysis, and the resulting set of connections is a subset of edges that have significant weight differences between the two groups. Additionally however TRACED also incorporates the information flow across the entire network in varied paths (because of all the source nodes considered). We aggregate this topological information across the entire network to describe the role that a specific network element (node or edge) plays in the network, and how that role is different between the two groups.

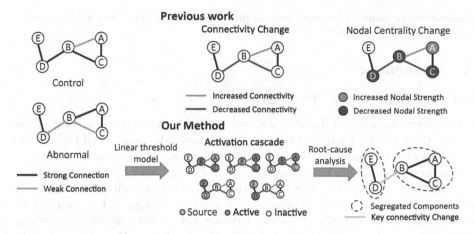

**Fig. 4.** Earlier work has mostly focused on brain connectivity differences using graph-theoretic metrics (e.g., node centrality metrics). TRACED associates connectivity changes with their impact on information transfer in the brain. It measures the impact of such changes on activation cascade differences, and identifies the specific connections that cause these differences through root-cause analysis.

Figure 4 illustrates typical node-level and edge-level network analysis metrics and compares them with TRACED. Compared to identifying solely edges with significant weight changes, TRACED associates a structural change (i.e., restoring the weight of a connection to its value in the other group) with functional changes (the node membership of the corresponding activation cascades). This is favorable for two reasons: it makes the results more interpretable, and less sensitive to variability across subjects. A significant difference in the weight of a connection between two networks may be simply due to subject variability. With TRACED, a connection is identified as causal not only based on its weight but also based on the topological role of that edge in the propagation of information (activation cascades) from different source nodes.

Compared to node-level analysis metrics, TRACED can provide higher spatial resolution because it identifies specific connections instead of entire brain regions. Additionally, some network analysis metrics often make implicit assumptions about information transfer in the brain (e.g., the betweenness centrality metric assumes that information travels through shortest paths, while the communicability metric assumes that information follows random-walks). These assumptions may not be realistic (e.g., shortest path routing requires information about the complete network stored in every node). It is also harder to interpret these metrics in terms of their associated localities in the brain (e.g., a node may have much lower communicability in one group but what is the corresponding set of affected information pathways?). TRACED makes an explicit assumption about information transfer, namely activation cascades based on the linear threshold model, and it associates structural connectivity changes with corresponding functional changes, making the results more transparent and informative.

**Acknowledgement.** This work was supported by the National Science Foundation (NSF) under award # 1822553.

# A    Appendix

## A.1    Optimization of TRACED

A key observation is that if adding a single edge $(x, y)$ into a solution set does not change the activation status of node $y$, we will inevitably need to add additional edges pointing to $y$ to build a final solution. Otherwise, for a solution $C$ with $(x, y)$, we can always find a better solution $C' = C - \{(x, y)\}$ with $U'_C(s) = U'_{C'}(s)$.

Therefore, we can improve the original TRACED algorithm, by adding a collection of edges in each iteration, so that $U'_C(s)$ changes when we create a new partial solution. This way we can reduce the number of partial solutions that we create during the search for the optimal solution. How do we find the collection of edges that can cause the change in $U_C(s)$? We know that we focus on change of activation status of nodes in $U'_C(s) \triangle U(s)$, and so we can discuss the case of nodes $U(s) \setminus U'_C(s)$ and $U'_C(s) \setminus U(s)$ separately.

1. For each node $v$ in $U(s) \setminus U'_C(s)$, we can check if there is an ensemble of edges from $U(s) \cap U'_C(s)$ pointing to this node, so that if we include the ensemble into the solution, $v$ would be active in the updated $U'_C(s)$. It is guaranteed that we can find at least one such collection of edges. Otherwise, we cannot explain why this $v$ could be active in $U(s)$.
2. For nodes in $U'_C(s) \setminus U(s)$, we can further find its subset $T_C(s)$ so that for each node $v \in T_C(s)$, $\sum_{u \in U(s) \cap U'_C(s)} w(u, v) \geq \theta$. We can prove that $U'_C(s) \setminus U(s)$ will no longer be in $U'_C(s)$ if and only if we add an ensemble of edges for each node in $T_C(s)$ into $C$. If for a node $v$ in $T_C(s)$ we do not add edges connecting to $v$ into $C$, $v$ will remain active and present in $U'_C(s)$. If we add edges connecting to $v$ for every node $v$ in $T_C(s)$, none of the nodes in $U'_C(s) \setminus U(s)$ receive an activation more than $\theta$, so that they will no longer be active.

With this modification, each partial solution $C$ corresponds to a state $U'_C(s)$, and it is guaranteed that there are no edges that can be removed from $C$ without changing that state. Therefore, all partial solutions corresponding to one state are equivalent, in terms of the edges that need to be added to the solution to reach another state. Therefore, we can construct a graph of solutions, where each node $x$ corresponds to a state, and each edge $(x, y, \{e_1, \dots \})$ corresponds to an ensemble of edges $\{e_1, \dots \}$ needed to be added into the partial solutions corresponding to state $x$ so that the new solution leads to state $y$. Such an edge is also weighted, with a weight that is equal to the number of edges in the collection. Notice that there can be multiple edges between two nodes, each corresponding to one collection of edges and may have a different weight different than other edges.

With such a graph of solutions, our goal is equivalent to finding the weighted shortest path between the initial state $U'(s)$ and the final state $U = U'_{\hat{C}}(s)$ in the graph. This is because the sum of the weights of edges along a path in the graph of solutions would be the number of actual edges we include in the final solution. We can find the shortest path using Dijkstra's algorithm since we have only positive weights. The major benefit of having this graph of solutions is that we can deal with the case of multiple optimal solutions more explicitly. They will be represented as multiple shortest paths from the initial state to the final state.

# References

1. Bassett, D.S., Bullmore, E.T.: Small-world brain networks revisited. Neuroscientist **23**(5), 499–516 (2017)
2. Berlot, R., Metzler-Baddeley, C., Ikram, M.A., Jones, D.K., O'Sullivan, M.J.: Global efficiency of structural networks mediates cognitive control in mild cognitive impairment. Front. Aging Neurosci. **8**, 292 (2016)
3. Choi, K.S., et al.: Reconciling variable findings of white matter integrity in major depressive disorder. Neuropsychopharmacology **39**(6), 1332–1339 (2014)
4. Dunlop, B.W., et al.: Predictors of remission in depression to individual and combined treatments (predict): study protocol for a randomized controlled trial. Trials **13**(1), 1–18 (2012)
5. Fan, L., et al.: The human brainnetome atlas: a new brain atlas based on connectional architecture. Cereb. Cortex **26**(8), 3508–3526 (2016)
6. Fischer, F.U., Wolf, D., Scheurich, A., Fellgiebel, A., Initiative, A.D.N., et al.: Altered whole-brain white matter networks in preclinical Alzheimer's disease. NeuroImage Clin. **8**, 660–666 (2015)
7. Fleischer, V., et al.: Graph theoretical framework of brain networks in multiple sclerosis: a review of concepts. Neuroscience **403**, 35–53 (2019)
8. Fornito, A., Zalesky, A., Pantelis, C., Bullmore, E.T.: Schizophrenia, neuroimaging and connectomics. Neuroimage **62**(4), 2296–2314 (2012)
9. Glasser, M.F., et al.: A multi-modal parcellation of human cerebral cortex. Nature **536**(7615), 171–178 (2016)
10. Grieve, S.M., Korgaonkar, M.S., Koslow, S.H., Gordon, E., Williams, L.M.: Widespread reductions in gray matter volume in depression. NeuroImage Clin. **3**, 332–339 (2013)
11. Hamilton, J.P., Farmer, M., Fogelman, P., Gotlib, I.H.: Depressive rumination, the default-mode network, and the dark matter of clinical neuroscience. Biol. Psychiat. **78**(4), 224–230 (2015)
12. Hwang, K., Hallquist, M.N., Luna, B.: The development of hub architecture in the human functional brain network. Cereb. Cortex **23**(10), 2380–2393 (2013)
13. Kerestes, R., et al.: Abnormal prefrontal activity subserving attentional control of emotion in remitted depressed patients during a working memory task with emotional distracters. Psychol. Med. **42**(1), 29–40 (2012). https://doi.org/10.1017/S0033291711001097
14. Korgaonkar, M.S., Fornito, A., Williams, L.M., Grieve, S.M.: Abnormal structural networks characterize major depressive disorder: a connectome analysis. Biol. Psychiat. **76**(7), 567–574 (2014)
15. Llufriu, S., et al.: Structural networks involved in attention and executive functions in multiple sclerosis. NeuroImage Clin. **13**, 288–296 (2017)

16. Long, Z., et al.: Disrupted structural connectivity network in treatment-naive depression. Prog. Neuropsychopharmacol. Biol. Psychiatry **56**, 18–26 (2015)
17. Qin, J., et al.: Abnormal brain anatomical topological organization of the cognitive-emotional and the frontoparietal circuitry in major depressive disorder. Magn. Reson. Med. **72**(5), 1397–1407 (2014)
18. Rajkowska, G., et al.: Morphometric evidence for neuronal and glial prefrontal cell pathology in major depression. Biol. Psychiat. **45**(9), 1085–1098 (1999)
19. Rehme, A.K., Grefkes, C.: Cerebral network disorders after stroke: evidence from imaging-based connectivity analyses of active and resting brain states in humans. J. Physiol. **591**(1), 17–31 (2013)
20. Riva-Posse, P., et al.: A connectomic approach for subcallosal cingulate deep brain stimulation surgery: prospective targeting in treatment-resistant depression. Mol. Psychiatry **23**(4), 843–849 (2018)
21. Shadi, K., Dyer, E., Dovrolis, C.: Multisensory integration in the mouse cortical connectome using a network diffusion model. Netw. Neurosci. **4**(4), 1030–1054 (2020)
22. Sporns, O., Betzel, R.F.: Modular brain networks. Annu. Rev. Psychol. **67**, 613–640 (2016)
23. Sporns, O., Tononi, G., Kötter, R.: The human connectome: a structural description of the human brain. PLoS Comput. Biol. **1**(4), e42 (2005)
24. Stam, C.J.: Modern network science of neurological disorders. Nat. Rev. Neurosci. **15**(10), 683–695 (2014)
25. Stam, C.J., Jones, B., Nolte, G., Breakspear, M., Scheltens, P.: Small-world networks and functional connectivity in Alzheimer's disease. Cereb. Cortex **17**(1), 92–99 (2007)
26. Van Hartevelt, T.J., et al.: Evidence from a rare case study for hebbian-like changes in structural connectivity induced by long-term deep brain stimulation. Front. Behav. Neurosci. **9**, 167 (2015)
27. Wen, M.C., et al.: Structural connectome alterations in prodromal and de novo Parkinson's disease patients. Parkinsonism Relat. Disord. **45**, 21–27 (2017)
28. Zeng, L.L., et al.: Identifying major depression using whole-brain functional connectivity: a multivariate pattern analysis. Brain **135**(5), 1498–1507 (2012)
29. Zhang, R., et al.: Rumination network dysfunction in major depression: a brain connectome study. Prog. Neuropsychopharmacol. Biol. Psychiatry **98**, 109819 (2020)

# Unstructured Categorization with Probabilistic Feedback: Learning Accuracy Versus Response Time

Bilyana Genova[✉] [ID], Nadejda Bocheva[ID], and Miroslava Stefanova[ID]

Institute of Neurobiology, Bulgarian Academy of Sciences, Sofia, Bulgaria

{b.genova,mirad_st}@abv.bg, nadya@percept.bas.bg

**Abstract.** Contradictory data exist whether the category number affects the learning performance in rule-based and integration-information classification tasks. When an effect is observed, the performance is better for a lower number of categories. We aimed to investigate the effect of the category number on the performance in the unstructured category learning tasks with probabilistic feedback. We conducted four experiments. The stimuli consisted of dot motion sequences. We presented eight motion directions ($0°$–$315°$ through $45°$) with motion direction coherence of 75% (Experiments 1, 3, and 4) and 20% (Experiment 2). We used the probabilistic rule of 79% (Experiments 1–3) or 75% (Experiment 4) correct answers. Eight observers classified the eight stimuli into 8 categories (Experiments 1–2); 2 categories (Experiment 3); 4 categories (Experiment 4). The results show: 1.) a wide variety of strategies adopted by the observers; 2.) Accuracy and response time changed at a different rate during learning; 3.) The rate of improvement differed between the experiments; 4.) The response time is a better characteristic of incremental category learning. The findings imply that the learning performance depends predominantly on the complexity of the rule of stimulus–response associations and to a lesser extent task's difficulty.

**Keywords:** Accuracy · Learning · Probabilistic feedback · Response time · Unstructured category learning

## 1 Introduction

Categorization is the process of sorting things into groups. In the categorization learning paradigm, the observer gives the same answer to all members of one category and different answers to members of other categories [1]. Categorization has an essential role for the individual to survive and succeed in unknown circumstances and in everyday life.

In an attempt to explain how unknown stimuli are classified and stored in memory and how the observer learns a new category, numerous categorization models were created [2]. The early theories proposed a single category-learning system for all types of categories [2, 3]. Later theories assume multiple category learning systems [2, 4–6]. It is usually assumed that two independent systems participate in category learning. One

© Springer Nature Switzerland AG 2022
M. Mahmud et al. (Eds.): BI 2022, LNAI 13406, pp. 99–113, 2022
https://doi.org/10.1007/978-3-031-15037-1_9

system, explicit (also named declarative, verbal, rule-based), relies on the medial temporal lobe (MTL) and uses working memory, executive control, attention, and hypothesis testing by application of simple rules [2, 7]. The other system, implicit (also procedural, nonverbal, or similarity-based), relies on the dorsal striatum and does not involve working memory or attention but learns associations between motor responses and category labels [2]. The learning from the implicit system is often assumed to be unavailable to awareness and/or impossible to verbalize [4, 8].

One approach to test whether single or multiple systems are involved in the classification process is to manipulate different characteristics of the classification task and evaluate whether these manipulations have a different effect depending on the category structures. Such approach is used in behavioral [9], neuropsychological [6], and neuroimaging investigations. Ashby and O'Brien [11] distinguished four different category structures: rule-based (RB), information-integration (II), prototype, and unstructured category. In rule-based category structures, the category can be learned via some logical reasoning process. The rule that maximizes accuracy is easy to describe verbally [3]. In information-integration category structures, the optimal strategy is difficult or impossible to describe verbally. Accuracy is maximized only if information from two or more stimulus dimensions is integrated at some pre-decisional stage [4]. In prototype type of structures, the exemplars of a category are created by randomly distorting a prototype [12, 13]; thus, the category members have high similarity. In unstructured category classification, the exemplars in a category are arbitrarily selected; they are not based on similarity as in prototype classification, on some abstract logical relationship as in rule-based classification, or the covariance of features as in information-integration.

Most studies show that certain manipulations affect either the outcome of the RB or the II classification studies but not both types, as predicted by multiple-system theories. One such manipulation is to change the number of categories in the classification task. The categories' learning accuracy deteriorates for RB classification when four instead of two categories are used. In contrast, II category learning is unaffected by category-number manipulations [9]. These results were taken as evidence for multiple-systems involved in category learning. However, Stanton and Nosofsky [14] conducted an II category learning similar to the work of Madox and colleagues and obtained significant deterioration in 4-category compared to 2-category classification for two different II category structures. Stanton and Nosofsky [14] see evidence in favor of single-system models in these contradictory results. Thus and so far, the case of single or multiple systems mediating category learning is still, to a great extent, open to debate.

Most of the existing studies used either RB or II structures, whereas the unstructured categories are extremely rarely studied and are among the most difficult categories to learn [15, 16]. Neuroimaging studies of unstructured-category learning have reported task-related activation in the striatum (in the body and tail of the caudate nucleus and the putamen), but typically not in the medial temporal lobe structures [17–19]. Together with a neuropsychological study of [20], these findings imply that unstructured-category learning is mediated by procedural memory, not by declarative one. Indeed, in a behavioral study of unstructured-category learning [21], the authors demonstrated that by switching the response keys' locations, unstructured-category learning recruits procedural memory. II tasks are also supposed to be mediated by procedural memory [4].

Except for the structure of the categories, the classification studies differ by the provided feedback. It could be incomplete, indicating only whether a response is correct or wrong, or it could provide full information showing the proper stimulus category. It could also be probabilistic, being inaccurate in a particular proportion of cases. The most used probabilistic classification task is the Weather Prediction task [8], in which, based on a combination of one to four cards (cues), the observers have to select one of two categories: "sun" or "rain." The classification outcome depends differently on the cards – two cards are highly predictive for the classification, while the other two are much less predictive. Hence, the classification is based on a combination of cues from the different cards, though the task could be performed with high accuracy using only the most predictive cards. Probabilistic category learning was developed to study procedural memory [10]. Still, some researchers suppose that a declarative component is also involved in the task [22] or that the task is entirely declarative [23].

The present study aims to investigate the effect of the number of categories on the performance of unstructured category tasks with probabilistic feedback. Contrary to the Weather prediction task, in our study, the classification is based on a single stimulus dimension – the direction of motion of dot patterns. A single stimulus was presented in each trial; thus, all stimuli were equally predictive for the outcome as they are associated with the same probability to their category. Also, in one of the experiments, we reduced the directions' coherence in the stimuli, making the categories less distinct. In this way, we expect to obtain new knowledge about the least studied type of category learning – the unstructured one, and a better understanding of the involvement of different processes and brain structures depending on the classification tasks.

The present research studies the learning processes in one of the least investigated classification tasks. It explores the effect of category number and distinctiveness in unstructured probabilistic classification using two different performance measures – response time and accuracy and their interrelation that allows evaluating better the contribution of the experimental manipulations revealing a potential competition between the explicit and implicit memory systems. Both the individual and the averaged learning curves were explored.

## 2   Materials and Methods

### 2.1   Stimuli

The stimuli consisted of 85-frame motion sequences of dots (diameter 0.16° and density 0.85 dots/deg$^2$) moving with constant speed at 5 deg/s in a circular aperture with a diameter of 15° positioned in the middle of a computer screen. Eight motion directions were presented: 0°, 45°, 90°, 135°, 180°, 225°, 270°, and 315°. Motion direction coherence was 20% in Experiment 2 and 75% in Experiments 1, 3, and 4. We varied stimulus–response association and randomly assigned one label (color) to each category by a probabilistic rule of 79% correct answers in Experiments 1, 2, and 3 and of 75% correct answers in Experiment 4. Each experiment was run on a separate day and consisted of two sessions, separated by a 2-min break.

The stimuli were binocularly viewed from 57 cm and presented on the computer screen (21" Dell Trinitron refresh rate 85 Hz; resolution 1280 × 1024 pixels). A custom program developed under Matlab PsychToolbox [24] generated stimuli and controlled the experiments.

## 2.2  Procedure

After a warning signal, a fixation point appeared in the center of the screen. A motion direction stimulus was presented for 1 s, followed by two circles of a diameter of 3° and different colors shown to the left and the right of the fixation point. The observer had to decide which of the colored circles corresponded to the correct answer and respond by clicking the mouse button. All combinations of different colors were presented an equal number of times. The colored circle corresponding to the correct response appeared as feedback on the screen center for 1 s. As not all colors are equally detectable in the retinal periphery [25], the colored circles were positioned at 10° from the screen center.

In Experiments 1 and 2, the observers had to classify the eight motion directions into eight categories with one exemplar in each. In Experiment 3, they had to classify the eight motion directions into two categories, each with four exemplars, and in Experiment 4 – into four categories, each with two exemplars. Before each experiment, the observers were informed of the number of categories.

Full feedback was provided after every response, and thus observers learned to associate each of the motion directions with the appropriate response through trial and error. The observers were told that at the beginning of each task, they could not know which stimulus belonged to which category, but by following the feedback, they could learn to categorize the stimuli and that in approximately 20% of the trials, the feedback would be false.

All observers were presented with the same random order of stimuli in each experiment. Several restrictions were used to generate the stimulus sequences: they consist of blocks with a random permutation of all possible stimulus–response combinations. An additional requirement is that the last stimulus–response combination differs from the starting one of the next block. This way of generating the sequences allows controlling to a certain degree, the effect of the memory processes by having an approximately equal separation between the presentations of each stimulus–response combination.

## 2.3  Observers

Eight healthy observers (mean age 30 years, range 22–39 years, 4 males, 4 females) participated in the study. The Ethics Board of the Institute of Neurobiology approved this study. All participants provided informed written consent to the approved protocol before the start of the investigation, according to the Declaration of Helsinki.

## 2.4  Statistical Analyses

All analyses were performed in the software R environment [26]. The package lme4 [27] was used to fit generalized linear mixed models to the observers' binary responses in the classification tasks. The package glmmTMB [28] was used for modeling the dependence of the response time on the experiment and the trial number. Model assumptions were verified by using the DHARMa package [29] to test for overdispersion, heteroscedasticity, and temporal dependency.

The mixed models consider the individual differences among the observers with the assumption that a common function relates the dependent variable and the experimental factors, the difference among the participants being in the value of the parameters.

# 3  Results

Large individual differences in the performance of the subjects both in the learning rate and the effect of the experimental conditions were observed. For 5 out of the 8 subjects, the highest proportion of correct responses is obtained in Experiment 1, but the worse performance varied greatly between them, with a slight prevalence for Experiment 2. The mean proportion of correct responses ranged from 0.48 to 0.98.

The large individual differences make the use of average learning curves and the assumptions of the generalized linear mixed models questionable. As shown in [30], averaging will lead to a misleading interpretation of the results if the learning is not gradual. To give credit to our analyses and conclusions, we applied the change-point algorithm of [30] to the individual learning curves. This algorithm uses the cumulative record to test whether the distribution of the different learning measures changes in the learning process. It is based on the insight that when the performance is stable, the cumulative record will approximate a straight line. In contrast, a change in the distribution will be apparent as a change in the cumulative record slope. The point of maximal deviation from a straight line is most likely a change point. The changes in performance reflected in a slope change of the cumulative records are evaluated on statistical grounds. A logarithm of the odds (logit) against the null hypothesis of no change is used as evidence that a particular putative point is a change point.

We applied the algorithm of [30] to each observer's responses in each condition using a logit of 2, corresponding approximately to a significance level of 0.01. The observers' binary responses were regarded as generated from a random rate process with a fixed probability. The cumulative records are presented in Fig. 1. The algorithm shows one or more change points from all 32 cumulative records, only in 6 cases (marked with black dots). No cumulative record indicates sharp changes in the learning curve. These results imply that while the individual data look quite diverse, the process of learning has similar characteristics.

Figure 2A presents the average learning curves obtained by calculating the number of correct responses in blocks of 28 presentations for Experiments 1–3 and in blocks of 32 presentations – for Experiment 4. The data imply performance improvement depending on the experiment; thus, the learning rates varied with the number of the categories and the induced noise.

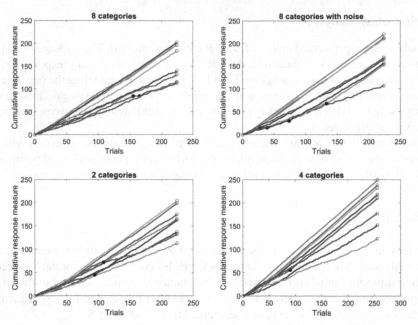

**Fig. 1.** The cumulative records of the observers' responses in the four experiments. The black dots show the presence of a change in the learning performance.

To evaluate the learning rate differences between the four experiments, we performed a generalized linear mixed model regression on the binary responses obtained in each experiment and each condition. A binomial distribution with a logit link was used (i.e., a mixed logistic regression). In this way, the learning curves are described by the following formula:

$$\pi_i = \frac{\exp(X_i\beta + Z_i u_i)}{1 + \exp(X_i\beta + Z_i u_i)} \tag{1}$$

In (1) $\pi_i$ is the probability of success on trial i (the number of successes at trial $i$ follows a binomial distribution), $X_i$ is $n_i \times p$ model matrix of the fixed effects, $Z_i$ is $n_i \times q$ model matrix for the random effects for trial $i$. The coefficient $\beta$ represents the $p - 1$ vector of the fixed-effect regression coefficients, $u_i$ is the $q - 1$ vector of the random-effects coefficients for trial $i$ distributed according to a normal probability distribution with mean zero and q × q covariance matrix D.

As fixed factors, we considered the experiment, the trial number treated as a continuous predictor, and their interaction. The trial number was scaled. We tested models with random slopes and intercepts and selected the model that best describes the experimental data based on the likelihood ratio test. The chosen model has a random slope and a random intercept that varies with the condition. Model validation indicated no problems. In the analysis, we used as a reference value the accuracy data from Experiment 3 in which the classification was with the least number (2) of categories.

The results of the analysis show that the trial number significantly affected the number of correct responses (Wald's $\chi 2(1) = 21.15$; $p < 0.001$). While the effect of the experiment was not significant at $p = 0.05$ (Wald's $\chi 2(1) = 3.12$; $p = 0.37$), the interaction between the trial number and the experiment is significant (Wald's $\chi 2(1) = 30.70$). This result implies differences in the learning rate depending on the number of categories or the presence of noise. However, the significant interaction is due only to the lower learning rate in Experiment 2 compared to the reference – the classification in 2 categories. This result implies no effect of category number but suggests that the increased noise in motion direction makes the difference between the categories less distinct. In this case, either the task requires more attention, or the classification performance becomes more similar to prototype categorization. Due to the random generation of the motion patterns and the reduced coherence of the motion directions, the performance might be based on the patterns' similarity. Most similar should be the patterns with the same motion direction, but some confusion between the neighboring categories could be expected. The fitted dependencies of the correct responses on the trial number are presented in Fig. 2B.

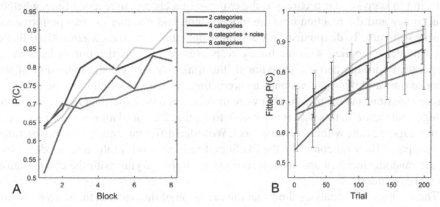

**Fig. 2.** A – The averaged learning curves for Experiments 1–4. B – The fitted dependence of the correct responses on the trial number

We next evaluated whether the reaction time also changes with the trial number and, if yes, whether this change is the same for all experimental tasks. One hypothesis is that when the observers learn the associations between the stimulus attributes and their corresponding category, the reaction time will decrease. To test this hypothesis, we performed a generalized linear mixed model with the response time as a dependent variable and the experiment, the trial number, and their interaction as predictors. In the model, the trial number was scaled and considered as a continuous predictor. We tested several distributions for the reaction time, as suggested by [31]. The model with Gamma distribution and identity link showed a lower Akaike information criterion and was applied to the data. The random effects included by-subject random intercept that varied with the classification task. Also, we included a dispersion model that varied with the subject, the classification task, and the trial number. Its inclusion specifies that the covariates' variance is not the same and changes with their value allowing to model heteroskedasticity.

The results of the analysis show a significant effect of the trial number (Wald's $\chi2(1) = 192.972$; $p < 0.001$). The estimated effect of the trial number on the reaction time is illustrated in Fig. 3A. It demonstrates the significant effect of the experiment (Wald's $\chi2(3) = 11.828$; $p < 0.05$) and the significant interaction between the experiment and the trial number (Wald's $\chi2(3) = 53.648$; $p < 0.001$). The figure clearly shows that the reaction time is longer in Experiment 2 and is almost independent of the trial number. In contrast, in the rest of the classification tasks, the reaction time decreases with the trial number. It is apparent that the reaction time increases with the number of categories for classification. Whereas the main effect of the experiment is due to the longer reaction times in Experiment 2, the interaction term significance is due to the different slopes in Experiment 4 (classification in 4 categories) and in Experiment 2. The reaction time decreases more sharply with the trial number for classification in 4 categories as compared to classification in 2 categories.

We also tried to evaluate the relationship between the accuracy and response time using a methodology proposed by [32]. Their approach estimates whether the observers are trying to keep similar accuracy at the expense of a change in reaction time, whether the accuracy and the reaction time are independent, and whether the two performance measures co-vary. To distinguish between these potential outcomes, a generalized linear mixed model is applied with the binary responses of the classification tasks used as a dependent variable and the experiment, the trial number, and the logarithm of the response time and their interactions - as predictors. Hence, two continuous predictors – the response time and the trial number were included, and the experiment was considered a categorical factor. In this way, it is possible to capture the correlation between accuracy and the response time within a given subject. We tested different random effects structures and compared their outcomes by the likelihood-ratio method. In the final model, a by-subject random intercept and by-subject random slope varying with the classification task were included.

The results of the analysis show that the inclusion of the reaction time as a predictor eliminated to a great extent the effect of the classification task. The main effect of the experiment (Wald's $\chi2(3) = 5.299$; $p = 0.15$); the interaction between the experiment and the trial number (Wald's $\chi2(3) = 4.902$; $p = 0.18$); the triple interaction between the trial number, the reaction time and the experiment (Wald's $\chi2(3) = 4.222$; $p = 0.24$) are insignificant at $p = 0.05$. The interaction between the trial number and the reaction time also turned insignificant (Wald's $\chi2(1) = 3.058$; $p = 0.08$). The only significant effects in the model remained the trial number (Wald's $\chi2(1) = 16.914$; $p < 0.001$), the effect of the logarithm of the reaction time (Wald's $\chi2(1) = 44.955$; $p < 0.001$), and the interaction between the experiment and the logarithm of the reaction time (Wald's $\chi2(3) = 11.936$; $p < 0.001$).

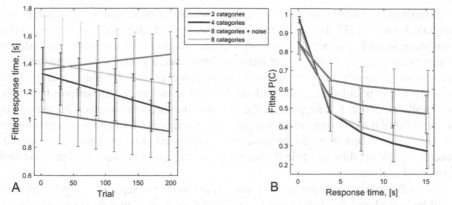

**Fig. 3. A** – The fitted dependence of the response times on the trial number; **B** – The fitted dependence of the correct responses on the response time

Figure 3B represents the accuracy changes depending on the reaction time's logarithm and the experiment. The figure shows that the accuracy declines with the increase in reaction time, opposite to the speed-accuracy trade-off that would imply a higher number of errors for shorter response times. The reduction in accuracy with reaction time seems most extreme for the classification tasks with 8 and 4 categories (Experiments 1 and 4) and least affected for the case when, due to the induction of noise in the stimulus motion, the discrimination of the stimuli deteriorates (Experiment 2). However, the estimated regression coefficients show a significant difference in the interaction term between the experiment and response time only for Experiment 4 compared to the reference (Experiment 3). Thus, the accuracy of the classification and the time needed for the task performance are related to each other. Significant differences are observed in the time needed to classify the stimuli in 4 and 2 categories.

## 4   Discussion

In the present study, we explored the effects of category number and their distinctiveness on the learning performance in unstructured classification tasks with probabilistic feedback. The manipulation of the category number is assumed to be a proper test, whether single or multiple systems are involved in the classification [9, 14]. In all experiments, we used the same 8 stimuli that differ in motion direction. The only difference is the number of categories they were randomly assigned to and the noise level induced in motion direction.

The use of probabilistic rule hampers the learning of the stimulus–response associations, allowing greater exploration of the learning processes and more observations before the learning maximum is reached. Our data show that learning the association between the stimuli and the response categories is very difficult, and not all subjects succeeded in achieving high performance. There are significant differences in learning ease, depending on the category number and the induced noise. While the average learning curves for the different experiments show improvement with the trial number, this is not the case for all participants and conditions.

Intuitively, we would assume that explicit memorization is involved in unstructured category learning [11]. However, there are fundamental differences between explicit memorization and unstructured-category learning. In a typical memorization task, the observers are presented with a list of things to remember, and they repeat them until they learn them. In unstructured-category learning, however, the stimulus–category label pairs are not explicitly presented and are learned from the accumulation of trial-by-trial feedback. Moreover, suppose all the classification tasks in our study are performed based on explicit memorization. In that case, no differences should be observed between the experimental conditions as the same stimuli are used in all of them, while our data indicate significant differences in the timing of the responses between the categorization in two and four categories.

As each stimulus in Experiments 1 and 2 is assigned to a separate category, this task could be considered an identification. It is logical to assume that there might be a difference between identification and categorization tasks. On the one hand, categorization might be expected to be easier than identification since the stimuli in a common category need not be discriminated from each other; thus, less information about a stimulus is required to classify it than to identify it. In this regard, it is worth mentioning the mapping hypothesis [15, 33] that considers the one-to-one mapping in the identification and many-to-one mapping of stimuli onto responses in categorization. According to it, all inter-stimulus confusions in the identification task that are within-class confusions would result in correct categorization responses. Only between-class confusions would result in categorization errors.

On the other hand, when using randomly grouped distinct stimuli (except for Experiment 2) in different categories, the categorization may be more difficult than identification since the observers must remember which stimuli are in a category; hence they have an additional task. This assumption would explain the deterioration of performance with the increase in category members as observed, for example, in RB classifications (e.g. [15]).

A winning strategy in unstructured category learning will be not to focus attention on remembering the members of a common category but to consider the task as identification with more identical answers, which would be an example of fast learning [34]. Indeed, based on the learning curves obtained in our study, it seems that the observers perform similarly both in the identification and the categorization tasks as if only an association between a single stimulus and its category is learned independently from the number of the rest members of this category. Whereas the average performance suggests significant differences between the experimental conditions with the best performance in Experiment 1 (the highest proportion of correct responses and steepest learning curves), this observation was not confirmed by the data's statistical analysis. Only in Experiment 2 (classification into 8 categories and lower coherence of motion direction), the learning rate turned to be significantly lower than in the rest of the classification tasks. The higher noise level in the stimuli could smear the motion directions' differences, making the task more similar to prototype learning. The unclear boundaries between the motion directions may prevent the generalization from previous experience with the stimuli.

The lack of differences in the learning curves depending on the number of categories in the unstructured categorization is similar to the II tasks that rely on procedural memory.

Most studies show that the increase in the number of categories does not affect the II classification performance (e.g. [9] but see [14]), though it affects the RB classification. Both unstructured and II tasks are based on gradual learning of the stimulus–response associations over many trials. It is generally assumed that the basal ganglia are involved in this type of learning (e.g. [10, 35]). Neurophysiological studies on the effects of basal ganglia damage on learning in tasks that involve incremental learning supposed to rely on procedural memory also support this hypothesis (e.g. [36, 37]).

The basal ganglia are also supposed to be involved in tasks with probabilistic feedback [38]. However, in probabilistic learning, the role of the basal ganglia seems to depend on task complexity. For multi-cue tasks like the Weather Prediction task, the basal ganglia are not involved in the initial stages of learning, but in its later stages, the learning switches to more subtle integrative rules of stimulus–response associations. Conversely, in single-cue probabilistic categorization, activity in the basal ganglia is observed in the initial phases of the learning process up to the moment when the association between the stimulus and the response is learned, and later on, their activity decreases [18, 39] replaced by activity in MTL [40], or prefrontal cortex (PFC) [39] that govern declarative strategies.

Hence, in an unstructured classification, it seems natural to expect no effect of the category number due to the similarity between this type of categorization and the II tasks. Due to the probabilistic feedback and the single-cue classification, it is possible to expect a switch from implicit learning supposed to be involved in this type of task to a more declarative explicit one. Do our data support such expectations? To answer this question we consider the differences in the response timing observed between the different classification tasks.

It is thought that the procedural system can learn almost any type of category structure. For example, pigeons, which are supposed to lack an explicit reasoning system, learn RB and II categories equally well using identical to human procedural strategies [41]. Some evidence suggests that in purely procedural tasks, people perform declaratively. The declarative strategy is included when the task is complex. We have an arbitrary structure of stimulus–response associations, so our task is complex, Experiment 1 being the most complex. Procedural memory will solve it, but slowly, by trial-by-trial information accumulation. When the declarative memory intervenes (this is an example of an optimization process), it inhibits the procedural system's ability to access motor output systems, though it does not exclude procedural learning [42]. This interference may explain the extension of the response time in Experiment 1.

Experiment 2 has similar complexity as Experiment 1, but in addition to it, the reduced coherence of motion direction makes the distinctiveness of the categories less clear. It is the only experiment in which the learning does not reduce the response time. This finding may imply that when the stimulus noise is high, and the difference between the categories is less clear, more time is needed for stimulus encoding, and this prolonged processing deteriorates previously learned associations.

Our data show a significant difference in response time for categorization in two and four categories, implying more effective learning for the case of four categories. Also, using the response time as a predictor of classification accuracy, we obtained differences for categorization in two and four categories. Usually, the response time analysis is taken as a complementary tool to confirm the results from the accuracy-based analysis of the experimental factors' effect. To our knowledge, only one study [43] analyzes the binary measurements that correspond to the sequences of correct and incorrect responses together with the continuous measurements representing the time needed to respond in a learning task. Its approach is quite different from ours, but it shows that the combined analysis provides evidence for more accurate and reliable estimates of the learning process and its dynamics than the separate analyses of the accuracy measurements and response time. It should be stressed that the response time for classification in two categories is shorter than that for classification in four categories, but it changes less in the process of learning. This finding would imply that the task of stimulus classification in two categories is not more difficult than the classification in four categories. One potential explanation of the less effective learning for the case of two categories may be that motion direction stimuli have natural categorization in different groupings like oblique and cardinal directions, or leftwards and rightward motions, upward and downward. In complex tasks like in the Weather Prediction tasks, the observers often use single-cue rules in the learning process that reflect memory operations dependent on interactions between the MTL and the PFC [38] before gradually shifting to a more optimal strategy that better reflects the relationship between the stimuli and their association with the responses. In classification in two categories, it might be easier to formulate simple rules between the stimuli in a category as rules-with-exceptions, thus delaying the involvement of the more optimal rules of categorization. Also, the rules' exceptions need memorization that might also affect the learning dynamics due to the additional cognitive load.

Future research is needed to understand the dissociation between the effect of category number on the response time and the accuracy of the classification, and the role of stimulus similarity on unstructured classification. Here, we used stimuli that have some inherent classification. It may have interfered with the random separation of the stimuli in groups and the different learning dynamics depending on category number.

Considerations of the results allude that in unstructured category learning with probabilistic feedback, the performance reflects the competition between the explicit and implicit memory systems. Unfortunately, there are not enough arguments in favor of this idea at this stage of the research. However, the study results provide new data about unstructured categories that are very rarely studied.

## 5   Conclusions

The results of the present study imply that in the unstructured category learning with probabilistic feedback the number of categories has diverse effects on the two characteristics used to represent the learning process. The classification accuracy is greatly unaffected by the category number, similar to the information-integration tasks. At the same time, the learning performance represented by the response time shows faster performance improvement for categorization in four than in two categories. Hence, the learning curves are less sensitive to the differences in the learning process. The response time is a better characteristic of incremental learning in these categorization tasks. When the boundaries between the classification categories are less distinct, the ability to generalize from the previous experience severely deteriorates. This result implies a role of similarity-based processes in unstructured classification tasks. The classification tasks with arbitrary stimulus–response associations and probabilistic feedback are challenging, showing great differences in learning rate when classification is based on a single cue. Future studies are needed to describe better the similarities and the differences in the performance and the processes involved in unstructured classification tasks.

**Acknowledgements.** This research was funded by the Bulgarian Science Fund, grant No KP-06-N52/6 from 12.11.2021.

# References

1. Ashby, F., Valentin, V.: The categorization experiment: experimental design and data analysis. In: Wixted, J.T., Wagenmakers, E.J. (eds.) The 'Stevens' Handbook of Experimental Psychology and Cognitive Neuroscience, vol. 5, 4th edn. Methodology. Wiley, New York (2017)
2. Ashby, F., Maddox, W.T.: Human category learning. Annu. Rev. Psychol. **56**, 149–178 (2005)
3. Ashby, F., Maddox, W.T.: Stimulus categorization. In: Birnbaum, M.H. (ed.) Handbook of Perception and Cognition: Measurement, Judgement and Decision Making, pp. 251–301. Academic, New York (1998).
4. Ashby, F., Alfonso-Reese, L., Turken, A., Waldron, E.: A neuropsychological theory of multiple systems in category learning. Psychol. Rev. **105**, 442–481 (1998)
5. Ashby, F., Ennis, J., Spiering, B.: A neurobiological theory of automaticity in perceptual categorization. Psychol. Rev. **114**(3), 632–656 (2007)
6. Poldrack, R., Foerde, K.: Category learning and the memory systems debate. Neurosci. Biobehav. Rev. **32**, 197–205 (2008). https://doi.org/10.1016/j.neurobiorev.2007.07.007
7. Minda, J., Miles, S.: The influence of verbal and nonverbal processing on category learning. In: Ross, B.H. (ed.) The Psychology of Learning and Motivation: Advances in Research and Theory, vol. 52, pp. 117–162. Academic Press, San Diego (2010)
8. Knowlton, B., Squire, L., Gluck, M.: Probabilistic classification learning in amnesia. Learn. Memory **1**(2), 106–120 (1994)
9. Maddox, W.T., Filoteo, J., Hejl, K., Ing, A.: Category number impacts rule-based but not information-integration category learning: further evidence for dissociable category-learning systems. J. Exp. Psychol. Learn. **30**, 227–245 (2004)
10. Knowlton, B., Mangels, J., Squire, L.: A neostriatal habit learning system in humans. Science **273**(5280), 1399–1402 (1996)
11. Ashby, F., O'Brien, J.: Category learning and multiple memory systems. Trends Cogn. Sci. **9**(2), 83–89 (2005)
12. Posner, M., Keele, S.: On the genesis of abstract ideas. J. Exp. Psychol. **77**(3p1), 353–363 (1968)
13. Posner, M., Keele, S.: Retention of abstract ideas. J. Exp. Psychol. **83**, 304–308 (1970)
14. Stanton, R., Nosofsky, R.: Category number impacts rule-based and information-integration category learning: a reassessment of evidence for dissociable category-learning systems. J. Exp. Psychol. Learn. **39**, 1174–1191 (2013)
15. Shepard, R., Hovland, C., Jenkins, H.: Learning and memorization of classifications. Psychol. Monogr Gen. Appl. **75**(13), 1–42 (1961)
16. Nosofsky, R., Gluck, M., Palmeri, T., McKinley, S., Glauthier, P.: Comparing models of rule-based classification learning: a replication and extension of Shepard, Hovland, and Jenkins (1961). Mem. Cognition **22**, 352–369 (1994). https://doi.org/10.3758/BF03200862

17. Lopez-Paniagua, D., Seger, C.: Interactions within and between corticostriatal loops during component processes of category learning. J. Cogn. Neurosci. **23**, 3068–3083 (2011)
18. Seger, C., Cincotta, C.: The roles of the caudate nucleus in human classification learning. J. Neurosci. **25**, 2941–2951 (2005). https://doi.org/10.1523/JNEUROSCI.3401-04.2005
19. Seger, C., Peterson, E., Cincotta, C., Lopez-Paniagua, D., Anderson, C.: Dissociating the contributions of independent corticostriatal systems to visual categorization learning through the use of reinforcement learning modeling and Granger causality modeling. Neuroimage **50**, 644–656 (2010)
20. Bayley, P., Frascino, J., Squire, L.: Robust habit learning in the absence of awareness and independent of the medial temporal lobe. Nature **436**, 550–553 (2005)
21. Crossley, M., Ashby, F.: Procedural learning during declarative control. J. Exp. Psychol. Learn. **41**, 1388–1403 (2015)
22. Meeter, M., Myers, C., Shohamy, D., Hopkins, R., Gluck, M.: Strategies in probabilistic categorization: results from a new way of analyzing performance. Learn. Memory **13**, 230–239 (2006)
23. Lagnado, D., Newell, B., Kahan, S., Shanks, D.: Insight and strategy in multiple-cue learning. J. Exp. Psychol. Gen. **135**, 162–183 (2006)
24. Brainard, D.: The psychophysics toolbox. Spat. Vis. **10**, 433–436 (1997)
25. Zlatkova, M., Racheva, K., Totev, T., Mihaylova, M., Hristov, I., Anderson, R.: Resolution acuity and spatial summation of chromatic mechanisms in the peripheral retina. J. Opt. Soc. Am. A. **38**(7), 1003–1014 (2021). https://doi.org/10.1364/JOSAA.418073
26. R Core Team R: A language and environment for statistical computing. R Foundation for Statistical Computing, 2021, Vienna, Austria. https://www.R-project.org. Accessed 11 Apr 2022
27. Bates, D., Maechler, M., Bolker, B., Walker, S.: Fitting linear mixed-effects models using lme4. J. Stat. Softw. **67**(1), 1–48 (2015). https://doi.org/10.18637/jss.v067.i0
28. Brooks, M., Kristensen, K., van Benthem, K., Magnusson, A., Berg, C., Nielsen, A., et al.: glmmTMB balances speed and flexibility among packages for zero-inflated generalized linear mixed modeling. R J. **9**(2), 378–400 (2017)
29. Hartig, F.: DHARMa: Residual diagnostics for hierarchical (multi-level/mixed) regression models. R package version 0.4.5, (2022). https://CRAN.R-project.org/package=DHARMa. Accessed 11 Apr 2022
30. Gallistel, C., Fairhurst, S., Balsam, P.: The learning curve: implications of a quantitative analysis. PNAS **101**(36), 13124–13131 (2004). https://doi.org/10.1073/pnas.0404965101
31. Lo, S., Andrews, S.: To transform or not to transform: using generalized linear mixed models to analyse reaction time data. Front. Psychol. **6**, 1171 (2015). https://doi.org/10.3389/fpsyg.2015.01171
32. Davidson, D., Martin, A.: Modeling accuracy as a function of response time with the generalized linear mixed effects model. Acta Psychol. **144**(1), 83–96 (2013). https://doi.org/10.1016/j.actpsy.2013.04.016
33. Nosofsky, R.: Attention, similarity, and the identification-categorization relationship. J. Exp. Psychol. Learn. **115**, 39–61 (1986)
34. Seger, C., Miller, E.: Category learning in the brain. Annu. Rev. Neurosci. **33**, 203–219 (2010)
35. Gabrieli, J.: Cognitive neuroscience of human memory. Annu. Rev. Psychol. **49**, 87–115 (1998)
36. Shohamy, D., Myers, C., Grossman, S., Sage, J., Gluck, M.: The role of dopamine in cognitive sequence learning: evidence from Parkinson's disease. Behav. Brain Res. **156**(2), 191–199 (2005)
37. Shohamy, D., Myers, C., Geghman, K., Sage, J., Gluck, M.: L-dopa impairs learning, but spares generalization. Parkinson's Dis. Neuropsychol. **44**(5), 774–784 (2006)

38. Shohamy, D., Myers, C., Kalanithi, J., Gluck, M.: Basal ganglia and dopamine contributions to probabilistic category learning. Neurosci. Biobehav. R. **32**, 219–236 (2008)
39. Delgado, M., Miller, M., Inati, S., Phelps, E.: An fMRI study of reward-related probability learning. Neuroimage **24**, 862–873 (2005)
40. Haruno, M., Kuroda, T., Doya, K., Toyama, K., Kimura, M., Samejima, K., et al.: A neural correlate of reward-based behavioral learning in caudate nucleus: a functional magnetic resonance imaging study of a stochastic decision task. J. Neurosci. **24**(7), 1660–1665 (2004)
41. Smith, J., Ashby, F., Berg, M., Murphy, M., Spiering, B., Cook, R.: Pigeons categorization may be exclusively nonanalytic. Psychon. B. Rev. **18**(2), 414–421 (2011). https://doi.org/10.3758/s13423-010-0047-8
42. Crossley, M., Madsen, N., Ashby, F.: Procedural learning of unstructured categories. Psychon. B. Rev. **19**(6), 1202–1209 (2012). https://doi.org/10.3758/s13423-012-0312-0
43. Prerau, M., Smith, A., Eden, U., Kubota, Y., Yanike, M., Suzuki, W., et al.: Characterizing learning by simultaneous analysis of continuous and binary measures of performance. J. Neurophysiol. **102**, 3060–3072 (2009)

# Brain Big Data Analytics, Curation and Management

# Optimizing Measures of Information Encoding in Astrocytic Calcium Signals

Jacopo Bonato[1,2](✉) , Sebastiano Curreli[3] , Tommaso Fellin[3] ,
and Stefano Panzeri[1,4]

[1] Neural Computation Laboratory, Istituto Italiano di Tecnologia,
38068 Rovereto, Italy
jacopo.bonato@iit.it
[2] Department of Pharmacy and Biotechnology, University of Bologna,
40126 Bologna, Italy
[3] Optical Approaches to Brain Function Laboratory, Istituto Italiano di Tecnologia,
16163 Genova, Italy
{sebastiano.curreli,tommaso.fellin}@iit.it
[4] Department of Excellence for Neural Information Processing, Center for Molecular
Neurobiology (ZMNH), University Medical Center Hamburg-Eppendorf (UKE),
20251 Hamburg, Germany
s.panzeri@uke.de

**Abstract.** While most models of brain information encoding focus on neurons, recent studies have shown that calcium dynamics of astrocytes, the major class of non-neural cells in the brain, can add information about key cognitive variables that is not found in the activity of nearby neurons. This raises the question of what could be the contribution of astrocytes in information processing, and calls for analysis tools to characterize this contribution. Here we construct simulations with realistic dependencies of astrocytic activity on external variables and we use these simulations to understand how to optimally set parameters of information theoretic analysis of astrocytic activities. Applications of our techniques to simulated and real astrocytic data show how to set parameters of information analyses that provide conservative, yet reliable, estimates of astrocytic calcium dynamics contribution to circuit-level brain information processing.

**Keywords:** Mutual information · Astrocytes · Significance testing · Information estimation

## 1 Introduction

Established models of how populations of brain cells encode information consider exclusively the encoding at the level of population of neurons [1,6,12,13]. However, this view has been recently challenged by studies of the activity of astrocytes [3]. Astrocytes, the most abundant glial cell type in the mammalian brain, are not electrically excitable but display excitability based on complex dynamics of

© Springer Nature Switzerland AG 2022
M. Mahmud et al. (Eds.): BI 2022, LNAI 13406, pp. 117–128, 2022
https://doi.org/10.1007/978-3-031-15037-1_10

intracellular calcium $(Ca^{2+})$ concentration. Astrocytic $Ca^{2+}$ dynamics can be recorded *in vivo* with high spatial resolution using functional two-photon microscopy [28]. Recordings of astrocytes in sensory areas have shown that these cells can encode sensory stimuli [10,21,24,25,27]. Recently, several laboratories [3,5,11] begun to investigate how astrocytes encode information about external variables. As an example, our work [3] has shown that astrocytes in hippocampal CA1 recorded during spatial navigation in a virtual environment encode spatial information that is complementary and synergistic to that carried by nearby "place cell" neurons. This additional non-neural reservoir of information suggests the possible presence of novel cellular mechanisms underlying how brain circuits encode information, and invites the inclusion of astrocytes in the models of brain information processing.

To improve our understanding of how astrocytes participate in information encoding it is important to have statistical tools that can be used to clarify whether astrocytes genuinely carry information about specific cognitive variables. Because little is known about how astrocytes encode information, nonparametric analyses that make little assumptions (e.g. linearity) about how information is encoded are particularly desirable at this stage. It has been recently proposed [3] that information theory [20,22] may be an ideal candidate to this aim. However, the use of information theory with limited size datasets and noisy biological cells is made difficult by statistical issues [9,18]. The neural literature has studied, using computer simulations, how to set optimally procedures and parameters of the analysis given the levels of information encoded by neurons and the size of the dataset available [9]. However, such studies have not been performed for astrocytes.

Here, we performed simulations of astrocytic $Ca^{2+}$ dynamics matching the statistical properties of signals recorded from real subcellular regions of interest (ROIs) of hippocampal astrocytes during virtual spatial navigation. We used these simulations to investigate how to optimally apply information theoretic methods to determine the presence and amounts of genuine information encoding by astrocytes. Last, we validated results and predictions of simulations by applying this methodology to *in vivo* recordings of hippocampal astrocytic subcellular $Ca^{2+}$ signals during spatial navigation.

## 2    Computing Amount and Significance of Information in Astrocytic Calcium Activity

Here we introduce the measures of information about external variables carried by astrocytic activity, and we define the parameters of its computation from real data. Suppose we have a two-photon microscopy calcium imaging experiment where a mouse is performing a task or is shown a certain set of sensory stimuli. In this scenario we can record $Ca^{2+}$ signals from astrocytic cellular compartments (for example, a soma or a process) defined as ROIs in a given field of view (FOV). We are interested in quantifying whether the $Ca^{2+}$ response $r$ of the astrocytic ROI, measured at given imaging time frame, encodes information about an external variable $s$ that varies during the task or a stimulus variable that is varied across the experiment. In the experimental dataset that we will use [3], the $Ca^{2+}$ dynamics of hippocampal CA1 astrocytes were recorded while a mouse was navigating in a linear track in a virtual reality environment. With this dataset we were interested in determining whether the astrocytic $Ca^{2+}$ response encoded the position of the mouse along the linear track, similarly to how neurons called place cells do in hippocampus [16]. How selective is an astrocytic ROI with respect to an external variables $s$ can be computed by using the mutual information $I(\mathbf{R}; \mathbf{S})$ between the set of astrocytic responses $\mathbf{R}$ and the set of external variables $\mathbf{S}$, defined as follows [22]:

$$I(\mathbf{R}; \mathbf{S}) = \sum_s P(s) \sum_r P(r|s) \log_2 \frac{P(r|s)}{P(r)} \tag{1}$$

where $P(s)$ is the probability of the external variable taking the value $s$, $P(r)$ is the probability of measuring an astrocytic response $r$ across all data points, and $P(r|s)$ is the probability of observing a responses $r$ given a value $s$ observed for the external variable. We assume that both astrocytic activity and the external variable take continuous values, and that we have discretized them into a number of bins $R$ and $S$, respectively. These probabilities can be estimated as normalized histograms of occurrences of discretized stimulus-response values. Such probabilities are computed from the finite number $N$ of experimentally available datapoints (denoted "trials" hereafter) measuring simultaneously $s$ and $r$. $I(\mathbf{R}; \mathbf{S})$ measures, in units of bits, how well we can infer the value of $s$ from a single trial observation of the astrocytic response $r$. Zero bits indicate that no information can be gained from observing $r$, whereas positive values of information indicate that it is possible to reconstruct with some precision the value of $s$ from the value of $r$. One bit means a reduction of uncertainty about $s$ of a factor of 2 from a single-trial observation of $r$.

A first important question that can be addressed with mutual information analysis of astrocytes regards individuating how many and which ROIs carry information about external variables. An information value can be greater than zero even when the considered ROI actually has no information. This can happen because of random fluctuations in probability values generated by the limited number of trials that were sampled [18]. The statistical significance of each mutual information value can be determined by creating a null-hypothesis distribution obtained from surrogate datasets in which the relationship between $s$ and $r$ is destroyed by randomly shuffling the values of $s$ and $r$ across trials. A second important question regards quantifying precisely how much information each ROI carries. This is made difficult by the fact that, because of the limited number of trials available, the "plugin" information measure obtained simply by plugging the experimental probabilities into Eq. 1 is affected by a systematic upward bias [19]. Several bias correction procedures can be used to obtain an unbiased estimate mutual information [14,15,17,18,26]. Two widely used methods are Panzeri-Treves bias correction (PT) method [19], which analytically estimates the bias, and the quadratic extrapolation (QE) method [26], which estimates bias through extrapolating the information values obtained with data subsampling.

Thus, free parameters and algorithmic choices of the information analysis include the number of bins $S$ and $R$, used to discretize the external variable $s$ and the astrocytic $Ca^{2+}$ activity, and the bias correction method used to compute information. Studies considering other types of brain signals have shown that computer simulations, characterized by realistic levels of information content and numerosity of trials, can be used to optimally set the information analysis parameters [9,18]. However, no such work has been performed for astrocytes. Here, we implemented data-driven simulations to identify optimal parameters to perform mutual information analysis of astrocytic data. To understand how to optimally set information estimation parameters, we simulated set of astrocytic $Ca^{2+}$ responses ($n = 20$) that realistically captured the dependency of astrocytic activity on the position of mouse during spatial navigation in virtual reality. (Astrocytic $Ca^{2+}$ signals simulation software and mutual information software can be found at github.com/jbonato1/AstroSimulation). $Ca^{2+}$ responses were modeled matching statistical parameters (mean and standard deviation) of $Ca^{2+}$ responses of real astrocytic ROIs recorded *in vivo* from the hippocampal CA1 area of mice navigating in a virtual environment [3]. Responses for each spatial position were drawn from a Gaussian distribution with the parameters found in the data. We evaluated the effects of trial numerosity, number of bins used to discretized the data, and information levels, by systematically modulating these parameters across simulations. The information level in the simulated responses was controlled by a parameter $\alpha$ [9] linearly rescaling the modulation of $r$ by $s$. $\alpha = 1$ (no rescaling) yields simulated responses with the same response properties and thus information levels as real data, whereas $0 < \alpha < 1$ corresponds to modeling responses with reduced information content, and $\alpha = 0$ (modulation of $r$ by $s$ completely rescaled away) corresponds to no information. We report results of simulations for $\alpha = 1$ (full-information, Fig. 1A), $\alpha = 0.5$ (Fig. 1B) and $\alpha = 0$ (no-information, Fig. 1C).

We first evaluated the performance of the non-parametric shuffling in classifying simulated responses as carrying significant information. We performed these numerical experiments as function of the number of trial per stimulus numerosity ($N_s$), and information content (Fig. 1D–F). For this first study, simulated astrocytic responses were discretized into $R = 4$ equally spaced bins and space in the linear track was discretized into $S = 12$ spatial bins. For each simulated response we computed a null-hypothesis distribution generating 100 shuffles and we set a significance level of $p < 0.05$. When using the *plugin* estimate of mutual information, we found that for the full-information model ($\alpha = 1$) the shuffling procedure classified correctly significance down to $N_s = 64$ ($\log_2(N_s/R) = 4$). When reducing the information content ($\alpha = 0.5$) the shuffling test required more samples to perform correct detection. Finally when the model had no-information we found that false positive rate was stable at the level of 5% set by our statistical threshold. The use of PT bias correction procedure did not affect the statistical power of the non-parametric shuffling test, while QE method resulted in reduced statistical power.

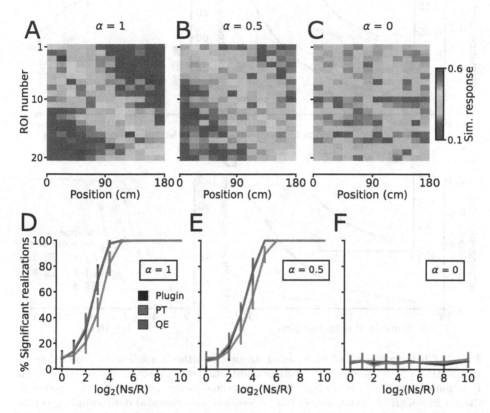

**Fig. 1.** Sensitivity of information content measures for realistic simulations of position encoding astrocytic $Ca^{2+}$ signals. (A–C) Mean $Ca^{2+}$ responses across trials as a function of position for simulated astrocytic ROIs (n = 20 ROIs) for $\alpha = (1, 0.5, 1)$ models, respectively. The number of trials per spatial positions (Sect. 2, here 64) was varied across simulations. (D–F) Percentage of significant realizations detected using different methods (*plugin*, PT, and QE) as a function of $N_s/R$ ratio for $\alpha = 1, 0.5, 1$ models. For each bias correction method, PT (red lines) and QE (green lines) information value was compared to the shuffled distribution of the corresponding values. 20 iterations of the simulation were generated for each number of trials used. (Color figure online)

Astrocytic $Ca^{2+}$ signals and position recorded during spatial navigation are continuous variables, and the number of bins into which they are discretized is one of the most delicate parameters of the analysis. A too coarse discretization may wash out all information, and a too fine discretization may make the measures too noisy especially when data are scarce. Thus, $S$ must be chosen to obtain to optimally trade off these two competing effects.

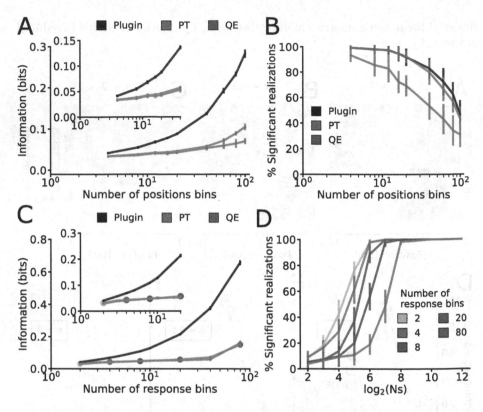

**Fig. 2.** Characterization of information theoretic methods applied on simulations of astrocytic $Ca^{2+}$ responses. (A) Average information estimate over 20 simulations as a function of the number of position bins. Simulations were repeated with fixed response discretization ($R = 4$), number of trials resembled experimental data sampling conditions. (B) Percentage of realizations classified as significant as a function of the number of position bins. (C) Average information estimate over 20 simulations as a function of the number of response bins. Simulations were repeated with fixed stimulus discretization ($S = 12$) and constant number of trials per stimulus $N_s = 68$. In (A–C) information computations were performed without bias correction (*plugin*, black line), PT (red line) or QE (green line) bias corrections. (D) Percentage of significant realizations as a function of $N_s$ for different values of number of response bins (no bias correction). The corresponding values of information for each R value are indicated by corresponding colored marks in panel (C). Data is shown as (mean ± std). (Color figure online)

We performed simulations using the full-information model ($\alpha = 1$) to generate data with a number of trials per stimulus resembling *in vivo* experimental data [3]. In these simulations we investigated the effect of position discretization while we kept the discretization of the response fixed at ($R = 4$). We found that (Fig. 2A) bias-corrected information measures (both PT and QE methods) plateaued for values of $S$ in the range (4–16). Conversely, *plugin* estimates monotonically increased with $S$, as their value contained an uncorrected upward bias component. For *plugin* estimates, we found that the fraction of realizations correctly detected as significantly informative (100 random shuffles, $p < 0.05$) decreased for $S$ values greater than 16 (Fig. 2B), thus indicating insufficient sampling. The PT bias correction procedure did not affect the statistical power of the non-parametric shuffling test, while the QE method resulted in reduced statistical power. Thus, for further statistical tests we used uncorrected *plugin* estimators.

We characterized the effect of response discretization performing numerical experiments in which we simulated a realistic number of trials per stimulus ($N_s = 68$, equal to the average number of trials per stimulus in real data, see Sect. 4), while the position discretization was set within the information estimate plateau identified before ($S = 12$). We found that (Fig. 2C) bias-corrected information measures (both PT and QE methods) plateaued over a large range of $R$, whereas *plugin* estimates were strongly affected by bias. Statistical power was strongly dependent on the selection of discretization parameters (Fig. 2D) showing, in these sampling conditions, adequate power up to $R = 8$. Further increasing $R$ would be possible only with much larger number of trials to avoid underestimation of significant astrocytes ROIs.

## 3  Measuring Conditional Mutual Information to Evaluate Genuine Information Encoding

In many cases, cognitive tasks rely on several correlated external variables. An important question is how to determine whether astrocytic activity is genuinely informative about each such correlated variable. For example, in the mentioned spatial navigation experiments different parts of the track have different visual cues to aid navigation [3,4,7], thus there is a correlation between position $s$ and visual cue identity $v$ (Fig. 3A). How do we determine for example if the astrocyte encodes genuinely spatial information above and beyond what can be explained by its possible tuning to the visual cue $v$? One way to address this issue it to compute the conditional mutual information (CMI) [9] of an astrocytic response $r$ about a stimulus $s$ conditioned on the value of a visual stimulus $v$. This quantifies the amount of information encoded in responses $\mathbf{R}$ about positions $\mathbf{S}$ that cannot be explained by the tuning to a set of visual stimuli $\mathbf{V}$ and it is defined as:

$$I(\mathbf{R}; \mathbf{S}|\mathbf{V}) = \sum_v P(v) \sum_{r,s} P(r,s|v) \log_2 \frac{P(r,s|v)}{P(r|v)P(s|v)} \tag{2}$$

where $P(r,s|v)$ is the joint probability of observing response $r$ and stimulus $s$ at fixed visual stimulus $v$. A non-zero value of CMI denotes genuine tuning of the astrocyte to $s$. The statistical significance of a CMI value can be assessed against a null-hypothesis distribution obtained shuffling the relationship between $r$ and $s$ within each specific $v$. We evaluated the performances of CMI statistical testing

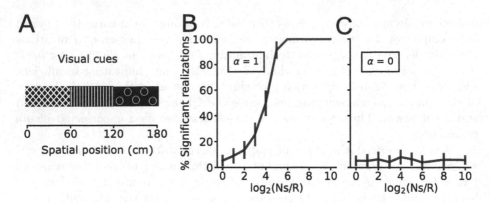

**Fig. 3.** Determining the significance of conditional mutual information. (A) Schematic of a virtual track containing three distinct visual patterns [3, 4, 7]. (B–C) Percentage of significant realizations classified with the shuffling test and without bias correction (*plugin*) for models with genuine spatial information (B) and without spatial information (C). Data is shown as (mean ± std).

in classifying simulated responses as bearing genuine spatial information. We used numerical experiments leveraging on the full information model ($\alpha = 1$), simulating astrocytic $Ca^{2+}$ signals bearing spatial information. We found that, to achieve robust CMI significance detection, it is required to sample approximately 256 trials per stimulus (Fig. 3B). Then, we quantified the extent of false positives reported by the CMI statistical testing. We performed numerical experiments generating astrocytic $Ca^{2+}$ signals devoid of spatial information ($\alpha = 0$). We found that the false positive rate was stable at 5% set by our statistical threshold (Fig. 3C).

## 4    Spatial Information in CA1 Astrocytes During Spatial Navigation

Here we apply the information theoretical formalism presented in Sects. 2 and 3 to investigate information encoding in astrocytic $Ca^{2+}$ dynamics using real two-photon functional imaging data. We used the dataset of [3], in which subcellular $Ca^{2+}$ dynamics of hippocampal CA1 astrocytes (specifically labeled with the genetically encoded $Ca^{2+}$ indicator GCaMP6f [2, 8, 23]) were recorded from head-fixed mice navigating in a monodirectional virtual corridor (Fig. 4A–B).

First, we investigated the influence of stimulus-response discretization on mutual information estimation and statistical significance detection on real data. We estimated the underlying probabilities for a grid of discretization parameters $S$ (8, 12, 16, 20, 40, 60, 80) and $R$ (2, 4, 6, 8, 10). We used a uniform-count binning procedure for positions and an equally-spaced binning procedure for responses. We found that correcting the information measures for the limited sampling bias

with PT method yield stable results over a wide range of discretization parameter S (4–16) (Fig. 4C), confirming the efficacy of the PT method in accurately
estimating the information value.

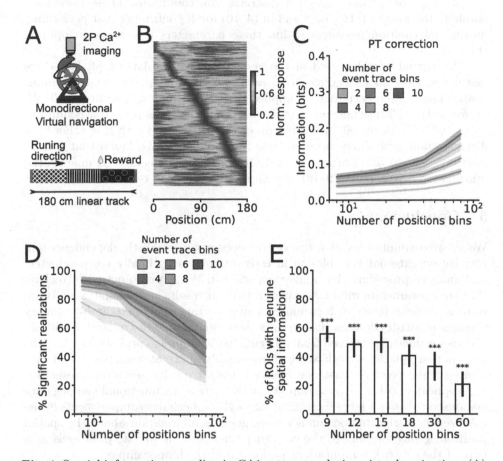

**Fig. 4.** Spatial information encoding in CA1 astrocytes during virtual navigation. (A)
2-photon $Ca^{2+}$ imaging was performed in head-fixed mice running along a 180 cm
virtual track [3]. (B) Normalized astrocytic $Ca^{2+}$ responses as a function of position
for ROIs with significant spatial information computed with R = 4 and S = 12 (n =
311 ROIs out of 356 total ROIs, 7 imaging sessions from 3 animals). Responses are
ordered according to the position of the maximum of the $Ca^{2+}$ responses. Vertical
scale: 50 ROIs. (C) Mutual information values with PT bias correction as a function of
the number of position bins. (D) Percentage of ROIs classified significant as a function
of the number of bins for the stimulus. (E) Fraction of astrocytic ROIs showing a
significant decrease in their information content when position is shuffled within the
same visual cue (Binomial test with 0.05 probability of success; *, p < 0.05; **, p ≤ 0.01;
***, p ≤ 0.001). Data are mean ± s.e.m. from 7 imaging sessions in 3 animals. (Color
figure online)

Significant realizations were affected by both $S$ and $R$ parameters. We found consistent results for $R > 2$ ($\sim$90% of significant realizations) over the range of $S$ (4–16) (Fig. 4D). This suggests that trial numerosity in this dataset limited the statistical power at more granular discretization conditions. These results are stable in the range (4–16) for $S$ and in (4–10) for $R$ confirming that performing mutual information measures within these parameters represents an optimal choice.

The virtual corridor used in the generation of this dataset [3] had three distinct visual cues extending 60 cm each (Fig. 4A). Thus, to test for genuine spatial information encoding, we applied the formalism described in Sect. 3. We performed the CMI significance test, for a set of position discretization conditions ($S = (9, 12, 15, 18, 30, 60)$) while responses were discretized with $R = 4$. For both discretization procedures we used equally spaced bins. We found that a large fraction ($\sim$40 to 55%) of astrocytic ROIs carried significantly genuine spatial information over a range (9–18) of position discretization conditions (Fig. 4E).

## 5    Conclusions

We created simulations of astrocytic responses with realistic dependencies of activity on external variables to investigate how to optimally set parameters and analyses procedures for a given experiment. While we do not wish to claim that such parameters will be always optimal, our results and simulation software provides a mean to set such parameters given certain easily measurable primary features of astrocytic data. Our results show that simple discretization and use of direct estimates, obtained from plugging in the empirical probabilities into the information equations, work well with reasonably high statistical power and with a rate of false positives that never exceeds the set p-value selection threshold.

Applications of these procedures to *in vivo* astrocytic functional imaging data demonstrated that a large fraction of astrocytic subcellular compartments in the CA1 region of the hippocampus carries genuine information about the spatial position, giving support to the emerging concept of astrocytic place cells as a part of the network computations performed in the hippocampus.

Future technical work includes investigating how to combine our information computations and selection criteria with other conservative criteria used for ruling out effects of data non-stationarities, such as reliability of $Ca^{2+}$ activity across trial blocks [3].

## References

1. Bellmund, J.L.S., Gärdenfors, P., Moser, E.I., Doeller, C.F.: Navigating cognition: spatial codes for human thinking. Science **362**(6415), eaat6766 (2018)
2. Chen, T.W., et al.: Ultrasensitive fluorescent proteins for imaging neuronal activity. Nature **499**(7458), 295–300 (2013)
3. Curreli, S., Bonato, J., Romanzi, S., Panzeri, S., Fellin, T.: Complementary encoding of spatial information in hippocampal astrocytes. PLoS Biol. **20**(3), e3001530 (2022)

4. Dombeck, D.A., Harvey, C.D., Tian, L., Looger, L.L., Tank, D.W.: Functional imaging of hippocampal place cells at cellular resolution during virtual navigation. Nat. Neurosci. **13**(11), 1433–1440 (2010)
5. Doron, A., et al.: Hippocampal astrocytes encode reward location. bioRxiv 2021.07.07.451434 (2021)
6. Hartley, T., Lever, C., Burgess, N., O'Keefe, J.: Space in the brain: how the hippocampal formation supports spatial cognition. Phil. Trans. R. Soc. B **369**(1635), 20120510 (2014)
7. Harvey, C.D., Collman, F., Dombeck, D.A., Tank, D.W.: Intracellular dynamics of hippocampal place cells during virtual navigation. Nature **461**(7266), 941–946 (2009)
8. Haustein, M.D., et al.: Conditions and constraints for astrocyte calcium signaling in the hippocampal mossy fiber pathway. Neuron **82**(2), 413–429 (2014)
9. Ince, R.A.A., Mazzoni, A., Bartels, A., Logothetis, N.K., Panzeri, S.: A novel test to determine the significance of neural selectivity to single and multiple potentially correlated stimulus features. J. Neurosci. Meth. **210**(1), 49–65 (2012)
10. Lines, J., Martin, E.D., Kofuji, P., Aguilar, J., Araque, A.: Astrocytes modulate sensory-evoked neuronal network activity. Nat. Commun. **11**(1), 3689 (2020)
11. Merten, K., Folk, R.W., Duarte, D., Nimmerjahn, A.: Astrocytes encode complex behaviorally relevant information. bioRxiv 2021.10.09.463784 (2021)
12. Moser, E.I., Moser, M.B., McNaughton, B.L.: Spatial representation in the hippocampal formation: a history. Nat. Neurosci. **20**(11), 1448–1464 (2017)
13. Moser, M.B., Rowland, D.C., Moser, E.I.: Place cells, grid cells, and memory. Cold Spring Harb. Perspect. Biol. **7**(2), a021808 (2015)
14. Nemenman, I., Bialek, W., de Ruyter van Steveninck, R.: Entropy and information in neural spike trains: progress on the sampling problem. Phys. Rev. E **69**(5), 056111 (2004)
15. Nemenman, I., Shafee, F., Bialek, W.: Entropy and inference. In: Dietterich, T.G., Becker, S., Ghahramani, Z. (eds.) Revisited Advances in Neural Information Processing Systems, vol. 14, pp. 95–100. MIT Press, Cambridge (2002)
16. O'Keefe, J., Dostrovsky, J.: The hippocampus as a spatial map: preliminary evidence from unit activity in the freely-moving rat. Brain Res. **34**(1), 171–175 (1971)
17. Paninski, L.: Estimation of entropy and mutual information. Neural Comput. **15**(6), 1191–1253 (2003)
18. Panzeri, S., Senatore, R., Montemurro, M.A., Petersen, R.S.: Correcting for the sampling bias problem in spike train information measures. J. Neurophysiol. **98**(3), 1064–1072 (2007)
19. Panzeri, S., Treves, A.: Analytical estimates of limited sampling biases in different information measures. Netw. Comput. Neural Syst. **7**(1), 87–107 (1996)
20. Quiroga, R.Q., Panzeri, S.: Extracting information from neuronal populations: information theory and decoding approaches. Nat. Rev. Neurosci. **10**(3), 173–185 (2009)
21. Schummers, J., Yu, H., Sur, M.: Tuned responses of astrocytes and their influence on hemodynamic signals in the visual cortex. Science **320**(5883), 1638–1643 (2008)
22. Shannon, C.E.: A mathematical theory of communication. Bell Syst. Tech. J. **27**(3), 379–423 (1948)
23. Shigetomi, E., et al.: Imaging calcium microdomains within entire astrocyte territories and endfeet with GCaMPs expressed using adeno-associated viruses. J. Gen. Physiol. **141**(5), 633–647 (2013)
24. Srinivasan, R., et al.: $Ca^{2+}$ signaling in astrocytes from $Ip3r2^{-/-}$ mice in brain slices and during startle responses in vivo. Nat. Neurosci. **18**(5), 708–717 (2015)

25. Stobart, J.L., et al.: Cortical circuit activity evokes rapid astrocyte calcium signals on a similar timescale to neurons. Neuron **98**(4), 726–735.e4 (2018)
26. Strong, S.P., Koberle, R., de Ruyter van Steveninck, R.R., Bialek, W.: Entropy and information in neural spike trains. Phys. Rev. Lett. **80**(1), 197–200 (1998)
27. Wang, X., et al.: Astrocytic $Ca^{2+}$ signaling evoked by sensory stimulation in vivo. Nat. Neurosci. **9**(6), 816–823 (2006)
28. Yu, X., Nagai, J., Khakh, B.S.: Improved tools to study astrocytes. Nat. Rev. Neurosci. **21**(3), 121–138 (2020)

# Introducing the Rank-Biased Overlap as Similarity Measure for Feature Importance in Explainable Machine Learning: A Case Study on Parkinson's Disease

Alessia Sarica[1]([✉]) [iD], Andrea Quattrone[2] [iD], and Aldo Quattrone[1,3] [iD]

[1] Neuroscience Research Center, Department of Medical and Surgical Sciences, Magna Graecia University, 88100 Catanzaro, Italy
sarica@unicz.it
[2] Department of Medical and Surgical Sciences, Institute of Neurology, Magna Graecia University, 88100 Catanzaro, Italy
[3] Neuroimaging Research Unit, Institute of Molecular Bioimaging and Physiology, National Research Council, 88100 Catanzaro, Italy

**Abstract.** Feature importance is one of the most common explanations provided by Machine Learning (ML). However, different classification algorithms or different training sets could produce different rankings of predictive features. Thus, the quantification of differences between feature importance is crucial for assessing model trustworthiness. Rank-biased Overlap (RBO) is a similarity measure between *incomplete*, *top-weighted* and *indefinite* rankings, which are all characteristics of feature importance. In RBO, tuning persistence $p$ allows to truncate rankings at any arbitrary depth, so to evaluate their overlapping size at increasing number of features. Classification of Parkinson's disease (PD) with Explainable Boosting Machine (EBM) was chosen here as case study for introducing RBO in ML. An imbalanced dataset, 168 healthy controls (HC) and 396 PD patients, with 178 among clinical and imaging features was obtained from PPMI. Imbalanced, undersampled (K-Medoids) and oversampled (SMOTE) datasets were used for training EBMs, obtaining their respective feature importance. RBO score was calculated between ranking pairs incrementally increasing the depth by five features, from 1 to 178. All classifiers reached excellent AUC-ROC (~1) on test set, demonstrating the EBM prediction stability when trained on imbalanced datasets. RBO revealed that the maximum size of overlapping (80%) among rankings was obtained truncating at top 40 features, while their similarity decreased asymptotically to 50% when more than 45 features were considered. Thanks to RBO it was possible to demonstrate that, for the same accuracy, the more similar are the feature importance, the more stable is the model and the more reliable is the ML interpretability.

**Keywords:** Explainable machine learning · Feature importance · Parkinson's disease · Rank-biased overlap

© Springer Nature Switzerland AG 2022
M. Mahmud et al. (Eds.): BI 2022, LNAI 13406, pp. 129–139, 2022
https://doi.org/10.1007/978-3-031-15037-1_11

# 1   Introduction

Explainable Artificial Intelligence (XAI) and interpretable Machine Learning (ML) is a recently born field, which aim is to maximize the explainability and interpretability of ML findings [1]. One of the most common explanations provided by ML algorithms is the feature importance [2], that is the contribution of each feature in the classification. The ordered list of features by their individual contribution is a *top-weighted* ranking where the variables on the top are more predictive than the variables in the tail [2, 3]. In the medical and clinical field, the feature importance provides to the researcher an immediate overview of the biological measures involved in a specific disease [4].

The predictive contribution of each feature depends on the ML algorithm used for the classification. Indeed, different models produce different rankings of importance and one highly predictive feature in a classifier could be unimportant in another classifier [2]. Moreover, the same ML classifier could show different feature importance rankings when trained on different folds/subsets of the same dataset [1]. Another example is the prediction of a rare disease with an imbalanced dataset [5] and there is the need to balance the classes through undersampling or oversampling. The balance of classes could improve the ML performance but could also provide a different feature importance than the one obtained with an imbalanced training set, thus preventing an exhaustive interpretation of the findings. For these reasons, the comparison of feature importance rankings is fundamental for understanding how different ML approaches or different training sets influence the reliability and trustworthiness of the findings. In other words, the main questions are: how similar are the feature importance lists produced by different ML methods or by the same classifier trained on different datasets? What statistics, measure or metric should be used?

The quantification of the dissimilarity or similarity of two rankings is usually performed with correlation coefficients calculated with the Kendall's $\tau$ [6], Spearman's $\rho$ [3] or their variants [7–9]. However, $\tau$, $\rho$ and their variants are unweighted measures and thus they are not able to emphasize the features on the top of the ranking [3]. Furthermore, these statistics are not applicable on indefinite and non-conjoint rankings, thus resulting not suitable for assessing the similarity of ML feature importance. On the contrary, the rank-biased overlap (RBO) [3] is a similarity measure that estimates the size of overlapping between indefinite ranked lists, representing a good candidate for comparing the classification feature importance. RBO score varies in a range from 0 to 1, where 1 indicates that the two rankings are identical, and zero indicates absence of similarity [3]. The weight given to the first $d$ (depth) features in a ranking can be modified by tuning the persistence ($p$), a probability parameter in the range [0,1]. A lower value of $p$ gives more importance to the top features, while a high value explores the ranking at a deeper depth [3].

The first aim of the present work is to introduce the RBO as a similarity measure for quantifying the differences between feature importance produced by explainable classification models. The Explainable Boosting Machine (EBM) [10] is a *glass*-box algorithm that showed high interpretability of ML findings, reaching excellent accuracies for example for the prediction of Alzheimer's disease [11] or for distinguishing between Parkinson's disease and SWEDD [12]. However, it has never been assessed whether and how EBM is able to deal with imbalanced datasets of neurodegenerative diseases. Thus, the second aim of the present study is to compare the performance of EBM models trained on imbalanced data and on balanced datasets obtained through undersampling with K-Medoids [13] and oversampling with Synthetic Minority Over-sampling Technique (SMOTE) [14]. The prediction of the Parkinson's disease (PD) was chosen here as case study, and for this purpose an imbalanced dataset with clinical and imaging features was obtained from the Parkinson's Progression Markers Initiative (PPMI). The third and last aim of this work is to use the RBO similarity measure for quantifying the differences among the three feature importance rankings produced by the EBM algorithm trained on the imbalanced, undersampled and oversampled dataset.

In summary, the three main contributions of the present study are: (i) introducing the RBO as measure for quantifying the similarity between feature importance rankings; (ii) building EBM classifiers on three different training sets - imbalanced, undersampled and oversampled datasets – and comparing their performance in predicting PD; (iii) assessing the similarity between feature importance rankings produced by the three EBM classifiers through the RBO score.

## 2    Materials and Methods

### 2.1    Participants

Data used in the preparation of this article were obtained from the Parkinson's Progression Markers Initiative (PPMI) database (www.ppmi-info.org/data). For up-to-date information on the study, visit www.ppmi-info.org. Table 1 reports the demographic, the clinical and imaging characteristics of the cohort, which consisted of 168 healthy controls (HC) and 396 PD. Only subjects without missing clinical and imaging features were considered and all data used for the analysis are acquired at the baseline visit.

### 2.2    Clinical and Imaging Features

The number of items per clinical assessment and the total number of features (178) used for training the ML models are reported in Table 1, and consisted in: Movement Disorder Society Unified Parkinson's Disease Rating Scale (MDS-UPDRS) [15], part I, II and III, Montreal Cognitive Assessment (MoCA), State-Trait Anxiety Inventory (STAI), Geriatric Depression Scale (GDS), Scales for Outcomes in Parkinson's Disease - Autonomic Dysfunction (SCOPA-AUT), Judgment of Line Orientation (JLO), the University of Pennsylvania Smell Identification Test (UPSIT), Epworth Sleepiness Scale (ESS), Hoen and Yahr (H&Y) scale for assessing the stage of PD (not included in the training features since it is not for diagnosis). The neuroimaging technique commonly used for the diagnosis PD is the dopamine transporter single-photon emission computed tomography (DaT-SPECT) of the striatum, the region comprising caudate and putamen. The specific binding ratio (SBR) of these two regions of interest (ROI) is calculated for each hemisphere from the count densities and normalized by the occipital cortex uptake. More details of the imaging protocol can be found on www.ppmi-info.org.

**Table 1.** Demographic, clinical and imaging data of the imbalanced PPMI dataset.

|  | HC (168) | PD (396) | #[a] |
|---|---|---|---|
| Age | 61.1 ± 11.3 | 61.7 ± 9.65 | – |
| Gender (M/F) | 109/59 | 260/136 | – |
| H&Y | 0.005 ± 0.07 | 1.57 ± 0.51 | – |
| MDS-UPDRS-I | 2.89 ± 2.76 | 5.61 ± 4.12 | 13 |
| MDS-UPDRS-II | 0.35 ± 0.95 | 5.39 ± 4.14 | 13 |
| MDS-UPDRS-III | 1.19 ± 2.06 | 20.9 ± 8.84 | 33 |
| MoCA | 28.1 ± 1.09 | 26.9 ± 2.38 | 26 |
| STAI | 47.7 ± 4.97 | 47.3 ± 5.32 | 40 |
| GDS | 5.17 ± 1.39 | 5.26 ± 1.45 | 15 |
| SCOPA-AUT | 5.11 ± 3.38 | 8.58 ± 6.51 | 21 |
| JLO | 13.1 ± 1.95 | 12.8 ± 2.1 | 1 |
| UPSIT | 34 ± 4.75 | 22.3 ± 8.34 | 4 |
| ESS | 5.66 ± 3.38 | 5.81 ± 3.42 | 8 |
| Left Caudate SBR | 3.0 ± 0.63 | 1.99 ± 0.59 | 1 |
| Right Caudate SBR | 2.9 ± 0.61 | 1.98 ± 0.59 | 1 |
| Left Putamen SBR | 2.14 ± 0.56 | 0.812 ± 0.35 | 1 |
| Right Putamen SBR | 2.16 ± 0.58 | 0.843 ± 0.36 | 1 |
|  |  | Tot: | 178 |

[a] Number of items per test, i.e. number of features used for training EBM models. Age, gender, and H&Y not included in the features space.

## 2.3 Sampling of the Dataset

The aim of sampling is to balance the dataset, thus, to obtain an equal sample size of the two classes. The original imbalanced dataset HC-PD$_{imb}$ (168-396) was randomly sampled by applying two different approaches, the first was an undersampling technique applied on the majority class (PD), the second one was an oversampling method applied on the minority class (HC), as described as follows.

**Undersampling.** The undersampling of the imbalanced dataset was done with the K-Medoids approach [13], which is an unsupervised method of clustering applied on the majority class (PD), where the number of clusters is equals the number of minority examples (HC = 168). The final dataset HC-PD$_{und}$ (168-168) is a combination of all data from the minority set and the cluster centers from the majority set. The undersampling was conducted with the Python package *sklearn_extra.cluster.KMedoids* of scikit-learn (v. 0.23) (metric "euclidean" and method "pam").

**Oversampling.** SMOTE [14] was applied on the minority class (HC), for generating new synthetic data by randomly interpolating pairs of nearest neighbors. The final dataset HC-PD$_{over}$ (396-396) is a combination of all data from the majority (PD) and minority set (HC) and, additionally, the new synthetic minority data such that final dataset is balanced. The oversampling was conducted with the Python package *imblearn.over_sampling.SMOTE* (v. 0.9.0).

The original imbalanced dataset and the two sampled datasets – HC-PD$_{imb}$, HC-PD$_{und}$ and HC-PD$_{over}$ – were then randomly split with a static seed into training and test sets with a percentage respectively of 80% and 20% by maintaining proportions between class distributions.

## 2.4  Machine Learning Analysis

The EBM algorithm [10] is based on standard Generalized Additive Models (GAMs) [16], which accuracy is improved by adding pairwise interactions [17], taking the name of GA$^2$Ms with the form:

$$g(E[y]) = \beta_0 + \sum f_j(x_j) + \sum f_{ij}(x_i, x_j), \tag{1}$$

where $E$ is the estimate of the additive model, $x_i = (x_{i1}, \ldots, x_{ip})$ is the feature vector with $p$ features, $y_i$ the response, $x_j$ denotes the $j$th variable in the feature space, $g$ is the *link function* that adapts the GAMs to regression ($g$ = identity) or classification ($g$ = logistic), $\beta_0$ is the intercept that adjusts the prediction from the model, and $f_j$ is the feature function, which could be plot for visualizing the contribution of each feature to the final prediction [17]. The feature importance is calculated after learning the best feature function $f_j$ by training the model on one feature at a time, so to obtain its contribution to the prediction [17].

In this work, three EBM models were built on the three training sets – imbalanced, undersampled and oversampled - and the performance was evaluated on the test set with the Area under the Curve of the Receiver Operating Characteristic (AUC-ROC). Moreover, the AUC-ROC (mean ± standard deviation) was calculated on the whole dataset with a 5-fold cross-validation (cv, *sklearn.model_selection.cross_val_score* of scikit-learn v. 0.23) for assessing overfitting. The pairwise interactions between features were not here considered to avoid complexity in the interpretation of the findings. The feature importance ranking of the three classifiers (FI[HC-PD$_{imb}$], FI[HC-PD$_{und}$], FI[HC-PD$_{over}$]) was obtained by ordering the features by their mean absolute contribution in the prediction of the training data, calculated as logit of the probability (logarithm of the odds) from the logistic link function $g$ (Eq. 1) [17]. Machine Learning analysis was conducted with the Python package *InterpretML* (v 0.2.7) [18] (implementation of EBM provided by Microsoft) on a MacOS 10.14.6 (2.9 GHz, 32 GB of RAM). The Python package *seaborn* (v. 0.11.2) was used for plotting the feature importance rankings.

## 2.5  Rank-Biased Overlap (RBO)

The feature importance produced by explainable ML algorithms is a *top-weighted* ranking, that is an ordered list of items where the variables on the top are more important than the variables in the tail [2, 3]. Other two characteristics of a feature importance ranking is that it could be *incomplete*, that is it could not cover all variables in the domain, and it could be *indefinite*, since the user's decision to stop the ranking at a particular depth is arbitrary [3]. One of the most used measure of rank similarity is the correlation that quantifies the direction (positive or negative) and the magnitude of the association between a pair of lists. The Kendall's $\tau$ [6] and Spearman's $\rho$ are two of the most widely used measures of correlation [3]. However, both $\tau$ and $\rho$ require that the two rankings are conjoint and since they are unweighted measures, they are not able to place more emphasis on the items on the top of the rank [3]. Several variants of the correlation measures were proposed for considering the weight of items in a list and for comparing non-conjoint ranks, for example the top-weighted variant of the Kendall's $\tau$, the $\tau_{AP}$ [7], the adaptations of Spearman's $\rho$ [9] and Spearman's footrules [8], or the Kolmogorov-Smirnov's $D$ [19]. However, all these variants do not fully satisfy the need to compare *indefinite* rankings, that is the need to truncate the feature importance at any particular and arbitrary depth [3]. To overcome this issue, a similarity measure was introduced, the rank-biased overlap (RBO), which is calculated as the expected average overlap between two indefinite rankings at incrementally increasing depths [3]. The depth of interest could be varied by tuning an input parameter of the RBO, called user's *persistence* ($p$). The persistence $p$ is a probability (in the range [0,1]) of continuing to the next rank in the list, while on the contrary, $1 - p$ is the probability that the user stops at a given depth $d$ of the ranking [3]. A lower value of $p$ gives more importance to top results, and when $p = 0$ only the first feature in the ranking is considered. Given two infinite rankings $S$ and $T$ to depth $d$ and the persistence $p$, the RBO is calculated as follows [3]:

$$RBO(S, T, p) = (1 - p) \sum p^{d-1} \cdot A_d, \tag{2}$$

where, $d = 1\,to\,\infty$ is the depth of the ranking to be examined, $A_d = X_d/d$ is the agreement between $S$ and $T$, i.e. the proportion of $S$ and $T$ that is overlapped, and $X_d = |S_{:d} \cap T_{:d}|$ is the size of overlap (intersection) between $S$ and $T$. The RBO varies in the range [0,1], where 0 means disjoint rankings and 1 means identical rankings [3].

In this work, the RBO was used for assessing the similarity between pairs of feature importance rankings ($RBO_{imb\_und}$, $RBO_{imb\_over}$, $RBO_{und\_over}$) that were obtained by training the EBM algorithm on the different datasets: imbalanced, undersampled and oversampled. Here, to investigate the similarity between feature importance rankings at different depths, the values of stopping depth $d$, i.e. the number of the top features in the ranking, were increased with a fixed step of 5 features in the range [1, 178]. Consequently, the value of persistence $p$ was automatically increased and calculated as $p = \frac{d-1}{d}$, assuming the values in the range [0, 0.9944]. The Python package *rbo* (v.0.1.2) was used as implementation of the RBO by Webber et al. [3].

## 3   Results

### 3.1   Machine Learning Analysis

The EBM models HC-PD$_{imb}$ and HC-PD$_{over}$ reached both an AUC-ROC of 1 ($1 \pm 0$ with 5-fold cv), while the classifier HC-PD$_{und}$ had an AUC-ROC of 0.99 ($0.998 \pm 0.004$ with

5-fold cv). The rankings of the first twenty most important features in the models HC-PD$_{imb}$, HC-PD$_{und}$ and HC-PD$_{over}$ are reported in Fig. 1A, B and C. Figure 1D reports the first fifty most important features ordered by their average importance across the three EBM models, where the first ten important features were NP2TRMR (MDS-UPRDS II item 2.10 Tremor), PUTAMEN_L (SBR of the left putamen), NP3FACXP (MDS-UPRDS III item 3.2 Facial expression), NP3BRADY (MDS-UPRDS III item 3.14 Global Spontaneity of movement) and NP3RTCON (MDS-UPRDS III item 3.18 Constancy of rest), PUTAMEN_R (SBR of the right putamen), NP2HWRT (MDS-UPRDS II item 2.7 Handwriting), NP3PRSPR (MDS-UPRDS III item 3.6a Pronation-Supination - Right Hand), NP3HMOVL (MDS-UPRDS III item 3.5b Hand movements - Left Hand) and NP3RIGRU (MDS-UPRDS III item 3.3b Rigidity - RUE).

## 3.2   RBO Scores

The RBO scores calculated by tuning the value of depth $d$ and consequently the persistence $p$ in each pair of comparisons (RBO$_{imb\_und}$, RBO$_{imb\_over}$, RBO$_{und\_over}$) are reported in Table 2. The maximum similarity (~1) was obtained when only the first item (NP2TRMR, MDS-UPRDS II item 2.10 Tremor) in the ranking was compared between FI[HC-PD$_{imb}$] and FI[HC-PD$_{und}$]. The maximum values RBO$_{imb\_over}$ = 0.802 and RBO$_{und\_over}$ = 0.74 were reached both when the first 40 features in the rankings were compared ($p = 0.975$, Table 2).

**Table 2.**  RBO of the pairwise comparisons of the feature importance rankings obtained by training the EBM models on the imbalanced, undersampled and oversampled datasets. Raising $p$ increases the depth $d$ of comparisons (number of features considered). In bold the maximum value.

| $p$ | $d$ | RBO$_{imb\_und}$ | RBO$_{imb\_over}$ | RBO$_{und\_over}$ |
|---|---|---|---|---|
| 0 | 1 | ~1 | ~0 | ~0 |
| 0.800 | 5 | 0.755 | 0.548 | 0.423 |
| 0.900 | 10 | 0.780 | 0.695 | 0.603 |
| 0.950 | 20 | 0.803 | 0.778 | 0.705 |
| 0.967 | 30 | 0.806 | 0.799 | 0.733 |
| 0.975 | 40 | 0.800 | **0.802** | **0.740** |
| 0.980 | 50 | 0.788 | 0.795 | 0.735 |
| 0.990 | 100 | 0.679 | 0.692 | 0.646 |
| 0.993 | 150 | 0.571 | 0.583 | 0.546 |
| 0.994 | 178 | 0.520 | 0.531 | 0.499 |

Abbreviations: $d$ = depth; $p$ = persistence; imb = imbalanced dataset (HC-PD$_{imb}$); und = undersampled dataset (HC-PD$_{und}$); over = oversampled dataset (HC-PD$_{over}$).

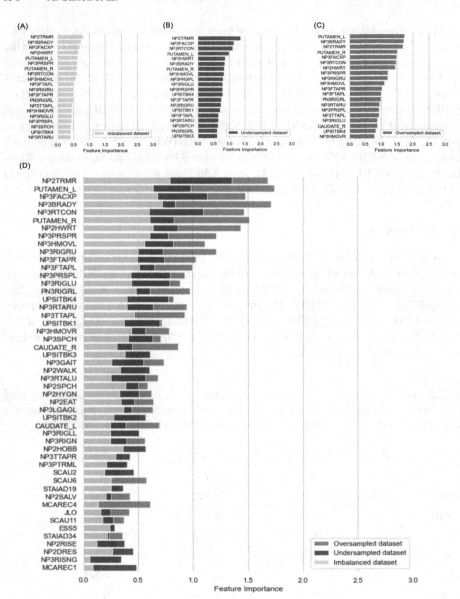

**Fig. 1.** Ranking of the first twenty most important features obtained by the EBM model trained (A) on the imbalanced dataset; (B) on the undersampled dataset; (C) on the oversampled dataset. (D) Feature importance (first fifty features) ordered by their average importance across the three classifiers trained on the imbalanced dataset (in green), on the undersampled dataset (in blue) and on the oversampled dataset (in red). (Color figure online)

Figure 2 depicts the RBO curves of the three ranking comparisons by raising the depth $d$, that is by considering a higher number of features as important. The $\text{RBO}_{\text{imb\_over}}$ and $\text{RBO}_{\text{und\_over}}$ curves show a similar increasing trend, moreover the three curves reach a plateau between $d = 20$ and $d = 40$, revealing that the maximum similarity among the three RBOs is obtained when the first 40 features are considered. For values $d > 45$ there is a decrease in the similarity among the three feature importance until the RBO curves asymptote to the final value of ~0.5.

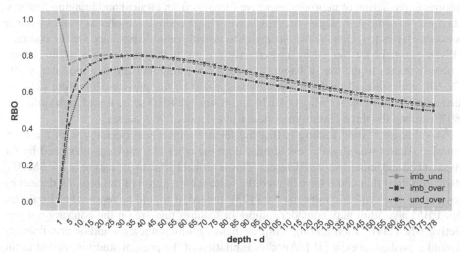

**Fig. 2.** RBO curves of the pairwise comparisons of feature importance rankings obtained by the EBM models HC-PD$_{\text{imb}}$, HC-PD$_{\text{und}}$ and HC-PD$_{\text{over}}$ for increasing values of depth $d$, that is for increasing number of important features considered.

## 4 Discussion and Conclusions

The purpose of this work was to introduce the RBO [3] score as similarity measure for comparing feature importance rankings produced by explainable ML. The classification of Parkinson's disease from clinical and imaging features was chosen as case study and conducted with the Explainable Boosting Machine [10, 17, 20] algorithm on three datasets, imbalanced, undersampled and oversampled. EBM models reached excellent accuracies (~1), thus demonstrating the robustness of EBM in dealing with imbalanced datasets. Interestingly, RBO allowed to reveal that the three feature importance rankings had the highest size of overlapping (~80%) when the depth was truncated at 40 features.

The classification task has two main goals: to obtain good accuracy in distinguishing classes and to provide the feature contribution in the prediction [1, 2, 21]. The classifier performance could be evaluated through several metrics (e.g. accuracy, precision recall) that are easy to compare both quantitatively and statistically (e.g. McNemar's test) [22]. However, when a multiplicity of models reach excellent accuracies, it is difficult to decide which one is better and what Breiman calls the *Rashomon Effect* takes place [21]. Indeed, for the same performance, a classifier can consider a feature more or less important than the importance given by another classifier. For this reason, it is crucial to quantify the differences between ML rankings, because if different models produce similar feature importance, "*it is more likely that these reflect genuine aspect of the data*" as stated by Saarela and Jauhiainen [2]. The present study faces the Rashomon Effect [21], given that all the three EBM models trained on the imbalanced, undersampled and oversampled datasets reach the highest accuracy (AUC-ROC ~1). The stability of the EBM performance in presence of imbalanced data is an important finding for the automatic prediction of neurodegenerative diseases from clinical and imaging features. The rarity of some pathologies prevents having large enough samples as well as balance between classes [5], thus the ML struggles to provide reliable findings. On the contrary, EBM seems to be unaffected by the perturbations due to the imbalance between classes, probably thanks to the use of bagging, gradient boosting and additive modularity [10, 17, 20], which are all methods strongly suggested by the previous literature [21]. As further evidence of the stability of EBM algorithm, the RBO score found high similarity (80%) among the three feature importance at a depth of 40 features.

Another interesting finding is that the feature importance obtained with the over-sampled dataset was slightly less similar than the other two rankings produced by the imbalanced and undersampled datasets. This is probably due to the nature of the SMOTE algorithm itself that could have altered the feature correlation of the original dataset by generating new synthetic minority data [23]. Indeed, it should be reported as limitation that EBM algorithm may consider important features that are on the contrary not predictive when correlation among features, heavy multicollinearity and/or non-linearity around a prediction exist [10]. Another limitation of the present study is related to the percent split of training and test sets (80-20); future works might assess whether the use of different proportion could produce different accuracies and feature importance. Further research might explore the application of RBO to compare the explanations produced by different ML algorithms, such as Random Forest [24]. It would be also interesting to investigate how the tuning of EBM hyperparameters, such as the outer bags or the learning rate, could affect the feature importance and the accuracy in this specific case study.

In conclusion, the present work demonstrated that RBO is a suitable similarity measure, allowing to state that, for the same classification accuracy, the more similar are the feature importance produced with different training sets, the more stable is the model and the more reliable is the interpretability and explainability of the ML findings.

# References

1. Molnar, C.: Interpretable machine learning. Lulu.com (2020)
2. Saarela, M., Jauhiainen, S.: Comparison of feature importance measures as explanations for classification models. SN Appl. Sci. **3**(2), 1–12 (2021). https://doi.org/10.1007/s42452-021-04148-9
3. Webber, W., Moffat, A., Zobel, J.: A similarity measure for indefinite rankings. ACM Trans. Inform. Syst. **28**, 1–38 (2010)
4. Sarica, A.: Editorial for the Special Issue on "Machine Learning in Healthcare and Biomedical Application", MDPI, vol. 15, p. 97 (2022)
5. Dubey, R., Zhou, J., Wang, Y., Thompson, P.M., Ye, J.: Initiative AsDN: analysis of sampling techniques for imbalanced data: an n= 648 ADNI study. Neuroimage **87**, 220–241 (2014)
6. Kendall, M.G.: Rank correlation methods (1948)

7. Yilmaz, E., Aslam, J.A., Robertson, S.: A new rank correlation coefficient for information retrieval. In: Proceedings of the 31st Annual International ACM SIGIR Conference on Research and Development in Information Retrieval, pp. 587–594 (2008)

8. Bar-Ilan, J., Mat-Hassan, M., Levene, M.: Methods for comparing rankings of search engine results. Comput. Netw. **50**, 1448–1463 (2006)

9. Bar-Ilan, J.: Comparing rankings of search results on the web. Inf. Process. Manage. **41**, 1511–1519 (2005)

10. Caruana, R., Lou, Y., Gehrke, J., Koch, P., Sturm, M., Elhadad, N: Intelligible models for healthcare: predicting pneumonia risk and hospital 30-day readmission. In: Proceedings of the 21th ACM SIGKDD International Conference on Knowledge Discovery and Data Mining, pp. 1721–1730 (2015)

11. Sarica, A., Quattrone, A., Quattrone, A.: Explainable boosting machine for predicting alzheimer's disease from MRI hippocampal subfields. In: Mufti Mahmud, M., Kaiser, S., Vassanelli, S., Dai, Q., Zhong, N. (eds.) BI 2021. LNCS (LNAI), vol. 12960, pp. 341–350. Springer, Cham (2021). https://doi.org/10.1007/978-3-030-86993-9_31

12. Sarica, A., Quattrone, A., Quattrone, A.: Explainable machine learning with pairwise interactions for the classification of Parkinson's disease and SWEDD from clinical and imaging features. Brain Imag. Behav. 1–11 (2022)

13. Park, H.-S., Jun, C.-H.: A simple and fast algorithm for K-medoids clustering. Expert Syst. Appl. **36**, 3336–3341 (2009)

14. Chawla, N.V., Bowyer, K.W., Hall, L.O., Kegelmeyer, W.P.: SMOTE: synthetic minority over-sampling technique. J. Artific. Intell. Res. **16**, 321–357 (2002)

15. Goetz, C.G., et al.: Movement disorder society URTF: movement disorder society-sponsored revision of the unified parkinson's disease rating scale (MDS-UPDRS): scale presentation and clinimetric testing results. Mov. Disord. **23**, 2129–2170 (2008)

16. Hastie, T.J., Tibshirani, R.J.: Generalized Additive Models. CRC Press (1990)

17. Lou, Y., Caruana, R., Gehrke, J., Hooker, G.: Accurate intelligible models with pairwise interactions. In: Proceedings of the 19th ACM SIGKDD International Conference on Knowledge Discovery and Data Mining, pp. 623–631 (2013)

18. Nori, H., Jenkins, S., Koch, P., Caruana, R.: Interpretml: A unified framework for machine learning interpretability. arXiv preprint arXiv:190909223 (2019)

19. Melucci, M.: Weighted rank correlation in information retrieval evaluation. In: Lee, G.G., et al. (eds.) Information Retrieval Technology, pp. 75–86. Springer, Heidelberg (2009). https://doi.org/10.1007/978-3-642-04769-5_7

20. Lou, Y., Caruana, R., Gehrke, J.: Intelligible models for classification and regression. In: Proceedings of the 18th ACM SIGKDD International Conference on Knowledge Discovery and Data Mining, pp. 150–158 (2012)

21. Breiman, L.: Statistical modeling: the two cultures (with comments and a rejoinder by the author). Stat. Sci. **16**, 199–231 (2001)

22. Jollans, L., et al.: Quantifying performance of machine learning methods for neuroimaging data. Neuroimage **199**, 351–365 (2019)

23. Patil, A., Framewala, A., Kazi, F.: Explainability of smote based oversampling for imbalanced dataset problems. In: 2020 3rd International Conference on Information and Computer Technologies (ICICT), pp. 41–45. IEEE (2020)

24. Sarica, A., Cerasa, A., Quattrone, A.: Random forest algorithm for the classification of neuroimaging data in Alzheimer's disease: a systematic review. Front. Aging Neurosci. **9**, 329 (2017)

# Prediction of Neuropsychological Scores from Functional Connectivity Matrices Using Deep Autoencoders

Delfina Irarte[1], Alberto Testolin[2](✉) [iD], Michele De Filippo De Grazia[2] [iD], and Marco Zorzi[2,3](✉) [iD]

[1] Department of Physics and Astronomy, University of Padova, 35141 Padua, Italy
[2] Department of General Psychology, University of Padova, 35141 Padua, Italy
{alberto.testolin,marco.zorzi}@unipd.it
[3] IRCCS San Camillo Hospital, 30126 Venice, Lido, Italy

**Abstract.** Deep learning models are being increasingly used in precision medicine thanks to their ability to provide accurate predictions of clinical outcome from large-scale datasets of patient's records. However, in many cases data scarcity has forced the adoption of simpler (linear) feature extraction methods, which are less prone to overfitting. In this work, we exploit data augmentation and transfer learning techniques to show that deep, non-linear autoencoders can in fact extract relevant features from resting state functional connectivity matrices of stroke patients, even when the available data is modest. The latent representations extracted by the autoencoders can then be given as input to regularized regression methods to predict neurophsychological scores, significantly outperforming recently proposed methods based on linear feature extraction.

**Keywords:** Resting state networks · Functional connectivity · Deep learning · Feature extraction · Predictive modeling

## 1 Introduction

Improvements in neuroimaging have provided physicians and radiologists with the ability to study the brain with unprecedented precision. In particular, Resting State functional Magnetic Resonance Imaging (RS-fMRI) measures spontaneous fluctuations in blood oxygen-level dependent neural activity and allows estimating the brain functional connectivity in the absence of any task-related activity [1].

Functional connectivity of resting state networks has shown to be a valuable predictor of individual neuropsychological scores in stroke survivors, making it a potentially useful tool in clinical practice [2–4]. However, building robust predictive models from such high-dimensional measurements requires a large number of training samples, which are not always available in clinical populations. Such limitation can be partially addressed by exploiting linear dimensionality reduction techniques such as Principal Component Analysis (PCA), Independent Component Analysis (ICA), or sparse coding in combination with regularized regression

© Springer Nature Switzerland AG 2022
M. Mahmud et al. (Eds.): BI 2022, LNAI 13406, pp. 140–151, 2022
https://doi.org/10.1007/978-3-031-15037-1_12

methods [5,6]. Nevertheless, the choice of the dimensionality reduction technique is non-trivial because it can affect performance of the predictive model [5,7].

Here we show that better performance can be achieved by exploiting the representational power of non-linear dimensionality reduction techniques, namely, deep autoencoders [8]. Autoencoders (AE) are becoming popular in functional neuroimaging thanks to their ability to disentangle the underlying brain dynamics in a completely unsupervised way [9,10] and have already been successfully used to build predictive models of psychiatric disorders [11,12]. Nevertheless, the application of such powerful deep learning models is often hindered by the limited size of clinical datasets. In this work we propose to mitigate this issue using two complementary approaches: data augmentation, which allows to expand the sample size by combining/distorting existing samples, and transfer learning, which allows to exploit additional large-scale datasets (in our case, from the Human Connectome Project [13]) containing functional connectivity data in order to pre-train the autoencoder.

The proposed approach is validated on a reference dataset containing functional connectivity matrices of stroke patients [3]. The features extracted by the autoencoder are used as predictors of the corresponding neurophsychological scores by means of regularized linear regression methods. The latter can limit multicollinearity and overfitting, which makes them particularly suitable for the analysis of neuroimaging data (for a recent review, see [14]). The performance of our method is benchmarked against other popular dimensionality reduction methods based on PCA and ICA, showing promising results.

## 2    Materials and Methods

### 2.1    Datasets

The main dataset used in our study consists of 100 resting state functional connectivity (RSFC) matrices from symptomatic stroke patients, taken from previous studies [3,5]. The patients underwent a 30-minute-long RS-fMRI acquisition, 1–2 weeks after the stroke occurred. Several scores were taken during the neuropsychological assessment: here we focus on language, verbal memory and spatial memory indexes, which are available for a subset of subjects (language: $N = 94$; memory: $N = 77$). In order to implement a transfer learning approach, we also used a dataset from the Human Connectome Project [13], consisting of RSFC matrices of 1050 healthy subjects. RSFC data represent the connectivity between brain regions that share functional properties and can be expressed as a symmetric matrix. In our case, the matrix of each subject is of size $324 \times 324$; following common practice [5], the data was vectorized by only considering the upper triangular matrix. Null values were converted to zero.

### 2.2    Dimensionality Reduction

Dimensionality reduction is the process of taking some input data in a high dimensional space and mapping it into a new "feature" space whose dimensionality is much smaller [15]. Our main focus was to test different variants of deep autoencoders in their ability to extract useful features from RSFC data, and compare their performance with standard linear dimensionality reduction methods [5]. The models were initially compared in terms of their reconstruction error, which corresponds to the mean squared error between the original matrix and the reconstructed one. During the unsupervised feature extraction process, the entire dataset (n = 100) was used regardless of the availability of neuropsychological scores.

Linear dimensionality reduction techniques, such as PCA and ICA, apply a linear transformation to the input data. That is, if the original data is in $\mathcal{R}^d$ and we want to embed it into $\mathcal{R}^n$ ($n < d$) then we would like to find a matrix $W \in \mathcal{R}^{n,d}$ that induces the mapping $x \to Wx$. A natural criterion for choosing $W$ is in a way that will enable a reasonable recovery of the original input $x$ [15]. Compared to deep autoencoders, the main drawback of PCA and ICA is that they cannot extract nonlinear structures modeled by higher than second-order statistics [16]. In the following, we will briefly review the main techniques used in the present study and their implementation.

**Principal Component Analysis.** Before performing PCA the data was standardized to obtain a distribution with zero mean and unit variance. This step was implemented using the predefined function **StandardScaler** from SKLEARN. PCA was then performed by using the function **PCA** from the same library, which performs linear dimensionality reduction using Singular Value Decomposition of the data to project it to a lower dimensional space.

**Independent Component Analysis.** ICA performs the decomposition step by imposing the constraint that the resulting components must be independent. In this work we used the **FastICA** algorithm from SKLEARN, which is a block fixed-point iteration algorithm based on negative entropy as a non-gaussianity measure, which converges faster than adaptive algorithms [9]. As in the case of PCA, data was first standardized.

**Autoencoders.** An autoencoder is an unsupervised neural-network based approach for learning latent representations of high-dimensional data that can be used to reconstruct the original input, while compressing it into a latent space that usually has much lower dimensionality [17]. Learning such "undercomplete" representations forces the autoencoder to capture the most salient features of the training data by discovering its latent factors of variation [18].

Let's consider a basic auto-encoder with a single hidden layer, $n$ neurons in the input/output layers and $m$ neurons in the hidden layer. The model takes an input $\mathbf{x} \in \mathcal{R}^n$ and first maps it into the latent representation $\mathbf{h} \in \mathcal{R}^m$ by using an encoding function $\mathbf{h} = g_\phi(\mathbf{x}) = \sigma(W\mathbf{x}+b)$ with parameters $\phi = \{W, b\}$, where $\sigma(\cdot)$ denotes the activation function of the neurons, $W$ denotes the connection weights and $b$ denotes the neurons' biases. Afterwards, a reconstruction of the input $\mathbf{x}'$ is obtained through the decoder function $\mathbf{x}' = f_\theta(\mathbf{h}) = \sigma(W'\mathbf{h} + b')$

with $\theta = \{W', b'\}$. The two parameter sets $(\theta, \phi)$ are usually constrained to be of the form $W \in \mathcal{R}^{n,m} = W'^T \in \mathcal{R}^{m,n}$, using the same weights for encoding the input and decoding the latent representation [19]. The parameters are learned by minimizing an appropriate cost function over the training set, which usually corresponds to the Mean Squared Error between the original input and the reconstructed output:

$$L_{\mathrm{AE}}(\theta, \phi) = \frac{1}{n} \sum_{i=1}^{n} (\mathbf{x}^{(i)} - f_\theta(g_\phi(\mathbf{x}^{(i)})))^2 \tag{1}$$

Fully connected AE do not have any spatial bias over the image structure. Convolutional autoencoders are an AE variant that exploits convolution filters to more efficiently capture local spatial structure. For a mono-channel input x the latent representation of the $k-th$ feature map is given by:

$$h^k = \sigma(x * W^k + b^k) \tag{2}$$

where the bias is broadcasted to the whole feature map, $\sigma$ is an activation function, and $*$ denotes a convolution. The reconstruction is obtained using:

$$y = \sigma(\sum_{k \in H} h^k * \hat{W}^k + c) \tag{3}$$

where $c$ represents the bias of the input channel, $H$ identifies the group of latent feature maps and $\hat{W}$ identifies the flip operation over both dimensions of the weights [19].

In this work we considered both fully-connected and Convolutional Autoencoder (CAE) architectures. As baselines, we implemented two simple, 1-layer AE with linear and non-linear activation functions. We then implemented a more sophisticated CAE architecture, as shown in Fig. 1. In the latter case, the encoder consisted of 3 convolutional layers followed by 2 fully connected layers, and the same structure was mirrored in the decoder. In order to overcome vanishing gradient the Leaky Rectified Linear activation function was used. Mean Square Error was used as loss function, which was minimized using the Adam optimizer with a learning rate of $1e-3$. Dropout was used as a further regularizer. Hyperparameters were automatically optimized using OPTUNA [20].

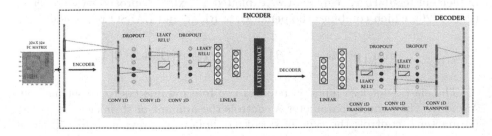

**Fig. 1.** Workflow and architecture of the deep convolutional autoencoder.

## 2.3   Data Augmentation and Transfer Learning

Deep networks perform remarkably well in many domains, but they are heavily reliant on big data to avoid overfitting. Given the limited size of our clinical dataset, we thus devised two approaches in order to promote a better generalization of the CAE during the feature extraction process.

The first method was based on *Data Augmentation*, which consists in combining and distorting each training sample in order to provide a more representative distribution as input to the autoencoder [21]. In particular, we designed a mix-up augmentation method that consists of a random convex combination of two input samples leading to a total of 7421 synthetic samples:

$$\hat{x} = \lambda x_i + (1 - \lambda) x_j$$

where $x_i$ and $x_j$ are raw input vectors and $\lambda$ are values sampled from the Beta distribution[1]. Following previous work [22], the choice of the parameters $\lambda \in [0, 1]$ was distributed accordingly to $\lambda \in Beta(\alpha, \alpha)$ for $\alpha \in (0, \inf)$. In the mix-up, the samples to be combined were chosen randomly from all available images. Isaksson et al. [23] tested the utility of the mix-up data augmentation technique for a medical image segmentation task using 100 MRI scans and observed an improvement when $\alpha = 0.5$. Although our dataset could be slightly different, we decided to use the same $\alpha$ value for consistency.

The second method was based on *Transfer Learning (TL)*, which consists in first training the autoencoder on a larger-scale dataset and subsequently tune it on the smaller dataset. In our case, we took advantage of the Human Connectome Project database for the pretraining phase. Afterwards, the model was fine-tuned using the stroke dataset freezing the weights of the convolutional layers.

## 2.4   Regularized Regression

The feature sets extracted by each method were used as regressors for the prediction of the neuropsychological scores.

Ridge regression [24] is a regularized regression method that controls the regression coefficients by adding the $L_2$ penalty term $\lambda \sum_{j=1}^{p} \beta_j^2$ to the objective function. The least absolute shrinkage and selection operator (LASSO) model [25] is an alternative method that adds the $L_1$ penalty term $\lambda \sum_{j=1}^{p} |\beta_j|$. To implement regularized regression we exploited a flexible approach based on elastic net [26], which combines the penalties of Ridge and LASSO regression:

$$\min_{(\beta_0, \beta)} \left( y - \beta_0 - X^T \beta \right)^2 + \lambda \left( \frac{1}{2} (1 - \alpha) \beta^2 + \alpha |\beta| \right), \tag{4}$$

The elastic-net loss function requires two free parameters to be set, namely $\lambda$ and $\alpha$. The penalty parameter $\lambda$ controls the amount of shrinkage, while the parameter $\alpha$ controls the type of shrinkage. Following previous work [5], these

---

[1] Note that although the extracted features were obtained using the synthetic data, the model performance was always measured on the final stroke dataset.

parameters were tuned using Leave-One-Out Cross validation (LOOCV). To evaluate the regression model we used R-squared ($R^2$), Mean Squared Error (MSE) and Bayesian information criterion (BIC).

# 3  Results

## 3.1  Dimensionality Reduction

Figure 2 shows the reconstruction error against the number of components/latent units for each method. The trend is similar across models: the larger the number of components, the better the reconstruction. The CAE trained directly on the stroke dataset obtained the worst reconstruction error, while the CAE trained on the augmented dataset achieved the best performance. This result highlights the importance of increasing the variability of the training distribution in order to improve the quality of the features extracted by complex convolutional architectures. The simple 1-layer AEs achieved an intermediate reconstruction error, comparable to those of PCA and ICA, which is no surprise given the intrinsic similarity between these techniques [27].

## 3.2  Regularized Regression

Table 1 presents the metrics obtained in the neuropsychological scores prediction task. As it can be observed, the $\lambda$ parameter is usually small. On the other hand, it can be seen that the $\alpha$ value mainly takes the two extremes: $\alpha \sim 1$, which corresponds to a ridge regression; and $\alpha \sim 0$, which corresponds to a LASSO penalization; an intermediate $\alpha \sim 0.75$ only happens in few cases. In order to have a better visualization, Fig. 3 presents the methods sorted by lowest $MSE$ error and highest $R^2$.

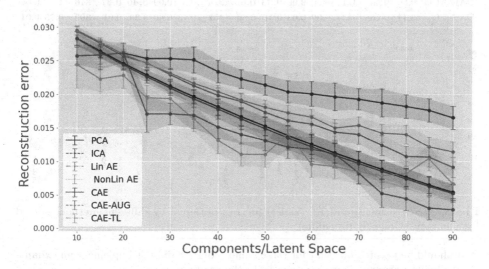

**Fig. 2.** Reconstruction error achieved by different feature extraction methods.

Concerning the metrics obtained for the language score, it can be observed that PCA slightly outperforms the other models in terms of $R^2$ and $MSE$, though the margin is fairly small. However, the CAE trained with Data Augmentation achieves the best performance in both spatial and memory scores, with a considerable margin over the other methods. Such remarkable performance is approached also by the CAE trained using Transfer Learning. Interestingly, the autoencoder with a single linear layer is often the one achieving the lowest BIC value, suggesting that such architecture is particularly useful to select a few representative components from the data distribution.

### 3.3 Getting Deeper on Augmentation and Transfer Techniques

Given the remarkable performance of the CAE trained using data augmentation and transfer learning, in a series of additional simulations we explored how the size of the augmented dataset could impact model performance, and whether a combination of data augmentation and transfer learning might further improve the predictive accuracy[2]. We thus designed four additional training regimens:

**Table 1.** Regression metrics and parameters obtained for the different feature extraction methods.

| | Language score (n = 94) | | | | | Spatial score (n = 77) | | | | | Memory score (n = 77) | | | | |
|---|---|---|---|---|---|---|---|---|---|---|---|---|---|---|---|
| | $R^2$ | $MSE$ | $BIC$ | $\alpha$ | $\lambda$ | $R^2$ | $MSE$ | $BIC$ | $\alpha$ | $\lambda$ | $R^2$ | $MSE$ | $BIC$ | $\alpha$ | $\lambda$ |
| PCA | **0.52** | **0.48** | 493 | 0.00 | 0.22 | 0.21 | 0.79 | **300** | 1 | 0.09 | 0.32 | 0.68 | 363 | 1 | 0.03 |
| ICA | 0.51 | 0.49 | 351 | 0.25 | 0.09 | 0.24 | 0.75 | 396 | 0.00 | 0.56 | 0.27 | 0.73 | 381 | 1 | 0.04 |
| Lin AE | 0.43 | 0.57 | **323** | 0.25 | 0.06 | 0.27 | 0.73 | 412 | 0.00 | 0.56 | 0.25 | 0.75 | **297** | 0.5 | 0.15 |
| NonLin AE | 0.50 | 0.50 | 357 | 0.75 | 0.00 | 0.26 | 0.74 | 456 | 0.00 | 0.22 | 0.26 | 0.74 | 369 | 0.75 | 0.01 |
| CAE | 0.42 | 0.57 | 624 | 0.25 | 0.01 | 0.27 | 0.73 | 390 | 0.5 | 0.01 | 0.27 | 0.73 | 759 | 0.00 | 0.7 |
| CAE-AUG | 0.50 | 0.50 | 421 | 0.50 | 0.06 | **0.33** | **0.65** | 315 | 0.5 | 0.09 | **0.40** | **0.61** | 316 | 1 | 0.04 |
| CAE-TL | 0.44 | 0.56 | 454 | 0.00 | 0.03 | 0.31 | 0.69 | 407 | 0.75 | 0.00 | 0.39 | 0.61 | 302 | 0.75 | 0.01 |

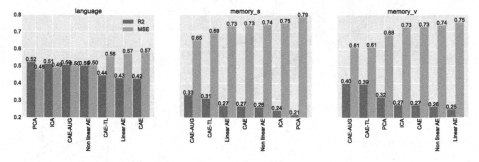

**Fig. 3.** $MSE$ (orange) and $R^2$ (violet) metrics obtained by different methods sorted by accuracy. (Color figure online)

---

[2] It should be pointed out that for these simulations we did not implement an exhaustive hyper-parameter optimization, as in the previous cases.

1. **Aug(15000):** Similarly as before, the CAE is trained with synthetic images obtained via the mix-up strategy; however this time the size of the augmented stroke dataset is increased to ∼15000 samples (i.e., twice the size used previously);
2. **TL-Aug:** The CAE is first trained over the HCP dataset, as done before for the Transfer Learning scenario. The model is then also trained on the initial augmented stroke dataset (∼7500 samples);
3. **AugTL-Aug:** The CAE is first trained over synthetic HCP data obtained by applying the same mix-up augmentation strategy (∼6000 samples). The model is then also trained on the initial augmented stroke data (∼7500 samples);
4. **AugTL-Stroke:** The CAE is first trained over synthetic HCP data obtained by applying the same mix-up augmentation strategy (∼6000 samples). The model is then also trained on the original stroke dataset.

Figure 4 shows the reconstruction error obtained by the four different regimens. The errors are comparable to that achieved previously by the simpler Data Augmentation technique, suggesting that also in these cases we achieve very good reconstructions.

At the same time, regression results reported in Table 2 and Fig. 5 clearly show that these improved data augmentation and transfer learning regimens further boosted the model's performance, both in terms of $R^2$ and MSE. All regimens generally enhance the CAE accuracy, however the most striking improvement is given by the TL-Aug regimen, which reaches significantly better performance compared to all methods previously investigated, establishing a new state-of-the-art for the stroke-prediction task. Interestingly, this improved model achieves such accurate predictions by relying, on average, on fewer components compared to other methods, which might be particularly relevant to improve interpretability of the resulting model.

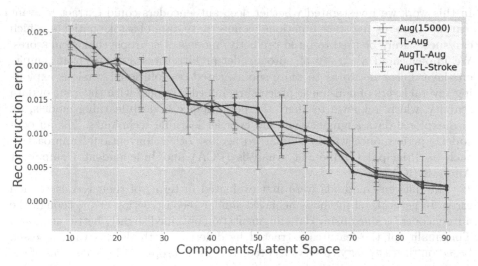

**Fig. 4.** Reconstruction error achieved by the four new augmentation/transfer regimens.

**Table 2.** Regression metrics and parameters obtained by the four augmentation/ transfer regimens.

| | Language score (n = 94) | | | | | Spatial score (n = 77) | | | | | Memory score (n = 77) | | | | |
|---|---|---|---|---|---|---|---|---|---|---|---|---|---|---|---|
| | $R^2$ | $MSE$ | $BIC$ | $\alpha$ | $\lambda$ | $R^2$ | $MSE$ | $BIC$ | $\alpha$ | $\lambda$ | $R^2$ | $MSE$ | $BIC$ | $\alpha$ | $\lambda$ |
| Aug (15000) | 0.51 | 0.49 | 421 | 0.5 | 0.06 | 0.36 | 0.58 | 570 | 0.00 | 0.05 | 0.41 | 0.59 | 570 | 0.00 | 0.05 |
| TL-Aug | **0.56** | **0.45** | 284 | 0.00 | 0.03 | **0.40** | **0.56** | 367 | 0.5 | 0.09 | **0.47** | **0.54** | 357 | 0.75 | 0.08 |
| AugTL-Aug | 0.53 | 0.46 | 421 | 0.5 | 0.06 | 0.23 | 0.77 | 247 | 1 | 0.16 | 0.43 | 0.57 | 239 | 1 | 0.08 |
| AugTL-Stroke | 0.47 | 0.53 | 433 | 1 | 0.02 | 0.28 | 0.72 | 380 | 0.00 | 0.81 | 0.42 | 0.58 | 242 | 1 | 0.16 |

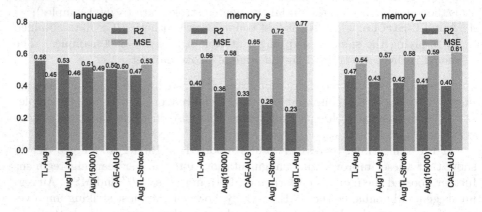

**Fig. 5.** $MSE$ and $R^2$ metrics obtained by augmentation/transfer regimens sorted by accuracy.

## 4   Conclusion

In this work we investigated whether deep autoencoders could extract relevant features from resting state functional connectivity data of stroke patients, which can successively be used to build predictive models of neuropsychological scores. We implemented a variety of autoencoder architectures, ranging from simple, one-layer linear networks to more sophisticated convolutional versions exploiting several layers of non-linear processing. In order to deal with the issue of data scarcity, which is known to affect the performance of deep learning models, we also explored data augmentation and transfer learning techniques. The autoencoder's performance was benchmarked against other conventional approaches, such as Principal Component Analysis (PCA) and Independent Component Analysis (ICA).

The different methods were first evaluated in terms of their reconstruction error. In general, all methods achieved similar reconstruction error, though the autoencoders trained using data augmentation obtained slightly better accuracy. The quality of the features extracted by different methods was then assessed based on their capacity to serve as predictors for neuropsychological scores of the patients in three cognitive domains (i.e., language, spatial memory, and verbal memory). To this aim, the extracted features were given as input to regularized regression models, and performance was evaluated in terms of coefficient of determination, mean squared error and Bayesian information criterion. Results showed that the performance of the basic autoencoders was overall comparable to that of traditional methods (ICA and PCA). However, more sophisticated convolutional architectures trained using data augmentation and transfer learning achieved a much higher performance, with considerable gains of 7% (language), 66% (spatial memory) and 47% (verbal memory) with respect to the previously reported state-of-the-art methods [5]. The larger accuracy gains for memory scores can be explained by the fact that prediction of language scores is likely close to ceiling. Memory has a more distributed neural basis and the prediction of deficits from structural lesions is relatively poor compared to other behavioral domains [4,6]. Therefore, predicting memory scores represents an important benchmark for RSFC-based machine learning methods.

In conclusion, our results demonstrate the great potential of deep learning models for the analysis of multi-dimensional neuroimaging data even in cases with limited data availability, which is often considered a critical limitation in clinical studies. Future work should aim at further consolidating our findings, for example by systematically evaluating the performance of deep learning models on the prediction of other neuropsychological and behavioral scores, or by increasing the sample size in order to allow testing model generalization on fully held-out data. The latter task calls for multi-centric, coordinated efforts for collection, harmonization and sharing of patients' functional imaging data. Moreover, a key research frontier would be to design and implement advanced techniques in order to interpret the features extracted by non-linear "black-box" models, such as deep networks. Although standard back-projection techniques [5] only work with linear dimensionality reduction, there is a growing interest in designing explainability techniques that can visualize the features that mostly influence the decision of deep networks (for a recent review, see [28]). Such techniques would be particularly relevant in the case of medical applications, since they could provide valuable insights to the clinicians for the design of more effective rehabilitation protocols.

**Acknowledgements.** This work was supported by grants from the Italian Ministry of Health (RF-2019-02359306 to MZ, Ricerca Corrente to IRCCS Ospedale San Camillo) and by MIUR (Dipartimenti di Eccellenza DM 11/05/2017 n. 262 to the Department of General Psychology). We are grateful to Prof. Maurizio Corbetta for providing the stroke dataset, which was collected in a study funded by grants R01 HD061117-05 and R01 NS095741. Healthy adults rs-fMRI data were provided by the Human Connectome Project, WU-Minn Consortium (Principal Investigators: David Van Essen and Kamil Ugurbil; 1U54MH091657) funded by the 16 NIH Institutes and Centers that support the NIH Blueprint for Neuroscience Research; and by the McDonnell Center for Systems Neuroscience at Washington University.

# References

1. Greicius, M., Supekar, K., Menon, V., Dougherty, R.: Resting-state functional connectivity reflects structural connectivity in the default mode network. Cereb. Cortex **19**, 72–8 (2008)
2. Meskaldji, D.E., et al.: Prediction of long-term memory scores in MCI based on resting-state FMRI. NeuroImage Clin. **12**, 785–795 (2016)
3. Siegel, J.S., et al.: Disruptions of network connectivity predict impairment in multiple behavioral domains after stroke. Proc. Natl. Acad. Sci. **113**(30), E4367–E4376 (2016)
4. Salvalaggio, A., De Filippo De Grazia, M., Zorzi, M., Thiebaut de Schotten, M., Corbetta, M.: Post-stroke deficit prediction from lesion and indirect structural and functional disconnection. Brain **143**(7), 2173–2188 (2020)
5. Calesella, F., Testolin, A., De Filippo De Grazia, M., Zorzi, M.: A comparison of feature extraction methods for prediction of neuropsychological scores from functional connectivity data of stroke patients. Brain Inform. **8**, 1–13 (2021)
6. Zorzi, M., De Filippo De Grazia, M., Blini, E., Testolin, A.: Assessment of machine learning pipelines for prediction of behavioral deficits from brain disconnectomes. In: Mahmud, M., Kaiser, M.S., Vassanelli, S., Dai, Q., Zhong, N. (eds.) BI 2021. LNCS (LNAI), vol. 12960, pp. 211–222. Springer, Cham (2021). https://doi.org/10.1007/978-3-030-86993-9_20
7. Jollans, L., et al.: Quantifying performance of machine learning methods for neuroimaging data. Neuroimage **199**, 351–365 (2019)
8. Bank, D., Koenigstein, N., Giryes, R.: Autoencoders. arXiv abs/2003.05991 (2020)
9. Kim, J.H., Zhang, Y., Han, K., Wen, Z., Choi, M., Liu, Z.: Representation learning of resting state fMRI with variational autoencoder. NeuroImage **241**, 118423 (2021)
10. Huang, H., et al.: Modeling task fMRI data via deep convolutional autoencoder. IEEE Trans. Med. Imaging **37**(7), 1551–1561 (2017)
11. Pinaya, W., Mechelli, A., Sato, J.: Using deep autoencoders to identify abnormal brain structural patterns in neuropsychiatric disorders: a large-scale multi-sample study. Hum. Brain Mapp. **40**, 944–954 (2018)
12. GENG, X.F., Xu, J.: Application of autoencoder in depression diagnosis. DEStech Trans. Comput. Sci. Eng. (2017)
13. Van Essen, D.C., et al.: The WU-Minn human connectome project: an overview. Neuroimage **80**, 62–79 (2013)
14. Cui, Z., Gong, G.: The effect of machine learning regression algorithms and sample size on individualized behavioral prediction with functional connectivity features. Neuroimage **178**, 622–637 (2018)
15. Shalev-Shwartz, S., Ben-David, S.: Understanding Machine Learning - From Theory to Algorithms. Cambridge University Press, Cambridge (2014)
16. Cai, B., et al.: Functional connectome fingerprinting: identifying individuals and predicting cognitive functions via autoencoder. Hum. Brain Mapp. **42**, 2691–2705 (2021)
17. Pedrycz, W., Chen, S.-M. (eds.): Deep Learning: Algorithms and Applications. SCI, vol. 865. Springer, Cham (2020). https://doi.org/10.1007/978-3-030-31760-7
18. Scholz, M., Vigário, R.: Nonlinear PCA: a new hierarchical approach. In: ESANN (2002)
19. Masci, J., Meier, U., Cireşan, D., Schmidhuber, J.: Stacked convolutional autoencoders for hierarchical feature extraction. In: Honkela, T., Duch, W., Girolami, M., Kaski, S. (eds.) ICANN 2011. LNCS, vol. 6791, pp. 52–59. Springer, Heidelberg (2011). https://doi.org/10.1007/978-3-642-21735-7_7

20. Akiba, T., Sano, S., Yanase, T., Ohta, T., Koyama, M.: Optuna: a next-generation hyperparameter optimization framework. In: Proceedings of the 25rd ACM SIGKDD International Conference on Knowledge Discovery and Data Mining (2019)
21. Shorten, C., Khoshgoftaar, T.: A survey on image data augmentation for deep learning. J. Big Data **6**, 1–48 (2019)
22. Zhang, H., Cissé, M., Dauphin, Y., Lopez-Paz, D.: Mixup: beyond empirical risk minimization. arXiv abs/1710.09412 (2018)
23. Isaksson, L., et al.: Mixup (sample pairing) can improve the performance of deep segmentation networks. J. Artif. Intell. Soft Comput. Res. **12**, 29–39 (2022)
24. Hoerl, A., Kennard, R.: Ridge regression: biased estimation for nonorthogonal problems. Technometrics **12**, 55–67 (2012)
25. Tibshirani, R.: Regression shrinkage selection via the lasso. J. Roy. Stat. Soc. Ser. B **73**, 273–282 (2011)
26. Zou, H., Hastie, T.: regularization and variable selection via the elastic net. J. Roy. Stat. Soc. B **67**(2), 301–320 (2005)
27. Baldi, P., Hornik, K.: Neural networks and principal component analysis: learning from examples without local minima. Neural Netw. **2**(1), 53–58 (1989)
28. Singh, A., Sengupta, S., Lakshminarayanan, V.: Explainable deep learning models in medical image analysis. J. Imaging **6**(6), 52 (2020)

# Classifying EEG Signals
# of Mind-Wandering Across Different
# Styles of Meditation

Shivam Chaudhary[1]([✉]), Pankaj Pandey[1], Krishna Prasad Miyapuram[1],
and Derek Lomas[2]

[1] Brain & Informatics Lab, Indian Institute of Technology Gandhinagar,
Gandhinagar, Gujarat, India
shivamchaudhary@iitgn.ac.in
[2] Vibe Research Lab, Delft University of Technology, Delft, Netherlands

**Abstract.** In the modern world, it is easy to get lost in thought, partly because of the vast knowledge available at our fingertips via smartphones that divide our cognitive resources and partly because of our intrinsic thoughts. In this work, we aim to find the differences in the neural signatures of mind-wandering and meditation that are common across different meditative styles. We use EEG recording done during meditation sessions by experts of different meditative styles, namely shamatha, zazen, dzogchen, and visualization. We evaluate the models using the leave-one-out validation technique to train on three meditative styles and test the fourth left-out style. With this method, we achieve an average classification accuracy of above 70%, suggesting that EEG signals of meditation techniques have a unique neural signature across meditative styles and can be differentiated from mind-wandering states. In addition, we generate lower-dimensional embeddings from higher-dimensional ones using t-SNE, PCA, and LLE algorithms and observe visual differences in embeddings between meditation and mind-wandering. We also discuss the general flow of the proposed design and contributions to the field of neuro-feedback-enabled mind-wandering detection and correction devices.

**Keywords:** Meditation · Mind-wandering · Classification · Machine learning · Deep learning · Cognition · Neuro-feedback · EEG

## 1 Introduction

Mind-wandering, also known as task-unrelated thought, daydreaming, fantasizing, zoning-out, unconscious thought, and undirected thought, is a common phenomenon, that most of us experience for approximately 50% of our daily waking time [11]. There are two types of mind-wandering, intentional or stimulus-independent or self-generated and unintentional or stimulus-driven [11]. Sometimes, these thoughts could be productive, i.e., used for *creative* thinking, *future planning*, and *problem-solving*, and sometimes could be detrimental to

© Springer Nature Switzerland AG 2022
M. Mahmud et al. (Eds.): BI 2022, LNAI 13406, pp. 152–163, 2022
https://doi.org/10.1007/978-3-031-15037-1_13

our mental health, leading to *depression* [2], *anxiety, schizophrenia* and *negative mood* [23].

In contemporary times, our mind wanders in anticipation of a text message, email, or social media notification, or thinking about how we can level up in the game in which we are stuck. Mind-wandering takes our attention away from the present, which we regret later, leading to an unending spiral of despair. However, all hope is not lost. Meditation is one of the many ways to control our thoughts. *Meditation* is a set of exercises that helps in the regulation of emotion, and attention [24]. It is also known as an exercise in which the person orients their attention to dwell upon a single sound, concept, or experience [22]. Meditation has positive effects on our mood and mental health by reducing unnecessary mind-wandering and enhancing our cognitive performance [15] (Fig. 1).

Although meditation has many benefits, it is hard to accomplish and sustain a state of mind where we must not get overwhelmed by our thoughts [8]. In some cases, meditators encountered troubling thoughts and, and in other cases, it aggravated mental health issues such as anxiety and depression [8].

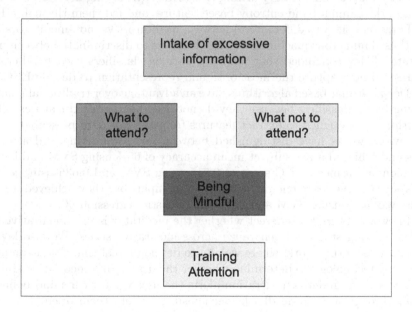

**Fig. 1.** Sustaining mind-full moments

The human brain generates movement by taking input from relevant sensory receptors, computing the desired inputs to stimulate motor neurons, which move the limbs. Brain-Computer Interface aims to capture the signals produced during these computations and process them to decode human intention to control external devices, say a joystick [4]. The decoding of human intentions is a difficult problem. The challenge here is to take a pattern of EEG signals and ascertain which brain regions contribute how much to the signal. In simpler terms, it is difficult to find out the representation of each brain region in the signal component, and an even more challenging task to model those contributions. Many recent papers aim to model this representation. In a recent paper, wavelet transformation-based feature extraction techniques were applied to capture the difference between expert and non-expert meditators. They used Bior3.5, Coif5 and db8 wavelets for this feature extraction [13]. Another approach to finding the representation of human intentions in EEG signals was to take topological maps generated from the EEG signals and feed them through a convolutional neural network [14]. Advancement in deep learning in the past two decades has ushered in an era of creating ever-larger networks to represent complex relationships. However, the problem arises when one questions on what basis the model is making these predictions. This is a problem highlighted by Riberio et al., wherein they discuss a model that performs well but has learned the wrong representation [17]. Recent work [12] uses the functional connectivity between brain regions as features to understand the significance and contribution of each region to the generated EEG signal. Previously, feature engineering-based methods were used to feed input to machine learning classifiers with varying degrees of success. [21] used the gamma-band entropy-based features and fed them through a Random Forest classifier to differentiate between meditators vs. non-meditators. [19] and [7] used numerous machine learning classifiers to discriminate between mental states. They concluded that machine learning classifiers used hand-crafted features did not capture the most optimum representation to decode EEG signals. Deep learning-based algorithms have an advantage over traditional machine learning-based classifiers because they do not need hand-crafted features. These algorithms are designed to extract features from the raw data presented.

Previous works have distinguished between mind-wandering and attentive states and achieved a per subject mean accuracy of 65% using SVM and logistic regression and a mean AUC score of 0.715 using SVM and 0.635 using logistic regression. On the leave-one-out participant comparison, they achieved a mean accuracy of 59% using SVM and 58% using logistic regression [3].

This work attempts to detect whether the meditator is in a meditative or a mind-wandering state and generalize across meditative styles. We also lay the foundation for future work, where we aim to develop a real-time brain-computer interfacing technology to determine whether the user is in a meditative state or not. The system under consideration alerts the user when their mind beings to wander through a neuro-feedback mechanism and help them orient back to a calm meditative state.

## 2    Motivation

### 2.1    Impact on Cognition

The rapid pace of software and hardware innovations [10] enables us to perform multiple tasks simultaneously. This ability granted to us by contemporary technological advancements has positive effects, such as communicating with distant people, getting news about what is going on halfway around the world, and much more. However, at the same time, it has detrimental effects, which include sensory overloading or simply taking in more information than we can process, leading to accidents due to the usage of mobile phones while walking and driving. Hence, we need to evolve with technology, the ability to focus our attention on the things that we can control and on the things that matter. Hence, we need to learn to focus our attention and not let our minds wander.

Mind-wandering, sometimes also referred to as daydreaming, fantasizing, zoning-out, unconscious thought, undirected thought, is defined as task-unrelated thought that occupies nearly 50% of our awake time daily. The benefits of focused attention or meditation has been highlighted by researchers throughout history [15]. Research on meditation has revealed that it is highly effective in regulating pain, insomnia, increasing calmness, bringing psychological balance, and improvement of general well-being and physical and mental health [1].

## 2.2 Technological Considerations

The work resulting from this paper can help create a device that helps the user improve their focused attention through a neuro-feedback mechanism. For a certain period, the user wears an EEG headband capable of producing high-quality data once a day. A mobile app reading and processing the data captured by the headband determines whether the user is in a meditative state or a mind-wandering state. While meditating, the user will get an audio-visual neuro-feedback from their mobile phone if their mind begins to wander (Fig. 2). Few neural markers for neuro-feedback have been discussed by Gupta et al. [16].

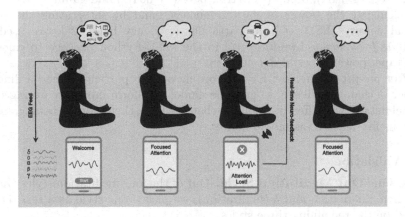

**Fig. 2.** A user is wearing a portable EEG headset while meditating. The real-time EEG signals are captured, processed, and meditative states sent to the user's mobile phone. When the user's mind begins to wander, an audio neuro-feedback is given to them, enabling them to reorient their focus away from task-irrelevant thoughts.

# 3   Dataset Description

We have used the publicly available EEG dataset [24]. Electroencephalographic (EEG) recordings were conducted on participants from meditative communities in India, Nepal, and the United States. Their respective instructors selected highly experienced and skilled meditators from each community. Each community provided space for recording the meditation sessions. Participants studied at least one of the different meditation practices - Zazen, Dzogchen, Shamatha, and Visualization. Some participants recorded sessions for a single meditative style and, in some cases, multiple meditative styles. EEG activity was recorded when the participants were sitting in their usual posture for meditation, and mind-wandering [24]. We used a pre-processed version of the dataset acquired from the author. The pre-processed data is sampled 128 Hz.

# 4   Methods

## 4.1   Feature Extraction

**Sliding Window.** We used the Yasa Sliding Window [20] library in python to create windows of 5 s for meditation recordings of 600 s each and a window of 5 s with a step size of 0.5 for the mind-wandering recordings of 60 s each. We obtained 1431 epochs of meditation and 1665 epochs of mind-wandering.

**Multitaper Bandpower.** The Multitaper method is an approach to determine the power of a signal at different frequencies [24]. We extracted the five frequency bands from each channel of the EEG signals, namely: delta (0.5–4 Hz), theta (4–7 Hz), alpha (8–13 Hz), beta (14–30 Hz) and gamma (31–50 Hz). We calculated the power of each frequency band by integrating the power spectral density (PSD) of that particular frequency band [25]. We used the *mne.time_frequency.psd_multitaper()* in the MNE-Python package to calculate multi taper power spectral density (PSD) [5].

After pre-processing, the EEG recording of each participant had a different number of channels. Hence, to give the model a uniform input, we averaged the channel data across different frequency bands (delta, theta, alpha, beta, gamma), giving us five features as model inputs.

## 4.2   Validation

**Leave One Out Meditation Style.** Out of the four meditation styles (Zazen, Dzogchen, Shamatha, and Visualization), we picked one style as a test set and trained on the remaining three styles.

## 4.3   Classifiers

**K Nearest Neighbors (KNN).** K nearest neighbors is a non-parametric classifier. They work by determining the K (specified by the user) number of training samples closest in the distance to the new point and predict the labels from these k training samples.

**Support Vector Machine (SVC):** A maximal margin classifier that attempts to maximize the distance between the closest training patterns known as support vectors. Maximal margin regularization parameter $C$, which denotes the trade-off between margin width and the number of misclassifications for linear SVM can be optimized from $[10^{-3}, 10^3]$ using grid search-based hyperparameter tuning on the validation set extracted from the training set.

**Decision Tree Classifier:** A Decision Tree Classifier is a predictive model used in statistics and machine learning. It creates a decision tree to iteratively go from the observations about an item to classify it into either of the given target labels.

**Random Forest Classifier:** It is an ensemble method that consists of a set of mutually independent and random trees. Each tree is populated using a random subset of features. Selection is based upon the majority voting over all the tree outputs.

**Multi Layered Perceptron (MLP):** The objective function (Cross-Entropy loss function) for this non-linear function approximator was optimized on our dataset, using first-order gradient-based optimization called Adam [6]. The binary prediction was performed using sigmoid as the output function.

**Ada Boost Classifier:** Ada Boost classifier is a meta estimator that initially fits a classifier to the dataset. In subsequent training, it makes copies of the model and puts more weight on instances that are hard to classify.

**Gaussian Naive Bayes:** It is a generative model that learns the actual data distribution by assuming that likelihood probabilities come from a multidimensional Gaussian distribution, and that all features are class-wise independent.

**Quadratic Discriminant Analysis (QDA):** QDA is a generative model, which assumes that each class follows a Gaussian distribution. These are used in cases where a non-linear decision boundary works best.

### 4.4   Visualization

**t-Distributed Stochastic Neighbor Embedding (t-SNE):** t-SNE is a statistical dimensionality reduction algorithm that reduces high dimensional data into dimensions, which aids in the visualization of the data [9]. We have employed the use of t-SNE to reduce five dimensional (five bands) data points into two-dimensional to visualize the difference between meditative and mind-wandering stages.

**Principal Components Analysis (PCA):** PCA is an unsupervised dimensionality-reduction machine learning algorithm. This algorithm generates new uncorrelated variables that successively maximize variance in the data. The algorithm helps reduce the dimensions of the data to visualize the data with the least information loss.

**Locally Linear Embedding (LLE):** LLE is an unsupervised method for dimensionality reduction. It does so by projecting the data to a lower dimension while preserving distance in the local neighborhoods [18].

## 5   Results

### 5.1   Classification Insights

We used the leave-one-out method to iteratively train on three meditative practices and test on the left-out practice. With this as our train and test sets, we applied various machine learning and neural network classifiers to separate meditation and mind-wandering states. The classification accuracies in Fig. 3 and Fig. 4 represent the testing accuracy on the left-out meditation style.

**Machine Learning Classifiers:** We achieved the best test accuracy on different machine learning models for meditation styles. For Shamatha meditation, we achieved the best accuracy of 77.7% using the K Nearest Neighbor classifier with k values as 2. For Visualization meditation, we achieved the best accuracy of 68.6% using the Random Forest classifier. For Zazen meditation, we achieved the best accuracy of 73.8% using the Quadratic Discriminant Analysis classifier. For Dzogchen meditation, we achieved the best accuracy of 74.7% using the K Nearest Neighbor classifier with k values as 2.

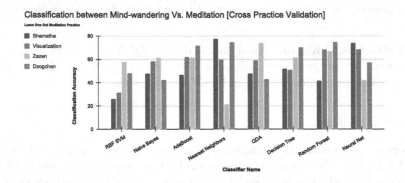

**Fig. 3.** Classification results for different machine learning classifiers.

**Neural Network Classifiers:** We achieved different classification accuracies for different network architecture sizes. We achieved the highest average classification accuracy using the network with the following configuration [80, 140, 100]. For Shamatha meditation, we achieved the best accuracy of 73.83% on most network architectures. For Visualization meditation, we achieved the best accuracy of 68.33% using the more extensive networks. For Zazen meditation, we achieved best the accuracy of 58.11% using the [40, 80, 60] architecture. For Dzogchen meditation, we achieved the best accuracy of 63.8% using the [40, 80, 60] architecture.

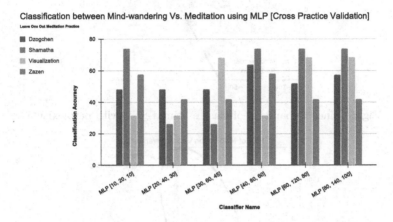

**Fig. 4.** Classification results for neural network classifiers with varying network architectures.

## 5.2  Lower Dimensional Visualization Insights

We used t-SNE, PCA, and LLE algorithms to reduce the dimensionality of our input feature space from five features to two features to plot them on a 2-D plane.

**t-Distributed Stochastic Neighbor Embedding (t-SNE):** As shown in the Fig. 5, we obtained a good separation of meditative and mind-wandering states using t-SNE, close to a linear separation. The perplexity measure for this reduction is 5.

**Principal Components Analysis (PCA):** Using the PCA algorithm, we were able to see a separation between the meditative vs. mind-wandering classes, as shown in Fig. 6. However, some portions of their representation were mixed and could not be easily separated. We were able to separate the 2-D representation using an ellipse manually.

**Locally Linear Embedding (LLE):** Using the LLE dimensionality reduction algorithm, we clustered the mind-wandering classes together. At the same time, the meditative state data points were spread out all over the 2-D plane, as shown in Fig. 7.

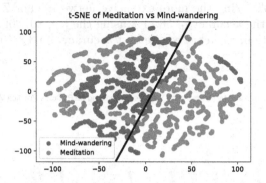

**Fig. 5.** Linear separation of classes using t-SNE with perplexity 5.

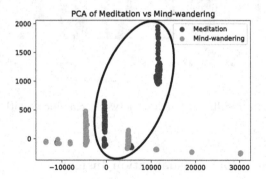

**Fig. 6.** Principal components analysis based dimensionality reduction.

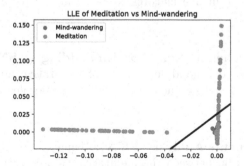

**Fig. 7.** Locally Linear Embedding based dimensionality reduction.

# 6  Discussion and Conclusion

Mind-wandering is often characterized as our attention being oriented away from the task at hand towards our internal, self-generated thoughts. This phenomenon is most often linked to a disruption in normal cognitive functions [3]. Too frequent mind-wandering can lead to depression, anxiety, insomnia, negative mood, and other detrimental effects. This study showed a difference in neural-signals between mind-wandering and meditation across meditation styles practices worldwide. We showed this difference by windowing the recordings and extracting the EEG signals' band-wise multi-taper power spectral density (PSD).

Using the machine learning models specified in Sect. 4.3, we got the highest classification accuracy using the KNN classifier for Shamatha and Dzogchen, QDA for Zazen, and Random Forest for Visualization styles when these were left-out as test sets. Using the Neural Network classifiers with architectures specified in Fig. 4, we achieved the highest average classification accuracy for all styles from the biggest network, i.e., [80, 140, 100]. We got good separation using t-SNE, PCA, and LLE with almost linear separation between mind-wandering and meditation sample points.

This research is essential since the computing power doubles every 18 months, and we have more and more devices with higher computational power. Each year, significant advancements are made towards technology, giving us everything at our fingertips. In these times, it is of utmost importance that we do not let our minds get lost in this sea of information, most of it not very important to us, leading to overuse and drain of sensory, perceptual, and cognitive resources. For this reason, practicing meditation may help us train our minds to gain control of our thoughts, focus our attention, and increase our metacognitive awareness and our propensity for compassion.

# 7  Limitation

This study is limited only to expert meditators and does not consider how the neural signatures differ between novice/non-meditators, which will be further investigated in future studies. We observed the classification outcome by varying only a few of the hyperparameters. Further experiments are needed to tune to the best hyperparameters. However, our results show a significant distinction between the two states, and future research can explore the involvement of region and frequency-specific discrimination.

**Acknowledgement.** We thank Science and Engineering Research Board (SERB), and PlayPower Labs for supporting the Prime Minister's Research Fellowship (PMRF) awarded to Pankaj Pandey. We thank the Federation of Indian Chambers of Commerce & Industry (FICCI) for facilitating this PMRF. We thank Jacob Young for providing the processed dataset.

# References

1. Meditation: In depth. https://www.nccih.nih.gov/health/meditation-in-depth
2. Deng, Y.Q., Li, S., Tang, Y.Y.: The relationship between wandering mind, depression and mindfulness. Mindfulness **5**(2), 124–128 (2014)
3. Dong, H.W., Mills, C., Knight, R.T., Kam, J.W.: Detection of mind wandering using EEG: within and across individuals. PLoS ONE **16**(5), e0251490 (2021)
4. Galway, L., Brennan, C., McCullagh, P., Lightbody, G.: BCI and eye gaze: collaboration at the interface. In: Schmorrow, D.D., Fidopiastis, C.M. (eds.) AC 2015. LNCS (LNAI), vol. 9183, pp. 199–210. Springer, Cham (2015). https://doi.org/10.1007/978-3-319-20816-9_20
5. Gramfort, A., et al.: MEG and EEG data analysis with MNE-Python. Front. Neurosci. **7**(267), 1–13 (2013). https://doi.org/10.3389/fnins.2013.00267
6. Kingma, D.P., Ba, J.: Adam: a method for stochastic optimization (2017)
7. Kora, P., Meenakshi, K., Swaraja, K., Rajani, A., Raju, M.S.: EEG based interpretation of human brain activity during yoga and meditation using machine learning: a systematic review. Complement. Ther. Clin. Pract. **43**, 101329 (2021)
8. Lomas, T., Cartwright, T., Edginton, T., Ridge, D.: A qualitative analysis of experiential challenges associated with meditation practice. Mindfulness **6**(4), 848–860 (2015)
9. Van der Maaten, L., Hinton, G.: Visualizing data using t-SNE. J. Mach. Learn. Res. **9**(11) (2008)
10. Mahmud, M., Kaiser, M.S., Hussain, A., Vassanelli, S.: Applications of deep learning and reinforcement learning to biological data. IEEE Trans. Neural Netw. Learn. Syst. **29**(6), 2063–2079 (2018). https://doi.org/10.1109/TNNLS.2018.2790388
11. Mooneyham, B.W., Schooler, J.W.: The costs and benefits of mind-wandering: a review. Can. J. Exp. Psychol./Revue canadienne de psychologie expérimentale **67**(1), 11 (2013)
12. Pandey, P., Gupta, P., Miyapuram, K.P.: Brain connectivity based classification of meditation expertise. In: Mahmud, M., Kaiser, M.S., Vassanelli, S., Dai, Q., Zhong, N. (eds.) BI 2021. LNCS (LNAI), vol. 12960, pp. 89–98. Springer, Cham (2021). https://doi.org/10.1007/978-3-030-86993-9_9
13. Pandey, P., Miyapuram, K.P.: Classifying oscillatory signatures of expert vs nonexpert meditators. In: 2020 International Joint Conference on Neural Networks (IJCNN), pp. 1–7. IEEE (2020)
14. Pandey, P., Miyapuram, K.P.: BRAIN2DEPTH: lightweight CNN model for classification of cognitive states from EEG recordings. In: Papież, B.W., Yaqub, M., Jiao, J., Namburete, A.I.L., Noble, J.A. (eds.) MIUA 2021. LNCS, vol. 12722, pp. 394–407. Springer, Cham (2021). https://doi.org/10.1007/978-3-030-80432-9_30
15. Pandey, P., Miyapuram, K.P.: Nonlinear EEG analysis of mindfulness training using interpretable machine learning. In: 2021 IEEE International Conference on Bioinformatics and Biomedicine (BIBM), pp. 3051–3057 (2021). https://doi.org/10.1109/BIBM52615.2021.9669457
16. Gupta, P., Pandey, P., Miyapuram, K.P.: Reliable EEG neuromarker to discriminate meditative states across practitioners (2022). https://doi.org/10.13140/RG.2.2.23937.94568
17. Ribeiro, M.T., Singh, S., Guestrin, C.: "Why should i trust you?" Explaining the predictions of any classifier. In: Proceedings of the 22nd ACM SIGKDD International Conference on Knowledge Discovery and Data Mining, pp. 1135–1144 (2016)

18. Roweis, S.T., Saul, L.K.: Nonlinear dimensionality reduction by locally linear embedding. Science **290**(5500), 2323–2326 (2000)
19. Sharma, H., Raj, R., Juneja, M.: An empirical comparison of machine learning algorithms for the classification of brain signals to assess the impact of combined yoga and sudarshan kriya. Comput. Methods Biomech. Biomed. Eng. **25**, 1–8 (2021)
20. Vallat, R., Walker, M.P.: An open-source, high-performance tool for automated sleep staging. eLife **10**, e70092 (2021). https://doi.org/10.7554/elife.70092
21. Vivot, R.M., Pallavicini, C., Zamberlan, F., Vigo, D., Tagliazucchi, E.: Meditation increases the entropy of brain oscillatory activity. Neuroscience **431**, 40–51 (2020)
22. West, M.: Meditation. Br. J. Psychiatry **135**(5), 457–467 (1979). https://doi.org/10.1192/bjp.135.5.457
23. Yamaoka, A., Yukawa, S.: Mind wandering in creative problem-solving: relationships with divergent thinking and mental health. PLoS ONE **15**(4), e0231946 (2020)
24. Young, J.H., Arterberry, M.E., Martin, J.P.: Contrasting electroencephalography-derived entropy and neural oscillations with highly skilled meditators. Front. Hum. Neurosci. **15**, 628417 (2021). https://doi.org/10.3389/fnhum.2021.628417. https://www.frontiersin.org/article/10.3389/fnhum.2021.628417
25. Zhang, Y., Zhang, Z., Luo, L., Tong, H., Chen, F., Hou, S.T.: 40 HZ light flicker alters human brain electroencephalography microstates and complexity implicated in brain diseases. Front. Neurosci. **15** (2021). https://doi.org/10.3389/fnins.2021.777183. https://www.frontiersin.org/article/10.3389/fnins.2021.777183

# Feature Fusion-Based Capsule Network for Cross-Subject Mental Workload Classification

Yinhu Yu[1] and Junhua Li[1,2(✉)]

[1] Wuyi University, Jiangmen 529020, China
[2] University of Essex, Colchester CO4 3SQ, UK
juhalee.bcmi@gmail.com, junhua.li@essex.ac.uk

**Abstract.** In a complex human-computer interaction system, estimating mental workload based on electroencephalogram (EEG) plays a vital role in the system adaption in accordance with users' mental state. Compared to within-subject classification, cross-subject classification is more challenging due to larger variation across subjects. In this paper, we targeted the cross-subject mental workload classification and attempted to improve the performance. A capsule network capturing structural relationships between features of power spectral density and brain connectivity was proposed. The comparison results showed that it achieved a cross-subject classification accuracy of 45.11%, which was superior to the compared methods (e.g., convolutional neural network and support vector machine). The results also demonstrated feature fusion positively contributed to the cross-subject workload classification. Our study could benefit the future development of a real-time workload detection system unspecific to subjects.

**Keywords:** Mental workload classification · Capsule network · Feature fusion · Cross-subject · EEG · Brain connectivity · Power spectral density

## 1 Introduction

With the prevalence of human-machine interactive systems, mental demand is dramatically increased to result in high mental workload. Excessive mental workload would quickly cause fatigue so that performance and accuracy are declined. In contrast, an extremely low mental workload would lead to inefficiency. Therefore, an appropriate level of mental workload should be maintained. In order to maintain the appropriate level of workload, we have to evaluate mental workload.

Traditional methods for evaluating mental workload include National Aeronautics and Space Administration-Task Load Index (NASA-TLX), subjective scale method, primary task performance method, and auxiliary task performance method. These methods rely on humans' self-feeling and the evaluation might be influenced by a few factors such as humans' emotions. Alternative ways based on physiological information have gradually become popular as they are objective for workload evaluation [1]. To date, electroencephalogram (EEG) [2], electrocardiogram (ECG) [3], eye movement [4], and

© Springer Nature Switzerland AG 2022
M. Mahmud et al. (Eds.): BI 2022, LNAI 13406, pp. 164–174, 2022
https://doi.org/10.1007/978-3-031-15037-1_14

functional near-infrared spectroscopy (fNIRS) [5] have been used for mental workload evaluation. Among them, EEG is a good choice because of its low cost, high temporal resolution, and portability.

Machine learning methods such as k-Nearest Neighbors (k-NN) [6], Random Forest (RF) [7], and Support Vector Machines (SVM) [8] were utilised to classify mental workload levels based on EEG. More recently, deep learning has shown advantages in the classification of mental workload. Convolutional neural network (CNN) is one of the deep learning models, which has been widely utilised for diverse applications, including P300 feature detection [9], seizure detection [10], and mental workload classification [11]. CNN exhibits advantages compared to the traditional machine learning methods. For example, Asgher et al. used CNN to analyse and classify mental workload levels in the n-back tasks, which outperformed SVM [12]. Although CNN has been applied to diverse applications successfully, it is not good at capturing spatial relationships between features. A new model called capsule network was proposed to overcome this drawback and is able to capture spatial relationships [13]. In addition, it is worth noting that the majority of studies performed within-subject classification for the mental workload, leaving less studies for cross-subject classification. The cross-subject classification is more difficult because there is a larger variation across subjects.

Features extracted from the time domain, spectral domain, and spatial domain can be used to classify mental workload. In the time domain, the decrease of event-related potential P300 in amplitude has been discovered to be associated with the increase of mental workload [14, 15]. In frequency domain, several studies have illustrated the associations between EEG signal frequencies and mental workload [16–22]. Band powers (including delta, theta, alpha, beta, and gamma bands) or their ratios have been used to evaluate the levels of mental workload. For instance, Ryu et al. found that the power in the alpha band was suppressed under the high mental workload conditions [18]. Moreover, the percentage of theta power at some brain regions was significantly increased with the increase of difficulty in the simulated air traffic control (ATC) task [19]. Besides, delta, beta, and gamma bands have also been reported to be related to mental workload [20–22]. In spatial domain, since the human brain has been considered to be a large-scale network composed of various brain regions [23], brain connectivity analysis may reveal the interactions between brain regions. For instance, brain connectivity has been found to be relevant to schizophrenia [24], attention-deficit/hyperactivity disorder (ADHD) [25], autism [26] and motor imagery (MI) [27]. For the mental workload studies, it has also been adopted [7, 28]. As shown in the assessment of driving drowsiness [29], functional connectivity can provide complementary information. It implies that the combination of features from different domains may benefit the classification.

In this study, we attempted to develop a feature fusion-based capsule network to capture structural relationships between features derived from the spectral domain and spatial domain for the cross-subject classification of mental workload. We compared it to other methods (i.e., k-NN; RF; SVM; and CNN) in terms of classification accuracy and showed the detailed results in this paper. Our study addresses the shortcomings mentioned above and provides a potential solution.

## 2  Methods

### 2.1  Experiment and Dataset

A total of seven subjects were recruited for the experiment. The subjects had not attended any EEG-related experiments or flight simulation experiments previously. The institutional ethics review committee of the National University of Singapore approved the experimental protocol. All subjects signed a consent form before the start of the experiment.

In the experiment, subjects experienced different levels of manipulation difficulty in controlling an aircraft by a joystick. Oculus Rift virtual reality headset was used to display virtual 3D aircraft. The subjects started with a low difficulty task and then performed the medium and high difficulty tasks, which corresponded to low, medium, and high levels of mental workload, respectively. Each task lasted 2 min, resulting in a total of 6 min for three tasks. And each subject repeated the tasks three times. Besides, 62 EEG channels were used to record EEG data at a sampling rate of 256 Hz.

### 2.2  Feature Extraction and Fusion

The recorded data were preprocessed to mitigate artifacts and then divided into segments with a length of two-second. This resulted in 540 segments for each subject. Each segment ($62 \times 512$) is a sample in the following classification evaluation. Short-time Fourier transform (STFT) with a one-second sliding time window and no overlapping was used to extract power features in five bands: delta (1–4 Hz), theta (4–8 Hz), alpha (8–12 Hz), beta (12–30 Hz), and gamma (30–45 Hz). This resulted in 2 features for each frequency band and each EEG channel. We collected all features to form a matrix of $62 \times 10$ (62 channels $\times$ 5 bands * 2).

Besides, we used phase locking value (PLV) to estimate phase synchronization between EEG channels. According to our previous study [7], the dominant frequency band for PLV is the gamma band. We, therefore, extracted PLV features from this band. PLV value ranges from 0 (reflecting no phase synchronization) to 1 (reflecting perfect phase synchronization) [30–32]. PLV value between channel $k$ and channel $l$ in the time span $t = \{t_1, t_2, ..., t_n\}$ can be calculated by

$$\text{PLV}_{k,l} = \left\langle e^{j(\varphi_k(t) - \varphi_l(t))} \right\rangle \tag{1}$$

where $\langle \cdot \rangle$ represents the arithmetic mean over the time span, $\varphi_k$ and $\varphi_l$ are the signal phases in channels $k$ and $l$. After estimating each pair of channels, we obtained a connectivity matrix of $62 \times 62$. Subsequently, we merged the band power matrix and connectivity matrix to form a larger feature matrix of $62 \times 72$. After that, the features were normalized to the range [0, 1] along with the channel dimension. For PLV features, elements on the diagonal were not included for the normalization because these elements represented self-connections.

### 2.3 Model Architecture

The model architecture is illustrated in Fig. 1. The proposed model consists of two convolutional layers, one primarycaps layer, and one digitcaps layer. The first convolutional layer has 8 convolution filters with the kernel size of 5 × 5 and the stride of 1. Rectified linear unit (ReLU) was used as an activation function. The settings of the second convolution layer were the same as the settings of the first layer except for the number of filters (16 for the second layer). The output size of the second layer was 16 × 54 × 64. This was followed by a primarycaps layer, where the number of filters was 32, the stride was 2, and the kernel size was 5 × 5. Each primary capsule was a vector with a depth of 4, of which the length and direction represent occurrence probability and associations to each workload level.

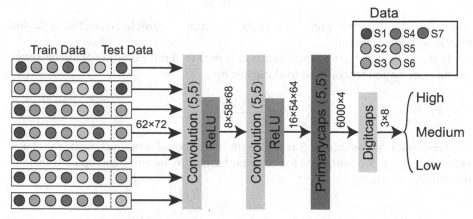

**Fig. 1.** The proposed model architecture. Colorful dots stand for subjects. The leave-one-subject-out was used to evaluate the model performance. The sizes of the outputs of each layer are shown in the figure.

The detailed operation process of the primarycaps layer is as follows. First, the layer used 32 filters to extract deeper features from the output of the upper layer. The features matrixes of 25 × 30 were achieved by 32 filters. Subsequently, we grouped the features with 4 as a unit to (32/4) * 25 * 30 primary capsules to encode the probability and low-level features related to mental workload level. We set three capsules with depth 8 in the digitcaps layer because there are three classes in our study. Capsules' length represents the probability of each mental workload level. Dynamic routing was used to train capsule layers.

### 2.4 Dynamic Routing

The dynamic routing mechanism [13, 33] is as follows. In the first step, the $i$-th primary capsule $u_i$ is transformed into a high-level mental workload "predicted vector" $\hat{u}_{j|i}$ through the weight matrix $W_{ij} (j = 1, 2, 3)$ by

$$\hat{u}_{j|i} = W_{ij} u_i \tag{2}$$

It represents the relative relationship between low-level mental workload features and high-level mental workload features.

In the second step, the "predicted vector" $\hat{u}_{j|i}$ is weighted and summed to obtain $s_j$ as follows

$$s_j = \Sigma_i c_{ij} \hat{u}_{j|i} \tag{3}$$

where $c_{ij}$ is the coupling coefficient between the $i$-th primary capsule and the $j$-th mental workload capsule, representing the probability that the $i$-th low-level primary capsule is connected to the $j$-th high-level mental workload capsule. The sum of all coupling coefficients is 1. The coupling coefficient $c_{ij}$ is calculated by

$$c_{ij} = \frac{\exp(b_{ij})}{\Sigma_k \exp(b_{ik})} \tag{4}$$

where $b_{ij}$ is the log prior probability of the $i$-th primary capsule connected to the $j$-th mental workload capsule.

In the third step, the nonlinear function is used to compress $s_j$ to obtain the vector output $v_j$ of the $j$-th mental workload capsule by

$$v_j = \frac{||s_j||^2}{1 + ||s_j||^2} \frac{s_j}{||s_j||} \tag{5}$$

This operation can ensure that the length of the mental workload capsule vector is between 0 and 1. We initialized log prior probability $b_{ij}$ by zeros and updated them in the routing process by

$$b_{ij} \leftarrow b_{ij} + \hat{u}_{j|i} \cdot v_j \tag{6}$$

where $\cdot$ stands for the scalar product. Iteration is stopped until the predefined maximum number of the iteration is reached. This iteration process can increase weights for the features closely associated with one mental workload level while decreasing the weights for the other features.

## 2.5 Loss Function

The margin loss and the reconstruction loss were used as the optimization objective of the model. The margin loss is calculated by

$$L_k = T_k \max\left(0, m^+ - ||v_k||\right)^2 + \lambda(1 - T_k) \max(0, ||v_k|| - m^-)^2 \tag{7}$$

where $T_k$ is an indicator of the class. When the mental workload of class $k$ is present, $T_k$ is equal to 1 (otherwise $T_k = 0$). $m^+$ and $m^-$ are set as 0.9 and 0.1, respectively. $\lambda$ is a coefficient for adjusting the proportion of the loss for absent mental workload classes and is set as 0.5 in our case.

A reconstruction loss was used additionally to encourage the mental workload capsules to encode the instantiation parameters of the input mental workload. The reconstruction loss is calculated by mean square error (MSE). We scaled down the reconstruction loss by 0.00001 so that it did not dominate the margin loss during training. In the end, the total loss was the sum of the margin losses of all mental workload capsules and the reconstruction losses.

Model training was terminated when the maximum number of iterations (i.e., 200) was reached or the average loss was less than $10^{-5}$. Moreover, we adopted a decaying learning rate. In other words, the learning rate was gradually reduced along with the iterations. This could help reduce the frequency of the fluctuation during the training, especially for the time around the minimum loss. The learning rate was changed after each iteration and was calculated by

$$lr = lr \times a^{epoch} \tag{8}$$

where $lr$ represents the learning rate, $a$ represents the base of the decaying learning rate, and $epoch$ represents the number of iterations until the current epoch.

## 3    Result

### 3.1    Methods Comparison

We performed a leave-one-subject-out scheme to evaluate the performance of the methods. Specifically, all data of a subject were used for testing while the data of the remaining subjects were used for training. This was repeated until every subject was in the testing set once. The final accuracies averaging across all subjects were reported in the format of mean $\pm$ standard deviation in this paper.

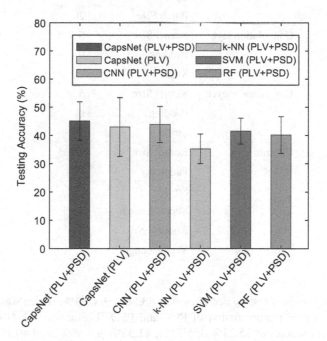

**Fig. 2.** Method comparisons in terms of testing accuracy

In this study, we not only compared different input features in the capsule network but also compared the capsule network with other mental workload classification methods (i.e., k-NN, SVM, RF, and CNN). CNN consists of convolutional layers, max-pooling layer, fully connected layer, and softmax. The input data were kept the same for all methods and the models were tuned to be as good as they can.

As shown in Fig. 2, the capsule network with the feature fusion of PLV and PSD achieved an average testing accuracy of 45.11% ± 6.82%, which was the best performance in the method comparison. The parameter settings of the model can be found in Table 1.

**Table 1.** Parameters of the capsule network model

| | | Name of the parameter | Value |
|---|---|---|---|
| Training settings | | Initial Learning Rate | 0.001 |
| | | Base of Decaying Learning Rate | 0.9 |
| | | Weight of Reconstruction Loss | 0.00001 |
| | | Maximum No. of Epochs | 200 |
| | | Batch Size | 20 |
| Convolution layer | | Kernel Size | $5 \times 5$ |
| | | Padding | 0 |
| | | Stride | 1 |
| Convolution layer | | Kernel Size | $5 \times 5$ |
| | | Padding | 0 |
| | | Stride | 1 |
| Capsule layers | 1 | Kernel Size | $5 \times 5$ |
| | | Padding | 0 |
| | | Stride | 2 |
| | | Vector Length | 4 |
| | 2 | Routing No | 3 |
| | | Vector Length | 8 |

The second-highest testing accuracy was 43.86% ± 6.41%, which was achieved by CNN in the case of feature fusion of PLV and PSD. The methods k-NN, SVM, and RF achieved accuracies of 35.21% ± 5.25%, 41.53% ± 4.59%, and 40.16% ± 6.50%, respectively (see Fig. 2). The detail of testing accuracies for each subject can be found in Table 2. The results showed that deep learning models outperformed the traditional methods. It implies that deep learning models have a high capacity to learn essential information from EEG data.

**Table 2.** Comparison of testing accuracies under different methods

| Methods (%) | S1 | S2 | S3 | S4 | S5 | S6 | S7 | Mean ± Standard deviation |
|---|---|---|---|---|---|---|---|---|
| CapsNet (PLV+PSD) | 57.04 | 43.15 | 41.11 | 47.78 | 34.81 | 47.04 | 44.81 | 45.11 ± 6.82 |
| CapsNet (PLV) | 64.07 | 41.30 | 38.33 | 44.44 | 36.11 | 31.48 | 45.37 | 43.01 ± 10.46 |
| CNN (PLV+PSD) | 50.00 | 43.89 | 33.15 | 44.81 | 38.33 | 45.19 | 51.67 | 43.86 ± 6.41 |
| k-NN (PLV+PSD) | 27.78 | 40.74 | 32.96 | 42.78 | 33.70 | 31.67 | 36.85 | 35.21 ± 5.25 |
| SVM (PLV+PSD) | 39.07 | 47.96 | 40.37 | 36.85 | 36.67 | 47.04 | 42.78 | 41.53 ± 4.59 |
| RF (PLV+PSD) | 51.48 | 38.15 | 35.37 | 38.70 | 33.33 | 37.41 | 46.67 | 40.16 ± 6.50 |

Better performance in the capsule network compared to CNN might be due to the capability of capturing structural relationships between features in the capsule network. We noticed that the standard deviation was smaller and the mean was higher in the case of feature fusion compared to the single feature category of PLV. This might be because the different kinds of features complement each other to improve the robustness so that there is a relatively robust performance across subjects.

In terms of the average training accuracy, the capsule network achieved the training accuracy of $98.72\% \pm 0.42\%$, while k-NN, SVM, RF, and CNN performed accuracies of $88.81\% \pm 0.63\%$, $100\%$, $100\%$, and $96.91\% \pm 0.79\%$ (see Fig. 3). The respective training accuracies for each subject are listed in Table 3. It was worth noting that SVM and RF had the highest training accuracy but the lower testing accuracy. It reflected that the overfitting was obvious in these two methods for the cross-subject mental workload classification. In the case of the same input features, in addition to SVM and RF, the training accuracy of the capsule network was also relatively high (see Fig. 3). However, the capsule network achieved a better testing accuracy. Taken together, the capsule network less suffers from overfitting. In this study, we observed that feature fusion of PLV and PSD was better than single category of features in both training accuracy and testing accuracy, showing the spectral features and connectivity features are complementary.

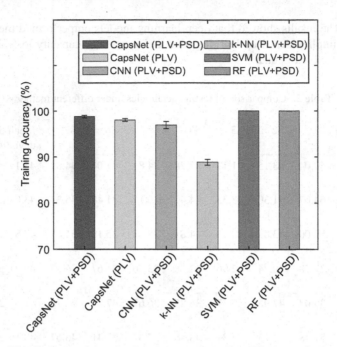

**Fig. 3.** Comparison of training accuracies under different methods

**Table 3.** Comparison of training accuracies under different methods

| Methods (%) | S1 | S2 | S3 | S4 | S5 | S6 | S7 | Mean ± Standard deviation |
|---|---|---|---|---|---|---|---|---|
| CapsNet (PLV + PSD) | 98.95 | 98.61 | 97.96 | 98.46 | 99.04 | 98.80 | 99.20 | 98.72 ± 0.42 |
| CapsNet (PLV) | 97.84 | 97.35 | 96.08 | 97.01 | 97.01 | 97.53 | 97.50 | 97.19 ± 0.57 |
| CNN (PLV + PSD) | 96.39 | 96.42 | 96.42 | 96.24 | 97.93 | 98.15 | 96.85 | 96.91 ± 0.79 |
| k-NN (PLV + PSD) | 88.30 | 89.32 | 87.62 | 88.95 | 89.38 | 89.01 | 89.04 | 88.81 ± 0.63 |
| SVM (PLV + PSD) | 100.00 | 100.00 | 100.00 | 100.00 | 100.00 | 100.00 | 100.00 | 100.00 ± 0.00 |
| RF (PLV + PSD) | 100.00 | 100.00 | 100.00 | 100.00 | 100.00 | 100.00 | 100.00 | 100.00 ± 0.00 |

## 4 Conclusion

In this study, we targeted the difficulty of the cross-subject mental workload classification. A feature fusion-based capsule network was proposed, which captured structural relationships between features of power spectral density and brain connectivity. We demonstrated that the feature fusion-based capsule network achieved the best performance in the cross-subject mental workload classification in terms of testing accuracy.

This study suggests that the feature fusion-based capsule network is relatively robust to the large variation across subjects and could be a good candidate way for the classification with large variations.

Although the feature fusion-based capsule network achieved the best performance in the cross-subject mental workload classification, the accuracy is not very adequate to make practical usage efficient. In the future, the accuracy should be further enhanced. We also noticed the training accuracies were much higher than the testing accuracies, implying the issue of model overfitting. A further study is required to mitigate this issue. Finally, it would be better to have a larger sample size for validating the performance of models.

# References

1. Radüntz, T.: Dual frequency head maps: a new method for indexing mental workload continuously during execution of cognitive tasks. Front. Physiol. **8**, 1019 (2017)
2. Bernhardt, K.A., Poltavski, D., Petros, T., et al.: The effects of dynamic workload and experience on commercially available EEG cognitive state metrics in a high-fidelity air traffic control environment. Appl. Ergon. **77**, 83–91 (2019)
3. Qu, H., Gao, X., Pang, L.: Classification of mental workload based on multiple features of ECG signals. Inform. Med. Unlocked **24**(8), 100575 (2021)
4. Yang, Y., Chen, Y., Wu, C., et al.: Effect of highway directional signs on driver mental workload and behavior using eye movement and brain wave. Accid. Anal. Prev. **146**, 105705 (2020)
5. Shimizu, T., Hirose, S., Obara, H., et al.: Measurement of frontal cortex brain activity attributable to the driving workload and increased attention. SAE Int. J. Passeng. Cars-Mech. Syst. **2**(1), 736–744 (2009)
6. Ko, L.W., Chikara, R.K., Lee, Y.C., Lin, W.C.: Exploration of user's mental state changes during performing brain-computer interface. Sensors **20**(11), 3169 (2020)
7. Pei, Z., Wang, H., Bezerianos, A., Li, J.: EEG-based multi-class workload identification using feature fusion and selection. IEEE Trans. Instrum. Meas. **99**, 1 (2020)
8. Lim, W.L., Sourina, O., Liu, Y., Wang, L.: EEG-based mental workload recognition related to multitasking. In: 2015 10th International Conference on Information, Communications and Signal Processing (ICICS), pp. 1–4. IEEE, Singapore (2015)
9. Cecotti, H., Gräser, A.: Convolutional neural networks for P300 detection with application to brain-computer Interfaces. IEEE Trans. Pattern Anal. Mach. Intell. **33**(3), 433–445 (2011)
10. Page A., Shea C., Mohsenin T.: Wearable seizure detection using convolutional neural networks with transfer learning. In: 2016 IEEE International Symposium on Circuits and Systems (ISCAS), pp. 1086–1089. IEEE, Montreal (2016)
11. Zhang, J., Li, S., Wang, R.: Pattern recognition of momentary mental workload based on multi-channel electrophysiological data and ensemble convolutional neural networks. Front. Neurosci. **11**, 310 (2017)
12. Asgher, U., Khalil, K., Ayaz, Y., Ahmad, R., Khan, M.J.: Classification of Mental Workload (MWL) using Support Vector Machines (SVM) and Convolutional Neural Networks (CNN). In: 2020 3rd International Conference on Computing Mathematics and Engineering Technologies, pp. 1–6. IEEE, Sukkur, Pakistan (2020)
13. Sabour, S., Frosst, N., Hinton, G.E.: Dynamic routing between capsules. In: Proceedings of 31st International Conference on Neural Information Processing Systems, pp. 3859–3869. Long Beach (2017)

14. Käthner, I., Wriessnegger, S.C., Müller-Putz, G.R., et al.: Effects of mental workload and fatigue on the P300, alpha and theta band power during operation of an ERP (P300) brain-computer interface. Biol. Psychol. **102**, 118–129 (2014)
15. Pergher, V., Wittevrongel, B., Tournoy, J., et al.: Mental workload of young and older adults gauged with ERPs and spectral power during N-Back task performance. Biol. Psychol. **146**, 107726 (2019)
16. Mühl, C., Jeunet, C., Lotte, F.: Eeg-based workload estimation across affective contexts. Front. Neurosci. **8**(8), 114 (2014)
17. Ke, Y., Qi, H., Zhang, L., et al.: Towards an effective cross-task mental workload recognition model using electroencephalography based on feature selection and support vector machine regression. Int. J. Psychophysiol. **98**(2), 157–166 (2015)
18. Ryu, K., Myung, R.: Evaluation of mental workload with a combined measure based on physiological indices during a dual task of tracking and mental arithmetic. Int. J. Ind. Ergon. **35**(11), 991–1009 (2005)
19. Brookings, J.B., Wilson, G.F., Swain, C.R.: Psychophysiological responses to changes in workload during simulated air traffic control. Biol. Psychol. **42**(3), 361–377 (1996)
20. Christensen, J.C., Estepp, J.R., Wilson, G.F., Russell, C.A.: The effects of day-to-day variability of physiological data on operator functional state classification. Neuroimage **59**(1), 57–63 (2012)
21. Pesonen, M., Hämäläinen, H., Krause, C.M.: Brain oscillatory 4–30 Hz responses during a visual n-back memory task with varying memory load. Brain Res. **1138**, 171–177 (2007)
22. Laine, T.I., Bauer, K.W., Lanning, J.W., et al.: Selection of input features across subjects for classifying crewmember workload using artificial neural networks. IEEE Trans. Syst. Man Cybern. Part A Syst. Hum. **32**(6), 691–704 (2002)
23. Bassett, D.S., Sporns, O.: Network neuroscience. Nat. Neurosci. **20**(3), 353–364 (2017)
24. Anticevic, A., Repovs, G., Krystal, J.H., et al.: A broken filter: prefrontal functional connectivity abnormalities in schizophrenia during working memory interference. Schizophr. Res. **141**(1), 8–14 (2012)
25. Mazaheri, A., Coffeycorina, S., Mangun, G.R., et al.: Functional disconnection of frontal cortex and visual cortex in attention-deficit/hyperactivity disorder. Biol. Psychiat. **67**(7), 617–623 (2010)
26. Jamal, W., Das, S., Oprescu, I.A., et al.: Classification of autism spectrum disorder using supervised learning of brain connectivity measures extracted from synchrostates. J. Neural Eng. **11**(4), 046019 (2014)
27. Wang, H., Xu, T., Tang, C., et al.: Diverse feature blend based on filter-bank common spatial pattern and brain functional connectivity for multiple motor imagery detection. IEEE Access **8**, 155590–155601 (2020)
28. Kakkos, I., Dimitrakopoulos, G.N., Sun, Y., et al.: EEG fingerprints of task-independent mental workload discrimination. IEEE J. Biomed. Health Inform. **25**(10), 3824–3833 (2021)
29. Harvy, J., Thakor, N., Bezerianos, A., Li, J.: Between-frequency topographical and dynamic high-order functional connectivity for driving drowsiness assessment. IEEE Trans. Neural Syst. Rehabil. Eng. **27**(3), 358–367 (2019)
30. Tass, P., Rosenblum, M., Weule, J., et al.: Detection of n: m phase locking from noisy data: application to magnetoencephalography. Phys. Rev. Lett. **81**(15), 3291 (1998)
31. Celka, P.: Statistical analysis of the phase-locking value". IEEE Signal Process. Lett. **14**(9), 577–580 (2007)
32. Aydore, S., Pantazis, D., Leahy, R.M.: A note on the phase locking value and its properties. Neuroimage **74**, 231–244 (2013)
33. Liu, Y., Ding, Y., Li, C.: Multi-channel EEG-based emotion recognition via a multi-level features guided capsule network. Comput. Biol. Med. **123**, 103927 (2020)

# Brain Source Reconstruction Solution Quality Assessment with Spatial Graph Frequency Features

Meng Jiao[1], Feng Liu[1(✉)], Onur Asan[1], Roshanak Nilchiani[1], Xinglong Ju[2], and Jing Xiang[3]

[1] School of Systems and Enterprises, Stevens Institute of Technology, Hoboken, NJ, USA
fliu22@stevens.edu
[2] Division of Management Information Systems, The University of Oklahoma, Norman, OK, USA
[3] MEG Center, Division of Neurology, Cincinnati Children's Hospital Medical Center, Cincinnati, OH, USA

**Abstract.** Different EEG/MEG source imaging (ESI) algorithms can render different reconstructions, so as to the same algorithm with different hyperparameters. Moreover, we found the locations of active sources also have an impact on the performance of ESI algorithms. For the real EEG/MEG source reconstruction, as the ground true activation is unknown, it is hard to validate which algorithm performs better. In this paper, we proposed to use statistical features from source space to predict whether the reconstruction is a satisfactory solution. The training data and testing data are from solutions from different algorithms based on synthetic EEG data where ground truth activations are available. The good and bad solutions are determined by Area Under Curve (AUC) and localization error (LE). We extract spatial and general statistical features from solutions, then we used machine learning models to classify good vs. bad solutions, and showed the feasibility of judging the quality of solution without knowing ground truth, which can serve as a feedback for further hyperparameter tuning.

**Keywords:** Brain source imaging · Solution quality · Graph fourier transform · EEG/MEG

## 1 Introduction

Brain source localization using the EEG/MEG measurement provides an important means to understand brain functions and to uncover the abnormal patterns for patients with brain disorders. EEG/MEG has a very high temporal resolution up to one millisecond compared to around one second of temporal resolution of fMRI. EEG or MEG devices also have the advantage of being inexpensive, easy portability and versatility. EEG is accepted as a powerful tool to capture the instantaneous brain functionality by measuring the neuronal processes [21]. However, one disadvantage of EEG is its poor spatial resolution as it measures the electric potential on the scalp rather than a direct

© Springer Nature Switzerland AG 2022
M. Mahmud et al. (Eds.): BI 2022, LNAI 13406, pp. 175–183, 2022
https://doi.org/10.1007/978-3-031-15037-1_15

measurement of the brain sources. EEG/MEG source imaging (ESI) bridges the gap between the scalp EEG measurement and the brain source activations as it infers the brain sources activation by solving the inverse problem based on the measurement of EEG or MEG [13,18]. However, given that the dimension of source signal significantly outnumbers the EEG/MEG sensors, the ESI is an ill-conditioned inverse problem that requires sophisticated design of regularizations that utilize the spatial-temporal assumptions on the source space [22,23].

Recently, numerous algorithms have been developed with different assumptions on the source structure. One seminal work is minimum norm estimate (MNE) where $\ell_2$ norm is used as a regularization [12]. Variants of MNE algorithm include dynamic statistical parametric mapping (dSPM) [6] and standardized low-resolution brain electromagnetic tomography (sLORETA) [24]. The $\ell_2$-norm based methods tend to render spatially-diffuse source estimation. To promote a sparse solution, Uutela *et al.* [28] introduced the $\ell_1$-norm, known as minimum current estimate (MCE). Also, Rao and Kreutz-Delgado proposed an affine scaling method [26] for a sparse ESI solution. Bore *et al.* proposed to use the $\ell_p$-norm regularization ($p < 1$) on the source signal and the $\ell_1$ norm on the data fitting error term [4]. Babadi *et al.* [1] demonstrated that sparse distributed solutions to event-related stimuli can be found using a greedy subspace-pursuit algorithm. Liu *et al.* proposed a dictionary learning framework to learn discriminative source activation patterns from different classes [16]. It is worth noting that the sparse constraint can be applied to the original source signal or the transformed spatial gradient domain [8,17,19]. As the brain is activated not discretely or pointwisely, an extended area of source estimation is preferred [2], and it has been used for multiple applications, such as somatosensory cortical mapping [5], and epileptogenic zone in focal epilepsy patients [3]. Recently, deep learning has been used to learn the mapping between EEG/MEG and source activation. Hecker *et al.* proposed a convolutional neural network approach for ESI and showed improved performance compared to traditional methods. Jiao and Liu proposed an unrolled optimization neural network based on iterative procedures in constrained optimization to solve ESI problem and achieved more accurate result [14].

However, different algorithms provide different solutions with varied quality, how to assess the solution quality given the statistical features of solution has not been explored. The contribution in this paper is to conduct a pilot study on how to distinguish when an algorithm provides a good solution vs a bad solution based on the statistical features. The correctly identified bad solution can be used to further guide the hyperparameter tuning process.

## 2 EEG/MEG Source Imaging Problem

EEG data are mostly generated by pyramidal cells in the gray matter with an orientation perpendicular to the cortex. The ESI forward model can be expressed as $Y = LS + E$, where $Y \in \mathbb{R}^{C \times T}$ is the EEG/MEG measurements, $C$ is the number of EEG/MEG channels, $T$ is the number of time points, $L \in \mathbb{R}^{C \times N}$ is the *leadfield* matrix which characterizes the mapping from brain source space to EEG/MEG channel space, $S \in \mathbb{R}^{N \times T}$ represents the electrical potentials in $N$ source locations for all the $T$ time points, and $E$ is the uncertainty/noise. The ESI inverse problem is to estimate $S$ given the

EEG/MEG measurements. Since channel number $C$ is much smaller than the number of sources $N$, estimating $S$ becomes ill-posed and has infinitely number of solutions. In order to find a unique solution, different regularizations were introduced by using prior assumptions of the source solution. More specifically, $S$ can be obtained by solving the following minimization problem:

$$\underset{S}{\operatorname{argmin}} \frac{1}{2} \|Y - LS\|_F^2 + \lambda R(S), \tag{1}$$

where $\| \cdot \|_F$ is the Frobenius norm. The first term of Eq. (1) is called *data fitting* which tries to explain the observed EEG data, and the second term is called *regularization* term which is imposed to find a unique solution of Eq. (1) by using the sparsity or other neurophysiology inspired regularizations. If $R(S)$ equals $\ell_2$ norm, the problem is called minimum norm estimate (MNE) [12]; if $R(S)$ is defined using $\ell_1$ norm, the problem becomes minimum current estimate (MCE) [28]. As the cortex is discretized with 3D meshes, simply employing $\ell_1$ norm on $S$ will result in an estimated discrete source located across the cortex instead of an extended continuous area in the cortex. In order to encourage source extents estimation, Ding proposed to use a sparse constraint in the transformed domain by introducing TV defined from the irregular 3D mesh [7]. Other researchers used the same TV definition such as [15, 18, 25, 27, 29]. The TV was defined to be the $\ell_1$ norm of the first order spatial gradient using a linear transform matrix $V \in \mathbb{R}^{P \times N}$ with its definition can be found in [7]. The use of TV regularization is especially useful when a focal area of brain sources are activated, which is common for epilepsy patients [9].

## 3 Method

The ESI algorithms usually render *dichotomous accuracy* illustrated in Fig. 3, where a long tail in the boxplot of both LE and AUC (defined later) representing bad reconstruction. The bad solutions typically lost the spatial structure as the left one in Fig. 2.

The solution quality assessment framework (SQAF) is illustrated in Fig. 1. It starts from collecting MRI scans from the subject and digitized locations of EEG or MEG sensors, and coregister the EEG/MEG sensors with the head model built from MRI images using boundary element method (BEM) or finite element method (FEM). Then we can build a forward model which characterizes the mapping from source space to the sensor space. The SQAF is to validate the quality of solutions from the ESI algorithms using spatial and general statistical features, which can further guide the ESI algorithm selection or parameter tuning.

Figure 2 provides an example of a good solution vs a bad solution, where the solution on the left represents a good recovery of an focal source extent activation, while the figure on the right has a bad reconstruction solution where sources are spatially over-diffused and non-continuous in the cortex.

**Feature Extraction:** We use basic statistical features of solution, including mean, variance, median, skewness, kurtosis, and the recently proposed spatial graph frequency (SGF) [15], and also the data fitting, which is defined by $\|y - Ls\|_2^2 / \|y\|_2^2$ to measure how the solution fits the measured EEG or MEG data. Specifically the SGF is defined as follows:

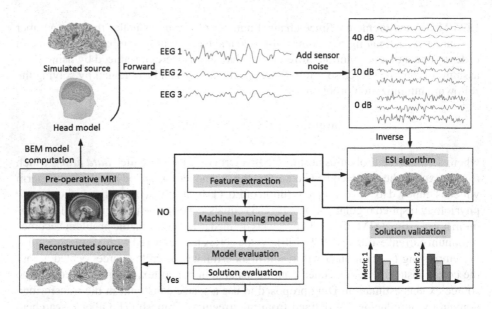

**Fig. 1.** ESI solution quality assessment framework.

**Definition 1.** Spatial Graph Frequency (SGF): $f_{\mathcal{G}}$ is a function of $s$, where $s$ is the signal defined on the irregular 3D mesh representing the brain source signal on the cortex, and SGF is defined as follows:

$$f_{\mathcal{G}}(s) = \sum_{m=1}^{N} \sum_{n \in \mathcal{N}(m)} \mathbb{I}(u_i(m)u_i(n) < 0)/2, \tag{2}$$

where $N$ is the number of nodes (sources), $\mathcal{N}(m)$ denotes all the neighbors of node $m$, and $\mathbb{I}(\cdot)$ is the indicator function to check if the values of $u_i$ at node $m$ and $n$ have a sign flip. The sign flip makes an analogy to counting the number of zero crossings of a basis signal within a given window for a time series data. The Laplacian matrix is constructed within the first order of neighbors. The SGF basically counts how many sign flips among neighboring nodes, measuring the level of spatial variations in the source space.

With the extracted features, we use several typical machine learning models, such as Support Vector Machine (SVM), Random Forest (RF), Decision Tree (DT), Naïve Bayesian (NB), K-Nearest Neighbors (KNN) and Logistic Regression (LR). The dataset was split into 70% for training and 30% for testing. In order to find the best hyperparameter for the machine learning models, we provide a range of hyperparameters and use 3-fold cross validation to select the best hyperparameters, and the hyperparameters are listed in Table 1. Using the training data, we conducted 3-fold cross validation to select the best hyperparameter, and then trained the model on the training dataset, and then tested on the testing dataset.

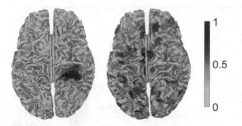

**Fig. 2.** A good solution with concentrated activation patches vs a bad activation where sources are reconstructed wide spread on the cortex.

**Table 1.** Hyperparameter tuning

| Model | Hyperparameter | Optimal value | Range |
|---|---|---|---|
| LR | $C$ | 1 | [0.01, 0.1, 1, 10] |
| | Penalty | $\ell_2$ | [$\ell_1$, $\ell_2$] |
| DT | Criterion | entropy | [entropy, gini] |
| | Max depth | 7 | [ 1 4 7 10 13 16 19] |
| RF | $N$ estimators | 40 | [10, 17, 25, 32, 40] |
| | Max features | auto | [auto, sqrt] |
| | Max depth | 8 | [2, 4, 6, 8] |
| GB | $N$ estimators | 95 | [10, 15, 20, 25, ..., 80, 85, 90, 95] |
| | Max depth | 4 | [2, 4] |
| | Learning rate | 0.1 | [0.001, 0.01, 0.1] |
| SVM | Gamma | 10 | [0.01, 0.05, 0.1, 1, 10] |
| | Kernel | rbf | [linear, rbf] |
| | $C$ | 10 | [0.01, 0.05, 0.1, 1, 10] |
| KNN | $N$ neighbors | 10 | [2, 4, 6, 8, 10] |
| | $P$ | 1 | [1, 2] |
| | Weights | distance | [uniform, distance] |

## 4   Result

**Synthetic Data Generation.** We first computed the BEM model based on the preoperative MRI images from a 26-year old male subject. Brain tissue segmentation and source surface reconstruction were conducted using FreeSurfer [10]. EEG signals were measured using a 128-channel BioSemi EEG cap. We coregistered EEG channels with the head model using Brainstorm and further validated on MNE-Python toolbox [11]. Then, the *leadfield* matrix $L$ can be calculated. The source space contains 2052 sources, so the dimension of $L$ is 128 by 2052. We used the forward model to generate scalp EEG data with simulated sources as the ground truth. The 2052 sources are activated in turn with 3 level of neighbors activated at the same time. The magnitudes of the center source, the first level neighbors, the second level neighbors, and the third level of

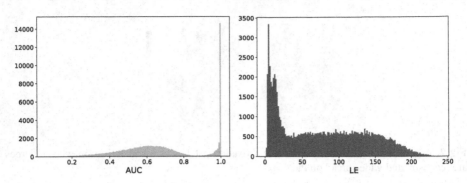

**Fig. 3.** Histogram for AUC (left) and LE (right).

neighbors are set to be 1, 0.8, 0.6, and 0.4, respectively. The SNR (signal-to-noise ratio) for the channel noise is set to be 10 dB, and each activation pattern is repeated 10 times subject to the randomness of the channel noise. Eventually, there are 20520 samples for ESI algorithms to reconstruct the source solutions.

Then we conducted source reconstruction with different ESI methods, including MNE [12], dSPM [6], sLORETA [24] and our recently proposed UONN [14]. The solutions are compared with the ground truth to calculate the performance metrics of all the solutions from the ESI algorithms. The performance metrics include localization error (LE) and AUC, which are defined as follows [20]:

(1) *Localization error (LE)*: it measures the geodesic distance between two source locations on the cortex meshes using the Dijkstra shortest path algorithm.
(2) *Area under curve (AUC)*: it is particularly useful to characterize the overlap of an extended source activation pattern.

The traditional ESI algorithms such as MNE, sLORETA, dSPM render over-diffused reconstructions, while our proposed algorithm [14] has a much higher probability of providing more reliable reconstructions. The histogram in terms of AUC and LE measured from the combined solutions from all the ESI algorithms is given in Fig. 3. We set the threshold for good solution when AUC $> 0.95$ and LE $< 15$ mm (flagged as 1), and bad solution otherwise (flagged as 0).

The selected best parameter setting based on 3-fold cross-validation for SVM is $C =10$, and penalty is $\ell_2$, the selected parameter for LR is $C = 10$, and $\ell_2$ penalty, the selected parameter for KNN is $K = 8$ and $p = 1$, and the weight is based on the distance. For DT, the best parameter setting is: splitting criterion: entropy, and max depth is 4. For RF, the max depth is 8, max features is set to be auto, and number of estimators is set to be 40. For GB, the max depth is set to be 4, and number of estimators is 40. We use the default setting for NB.

The feature importance evaluated by LR is given in Fig. 4. The SGF is the most important feature, followed by variance and EEG data fitting.

Finally, the AUC curves from different algorithms are given in Fig. 5. And all the classification results are given in Table 2. All the algorithms achieved very accurate performance with or without SGF. Given the performance for the models without SGF

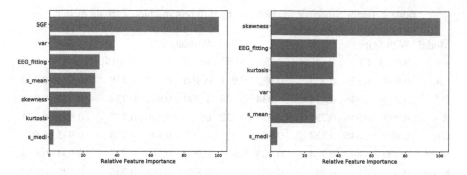

**Fig. 4.** Feature Importance evaluated by LR with SGF (left), and without SGF (right).

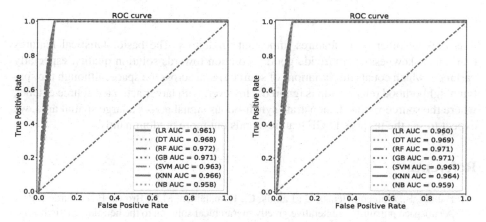

**Fig. 5.** Comparison of the AUC values between with feature frequency (on the left) and without feature frequency (on the right).

feature already achieved very high accuracy, adding SGF didn't show a significant improvement.

## 5   Discussion and Limitation

This research provides a simple yet important pilot study to distinguish the good vs bad solutions rendered by different ESI algorithms. The key features are based on spatial graph Fourier transform which has not been much explored in the ESI context. We found the SGF is the top one feature to distinguish the good vs. bad solutions. This research demonstrates the feasibility of solution quality check with simple machine learning models and statistical features, which can help to find an enhanced design of hyperparameters of the ESI algorithms.

This paper has some limitations, for example, there is only one activated source, and the activated area is still a much smaller region compared to the whole cortex,

**Table 2.** Performance comparison among different machine learning models

| Model | With SGF | | | | | Without SGF | | | | |
|-------|--------|-------|-----------|-------|-------|--------|-------|-----------|-------|-------|
|       | Recall | F1    | Precision | ACC   | AUC   | Recall | F1    | Precision | ACC   | AUC   |
| LR    | 0.981  | 0.839 | 0.733     | 0.932 | 0.961 | 0.866  | 0.797 | 0.738     | 0.920 | 0.960 |
| DT    | 0.999  | 0.846 | 0.734     | 0.934 | 0.968 | 1.000  | 0.847 | 0.734     | 0.935 | 0.968 |
| RF    | 0.993  | 0.846 | 0.737     | 0.935 | 0.972 | 0.992  | 0.846 | 0.737     | 0.935 | 0.971 |
| GB    | 0.990  | 0.846 | 0.738     | 0.935 | 0.971 | 0.991  | 0.846 | 0.738     | 0.935 | 0.971 |
| SVM   | 1.000  | 0.847 | 0.734     | 0.934 | 0.963 | 0.999  | 0.846 | 0.733     | 0.934 | 0.963 |
| KNN   | 0.901  | 0.816 | 0.746     | 0.927 | 0.966 | 0.882  | 0.808 | 0.746     | 0.925 | 0.964 |
| NB    | 0.990  | 0.843 | 0.733     | 0.933 | 0.958 | 0.992  | 0.844 | 0.734     | 0.934 | 0.959 |

thus making other basic features important predictors. The basic statistical features (variance, skewness) can provide good prediction towards solution quality, especially variance, which counts the variations of source signal across the space, although the spatial neighborhood relationship is ignored. However, with larger activated source extents, where the source voxels demonstrate synchronous signal across a large spatial area, we expect to see the proposed SGF feature stands out more predominantly.

# References

1. Babadi, B., Obregon-Henao, G., Lamus, C., Hämäläinen, M.S., Brown, E.N., Purdon, P.L.: A subspace pursuit-based iterative greedy hierarchical solution to the neuromagnetic inverse problem. Neuroimage **87**, 427–443 (2014)
2. Baillet, S., Mosher, J.C., Leahy, R.M.: Electromagnetic brain mapping. IEEE Signal Process. Mag. **18**(6), 14–30 (2001)
3. Becker, H., et al.: EEG extended source localization: tensor-based vs. conventional methods. NeuroImage **96**, 143–157 (2014)
4. Bore, J.C., et al.: Sparse EEG source localization using LAPPS: least absolute lP $(0 < p < 1)$ penalized solution. IEEE Trans. Biomed. Eng. **66**(7), 1927–1939 (2018)
5. Cai, C., Diwakar, M., Chen, D., Sekihara, K., Nagarajan, S.S.: Robust empirical Bayesian reconstruction of distributed sources for electromagnetic brain imaging. IEEE Trans. Med. Imaging **39**(3), 567–577 (2019)
6. Dale, A.M., et al.: Dynamic statistical parametric mapping: combining fMRI and MEG for high-resolution imaging of cortical activity. Neuron **26**(1), 55–67 (2000)
7. Ding, L.: Reconstructing cortical current density by exploring sparseness in the transform domain. Phys. Med. Biol. **54**(9), 2683 (2009)
8. Ding, L., He, B.: Sparse source imaging in electroencephalography with accurate field modeling. Hum. Brain Mapp. **29**(9), 1053–1067 (2008). https://doi.org/10.1002/hbm.20448
9. Ebersole, J., Squires, K., Eliashiv, S., Smith, J.: Applications of magnetic source imaging in evaluation of candidates for epilepsy surgery. Neuroimaging Clin. N. Am. **5**(2), 267–288 (1995)
10. Fischl, B.: Freesurfer. Neuroimage **62**(2), 774–781 (2012)
11. Gramfort, A., et al.: MNE software for processing MEG and EEG data. Neuroimage **86**, 446–460 (2014)

12. Hämäläinen, M.S., Ilmoniemi, R.J.: Interpreting magnetic fields of the brain: minimum norm estimates. Med. Biol. Eng. Comput. **32**(1), 35–42 (1994)
13. He, B., Sohrabpour, A., et al.: Electrophysiological source imaging: a noninvasive window to brain dynamics. Annu. Rev. Biomed. Eng. **20**, 171 (2018)
14. Jiao, M., Liu, F.: Extended brain sources estimation via unrolled optimization neural network. bioRxiv (2022)
15. Jiao, M., et al.: A graph fourier transform based bidirectional LSTM neural network for EEG source imaging. Front. Neurosci. 447 (2022)
16. Liu, F., Wang, S., Rosenberger, J., Su, J., Liu, H.: A sparse dictionary learning framework to discover discriminative source activations in EEG brain mapping. In: AAAI, pp. 1431–1437 (2017)
17. Liu, F., Hosseini, R., Rosenberger, J., Wang, S., Su, J.: Supervised discriminative EEG brain source imaging with graph regularization. In: Descoteaux, M., Maier-Hein, L., Franz, A., Jannin, P., Collins, D.L., Duchesne, S. (eds.) MICCAI 2017. LNCS, vol. 10433, pp. 495–504. Springer, Cham (2017). https://doi.org/10.1007/978-3-319-66182-7_57
18. Liu, F., Rosenberger, J., Lou, Y., Hosseini, R., Su, J., Wang, S.: Graph regularized EEG source imaging with in-class consistency and out-class discrimination. IEEE Trans. Big Data **3**(4), 378–391 (2017)
19. Liu, F., Wan, G., Purdon, P.: Extended electrophysiological source imaging with spatial graph filters. In: International Conference on Medical Image Computing and Computer-Assisted Intervention (2022)
20. Liu, F., Wang, L., Lou, Y., Li, R.C., Purdon, P.L.: Probabilistic structure learning for EEG/MEG source imaging with hierarchical graph priors. IEEE Trans. Med. Imaging **40**(1), 321–334 (2020)
21. Michel, C.M., Brunet, D.: EEG source imaging: a practical review of the analysis steps. Front. Neurol. **10**, 325 (2019)
22. Michel, C.M., Murray, M.M., Lantz, G., Gonzalez, S., Spinelli, L., de Peralta, R.G.: EEG source imaging. Clin. Neurophysiol. **115**(10), 2195–2222 (2004)
23. Ou, W., Hämäläinen, M.S., Golland, P.: A distributed spatio-temporal EEG/MEG inverse solver. Neuroimage **44**(3), 932–946 (2009)
24. Pascual-Marqui, R.D., et al.: Standardized low-resolution brain electromagnetic tomography (sLORETA): technical details. Methods Find. Exp. Clin. Pharmacol. **24**(Suppl. D), 5–12 (2002)
25. Qin, J., Liu, F., Wang, S., Rosenberger, J.: EEG source imaging based on spatial and temporal graph structures. In: International Conference on Image Processing Theory, Tools and Applications (2017)
26. Rao, B.D., Kreutz-Delgado, K.: An affine scaling methodology for best basis selection. IEEE Trans. Signal Process. **47**(1), 187–200 (1999)
27. Sohrabpour, A., Lu, Y., Worrell, G., He, B.: Imaging brain source extent from EEG/MEG by means of an iteratively reweighted edge sparsity minimization (IRES) strategy. Neuroimage **142**, 27–42 (2016)
28. Uutela, K., Hämäläinen, M., Somersalo, E.: Visualization of magnetoencephalographic data using minimum current estimates. Neuroimage **10**(2), 173–180 (1999)
29. Zhu, M., Zhang, W., Dickens, D.L., Ding, L.: Reconstructing spatially extended brain sources via enforcing multiple transform sparseness. Neuroimage **86**, 280–293 (2014)

# Enhancing the MR Neuroimaging by Using the Deep Super-Resolution Reconstruction

Yu Cao[1,3], Hongzhi Kuai[2,3(✉)], and Guanqiao Peng[4]

[1] Information Department, Beijing University of Technology, Beijing, China
[2] Graduate School of Engineering, Maebashi Institute of Technology, Maebashi, Gunma, Japan
hongzhi.kuai@gmail.com
[3] International WIC Institute, Beijing University of Technology, Beijing, China
[4] Beijing 101 Middle School, Beijing, China

**Abstract.** As brain investigation progresses, the need has become urgent from acquiring the higher resolution neuroimaging data to give a more detailed interpretation. In particular, the technological development and innovation of the Magnetic Resonance Imaging (MRI) machine, through increasing the magnetic field from low (such as 3T) to high (such as 7T), has revealed significant advantages regarding the image quality enhancement, etc. Currently, due to the limitations of hardware, physics and physiology, the large-scale acquisition of the high-resolution MRI neuroimages is still running on the road. Hence, enhancing the quality of the low-field MRI data is critical by using the advanced artificial intelligence technology. In this study, we propose a novel image enhancement framework, namely SR-MRI, trying to improve the quality of the low-resolution neuroimage: (1) combining with the Real-ESRGAN deep learning model; (2) bridging the 3T-MRI and the 7T-MRI within the same analysis scale; and (3) systematically comparing multiple evaluation indicators, including Brenner, SMD, SMD2, Variance, Vollath, Entropy, and NIQE. The experimental results suggest that the edge, fineness and texture features of the low-resolution neuroimages are restored to a great extent from the SR-MRI framework. In addition, the evaluation results of multiple indicators show that the processed 3T-MRI can achieve the similar effect from the 7T-MRI machine.

**Keywords:** Magnetic Resonance Imaging (MRI) · Super-resolution · Brain informatics · Deep learning · Real-ESRGAN model

## 1 Introduction

As the most important information processing and control center in the human body, the brain is closely related to cognitive, emotional, psychological and behavioral functions [1]. With the rapid development of medical informatization and the popularization of medical neuroimages in this digital age, Magnetic Resonance Imaging (MRI) plays an increasingly significant role in the detection and diagnosis of various diseases for smart health [2]. The quality of MR neuroimages, as the carrier of patients' pathological

© Springer Nature Switzerland AG 2022
M. Mahmud et al. (Eds.): BI 2022, LNAI 13406, pp. 184–194, 2022
https://doi.org/10.1007/978-3-031-15037-1_16

information, can influence doctors' perception, reception, comprehension and diagnosis of patients' pathological information.

The magnetic resonance phenomenon is produced by using a high magnetic field and a radio signal to excite hydrogen protons in the human body. By changing the intensity of external gradient magnetic field "T", different tissues of the body can resonate at different frequencies and draw structural images in human body [3]. The letter "T" indicates Tesla in the magnetic resonance, which is the magnitude of the field strength. Theoretically, the stronger the field intensity is used, the higher the signal to noise ratio (SNR) is given, implying that more image resolution can be offered. From the hardware perspective, the 7T-MRI machine, even the machine with the higher Tesla, is developed to obtain the higher-resolution MRI data. However, due to the limitations of hardware and physics, the acquisition system cost of the high-resolution (HR) 7T MRI is high [4]. Therefore, the current mainstream still depends on the 3T-MRI technology, which has generated massive amounts of data. Furthermore, from the method perspective, the super-resolution (SR) reconstruction of low-resolution (LR) MR neuroimages is attracting greater attention, which can reduce the requirements of hardware equipment without increasing the cost of imaging technology. The reconstructed high-resolution MR neuroimages can help doctors make accurate diagnosis of patients' condition.

So far, the natural images have been the focus of academic super-resolution network processing. However, as the super-resolution advances and the medical industry's demand of high-resolution images grow, more network structures and associated approaches for medical images are being presented [5]. For instance, Liu [6] proposed a multi-scale fusion convolution network to conduct super-resolution for MRI reconstruction in order to investigate the various edge responses utilizing various convolution kernel sizes. Shi [7] put forward a new residual learning-based SR technique for MRI by combining local residual block with global residual network. Furthermore, numerous researchers have focused on different improved methods, such as the modified SRCNN (Super-Resolution Convolutional Neural Network) based global residual learning strategy [8] and the GAN based common algorithms [9]. As a result, in this paper, we introduce a novel super-resolution reconstruction framework for enhancing the MR neuroimaging quality from 3T to 7T, combining with different deep learning algorithms. Different from the common pipeline of the super-resolution reconstruction, the current work builds flexible components to process different scale neuroimaging data within a unified framework towards the goal of greater practice. In addition, considering the necessity of the systematic analysis from the Brain Informatics methodology [10], multiple evaluation indicators are calculated to verify the effectiveness of the enhanced 3T-MRI.

## 2  Method

In this section, we introduce a novel super-resolution framework, namely SR-MRI, for enhancing MR neuroimaging from 3T to 7T. Figure 1 depicts the image enhancement framework, which is made up of three components: the preprocessing component, the super-resolution component and the evaluation component.

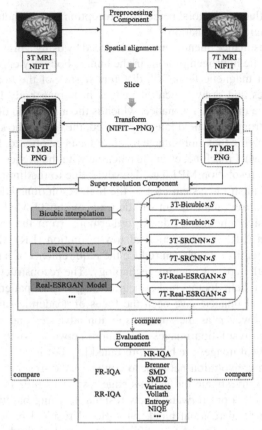

**Fig. 1.** The detailed components and their workflows in the SR-MRI framework. ($S$ is the magnification of neuroimaging reconstruction. FR: Full Reference; RR: Reduced Reference; NR: No Reference.)

## 2.1 The Preprocessing Component

In the preprocessing component, through the operation of spatial alignment, the images have been aligned into the template derived from 555 healthy subjects of the IXI database (http://www.brain-development.org) [11]. To execute the nonlinear registration properly, we also need to initialize it by a linear registration to acquire the image's orientation and size close enough for the nonlinear registration. The significance of spatial alignment is to align images to the same template space for comparison, as well as to eliminate noise that may arise during PNG conversion. Subsequently, we slice both 3T and 7T MR neuroimages along the Z axis, and convert them from 3D NIfTI format to PNG format.

## 2.2 The Super-Resolution Component

In the component of super-resolution, three super-resolution methods are integrated into this framework, including the bicubic interpolation algorithm, and the SRCNN and Real-ESRGAN models based on deep learning. These methods are performed to reconstruct low-resolution images, respectively. Meanwhile, images can be magnified with different scales in these three various methods. Obviously, more effective super-resolution algorithms can be added to the framework to improve the image quality.

SRCNN technology is the first time to apply the deep learning model of convolutional neural network in the field of super-resolution reconstruction [12]. Its network structure is shown in Fig. 2. The supplied low-resolution image is first enlarged to the intended size using bicubic interpolation. Secondly, to match the non-linear mapping between LR and HR images, a three-layer convolutional neural network is utilized. Finally, the output of the network is the reconstructed HR image.

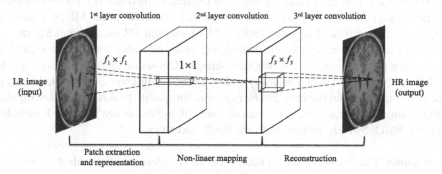

**Fig. 2.** The network structure of SRCNN.

Real-ESRGAN (Real-Enhanced Super-Resolution Generative Adversarial Networks) is one of the top SR technologies in recent years including the Generative Network and the Discriminator Network [13]. The model manages to achieve a decent mix between image improvement and artifact reduction. The study proposes a high-order degradation procedure, and uses the 'sinc' filters to the mimic typical ringing and overshoot problems in order to synthesize more realistic degradations. The Generative Network (as shown in Fig. 3) is a deep network constructed by several residual-in-residual dense blocks (RRDB) without batch normalization, making it easier to train deeper and more complicated network architectures. Meanwhile, to improve discriminator capabilities and stabilize training dynamics, the researchers used a U-Net discriminator with spectral normalization regularizations. For most real-world images, Real-ESRGAN trained on synthetic data is able to increase details while reducing annoying artifacts.

### 2.3 The Evaluation Component

There exist two types of image quality evaluation methods: subjective and objective [14]. The former relies on the subjective perception of the experimenter, while the latter measures the image quality according to the quantitative index. The use of one or more image indicators creates a mathematical model, ensuring that the outcomes of objective evaluations are congruent with people's subjective sentiments. According to whether the

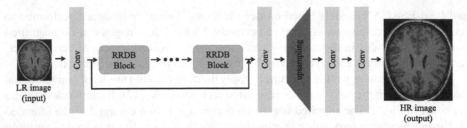

**Fig. 3.** The structure of Generative Network of Real-ESRGAN.

original image is referenced and the degree of reference, the objective quality evaluation can be divided into the following three types: (a) Full Reference (FR), (b) Reduced Reference (RR), (c) No Reference (NR) [15]. Since both FR method and RR method require the information from the original images as the reference for assessment, and the data used in this article is not HR MR neuroimages. Consequently, this research opts for the NR method [16], which does away with the need for reference images and relies on some information from the image to be reviewed for quality evaluation. Following that, in the evaluation component, numerous distinct NR indicators are integrated, including Brenner, SMD, SMD2, Vollath, Entropy, NIQE and so on

1. **Brenner**. The Brenner gradient function is the simplest gradient evaluation function. It simply calculates the square of the gray difference between two adjacent pixels, which is given by:

$$D\left(f^{Brenner}\right) = \sum_y \sum_x |f(x+2, y) - f(x, y)|^2 \tag{1}$$

where $D\left(f^{Brenner}\right)$ is the index calculated by the Brenner gradient function, and $f(x, y)$ represents the gray value of the pixel $(x, y)$ corresponding to image $f$.

2. **SMD**. The Sum of Modulus of gray Difference (SMD) function takes the gray change as the basis for focus evaluation. SMD extracts the change size of the gray value of point $(x, y)$ and its adjacent points by performing a differential operation on the gray level of the point $(x, y)$ and its neighboring points, which is given by:

$$D\left(f^{SMD}\right) = \sum_y \sum_x (|f(x, y) - f(x, y-1)| + |f(x, y) - f(x+1, y)|) \tag{2}$$

where $D\left(f^{SMD}\right)$ is the index calculated by the Sum of Modulus of gray Difference function.

3. **SMD2**. The SMD2 function is the product of modulus of gray difference. That is, the two gray differences in each pixel field are multiplied and then accumulated pixel by pixel, which is given by:

$$D\left(f^{SMD2}\right) = \sum_y \sum_x |f(x, y) - f(x+1, y)| * |f(x, y) - f(x, y+1)| \tag{3}$$

where $D\left(f^{SMD2}\right)$ is the index calculated by the SMD2 function.

4. **Variance**. The Variance function may be utilized as the evaluation function since the sharply focused image has a bigger gray difference than the unfocused image, which is given by:

$$D\left(f^{Variance}\right) = \sum_y \sum_x |f(x, y) - \mu|^2 \tag{4}$$

where $D\left(f^{Variance}\right)$ is the index calculated by the Variance function.

5. **Vollath**. The Vollath function is based on the image cross-correlation function, which efficiently suppresses noise and reduces interference from impurities. The function is defined as follows:

$$D\left(f^{Vollath}\right) = \sum_y \sum_x f(x, y) * f(x + 1, y) - M * N * \mu \tag{5}$$

where $D\left(f^{Vollath}\right)$ is the index calculated by the Vollath function, and $\mu$ indicates the average gray value of the whole image, and $M$ and $N$ are the image's width and height, respectively.

6. **Entropy**. The Entropy function, which is based on statistical characteristics, is a useful metric for assessing the richness of visual data. According to information theory, the information quantity of an image is measured by the information entropy of the image, which is given by:

$$D\left(f^{Entropy}\right) = -\sum_{I=0}^{L-1} P_i \ln(P_i) \tag{6}$$

where $D\left(f^{Entropy}\right)$ is the index calculated by the Entropy function, and $P_i$ is the probability of pixels with gray value $I$ in the image, and $L$ is the total number of gray levels (usually 256).

7. **NIQE**. The Natural Image Quality Evaluator (NIQE) [17] is the evaluation index of ECCV's PIRM competition in 2018. The NIQE first extracts the region of interest from the image when extracting the statistical features of the image. It stems from the fact that the human eye prefers to judge the image quality by the clearer part of the image. When using the collected 36 features for image quality evaluation, the Multivariate Gaussian Model (MVG) is used to fit, which is given by:

$$f_X(x_1, ..., x_k) = \frac{1}{(2\pi)^{k/2}|\Sigma|^{1/2}} \exp\left(-\frac{1}{2}(x - v)^T \Sigma^{-1}(x - v)\right) \tag{7}$$

where $(x_1, ..., x_k)$ are the 36 features collected, $v$ and $\Sigma$ are the mean and covariance matrix of MVG, which can be obtained by maximum likelihood estimation.

The value of NIQE is obtained by calculating the distance of the MVG parameters between the natural image and the distorted image:

$$D\left(f^{NIQE}\right) = D(v_1, v_2, \Sigma_1, \Sigma_2) = \sqrt{(v_1 - v_2)^T \left(\frac{\Sigma_1 + \Sigma_2}{2}\right)^{-1} (v_1 - v_2)} \tag{8}$$

where $D\left(f^{NIQE}\right)$ is the index calculated by the NIQE.

## 3    Results and Discussions

### 3.1    MR Neuroimage Acquisition and Preprocessing

In this work, two datasets with the accession numbers of ds001553 and ds001555 are obtained from the OpenNeuro platform (https://openneuro.org). Each study was performed by three people with no known history of neurological diseases (5 females; age = $25 \pm 5$ years). All participants gave informed consent in compliance with a protocol approved by the Institutional Review Board of the National Institute of Mental Health in Bethesda, MD, USA. For 3T images, its accession number is ds001553. 372 coronal slices were obtained in a General Electric 3T MRI scanner using image parameters: TR = 7240 ms, TE = 2.7 ms, TI = 725 ms, Flip angle = 12°, and resolution = $1 \times 1 \times 1$ mm$^3$. For 7T images, its accession number is ds001555. 354 coronal slices were obtained in a Siemens 7T MRI scanner equipped with a 32-element receive coil using image parameters: TR = 3000 ms, TE = 3.88 ms, TI = 1500 ms, Flip angle = 6°, and resolution = $1 \times 1 \times 1$ mm$^3$. As for spatial alignment, we registered the corresponding 3T and 7T images using Matlab SPM12 toolbox, to minimize the possible global distortions. To do so, all the images were linearly aligned to the MNI space by using an individual template [18]. After one subject's MRI data is aligned to the MNI standard space, the NIfTI file is converted to 78 images of PNG format by slicing. Finally, we obtained 234 normalized images from three subjects, with respect to the 3T scale, and the same number of normalized images at the 7T scale. As individual differences are not concerned about the core point in this paper, the average effectiveness of all super-resolution images corresponding to different scale is evaluated respectively in the following evaluation phase.

### 3.2    The Super-Resolution Results of the MR Neuroimaging

From Fig. 4, it can be seen that the resolution of MR neuroimages has been greatly increased by using the proposed SR-MRI framework.

In this framework, the super-resolution images using the bicubic interpolation algorithm have relatively higher ambiguity compared with the results from the SRCNN and Real-ESRGAN methods, not only on the edge, but also in the region. The image rebuilt using the SRCNN model has somewhat enhanced intra-regional resolution, however it still falls short of the image recovered by the Real-ESRGAN model. By using the Real-ESRGAN reconstruction, the images are clearest at the junction of white matter and gray matter, and the edge, fineness and texture characteristics are recovered to a large extent. Therefore, the Real-ESRGAN method is embedded into the current framework with stronger recommendation. In the next section, we compare the performance of super-resolution results from both 3T and 7T MRI using quality evaluation of no reference.

### 3.3    Quantitative Analysis Based on No-Reference Indicators

As shown in Table 1, the evaluation value of each index is given by averaging all values from a group of images (234 slices). Apart from the NIQE index of the seven indexes in this article, the greater an index value is, the higher an image quality has.

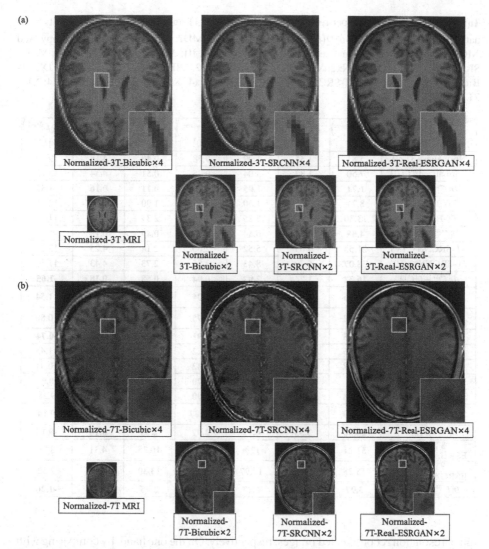

**Fig. 4.** The reconstructed MRI results based on the proposed SR-MRI framework. (a) shows the reconstructed results based on the normalized-3T MR neuroimages; (b) shows the reconstructed results based on the normalized-7T MR neuroimages. (×2 is the two times magnification for super-resolution reconstructed images, and ×4 is the four times magnification.)

In Table 1, it is found that all indicators of 7T MRI are superior than those of 3T MRI. When comparing the image quality of three alternative processing algorithms in this SR-MRI framework, the Real-ESRGAN method outperforms the SRCNN and bicubic interpolation methods. Meanwhile, the four times magnification produces a superior visual quality than the two times magnification. In addition, to evaluate the enhanced scale before and after running this SR-MRI framework, the difference of indictors is calculated between both 3T and 7T normalized MR neuroimaging and the

**Table 1.** Comparison of super-resolution results between 3T and 7T MRI based on quality evaluation of no reference. ($*$ in $D(f^*)$ is Brenner, SMD, SMD2, Variance, Vollath, Entropy, and NIQE, respectively. I: Normalized 3T; II: Normalized 7T; III: 3T-Bic ×2; IV: 7T-Bicx2; V: 3T-SRCNN×2; VI: 7T-SRCNNx2; VII: 3T-Real-ESRGAN×2; VIII: 7T-Real-ESRGANx2; IX: 3T-Bic×4; X: 7T-Bicx4; XI: 3T-SRCNN×4; XII: 7T-SRCNNx4; XIII: 3T-Real-ESRGAN ×4; XIV: 7T-Real-ESRGANx4.)

| Index / Image | $D(f^{Brenner})$ /$10^6$ | $D(f^{SMD})$ /$10^5$ | $D(f^{SMD2})$ /$10^6$ | $D(f^{Variance})$ /$10^7$ | $D(f^{Vollath})$ /$10^7$ | $D(f^{Entropy})$ /$10^0$ | $D(f^{NIQE})$ /$10^0$ |
|---|---|---|---|---|---|---|---|
| Normalized 3T (I) | 5.81 | 1.35 | 1.99 | 0.58 | 0.40 | 4.18 | 19.79 |
| Normalized 7T (II) | 7.50 | 1.87 | 3.04 | 0.75 | 0.51 | 4.34 | 15.22 |
| $D(f^{*,II})-D(f^{*,I})$ | **1.71** | **0.53** | **1.05** | **0.18** | **0.11** | **0.16** | **-4.57** |
| 3T-Bic×2 (III) | 8.71 | 2.56 | 1.60 | 2.07 | 1.90 | 4.20 | 12.08 |
| 7T-Bicx2 (IV) | 13.30 | 3.44 | 2.25 | 2.63 | 2.39 | 4.33 | 11.03 |
| $D(f^{*,IV})-D(f^{*,III})$ | **4.58** | **0.87** | **0.64** | **0.56** | **0.49** | **0.13** | **-1.05** |
| 3T-SRCNN×2 (V) | 21.55 | 4.05 | 5.52 | 2.60 | 2.14 | 4.25 | 13.21 |
| 7T-SRCNNx2 (VI) | 38.07 | 5.79 | 8.43 | 3.55 | 2.73 | 4.43 | 11.56 |
| $D(f^{*,VI})-D(f^{*,V})$ | **16.52** | **1.74** | **2.92** | **0.94** | **0.58** | **0.18** | **-1.65** |
| 3T-Real-ESRGAN×2 (VII) | 16.46 | 3.43 | 3.65 | 3.04 | 2.72 | 4.30 | 11.54 |
| 7T-Real-ESRGANx2 (VIII) | 28.72 | 4.71 | 5.77 | 3.95 | 3.38 | 4.45 | 10.80 |
| $D(f^{*,VIII})-D(f^{*,VII})$ | **12.25** | **1.27** | **2.12** | **0.91** | **0.65** | **0.15** | **-0.74** |
| 3T-Bic×4 (IX) | 10.56 | 5.07 | 1.65 | 7.72 | 7.52 | 4.23 | 11.45 |
| 7T-Bicx4 (X) | 16.27 | 6.74 | 2.30 | 9.42 | 9.15 | 4.34 | 10.91 |
| $D(f^{*,X})-D(f^{*,IX})$ | **5.71** | **1.67** | **0.64** | **1.70** | **1.63** | **0.11** | **-0.54** |
| 3T-SRCNN×4 (XI) | 34.68 | 8.08 | 7.09 | 9.90 | 9.32 | 4.27 | 9.28 |
| 7T-SRCNNx4 (XII) | 63.29 | 11.41 | 11.20 | 12.87 | 11.90 | 4.45 | 9.14 |
| $D(f^{*,XII})-D(f^{*,XI})$ | **28.60** | **3.33** | **4.12** | **2.97** | **2.53** | **0.18** | **-0.14** |
| 3T-Real-ESRGAN×4 (XIII) | 51.21 | 9.15 | 12.8 | 11.21 | 10.25 | 4.31 | 8.78 |
| 7T-Real-ESRGANx4 (XIV) | 55.28 | 9.74 | 12.97 | 14.16 | 13.30 | 4.48 | 7.52 |
| $D(f^{*,XIV})-D(f^{*,XIII})$ | **3.97** | **0.59** | **0.17** | **2.95** | **3.05** | **0.17** | **-1.26** |

super-resolution reconstructed images, respectively. On the one hand, by comparing with the NIQE difference of $|D(f^{*,II}) - D(f^{*,I})| = 4.57$ calculated by the normalized 3T and 7T images, the NIQE difference after the super-resolution reconstruction processes is reduced obviously. On the other hand, the difference calculated by the other six indicators is increased after running this framework. It is found that the SR-MRI framework can enhance the performance of images, and even the enhanced 3T-MRI could achieve the similar effect from the 7T-MRI machine.

## 4   Conclusion

In this paper, by developing a novel super-resolution framework, namely SR-MRI, combined with the pre-trained SRCNN and Real-ESRGAN models, we apply the image super-resolution reconstruction technology based on deep neural network to enhance the

MR neuroimages. The effectiveness of the deep super-resolution model is verified by comparing multi-scale MRI data from 3T to 7T. It has been shown that when the 3T MR neuroimages are processed using the current framework, the image quality is increased considerably, and the effect from a 7T MRI machine could be achieved similarly. In the future, the further research is needed to integrate more super-resolution techniques into this framework and apply it to more potential scenarios towards accelerating the clinical practice.

# References

1. Kuai, H., Zhong, N.: The extensible data-brain model: architecture, applications and directions. J. Comput. Sci. 101103 (2020)
2. Kuai, H., Zhong, N., Chen, J., Yang, Y.: Multi-source brain computing with systematic fusion for smart health. Inform. Fus. **75**, 150–167 (2021)
3. Weiskopf, N., Edwards, L.J., Helms, G.: Quantitative magnetic resonance imaging of brain anatomy and in vivo histology. Nat. Rev. Phys. **3**(8), 570–588 (2021)
4. Stucht, D., Danishad, K.A., Schulze, P.: Highest resolution in vivo human brain MRI using prospective motion correction. PLoS ONE **10**(7), e0133921 (2015)
5. Yang, W., Zhang, X., Tian, Y., Wang, W.: Deep learning for single image super-resolution: a brief review. IEEE Trans. Multimedia **21**(12), 3106–3121 (2019)
6. Liu, C., Wu, X., Yu, X., Tang, Y.: Fusing multi-scale information in convolution network for MR image super-resolution reconstruction. Biomed. Eng. Online **17**(1), 1–23 (2018)
7. Shi, J., Liu, Q., Wang, C., Zhang, Q.: Super-resolution reconstruction of MR image with a novel residual learning network algorithm. Phys. Med. Biol. **63**(8) (2018)
8. Qiu, D., Zheng, L., Zhu, J., Huang, D.: Multiple improved residual networks for medical image super-resolution. Futur. Gener. Comput. Syst. **116**, 200–208 (2021)
9. Lv, J., Zhu, J., Yang, G.: Which GAN? A comparative study of generative adversarial network-based fast MRI reconstruction. Phil. Trans. R. Soc. A **379**(2200), 20200203 (2021)
10. Zhong, N., Bradshaw, J.M., Liu, J., Taylor, J.G.: Brain informatics. IEEE Intell. Syst. **26**(5), 16–21 (2011)
11. Tavares, V., Prata, D., Ferreira, H.A.: Comparing SPM12 and CAT12 segmentation pipelines: a brain tissue volume-based age and Alzheimer's disease study. J. Neurosci. Methods **334**, 108565 (2020)
12. Dong, C., Loy, C.C., He, K.: Learning a deep convolutional network for image super-resolution. In: Fleet, D., Pajdla, T., Schiele, B., Tuytelaars, T. (eds.) European Conference on Computer Vision, LNIP, vol. 8692, pp. 184–199. Springer, Cham (2014). https://doi.org/10.1007/978-3-319-10593-2_13
13. Wang, X., Xie, L., Dong, C., Shan, Y.: Real-esrgan: Training real-world blind super-resolution with pure synthetic data. In: Proceedings of the IEEE/CVF International Conference on Computer Vision, pp. 1905–1914 (2021)
14. Mohammadi, P., Ebrahimi-Moghadam, A., Shirani, S.: Subjective and objective quality assessment of image: a survey. Majlesi J. Electric. Eng. **9**(1) (2014)
15. Yang, J., Zhao, Y., Liu, J., Jiang, B.: No reference quality assessment for screen content images using stacked autoencoders in pictorial and textual regions. IEEE Trans. Cybern. **99**, 1–13 (2020)
16. Hu, S., Wang, X., Wu, H., Luan, X.: Unified diagnosis framework for automated nuclear cataract grading based on smartphone slit-lamp images. IEEE Access **8**, 174169–174178 (2020)

17. Mittal, A., Soundararajan, R., Bovik, A.C.: Making a "completely blind" image quality analyzer. IEEE Signal Process. Lett. **20**(3), 209–212 (2012)
18. Holmes, C.J., Hoge, R., Collins, L., Woods, R.: Enhancement of MR images using registration for signal averaging. J. Comput. Assist. Tomogr. **22**(2), 324–333 (1998)

# Towards Machine Learning Driven Self-guided Virtual Reality Exposure Therapy Based on Arousal State Detection from Multimodal Data

Muhammad Arifur Rahman[1]([✉])[iD], David J. Brown[1,2][iD], Nicholas Shopland[1][iD], Matthew C. Harris[1][iD], Zakia Batool Turabee[1][iD], Nadja Heym[3][iD], Alexander Sumich[3][iD], Brad Standen[3][iD], David Downes[4][iD], Yangang Xing[5][iD], Carolyn Thomas[5][iD], Sean Haddick[1][iD], Preethi Premkumar[6][iD], Simona Nastase[7][iD], Andrew Burton[1][iD], James Lewis[1][iD], and Mufti Mahmud[1,2]([✉])[iD]

[1] Department of Computer Science, Nottingham Trent University, Nottingham NG11 8NS, UK
{muhammad.rahman02,mufti.mahmud}@ntu.ac.uk, arif@juniv.edu, mufti.mahmud@gmail.com
[2] CIRC and MTIF, Nottingham Trent University, Nottingham NG11 8NS, UK
[3] School of Social Sciences, Nottingham Trent University, Nottingham NG1 4FQ, UK
[4] Nottingham School of Art and Design, Nottingham Trent University, Nottingham, NG1 4FQ, UK
[5] School of ADBE, Nottingham Trent University, Nottingham NG1 4FQ, UK
[6] Division of Psychology, London South Bank University, London SE1 0AA, UK
[7] London, UK

**Abstract.** Virtual-reality exposure therapy (VRET) is a novel intervention technique that allows individuals to experience anxiety evoking stimuli in a safe environment, to recognise specific triggers and gradually increase their exposure to perceived threats. Public-speaking anxiety (PSA) is very common form of social anxiety, characterised by stressful arousal and anxiety generated when presenting to an audience. In self-guided VRET participants can gradually increase their tolerance to exposure and reduce anxiety induced arousal and PSA over time. However, creating such a VR environment and determining physiological indices of anxiety induced arousal or distress is an open challenge. Environment modelling, character creation and animation, psychological state determination and the use of machine learning models for anxiety or stress detection are equally important, and multi-disciplinary expertise is required. In this work, we have explored a series of machine learning models with publicly available data sets (using electroencephalogram and heart rate variability) to predict arousal states. If we can detect anxiety-induced arousal, we can trigger calming activities to allow individuals to cope with and overcome the distress. Here, we discuss the means of effective selection of machine learning models and parameters in arousal

---

S. Nastase—Independent Clinical Psychologist.

© Springer Nature Switzerland AG 2022
M. Mahmud et al. (Eds.): BI 2022, LNAI 13406, pp. 195–209, 2022
https://doi.org/10.1007/978-3-031-15037-1_17

detection. We propose a pipeline to overcome the model selection problem with different parameter settings in the context of Virtual Reality Exposure Therapy. This pipeline can be extended to many other domains of interest, where arousal detection is crucial.

**Keywords:** Arousal · EEG · HRV · Random forest · Glossophobia · Stress · VRET

# 1    Introduction

Anxiety is an emotional state characterised by negative affect and worry, heightened arousal, careful environmental monitoring, rumination and avoidance behaviour, ranging from mild to severe. Intense states of anxiety, or even fear - a more rudimentary physiological response to a perceived threat that can lead to fight/flight/freeze reactions and panic behaviour - can be symptoms of different psychological disorders. For example, phobias are defined by an exaggerated fear or unrealistic sense of threat to a situation or object, which appear in many forms. In the Diagnostic and Statistical Manual of Mental Disorders (DSM-5, 2013) [18,23], the American Psychiatric Association defines five types of phobia, related to natural environments (e.g., heights), animals (e.g., spiders), specific situations (e.g., public spaces), blood/injury or medical issues, and other types (e.g. loud noise, vomiting, choking). These debilitating disorders affect about 13% of the world's total population. Research is ongoing for contributing factors to the onset, development, and maintenance of phobias and anxiety-related disorders, their underlying cognitive and behavioural processes, physical manifestation, and treatment methods [4,5,26,31]. Traditional treatments of such disorders include *in-vivo* exposure, interoceptive exposure, cognitive behavioural therapy (CBT), applied muscle tension, supportive psychotherapy, hypnotherapy, and medications such as beta-blockers or sedatives [9].

Virtual reality exposure therapy (VRET) is one of the most promising novel treatments, enabled by its superior immersive capabilities that generate a greater sense of presence and enhance user effects, especially for negatively valenced, high arousal stimuli [37]. Over the last two decades VRET, encompassing psychological treatment principles and enabled by advancing display and computing technology developments, has become a popular digital intervention for various psychological disorders [6,38], being as effective as in-vivo (i.e., face-to-face) exposure therapy post-intervention [20]. For example, a meta-analysis showed VRET for Social Anxiety Disorder (encompassing an exaggerated fear of being rejected, negatively evaluated or humiliated during social interactions, observations and/or in performance situations) to be more effective than wait-list controls (with large effect sizes), and even therapist-led in-vivo exposure therapy (though only small effect size) [6]. It shows good acceptability in users due to its safe, controlled and empowering means of exposure. A vital part of the development of VRET is the integration of bio-signals, such as heart rate variability or cortical arousal, to assess and ameliorate physiological distress states (e.g., fear or anxiety induced arousal) during exposure. Here, correct detection of physiological states through robust models for effective management of anxiety-induced arousal or stress is pivotal to facilitating intervention and enhancing psychological health and well-being.

## 2  Related Work

Arousal detection, a noninvasive intervention, requires a multi-disciplinary approach, where psychological state determination, machine learning models for arousal or stress detection, and exploration of the related domains for model implementation are equally important. In this paper, we narrow down the areas and present an overview of the state of the art scenarios.

*Emotion/Stress Detection:* Koelstra et al. (2012) presented a multimodal dataset for the analysis of human affective states [21]. They collected physiological signals, including electroencephalographic (EEG) data from participants watching music videos and rated each video in terms of excitement, stress, arousal, flaws, valence, like, dislike. The data has been widely used for developing various machine learning models for arousal, anxiety and stress detection. Ahuja and Banga (2019) created another dataset from the Jaypee Institute of Information Technology where they classified mental stress in 206 students [2]. They used Linear Regression (LR), Support Vector Machine (SVM), Naïve Bayes (NB) and Random Forest (RF) machine learning classification algorithms [10,11,15,25,28,32–34] to determine mental stress. Using SVM and 10-Fold cross-validation, they claimed an 85.71% accuracy. Ghaderi et al. (2015) used respiration, galvanic skin response (GSR) from hand and foot, heart rate (HR) and electromyography (EMG) at different time intervals to examine different stress levels. Then they used k-nearest neighbour (k-NN) and the SVM machine learning model for stress detection [16].

*Emotion/Stress Detection using EEG:* EEG is a non-invasive way to measure electrical responses generated by the outer layers of the cortex, primarily pyramidal cells. It has been used to investigate neural activity during arousal, stress, depression, anxiety or various other emotions. Several studies have applied machine learning methods to classify and/or predict emotional brain states based on EEG activity [12,13]. For example, Chen et al. (2020) designed a neural feedback system to predict and classify anxiety states using EEG signals during the resting state from 34 subjects [8]. Anxiety was calculated using power spectral density (PSD), and then SVM was used to classify anxious and non-anxious states. Shon et al. (2018) integrated genetic algorithm (GA)-based features in the machine learning pipeline along with a k-NN classifier to detect stress in EEG signals [36]. The model was evaluated using DEAP data set [21] for the identification of emotional stress state. Other work also used the publicly available DEAP data set for emotion recognition in virtual environments [27]. Based on Russell's circumplex model, statistical features, high order crossing (HOC) features and powerbands were extracted from the EEG signals, and affective state classification was performed using SVM and RF. In major depressive disorder (MDD, n = 32), Duan et al. (2020) [14] extracted interhemispheric asymmetry and cross-correlation features from EEG signals and combined these in a classification using $k$-NN, SVM and convolutional neural networks (CNN). Similarly, in other research by Omar [3] frontal lobe EEG data was used to identify stressed patients. Fast Fourier Transformation (FFT) was applied to extract features from the signal, which were then passed to machine learning models, such as SVM and NB for subject-wise classification of control and stress groups. Table 1 shows a summary of ML models used for arousal detection and their performance.

*Machine Learning and VRET:* Balan et al. (2020) used the publicly available DEAP [21] database and applied various machine learning algorithms for classifying the six basic emotions joy, anger, sadness, disgust, surprise and fear, based on the physiological data [5]. They presented the stages of model development and its evaluation in a virtual environment with gradual stimulus exposure for acrophobia treatment, accompanied by physiological signals monitoring. In [39], authors used a hybrid machine learning technique using $k$-Means++ clustering algorithm and principal component analysis (PCA) to cluster drug addicts to find out the relationship between cardiac physiological characteristic data and treatment effect. The author showed the relationship between cardiac

**Table 1.** Machine learning models of arousal detection.

| Ref. | Domain | Data type | Model | Performance | Modality |
|------|--------|-----------|-------|-------------|----------|
| [5] | Acrophobia | GSR, HR, BVR | SVM, RF, kNN | SVM-42.6% kNN-89.5%, RF-99% | Unimodal |
| [39] | Drug addiction | HRV | PCA, $k$-Means++ | ... | Unimodal |
| [24] | Spider phobia | Clinical characteristics | RF, Permutation Test | $*p < 0.05$; $**p < 0.01$; $***p < 0.001$ | Unimodal |
| [35] | Spider phobia | fMRI, Genetic Data | SVM, GPC | ... | Unimodal |
| [31] | PSA | ... | ... | ... | Unimodal |
| [7] | Anxiety disorder | EEG | SVM | Healthy subjects-97.70 ± 3.32%, Anxious subjects-92.29 ± 4.44% | Unimodal |
| [36] | Stress | EEG | k-NN with GA Based Feature Selection | k-NN 71.76% | Unimodal |
| [27] | Emotion Recognition | EEG | SVM,RF | RF-74.0%, SVM-57.2% | Unimodal |
| [14] | Major depressive disorder | EEG | KNN, SVM, CNN | CNN-94.13%, SVM-88.22%, KNN-83.15% | Unimodal |
| [3] | Stress | EEG | SVM, NB | SVM-90%, NB-81.7% | Unimodal |
| [21] | Human affective state | EEG | LR, SVM, NB | | Multimodal |
| [2] | Metal stress | EEG | LR, SVM, NB | 85.71% | Unimodal |

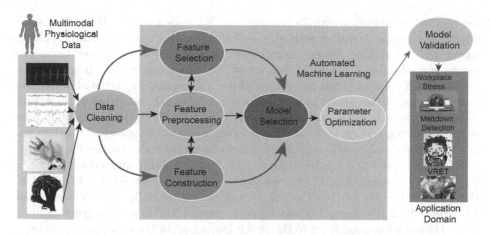

**Fig. 1.** Proposed Machine Learning Pipeline: We collect EEG and multimodal physiological data from suitable sensors. To clean the data for further processing we used individual phases of feature selection, feature prepossessing and feature constructions for model selection which was used for parameter optimisation. This process was repeated using automated machine learning for the best possible outcome from the collected data set. After model validation, we use our trained model for meltdown moment detection, workplace stress detection, VRET and/or other domains where arousal detection is crucial.

physiological characteristics and treatment effects using virtual reality. Other research [35] used a single session VRET for patients with spider phobia, including clinical, neuroimaging (functional magnetic resonance imaging, fMRI), and genetic data for baseline and post-treatment (after six months) analysis. They claimed a 30% reduction in spider phobia, assessed psychometrically, and a 50% reduction in individual distance avoidance tests using behavioural patterns.

## 3    ML Model Pipeline and Data Set

First, we collected EEG and multimodal physiological data from suitable sensors. Then we cleaned the data for further processing. Here we used individual phases of feature selection, feature prepossessing and feature constructions for model selection used for parameter optimisation. This process was repeated using automated machine learning for the best possible outcome from the collected data set. After the model validation, we apply our trained model to VRET and/or other domains where arousal detection is crucial. Figure 1 shows the proposed machine learning pipeline.

*Data Set:* For this research, we explored three publicly available data sets. The first one is the SWELL data set of [22]. The authors calculated the inter-beat interval (IBI) between peaks in electrocardiographic (ECG) signals. Then, the heart rate variability (HRV) index was computed on a five minutes IBI array by appending the new IBI sample to the array in a repeated manner. The data set was manually annotated with the conditions under which the data was collected. This data set has 204885 samples with 75 features and 3 labelled classes. Here, 25 people performed regular cognitive activities, including reading e-mails, writing reports, searching, and making presentations under manipulated working conditions. We used a second publicly available data set of [30], which was initially inspired from [19], with HRV data to train our proposed machine learning model and determine arousal levels. We also used a third publicly available data set titled 'EEG during Mental Arithmetic Task Performance' [40] to explore EEG recordings of 36 participants during resting state and while doing an arithmetic task. This data set has been commonly used to identify anxiety in individuals triggered while performing arithmetic tasks. It has been collected using a Neurocom monopolar EEG 23-channel system device. Electrodes (Fp1, Fp2, F3, F4, Fz, F7, F8, C3, C4, Cz, P3, P4, Pz, O1, O2, T3, T4, T5, T6) were placed on the scalp using international 10/20 standard. The sampling rate for each channel 500 Hz with a high-pass filter of 0.5 Hz and a low-pass filter 45 Hz cut-off frequency. In the experimental manipulation, participants were asked to solve mental arithmetic questions to increase cognitive load and induce stress, thus, evoking higher arousal states.

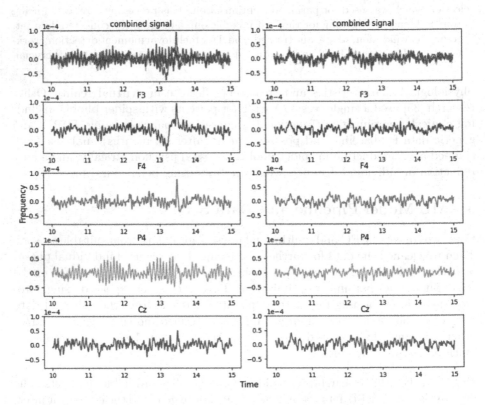

**Fig. 2.** The time domain representation of EEG data of [40]. The top Figures show the combined representations. Figures on the left show the initial condition and figures on the right show the stressed condition in channels F3, F4, Fz, Cz. We can clearly see the increase of oscillatory patterns of the signal from initial to stressful condition.

## 4    Result Analysis

In this study, we took the data set of EEG signals during mental arithmetic tasks[1] [40]. Decomposed EEG signals for a duration of 5 s before and during an arithmetic task are shown in Fig. 2. The signals were in edf format, which were converted to epochs and their statistical features (mean, std, ptp, var,

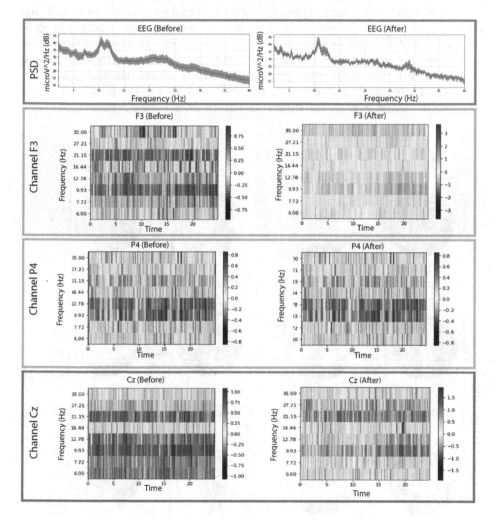

**Fig. 3.** Average frequency content of signal before and during the arithmetic task using [40] data set. We can clearly see changes in excitation levels. The figure on the left shows the initial level, whereas the right figure shows the stressed condition during mathematical problem solving. The figures were generated using the open source python package MNE-Python [17].

---

[1] https://physionet.org/content/eegmat/1.0.0/.

minim, maxim, argminim, argmaxim, skewness and kurtosis) were calculated. These were then used for the classification of the signals. RF model was used for this purpose which gave an accuracy of 87.5%. Figure 2 shows the time-domain representation of EEG signal of [40]. In this figure, plots on the left show recordings during the initial condition and plots on the right during stressed condition in channels F3, F4, Fz, Cz. We can clearly see the increase of oscillatory patterns of the signal from initial to stressful condition (Fig. 4).

Figure 3 shows average frequency content of signal epochs before and during solving arithmetic tasks using [40] data set. We can see some changes in excitation levels. The figures on the left show the signal in a relaxed state, whereas figures on the right depict the signals under stress while performing mental arithmetic task. Similarly, subsequent images in Fig. 3 show the time-frequency analysis of individual channels (F3, Cz, P4) generated using power plots and topographic maps. Significant difference can be seen between plots before and

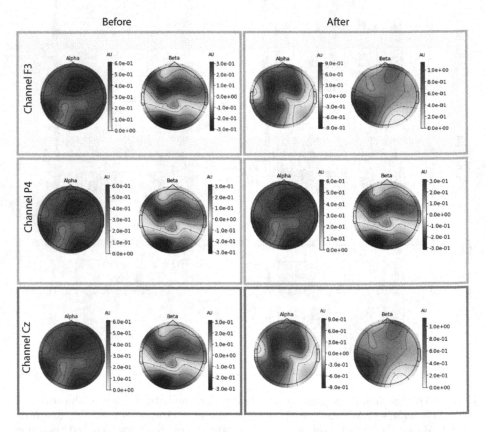

**Fig. 4.** Images above show the time frequency representations plotted using power plot topographic maps. Changes in Power Spectral Density can be seen for individual channels before and during the stressed conditions. The figures were generated using the open source python package MNE-Python [17].

during evoked stress states. The Fig. 5 shows the pair plot of few notable features MEAN-RR, MEDIAN-RR, SDRR-RMSSD, MEDIAN-REL-RR, SDRR-RMSSD-REL-RR, VLF, VLF-PCT from SWELL dataset [22]. These statistical features have been used to classify the signals aiming for arousal detection. This publicly available HRV dataset has been used to train our machine learning models. The Fig. 6 shows the prediction of stressful moments from the HRV data set generated by [30] inspired from [19]. We used the publicly available data set of [30] to train our proposed machine learning model and determine momentary stressful states. Figure 7 shows the performance (accuracy, precision, recall

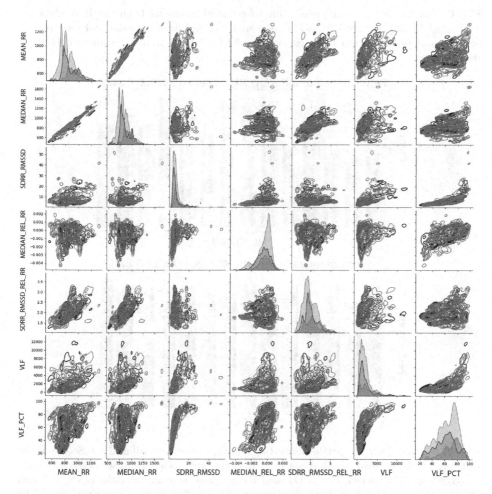

**Fig. 5.** The figure shows the pairplot of a few notable features MEAN-RR, MEDIAN-RR, SDRR-RMSSD, MEDIAN-REL-RR, SDRR-RMSSD-REL-RR, VLF, VLF-PCT from SWELL dataset [22]. These statistical features have been used for the classification of the signals aiming at arousal detection. This publicly available HRV dataset has been used to train our machine learning models.

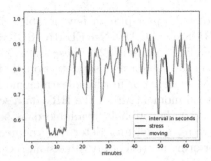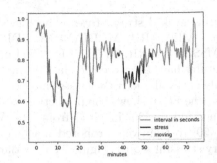

**Fig. 6.** The figure shows the prediction of stressful moments from the HRV data set generated by [30] inspired from [19]. We used the publicly available data set of [30] to train our proposed machine learning model for VRET and determine momentary stress states.

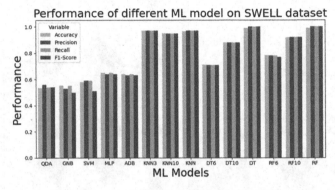

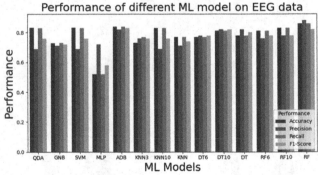

**Fig. 7.** Figures show the performance (accuracy, precision, recall and *F1*-Score) of the publicly available data set that we used to train our model. Here we consider QDA, GNB, SVM, MLP, ADB, KNN, DT and RF machine learning models. KNN, DT and RF has been used with multiple parameter settings. The figure on the top shows the performance on SWELL [22] data set and figure on the bottom shows the performance on EEG data set of [40].

and *F1*-Score) of the publicly available data set that we have used to train our model. Here we consider Gaussian Naïve Bayes (GNB), Quadratic Discriminant Analysis (QDA), Support Vector Machine (SVM), Multilayer Perceptron (MLP), AdaBoost (ADB), *k*-nearhood neighbour (KNN), Decision Tree(DT) and random Forest (RF) machine learning models. KNN, DT and RF have been used with multiple parameter settings. The figure on the top shows the performance of the SWELL [22] data set and figure on the bottom shows the performance on the EEG data set of [40]. If we use a different set of data then they results may vary slightly as showed by [1].

## 5   Challenges and Future Research Directions

As we mentioned in the Related Work section (Sect. 2) this work is derived through multidisciplinary research. So, diverse open domain challenges have been identified. Some of the key issues are-

- The real-time analysis of the machine learning data. Stream processing will be one of the next challenges that we want to overcome for the same problem.
- The placement of the BCI electrodes is an important consideration, and interesting to investigate further to determine the most relevant regions of the brain to monitor arousal.
- In future, additional sensor/polar devices, chest-straps and/or wrist bands could be used to collect further types of signals. Moreover, additional data should be collected from different experimental conditions to further improve efficacy.

## 6   Conclusion

In self-guided VRET, participants can gradually increase their own exposure to anxiety evoking stimuli (like audience size, audience reaction, salience of self etc.) to desensitise and reduce momentary anxiety and arousal states, facilitating amelioration of PSA over time. However, creating this VR environment and determining anxiety induced arousal or momentary stress states is an open challenge. In this work, we showed which selection of parameters and machine learning models can facilitate arousal detection. As such, we propose a machine learning pipeline for effective arousal detection. We trained our model with three publicly available data sets where we particularly focused on EEG and HRV data. Considering the scenarios, our proposed automated machine learning pipeline will overcome the model selection problem for arousal detection. Our trained machine learning model can be used for further development in VRET to overcome psychological distress in anxiety and fear related disorders. Further useful applications of the model can be seen in meltdown moment detection in Autism Spectrum Disorder (ASD) and other scenarios where stress and arousal play a significant role and early intervention will be helpful for physiological amelioration. For example, early identification and signalling of a meltdown moment, can facilitate initiation of targeted interventions preventing meltdowns, which will help parents, carers and supporting staff deal with such occurrences and reduce distress and harm in individuals with ASD. Finally, arousal and increasing stress have become buzzwords of recent times, adversely affecting a vast range of populations across the globe regardless of age group, ethnicity, gender, or work profile. Due to the long ongoing COVID-19 pandemic, changing scenarios, work patterns and lifestyles, increasing pressures, and technological advancements are a few possible reasons for this trend [16,21,29,30]. Thus, accurate detection of distress related arousal levels across the general population (e.g., in educational settings or the workplace) may help to avoid associated adverse impacts through effective interventions, prevent long-term mental health issues and improve overall well-being.

**Acknowledgement.** Funding for the VRET study is provided by the Higher Education Funding Council for England quality-related research (QR) funding awarded to Nottingham Trent University. Additionally, this work is supported by the AI-TOP (2020-1-UK01-KA201-079167) and DIVERSASIA (618615-EPP-1-2020-1-UKEPPKA 2-CBHEJP) projects, supported by the European Commission under the Erasmus+ programme.

# References

1. Adiba, F.I., Islam, T., Kaiser, M.S., Mahmud, M., Rahman, M.A.: Effect of corpora on classification of fake news using Naive Bayes classifier. Int. J. Autom. Artif. Intell. Mach. Learn. **1**(1), 80–92 (2020). https://researchlakejournals.com/index. php/AAIML/article/view/45
2. Ahuja, R., Banga, A.: Mental stress detection in university students using machine learning algorithms. Procedia Comput. Sci. **152**, 349–353 (2019). https://doi. org/10.1016/j.procs.2019.05.007. https://www.sciencedirect.com/science/article/ pii/S1877050919306581
3. Alshorman, O., et al.: Frontal lobe real-time EEG analysis using machine learning techniques for mental stress detection. J. Integr. Neurosci. 1–11 (2021)
4. Biswas, M., Kaiser, M.S., Mahmud, M., Al Mamun, S., Hossain, M.S., Rahman, M.A.: An XAI based autism detection: the context behind the detection. In: Mahmud, M., Kaiser, M.S., Vassanelli, S., Dai, Q., Zhong, N. (eds.) BI 2021. LNCS (LNAI), vol. 12960, pp. 448–459. Springer, Cham (2021). https://doi.org/10.1007/ 978-3-030-86993-9_40
5. Bălan, O., Moldoveanu, A., Leordeanu, M.: A machine learning approach to automatic phobia therapy with virtual reality. In: Opris, I., Lebedev, M.A., Casanova, M.F. (eds.) Modern Approaches to Augmentation of Brain Function. CCN, pp. 607–636. Springer, Cham (2021). https://doi.org/10.1007/978-3-030-54564-2_27
6. Carl, E., et al.: Virtual reality exposure therapy for anxiety and related disorders: a meta-analysis of randomized controlled trials. J. Anxiety Disord. **61**, 27–36 (2019)
7. Chen, C., et al.: EEG-based anxious states classification using affective BCI-based closed neurofeedback system. J. Med. Biol. Eng. **41**(2), 155–164 (2021)
8. Chen, L., Yan, J., Chen, J., Sheng, Y., Xu, Z., Mahmud, M.: An event based topic learning pipeline for neuroimaging literature mining. Brain Inform. **7**(1), 1–14 (2020)

9. Choy, Y., Fyer, A.J., Lipsitz, J.D.: Treatment of specific phobia in adults. Clin. Psychol. Rev. **27**(3), 266–286 (2007). https://doi.org/10.1016/j.cpr.2006.10.002. https://www.sciencedirect.com/science/article/pii/S0272735806001164
10. Das, S., Yasmin, M.R., Arefin, M., Taher, K.A., Uddin, M.N., Rahman, M.A.: Mixed Bangla-English spoken digit classification using convolutional neural network. In: Mahmud, M., Kaiser, M.S., Kasabov, N., Iftekharuddin, K., Zhong, N. (eds.) AII 2021. CCIS, vol. 1435, pp. 371–383. Springer, Cham (2021). https://doi.org/10.1007/978-3-030-82269-9_29
11. Das, T.R., Hasan, S., Sarwar, S.M., Das, J.K., Rahman, M.A.: Facial spoof detection using support vector machine. In: Kaiser, M.S., Bandyopadhyay, A., Mahmud, M., Ray, K. (eds.) Proceedings of International Conference on Trends in Computational and Cognitive Engineering. AISC, vol. 1309, pp. 615–625. Springer, Singapore (2021). https://doi.org/10.1007/978-981-33-4673-4_50
12. Doborjeh, Z., et al.: Interpretability of spatiotemporal dynamics of the brain processes followed by mindfulness intervention in a brain-inspired spiking neural network architecture. Sensors **20**(24), 7354 (2020)
13. Doborjeh, Z., et al.: Spiking neural network modelling approach reveals how mindfulness training rewires the brain. Sci. Rep. **9**(1), 1–15 (2019)
14. Duan, L., et al.: Machine learning approaches for MDD detection and emotion decoding using EEG signals. Front. Hum. Neurosci. **14**, 284 (2020)
15. Ferdous, H., Siraj, T., Setu, S.J., Anwar, M.M., Rahman, M.A.: Machine learning approach towards satellite image classification. In: Kaiser, M.S., Bandyopadhyay, A., Mahmud, M., Ray, K. (eds.) Proceedings of International Conference on Trends in Computational and Cognitive Engineering. AISC, vol. 1309, pp. 627–637. Springer, Singapore (2021). https://doi.org/10.1007/978-981-33-4673-4_51
16. Ghaderi, A., Frounchi, J., Farnam, A.: Machine learning-based signal processing using physiological signals for stress detection. In: 2015 22nd Iranian Conference on Biomedical Engineering (ICBME), pp. 93–98, November 2015. https://doi.org/10.1109/ICBME.2015.7404123
17. Gramfort, A., et al.: MEG and EEG data analysis with MNE-Python. Front. Neurosci. **7**(267), 1–13 (2013). https://doi.org/10.3389/fnins.2013.00267
18. Grzadzinski, R., Huerta, M., Lord, C.: DSM-5 and autism spectrum disorders (ASDs): an opportunity for identifying ASD subtypes. Mol. Autism **4**(1), 1–6 (2013)
19. Healey, J.A.: Wearable and automotive systems for affect recognition from physiology. Thesis, Massachusetts Institute of Technology (2000). https://dspace.mit.edu/handle/1721.1/9067. Accepted 24 Aug 2005
20. Horigome, T., et al.: Virtual reality exposure therapy for social anxiety disorder: a systematic review and meta-analysis. Psychol. Med. **50**(15), 2487–2497 (2020)
21. Koelstra, S., et al.: DEAP: a database for emotion analysis; using physiological signals. IEEE Trans. Affect. Comput. **3**(1), 18–31 (2012). https://doi.org/10.1109/T-AFFC.2011.15. http://ieeexplore.ieee.org/document/5871728/
22. Koldijk, S., Neerincx, M.A., Kraaij, W.: Detecting work stress in offices by combining unobtrusive sensors. IEEE Trans. Affect. Comput. **9**(2), 227–239 (2018). https://doi.org/10.1109/TAFFC.2016.2610975
23. LeBeau, R.T., et al.: Specific phobia: a review of DSM-IV specific phobia and preliminary recommendations for DSM-V. Depress. Anxiety **27**(2), 148–167 (2010). https://doi.org/10.1002/da.20655

24. Leehr, E.J., Roesmann, K.: Clinical predictors of treatment response towards exposure therapy in virtuo in spider phobia: a machine learning and external cross-validation approach. J. Anxiety Disord. **83**, 102448 (2021). https://doi.org/10.1016/j.janxdis.2021.102448

25. Mahmud, M., et al.: A brain-inspired trust management model to assure security in a cloud based IoT framework for neuroscience applications. Cogn. Comput. **10**(5), 864–873 (2018)

26. Mahmud, M., Kaiser, M.S., Rahman, M.A.: Towards explainable and privacy-preserving artificial intelligence for personalisation in autism spectrum disorder. In: Antona, M., Stephanidis, C. (eds.) Universal Access in Human-Computer Interaction. User and Context Diversity. LNCS, pp. 356–370. Springer, Cham (2022). https://doi.org/10.1007/978-3-031-05039-8_26

27. Menezes, M.L.R., et al.: Towards emotion recognition for virtual environments: an evaluation of EEG features on benchmark dataset. Pers. Ubiquit. Comput. **21**(6), 1003–1013 (2017). https://doi.org/10.1007/s00779-017-1072-7

28. Nasrin, F., Ahmed, N.I., Rahman, M.A.: Auditory attention state decoding for the quiet and hypothetical environment: a comparison between bLSTM and SVM. In: Kaiser, M.S., Bandyopadhyay, A., Mahmud, M., Ray, K. (eds.) Proceedings of International Conference on Trends in Computational and Cognitive Engineering. AISC, vol. 1309, pp. 291–301. Springer, Singapore (2021). https://doi.org/10.1007/978-981-33-4673-4_23

29. Newman, M.G., Szkodny, L.E., Llera, S.J., Przeworski, A.: A review of technology-assisted self-help and minimal contact therapies for anxiety and depression: is human contact necessary for therapeutic efficacy? Clin. Psychol. Rev. **31**(1), 89–103 (2011). https://doi.org/10.1016/j.cpr.2010.09.008

30. Ottesen, C.: Stress classifier with AutoML, January 2022. https://github.com/chriotte/wearable_stress_classification. Accessed 03 July 2018

31. Premkumar, P., et al.: The effectiveness of self-guided virtual-reality exposure therapy for public-speaking anxiety. Front. Psychiatry **12** (2021)

32. Rahman, M.A.: Gaussian process in computational biology: covariance functions for transcriptomics. Ph.D., University of Sheffield, February 2018. https://etheses.whiterose.ac.uk/19460/

33. Rahman, M.A., Brown, D.J., Shopland, N., Burton, A., Mahmud, M.: Explainable multimodal machine learning for engagement analysis by continuous performance test. In: Antona, M., Stephanidis, C. (eds.) Universal Access in Human-Computer Interaction. User and Context Diversity. LNCS, vol. 13309, pp. 386–399. Springer, Cham (2022). https://doi.org/10.1007/978-3-031-05039-8_28

34. Sadik, R., Reza, M.L., Al Noman, A., Al Mamun, S., Kaiser, M.S., Rahman, M.A.: Covid-19 pandemic: a comparative prediction using machine learning. Int. J. Autom. Artif. Intell. Mach. Learn. **1**(1), 1–16 (2020)

35. Schwarzmeier, H., Leehr, E.J.: Theranostic markers for personalized therapy of spider phobia: methods of a bicentric external cross-validation machine learning approach. Int. J. Methods Psychiatric Res. **29**(2), e1812 (2020). https://doi.org/10.1002/mpr.1812. https://onlinelibrary.wiley.com/doi/abs/10.1002/mpr.1812

36. Shon, D., Im, K., Park, J.H., Lim, D.S., Jang, B., Kim, J.M.: Emotional stress state detection using genetic algorithm-based feature selection on EEG signals. Int. J. Environ. Res. Public Health **15**(11), 2461 (2018)

37. Standen, B., Anderson, J., Sumich, A., Heym, N.: Effects of system- and media-driven immersive capabilities on presence and affective experience. Virtual Reality (2021). https://doi.org/10.1007/s10055-021-00579-2

38. Valmaggia, L.R., Latif, L., Kempton, M.J., Rus-Calafell, M.: Virtual reality in the psychological treatment for mental health problems: an systematic review of recent evidence. Psychiatry Res. **236**, 189–195 (2016)
39. Yuan, Y., Huang, J., Yan, K.: Virtual reality therapy and machine learning techniques in drug addiction treatment. In: 2019 10th International Conference on Information Technology in Medicine and Education (ITME), pp. 241–245, August 2019. https://doi.org/10.1109/ITME.2019.00062. ISSN 2474-3828
40. Zyma, I., et al.: Electroencephalograms during mental arithmetic task performance. Data **4**(1), 14 (2019). https://doi.org/10.3390/data4010014

# Convex Hull in Brain Tumor Segmentation

Kashfia Sailunaz[1], Deniz Bestepe[2], Sleiman Alhajj[3], Tansel Özyer[4],
Jon Rokne[1], and Reda Alhajj[1,2,5(✉)]

[1] Department of Computer Science, University of Calgary, Calgary, AB, Canada
rsalhajj@gmail.com
[2] Department of Computer Engineering, Istanbul Medipol University,
Istanbul, Turkey
[3] International School of Medicine, Istanbul Medipol University, Istanbul, Turkey
[4] Department of Computer Engineering, Ankara Medipol University, Ankara, Turkey
[5] Department of Health Informatics, University of Southern Denmark,
Odense, Denmark

**Abstract.** Tumors are the second leading cause of death. Among the
tumors, brain tumors constitute one of the most complex tumor categories with a high mortality rate. Therefore, brain tumor detection
and segmentation from non-invasive imaging like MRI is an important
research area. Although most recent researches for brain tumor detection are focused on deep learning methods, machine learning, geometrical
approaches, thresholding and hybrid models are also explored frequently.
In this paper, a novel brain tumor segmentation method containing
thresholding, computational geometry and heuristics is proposed. The
proposed model is tested with two brain tumor datasets to show comparative results for brain tumor segmentation with thresholding, convex
hull and an area heuristic. The application of different filtering on a direct
convex hull model and a heuristic-based convex hull model shows that
the convex area based heuristic with the convex hull approach is able to
segment brain tumors more accurately than previous approaches.

**Keywords:** Brain tumor · Image analysis · Convex hull ·
Segmentation

## 1 Introduction

Cells are the building blocks of the human body and they have a certain lifespan
where they grow, mature and eventually die. New cells replace the dead cells and
the normal cell life-cycle continues. However, in some cases, due to some genetic
abnormalities, some cells do not die in time or they have unnecessary growth
creating an abnormal shape with excessive cells. These structures are called
'tumors'. Tumors are normally named according to the organ of their origin.
Tumors can be either non-cancerous (i.e. benign) or cancerous (i.e. malignant).

Brain tumors are tumors that originate from any brain or skull component
(i.e. skull bones/muscles, brain membranes, brain nerves, brain tissues etc.).
There are more than 150 types of brain tumors based on their locations [9,11,22].

© Springer Nature Switzerland AG 2022
M. Mahmud et al. (Eds.): BI 2022, LNAI 13406, pp. 210–225, 2022
https://doi.org/10.1007/978-3-031-15037-1_18

About 4.25 malignant brain tumor cases exist globally per 100,000 person-years [15] with Europe and North America having the highest numbers of cases. More than 1,400,000 people suffer from malignant brain tumors worldwide and 9 out of 10 patients generally die within 5 years of their disease being diagnosed [7]. If a brain tumor is detected at an early stage it may be possible to remove it and the patient might eventually be tumor free.

Researchers from both medical and technological backgrounds have therefore been working on brain tumor detection, segmentation and diagnosis for a long time. Brain tumor analysis from medical images like Magnetic Resonance Imaging (MRI), Computed Tomography (CT), Positron Emission Tomography (PET), Cerebral Angiography, Myelography etc. have been studied by researchers with different image recognition, segmentation, machine learning and deep learning techniques. MRIs have been used in most of the recent studies because of their clarity. Various types of frequencies can be used in MRI imaging with different response times and echo times of the pulse signals that are used to produce multiple types or modalities of image sequences (i.e. T1-weighted, T2-weighted, Fluid Attenuated Inversion Recovery (Flair) etc.).

The brain tumor analysis problem has also been explored from a geometric perspective. Various fractal and computational geometry approaches have been proposed and tested for automatic brain tumor detection, tumor segmentation, 3D tumor reconstruction, tumor area/volume calculation etc. Fractal features and algorithms have been applied in most of these works. Some researches have used computational geometry techniques like 'Convex Hull Computation' and 'Delaunay Triangulation' for brain tumor analysis. Delaunay triangulation has been used for 3D brain tumor reconstruction from 2D slices [1]. Convex hull computations have been used for brain tumor segmentation [27], tumor area or volume calculation [10] and artefact removal from brain tumor images [29].

Convex hull computation [25] is one of the most well-known topic in computational geometry. In the 2D case, it calculates the minimum or smallest convex area containing a given set of points. The 2D convex hull computation problem has been solved with algorithms like Gift wrapping, Graham scan, Quickhull, Divide and Conquer each having different time complexities [23]. Convex hull algorithms generate a minimum convex polygon enclosing a set of points, and hence graph-based and image-based researches have been using convex hull computation for object detection problems in regular images [21], medical images [10,27,29], gaming platforms [26] and many other types of images. The brain tumor detection from MRIs can be represented as an object (i.e. tumor) detection problem from an image (i.e. MRI) by calculating the convex hull for the tumor.

In this paper, a convex hull computation based approach is used for brain tumor segmentation. A convex hull algorithm is used to detect the tumor area from brain MRIs with different filtering and thresholding methods. The proposed system uses brain MRIs as inputs and produces the convex hull for the tumor regions as outputs. The input images are pre-processed by basic image preprocessing methods to resize and normalize the images and redefine them to achieve homogeneity. The system then focuses on the abnormal regions of the brain by removing pixels containing healthy brain tissues using a thresholding method, such as Yen's thresholding, adaptive thresholding, anisotropic filtering or a customized (manually defined) thresholding which is then applied to each pre-processed image to highlight the tumor region. As the intensities of the pixels from the tumor region are generally higher than pixels containing healthy tissues, region-labeling is used to identify all connected high intensity pixels regions and extract the major remaining region as the tumor region from the image. The key-points of the abnormal area (i.e. tumor area or major region) are extracted based on their intensity-level. A convex hull algorithm is used to define the specific tumor boundary using the hull area with the extracted key-points. The method is applied separately on region-segmentation with Yen's filters, adaptive thresholding, anisotropic filtering and customized or manual thresholding. An area-based heuristic is added to the methods that calculates the convex area of the extracted major region to check if it is a part of non-tumor region or not. For each image, the area-heuristic is also separately applied to the region-segmentation with the mentioned thresholdings and filtering to generate an area-heuristic region-segmentation for each of them. The brain tumor image segmentation is therefore viewed as a problem from a (computational) geometry perspective.

The major contributions of this paper include - i) applying various existing thresholding, filtering, region-growing methods (i.e. Yen filters, adaptive thresholds, anisotropic filtering, customized thresholds, region-based segmentation etc.) on different types of brain MRIs from two brain tumor MRI datasets to decide on the best thresholding for brain MRIs, ii) defining a convex area based measurement (i.e. area-heuristic) to detect the tumor area more accurately, iii) generating the convex hulls for the detected tumor region using each method, and iv) finally analyzing the results produced by each method.

The next sections are organized as follows: some related works are mentioned in Sect. 2, the methodology is summarized in Sect. 3, the experimental setup with results are mentioned in Sect. 4 and the conclusion is provided in Sect. 5.

## 2    Literature Review

Medical image data analysis is the research area of computer science that works with machine learning, deep learning, image processing and many other relevant methods to extract meaningful medical image objects. Brain tumor image analysis is a subset of medical image analysis that specifically analyzes images of the brain to detect tumors. It has also been explored for decades due to the complexity and variation of brain images.

Researchers have been reviewing existing works of brain tumor analysis for understanding past and new challenges and scopes. A recent survey [2] included detail definitions and explanations of MRI techniques, MRI image types, brain tumors, brain tumor types and characteristics. They focused on machine learning models of brain tumor segmentations and classifications. Their detail study also mentioned statistics on publications, performance metrics and datasets. Most commonly used brain tumor segmentation methods like various thresholding, supervised MLs (i.e. Artificial Neural Networks (ANN), Support Vector

Machines (SVM), K-Nearest Neighbors (KNN), Random Forests etc.), unsupervised MLs (i.e. clustering, active contour models etc.) were discussed. They also described future possible uses of Deep Neural Network (DNN), Fuzzy C-means Clustering (FCM) and Particle Swarm Optimization (PSO) for brain tumor analysis research.

Saman et al. [30] reviewed the existing researches on brain tumor segmentation and feature extraction and explained every step of the procedure in detail. Various machine learning and thresholding approaches were discussed for different types of segmentations (i.e. intensity-based, manual, atlas-based, surface-based, and hybrid). Feature extraction models like texture-based, intensity-based and shape-based methods were also discussed. They also briefly mentioned the recent focus on DNNs. Abd-Ellah et al. [19] listed recent works and their applications on brain tumor segmentation and classification with Fuzzy Hopfield Neural Network (FHNN), Convolution Neural Network (CNN), Cascaded Correlation Artificial Neural Network (CCANN), Backpropagation Neural Network (BPNN), Feedforward Backpropagation Neural Network (FFBPNN), Probabilistic Neural Network (PNN), and other Deep Learning (DL) models. Because of their significantly higher performances, most recent researches on brain tumor analysis used different Deep Neural Networks (DNN).

Geometry has been one of the areas contributing to brain image analysis. 'Fractal Geometry' was mostly used for brain tumor analysis from brain images in [6]. Fractal geometry is a non-Euclidean geometry that is used to describe complex structures found in nature. Generally, the components present in nature or in human/animal bodies do not have simple shapes that can be described by euclidean geometry. Fractal geometry therefore defines self-similar structures that are able to create infinitely complex objects by magnification of the structure recursively with self-similarity. Fractal geometry features and algorithms have been long used by researchers for brain tumor image analysis. Iftekharuddin et al. [17] extracted fractal features for brain tumor segmentation and classification in pediatric brain images. Fractal features were extracted with the Piece-wise Triangular Prism Surface Area (PTPSA) algorithm. They used a novel fractional Brownian motion framework to extract fractal wavelet features from 204 MRIs of T1, T2 and FLAIR sequences. The fractal features were fused with intensity values and the feature set was able to detect tumors from single and multimodal MRIs where only the tumor region had the highest intensities. Although the model outperformed other existing fractal feature based systems, it performed poorly for MRIs that contained other parts of the brain with similar intensities as tumor pixels.

Fractal algorithms like PTPSA, Piece-wise Modified Box Counting (PMBC) and Blanket algorithm were also used in brain tumor segmentation research [14,18]. Each MRI was divided into multiple pieces and these algorithms were applied to the pixel intensities of every piece of MRI. Fractal dimension (FD) and cumulative histograms were generated with different thresholding and filtering. PMBC algorithm for tumor detection outperformed other similar methods in [18]. FD was calculated for 80 MRI and CT images in [14] for statistical validation.

FD was proven as an effective measure for brain tumor detection from the comparisons of average tumor FD and non-tumor FD for all of the images in the dataset, negative and positive FD differences of half images for Blanket, PMBC and PTPSA algorithms. The FD scores for the tumor areas and the non-tumor areas had very distinguishable characteristics that helped segmenting a tumor accurately from the rest of a brain.

Computational geometry, another well-known field of geometry, has also been used in brain tumor detection and segmentation. Bharathi et al. [1] used Delaunay triangulation for 3D tumor reconstruction by using stacks of 2D parallel cross-sectional segmented slices. Pre-processing and tumor boundary detection were done by Sobel operators and morphological operations. Then Delaunay triangulation was applied between points of two consecutive 2D planes. The connected 2D slices were used to reconstruct the 3D tumor using a stacking algorithm. The proposed novel idea of 3D reconstruction improved the quality of tumor segmentation. The datasets and proper experimental results representing their performance were absent in the published work. As a result, their claim of 'proposed method was better than other segmentations' needed to be justified by experiments on benchmark datasets. The proposed method also specified the tumor location, size and calculated the volume of the segmented tumor.

'Convex hull computation', another primary topic of computational geometry was also used for brain tumor segmentation in multiple researches. Shivhare et al. [27] generated the convex hull of the tumor region and used it as the input for an active contour model. One of the benchmark datasets for brain image analysis BRATS2015 [3] was used in their experiments. The key points were extracted from high energy regions of the image according to the assumption that tumor was the highest energy region of the image. The key points were used to draw the convex hull of the brain tumor. The convex hull of the tumor was then used to create a more accurate tumor segmentation with the active contour model. The model segmented the tumor into the tumor core, the complete tumor and the enhanced tumor. The proposed method achieved 81% to 92% Dice similarity coefficient and outperformed the other state-of-the-art image segmentation models. The convex hull computation was also used in another brain tumor research for the tumor convex area generation [10]. The proposed tumor segmentation model generated a similarity graph of each MRI and applied a spectral clustering-based segmentation algorithm. All connected regions were found using a connected component labeling algorithm and the largest component was identified as the tumor. The convex hull was generated for the tumor and the convex area was measured. The tumor volume was then calculated from the convex area and both the tumor segmentation and tumor volume were produced as final outputs.

A number of image processing and deep-learning based methods are being used for brain tumor segmentation with high accuracy in recent years. But there is an absence of research describing euclidean geometric approaches to address brain tumor detection and segmentation. Hence, this paper will focus on thresholding approaches to analyze the pixel intensities and represent the brain tumor segmentation as a computational geometry problem to be solved by computing the convex hull of the detected tumor region.

## 3    Methodology

The methodology of the proposed framework follows a sequence of steps to process the input MRIs for finding the tumor convex hulls. Figure 1 shows the framework for the implemented system for brain tumor detection. Each MRI input is pre-processed and then filtering and thresholding are applied on the pre-processed image. After that, region-based segmentation and area-heuristic region-based segmentation are applied on the image separately to extract the possible tumor region. Finally, a convex hull is generated for the extracted region which is compared to the original tumor to check the accuracy of the segmented tumor convex hull.

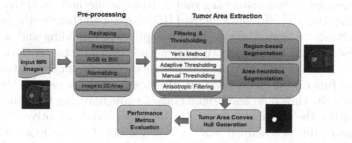

**Fig. 1.** Workflow of the proposed brain tumor segmentation system.

### 3.1    Pre-processing

The first step of the methodology is image pre-processing. As the dimensions of the MRIs are not consistent, the first step of image pre-processing is 'Image Reshaping'. Each image is checked for its' dimensions and then it is converted into 2D. Also, the images have different heights and widths which creates inconsistencies in the pixel intensity calculations and locations. Therefore, every image is resized to height of 300 pixels height and 250 pixels width. Then the images are converted from RGB (i.e. color) to grayscale for further processing. The original pixel values of each image are from 0 to 255 where 0 represents black pixels (i.e. lowest intensity pixels) and 255 represents white pixels (i.e. highest intensity pixels). To ensure the consistency and ease of calculation, the images are normalized to the range of 0 to 1 (fractional values) after reshaping and resizing. The original pixel values varied from 0 to 255 with 0 being the value for black pixel and 255 for white pixel. To normalize the pixel values within the range of 0 to 1, the min-max normalization is used according to Eq. 1. $Z_i$ is the normalized pixel value, $P_i$ is the original pixel value, $Max$ is the maximum range and $Min$ is the minimum range. As Max = 255 and Min = 0, the normalized pixels values are calculated with dividing the original pixel values by 255. Finally, each image is converted into a 2D array storing the pixel intensity for each corresponding cell of the array.

$$Z_i = \frac{P_i - Min}{Max - Min} = \frac{P_i}{Max} = \frac{P_i}{255} \tag{1}$$

## 3.2    Tumor Area Extraction

The tumor area is extracted using filtering, thresholding, region extraction and area-heuristic methods. All of the input images are tested individually with every region-based and area-heuristic region-based segmentation methods.

**Filtering and Thresholding.** Different image equalization and filtering methods are applied on the images so that the best method can be chosen. Thresholding is applied on the images to convert the grayscale images into binary images while removing the non-ROI areas. Thresholds are applied using Otsu's method [20], Ridler-Calvard method [31], Li's iterative method [4], mean of grayscale values, minimum of the histogram values, triangle method, adaptive method, anisotropic method [8] and Yen's method [16]. Among all these methods, filtering using the threshold from Yen's method, adaptive thresholding and anisotropic filtering produces the best results that highlights the tumor better than the other filters. Yen's method uses bilevel thresholding on maximum correlation criteria where a cost function is optimized until the threshold value reduces the discrepancy between the threshold and original image while reducing the number of bits for representing the threshold image. On the other hand, adaptive thresholding uses the mean value of a defined number of neighbors of a pixel as a threshold for the pixel. The anisotropic filtering mentioned above is a texture based filtering.

Another customized (manual) thresholding is also applied to the images. After converting the images into 2D arrays, each pixel intensity is manually checked with a customized threshold value which is varied from 0.3 to 0.9 to find the perfect customized threshold for the images. Most of the time, the whole tumor area does not have the same intensity and some parts of the tumor have intensity value less than 0.6. Therefore, choosing any threshold value less than 0.5 or greater than 0.5 results in either including non-tumor regions or loosing some parts of the tumor area. So, a customized threshold value 0.5 is applied on each pixel of the converted 2D array. If the pixel value is less than 0.5 then it is replaced by 0, otherwise the original value is kept.

**Region-Based Segmentation.** After applying the Yen, anisotropic, customized and adaptive thresholding, the tumor area is extracted from the image using region labeling. All of the connected sets of pixels are identified as individual regions and a label is assigned to each of them after removing artefacts from the image borders. Each region label is then associated with properties of that region like area, centroid, axis lengths etc. Then an overlay is stacked on the original grayscale image to plot each region with a colored rectangle bounding box. Generally, the tumor region is the largest high intensity region. So, the region with the maximum area (i.e. maximum number of connected pixels) is identified as the major region from the image and is considered to be the tumor region.

**Area-Based Heuristic.** One common problem after analyzing the detected major regions from the MRIs, is that the system might detect a non-tumor area of the image that has a connected set of pixels with similar intensities but higher number of pixels. To solve this problem, an area-based heuristic approach is used. The major region collected from the previous part is the largest connected component in the image with the region area possessing the highest number of connected pixels. Therefore, checking only the region area is not enough to find the tumor. Checking the co-ordinates of the centers of the regions is not a valid approach either as the tumor can be located at any place of the image. After assessing all the properties (i.e. Area, Bounding Box, Centroid, Major Axis Length, Minor Axis Length, Convex Area etc.) for each region in a region-based segmentation, the convex area is the most appropriate one to consider for the tumor.

The convex area computation returns the area defined. Due to the finite resolution (i.e., pixels) of the display device, this area is a set of connected pixels. As the images are resized with height of 300 pixels and width of 250 pixels, the complete image is a convex area defined by 75,000 pixels. In most cases, the tumor occupies at most 20% to 30% of the total area. So, the area-based heuristic checks if the extracted major region has a convex area of 22,500 pixels or more (i.e., 30% or more of the total area). To achieve that, the regions are sorted in a separate dictionary according to their convex areas after labeling. Then, the major region is extracted with it's label. The system checks the convex area corresponding to that label and if the convex area is more than 30% of the total area, the sorted dictionary is used to find the label of the next region that has a convex area of less than 22,500 pixels. Then the label for the latter region is used to extract the corresponding characteristics from the properties dictionary to define that as the tumor area.

### 3.3   Convex Hull Generation

Each method explained in the previous part extracts a region from the processed image and detects that as a tumor area which is a connected set of pixels that represents the tumor. As the convex hull is the minimum convex area enclosing a set of points, the pixels are needed to be extracted from the detected area to create the set of points for convex hull algorithm. After extracting all of the tumor pixels from the tumor area, each pixel is considered as a point with x and y coordinates as its' location on a 2D logical matrix. The convex hull algorithm then uses the set of pixel coordinates as the input points and generates the minimum convex area by defining the convex hull enclosing the detected tumor pixels.

### 3.4   Convex Hull Accuracy Detection

The images containing only the convex hulls of the segmented tumor using all of the methods are collected for comparison analysis. Each generated convex hull image is compared to the original tumor image (containing only the tumor) to check the accuracy of the detected tumor convex hull. Different metrics are used on these two images to check which method works better. The details about the performance metrics are included in the next section.

## 4   Experimental Results

### 4.1   Datasets

Two different datasets were used for the experiments. Dataset1 (i.e. the Kaggle brain tumor dataset) [28] includes 253 axial (i.e. horizontal intersection) view MRIs and Dataset2 (i.e. the CjData or Figshare brain tumor dataset) [12,13] includes 3064 axial, coronal (or frontal) and sagittal (or longitudinal) .views of T1-weighted MRIs [5,24]. Table 1 shows the information on the datasets with references.

**Table 1.** The datasets

| Datasets | #Images | View | Type |
|---|---|---|---|
| Dataset1:  Kaggle [28] | 253 | Axial | 2D or 3D |
| Dataset2:  CjData [12,13] | 3064 | Axial, Coronal, Sagittal | 2D (T1) |

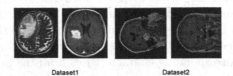

Dataset1                              Dataset2

**Fig. 2.** Sample MRIs from the datasets.

Figure 2 show some sample MRIs from Dataset1 and Dataset2. As all of the images in Dataset1 were axial view images and the experiments could detect the brain tumors more accurately for Dataset1 than for Dataset2. Also, in most cases, the brain tumor images in Dataset1 had higher intensity pixels than the other parts of the brain. Dataset2 included more complex images with horizontal, vertical and cross-sectional views of the skull. The tumors in Dataset2 images were not as clear as the tumors in Dataset1 and the pixel intensities of the tumor regions were similar to the other parts of the brain and sometimes were even lower. All the files of Dataset2 were in .mat format. Each file included an integer label for the tumor type, a patient ID, the MRI data, a vector with coordinates of tumor border and a tumor mask.

### 4.2   Performance Metrics

The performance metrics used to compare the actual tumor and the convex hull of detected tumor region included the commonly used brain tumor segmentation performance measures. The resultant convex hulls were used to calculate the Dice Coefficient ($DCC$), Jaccard Coefficient ($JCC$), *precision*, *recall* and *specificity*. All these metrics work with two images - the reference image and the resultant image.

Let, A be the resulting image (i.e. convex hull of detected tumor region) and B be the reference image (i.e. tumor ground truth). $DCC$ measures the similarity between A and B with Eq. 2. As $DCC$ does not satisfy the triangle inequality, $JCC$ provides a more proper distance metric with Eq. 3.

$$DCC(A, B) = \frac{2|A \cap B|}{|A| + |B|} \tag{2}$$

$$JCC(A, B) = \frac{|A \cap B|}{|A \cup B|} \tag{3}$$

Table 2 and 3 report the results of the various performance metrics applied to Dataset1 and Dataset2, respectively.

### 4.3   Results and Discussion

The *DCC, JCC, precision, recall* and *specificity* were calculated for all MRIs from both datasets and the results are included in Table 2 and 3. The 'Region' result represents the result of the convex hull generated by region-based segmentation after applying Yen filter whereas 'Region (Anisotropic+Yen)' is the region-based segmentation with a combination of Yen and anisotropic filtering. 'Region (Adaptive)' represents the result of region-based segmentation with adaptive thresholding and 'Region (Manual)' is the region-based segmentation with customized thresholding. Similarly, 'ConvexArea' represents the result for region-based segmentation with area heuristic using Yen's method. 'Convex (Anisotropic+Yen)', 'ConvexArea (Adaptive)' and 'ConvexArea (Manual)' are the results for region-based segmentation with area heuristic using anisotropic filtering, adaptive thresholding and customized thresholding respectively.

**Table 2.** Comparisons of segmentation results on Dataset1.

| Method | DCC | JCC | Prec. | Rec. | Spec. |
|---|---|---|---|---|---|
| Region | 0.61 | 0.50 | 0.52 | 0.87 | 0.76 |
| Region (Adaptive) | **0.67** | **0.55** | **0.57** | **0.90** | **0.81** |
| Region (Manual) | 0.57 | 0.46 | 0.48 | 0.86 | 0.75 |
| Region (Anisotropic) | 0.59 | 0.49 | 0.51 | 0.85 | 0.73 |
| ConvexArea | 0.77 | 0.65 | 0.68 | **0.93** | 0.97 |
| ConvexArea (Adaptive) | 0.74 | 0.61 | 0.64 | 0.92 | 0.96 |
| ConvexArea (Manual) | 0.75 | 0.62 | 0.65 | 0.92 | 0.97 |
| ConvexArea (Anisotropic) | **0.79** | **0.69** | **0.70** | **0.93** | **0.98** |

**Table 3.** Comparisons of segmentation results on Dataset2.

| Method | DCC | JCC | Prec. | Rec. | Spec. |
|---|---|---|---|---|---|
| Region | 0.10 | 0.06 | 0.06 | **0.86** | 0.64 |
| Region (Adaptive) | **0.14** | **0.10** | **0.12** | 0.53 | **0.79** |
| Region (Manual) | 0.09 | 0.05 | 0.06 | 0.74 | 0.69 |
| Region (Anisotropic) | 0.09 | 0.05 | 0.05 | **0.86** | 0.63 |
| ConvexArea | 0.13 | 0.10 | 0.16 | 0.16 | **0.97** |
| ConvexArea (Adaptive) | **0.16** | **0.12** | **0.17** | **0.20** | 0.96 |
| ConvexArea (Manual) | 0.10 | 0.08 | 0.13 | 0.14 | 0.96 |
| ConvexArea (Anisotropic) | 0.12 | 0.09 | 0.15 | 0.14 | **0.97** |

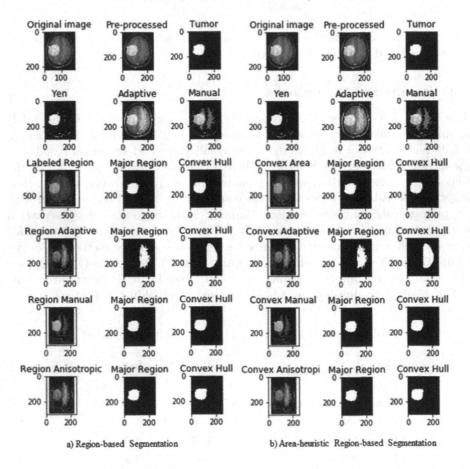

a) Region-based Segmentation          b) Area-heuristic Region-based Segmentation

**Fig. 3.** Sample segmentation execution of an image (Y1.jpg) from Dataset1.

The results reported in Table 2 show that the area-heuristic based region-segmentation generated better results than the region-based segmentation considering all the performance metrics values for Dataset1. These results have been

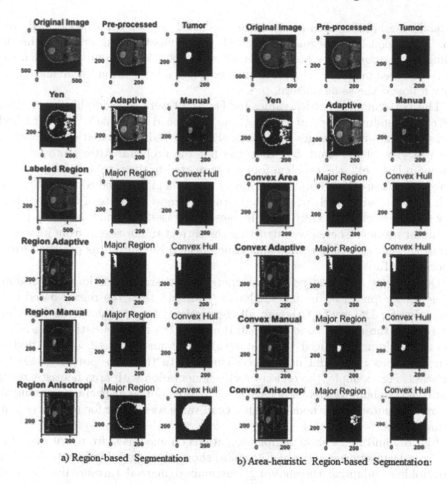

a) Region-based Segmentation          b) Area-heuristic Region-based Segmentation

**Fig. 4.** Sample segmentation execution of an image (222.jpg) from Dataset2.

validated by a domain expert who confirmed that the developed approach is promising and could lead to a stable solution which will guide pathologists and may act as a seed for developing a learning tool for juniors to benefit from their seniors. Among the methods of normal region-based segmentations, region-segmentation with adaptive thresholding achieved the best results in terms of all the performance metrics. In case of the area-heuristic methods, the anisotropic filtering with area heuristic showed the best results for tumor segmentation. The region-based segmentation with area heuristic produced the convex hulls with second highest dice coefficient values and region-based segmentation with area heuristic using customized thresholding had the third highest DCC values.

The same thing was true for JCC which means the convex hull generated from the extracted area was very similar to the original tumor using area-heuristic anisotropic filtering, area-heuristic region-based segmentation while manual thresholding area-heuristic region-based segmentation performed well too. The region-based segmentation with area heuristic using adaptive thresholding also performed well and had a difference of 1%–4% from the other area-heuristic based methods. The other metrics values like precision, recall and specificity followed the same pattern.

The performance metrics values for Dataset2 were considerably lower than the corresponding values of Dataset1 as mentioned in Table 3. Dataset2 had almost 12 times more images than Dataset1 and it had a combination of different types of view of the skull, but that was not the problem. After analyzing the images in Dataset2, the problem found was related to the pixel intensities of the images. In Dataset1, the tumor region was mostly a highlighted connected region with high-intensity pixels whereas in Dataset2 almost all parts of the image had very similar intensities. Only a few images in Dataset2 had high intensity pixels for tumor regions. Therefore, extracting the correct tumor region from images of Dataset2 was very challenging. This issue affected the output as per the results reported in Table 3.

Despite the lower values for the metrics, the area-heuristic based region-segmentation produced better results for Dataset1 than the region-based segmentation for Dataset2. Although all the methods for area-heuristics had similar results, the region-based segmentation with the area heuristic using adaptive thresholding produced the best results. But for Dataset2, all the performance metrics values did not behave similarly to the corresponding ones for Dataset1. For example, the region-based segmentation with area heuristic using adaptive thresholding had higher DCC, JCC, precision and specificity among all region-segmentation methods, but the recall value was higher for regular region-segmentation.

Figure 3 and Fig. 4 show sample executions on one image from Dataset1 and one from Dataset2 respectively. Figure 3a) shows the original image, tumor, Yen thresholding, adaptive thresholding, customized/manual thresholding, and all four region-segmentation and Fig. 3b) shows area-heuristic region-segmentation for the same image. Similarly, Fig. 4a) and 4b) are samples of all eight methods on an image from Dataset2.

For Fig. 3, region-segmentation, region-segmentation with anisotropic filtering and region-segmentation with manual thresholding were very similar for both datasets and had very similar convex hulls whereas region-segmentation with adaptive thresholding extracted an incorrect area in both cases. Figure 4 shows the results for an image from Dataset2. Only adaptive thresholding and anisotropic filtering produced incorrect regions whereas manual thresholding had the most accurate tumor convex hulls. The problem with lower intensity tumor pixels can be seen in the Dataset2 images. As other parts of the image included a large set of connected high intensity pixels (i.e. part of skull or part of other healthy brain tissues) and the tumor pixels had lower intensities with a smaller connected set of pixels, the system picked the major region from the skull image and detected that as the tumor region.

The intensity overlapping issue was a common problem for many images in Dataset2 that had large set of connected high intensity pixels from parts of the brain or skull and the tumor had a small set of connected low intensity pixels. Hence, the system detected non-tumors parts as tumors. After applying the convex area heuristic condition, the system detected the correct tumor region with area-heuristic region-based segmentation. The area heuristic could not detect the correct tumor region for manual thresholding and anisotropic filtering, but it at least stopped detecting a large part of skull as tumor and concentrated on smaller connected high intensity regions.

## 5  Conclusion

Brain tumor image segmentation is a well-known research area that have been explored using thresholding, supervised/unsupervised machine learning and deep learning methods for a long time and achieved high accuracy. The goal of this research was to solve the same problem from a geometric perspective - 'Brain tumor segmentation from MRIs as an application of convex hull generation'. The main focus of this research was to explore further possibilities of applying computational geometry tools for brain tumor segmentation. Experiments done on different thresholding and filtering methods and their combination with region-based segmentation showed that tumor pixels could be identified and distinguished from the other parts of the image with certain threshold conditions. But applying a more directed convex area based heuristic on the thresholdings and region-segmentation improved the tumor detection considerably. The major limitation of the system was that it could not extract the tumor area from many images where the tumor area pixels were not the only high intensity connected set of pixels. A possible future extension of this research would be to define a better heuristic-based approach using other region properties and their combinations to extract only the tumor region from the image. This would include other image properties like texture, shape and applying brain-based pre-processing as skull stripping.

## References

1. Bharathi, A.S., Manimegalai, D.: 3D digital reconstruction of brain tumor from MRI scans using Delaunay triangulation and patches. ARPN J. Eng. Appl. Sci **10**, 9227–9232 (2015)
2. Tiwari, A., Srivastava, S., Pant, M.: Brain tumor segmentation and classification from magnetic resonance images: review of selected methods from 2014 to 2019. Pattern Recogn. Lett. **131**, 244–260 (2020)
3. Menze, B.H., et al.: The multimodal brain tumor image segmentation benchmark (BRATS). IEEE Trans. Med. Imaging **34**(10), 1993–2024 (2014)
4. Li, C.H., Tam, P.K.: An iterative algorithm for minimum cross entropy thresholding. Pattern Recogn. Lett. **19**(8), 771–776 (1998)
5. Clare, S.: Magnetic resonance imaging of brain function. https://users.fmrib.ox.ac.uk/~stuart/thesis/chapter_3/section3_2.html

6. Di Ieva, A. (ed.): The Fractal Geometry of the Brain. Springer, New York (2016). https://doi.org/10.1007/978-1-4939-3995-4
7. Barrow Neurological Foundation: Research to cure brain cancer within the next decade. https://www.supportbarrow.org/programs-that-save-lives/brain-tumor/
8. Gerig, G., Kubler, O., Kikinis, R., Jolesz, F.A.: Nonlinear anisotropic filtering of MRI data. IEEE Trans. Med. Imaging 11(2), 221–232 (1992)
9. Mohsen, H., et al.: Classification using deep learning neural networks for brain tumors. Future Comput. Inform. J. 3(1), 68–71 (2018)
10. Shally, H.R., Chitharanjan, K.: Tumor volume calculation of brain from MRI slices. Int. J. Comput. Sci. Eng. Technol. (IJCSET) 4(8), 1126–1132 (2013)
11. Ali, H.M., Kaiser, M.S., Mahmud, M.: Application of convolutional neural network in segmenting brain regions from MRI data. In: Liang, P., Goel, V., Shan, C. (eds.) BI 2019. LNAI, vol. 11976, pp. 136–146. Springer, Cham (2019). https://doi.org/10.1007/978-3-030-37078-7_14
12. Cheng, J., et al.: Enhanced performance of brain tumor classification via tumor region augmentation and partition. PLoS ONE 10(10), e0140381 (2015)
13. Cheng, J., et al.: Retrieval of brain tumors by adaptive spatial pooling and fisher vector representation. PLoS ONE 11(6), e0157112 (2016)
14. Zook, J.M., Iftekharuddin, K.M.: Statistical analysis of fractal-based brain tumor detection algorithms. Magn. Reson. Imaging 23(5), 671–678 (2005)
15. Bell, J.S., et al.: Global incidence of brain and spinal tumors by geographic region and income level based on cancer registry data. J. Clin. Neurosci. 66, 121–127 (2019)
16. Yen, J., Chang, F., Chang, S.: A new criterion for automatic multilevel thresholding. IEEE Trans. Image Process. 4(3), 370–378 (1995)
17. Iftekharuddin, K.M., et al.: Fractal-based brain tumor detection in multimodal MRI. Appl. Math. Comput. 207(1), 23–41 (2009)
18. Iftekharuddin, K.M., Jia, W., Marsh, R.: Fractal analysis of tumor in brain MR images. Mach. Vis. Appl. 13(5), 352–362 (2003). https://doi.org/10.1007/s00138-002-0087-9
19. Abd-Ellah, M.K., et al.: A review on brain tumor diagnosis from MRI images: practical implications, key achievements, and lessons learned. Magn. Reson. Imaging 61, 300–318 (2019)
20. Otsu, N.: A threshold selection method from gray-level histograms. IEEE Trans. Syst. Man Cybern. 9(1), 62–66 (1979)
21. Singh, N., Arya, R., Agrawal, R.K.: A convex hull approach in conjunction with Gaussian mixture model for salient object detection. Digit. Sig. Process. 55, 22–31 (2016)
22. American Association of Neurological Surgeons (AANS): Brain tumors. https://www.aans.org/en/Patients/Neurosurgical-Conditions-and-Treatments/Brain-Tumors
23. Preparata, F.P., Shamos, M.I.: Computational Geometry: An Introduction. Springer, New York (2012)
24. Cambridge University Press: Cognitive neuroscience methods to study the adolescent brain. https://www.cambridge.org/core/books/neuroscience-of-adolescence/cognitive-neuroscience-methods-to-study-the-adolescent-brain/FC6F05A89E2A35EBE37E686BA7BE489D
25. Graham, R.L., Yao, F.F.: Finding the convex hull of a simple polygon. J. Algorithms 4(4), 324–331 (1983)
26. Liu, R., Zhang, H., Busby, J.: Convex hull covering of polygonal scenes for accurate collision detection in games. In: Graphics Interface, pp. 203–210 (2008)

27. Shivhare, S.N., Kumar, N., Singh, N.: A hybrid of active contour model and convex hull for automated brain tumor segmentation in multimodal MRI. Multimed. Tools Appl. **78**(24), 34207–34229 (2019). https://doi.org/10.1007/s11042-019-08048-4
28. Rai, S., et al.: A hybrid approach to brain tumor detection from MRI images using computer vision. J. Innov. Comput. Sci. Eng. **8**(2), 8–12 (2019)
29. Roy, S., et al.: Artefact removal and skull elimination from MRI of brain image. Int. J. Sci. Eng. Res. **4**(6), 163–170 (2013)
30. Saman, S., Narayanan, S.J.: Survey on brain tumor segmentation and feature extraction of MR images. Int. J. Multimed. Inf. Retrieval **8**(2), 79–99 (2019). https://doi.org/10.1007/s13735-018-0162-2
31. Ridler, T.W., Calvard, S.: Picture thresholding using an iterative selection method. IEEE Trans. Syst. Man Cybern. **8**(8), 630–632 (1978)

# Informatics Paradigms for Brain and Mental Health Research

# Computer-Aided Diagnosis Framework
# for ADHD Detection Using Quantitative EEG

Ruchi Holker$^{(\boxtimes)}$ ⓘ and Seba Susan ⓘ

Delhi Technological University, New Delhi, India
ruchi.holker@gmail.com

**Abstract.** Attention Deficit Hyperactivity Disorder (ADHD) is a mental disorder that is marked by abnormally high levels of impulsivity, hyperactivity and inattention. One of the methods to detect and diagnose brain disorders is Electroencephalogram (EEG). This paper proposes a framework that uses Quantitative Electroencephalogram (QEEG) features to diagnose ADHD in children. A 19-channel EEG signal is used to extract the spectral, amplitude, functional connectivity and Range EEG (rEEG) features from five frequency bands to diagnose ADHD children. Four feature selection methods: ANOVA, Chi-square, Gini Index and Information Gain are used to rank the QEEG features based on their relative importance to the classification task. The feature ranks are then averaged and the top-600 most discriminative features are passed as the input to an array of classifiers. We carried out experiments on a benchmark ADHD dataset and proved that our proposed framework gives better accuracy as compared to the state of the art. The highest accuracy of 81.82% is obtained with the Random Forest classifier, while the KNN, SVM and ANN classifiers yield accuracies of 78.51%, 76.86% and 76.93%, respectively.

**Keywords:** Attention Deficit Hyperactivity Disorder · Quantitative EEG features · Range EEG features · Functional connectivity features · Amplitude features · Spectral features

## 1 Introduction

Attention-deficit hyperactivity disorder (ADHD) is a long-term mental health condition that is marked by inattention and/or hyperactivity-impulsivity. It affects how people work and their intellectual growth. ADHD is estimated to impact 5% of children globally and is one of the most frequent mental disorders affecting children and adults [1]. Affected children/people lack the cognitive ability to follow brief talks and operate in a goal-oriented manner. As a result, despite having an IQ above average, their education and work performance is below average. The constant feeling of failure causes most afflicted people to develop further psychological issues, such as anxiety disorders, depression, and drug usage. Two gene mutations: dopamine transporter (DAT1) and dopamine D4 receptor are linked to the ADHD phenotype [11]. Dopamine and noradrenalin metabolism and neurotransmission in the prefrontal cortex and other subcortical areas are all dysfunctional in adults. Three clinical presentations of ADHD are characterized based on the

© Springer Nature Switzerland AG 2022
M. Mahmud et al. (Eds.): BI 2022, LNAI 13406, pp. 229–240, 2022
https://doi.org/10.1007/978-3-031-15037-1_19

most prevalent features: mainly ADHD-I: inattentive type, ADHD-H: predominantly hyperactive impulsive type, and ADHD-C: mixed type clinical presentations [2, 3].

In the last two decades, several studies have explored the usage of different types of QEEG features belonging to the frequency, spatial, temporal, and spectral domains to distinguish between ADHD and healthy individuals [22, 23]. Absolute power and relative power of a EEG signal were used as QEEG features in [18], with t-test and Principal Component Analysis (PCA) being employed for feature selection. The NEURAL toolbox that includes Range EEG (rEEG) features was proposed by Toole et al. to classify EEG signals [17]. The Approximate entropy (ApEn) as a nonlinear information-theoretic metric and spectral analysis of each band was utilized to analyze the EEG signal in [4]. The results of this investigation demonstrated that the mean approximate entropy of the ADHD patients was considerably lower than that of the healthy individuals over the right frontal regions (Fp2 and F8) while doing a cognitive activity, but not while the subjects were at rest state. Ghassemi et al. conducted a study to investigate EEG signals in adults while performing a Continuous Performance Test (CPT) using three nonlinear features: wavelet entropy (WE), correlation dimension (CD) and Lyapunov exponent (LE), and classified them using the K-Nearest Neighbor (KNN) classifier [5]. Another study by the same authors explores several frequency domain features from Event Related Potentials obtained from Independent Components of EEG (ERPIC), for an adult performing a CPT task [12]. They revealed a significant correlation between the clinical situation of the ADHD and normal adult participants, and several features were selected from independent components of EEG signals for the classification. The chaotic nonlinear dynamics of EEG signals was quantified using the multifractal singularity spectrum, the maximum Lyapunov exponent, and approximate entropy in another research [6]. Features that were highly associated were extracted through the application of PCA. They also analyzed that the greatest Lyapunov exponent (LE) over the left frontal-central cortex was significantly different between ADHD and age-matched control groups. In addition, in the prefrontal cortex of ADHD patients, mean approximation entropy was considerably lower. Finally, they found that nonlinear characteristics were more effective than band power features in distinguishing between ADHD and normal behavior. In another study, fractal dimension (FD), ApEn and LE nonlinear features were used for classification using a multilayer perceptron (MLP) neural network [7]. Double input symmetrical relevance (DISR) and minimum Redundancy Maximum Relevance (mRMR) approaches were used to select the best features for classification. Region-wise nonlinear properties (LE, Higuchi fractal dimension, Katz fractal dimension, and Sevcik fractal dimension) of EEG signals were classified by using a multilayer perceptron neural network in [8].

A novel idea was proposed by TaghiBeyglou et al. in [9] to combine the nonlinear EEG features with temporal and spectral analysis. This work used a combination of filter banks, time windowing techniques, Common spatial pattern (CSP) and nonlinear features for the analysis of ADHD data. Rezaeezadeh et al. developed two classification methods based on univariate data derived from individual EEG recording channels, and multivariate features collected from brain lobes for distinguishing ADHD children from normal children [10]. Entropy measurements were employed as nonlinear univariate and multivariate characteristics in [10]; the authors proved that entropy mapping could be a useful tool to visually track the changes in the brain region. The nonlinear features and decomposition method were recently combined to extract the features from EEG signals for ADHD detection [13]. The EEG signals were decomposed using empirical mode decomposition (EMD) and discrete wavelet transform (DWT), and the autoregressive modelling coefficient and relative wavelet energy were calculated. From the decomposed coefficient, a number of nonlinear features were retrieved for the classification. Several EEG features from different domains are used to diagnose ADHD and healthy individuals. The authors in their previous work have used a mix of amplitude, spectral, range and connectivity QEEG features for alcoholism diagnosis [32].

Several studies have explored the ADHD disorder and their impact on child brain functioning by using EEG. ADHD children show a significant difference in the direct information transfers from one electrode to other as compared to healthy children [20]. Coherence features have been used to find the functional connectivity and synchronization between brain regions of ADHD and healthy subjects [29–31]. The direct phase transfer entropy was used to find the flow of information transfer between the brain regions of ADHD and healthy children [21]. To investigate the structural and functional information of ADHD subjects, graph signal processing and graph learning techniques have recently become popular [24]. Deep learning and Convolutional Neural network (CNN) are also some of the recent techniques that have been applied to distinguish between ADHD and healthy children [25, 26]. Our paper proposes a framework that extracts a set of discriminative quantitative EEG features from spectral, amplitude, rEEG and functional connectivity domains to design an automated computer-aided diagnosis system for ADHD children. In this paper, Sect. 2 describes the materials and method for the proposed framework. Section 3 discusses the experimentation results, and Sect. 4 concludes the paper.

## 2 Materials and Method

### 2.1 Dataset

We have used a recently introduced ADHD dataset of raw EEG recordings of ADHD and healthy children, available online at [35]. A total of 121 children participated in this study; from these, 61 children were diagnosed with ADHD and 60 were healthy. Out of 61 ADHD participants, there were 48 boys and 13 girls, and the mean age was 9.62 ± 1.75 years. Similarly, among the 60 healthy children there were 50 boys and ten girls, with a mean age of 9.85 ± 1.77 years. An experienced child and adolescent psychiatrist used the DSM-IV criteria listed in [36] to classify children with ADHD. DSM-IV has listed some scales for inattention and hyperactivity-impulsivity symptoms. Some criteria for rating scales of inattention are; - failing to pay attention to schoolwork, less attention in play activity, lack awareness in listing, having difficulties in organizing a task, avoiding the task that requires attention, forgetting daily activities, and getting easily distracted by extraneous stimuli. Some of the criteria for rating scales of hyperactivity-impulsivity are: - difficulty in awaiting a turn in any task, frequently interrupting or intruding on others, fidgeting with hands or feet or squirming in the seat, often leaving the seat in the classroom, and talking excessively.

The patients were referred to the Roozbeh Hospital's psychiatric clinic in Tehran, Iran, for an ADHD evaluation. EEG signals were acquired using a digital instrument (SD-C24, Sholeh Danesh Co., Tehran, Iran) (Tehran, Iran). The visual attention task was used to develop the EEG recording procedure. The children were given a task in which they were presented with 20 photos of various characters, and were instructed to count them. The images were picked at random, in sizes large enough to be seen, and the number of characters in each picture was calculated at random between 5 and 16. Each image was presented immediately after the child's response to ensure constant stimulation during the EEG recording. As a result, the length of the EEG recording is determined by the child's performance. The correct and incorrect replies were not taken into account, and the activity was not developed with rewards in mind. During this experiment, 19 electrodes: Fz, Cz, Pz, C3, T3, C4, T4, Fp1, Fp2, F3, F4, F7, F8, P3, P4, T5, T6, O1, O2, were put on the scalp using the 10–20 system as displayed in Fig. 1. The data is recorded at a 128 Hz sampling frequency with 16 bits EEG resolution. Electrodes A1 and A2 are used as earlobe references.

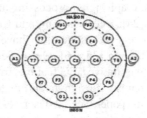

**Fig. 1.** 19 electrode positions on the brain scalp according to the 10–20 system.

## 2.2 Proposed Method

The proposed method is divided into four steps. In the first step, we pre-process the raw EEG data and decompose the EEG signal into five frequency bands. After the pre-processing, we extract 540 features from the amplitude domain, 714 features from the spectral domain, 720 features from rEEG and 450 functional connectivity QEEG features for classification. In the spectral domain, we extracted four features (Absolute and relative power, approximate and permutation entropy) using the common average reference montage with respect to the entire signal and the remaining features were extracted using bipolar montage. So, the feature vector used for the classification has 2424 features from spectral, amplitude, rEEG and functional connectivity domains. In third step, we identified the most discriminative 600 features by averaging the feature ranks given by four popular feature selection techniques. The final step is to classify the selected QEEG features using Random Forest, SVM, KNN and ANN classifiers. Figure 2 shows the pipeline of the proposed framework. Each step is described in detail as follows.

**Pre-processing.** All EEG signals were digitized at 128 Hz sampling frequency in the pre-processing stage. Then each signal is filtered using bandpass filter to generate five

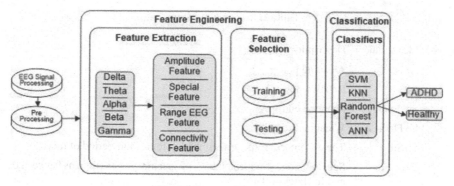

**Fig. 2.** Proposed framework.

frequency bands corresponding to *delta* ($\delta$: 0–3 Hz), *theta* ($\theta$: 4–7 Hz), *alpha* ($\alpha$: 8–12 Hz), *beta* ($\beta$: 13–30 Hz), and *gamma* ($\gamma$: 30–100 Hz) [14, 14].

**The topographic map represents** the activity across the scalp. Figure 3 displays the band-wise topographic map of an ADHD and a healthy participant. In this representation, the blue colour across the scalp represents less activity and the red colour represents high activity. As observed from Fig. 3, the *delta* band (Fig. 3(a)) shows low activity for ADHD children while performing the task while the *gamma* band (Fig. 3 (e)) shows high activity.

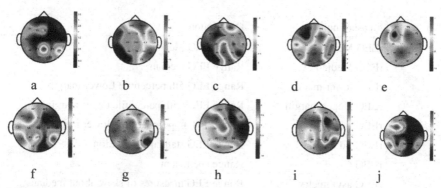

**Fig. 3.** Topographic map of ADHD and healthy participants. ADHD band-wise topographic map is displayed from (a) to (e), and the healthy participant band-wise topographic map is displayed from (f) to (j). The blue colour represents less activity and the red colour represents high activity across the scalp. (Color figure online)

**Feature Extraction.** In this step, we extract twenty-six QEEG features from each of the 19 channels in each frequency band. Tables 1, 2, 3 and 4 list the extracted features from four different quantitative measurements. Table 1 lists all the features extracted from the spectral domain. Spectral features are obtained by converting the EEG signal into the frequency domain, with frequencies ranging from 0 to 100 Hz at a resolution of 0.5 Hz using the Fast Fourier transformation (FFT). Afterwards, all the features are extracted from each of the five bands for the 19 EEG channels.

**Table 1.** Spectral measures.

| S. No. | Measurement | Description |
|---|---|---|
| 1 | AP | Absolute power |
| 2 | RP | Relative power |
| 3 | Sp_En | Shannon entropy |
| 4 | Sp Flatness | Wiener entropy |
| 5 | Sp Sd | The difference in spectral estimation for a short period of time |
| 6 | Edge Freq | Spectral_edge_frequency: 95% of spectral-power contains between 0.5 and fc Hz(cut-off-frq) |
| 7 | Fd | Fractal-dimension |
| 8 | ApEn | Approximate entropy |
| 9 | PeEn | Permutation entropy |

Table 2 lists all the range EEG (rEEG) measurements [16, 16] that are similar to amplitude-integrated EEG and measure the peak-to-peak amplitude of EEG signal.

**Table 2.** rEEG measures.

| S. No. | Measurement | Description |
|---|---|---|
| 1 | rEEG Mean | Range EEG Mean |
| 2 | rEEG Median | Range EEG median |
| 3 | rEEG lower margin | Range EEG:5th percentile Lower margin |
| 4 | rEEG Upper margin | Range EEG 95th percentile upper margin |
| 5 | rEEG width | Rang EEG: upper margin – lower margin |
| 6 | rEEG Sd | Range EEG standard Deviation |
| 7 | rEEG Cv | Range coefficient |
| 8 | rEEG asymmetry | Range EEG measures of skew about median |

Similarly, Table 3 lists all the functional connectivity measurements. Functional connectivity (FC) refers to features that measure how the neural activity in one brain area interacts with other brain regions. To find the FC features of a brain, we have to arrange the EEG signal in a particular montage. So here, we use the bipolar montage to extract the FC features. Table 4 lists all the amplitude features computed from signal power and signal envelope.

**Feature Selection.** Feature selection is a technique to reduce the input vector dimension for classification. In the proposed framework, we used the ensemble feature ranking method to select the most discriminative features for classification. We used four feature selection techniques: -ANOVA, Chi-square test, Information Gain and Gini Index (GI)

**Table 3.** Functional connectivity measures.

| S.No | Measurement | Description |
|------|-------------|-------------|
| 1 | Connectivity BSI | Brain Symmetry Index |
| 2 | Connectivity Corr | Pearson Correlation-between envelopes of hemisphere-paired channels |
| 3 | Connectivity Coh_mean | Coherence-mean value |
| 4 | Connectivity coh_freqmax | Coherence-frequency of maximum value |
| 5 | Connectivity con_max | Coherence-maximum value |

**Table 4.** Amplitude measures

| S. No | Measurement | Description |
|-------|-------------|-------------|
| 1 | Total power | Total power of a signal |
| 2 | SD | Standard-Deviation |
| 3 | SK | Skewness |
| 4 | KU | Kurtosis |
| 5 | Env Mean | Envelop Mean Value |
| 6 | Env SD | Envelop standard deviation |

to obtain the feature ranks which were then averaged and sorted in the ascending order. The top-600 features were thus obtained from the averaged feature ranks.

**Classifiers.** In our experiments, four classifiers are used to predict the accuracies of various methods. These are explained below. The Random Forest (RF) classifier is a collection of individual decision trees, and each tree makes an individual prediction. The most voted class is the final prediction of the classifier. The KNN classifier assigns class labels to the test samples based on their similarity to those in the training set. A distance function is used to find the distance from the nearest neighbours. Support Vector Machine (SVM) classifier separates the classes by finding the best hyperplane for dividing the multidimensional space into categories. The artificial Neural Network (ANN) is a brain-inspired network that consists of an input layer, one or more hidden layers, and an output layer. A weight is associated with each connection and the performance of the network may be improved repeatedly by adjusting the network weights.

## 3   Results and Discussions

The machine configuration in this study has an Intel(R) Core (TM) i5-8265U CPU running at 1.80 GHz, 8 GB of RAM, with Windows 10 Professional K 64 bit installed. To conduct the experiments and analysis, we used the MATLAB R2019a version.

This section summarizes the findings of this study. A comprehensive evaluation has been conducted to evaluate the proposed framework for classifying the EEG signals of ADHD and healthy children. The accuracy of the proposed method and three state-of-art methods are shown in Table 5. Using the Random Forest classifier, we achieved the best accuracy of 81.82% for the proposed method.

Our feature vector comprises of 2424 features obtained from five frequency bands corresponding to the 19 EEG channels, and ranked separately using Information gain, Chi-square, ANOVA and GI feature selection techniques. Next, we averaged the feature ranks to yield the top-600 discriminative features that are passed as the input to an array of classifiers. We performed five-fold (split the data into 80–20 ratio) cross-validation to train the model. The k-value determines the number of nearest neighbours in KNN. We used $k = 8$ and the Manhattan function to calculate the distance. We used a RF classifier having 500 trees of depth 8 with six nodes in each subtree. For SVM, we employed an RBF kernel with a penalty value of 10 and an eps of 0.1. We use a rectifying linear unit activation function (ReLU) and two hidden layers with 90 and 10 neurons, respectively, in the ANN classifier. The Adam optimizer, which is a stochastic gradient-based optimizer for network weight optimization is used with 100 iterations. Table 5 presents the findings of the proposed technique for all four classifiers (KNN, SVM, RF, and ANN) in terms of accuracy, F1-score, precision, and recall. We compare our findings to those of [17–19], which are state-of-the-art techniques for QEEG-based classifications.

**Table 5.** Comparison of the classification accuracy of the proposed method and existing work

| Existing method | Model | Accuracy | F1-score | Precision | Recall |
|---|---|---|---|---|---|
| Mumtaz et al. 2016 [18] | KNN | 69.42% | 0.6942 | 0.6948 | 0.6942 |
| | SVM | 70.25% | 0.7024 | 0.7028 | 0.7025 |
| | RF | 69.42% | 0.6940 | 0.6780 | 0.6842 |
| | ANN | 67.77% | 0.6774 | 0.7678 | 0.6777 |
| Toole et al. 2016 [17] | KNN | 71.90% | 0.7048 | 0.7678 | 0.7190 |
| | SVM | 73.55% | 0.7353 | 0.7367 | 0.7355 |
| | RF | 79.34% | 0.7934 | 0.7934 | 0.7934 |
| | ANN | 79.34% | 0.7931 | 0.7955 | 0.7934 |
| Huang et al. 2020 [19] | KNN | 63.64% | 0.6356 | 0.6380 | 0.6364 |
| | SVM | 67.77% | 0.6770 | 0.6787 | 0.6777 |
| | RF | 75.21% | 0.7520 | 0.7523 | 0.7521 |
| | ANN | 74.38% | 0.7436 | 0.7443 | 0.7438 |
| Proposed method | KNN | 78.51% | 0.7820 | 0.8009 | 0.7851 |
| | SVM | 76.86% | 0.7685 | 0.7688 | 0.7686 |
| | RF | 81.82% | 0.8179 | 0.8195 | 0.8182 |
| | ANN | 76.93% | 0.7692 | 0.7691 | 0.7693 |

We also find the band-wise number of features shortlisted in the top-600 selected features for EEG classification. When we carefully examine the result, it is found that bands *delta, alpha* and *gamma* are equally important for ADHD classification among all the bands, as we observe in Fig. 4. Similarly, we also compute the participation of each electrode in the top-600 selected features for classification. Figure 5 displays a detailed analysis of the electrode participation for classification. The feature count for a pair of electrodes in bipolar montage is incremented by one for both the electrodes, for visualization purpose only.

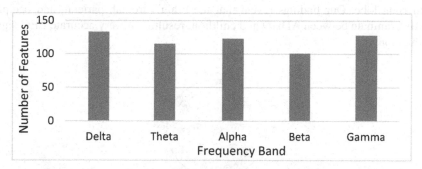

**Fig. 4.** Number of features belonging to the five frequency bands in the top-600 feature subset.

Though all the 19 electrodes contribute to the shortlisted set of features for classification, but FP2, O2, F7 and F8 are slightly more important, as observed from Fig. 5. In [28], it is mentioned that for the eyes open resting state, the frontal and central region, especially electrode FP2, shows some significant activity, and for the eye closing state, the O1 electrode shows significant changes. Similarly, both the frontal and parietal regions are implicated in ADHD and involve brain networks and attention [27]. This evidence indicates that our framework is informative and gives accurate analysis. Our work has some limitations, though, such as it requires a fixed setup where the number of bands is fixed. We may try adaptive sub-bands with more advanced features in future.

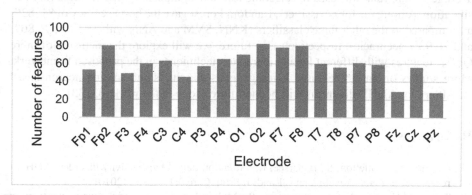

**Fig. 5.** The number of features associated with different electrodes in the top-600 feature subset.

We also tried to find out the more affected part of the brain in ADHD children by examining a reduced feature set comprising of the top-100 ranked features. Figure 6 displays the electrodes contributing to the maximum number of features in the reduced feature set. The O2, P8 and T7 electrodes are related to the right occipital region, right parietal lobe and the left temporal lobe, respectively. Two electrodes are selected from the frontal lobe, F7 associated with the left frontal region, and FP2 associated with the frontal right lobe. Our findings reveal that the brain's frontal, parietal, and occipital areas discriminate between ADHD and children, resulting in very accurate EEG signal classification.

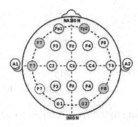

**Fig. 6.** The most discriminative electrodes for ADHD detection.

## 4    Conclusion

In this paper, we designed and implemented a QEEG features based classification framework for identifying ADHD and healthy children. After pre-processing the data, 19 electrodes' EEG signals were divided into five frequency bands. The spectral, amplitude, rEEG and functional connectivity features were extracted from each frequency band. The average feature rank was used to select the top-600 significant QEEG features for classification. Among the four classifiers, Random Forest gave the best accuracy of 81.82% as compared to the other three classifiers (KNN, SVM and ANN with 78.51%, 76.86% and 76.93% accuracies, respectively). In future, we will explore the inclusion of more QEEG features with different feature extraction techniques in the proposed framework. More studies on ensemble-based heterogeneous classifiers and spiking neuron-based classifiers for ADHD diagnosis will be the future scope of the work [33, 33].

## References

1. Ougrin, D., Chatterton, S., Banarsee, R.: Attention deficit hyperactivity disorder (ADHD): review for primary care clinicians. Lond. J. Prim. Care **3**(1), 45–51 (2010)
2. Tosto, M.G., Momi, S.K., Asherson, P., Malki, K.: A systematic review of attention deficit hyperactivity disorder (ADHD) and mathematical ability: current findings and future implications. BMC Med. **13**(1), 1–14 (2015)
3. Guha, M.: Diagnostic and statistical manual of mental disorders: DSM-5. Ref. Rev. **28**, 36–37 (2014)

4. Sohn, H., et al.: Linear and nonlinear EEG analysis of adolescents with attention-deficit/hyperactivity disorder during a cognitive task. Clin. Neurophysiol. **121**(11), 1863–1870 (2010)
5. Ghassemi, F., Hassan_Moradi, M., Tehrani-Doost, M., Abootalebi, V.: Using nonlinear features of EEG for ADHD/normal participants' classification. Procedia-Soc. Behav. Sci. **32**, 148–152 (2012)
6. Khoshnoud, S., Nazari, M.A., Shamsi, M.: Functional brain dynamic analysis of ADHD and control children using nonlinear dynamical features of EEG signals. J. Integr. Neurosci. **17**(1), 17–30 (2018)
7. Mohammadi, M.R., Khaleghi, A., Nasrabadi, A.M., Rafieivand, S., Begol, M., Zarafshan, H.: EEG classification of ADHD and normal children using nonlinear features and neural network. Biomed. Eng. Lett. **6**(2), 66–73 (2016)
8. Allahverdy, A., Moghadam, AK., Mohammadi, M.R., Nasrabadi, A.M.: Detecting ADHD children using the attention continuity as nonlinear feature of EEG. Front. Biomed. Technol. **3**, 1–2, 28–33 (2016)
9. TaghiBeyglou, B., Hasanzadeh, N., Bagheri, F., Jahed, M.: ADHD diagnosis in children using common spatial pattern and nonlinear analysis of filter banked EEG. In: 2020 28th Iranian Conference on Electrical Engineering (ICEE), pp. 1–5. IEEE (2020)
10. Rezaeezadeh, M., Shamekhi, S., Shamsi, M.: Attention deficit hyperactivity disorder diagnosis using nonlinear univariate and multivariate EEG measurements: a preliminary study. Phys. Eng. Sci. Med. **43**(2), 577–592 (2020). https://doi.org/10.1007/s13246-020-00858-3
11. Singh, A., Yeh, C.J., Verma, N., Das, A.K.: Overview of attention deficit hyperactivity disorder in young children. Health Psychol. Res. **3**(2) (2015)
12. Ghassemi, F., Moradi, M.H., Tehrani-Doost, M., Abootalebi, V.: Classification of ADHD/normal participants using frequency features of ERP's Independent Components. In: 2010 17th Iranian Conference of Biomedical Engineering (ICBME), pp. 1–4. IEEE (2010)
13. Tor, H.T., et al.: Automated detection of conduct disorder and attention deficit hyperactivity disorder using decomposition and nonlinear techniques with EEG signals. Comput. Methods Programs Biomed. **200**, 105941 (2021)
14. Saby, J.N., Marshall, P.J.: The utility of EEG band power analysis in the study of infancy and early childhood. Dev. Neuropsychol. **37**(3), 253–273 (2012)
15. https://en.wikipedia.org/wiki/Gamma_wave. Accessed 14 June 2022
16. O'Reilly, D., Navakatikyan, M.A., Filip, M., Greene, D., Van Marter, L.J.: Peak-to-peak amplitude in neonatal brain monitoring of premature infants. Clin. Neurophysiol. **123**(11), 2139–2153 (2012)
17. Toole, J.M.O., Boylan, G.B.: NEURAL: quantitative features for newborn EEG using Matlab. arXiv preprint arXiv:1704.05694 (2017)
18. Mumtaz, W., Vuong, P.L., Xia, L., Malik, A.S., Abd Rashid, R.B.: Automatic diagnosis of alcohol use disorder using EEG features. Knowl. Based Syst. **105**, 48–59 (2016)
19. Huang, H., et al.: Early consciousness disorder in acute large hemispheric infarction: an analysis based on quantitative EEG and brain network characteristics. Neurocrit. Care **33**(2), 376–388 (2020)
20. Abbas, A.K., Azemi, G., Amiri, S., Ravanshadi, S., Omidvarnia, A.: Effective connectivity in brain networks estimated using EEG signals is altered in children with ADHD. Comput. Biol. Med. **134**, 104515 (2021)
21. Ekhlasi, A., Nasrabadi, A.M., Mohammadi, M.R.: Direction of information flow between brain regions in ADHD and healthy children based on EEG by using directed phase transfer entropy. Cogn. Neurodyn. **15**(6), 975–986 (2021). https://doi.org/10.1007/s11571-021-09680-3

22. Khaleghi, A., Birgani, P.M., Fooladi, M.F., Mohammadi, M.R.: Applicable features of electroencephalogram for ADHD diagnosis. Res. Biomed. Eng. **36**(1), 1–11 (2020). https://doi.org/10.1007/s42600-019-00036-9
23. Lenartowicz, A., Loo, S.K.: Use of EEG to diagnose ADHD. Curr. Psychiatry Rep. **16**(11), 1–11 (2014)
24. Einizade, A., Mozafari, M., Rezaei-Dastjerdehei, M., Aghdaei, E., Mijani, A.M., Sardouie, S.H.: Detecting ADHD children based on EEG signals using Graph Signal Processing techniques. In: 2020 27th National and 5th International Iranian Conference on Biomedical Engineering (ICBME), pp. 264–270. IEEE (2020)
25. Ahmadi, A., Kashefi, M., Shahrokhi, H., Nazari, M.A.: Computer aided diagnosis system using deep convolutional neural networks for ADHD subtypes. Biomed. Signal Process. Control **63**, 102227 (2021)
26. Chen, H., Song, Y., Li, X.: A deep learning framework for identifying children with ADHD using an EEG-based brain network. Neurocomputing **356**, 83–96 (2019)
27. Marcano, J.L.L., Bell, M.A., Louis Beex, A.A.: EEG channel selection for AR model based ADHD classification. In: 2016 IEEE Signal Processing in Medicine and Biology Symposium (SPMB), pp. 1–6. IEEE (2016)
28. Kaur, S., Arun, P., Singh, S., Kaur, D.: EEG based decision support system to diagnose adults with ADHD. In: 2018 IEEE Applied Signal Processing Conference (ASPCON), pp. 87–91. IEEE (2018)
29. Barttfeld, P., et al.: Functional connectivity and temporal variability of brain connections in adults with attention deficit/hyperactivity disorder and bipolar disorder. Neuropsychobiology **69**(2), 65–75 (2014)
30. Rodrak, S., Wongsawat, Y.: EEG brain mapping and brain connectivity index for subtypes classification of attention deficit hyperactivity disorder children during the eye-opened period. In: 2013 35th Annual International Conference of the IEEE Engineering in Medicine and Biology Society (EMBC), pp. 7400–7403. IEEE (2013)
31. González, J.J., Alba, G., Mañas, S., González, A., Pereda, E.: Assessment of ADHD through electroencephalographic measures of functional connectivity. ADHD-New Dir. Diagn. Treat 35–54 (2017)
32. Holker, R., Susan, S.: Quantitative EEG feature selection by majority voting for alcohol use disorder detection. In: 2021 IEEE EMBS International Conference on Biomedical and Health Informatics (BHI), pp. 1–4. IEEE (2021)
33. Susan, S., Kumar, A., Jain, A.: Evaluating heterogeneous ensembles with boosting meta-learner. In: Ranganathan, G., Chen, J., Rocha, Á. (eds.) Inventive Communication and Computational Technologies. LNNS, vol. 145, pp. 699–710. Springer, Singapore (2021). https://doi.org/10.1007/978-981-15-7345-3_60
34. Holker, R., Susan, S.: Neuroscience-inspired parameter selection of spiking neuron using Hodgkin Huxley model. Int. J. Softw. Sci. Comput. Intell. (IJSSCI) **13**(2), 89–106 (2021)
35. https://ieee-dataport.org/open-access/eeg-data-adhd-control-children. Accessed 14 June 2022
36. https://www.ncbi.nlm.nih.gov/books/NBK519712/table/ch3.t3/. Accessed 14 June 2022

# A Machine Learning Approach for Early Detection of Postpartum Depression in Bangladesh

Jasiya Fairiz Raisa[1]([⊠]) [iD], M. Shamim Kaiser[2][iD], and Mufti Mahmud[3,4,5][iD]

[1] Information and Communication Technology, Bangladesh University
of Professionals, Dhaka 1216, Bangladesh
jasiyafairiz@gmail.com
[2] Institute of Information Technology, Jahangirnagar University,
Savar, Dhaka 1342, Bangladesh
mskaiser@juniv.edu
[3] Department of Computer Science, Nottingham Trent University, Clifton Campus,
Nottingham NG11 8NS, UK
[4] Medical Technologies Innovation Facility, Nottingham Trent University,
Clifton Campus, Nottingham NG11 8NS, UK
[5] Computing and Informatics Research Centre, Nottingham Trent University,
Clifton Campus, Nottingham NG11 8NS, UK
mufti.mahmud@ntu.ac.uk

**Abstract.** Postpartum depression is a severe mental health issue exhibited among perinatal women after the childbirth process. While the negative impact of postpartum depression is extensive in developing countries, there is a significant lack of proper tools and techniques to predict the disorder due to negligence. This work proposes a machine learning-based system for finding the risk factors and prevalence of postpartum depression in Bangladesh. We developed a survey of different socio-demographic questions and modified questions from two standard postpartum depression screening scales (EPDS, PHQ-2). Data from 150 women have been collected, processed, and implemented in different machine learning models to find—the best performing models. Based on the collected data of the perinatal women in Bangladesh, the best performing machine learning model was Random Forest. The performance metrics for the best model were AUC: 98%, Accuracy: 89%, and Sensitivity: 89%. The performance of the models varies from 88%–98% (AUC), 82%–89% (Accuracy), and 81%–89% (Sensitivity). We have also found the top risk factors for causing PPD. According to this work, the prevalence of PPD in Bangladesh is 66.7% (Considering the medium and high chance of PPD). This proposed work is the first to detect the risk factors and prevalence of PPD in Bangladesh using a machine learning approach.

**Keywords:** Depression · Postpartum depression · Machine learning · Detection model · Mental health

© Springer Nature Switzerland AG 2022
M. Mahmud et al. (Eds.): BI 2022, LNAI 13406, pp. 241–252, 2022
https://doi.org/10.1007/978-3-031-15037-1_20

# 1    Introduction

Postpartum depression (PPD) is a non-psychotic mental disorder that is commonly seen in mothers within the first year of delivery [12,22]. PPD often goes undiagnosed in most cases, and it can lead to severe complications and should be managed promptly [1]. Women with PPD may experience significant difficulties in cognitive and emotional processes that impact mother-infant attachment. Globally, the prevalence of postpartum depression among perinatal women varies between 0.5 and 60.8% [12]. The prevalence of PPD in Bangladesh is 39.4% in the first twelve months after childbirth [4]. Identifying women at risk of having PPD is essential for clinical practice because it enables targeted prevention treatments [23]. A robust PPD classifier can assist health care practitioners in identifying and effectively managing at-risk individuals [19], as evidenced by recent studies examining this prospect and feasibility [17].

Machine learning (ML) assists in making precise estimates using data from numerous sources and has been utilized in recent years in prediction studies [20]. ML is thought to assist mental health practitioners in more objectively defining mental diseases than the Diagnostic and Statistical Manual of Mental Disorders [25] and identifying these illnesses to improve the efficacy of therapies [11].

Considering the effectiveness of ML in predictive studies and the unique case of PPD, ML-based classification can be applied for prevalence and risk factors detection for PPD, providing benefit to the mothers and their families.

Given the severity of the problem of PPD, the number of existing works for detecting it is not significant. Furthermore, most of the existing works are from the perspective of developed countries, which might not be effective from the perspective of developing countries such as Bangladesh. To our knowledge, no such work currently exists that detects PPD in Bangladesh using machine learning approaches.

The work aims to develop a machine learning-based system for risk analysis and detection of postpartum depression among Bangladeshi perinatal women and a survey questionnaire prior to data collection.

The contribution of the study can be summarized as follows:

1. Development and comparison of different machine learning models for detecting PPD among Bangladeshi women
2. Finding the correlation between demographic factors and postpartum depression in Bangladesh

# 2    Related Works

The number of existing works to detect postpartum depression among women is not significantly rich. In the perspective of Bangladesh, some research works presented the prevalence and risk factors from a sociological perspective. While narrowing down the existing works in the machine learning perspective, the number of works drops low in numbers accordingly. The existing works in this field are primarily from the perspective of developed countries [2,21,23,27].

A significant number of the existing works are developed using data collected from the hospital or any cohort studies. In this section, we have reviewed existing works for PPD detection, first from the Bangladesh perspective. Later, some significant works on machine learning-based PPD detection are reviewed.

## 2.1  PPD in Bangladesh Perspective

Postpartum depression is one of the understudied research topics in Bangladesh. Several studies have analyzed the prevalence and risk factors among Bangladeshi perinatal women.

The study developed by Gausia et al. [9] has reported the prevalence and associated factors of postpartum depression in the rural areas of Bangladesh. The authors found the prevalence of PPD at 22% and the incidence of postpartum depressive symptoms at 9.8% at 6–8 weeks postpartum.

Using a cohort study approach, Edhborg et al. [15] studied the incidence and risk factors of PPD in Bangladesh. The researchers analyzed the mental and socio-economic conditions of 588 women during pregnancy and after childbirth. After implementing multiple Cox's regression, it was found that 18.58% of the participants were at risk of postpartum depression. The socio-economic status, history of abuse and anxiety during pregnancy, and previous depressive symptoms are the most critical risk factors for postnatal depression.

Azad et al. [4] developed a cross-sectional study to find the prevalence and related risk factors in the slum areas of Dhaka city. The research shows that the prevalence of PPD among the participants is 39.4% within the first 12 months after childbirth. The authors used EPDS as the standard scale for measuring the risk of PPD. The risk factors with the highest impact were found to the job status.

A study [18] developed using hospital data found that 65.22% of the participants were at risk of PPD. They found that the mother's age, multigravida, newborn's gender, and congenital anomalies are the most critical factors responsible for the prevalence of PPD.

## 2.2  Machine Learning for PPD Detection

Researchers are now approaching to predict and classify many health problems with machine learning, including postpartum depression is one. Some notable works are reviewed to analyze their implemented techniques and PPD classification accuracy.

Zhang et al. [26] proposed that SVM and FFS-RF were found to have the best prediction effects for PPD. They performed a longitudinal survey to collect data from 508 women and used EPDS for measuring the risk of PPD.

Zhang et al. [27] implemented EHR datasets for detecting PPD among perinatal women. They found that logistic regression with L2 regularization was the best performing algorithm using data up to childbirth. For the data after childbirth, MLP performed the best.

The PRAMS 2012–2013 dataset and the PHQ-2 questionnaire were proposed to be implemented in several machine learning algorithms by Shin et al. [21] to find the prevalence of PPD. The authors found Random Forest to be the best-performing algorithm for predicting postpartum depression.

Andersson et al. [2] developed several machine learning models and used data collected from hospitals in Sweden. The extremely Randomized Trees model was the best performing model for this large population-based study.

Another research work was developed using data collected from hospitals by Tortajada et al. [23]. The proposed work used MLP for predicting PPD and achieved 81% accuracy. De Choudhury [8] performed a longitudinal online survey on postpartum women and experimented with different regression models on the dataset.

A comparison among Functional-gradient boosting, Decision-trees, Naive Bayes and SVM for PPD detection is shown by Nataranjan et al. [16]. The authors developed a longitudinal dataset for this research work and showed that Functional-gradient boosting performed best among the implemented algorithms. Wang et al. [24] developed a machine learning-based model on EHR data and found that SVM performed best with their dataset.

## 3  Materials and Methodology

The development of the PPD screening survey and the methodology of the proposed work are discussed in this section. The whole workflow of the model is depicted in Fig. 1.

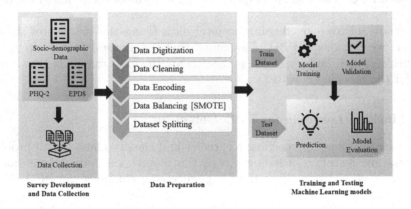

**Fig. 1.** Proposed workflow of the PPD detection model

### 3.1  Sampling

**Study Population.** All reproductive age group women who gave birth in the last 24 months in Bangladesh.

**Study Location.** The data collection was performed in different regions of Bangladesh. We included women from separate residences, education, and income level.

**Study Type.** A cross-sectional study was performed by interviewing 150 postpartum women. The complete questionnaire is developed in Bangla for the ease of the participants.

**Time Period.** The data was collected from January 2022 to February 2022 in different geographical locations in Bangladesh.

**Inclusion and Exclusion Criteria.** All mothers who gave birth before the interview and their latest born child is alive and not more than two years old were included in the study. The study only included postpartum women who gave their consent to this interview. Those mothers who are seriously ill and unable to respond during data collection were excluded from this study.

### 3.2 Measures

The interview questionnaire contained socio-demographic questions, a PHQ-2 questionnaire, and the EPDS questionnaire.

**Socio-demographic Questionnaire.** Questions about general health, relationships, education, income level, and history of abuse are developed and added to the questionnaire.

**PHQ-2.** The Patient Health Questionnaire-2 [14] is used to determine the mothers' mental health condition before, during, and after their latest childbirth using only two questions for each time period.

**EPDS.** The Edinburgh Postnatal Depression Scale [7] is a ten-item self-report assessment, that is used for in-depth screening for PPD among the participants. This self-screening survey has been verified as a clinical screening tool for postpartum depression in Bangladeshi women aged 6–8 weeks [7,10]. Several psychologists validated the questionnaire before starting the data collection process.

### 3.3 Data Collection Procedure

A pilot study was performed on 8 participants (5% of the 150 participants), and the data from the pilot study were excluded from the original dataset. The data was collected in person from different areas of Bangladesh, including different cities and villages. However, in some cases, we had to collect data from appropriate participants online since it was hard to reach postpartum women during the lockdown. The collected data were cross-checked to ensure the completeness of the questionnaire by the participants.

## 3.4   Data Preparation

At first, the collected data was transferred in digital format. Since the data were cross-checked for completeness, no missing-value entries were found in the raw dataset. We translated the data from Bangla to English to fit the model. The data were encoded into numeric values. The PHQ2 questionnaire for the different time periods of mothers' lives was labelled "likely depressive" or "not likely depressive" based on their results and the cutoff score. Similarly, the data of the EPDS questionnaire were scored and added to calculate their sum for getting the final EPDS score. In this study, we have considered three levels of likely to have postpartum depression:

1. Score 0 to 8: Less likely to have PPD (Marked as "Low")
2. Score 9–12: Likely to have PPD (Marked as "Medium")
3. Score 13–30: Highly likely to have PPD (Marked as "High")

## 3.5   Statistical Approach for Data Analysis

The processed data were analyzed, grouped by the level of EPDS score range, using the statistical analysis tool, SPSS. Independent sample T-test assuming unequal variances and Chi-Square test were used for numerical and categorical variables as appropriate.

## 3.6   Machine Learning Approach for PPD Detection

**Resampling to Address Dataset Imbalance.** Unbalanced data can reduce the accuracy of ML-based classification [6]. To correct the data imbalance, we employed the widely used synthetic minority oversampling approach (SMOTE) [5]. Instead of reproducing existing minority members, SMOTE develops synthetic members based on Euclidean distances between data points in feature space.

**Model Development.** We have implemented several supervised machine learning algorithms and ensemble models for PPD detection in the proposed work. After reviewing the existing works, we have selected some of the most common and best-performing models for the detection of postpartum depression. We have used SVM, Random Forest, and Logistic Regression from the supervised techniques and boosting classifiers as the ensemble methods, such as Gradient Boosting and Extreme Gradient Boosting for PPD detection in this work. The algorithms were selected in such a way that over-fitting or under-fitting problems don't affect the result. Both classical and ensemble algorithms were implemented to ensure the validity of the performance of the model using the collected dataset.

**Model Training for Classification.** The processed dataset is split into an 80-20 ratio as training and testing datasets. Five ML algorithms were individually implemented to detect PPD in this proposed work. A 10-fold cross-validation strategy was used to evaluate the classification models. The original samples were randomly partitioned into ten equal-sized subsamples, and a single subsample was retained as validation data for testing the model built using the other nine subsamples.

**Model Performance Evaluation.** The test dataset was fed into the trained machine learning models for prediction. The original and the predicted data were compared to develop a confusion matrix. A series of performance metrics were obtained for each model, including Area under Curve, Sensitivity, Accuracy, Precision, F1 Score, and Geometric Mean. Among these metrics, Area Under Curve (AUC), accuracy, and sensitivity are the three most important metrics for PPD detection. These are used to evaluate the effects of each model and choose the best prediction model.

**Table 1.** Risk factors for postpartum depression

| Risk factor | $\chi^2$ (df) | p-value | Risk factor | $\chi^2$ (df) | p-value |
|---|---|---|---|---|---|
| Age range | 6.77(6) | 0.342 | Loss during pregnancy | 15.6(14) | 0.337 |
| Residence | 0.931(2) | 63% | Abuse | 15.0(2) | <.001 |
| Education level | 4.61(6) | 60% | Sharing feeling with friends | 5.26(2) | 0.072 |
| Marital status | NaN | NaN | Number of latest pregnancy | 6.96(8) | 0.541 |
| Job before pregnancy | 7.74(12) | 0.805 | Pregnancy length | 8.72(10) | 0.558 |
| Income before pregnancy | 5.83(8) | 67% | Pregnancy planned | 1.33(2) | 0.515 |
| Current job | 11.2(12) | 0.509 | Checkup | 1.63(2) | 0.443 |
| Current income | 4.80(8) | 0.779 | Fear of pregnancy | 6.04(2) | 0.049 |
| Husband's education | 8.03(6) | 0.236 | Diseases during pregnancy | 9.08(4) | 6% |
| Husband's income | 6.02(8) | 0.645 | Age of latest child | 3.94(6) | 0.685 |
| Addiction | 2.01(2) | 0.365 | Age of previous baby | 23.3(18) | 18% |
| Number of children | 4.57(6) | 0.6 | Delivery mode | 1.64(2) | 44% |
| Disease before pregnancy | 3.05(4) | 0.549 | Birth complicay | 2.43(2) | 0.296 |
| Pregnancy loss | 2.81(4) | 0.59 | Gender | 0.539(2) | 0.764 |
| Family type | 0.354(2) | 0.838 | Breastfeed | 4.69(2) | 0.096 |
| Number of family member | 12.7(20) | 0.89 | Illness of the baby | 14.5(2) | <.001 |
| Relation with in-laws | 16.1(4) | 0% | Worry for baby | 5.62(2) | 0.06 |
| Relation with husband | 20.3(4) | <.001 | Rest while baby is monitored | 2.25(2) | 0.325 |
| Relation with baby | 4.00(4) | 0.406 | Rest when baby sleeps | 12.4(2) | 0.002 |
| Husband and baby relation | 9.06(4) | 6% | Anger after delivery | 44.0(2) | <.001 |
| Motherhood feeling | 11.1(4) | 3% | Work feeling after delivery | 13.3(6) | 0.039 |
| Received support | 25.0(16) | 0.07 | PHQ 2 (before pregnancy) | 1.13(2) | 0.567 |
| Want support | 33.7(8) | <.001 | PHQ 2 (during pregnancy) | 6.68(2) | 0.035 |

## 4   Result

### 4.1   Correlation of the Socio-demographic Features with PPD

The status of postpartum depression significantly differed by many factors [3,13]. We have collected 46 socio-demographic features of postpartum women for this research work. These factors were statistically analyzed to understand better these features and their effect on the occurrence of PPD. The distribution of predictor variables are summarized in Table 1. From the analysis, it is found that factors like relation with husband, need for support, history of abuse, illness of the newborn, depression prior to pregnancy, etc., influence the occurrence of PPD among women.

### 4.2   Prevalence of PPD

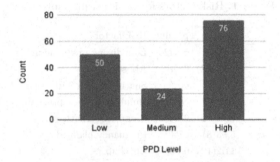

**Fig. 2.** Prevalence of PPD in Bangladesh

Using the trained model to predict PPD in the test dataset yielded the highest AUC-ROC of 98% and the highest accuracy of 89% with the Random Forest model. Among the 150 participants, 100 (66.7% of the total) were regarded as likely to have PPD, considering the EPDS score over the cutoff score (medium and high risk). The data distribution is shown in Fig. 2 15.33% of the participants were at risk of depression prior to their latest pregnancy, and 25.33% were at risk of depression during pregnancy. Participants with previous depressive symptoms had a higher chance of PPD (73.91% more in the participants with previous depression before pregnancy and 76.32% more in the participants with previous depression during pregnancy) than women with no history of depression.

### 4.3   Effect of Machine Learning Classifier Models

Classification models were developed to predict the multiclass of postpartum depression (High, Medium, Low). The classification process was performed in the balanced dataset developed using SMOTE technology. The PPD prediction models were established using five ML algorithms Random Forest, Extreme Gradient

Boosting, SVM, Gradient Boosting, and Logistic Regression. The algorithms were applied to the training data set, and later test data set was fed into the model to predict the PPD level. The performance metrics for the implemented models are shown in the Table 2, and the ROC-AUC curve and the confusion metrics of the best performing model, Random Forest, are illustrated in the Fig. 3.

**Table 2.** Performance metrics of the top five machine learning models

| Classifier | AUC | Acc | Sens | Prec | F1 score | G-mean | Cross val |
|---|---|---|---|---|---|---|---|
| Random Forest | 98% | 89% | 89% | 89% | 89% | 89% | 63% |
| Extreme Gradient Boosting | 94% | 86% | 85% | 86% | 85% | 85% | 55% |
| SVM | 88% | 84% | 84% | 86% | 84% | 84% | 63% |
| Gradient Boosting | 91% | 84% | 81% | 83% | 82% | 81% | 66% |
| Logistic Regression | 91% | 82% | 83% | 82% | 82% | 83% | 57% |

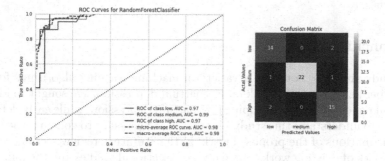

**Fig. 3.** Performance metrics of the Random Forest model

## 5    Discussion

### 5.1    Key Findings and Contributions

In the current work, we implemented supervised and ensemble techniques with the data of postpartum women from Bangladesh. All the implemented algorithms achieved similar performance, among which the Random Forest and the Extreme gradient boosting algorithms had the best performance. The overall performance of the machine learning algorithms ensures that the data properly fit into the model.

The prevalence of postpartum depression among the studied women is found to be about 66.67%, considering the medium and high probability of PPD based on the EPDS scale. The random forest algorithm calculated the prevalence of PPD as 70.17%.

From the provided statistical analysis of the dataset, the correlation between the demographic factors and PPD can be measured. The features can be categorized based on feature importance calculated from their p-value.

With significantly high-performance metrics, (Accuracy: 89%, AUC: 98%, Sensitivity: 89%), the proposed model can be said to be significant and promising in predicting postpartum depression. To our best knowledge, this is the first machine learning-based model to predict postpartum depression among Bangladeshi perinatal women.

## 5.2   Limitations

It is important to compare the proposed work with the existing relevant works for performance validation of the prior work. However, because earlier studies employed various types of data and offered various machine learning algorithms to detect the prevalence of PPD, the model prediction impacts cannot simply be compared. Additionally, potential selection bias, small sample size, and the requirement of more extended validation may have affected the performance of the models.

## 6   Conclusion

This study aimed to compare a variety of machine learning algorithms for predicting perinatal women at risk of postpartum depression. We sought to identify potential risk factors for developing postpartum depression, while early detection of PPD. To understand this study's quality, it is necessary to compare the results and contributions of the proposed work. In the literature review section, we have seen the lack of existing works based on cross-sectional studies and the implementation of several standardized scales for PPD screening. Drawing a comparison among the existing works with this study, it can be said that this research work has addressed these gaps in the existing works accordingly. Despite the novelty of the current work, there are some limitations pointed out in the discussion section. Further studies should develop to address these gaps. It is evident that machine learning can considerably improve the early diagnosis of PPD. The proposed work's findings imply a potential benefit of utilizing machine learning to screen new mothers for PPD in the perspective of Bangladesh. This work's data-driven, machine learning-based strategy can be expanded to create an accurate and scalable system for cost-effectively offering preventive treatments, assuring improved mental healthcare and support for postpartum mothers in Bangladesh.

## References

1. Aliani, R., Khuwaja, B.: Epidemiology of postpartum depression in pakistan: a review of literature. Natl. J. Health Sci. **2**(1), 24–30 (2017). https://doi.org/10.21089/njhs.21.0024, http://njhsciences.com/wp-content/uploads/2017/02/6-Razia-Alini_MS.pdf

2. Andersson, S., Bathula, D.R., Iliadis, S.I., Walter, M., Skalkidou, A.: Predicting women with depressive symptoms postpartum with machine learning methods. Sci. Rep. **11**(1), 7877 (2021). https://doi.org/10.1038/s41598-021-86368-y, http://www.nature.com/articles/s41598-021-86368-y

3. Ay, F.: Postpartum depression and the factors affecting It: 2000–2017 study results. J. Psychiatr. Nurs. **93**, 147–152 (2018). https://doi.org/10.14744/phd.2018.31549, https://www.journalagent.com/phd/pdfs/PHD-31549-RESEARCH_ARTICLE-AY.pdf

4. Azad, R., et al.: Prevalence and risk factors of postpartum depression within one year after birth in urban slums of Dhaka, Bangladesh. PLOS ONE **14**(5), e0215735 (2019). https://doi.org/10.1371/journal.pone.0215735, https://dx.plos.org/10.1371/journal.pone.0215735

5. Chawla, N.V., Bowyer, K.W., Hall, L.O., Kegelmeyer, W.P.: SMOTE: synthetic minority over-sampling technique. J. Artif. Intell. Res. **16**, 321–357 (2002). https://doi.org/10.1613/jair.953, arXiv: 1106.1813

6. Chawla, N.V.: Data Mining For Imbalanced Datasets: An Overview. In: Maimon, O., Rokach, L. (eds) Data Mining and Knowledge Discovery Handbook, pp. 853–867. Springer, Boston, MA (2005). https://doi.org/10.1007/0-387-25465-X_40

7. Cox, J.L., Holden, J.M., Sagovsky, R.: Detection of postnatal depression. Development of the 10-item Edinburgh postnatal depression scale. Br. J. Psychiatr. J. Mental Sci. **150**, 782–786 (1987). https://doi.org/10.1192/bjp.150.6.782

8. De Choudhury, M., Counts, S., Horvitz, E.J., Hoff, A.: Characterizing and predicting postpartum depression from shared Facebook data. In: Proceedings of the 17th ACM Conference on Computer Supported Cooperative Work & Social Computing, pp. 626–638. CSCW 2014, Association for Computing Machinery, New York, NY, USA (2014). https://doi.org/10.1145/2531602.2531675

9. Gausia, K., Fisher, C., Ali, M., Oosthuizen, J.: Magnitude and contributory factors of postnatal depression: a community-based cohort study from a rural subdistrict of Bangladesh. Psychol. Med. **39**(6), 999–1007 (2009). https://doi.org/10.1017/S0033291708004455

10. Gausia, K., Fisher, C., Algin, S., Oosthuizen, J.: Validation of the Bangla version of the Edinburgh postnatal depression scale for a Bangladeshi sample. J. Reprod. Infant Psychol. **25**, 308–315 (2007). https://doi.org/10.1080/02646830701644896

11. Graham, S., et al.: Artificial intelligence for mental health and mental illnesses: an overview. Current Psychiatry Rep. **21**(11), 1–18 (2019). https://doi.org/10.1007/s11920-019-1094-0

12. Halbreich, U., Karkun, S.: Cross-cultural and social diversity of prevalence of postpartum depression and depressive symptoms. J. Affect. Disord. **91**(2–3), 97–111 (2006). https://doi.org/10.1016/j.jad.2005.12.051

13. Insan, N., Weke, A., Forrest, S., Rankin, J.: Social determinants of antenatal depression and anxiety among women in South Asia: a systematic review & meta-analysis. PLOS ONE **17**, e0263760 (2022). https://doi.org/10.1371/journal.pone.0263760

14. Kroenke, K., Spitzer, R.L., Williams, J.B.W.: The patient health questionnaire-2: validity of a two-item depression screener. Med. Care **41**(11), 1284–1292 (2003). https://doi.org/10.1097/01.MLR.0000093487.78664.3C

15. Maigun Edhborg, H.E.N.: Incidence and risk factor of postpartum depressive symptoms in women: a population based prospective cohort study in a rural district in Bangladesh. J. Depress. Anxiety **04**(02), 2167–1044 (2015). https://doi.org/10.4172/2167-1044.1000180, http://www.omicsgroup.org/journals/incidence-and-risk-factor-of-postpartum-depressive-symptoms-in-women-a-population-based-prospective-cohort-study-in-a-rural-district-in-bangladesh-2167-1044-1000180.php?aid=51561

16. Natarajan, S., Prabhakar, A., Ramanan, N., Bagilone, A., Siek, K., Connelly, K.: Boosting for postpartum depression prediction. In: 2017 IEEE/ACM International Conference on Connected Health: Applications, Systems and Engineering Technologies (CHASE), pp. 232–240. IEEE, Philadelphia, PA, USA, Jul 2017. https://doi.org/10.1109/CHASE.2017.82, http://ieeexplore.ieee.org/document/8010637/

17. Righetti-Veltema, M., Conne-Perréard, E., Bousquet, A., Manzano, J.: Risk factors and predictive signs of postpartum depression. J. Affect. Disord. **49**(3), 167–180 (1998). https://doi.org/10.1016/s0165-0327(97)00110-9

18. Rn, D.R.M., Rn, M.: Depression Among Postnatal Mothers in Bangladesh p. 8

19. Robertson, E., Grace, S., Wallington, T., Stewart, D.E.: Antenatal risk factors for postpartum depression: a synthesis of recent literature. Gener. Hosp. Psychiatry **26**(4), 289–295 (2004). https://doi.org/10.1016/j.genhosppsych.2004.02.006

20. Shatte, A.B.R., Hutchinson, D.M., Teague, S.J.: Machine learning in mental health: a scoping review of methods and applications. Psychol. Med. **49**(9), 1426–1448 (2019). https://doi.org/10.1017/S0033291719000151

21. Shin, D., Lee, K.J., Adeluwa, T., Hur, J.: Machine learning-based predictive modeling of postpartum depression. J. Clin. Med. **9**(9), 2899 (2020). https://doi.org/10.3390/jcm9092899, https://www.mdpi.com/2077-0383/9/9/2899

22. Stewart, D.E., Robertson, E., Phil, M., Dennis, C.L., Grace, S.L., Wallington, T.: Postpartum depression: literature review of risk factors and interventions, p. 289 (2003)

23. Tortajada, S., et al.: Prediction of postpartum depression using multilayer perceptrons and pruning. Methods Inform. Med. **48**(03), 291–298 (2009). https://doi.org/10.3414/ME0562, http://www.thieme-connect.de/DOI/DOI?10.3414/ME0562

24. Wang, S., Pathak, J., Zhang, Y.: Using electronic health records and machine learning to predict postpartum depression. Stud. Health Technol. Inform. **264**, 888–892 (2019). https://doi.org/10.3233/SHTI190351

25. Wisner, K.L., Moses-Kolko, E.L., Sit, D.K.Y.: Postpartum depression: a disorder in search of a definition. Arch. Women's Mental Health. **13**(1), 37–40 (2010). https://doi.org/10.1007/s00737-009-0119-9, https://www.ncbi.nlm.nih.gov/pmc/articles/PMC4426488/

26. Zhang, W., Liu, H., Silenzio, V.M.B., Qiu, P., Gong, W.: Machine learning models for the prediction of postpartum depression: application and comparison based on a cohort study. JMIR Med. Inform. **8**(4), e15516 (2020). https://doi.org/10.2196/15516, http://medinform.jmir.org/2020/4/e15516/

27. Zhang, Y., Wang, S., Hermann, A., Joly, R., Pathak, J.: Development and validation of a machine learning algorithm for predicting the risk of postpartum depression among pregnant women. J. Affect. Disord. **279**, 1–8 (2021). https://doi.org/10.1016/j.jad.2020.09.113, https://linkinghub.elsevier.com/retrieve/pii/S0165032720328093

# Epilepsy Detection from EEG Data Using a Hybrid CNN-LSTM Model

Md. Arif Istiak Neloy[1]📧, Anik Biswas[1]📧, Nazmun Nahar[2]📧,
Mohammad Shahadat Hossain[3(📧)]📧, and Karl Andersson[4]📧

[1] BGC Trust University Bangladesh Bidyanagar, Chandanaish, Bangladesh
[2] Noakhali Science and Technology University, Noakhali, Bangladesh
nazmun@nstu.edu.bd
[3] University of Chittagong, Chittagong, Bangladesh
hossain_ms@cu.ac.bd
[4] Lulea University of Technology, 931 87 Skellefteå, Sweden
Karl.andersson@ltu.se

**Abstract.** 'An epileptic seizure', a neurological disorder, occurs when electric burst travel over the brain, causing the person to lose control or consciousness. Anticipating epilepsy when the event happen is beneficial for epileptic control with medication or neurological pre-surgical planning. To detect epilepsy using electroencephalogram (EEG) data, machine learning and computational approaches are applied. Because of their better categorization skills, deep learning (DL) and machine learning (ML) approaches have recently been applied in the automated identification of epileptic events. ML and DL models can reliably diagnose diverse seizure disorders from vast EEG data and supply relevant findings for neurologists. To detect epilepsy, we developed a hybrid network that combines a 'Convolutional Neural Network (CNN)' and a 'Long Term Short Term Memory (LSTM)'. Our dataset is divided into two categories: epilepsy and normal. CNN-LSTM has been used to train our algorithm. With the Adam optimizer, our proposed CNN-LSTM model achieves 94.98% training accuracy and 82.21% validation accuracy. We also evaluate our results to those of machine learning methods such as Decision Tree, Logistic Regression and Naive Bayes. The comparative results clearly reveal that our suggested CNN-LSTM classifier outperforms the other learners.

**Keywords:** Epilepsy detection · EEG · CNN-LSTM

## 1 Introduction

Machine Learning (ML) has recently become popular for detecting diseases in advance. This trend isn't just about detection; it's also about gaining a better knowledge of the condition and working on treatments. In recent years, brain research has become a trendy topic. ML is demonstrating a high level of proficiency

© Springer Nature Switzerland AG 2022
M. Mahmud et al. (Eds.): BI 2022, LNAI 13406, pp. 253–263, 2022
https://doi.org/10.1007/978-3-031-15037-1_21

in diagnosing disorders involving the brain and its functions. Following that line of thought, this research focuses on the use of deep learning to detect epilepsy.

Epilepsy is a well-known neurological condition. Being an epilepsy sufferer results in sudden seizure attacks, which involve loss of awareness, difficulty moving, muscle contraction, and other symptoms. Epilepsy can affect people of any age, race, or origin. According to the World Health Organization (WHO), this condition affects around 50 million individuals worldwide. This neurological disorder not only affects a person's bodily well-being, but it can also lead to a lack of social standing and support [26]. That is why it is critical to recognize epilepsy early.

The main reason epilepsy is considered one of the most severe diseases is because of sudden seizure attacks. The risk of mortality or physical injury can be lowered if treatment is given promptly after the seizure occurs. However, as one of the most common neurological illnesses, the exact cause is still mostly unknown. Injury to the head or brain, on the other hand, has been discovered to be a reliable cause of epilepsy. This also covers things like brain tumors and strokes.

Electroencephalography is the most common method of detecting epilepsy (EEG). The electroencephalogram (EEG) is a measurement of the electrical activity of the brain [15]. The voltage change was measured by two electrodes placed in human scruples while measuring the EEG. If there is any anomalous brain activity in the EEG data, it suggests the presence of a neurological condition. However, it is time-consuming, and it is not the only approach to diagnosing epilepsy [10].

In the identification of epilepsy, machine learning is providing better results. Researchers are experimenting with various ways in an attempt to identify seizures early enough to save the patient's life. To detect epilepsy, EEG recordings are frequently combined with machine learning algorithms [10,16]. Even the usage of wearables can improve efficiency to some extent because the patient does not have to stay in the hospital all of the time. This is also something that researchers are working on [25]. However, when it comes to utilizing machine learning to diagnose epilepsy, EEG data appears to be the most useful.

In this paper, we will be using deep learning to detect epilepsy from EEG data. We propose a hybrid model for detecting epilepsy. The LSTM method is capable of retaining patterns for an extended period of time. The suggested 1D-CNN + LSTM architecture is then applied to data from EEG time series.

The following is the rest of the paper's structure. Section 2 focuses on the present field's literature evaluation. The methodology is described in Sect. 3. Section 4 contains the experiment's findings as well as a comparison of several methods. Section 5 concludes with future work.

## 2 Related Work

Numerous existing approach that have been used for detecting epilepsy disease detection can be found. They are discussed in the following.

EEG data were utilized to detect epilepsy in a study published in 2017. They used an Artificial Neural Network (ANN) to diagnose the disease in that study and were able to do so with 100% accuracy using a dataset of 170,502 entries [26]. The dataset they utilized was far larger than the studies with which they compared it.

Researchers employed a Wavelet-based deep learning technique to detect epilepsy in another work published in 2019. They claim to overcome two fundamental problems by eliminating the need for feature extraction and working effectively with limited datasets. Using the deep learning technique (CNN), they were able to obtain 100% accuracy in binary classification and 99.4% in ternary classification [4].

In 2017, a publication used the frequency domain to extract features from EEG data in order to detect seizure events. They employed a deep learning technique using multilayer senses to increase detection accuracy. And they have a 95% accuracy rate [8].

A group of academics applied the Support Vector Machine (SVM) algorithm on EEG data in a recent work published in 2019 to detect epilepsy. To find the best parameters, they employed a genetic algorithm (GA) and particle swarm optimization (PSO). In comparison to the GA approach, the PSO-based strategy has a higher accuracy of 99.38% [29].

In 2020, a study was conducted with the goal of improving epilepsy detection accuracy, and a generic algorithm was combined with four other algorithms: Support Vector Machine (SVM), K-Nearest Neighbors (KNN), Artificial Neural Network (ANN), and Naive Bayes (NB), with the ANN achieving the highest accuracy [17].

In a separate study, researchers analyzed EEG data in two distinct ways to detect seizure attacks. The ML-based K-Nearest Neighbor (KNN) and the Fuzzy-based Fuzzy Rough Nearest Neighbor (FRNN) are two examples (FRNN). And, accordingly, 99.63 and 99.81% accuracy [24].

The popular deep learning model Convolutional Neural Network (CNN) was used to detect seizure attacks from EEG data in a paper published in 2019. They claimed to be able to extract spectral and temporal information from EEG data using their deep learning model. The accuracy of their seizure detection was 99.46% [13].

In a paper published in 2019, deep learning was utilized to detect epilepsy seizures automatically. This model is more accurate than ML models because it does not require feature extraction. They have, however, employed feature sealing to improve accuracy. They achieved 97.21% and 97.60% accuracy with StandardScaler and RobustScaler, respectively [31].

In a report published in 2018, the Long Short-Term Memory (LSTM) network was combined with convolutional neural networks (CNN) to detect epilepsy seizures from EEG data. Their proposed technique has successfully recognized 185 seizures with no false positives [32].

# 3   Methodology

The approach for this analysis is demonstrated in this section. Each component revealed how the research was carried out in order to discover epilepsy. This research's methodology is shown in Fig. 1.

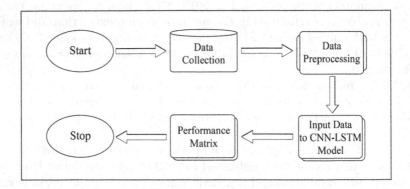

**Fig. 1.** Methodology steps.

## 3.1   Data Collection

There is accumulating evidence that indicates the temporal aspects of brain function may be categorized into four states: interictal (between seizures, or baseline), preictal (before to seizure), ictal (seizure), and post-ictal (after seizures). Seizure forecasting necessitates the capacity to distinguish a preictal state from the interictal, ictal, and postictal states. The fundamental difficulty in seizure forecasting is distinguishing between preictal and interictal stages. Human brains function was captured using intracranial EEG (iEEG), which comprises electrodes placed on the cerebral cortex's surface and the capturing of electrical signals using an ambient monitoring device. At 400 Hz, iEEG was collected from 16 electrodes, and captured voltages were compared to the electrode overall average. These are long-term recordings that might last months or years, and they capture a substantial number of seizures in certain persons.

## 3.2   Convolutional Neural Network (CNN)

CNN, often known as ConvNet, is a deep learning method that is mostly used for image classification. The CNN framework was influenced by the Visual Cortex, which is analogous to the pattern of interconnection in the nervous system. Convolution, max pooling and fully connected-Relu are among the different stages used to categorize the dataset. Convolution is necessary for extracting features and data resizing after many stages.

### 3.3  Long Term Short Term Memory (LSTM)

LSTM is a deep learning artificial recurrent neural network variant (RNN). LSTMs, unlike traditional neural networks, have input connections. It is capable of handling both large data streams and single data points (such as images). LSTM is used in non-segmented handwriting recognition, speech recognition, network traffic anomaly detection, and emotion recognition. A standard LSTM unit includes a cell, an entry gate, an exit gate, and a forgetfulness door. The information flows within and out of the cell are regulated by the three gates, and the cell's time scores are uncertain. Because of it's ambiguity in delay periods, time series data-based LSTM networks are suitable for classification, analysis, and forecasting. LSTMs are often used to fix the break - down and vanishing gradient issues that are common in regular RNNs.

### 3.4  Proposed Hybrid CNN-LSTM Model

In contrast to conventional CNNs, RNNs enable the formation of associations between input series, providing a new approach to hybrid features [12, 33]. Researchers developed methods to integrate functionalities using LSTM (a variant of the RNN), which can evaluate the data's long-term dependence to enhance detection performance. A contemporary but similar strategy to extracting features has been established in the function of this research by using many convolutional kernels. Our method is divided into two parts: a feature extraction segment based on CNN and a feature fusion segment based on LSTM.

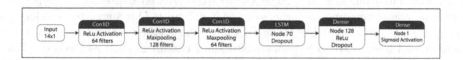

**Fig. 2.** Proposed CNN-LSTM model.

Figure 2 depicts our suggested CNN-LSTM model. In the proposed model, two 1D convolutional layers are separated by a max-pooling layer and after which a further 1D convolutional layer. An LSTM layer follows the third convolutional layer, followed by a dropout layer, and finally a dense layer or output layer. The output layer contains loss and accuracy parameters such as optimizer functions, learning rates, and matrices.

The first convolution layer consists of 64 filters with a 3 by 3 kernel size. The input layer sends data to the output layer. A Rectied Linear Unit activation function is also present in the convolution layers (ReLU). ReLU aids the model in reducing the problem of disappearing gradients [20]. After the convolution layer, there is a max-pooling and dropout layer. With a max-pooling layer, the feature map extracts the most features.

To save the features in the feature map, this max-pooling layer fits them into a two-by-two slot. Several convolution layers are dropped out by the dropout layer, which removes 25% of the nodes. Dropout layers avoid overfitting [28] while also reducing model loss. After that, an LSTM layer is added to the CNN model. The LSTM layers contain 70 nodes. Its primary objective is to derive definition from the CNN layer's extracted features. The model is then placed in an output layer. In the output layers, there are one nodes. The one nodes correspond to two distinct classes. A sigmoid activation function is also included in the output layer.

## 4   Result and Discussion

In this section, we'll look at how the proposed model determines epilepsy. We have used two classes in our research which are epilepsy and normal The EEG was used to obtain data for this experiment. The dataset was split into two parts, each with a train-test ratio of 80-20%. We utilized 80% of our data for training our Cnn architecture, and the rest 20% had been used to verify it once it had been trained.

### 4.1   System Configuration

We employed a GPU [1] with tensor flow capabilities to implement CNN-LSTM. Because the CNN-LSTM model involves a lot of matrix multiplication operations, a powerful GPU is required for training. TBecause of the processing power constraints of a CPU, the suggested CNN-LSTM architecture is intended for training on the Google Colaboratory cloud server. The GPU and Jupyter Notebook environments in Google Colab were created expressly to help computer learners overcome the processing unit difficulty. Our suggested model was trained and validated using Google Colab. The Python scikit-learn [23] component had been used to implement standard classifiers such as Decision Tree, Logistic Regression, and Support Vector Machine.

### 4.2   Hyperpararmeters Tuning

Because hyperparameters have a direct influence on the model's behavior, they are mandatory. We've trained our proposed model with a variety of optimizers, including Adam, SGD, RMSProp, and Adamax, to examine how it reacts to different optimization techniques. For training the model, we employed 16 batch sizes and 200 epochs, as well as a learning rate of 0.001. The probability loss of the class predicted by the sigmoid function is measured by the binary crossentropy loss function as well.

### 4.3   Performance Matrix

We employed Accuracy, Loss, and MAE (mean absolute error) [27] to evaluate epilepsy detection in this study. We also compared the proposed model's performance to that of existing machine learning classifiers using three metrics: precision, recall, and F1-score.

## 4.4  Result

The outcomes of our suggested model employing various optimizers are shown in Table 1. The Adam optimizer has a 94.98% training accuracy and an 82.21% testing accuracy. It also has a testing loss of 0.249 and a training loss of 0.12. The RMSProp optimizer, on the other hand, has training accuracy and training loss of 93.96% and 0.148%, respectively. RMSProp has a testing accuracy of 81.08% and a training loss of 0.803. SGD, the Next optimizer, has a training accuracy of 70.65% and a testing accuracy of 72.97%. The training loss of the SGD optimizer is 0.584, and the testing loss is 0.539. Finally, the Adamax optimizer has a training accuracy of 98.80% and a training loss of 0.047, as well as a testing accuracy of 79.97% and a testing loss of 1.323%.

**Table 1.** CNN-LSTM model performance.

| Optimizer | Training accuracy | Training loss | Validation accuracy | Validation loss |
|-----------|-------------------|---------------|---------------------|-----------------|
| Adam      | 94.98%            | 0.120         | 82.21%              | 0.249           |
| RMSProp   | 93.96%            | 0.148         | 81.08%              | 0.803           |
| SGD       | 70.65%            | 0.584         | 72.97%              | 0.539           |
| Adamax    | 98.80%            | 0.047         | 79.97%              | 1.323           |

Table 2 compares the performance of our proposed CNN-LSTM model with three existing machine learning techniques. Decision Tree, Naive Bayes, and Logistic Regression are the three methods. Accuracy, precision, recall, f-score, RMSE, and MSE are the parameters we utilized to compare. CNN-LSTM has a precision of 0.84 and an accuracy of 82.21%, with recall, f-score, RMSE, and MSE of 0.82, 0.83, 0.421, and 0.178, respectively. In every sector, it clearly outperforms the other three algorithms.

**Table 2.** Comparisons among proposed CNN-LSTM and machine learning classifier.

| Algorithm | Accuracy | Precision | Recall | F-score | RMSE | MSE |
|-----------|----------|-----------|--------|---------|------|-----|
| CNN-LSTM            | 82.21% | 0.84 | 0.82 | 0.83 | 0.421 | 0.178 |
| CNN                | 81.08% | 0.81 | 0.83 | 0.82 | 0.568 | 0.205 |
| Decision Tree      | 75.21% | 0.74 | 0.79 | 0.77 | 0.504 | 0.254 |
| Naïve Bayes        | 67.34% | 0.72 | 0.61 | 0.66 | 0.577 | 0.334 |
| Logistic Regression | 80.00% | 0.79 | 0.81 | 0.82 | 0.447 | 0.204 |

Figure 3 depicts the proposed CNN-LSTM algorithm's training and validation accuracy. The training accuracy is shown in red, while the validation accuracy is shown in blue. From epoch 20 onwards, we can see that the training accuracy is ahead of the validation accuracy. The accuracy of training and validation is almost 70% in the first epoch, as seen in this graph. As the number of epochs increases, so does the accuracy. The training accuracy is almost 83% at epoch 50, whereas the validation accuracy is 80%. Training accuracy is 94% in Epoch 200, whereas testing accuracy is 82%.

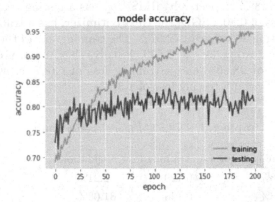

**Fig. 3.** Training and validation accuracy of the proposed CNN-LSTM.

The training and validation losses of our proposed CNN-LSTM method are shown in Fig. 4. The training loss is shown in red, while the validation loss is shown in blue. With the first epoch, the suggested CNN-LSTM algorithm's training and validation loss is near 0.6. When the epoch number is raised, the training loss decreases. And it continues to fall until it reaches 0.2 at epoch 200. The loss value for testing, on the other hand, continues to rise, reaching 0.9 at epoch level 200.

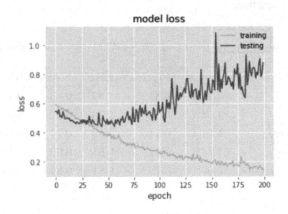

**Fig. 4.** Training and validation loss of the proposed CNN-LSTM.

# 5    Conclusion and Future Work

We proposed a new method for detecting epilepsy using EEG in this research. To identify epilepsy from EEG data, a hybrid CNN-LSTM approach is used. The proposed approach has a high accuracy, according to the results of the experiments. Our suggested technique was also compared to various machine learning classifiers. Data, on the other hand, is insufficient. In the future, we will use additional data to train our model. We also apply some technique for avoiding the overfitting problem. We also try to apply some other method [2, 3, 5–7, 9, 11, 14, 18–22, 30] to detect epilepsy.

# References

1. Abadi, M., et al.: Tensorflow: a system for large-scale machine learning. In: 12th USENIX Symposium on Operating Systems Design and Implementation (OSDI 2016), pp. 265–283 (2016)
2. Afroze, T., Akther, S., Chowdhury, M.A., Hossain, E., Hossain, M.S., Andersson, K.: Glaucoma detection using inception convolutional neural network V3. In: Mahmud, M., Kaiser, M.S., Kasabov, N., Iftekharuddin, K., Zhong, N. (eds.) Glaucoma detection using inception convolutional neural network v3. CCIS, vol. 1435, pp. 17–28. Springer, Cham (2021). https://doi.org/10.1007/978-3-030-82269-9_2
3. Ahmed, F., Hossain, M.S., Islam, R.U., Andersson, K.: An evolutionary belief rule-based clinical decision support system to predict COVID-19 severity under uncertainty. Appl. Sci. **11**(13), 5810 (2021)
4. Akut, R.: Wavelet based deep learning approach for epilepsy detection. Health Inf. Sci. Syst. **7**(1), 1–9 (2019). https://doi.org/10.1007/s13755-019-0069-1
5. Basnin, N., Nahar, L., Hossain, M.S.: An integrated CNN-LSTM model for micro hand gesture recognition. In: Vasant, P., Zelinka, I., Weber, G.-W. (eds.) ICO 2020. AISC, vol. 1324, pp. 379–392. Springer, Cham (2021). https://doi.org/10.1007/978-3-030-68154-8_35
6. Basnin, N., Nahar, N., Anika, F.A., Hossain, M.S., Andersson, K.: Deep learning approach to classify Parkinson's disease from MRI samples. In: Mahmud, M., Kaiser, M.S., Vassanelli, S., Dai, Q., Zhong, N. (eds.) BI 2021. LNCS (LNAI), vol. 12960, pp. 536–547. Springer, Cham (2021). https://doi.org/10.1007/978-3-030-86993-9_48
7. Basnin, N., Sumi, T.A., Hossain, M.S., Andersson, K.: Early detection of Parkinson's disease from micrographic static hand drawings. In: Mahmud, M., Kaiser, M.S., Vassanelli, S., Dai, Q., Zhong, N. (eds.) BI 2021. LNCS (LNAI), vol. 12960, pp. 433–447. Springer, Cham (2021). https://doi.org/10.1007/978-3-030-86993-9_39
8. Birjandtalab, J., Heydarzadeh, M., Nourani, M.: Automated EEG-based epileptic seizure detection using deep neural networks. In: 2017 IEEE International Conference on Healthcare Informatics (ICHI), pp. 552–555. IEEE (2017)
9. Biswas, M., Chowdhury, S.U., Nahar, N., Hossain, M.S., Andersson, K.: A belief rule base expert system for staging non-small cell lung cancer under uncertainty. In: 2019 IEEE International Conference on Biomedical Engineering, Computer and Information Technology for Health (BECITHCON), pp. 47–52. IEEE (2019)

10. Chakraborti, S., Choudhary, A., Singh, A., Kumar, R., Swetapadma, A.: A machine learning based method to detect epilepsy. Int. J. Inf. Technol. **10**(3), 257–263 (2018). https://doi.org/10.1007/s41870-018-0088-1

11. Gosh, S., Nahar, N., Wahab, M.A., Biswas, M., Hossain, M.S., Andersson, K.: Recommendation system for e-commerce using alternating least squares (ALS) on apache spark. In: Vasant, P., Zelinka, I., Weber, G.-W. (eds.) ICO 2020. AISC, vol. 1324, pp. 880–893. Springer, Cham (2021). https://doi.org/10.1007/978-3-030-68154-8_75

12. Greff, K., Srivastava, R.K., Koutník, J., Steunebrink, B.R., Schmidhuber, J.: LSTM: a search space odyssey. IEEE Trans. Neural Netw. Learn. Syst. **28**(10), 2222–2232 (2016)

13. Hossain, M.S., Amin, S.U., Alsulaiman, M., Muhammad, G.: Applying deep learning for epilepsy seizure detection and brain mapping visualization. ACM Trans. Multimed. Comput. Commun. App. (TOMM) **15**(1s), 1–17 (2019)

14. Islam, R.U., Ruci, X., Hossain, M.S., Andersson, K., Kor, A.L.: Capacity management of hyperscale data centers using predictive modelling. Energies **12**(18), 3438 (2019)

15. Kumar, J.S., Bhuvaneswari, P.: Analysis of electroencephalography (EEG) signals and its categorization-a study. Proc. Eng. **38**, 2525–2536 (2012)

16. Liu, J., Woodson, B.: Deep learning classification for epilepsy detection using a single channel electroencephalography (EEG). In: Proceedings of the 2019 3rd International Conference on Deep Learning Technologies, pp. 23–26 (2019)

17. Mardini, W., Yassein, M.M.B., Al-Rawashdeh, R., Aljawarneh, S., Khamayseh, Y., Meqdadi, O.: Enhanced detection of epileptic seizure using EEG signals in combination with machine learning classifiers. IEEE Access **8**, 24046–24055 (2020)

18. Nahar, N., Ara, F., Neloy, M.A.I., Biswas, A., Hossain, M.S., Andersson, K.: Feature selection based machine learning to improve prediction of Parkinson disease. In: Mahmud, M., Kaiser, M.S., Vassanelli, S., Dai, Q., Zhong, N. (eds.) .: Feature selection based machine learning to improve prediction of parkinson disease. LNCS (LNAI), vol. 12960, pp. 496–508. Springer, Cham (2021). https://doi.org/10.1007/978-3-030-86993-9_44

19. Nahar, N., Ara, F., Neloy, M.A.I., Barua, V., Hossain, M.S., Andersson, K.: A comparative analysis of the ensemble method for liver disease prediction. In: 2019 2nd International Conference on Innovation in Engineering and Technology (ICIET), pp. 1–6. IEEE (2019)

20. Nahar, N., Hossain, M.S., Andersson, K.: A machine learning based fall detection for elderly people with neurodegenerative disorders. In: Mahmud, M., Vassanelli, S., Kaiser, M.S., Zhong, N. (eds.) BI 2020. LNCS (LNAI), vol. 12241, pp. 194–203. Springer, Cham (2020). https://doi.org/10.1007/978-3-030-59277-6_18

21. Pathan, R.K., Uddin, M.A., Nahar, N., Ara, F., Hossain, M.S., Andersson, K.: Gender classification from inertial sensor-based gait dataset. In: Vasant, P., Zelinka, I., Weber, G.-W. (eds.) ICO 2020. AISC, vol. 1324, pp. 583–596. Springer, Cham (2021). https://doi.org/10.1007/978-3-030-68154-8_51

22. Pathan, R.K., Uddin, M.A., Nahar, N., Ara, F., Hossain, M.S., Andersson, K.: Human age estimation using deep learning from gait data. In: Mahmud, M., Kaiser, M.S., Kasabov, N., Iftekharuddin, K., Zhong, N. (eds.) AII 2021. CCIS, vol. 1435, pp. 281–294. Springer, Cham (2021). https://doi.org/10.1007/978-3-030-82269-9_22

23. Pedregosa, F., et al.: Scikit-learn: Machine learning in python. J. Mach. Learn. Res. **12**, 2825–2830 (2011)

24. Qureshi, M.B., et al.: Machine learning-based EEG signals classification model for epileptic seizure detection. Multimed. Tools App. **80**(12), 17849–17877 (2021)
25. Resque, P., Barros, A., Rosário, D., Cerqueira, E.: An investigation of different machine learning approaches for epileptic seizure detection. In: 2019 15th International Wireless Communications & Mobile Computing Conference (IWCMC), pp. 301–306. IEEE (2019)
26. Shoeibi, A., et al.: Epileptic seizures detection using deep learning techniques: a review. Int. J. Environ. Res. Publ. Health **18**(11), 5780 (2021)
27. Sokolova, M., Lapalme, G.: A systematic analysis of performance measures for classification tasks. Inf. Process. Manag. **45**(4), 427–437 (2009)
28. Srivastava, N., Hinton, G., Krizhevsky, A., Sutskever, I., Salakhutdinov, R.: Dropout: a simple way to prevent neural networks from overfitting. J. Mach. Learn. Res. **15**(1), 1929–1958 (2014)
29. Subasi, A., Kevric, J., Abdullah Canbaz, M.: Epileptic seizure detection using hybrid machine learning methods. Neural Comput. App. **31**(1), 317–325 (2017). https://doi.org/10.1007/s00521-017-3003-y
30. Sultana, Z., Nahar, L., Basnin, N., Hossain, M.S.: Inference and learning methodology of belief rule based expert system to assess Chikungunya. In: Mahmud, M., Kaiser, M.S., Kasabov, N., Iftekharuddin, K., Zhong, N. (eds.) AII 2021. CCIS, vol. 1435, pp. 3–16. Springer, Cham (2021). https://doi.org/10.1007/978-3-030-82269-9_1
31. Thara, D., PremaSudha, B., Xiong, F.: Auto-detection of epileptic seizure events using deep neural network with different feature scaling techniques. Pattern Recogn. Lett. **128**, 544–550 (2019)
32. Tsiouris, K.M., Pezoulas, V.C., Zervakis, M., Konitsiotis, S., Koutsouris, D.D., Fotiadis, D.I.: A long short-term memory deep learning network for the prediction of epileptic seizures using EEG signals. Comput. Biol. Med. **99**, 24–37 (2018)
33. Wang, J., Zhang, J., Wang, X.: Bilateral LSTM: a two-dimensional long short-term memory model with multiply memory units for short-term cycle time forecasting in re-entrant manufacturing systems. IEEE Trans. Ind. Inform. **14**(2), 748–758 (2017)

# Classifying Brain Tumor from MRI Images Using Parallel CNN Model

Tahmina Akter Sumi[1]([✉])(iD), Tanuja Nath[1](iD), Nazmun Nahar[2](iD),
Mohammad Shahadat Hossain[1](iD), and Karl Andersson[3](iD)

[1] University of Chittagong, Chittagong, Bangladesh
tahminashumi1997@gmail.com, hossain_ms@cu.ac.bd
[2] Noakhali Science and Technology University, Noakhali, Bangladesh
nammun@nstu.edu.bd
[3] Lulea University of Technology, Skelleftea, Sweden
karl.andersson@ltu.se

**Abstract.** Brain tumor, commonly known as intracranial tumor, is the most general and deadly disease which leads to a very short lifespan. It occurs due to the uncontrollable growth of cells which is unchecked by the process that is engaged in monitoring the normal cells. The survival rate due to this disease is the lowest and consequently the detection and classification of brain tumor has become crucial in early stages. In manual approach, brain tumors are diagnosed using (MRI). After the MRI displays the tumor in brain, the type of the tumor is identified by examining the result of biopsy of sample tissue. But having some limitations such as accurate measurement is achieved for finite number of image and also being time consuming matter, the automated computer aided diagnosis play a crucial rule in the detection of brain tumor. Several supervised and unsupervised machine learning algorithms have been established for the classification of brain tumor for years. In this paper, we have utilized both image processing and deep learning for successful classification of brain tumor from the MRI images. At first in the image preprocessing step, the MRI images are normalized and through image augmentation the number of images is enriched. Further the preprocessed images are passed through a parallel CNN network where the features of the images are extracted and classified. Our experimental result shows an accuracy of 89% that is promising.

**Keywords:** Brain tumor · Data augmentation · Convolution neural network · Deep learning

## 1 Introduction

An extracellular growth in the brain, also known as a brain tumor, an anomalous living tissue in which cells proliferate and multiply uncontrolled, appearing unrestrained by the module controls normal cells. There are many more over 150 different types of brain tumors, but the two most common types are

© Springer Nature Switzerland AG 2022
M. Mahmud et al. (Eds.): BI 2022, LNAI 13406, pp. 264–276, 2022
https://doi.org/10.1007/978-3-031-15037-1_22

primary and metastatic. Tumors that arise from the brain's tissues or the brain's surrounding are known as primary brain tumors. Glial and non-glial primary tumors are classified as benign or malignant. Tumors that start somewhere else in the body (such as the lungs) and spread to the brain via the circulation are known as metastatic brain tumors. Cancerous tumors that have spread to other parts of the body are known as metastatic tumors.

There are different treatment procedures for different type of tumor. So, it is also obvious to classify what type of tumor it is. In this research, first we focused on detecting the tumor and then classify the tumor according to their type whether the tumor is Meningioma or Glioma or Pituitary or No Tumor.

The major tasks regarding medical image processing can be categorized in many ways. It has been researched by many scientists for a long time from now. Different researchers approached this problem in different ways and tried to solve them efficiently. Yet there is scope to improve the prediction task and contribute in health care. Many have done this research using MRI, many have used CT scan image of brain tumor.

Magnetic Resonance Image (MRI) of brain is widely used. Because Magnetic resonance imaging (MRI) may be a powerful imaging technique that makes prime quality images of the carnal structures of the human body, particularly within the brain, and produces much high information for medical diagnosis and clinical research [7,16,17,29]. The characteristic values of MRI are greatly augmented by the computerized and proper classification technique [22].

So in this paper for classifying brain tumor, we have utilized the MRI images that has been collected from kaggle website to develop a statistical and efficient model to make our classification accurate. In this regard at first we have normalised the images as preprocessing step. After that, the images have been augmented that helps to enrich and increase the size of the data. Once the preprocessing and augmentation is done, the dataset is now ready to pass through deep learning model. We have applied a parallel CNN model on the dataset that perform the feature extraction and the classification that finally classify the images into four brain tumor category that are "Meningioma", "Glioma" and "Pituitary" and "No tumor".

The following are the portions of this document in order of appearance: The past works on brain tumor detection and classification are described in Sect. 2. The Parallel Convolution Neural Network model has been discussed comprehensively in Sect. 3, which displays the complete process. The outcomes of our work are discussed in Sect. 4, and the conclusion and future work of this research are shown in Sect. 5.

## 2   Literature Review

Recent advancements in technological clinical applications have led to an improved functioning of the incorporation of deep learning concepts.

A method, proposed by Cheng et al. [6], for extracting characteristics from the selected area of T-1 MRI images based on manually defined tumor borders, with the best findings acquired using an SVM model incorporating bag of words (BOW) features. One of the first assessments of the figshare brain MRI image collection has been published in this research work.

A Gabor filter and discrete wavelet transform feature extraction method, proceeded by a algorithm named multi-layer perceptron algorithm for classifying the images , has been introduced in A. Qadar et al. [11]'s research work. The shortcoming of both of these approaches is that feature extraction is done through semi-manual techniques. CNNs offer a clear benefit in this situation because they do not require human occupied segmentation and are capable of extracting key characteristics through their own.

Using the transfer learning technique, K. Swati et al. [25] constructed a VGG-19 model that's been pre-trained to diagnose brain cancers out of a figshare brain MRI image dataset. S. Deepak et al. [25] used the same transfer learning technique to execute an extended GoogLeNet model on the equivalent figshare dataset.

In the past, Justin Ker et al. [15] employed the InceptionV3 model to classify brain histology slices, as well as histology slices from the tissues of brain and breast.

A CNN-based deep learning network was satisfactorily used to solve the problem of brain tumor categorization [?]. CNN-based classifier systems offer the advantage of not requiring manually segmented tumor regions and giving a fully automated classifier.

A CNN structure turned into designed through Pashaei et al. [18] to extract attributes from mind MRI samples. The version blanketed 5 learnable layers with $3 \times 3$ filter sizes throughout all of them. The version contained 5 learnable layers with $3 \times 3$ filter sizes throughout all of them. The class accuracy of the CNN version turned into 81%. The overall performance turned into advanced with the aid of using combining CNN capabilities with an excessive getting to know system classifier version (ELM). In this research, the recall measures for pituitary tumors had been pretty high, whilst the ones for meningioma had been pretty poor. This suggests that the classifier's discrimination capability is not unlimited.

To categorize brain tumors, Afshar et al. [1] constructed a CNN model which is modified and known as a capsule network (CapsNet). CapsNet took into account the tumor's spatial relationship with its muscle tissue. Despite this, there was only a slight improvement in performance.

Talo et al. [26] introduced a deep transfer learning to obtain effective classification results for finding brain tumor abnormalities categorization. They have used ResNet-34 in their study, including comprised improved dense layer training, data augmentation during training, plus fine tuning of model named transfer learning model. The studies revealed that a model which is based on deep transfer may be utilized to classify medical photos with little or no pre-processing.

In their study, Yang et al. [28] used AlexNet and GoogLeNet to assess gliomas from MRI data. On the reported performance criteria, GoogLeNet outperformed AlexNet for the task. Transfer learning was used to detect brain tumors in content-based image retrieval (CBIR) [25]. The experiment was carried out with the use of a freely released dataset, and the findings were positive.

## 3    Methodology

Biological systems have been highly inspired by the CNN which mainly contains three neural layers that construct the architecture [4,9,19,23,24]. These layers are- Convolutional, Pooling, and Fully Connected (FC) layer [2,5,31]. This section will broadly discuss the architecture of our model. Our proposed model mainly covers two basic parts feature extraction and classification. Firstly, convolution and pooling layers are implemented simultaneously. After that in the function level we adjoin the parallel layers. There after the flatten layers contain Multi Layer Perceptrons into 2 levels. However, the neurons at each layers that drop are needed to be calculated for preventing the overfitting problem. Finally the classification is done using softmax function.

### 3.1    Dataset

The dataset has been collected from the kaggle website which is an open source resource. There are total 3,264 numbers of T2 weighted contrast images which are divided into four different classes where one class depicts the MRI images with no tumor and other classes depict three different types of brain tumor namely Meningioma, Glioma and Pituitary tumor. Here among all the 3024 images, Glioma contains 926 images, Meningioma contains 937, Pituitary holds 901 images and finally 500 images contains MRI images with no tumor. The MRI brain images vary in "Axial", "Coronal", and "Sagittal" aspects. The resolution of the MRI images is $512 \times 512$ pixels which follows a matrix form. A sample view of the dataset used in this research is given in Fig. 1 where four different type of images has been shown of four different class tumor. In this figure the first image is the sample example of Glioma tumor. The second image illustrates the sample of Meningioma tumor. The third one is collected from the Pituitary tumor class and finally the last one is the MRI image that contains no tumor.

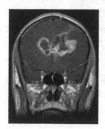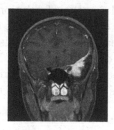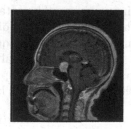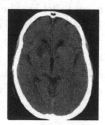

**Fig. 1.** MRI images of 4 different types of brain tumor

## 3.2  Data Preprocessing

Preprocessing technique is mainly applied on images to reduce the low frequency background noise and normalize the data so that it can be prepared for better feature extraction. Here in the preprocessing stage at first we have resized all the images into $224 \times 224$ pixels. The Z-score normalization has been used to standardize the intensity of the images. After applying the normalization technique, the range of the pixel values of the images will be within 0 and 1. The normalization can be calculated by the equation given below where x refers the training sample and s denotes the standard deviation of training sample.

$$z = \frac{x - b}{s} \tag{1}$$

## 3.3  Data Augmentation

Data augmentation is a process that helps to enhance the performance of a model by enriching the dataset to a great extant. Usually by the data augmentation process, more copies of data from the existing dataset are generated. It is about fabricating more data from the existing dataset without losing the data information. This process is efficient in case of smaller size of dataset as it helps to increase the number of data and thus lessen the risk of overfitting problem.

As stated earlier, in this study we have used total 3264 MRI images of four different types of brain tumor which is relatively smaller for assuring the neural network model's stability. For this reason we implemented the data augmentation process on the MRI images before training the model. In case of this, we applied the ImageDataGenerator. Here rotation, width shift, height shift, zoom has been kept as 25, 0.10, 0.10, 0.10 respectively. The horizontal flip has been kept as true and fill mode is nearest.

## 3.4  Feature Extraction

In the first phase of our model, it holds 5 convolution layers as CBr = iconv where the values of n are 64, 128, 256, 512, 512 respectively that is followed by max pooling layer. As we can see in Fig. 2, two CBr = iConv blocks are rendered in parallel by the input image. The total number of dilation for example $d_i = 1, 2, 3, ..., N$ are changed. As the rate of dilation increases, the performance of convolution layer improves and attains quality picture details. As per definition, the dilation rate 1 indicates the normal convolution layer. However, when the dilation rate is two, each input will skip a pixel. The following Eq. 2 illustrates the receptive file when the kernel size is ks that is dilated by the dilation rate $d_i$.

$$r_f = d_i(k_1) + 1 \tag{2}$$

And Eq. 3 illustrates the size of the output O for ixi input image along with dialation factor $d_i$, padding $p_d$ and the stride is $s_t$ respectively.

$$O = i + 2p_{d}r_{f}s_{t} + 1 \tag{3}$$

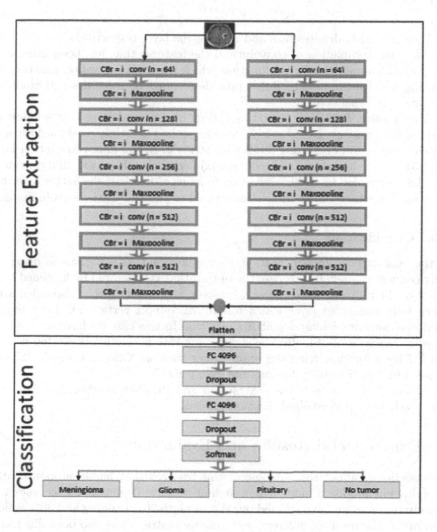

**Fig. 2.** A full schematic diagram of network architecture

Each of the 1st CBr = iconv block contains 2 convolution and activation layers whereas the last 3 blocks contains 4 convolution and activation layers with $(3 \times 3)$ filter size. The equation for convolution layer with filters as following:

$$F_s = f_1^{j \times j} f_2^{j \times j} ... f_n^{j \times j} \tag{4}$$

For the layer 1, the convolution network yield feature maps from the inputs where the $d_i$ denotes the dilation rate and $m_f \times m_f$ is considered as input feature map.

$$Y_l^{o \times o} = Y_{l_1, d_i=k}^{m_f \times m_f} \times l_f + l_b \tag{5}$$

Here, $l_b$ and $l_f$ denotes bias and filter of the layer respectively.

After the completion of convolution, the features that has been generated, are passed through the ReLU function which works as activation function for creating new feature map as ReLU provides a range of amenities and gradients can be easily expanded.

Max pooling layer is designed as 5 time incremental form that supports a block of CBr = iconv. In our study, the maxpooling is mainly used for downscaling the strained images using $2 \times 2$ with stride 2. In the final convolution layer total 512 filters have been utilized with jxj kernel size. Here the dilation rate is one that is pursued by ReLU activation function. Afterthat, the flatten layer has been applied where the architecture revealed to transforms the feature maps.

## 3.5    Classification

In the final stage of implementation, a classification task is performed using the fully connected layer. In this case the output that is generated by flattened layer is fed to the fully connected layer. Moreover, a dropout layer is appended after every fully connected layer which mainly disconnect certain FC layer weight randomly for diminishing overfitting problem. In this case we have selected the dropout range as 0.5. Finally, the sigmoid activation function is exerted next to the FC layer for classifying the brain tumor such as "Glioma tumor", "Meningioma tumor", "Pituitary tumor" and "No tumor".

In Fig. 2, the whole feature extraction and the classification that has been discussed above is illustrated diagrammatically.

# 4    Experimental Results and Evaluation

This section is about the outcome of this research that has been gained after applying our proposed model. Here at first we have depicted the accuracy and loss curve. Here, we have splitted our dataset into 70% training and 30% validation ratio. The result of different performance matrices has also been illustrated in the following subsection. Finally, we have shown a comparison of our proposed model with other pretrained model and also with some recent works.

## 4.1    Result

Figure 3 graphically illustrates the performance of accuracy as well as loss for the parallel CNN model on the MRI images. Here the left image shows the training and testing accuracy curve whereas the right image indicates the training and testing loss curve. It is clear from the graph that the both training and testing accuracy follows an upward trend. On the other hand, the loss curve decrease.

According to Fig. 3(a), it is appeared that the X axis indicates the total epoch for train dataset whereas the Y axis depicts the accuracy and loss respectively. From Fig. 3(a) it can be summarised by saying that the training accuracy rises from 73% upto 92% and testing accuracy rises from 70% to 89% respectively after the completion of 50 epochs.

According to Fig 3(b), the training loss decreases from 1.6 to .5 and testing loss decreases from 1.6 to .6 respectively after the implementation of 50 epochs. It is clear from both graph that the both training and testing accuracy follows an upward trend whereas the loss decreases with time.

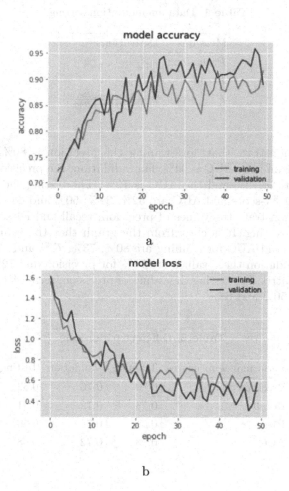

**Fig. 3.** Accuracy and loss curve: (a) accuracy vs epoch (b) loss vs epoch

## 4.2  Performance Matrix

To evaluate the overall performance of our model and also to test the efficacy, several performance matrix for example Recall, Precision and F1 score has been calculated here. In Table 2, equation for each of the performance matrix utilized in this research has been illustrated. Here, TP indicates true positive rate, FP indicates false positive rate, TN indicates true negative rate and FN indicates false negative rate.

**Table 1.** Data augmentation settings

| Measures | Derivations |
|----------|-------------|
| $Precision$ | $\frac{TP}{TP+FN}$ |
| $Recall$ | $\frac{TP}{TP+FN}$ |
| $F1 - score$ | $2. \frac{Precision\,.\,Recall}{Precision+Recall}$ |

Table 3 demonstrate that, for training the precision is 80%, recall is 73%, F1-score is 77% and the AUC is 93%. For validation, the precision is 76%, recall is 72%, F1-score is 72% and the AUC is 72%. The testing shows the value of precision, recall F1-score and AUC are 52%, 31%, 50% and 68% respectively.

Table 3 demonstrate the values of precision, recall and F1-score of training, validation and testing. It is clear from the graph that the values of precision, recall, F1-score and AUC for training are 80%, 73%, 77% and 93% respectively whereas for validation these values are 76% for precision and 72% for the other performance matrix. For testing the values of precision, recall, F1-score and AUC are 52%, 31%, 50% and 68%.

**Table 2.** Different parameters

| Performance measures | Training | Validation | Testing |
|----------------------|----------|------------|---------|
| Precision | 0.80 | 0.76 | 0.52 |
| Recall | 0.73 | 0.72 | 0.31 |
| F1-score | 0.77 | 0.72 | 0.50 |
| AUC | 0.93 | 0.72 | 0.68 |

## 4.3  Comparison of Different Models

In this paper, several pretrained model have been used to train our dataset so that we can compare our model with other pretrained model. Here, the pretrained model (VGG19, ResNet50, EfficientNetB0) have been used in this respect. After implementing all this models we have observed that out proposed parallel CNN model outperforms the other models. Table 4 illustrates the training and testing accuracy as well as the training and testing loss of the other models.

**Table 3.** Comparison of results

| Models | Accuracy | Loss |
|---|---|---|
| Proposed model | .89 | 0.6 |
| VGG-19 | 0.74 | 1.43 |
| ResNet50 | 0.73 | 1.6 |
| EfficientNetB0 | 0.75 | 1.46 |

In Table 4, we have compared our proposed method with other works. Here, we have illustrated the classification technique that has been used in the previous research as well as the accuracy of the work. As we can see, our proposed methods outperforms all the previous works with 89% accuracy.

**Table 4.** Comparison with previous works

| Reference | Classifier | Accuracy |
|---|---|---|
| Sajid S. et al. [21] | CNN | 86% |
| Iqbal S. et al. [8] | Ensemble fusion | 82.29% |
| Amian M. et al. [3] | Random forest | 55% |
| Our proposed model | Parallel CNN | 89% |

## 5   Conclusion and Future Work

In this research work, the main objectives is to develop a system to classify brain tumor type which works in the same line of work of a physician or medical diagnosis. This research paper presented a step-by-step methodology for the MRI brain tumor classification using Deep learning. This automated system of classifying brain tumor holds some benefits of quick classification, effective and time saving process. In this research we have employed deep neural network for training dataset. Here, we classify four types brain tumor using our pretrained model. However as the dataset used is this research is limited, there an overfitting problem has been occured. So, in future, we aim at collecting more images to train our model. Also, as the k fold cross validation has not been performed in this work, so in future we aim at applying k fold cross validation to asses our model. Moreover, it would be very interesting if we can include additional feature information from locations or more from textures to make the system more sensitive. And we intent to improve our proposed model applying the BRBaDE. Thus we can ameliorate the performance by conducting parameter and structure optimization [10, 12–14, 20, 27, 30].

# References

1. Afshar, P., Plataniotis, K.N., Mohammadi, A.: Capsule networks for brain tumor classification based on MRI images and coarse tumor boundaries. In: ICASSP 2019–2019 IEEE International Conference on Acoustics, Speech and Signal Processing (ICASSP), pp. 1368–1372. IEEE (2019)
2. Ahmed, T.U., Hossain, S., Hossain, M.S., ul Islam, R., Andersson, K.: Facial expression recognition using convolutional neural network with data augmentation. In: 2019 Joint 8th International Conference on Informatics, Electronics & Vision (ICIEV) and 2019 3rd International Conference on Imaging, Vision & Pattern Recognition (icIVPR), pp. 336–341. IEEE (2019)
3. Amian, M., Soltaninejad, M.: Multi-resolution 3D CNN for MRI brain tumor segmentation and survival prediction. In: Crimi, A., Bakas, S. (eds.) BrainLes 2019. LNCS, vol. 11992, pp. 221–230. Springer, Cham (2020). https://doi.org/10.1007/978-3-030-46640-4_21
4. Basnin, N., Nahar, L., Hossain, M.S.: An integrated CNN-LSTM model for micro hand gesture recognition. In: Vasant, P., Zelinka, I., Weber, GW. (eds) Intelligent Computing and Optimization. ICO 2020. Advances in Intelligent Systems and Computing, vol. 1324, pp. 379–392. Springer, Cham (2020). https://doi.org/10.1007/978-3-030-68154-8_35
5. Basnin, N., Sumi, T.A., Hossain, M.S., Andersson, K.: Early detection of Parkinson's disease from micrographic static hand drawings. In: Mahmud, M., Kaiser, M.S., Vassanelli, S., Dai, Q., Zhong, N. (eds.) BI 2021. LNCS (LNAI), vol. 12960, pp. 433–447. Springer, Cham (2021). https://doi.org/10.1007/978-3-030-86993-9_39
6. Cheng, J., et al.: Enhanced performance of brain tumor classification via tumor region augmentation and partition. PloS ONE **10**(10), e0140381 (2015)
7. Golestanirad, L., Izquierdo, A.P., Graham, S.J., Mosig, J., Pollo, C.: Effect of realistic modeling of deep brain stimulation on the prediction of volume of activated tissue. Progr. Electromagn. Res. **126**, 1–16 (2012)
8. Iqbal, S., et al.: Deep learning model integrating features and novel classifiers fusion for brain tumor segmentation. Microsc. Res. Techn. **82**(8), 1302–1315 (2019)
9. Islam, M.Z., Hossain, M.S., ul Islam, R., Andersson, K.: Static hand gesture recognition using convolutional neural network with data augmentation. In: 2019 Joint 8th International Conference on Informatics, Electronics & Vision (ICIEV) and 2019 3rd International Conference on Imaging, Vision & Pattern Recognition (icIVPR), pp. 324–329. IEEE (2019)
10. Islam, R.U., Hossain, M.S., Andersson, K.: A deep learning inspired belief rule-based expert system. IEEE Access **8**, 190637–190651 (2020)
11. Ismael, M.R., Abdel-Qader, I.: Brain tumor classification via statistical features and back-propagation neural network. In: 2018 IEEE international conference on electro/information technology (EIT), pp. 0252–0257. IEEE (2018)
12. Jamil, M.N., Hossain, M.S., ul Islam, R., Andersson, K.: A belief rule based expert system for evaluating technological innovation capability of high-tech firms under uncertainty. In: 2019 Joint 8th International Conference on Informatics, Electronics & Vision (ICIEV) and 2019 3rd International Conference on Imaging, Vision & Pattern Recognition (icIVPR), pp. 330–335. IEEE (2019)
13. Kabir, S., Islam, R.U., Hossain, M.S., Andersson, K.: An integrated approach of belief rule base and deep learning to predict air pollution. Sensors **20**(7), 1956 (2020)

14. Karim, R., Andersson, K., Hossain, M.S., Uddin, M.J., Meah, M.P.: A belief rule based expert system to assess clinical bronchopneumonia suspicion. In: 2016 Future Technologies Conference (FTC), pp. 655–660. IEEE (2016)
15. Ker, J., Bai, Y., Lee, H.Y., Rao, J., Wang, L.: Automated brain histology classification using machine learning. J. Clin. Neurosci. **66**, 239–245 (2019)
16. Mohsin, S.: Concentration of the specific absorption rate around deep brain stimulation electrodes during MRI. Progr. Electromagn. Res. **121**, 469–484 (2011)
17. Mohsin, S., Sheikh, N., Saeed, U.: MRI induced heating of deep brain stimulation leads: effect of the air-tissue interface. Progr. Electromagn. Res. **83**, 81–91 (2008)
18. Pashaei, A., Sajedi, H., Jazayeri, N.: Brain tumor classification via convolutional neural network and extreme learning machines. In: 2018 8th International Conference on Computer and Knowledge engineering (ICCKE), pp. 314–319. IEEE (2018)
19. Progga, N.I., Hossain, M.S., Andersson, K.: A deep transfer learning approach to diagnose covid-19 using x-ray images. In: 2020 IEEE International Women in Engineering (WIE) Conference on Electrical and Computer Engineering (WIECON-ECE), pp. 177–182. IEEE (2020)
20. Rahaman, S., Hossain, M.S.: A belief rule based clinical decision support system to assess suspicion of heart failure from signs, symptoms and risk factors. In: 2013 International Conference on Informatics, Electronics and Vision (ICIEV), pp. 1–6. IEEE (2013)
21. Sajid, S., Hussain, S., Sarwar, A.: Brain tumor detection and segmentation in MR images using deep learning. Arab. J. Sci. Eng. **44**(11), 9249–9261 (2019)
22. Scapaticci, R., Di Donato, L., Catapano, I., Crocco, L.: A feasibility study on microwave imaging for brain stroke monitoring. Progr. Electromagn. Res. B **40**, 305–324 (2012)
23. Sumi, T.A., Hossain, M.S., Andersson, K.: Automated acute lymphocytic leukemia (all) detection using microscopic images: an efficient cad approach. In: Kaiser, M.S., Bandyopadhyay, A., Ray, K., Singh, R., Nagar, V. (eds.) Proceedings of Trends in Electronics and Health Informatics. LNNS, vol. 376, pp. 363–376. Springer, Singapore (2022). https://doi.org/10.1007/978-981-16-8826-3_31
24. Sumi, T.A., Hossain, M.S., Islam, R.U., Andersson, K.: Human gender detection from facial images using convolution neural network. In: Mahmud, M., Kaiser, M.S., Kasabov, N., Iftekharuddin, K., Zhong, N. (eds.) AII 2021. CCIS, vol. 1435, pp. 188–203. Springer, Cham (2021). https://doi.org/10.1007/978-3-030-82269-9_15
25. Swati, Z.N.K., et al.: Brain tumor classification for MR images using transfer learning and fine-tuning. Comput. Med. Imaging Graph. **75**, 34–46 (2019)
26. Talo, M., Baloglu, U.B., Yıldırım, Ö., Acharya, U.R.: Application of deep transfer learning for automated brain abnormality classification using MR images. Cogn. Syst. Res. **54**, 176–188 (2019)
27. Uddin Ahmed, T., Jamil, M.N., Hossain, M.S., Andersson, K., Hossain, M.S.: An integrated real-time deep learning and belief rule base intelligent system to assess facial expression under uncertainty. In: 9th International Conference on Informatics, Electronics & Vision (ICIEV). IEEE Computer Society (2020)
28. Yang, Y., et al.: Glioma grading on conventional MR images: a deep learning study with transfer learning. Front. Neurosci. **12**, 804 (2018)
29. Zhang, Y.D., Wu, L., Wang, S.: Magnetic resonance brain image classification by an improved artificial bee colony algorithm. Progr. Electromagn. Res. **116**, 65–79 (2011)

30. Zisad, S.N., Chowdhury, E., Hossain, M.S., Islam, R.U., Andersson, K.: An integrated deep learning and belief rule-based expert system for visual sentiment analysis under uncertainty. Algorithms **14**(7), 213 (2021)
31. Zisad, S.N., Hossain, M.S., Andersson, K.: Speech emotion recognition in neurological disorders using convolutional neural network. In: Mahmud, M., Vassanelli, S., Kaiser, M.S., Zhong, N. (eds.) BI 2020. LNCS (LNAI), vol. 12241, pp. 287–296. Springer, Cham (2020). https://doi.org/10.1007/978-3-030-59277-6_26

# Triplet-Loss Based Siamese Convolutional Neural Network for 4-Way Classification of Alzheimer's Disease

Noushath Shaffi[1(✉)], Faizal Hajamohideen[1], Mufti Mahmud[2,3],
Abdelhamid Abdesselam[4], Karthikeyan Subramanian[1],
and Arwa Al Sariri[1]

[1] Department of Information Technology, University of Technology and Applied
Sciences-Sohar, Sohar 311, Sultanate of Oman
noushath.soh@cas.edu.om
[2] Department of Computer Science, Nottingham Trent University,
Nottingham NG11 8NS, UK
[3] CIRC and MTIF, Nottingham Trent University, Nottingham NG11 8NS, UK
[4] Department of Computer Science, Sultan Qaboos University, Muscat 123,
Sultanate of Oman

**Abstract.** Alzheimer's disease (AD) is a neurodegenerative disease that causes irreversible damage to several brain regions including the hippocampus causing impairment in cognition, function and behaviour. Earlier diagnosis of the disease will reduce the suffering of the patients and their family members. Towards that aim, this paper presents a Siamese Convolutional Neural Network (CNN) based model using the Triplet-loss function for the 4-way classification of AD. We evaluated our models using both pre-trained and non-pre-trained CNNs. The models' efficacy was tested on the OASIS dataset and obtained satisfactory results under a data-scarce real-time environment.

**Keywords:** Structural magnetic resonance imaging · Alzheimer's disease · Mild cognitive impairment · Triplet-loss · Siamese CNN

## 1 Introduction

Nerve system disorders or Neurological Disorders (NLD) are diseases that affect the central and peripheral nervous systems. This includes the brain, the spinal cord, nerves (cranial and peripheral), autonomic nervous system, etc. Any disruption in the functionality of these will manifest in the form of fatal physiological disorders. Alzheimer's Disease (AD) is one such incurable life-threatening/life-altering disorder. Out of several NLD, Alzheimer's disease (AD) is the most prevalent and affects sizeable populations around the globe [2,11].

This work is funded by the Ministry of Higher Education, Research and Innovation (MoHERI) of the sultanate of Oman under the Block Funding Program (Grant number-MoHERI/BFP/UoTAS/01/2021).

The World Health Organization (WHO) has estimated that there are about 47.5 million cases of dementia with 7.7 million emerging cases every year. Out of these, 60–70% of cases contribute to the prevalence of AD alone.

It takes a heavy toll on the emotional and physical well-being of family members of those who got affected with such NLD. Moreover, the knowledge of family members about these diseases is very limited to cope with the patient. Public health care systems which are meant to provide supportive and complementary therapies are not accessible to everyone for various reasons. As a result, the patient and the family members will undergo immense distress mentally, physically, and emotionally. Hence it becomes vitally important to detect AD at the earliest possible stage so that the suffering of the patient and family can be curtailed to a greater extent.

Deep learning (DL) techniques have permeated the healthcare industry in the last several years not only because they are accurate, fast, and efficient but also because they are able to learn end-to-end models using compound data [6,7]. This has opened up possibilities for the accurate identification of neurological disorders in an unprecedented manner. Neuroimaging, when coupled with DL techniques, provides vital clues in the perception of brain activity and relevant disorders [13]. These high-definition image data along with DL's powerful modelling technique extract features which can be elucidated by clinicians for medical decision-making in complex AD disorders.

In this paper, we propose deep Siamese network architecture using both pretrained and non-pretrained convolutional neural networks (CNN) for the diagnosis of AD stages. The model is developed using Magnetic Resonance Imaging (MRI) images extracted from the Open Access Series of Imaging Studies (OASIS) [4] dataset. The proposed model does a 4-way classification of MRI images which are categorized based on the Clinical Dementia Rating (CDR) score: CDR-0 (No Dementia), CDR-0.5 (Very Mild Dementia), CDR-1 (Mild-Dementia), and CDR-2 (Moderate AD) (CDR-0 vs CDR-0.5 vs CDR-1 vs CDR-2).

In the rest of this paper, Sect. 2 presents the review of related literature, Sect. 3 formulates the triplet-loss-based Siamese-CNN, Sect. 4 presents the experimental results followed by conclusion and future work in Sect. 5.

## 2    Review of Recent Literature

The Siamese CNN (SCNN) is proven to be an effective model for the classification of data points whenever the samples in the dataset are limited or imbalanced [15,19]. The concept of the Siamese network for similarity computation was originally proposed by Tiagman et al. [19] for efficient recognition of face images that resulted in a performance on par with human-level performance. Ever since there have been numerous applications of SCNN in various domains of pattern recognition and computer vision [17]. In [15], a new framework was proposed where the triplet loss function was introduced that leverages the concept of the Siamese network for optimal classification of facial images. In this section, we briefly outline some of the work carried out using various S-CNN for the classification of AD using different modalities.

In [5], the deep Siamese neural network was used to enhance the discriminatory feature of whole-brain volumetric asymmetry. This paper demonstrated the performance to be on par with the model that utilises whole-brain MRI images. In [8], the authors have used the pre-trained VGG-16 model for the classification of AD using the OASIS dataset. They have achieved a test accuracy of 99.05%. In [12], authors have proposed multimodal data for training to predict the evolution of the disease. This achieved an accuracy of 92.5% on the Alzheimer's Disease Neuroimaging Initiative (ADNI) dataset that was curated to consider the baseline and 12-month MRI. Mehmood et al. [9] have proposed a transfer learning-based CNN classification to diagnose the early stage of AD, namely Alzheimer's Disease (AD) vs Healthy Control (CN) vs Early Mild Cognitive Impairment (EMCI) vs Late Cognitive Impairment (LMCI), using the ADNI dataset. Authors have provided a 2-way classification (AD vs CN & EMCI vs LMCI) using this method and obtained an accuracy of 98.37% and 83.72% respectively. In [14], authors have applied CNN for the classification of AD using MRI images collected using the ADNI dataset. The algorithm applies specifically preprocessing to the images of MRI to aid in the efficient diagnosis of AD. In another study, [10], authors have used the popular AlexNet model for the feature extraction from the brain MRI images for subsequent classification by popular tools such as Random Forest (RF), Support Vector Machine (SVM), k-Nearest Neighbour (KNN) etc. The proposed approach resulted in good accuracy in the classification of AD disease. Arifa et al. [16] propose a hybrid approach to train a deep neural network that combines the features from MRI and EEG signals. The main idea of this approach is in the consideration of multi-modal data in training the classifier. Chitradevi et al. [1] presented an approach to segment the cerebral sub-regions for efficient classification of AD. The segmentation output is fed to machine learning classifiers for the diagnosis of AD which resulted in 98% accuracy using the Grey-Wolf optimisation approach.

Based on this recent brief review of the research, we can conclude that:

1. Many works have been reported that leverage the CNN architecture for the AD classification purposes either by the usage of pretrained models or a minimalist non-pretrained CNN model. These models have obtained satisfactory results.
2. Not many works reported the use of Siamese in the recent past for the classification of AD except for a few works [5, 8, 12].
3. Pretrained models have been successfully utilised for the AD classification [8].
4. Although there has been reported use of Siamese for the classification of AD, employing the triplet-loss function for the learning of the underlying CNN for optimal separation of classes is not done to the best of our knowledge.

Furthermore, the CNN architectures mentioned in the literature have performed well but these algorithms when presented with limited samples or imbalance data points, the underlying model will be severely affected. We overcome these limitations in two ways in our work: i) Adopting the Siamese model that learns the similarity mapping with limited samples ii) Using pretrained architectures will allow better model convergence as it offers a good starting point through optimal filter weights.

In our work, we employed both the pretrained VGG16 model and non-trained CNN for the Siamese architecture for feature extraction using the triplet loss function for the classification of AD. Adopting the Siamese architecture using VGG16 has the inherent advantage of addressing the limitedness of the AD dataset. Hence, the model proposed will not suffer from the problem of overfitting or issues related to class imbalanceness. We have tested the performance of this on OASIS dataset [4] and set the baseline accuracy. We believe that this work will serve as a prelude for many work that exploits the benefit of triplet-loss coupled with various DeepNet architectures in the literature.

## 3    A Brief Overview of the Triplet-Loss Siamese CNN

In this section, we present the overall architecture in building the Siamese CNN using the Triplet loss function for the 4-way classification of AD.

### 3.1    Siamese CNN Architecture

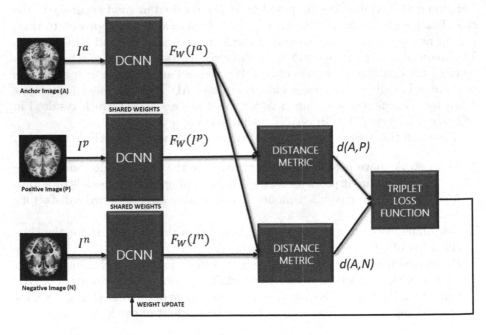

**Fig. 1.** The Siamese architecture

The Siamese Convolutional Neural Network (SCNN), which has two or more identical sub-networks, works in tandem to produce feature vectors for input images and helps to compute similarity scores as shown in Fig. 1. The objective of this learning process is to learn a similarity model that produces distinctive embedding for input images that optimally distinguishes them from images belonging to the same or different classes. The model will be provided with three images (triplets): where two images (anchor and positive) will be from the same class whereas the third image (negative) will be from a different class. The objective of this model is to learn similarities between (A, P) and (A, N) images as depicted in Fig. 1.

It can be seen from Fig. 1 that the input of the SCNN is a triplet of images: Anchor (A), Positive (P) and Negative (N). The objective of SCNN is to produce embeddings for every image in the triplet: A, P, and N in such a way that the distance from the anchor image to the positive image becomes closer than the anchor to the negative image.

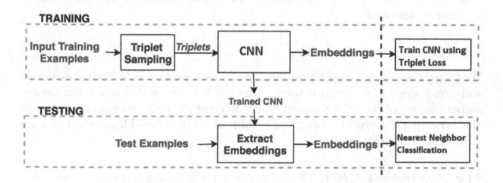

**Fig. 2.** The training and testing phases

The triplets $(A, P, N)$ will pass through these similarly-weighted ConvNet encoders that transform the triplet images into an embedding space $F_w(I^a)$, $F_w(I^p)$, $F_w(I^n)$. These ConvNet encoders represent the Siamese architecture. It is to be noted that the SCNN, although depicted as having separate branches, essentially has a single ConvNet encoder that sequentially extracts features of $A$, $P$, and $N$ images. The final layer of the ConvNet encoder is a fully connected (FC) layer which represents the embeddings for the input image. The L2 distance metric can be used to measure the distance between (A,P) and (A,N) pairs as: $d(A, P) = ||F_w(I^a) - F_w(I^p)||$ and $d(A, N) = ||F_w(I^a) - F_w(I^n)||$.

The triplet-loss function can be used at this stage using the $d(A, P)$ and $d(A, N)$ to compute the loss of the model being learned. Finally, the cosine similarity measure will be used to transform the similarity score to a value in the range of 0 to 1. Cosine similarity of Anchor image A with positive and negative images will be computed separately. It is expected that the similarity of $(A, P)$ is larger than the similarity of $(A, N)$.

## 3.2   Triplet Loss

This is a loss function-based distance measure that needs three inputs, Given $A$, $P$, and $N$ images:

$$\mathcal{L}(A, P, N) = max(d(A, P) - d(A, N) + \alpha, 0) \tag{1}$$

If there are $m$ training triplet images, the overall cost function for the SCNN would be:

$$\mathcal{J}(L(A, P, N)) = \sum_{i=1}^{m} \mathcal{L}(A_i, P_i, N_i) \tag{2}$$

The constraint $d(A, P) - d(A, N) + \alpha$ can be easily satisfied. Hence, we need to choose triplets that are hard to train on such as the ones where $d(A, P) \approx d(A, N)$. The subsequent Gradient Descent process will then minimise the loss function such that $d(x^{(i)}, x^{(j)})$ is smaller for similar pairs, typically for A and P, and larger otherwise.

## 3.3   The ConvNet Encoders

We tested the efficacy of the proposed model by making use of both pre-trained and non-trained CNN architectures. This will help us to determine the performance efficacy of the SCNN model under different scenarios such as the presence of a very deep ConvNet encoder and its impact on the embeddings, the influence of pretrained weights, etc.

**The Non-trained CNN.** The non-trained CNN architecture we used has three Convolutional layers, 2 pooling layers, and 2 Fully Connected (FC) or Dense layers. This architecture is used as a ConvNet encoder to transform the input image into the embedding space. This architecture can be represented as: $64C7 - MP2 - 64C3 - MP2 - 128C3 - FC1024 - FC48$, where $nCj$ denotes $n$ Convolutional layer with $j \times j$ filters, $MPk$ indicates a Maxpooling layer with $k \times k$ kernel, and $FCn$ indicates a FC layer. This way every image (A, P, N) is transformed into a $k$-dimensional embedding/feature vector.

**The Pre-trained VGG16 Model.** The VGG16 model [18] has been successfully applied in solving many computer vision problems [17]. Inspired by its success, we have used this architecture in our proposed work in two ways: i) as a feature extractor for the Siamese architecture and ii) as a traditional classifier. The architecture of the VGG16 model is as shown in Fig. 3. The top layer constituting 3 dense layers will be removed and replaced by one or two Dense layers catering for our requirements. When used as a ConvNet encoder, we use a single Dense layer to extract a 1-dimensional feature vector of length $k$. When used as a classifier, the top layers were replaced by two dense layers of dimensions 256 and 4 respectively.

The overall process involved in the triplet-loss-based Siamese-CNN training and subsequent classification of AD can be outlined in Fig. 2.

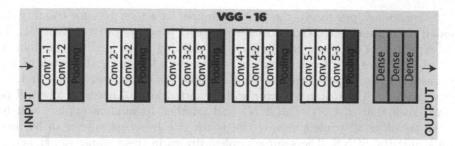

**Fig. 3.** The VGG16 architecture

# 4  Experimental Results

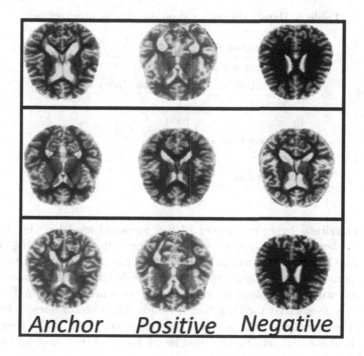

**Fig. 4.** Sample triplets formation

In this section, we present the results of experiments carried out to demonstrate the efficacy of the proposed model using the OASIS-3 dataset [4]. The dataset can be categorized into 4 classes based on the CDR score as mentioned previously. The number of samples in CDR-0, CDR-0.5, CDR-1, and CDR-2.0 are respectively, 3200, 2240, 896, and 64 images. The imbalance in the dataset is not a cause of concern for the underlying SCNN model and represents the real-time data-scarce scenario where our proposed model is expected to perform well.

As mentioned previously, the SCNN requires triplet samples for training the model: an anchor image (A), positive image (P), and negative image (N). In our experiments, we draw hard triplets by drawing a batch of 200 random A, P, and N images at a time. We then extract embeddings for the batch of 200 images using the ConvNet encoder and compute the distance $d(A, P) - d(A, N)$ between them. The distance vector will be sorted and 16 hard triplets will be drawn such that $d(A, P) \approx d(A, N)$ and another 16 random triplets will be drawn totalling 32 triplets suiting the batch size hyper-parameter of 32 used in learning the SCNN. The sample triplets drawn in this manner are shown in Fig. 4. The SCNN will update its weights in such a manner for 1000 iterations.

The hyperparameters used in learning the SCNN are tabulated as shown in Table 1. For the remainder of this experimental section, unless it is mentioned explicitly, the hyperparameter values conform to the values shown in this table.

**Table 1.** Hyperparameter values used in the architecture

| Hyperparameter | Value |
| --- | --- |
| Embedding size | 48 |
| Loss function | Triplet-loss (refer Eq. 2) |
| Batch size | 32 |
| Epochs | 1000 |
| Activation function | ReLU |
| Optimizer | Adam |
| Learning rate | 0.00001 |

Another critical hyper-parameter of the proposed model is the embedding size($k$) – the length of the feature vector obtained after transforming the image through the ConvNet encoder. In order to determine the optimal value for $k$, we ran a series of experiments by varying the length of the embedding size and corresponding loss values over 1000 iterations are plotted in Fig. 5. This experiment suggests that the length of the embedding vector doesn't have much impact on the convergence of the model or the loss value. As can be seen that the $k = 16$ yielded optimal performance and hence We fixed this value for embedding size for the rest of our experiments.

**Table 2.** Results outcome of proposed models

| Models | Accuracy | FPR | TPR | F1-score |
| --- | --- | --- | --- | --- |
| Proposed method | 93.46 | 0.0004 | 0.9345 | 0.9344 |
| Proposed method with VGG16 | 92.17 | 0.0004 | 0.9216 | 0.9217 |
| VGG16 | 87.29 | 0.0008 | 0.8717 | 0.8719 |

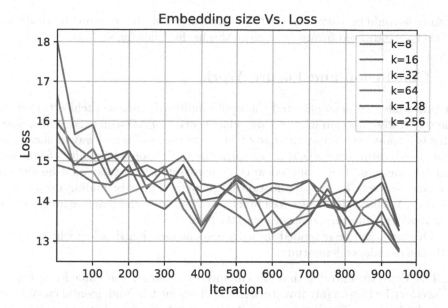

**Fig. 5.** Effect of embedding length on model's performance

The result findings of the proposed model are shown in Table 2. Some important observations from this experiment are:

1. The proposed model for the 4-way classification of AD achieves overall a good recognition accuracy considering the limited samples and class imbalance that exists in the dataset we considered. This is the true benefit of using Siamese architecture. The usage of the triplet-loss function further enhances the class separability among the four classes where samples of some classes have finer distinctive features (for instance CDR-0.5 and CDR-1.0 MRI images).

2. Although the deep ConvNet models are known to perform well, their performance on test data is lesser than the basic ConvNet encoder we proposed. This may be due to the fact of using pretrained weights in the frozen layers. If we set those layers to trainable option with an empirically determined learning rate would yield probably the best results [3].

3. Inspired by the success of the VGG16 model in solving many computer vision problems, we leveraged the pretrained VGG16 model as a traditional classifier for the 4-way classification of the AD. Firstly, the input samples were resized to $64 \times 64 \times 3$ in order to be compatible with its architecture. The VGG16 model was trained using the ImageNet weights and by removing the top layer. Two dense layers were added with the final layer being the output 4-neuron layer to classify the AD. The results of this model are not better than the proposed Siamese based one. There could be many reasons for this but the main point here is that we have insufficient samples to train the model. The reasonable accuracy it managed to obtain was probably due to the immense training the model originally underwent for the ImageNet competition. Those convolutional

kernels could have contributed to the accuracy. This deserves further study and we have indicated future avenues on this in the following section.

## 5   Conclusion and Future Work

In this study, we demonstrated the applicability of Siamese architecture using the triplet loss function for the 4-way classification of AD using the MRI images. This is a real-world data-scarce problem where the traditional way of classifying using deep neural networks is impractical due to the non-availability of sufficient training samples. The proposed work demonstrated that this could be circumvented effectively by the application of Siamese similarity finding deep neural network. We used the triplet-loss function to calibrate the Siamese architecture. The model resulted in an accuracy of 93.46%.

This work can be extended in many ways as mentioned below which deserve a thorough independent study:

1. The ConvNet encoder that we employed to extract the embedding feature needs to be thoroughly investigated to determine the fundamental capabilities or limitations. The Siamese architecture produces even better results when provided with a deep neural network for feature extraction. We could utilise popular pretrained networks and analyse the best-performing model with the goal in mind of the data-scarce real-world environment.
2. The ADNI dataset could be utilised and MRI images from different planes (sagittal or axial) could be considered to see the applicability of the proposed model.

The Siamese architecture using the triplet-loss function has not seen wider applicability in the field of AD classification. We believe that our work presented here would serve as good reference material for many such works in the future.

## References

1. Chitradevi, D., Prabha, S.: Analysis of brain sub regions using optimization techniques and deep learning method in Alzheimer disease. Appl. Soft Comput. **86**, 105857 (2020)
2. Jahan, S., et al.: Explainable AI-based Alzheimer's prediction and management using multimodal data. Preprints, pp. 1–16 (2022)
3. Kornblith, S., Shlens, J., Le, Q.V.: Do better ImageNet models transfer better? In: Proceedings of the IEEE/CVF Conference on Computer Vision and Pattern Recognition, pp. 2661–2671 (2019)
4. LaMontagne, P.J., et al.: OASIS-3: longitudinal neuroimaging, clinical, and cognitive dataset for normal aging and Alzheimer disease. medRxiv (2019). https://doi.org/10.1101/2019.12.13.19014902. https://www.medrxiv.org/content/early/2019/12/15/2019.12.13.19014902
5. Liu, C.F., et al.: Using deep Siamese neural networks for detection of brain asymmetries associated with Alzheimer's disease and mild cognitive impairment. Magn. Reson. Imaging **64**, 190–199 (2019)

6. Mahmud, M., Kaiser, M.S., McGinnity, T.M., Hussain, A.: Deep learning in mining biological data. Cogn. Comput. **13**(1), 1–33 (2021). https://doi.org/10.1007/s12559-020-09773-x

7. Mahmud, M., Kaiser, M.S., Hussain, A., Vassanelli, S.: Applications of deep learning and reinforcement learning to biological data. IEEE Trans. Neural Netw. Learn. Syst. **29**(6), 2063–2079 (2018)

8. Mehmood, A., Maqsood, M., Bashir, M.: A deep Siamese convolution neural network for multi-class classification of Alzheimer disease. Brain Sci. (2020) https://doi.org/10.3390/brainsci10020084

9. Mehmood, A., et al.: A transfer learning approach for early diagnosis of Alzheimer's disease on MRI images. Neuroscience **460**, 43–52 (2021)

10. Nawaz, H., Maqsood, M., Afzal, S., Aadil, F., Mehmood, I., Rho, S.: A deep feature-based real-time system for Alzheimer disease stage detection. Multimed. Tools Appl. **80**(28), 35789–35807 (2021). https://doi.org/10.1007/s11042-020-09087-y

11. Noor, M.B.T., Zenia, N.Z., Kaiser, M.S., Mamun, S.A., Mahmud, M.: Application of deep learning in detecting neurological disorders from magnetic resonance images: a survey on the detection of Alzheimer's disease, Parkinson's disease and schizophrenia. Brain Inform. **7**(1), 1–21 (2020). https://doi.org/10.1186/s40708-020-00112-2

12. Ostertag, C., Beurton-Aimar, M., Visani, M., Urruty, T., Bertet, K.: Predicting brain degeneration with a multimodal Siamese neural network. In: 2020 Tenth International Conference on Image Processing Theory, Tools and Applications (IPTA), pp. 1–6. IEEE (2020)

13. Ruiz, J., Mahmud, M., Modasshir, M., Shamim Kaiser, M., For the Alzheimer's Disease Neuroimaging Initiative: 3D DenseNet ensemble in 4-way classification of Alzheimer's disease. In: Mahmud, M., Vassanelli, S., Kaiser, M.S., Zhong, N. (eds.) BI 2020. LNCS (LNAI), vol. 12241, pp. 85–96. Springer, Cham (2020). https://doi.org/10.1007/978-3-030-59277-6_8

14. Sathiyamoorthi, V., Ilavarasi, A., Murugeswari, K., Ahmed, S.T., Devi, B.A., Kalipindi, M.: A deep convolutional neural network based computer aided diagnosis system for the prediction of Alzheimer's disease in MRI images. Measurement **171**, 108838 (2021)

15. Schroff, F., Kalenichenko, D., Philbin, J.: FaceNet: a unified embedding for face recognition and clustering. In: Proceedings of the IEEE Conference on Computer Vision and Pattern Recognition, pp. 815–823 (2015)

16. Shikalgar, A., Sonavane, S.: Hybrid deep learning approach for classifying Alzheimer disease based on multimodal data. In: Iyer, B., Deshpande, P.S., Sharma, S.C., Shiurkar, U. (eds.) Computing in Engineering and Technology. AISC, vol. 1025, pp. 511–520. Springer, Singapore (2020). https://doi.org/10.1007/978-981-32-9515-5_49

17. Shorfuzzaman, M., Hossain, M.S.: MetaCOVID: a Siamese neural network framework with contrastive loss for n-shot diagnosis of COVID-19 patients. Pattern Recogn. **113**, 107700 (2021)

18. Simonyan, K., Zisserman, A.: Very deep convolutional networks for large-scale image recognition. arXiv preprint arXiv:1409.1556 (2014)

19. Taigman, Y., Yang, M., Ranzato, M., Wolf, L.: DeepFace: closing the gap to human-level performance in face verification. In: Proceedings of the IEEE Conference on Computer Vision and Pattern Recognition, pp. 1701–1708 (2014)

# Understanding Syntax Structure of Language After a Head Injury

Marisol Roldán-Palacios and Aurelio López-López[✉]

Instituto Nacional de Astrofísica, Óptica y Electrónica,
Luis Enrique Erro No. 1, Sta. María Tonantzintla, 72840 Puebla, Mexico
{marppalacios,allopez}@inaoep.mx
https://ccc.inaoep.mx/

**Abstract.** Cognitive-communication disorder is a type of language alteration generally associated with a traumatic brain injury, but could also be a sequelae from a disease. There is a latent possibility of establishing a connection between the ongoing epidemic language alterations sequelae with those reorganization in language after a head trauma that includes modifications in syntax production process.

From a set of syntax indices previously elaborated to study language development, we propose a grammar-based analysis of such indices allowing a depiction in terms of a triangle-segmented polygon. A finding of the analysis is that the suggested context-free grammar gives the resources to have a suitable representation of the construction of the syntax production in individuals after a traumatic brain injury, in a post-recovery stage. The produced maps could serve to interpret how rules, when demanding more complexity, progress in contrast with a negative sample.

**Keywords:** Cognitive-communication disorder · Traumatic brain injury · Syntax · Context-free grammar · Triangle-segmented polygon maps

## 1 Introduction

A disorder in *cognitive communication* is within the ambit of faculty communication disruptions, a type of acquired language deficit that can follow a traumatic brain injury (TBI) [17]. This type of sequelae has a group of intricate consequences in different aspects of people living with this acquired alteration that can go from the loss of friends to the risk of depression, anxiety, delirium and psychotic behaviors [1,6]. Circumstances like these situate patients in an uninterrupted cycle of drop backs.

Final outcomes depend on several factors, but works analyzing numerical data observe that a TBI represents a worldwide leading cause of death and disability [2,5,23]. Moreover, a common factor strongly associated with SARSCOV-II, i.e. the deprivation of oxygen, is causing a number of alterations on communication at

Supported by Conacyt and partially by SNI, México.

cognitive level [14]. Considering that this is a global scenario, along with an also global increasing tendency [23] in the incidence of TBI, the context is intensified and an increasing number of cases revealing language alterations can be expected.

Any communication attribute disrupted in cognition, such as executive functioning or memory can lead to deficiencies in communication or even the daily exchange of information [13]. Within the ongoing epidemic, information already documented can be indirectly associated to those symptoms centered on the analysis of attributes to trace cognitive communication disorders often related to TBI [14]. Deficits in language such as syntax comprehension and production, or in *micro level*, as in lexis, and *macro level* (pragmatic) [14], can also occur.

Syntax dictates the valid combinations of words that make sense for each language [26]. In this study, we are not working on modeling those rules that have accumulated varied abstraction approaches [12]. Instead, we look for the depiction of indices, i.e. a set of assigned marks based on rules, as a result of a prior evaluation, to have an index of syntax production of participants. This is a way to discern the behavior of syntax features on atypical language. Previous work showed that a subset of our current analyzed features has appropriate levels of discrimination to recognize study cases, after assessing them with learning methods [18,19]. However, we are looking for additional understanding about the information that the entire feature set comprises.

The design of computational tools that add or complement information for supporting clinical decision are proposed and explored in this work. We are proposing triangular maps for representing the syntax indices evaluation from participants recovering of a head trauma. This, with a purpose that go beyond the prevalent objective of classification. We look for understanding the pattern evolution of the studied language restructuring. For this, a context free grammar (cfg) is specified to generate the maps and reveal what attributes can show. Our principal finding, a descriptive cfg is proposed and related to a triangular graph representation that seems to support the identification of evolving patterns within features that assess syntax production.

The rest of the work is organized as follows. The closest works are briefly described in previous research section. In Sect. 3 we mainly describe TBI corpus and its feature set. Next, the proposed approach is detailed in Sect. 4 with an explanation of the rationale behind it. The experimental setting is described in Sect. 5 followed by results in Sect. 6, including the discussion, and the advantage and limitations of the approach. Closing the paper with conclusions and further work.

## 2  Previous Research

Language and its generation process have demanded the attention of several research fields that, at first, studied ordinary language from their own perspectives, achieving some understanding and worked on initial theories or models. Then, the analysis of disorders in language, environmental or acquired, started. Part of the efforts were addressed to defining subareas of study, exploring language features sets delimitation, or approaching assessment methods, introducing some measures for that purpose.

For instance, during the last forty five years, solely for aphasia, a language impairment partially sharing some descriptive attributes with those of communication deficits presented in language after a TBI [8], around 550 measurements were proposed [3]. With the advancement of language studies along other interrelated fields as in clinic and technology disciplines, a variety of language disorders are being identified, with the consequent growing efforts to advance their understanding.

However, inconsistencies in findings have been reported due to contexts or conditions faced in the execution of researches, with some recommendations to consider in the employed methodology [9], such as analyses running on *narrative language samples* [8–10]. We have the intrinsic and natural intervention of linguistics, defining relations to standardize assessments of the development, state, or restructuring of language [11]. Also the computational analyses that are mostly addressed to assign a polarity, positive or negative, to the examined instances [16].

The investigation of interventions of narrative-based discourse can represent the starting point in the design of treatment focused on the improvement of day-to-day communication competence. Though, the works addressing the recovery of basic communication are limited, solely three recent efforts were identified [21]. For this purpose, a suitable representation often results convenient to gain comprehension on the development of the inspected phenomenon.

Geometrically speaking, counting with three discrete values, an intuitive association can be established with a triangular depiction. Gross and Lentin [7] associated a *free-context grammar* with the formulation of a triangle, making possible the generation of a polygon segmented in triangles, indeed associated with graphs [15]. In the present work, this representation allows to depict variables (features) extracted from narrative samples at a few consecutive time points (recovery stages).

## 3   TBI Corpus

The availability of the traumatic brain injury corpus [24] is a substantial efforts of more than one institution. Carnegie Mellon and Sydney Universities collaborated in a longitudinal project accounting for four periodic time points every three months, and one more at twenty-four months, for the recovery stage following a TBI, dealing with a cohort group of 42 members, in average, per recovery point [25].

The sample consists of different narrative tasks, such as storytelling of *Cinderella* or *an important event*, that are examined in this paper. The noticeable scarcity of instances for the last time point caused to treat together Cinderella and an important event instances, as a single sample per time points reported in this study. This was done to maintain conditions as similar as possible, for the reported analysis. An extensive description of the examined characteristics can be found in [11,16,20]. The studied features are divided in four subgroups as explained next.

## 3.1 Data Description and Feature Set

TBI corpus has a set of markers called *IPSYN*, abbreviation of the *Index of Productive SYNtax*. The indices are an implementation [11] of those variables delineated by [20]. The scores are organized in 11 *noun-phrase*, 17 *verb-phrase*, 11 *question & answer*, and 20 *sentence-structure* rules, indeed the global densities that are accumulating the individual rates per subgroup. These last, i.e., the overall grades are not considered here since we focus on individual markers as they are calculated, taking values from the set $\{0, 1, 2\}$ where a grammar is defined. According to the target of each rule, a punctuation is assigned to every variable, that takes the previously mentioned values. All the variables are started in zero, if a sequence of terms in the narrative meets the defined rule, then the variable receives a point. With the presence of two different word stems, a second point is added. The variables remain with their initial null value if the narrative sample does not contain the sequence of the defined respective rule. We observe that, by their rules definition, the domain is restricted to these three discrete values.

# 4 The Approach

In a *context-free grammar* definition, *terminal* and *non-terminal* symbols are involved. The idea behind the approach of Gross & Lentin is that the *non-terminal* **S** associated with the variable of the grammar definition is connected to what they call a *virtual* side. The *terminal* symbols in the grammar, i.e. **a**, **b**, are linked with *real* sides, where by real we mean a side value that is fix once is set. This is contrary to *virtual* sides that can be replaced according to what was defined for the non terminal symbol **S**, dictating the further development of the polygon.

More recently, this idea was brought into a graph framework [15], allowing a map generation to decipher the full trajectory to show all the called faces in a flexible device, while they are stepping on the depth levels of its *parse tree* connected with its triangle map related to the generated graph.

In an effort to gain understanding about the reconfiguration of the group of language features (detailed in Sect. 3.1), a visual depiction of data is developed. We hypothesized an existing restructuring of the examined language given the sample discrimination capacity showed in recent analysis [16,19]. An understandable decoded representation is the target, and we are looking for a language behavior depiction where it is possible to recognize breaks, reconnections, or remanent adaptations on the syntax attributes belonging to the reshaped language after a traumatic brain injury. For that purpose, we defined a `cfg` to trace syntax progression of this language. We already mentioned that IPSYN scores, i.e. the *syntax attributes* we are working on, take values in $\{0, 1, 2\}$. Besides, a poor punctuation prevails on the subgroups of IPSYN set when directives are assessed on the narrative discourse samples, per participant. With this in mind, we elaborate the grammar to include every case presented in our examined sample, that resulted in the formal definition of the *context-free grammar*.

DEFINITION. Let set $G = (V, \Sigma, S, P)$, where $\Sigma = \{\emptyset_2, 0, 1, 2\}$ is the finite terminal symbol set, where $\emptyset_2$ specifies the absence of the base to generate the next triangle. $V = \{S\}$ is the non-terminal or variable set. The finite set $P$ of productions is given by:

$$S \rightarrow 2SS \qquad (1)$$
$$S \rightarrow \emptyset_2 SS$$
$$S \rightarrow 0|1$$

The unique symbol $S \in V$ also denotes the start variable.

### 4.1   The Rationale Behind Grammar Productions

As detailed previously (Sect. 3.1), IPSYN set is divided in four directive sub-groups, but here we report results of three of them, for the *noun-phrase, verb-phrase* and *structure-sentence* segments. The assessment for the *question & negation* subgroup was not included since, in previous analysis [19], this set showed to bring limited information.

We explored the responses corresponding to the first sample, at three months after the head injury. We traced the possible sequences presented in the examined instances to determine a set of *directives* to produce the corresponding *grammar* for each set of variables per participant, automatically.

Let call the current queue and entry as $Q_c$ and $E_c$, respectively, where $E_c$ is the character in the head of $Q_c$. The process to analyse (parse) the sequence of variables and generate a map is as follows:

1. While $Q_c$ is non-empty.
2. If $E_c == 2$,
      then rule $S \Longrightarrow S \rightarrow 2SS$ applies.
      The array is divided in three parts.
      The first one is the terminal 2,
            the second entry applies $S_2 \Longrightarrow 0|1$,
            and the remaining will be assigned as the current queue, $Q_c = S_3$.
      Subscripts $2, 3$ are used to emphasize that correspond to the second
            and third segmentation of $Q_c$.
3. Otherwise, the rule $S \rightarrow \emptyset_2 SS$ applies.
      $Q_c$ is divided in two parts.
      A $\emptyset_2$ is fed.
      The first segment is the next entry, applying $S_2 \Longrightarrow 0|1$
      The second part is reassigned, $Q_c = S_3$

The absence of the base, the *real* side, allows the continuation of more complex syntax composition and is remarked with the introduction of a $\emptyset_2$ symbol, represented in the recognized response chain as a $-1$ value.

## 5   Experiments

### 5.1   Experimental Setting

The variables were extracted for a sample of participants [22] registered during the post-recovery period at periodic times, and these are analyzed comparatively against a negative sample recorded only once [4]. We observe that though the examined sample has five times, the last corresponding to twenty-four months, this is not as extent as the other, counting merely with eight transcripts for the used narratives. To deal with this situation, we extended the sample of *Cinderella* story recount, the task we initially considered, with another exercise of *an important event* narrative, replicating this composition, as possible, for the same sub sample of participants. In the same way, we built the samples for the other two time points (three and twelve months) to have similar conditions of comparison.

The negative cases (control group) count with individual instances per task. Hence, we selected the instances from the sub sample as those as closer as possible in age and years of education, to those in the study group.

# 6    Results

The definition of the `cfg` for IPSYN response attributes expresses them as a triangle-partitioned polygon representation, and consequently allowing to look through the data via its corresponding plot. As we previously explained, the available data at twenty-four months is more restricted than for the other samples. After determining the instances we worked on, we have samples of sixteen instances per time-point, whose polygonal representations are grouped by IPSYN subset and by period. The generated maps are included in Figs. 1, 2 and 3, corresponding to noun phrase, verb phrase, and sentence structure, respectively. In each figure, the first graph (a) represents the negative instances (i.e. NonTBI), (b) the first sample at three months, and (c) and (d) to the twelve and twenty-four months, respectively, where each row corresponds to scores of an individual. Terminals are depicted as arrows in: light blue 2, blue 1, green 0, and red $-1$.

## 6.1    Discussion

An important property of the studied features is that they were defined grounded on Linguistics. Also, we noted that the complexity of the rules, determining the IPSYN indices, increases with their subsequent definition, including some dependencies, that were called *conditional rules* [16, 19]. Considering those facts, for the present analysis we hypothesized that posterior markers are built on the basis of those preceding. This justifies the connection of the suggested `cfg` with the previously described *triangular* polygon map representation. Looking at the real side as *the base* on which the subsequent syntax structures are built and its absence to continue assembling the syntax could represent a signal of the intended restructuring of the examined language. For this reason the $\emptyset_2$[1] symbol was introduced in the specification of the grammar. So, this is associated with the $-1$ value (red arrow).

---

[1] Read as: *empty two*.

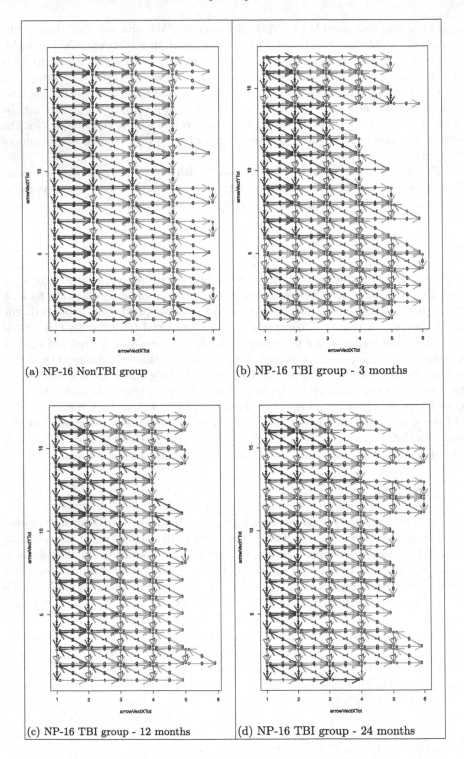

(a) NP-16 NonTBI group

(b) NP-16 TBI group - 3 months

(c) NP-16 TBI group - 12 months

(d) NP-16 TBI group - 24 months

**Fig. 1.** Maps for noun phrase (Color figure online)

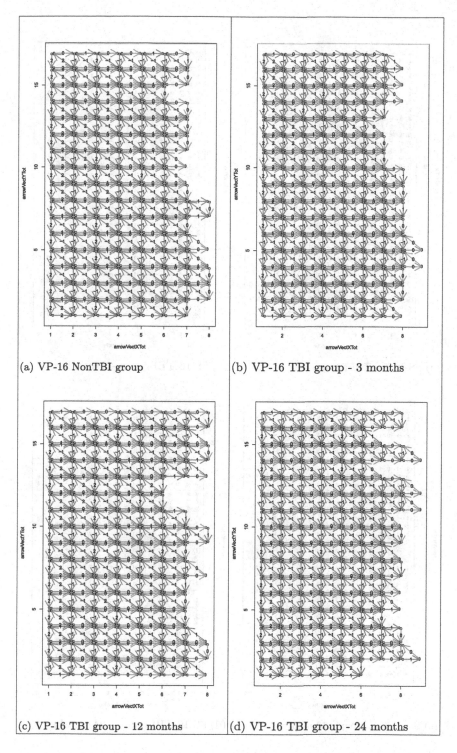

(a) VP-16 NonTBI group

(b) VP-16 TBI group - 3 months

(c) VP-16 TBI group - 12 months

(d) VP-16 TBI group - 24 months

**Fig. 2.** Maps for verb phrase (Color figure online)

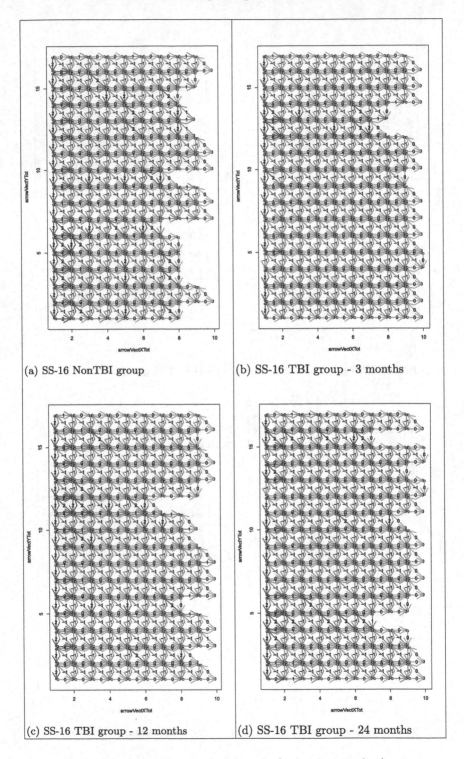

(a) SS-16 NonTBI group

(b) SS-16 TBI group - 3 months

(c) SS-16 TBI group - 12 months

(d) SS-16 TBI group - 24 months

**Fig. 3.** Maps for sentence structure (Color figure online)

A three bar pattern is evident from Figs. 1a to 1d, that correspond to the *noun-phrase* group, though a more dominant completeness of the syntax structure on negative group (Fig. 1a) can be noticed. Note at the start of the feature responses production chain, the grammar rule $S \rightarrow 2SS$ is mostly applied. That is in agreement to our hypothesis, and suggests that the basis directives of the grammar are satisfied, moreover with a notable favorable outcome for the control group in comparison to the response for the three and twenty-four months. However, the maps for twelve months sample could indicate an amelioration on language of affected group, in the construction of the *noun-phrase* basis rules.

On the second colored delimited block, the grammar rule $S \rightarrow \emptyset_2 SS$ predominates on both groups. However, according to the defined *noun-phrase* policies, the syntax structure is still more consistent on control group than on restructured studied set, given that the density of the execution of the rule is minor on the former than on the latter. As a consequence of this, the last block is extended to two columns for the three, twelve and twenty-four months samples, where for negative set, it consists of only one, with insertions of $\emptyset_2$ being more recurrent to our study group than on the negative set. This could be a possible sign of the difficulty in the construction of elaborated noun phrase directives in those cases.

Observing this same time point at three months, we notice that these results seem to be in agreement with those coming from the assessment of the complete sample for the independent Cinderella task with some learning methods as *Random Forest*, SPAARC, *Bayes Net*, and CVR, where the macro F1-score fluctuates in the [0.87, 1.00] interval [19]. Going from the highest to lower scores as we advanced through the individual evaluations of the subsequent features, until the performance moved around 0.5 for the last two, i.e. $N10$ and $N11$.

In the case of *verb-phrase* (Figs. 2a to 2d), the particularities for each group are not as delimited as for the NP set. However, at a global level, we note a variation in density color, as well as in length of the generated productions. At three-months, we perceive a red-toned and longer derivations in comparison to the negative graph. The same is replicated if we compare it against the plot for twelve months, which in fact gives the appearance of an existing amelioration in restructuring language. But, the achieved improvement seems to vanish at the twenty-four months. This same behavior is reproduced by the *sentence-structure* feature group (Figs. 3a to 3d). Locally, compared individually, we can notice particular cases. The maps corresponding to the verb phrases rules indicate, for example, that the instance number four is achieving and maintaining subtle improvement. Fact that seems to be clearer in the development of the sentence structure policy map, shorter and bluer in the twenty-four time point. In other words, we have a notable reduced insertion of $\emptyset_2$ rule, probably because of a more appropriate construction of the sentence structure.

One last but not the least note is that there are few cases in *noun-phrase* group responses where the diagram closing triangle showed a 2 value in the second or third side, a fact that is in conflict with the specified cfg. The cfg was formulated according to the facts considered to establish the hypothesis we base on. Considering this framework, we conjecture that these instances could represent a singular behavior, suggesting a closer treatment of those examples.

Notice that any interpretation coming from the exposed rules has to be clinically validated. The variation in the evolution of the maps and in consequence on the examined language could give some hints to language pathologist to consider in the rehabilitation therapies, but any recommendation about them is out of the scope of this work.

## 6.2    Advantages and Limitations

The directives to automatize the processing of the fed entry is a double edge resource. On one side, the linearity of the triangular polygon maps produced from the automatized analysis of the worked groups response instances is convenient to have a clustered arrangement of them and to observe the progression in the syntax construction per participant. However, on the other side, we have to keep in mind that they are restricting the sort of the produced map.

We build our framework and experimental setting based on a hypothesis of a growing and dependable complexity in the syntax production defined by the variables which were considered consecutively. This conjecture along with the convenience of the current suggested representation need to be analyzed, assessed and supported or rejected by specialists.

## 7    Conclusions and Further Work

We described a `cfg` that mostly define the responses to the *noun-phrase, verb-phrase* and *sentence-structure* subgroup directives evaluation. These of language instances belonging to participants at different time points, considering the three, twelve and twenty-four months samples of the recovery stage after a traumatic brain injury, whose evolution was contrasted with a negative set. This enabled a triangle-segmented polygon diagram to decipher the syntax construction of the analyzed groups. However, few cases were observed that do not seem to adhere to it, closing the triangular representation with a 2 value. This fact requires to study in depth data and participant profile, to determine how these cases, more present on study sample than in negative group, should be attended.

This analysis could be directly extended to the *question&negation* group, exploration that could bring us to a particularly practical context when comparing with their modest power of discrimination [19], when they are evaluated with learning methods. It is desirable to count with the full transcriptions for the considered tasks, that enable us to replicate this analysis on the entire samples of the complete recovery stage and compare against the results in syntax production of the current results using blended instances to gain ground in the understanding about the presented alterations around the TBI affected language.

# References

1. Ahmed, S., Venigalla, H., Mekala, H.M., Dar, S., Hassan, M., Ayub, S.: Traumatic brain injury and neuropsychiatric complications. Indian J. Psychol. Med. **39**, 11–121 (2017)
2. Brazinova, A., et al.: Epidemiology of traumatic brain injury in Europe: a living systematic review. J. Neurotrauma **38**, 1411–1440 (2021)
3. Bryant, L., Ferguson, A., Spencer, E.: Linguistic analysis of discourse in aphasia: a review of the literature. Clin. Linguist. Phonetics **30**(7), 489–518 (2016)
4. Coelho, C.A., Grela, B., Corso, M., Gamble, A., Feinn, R.: Microlinguistic deficits in the narrative discourse of adults with traumatic brain injury. Brain Inj. **19**(13), 1139–1145 (2005)
5. Dewan, M.C., et al.: Estimating the global incidence of traumatic brain injury. Neurosurgery **130**, 1080–1097 (2019). https://doi.org/10.3171/2017.10.JNS17352
6. Douglas, J.: Loss of friendship following traumatic brain injury: a model grounded in the experience of adults with severe injury. Neuropsychol. Rehabil. **30**(7), 1277–1302 (2020)
7. Gross, M., Lentin, A.: Introduction to Formal Grammars. Springer, Heidelberg (1970). https://doi.org/10.1007/978-3-642-87129-0
8. Hegde, M.N., Freed, D.: Assessment of Communication Disorders in Adults Resources and Protocols. Plural Publishing, Inc. (2022)
9. Linnik, A., Bastiaanse, R., Höhle, B.: Discourse production in aphasia: a current review of theoretical and methodological challenges. Aphasiology **30**(7), 765–800 (2015)
10. MacWhinney, B.: The CHILDES Project: Tools for Analyzing Talk, 3rd edn. Lawrence Erlbaum Associates, Mahwah (2000)
11. MacWhinney, B.: Tools for Analyzing Talk - Part 2: The CLAN Programs. Electronic edn. Carnegie Mellon University (2020). https://doi.org/10.21415/T5G10R
12. Mitkov, R. (ed.): The Oxford Handbook of Computational Linguistics. Oxford University Press Inc., New York (2003)
13. Morrow, E.L., Turkstra, L.S., Duff, M.C.: Confidence and training of speech-language pathologists in cognitive- communication disorders: time to rethink graduate education models? Am. J. Speech-Lang. Pathol. **30**, 986–992 (2020)
14. Ramage, A.E.: Potential for cognitive communication impairment in COVID-19 survivors: a call to action for speech-language pathologists. Am. J. Speech-Lang. Pathol. **29**, 1821–1832 (2020)
15. Roldán-Palacios, M.: Closure under substitution to proper flexagons. Bachelor thesis, BUAP (2018)
16. Roldán-Palacios, M.: A multi-level analysis of language production: features compromised by traumatic brain injury. Master thesis, INAOE (2021)
17. Power, E., et al.: Patterns of narrative discourse in early recovery following severe traumatic brain injury. Brain Inj. **34**(1), 98–109 (2020)
18. Roldán-Palacios, M., López-López, A.: Feature analysis for aphasic or abnormal language caused by injury. In: Arai, K. (ed.) Intelligent Computing. LNNS, vol. 285, pp. 1–16. Springer, Cham (2021). https://doi.org/10.1007/978-3-030-80129-8_1
19. Roldán-Palacios, M., López-López, A.: Feature analysis and classification of impaired language caused by brain injury. In: Natural Language Processing in Healthcare: A Special Focus on Low Resource Languages. CRC-Press (in-press)

20. Scarborough, H.S.: Index of productive syntax. Appl. Psycholinguist. **11**(1), 1–22 (1990)
21. Steel, J., Elbourn, E., Togher, L.: Narrative discourse intervention after traumatic brain injury: a systematic review of the literature. Top. Lang. Disord. **41**(1), 47–72 (2021)
22. Stubbs, E., et al.: Procedural discourse performance in adults with severe traumatic brain injury at 3 and 6 months post injury. Brain Inj. **32**(2), 167–181 (2018)
23. James, S.L., et al.: Global, regional, and national burden of traumatic brain injury and spinal cord injury, 1990–2016: a systematic analysis for the global burden of disease study 2016. Lancet Neurol. **18**(1), 56–87 (2019)
24. TBIBank. https://tbi.talkbank.org/. Accessed Sept 2021
25. Togher, L., et al.: TBI Bank is a feasible assessment protocol to evaluate the cognitive communication skills of people with severe TBI during the subacute stage of recovery. In: Brain Injury, vol. 28, no. 5–6, pp. 723–723, May 2014
26. Harley, T.: Talking the Talk: Language, Psychology and Science. Psychology Press, London (2010)

# A Belief Rule Based Expert System to Diagnose Alzheimer's Disease Using Whole Blood Gene Expression Data

S. M. Shafkat Raihan[1] , Mumtahina Ahmed[2] , Angel Sharma[1] ,
Mohammad Shahadat Hossain[1(✉)] , Raihan Ul Islam[3] ,
and Karl Andersson[3]

[1] Department of Computer Science and Engineering, University of Chittagong,
Chittagong 4331, Bangladesh
hossainms@cu.ac.bd
[2] Port City International University, Chittagong, Bangladesh
[3] Pervasive and Mobile Computing Laboratory, Lulea University of Technology,
Lulea, Sweden
{raihan.ul.islam,karl.andersson}@ltu.se

**Abstract.** Alzheimer's disease (AD) is a degenerative neurological disease that is the most common cause of dementia. It is also the fifth-greatest reason for death in adults aged 65 and over. However, there is no accurate way of diagnosing neurological Alzheimer's disorders in medical research. Blood gene expression analysis offers a realistic option for identifying those at risk of AD. Blood gene expression patterns have previously proved beneficial in diagnosing several brain disorders, despite the blood-brain barrier's restricted permeability. The most extensively used statistical machine learning and deep learning algorithms are data-driven and do not address data uncertainty. Belief Rule-Based Expert System (BRBES) is an approach that can identify various forms of uncertainty in data and reason using evidential reasoning. No previous research studies have examined BRBES' performance in diagnosing AD. As a result, this study aims to identify how effective BRBES is at diagnosing Alzheimer's disease from blood gene expression data. We used a gradient-free technique to optimize the BRBES because prior research had shown the limits of gradient-based optimization. We have also attempted to address the class imbalance problem using BRBES' consequent utility parameters. Finally, after 5-fold cross-validation, we compared our model to three classic ML models, finding that our model had a greater specificity than the other three models across all folds. The average specificity of our models for all folds was 32%

**Keywords:** BRBES · Alzheimer's disease · Gene expression data · Disjunctive BRBES · Class imbalance

## 1 Introduction

Alzheimer's disease (AD), the most common form of dementia, is estimated to affect 13.8 million individuals in the United States by 2050. [11]. The shift from

© Springer Nature Switzerland AG 2022
M. Mahmud et al. (Eds.): BI 2022, LNAI 13406, pp. 301–315, 2022
https://doi.org/10.1007/978-3-031-15037-1_25

symptom-based to pathophysiology-based AD diagnosis revealed that structural brain changes (MRI), molecular neuroimaging changes, and alterations in cerebral spinal fluid biomarkers are the most significant factors in AD diagnosis [6]. However, more research is required on the changes that cause symptoms and how to mitigate, stop, or reduce the disease. Biological data are currently being produced at a faster rate than it is being understood. As a result, the task is to derive new information from existing data. In comparison to individual research, a meta-analysis integrates many studies to enhance sample size [19]. In 2009, a large-scale genome-wide association study (GWAS) involving 2,032 people with Alzheimer's disease and 5,328 healthy people found mutations at CLU and CR1 that were related to the disease [12]. In addition, a meta-analysis of four previously published GWAS dataset identified 11 additional susceptibility loci for Alzheimer's disease [24].

The demand for novel healthcare solutions, as well as continued efforts to understand the biological basis of disease, necessitate extensive research in the life sciences [27]. Recent advancements in the life sciences have allowed researchers to get insights into the molecular characteristics of living organisms, allowing them to explore biological systems comprehensively. Alzheimer's disease (AD), Parkinson's disease (PD), and schizophrenia (SZ) are three of the most common neurological disorders in which normal brain functions are interrupted. As a result, a variety of neuroimaging techniques and deep learning-based analysis approaches contribute to establishing effective treatment strategies for the classification and early identification of diseases [28]. Recently, the detection of COVID-19 is performed using a nucleic acid-based diagnostic approach known as RT-PCR. PCR has become the most widely used technology for several clinical applications, including disease evaluation, surveillance, early detection of biothreat substances, and antibiotic resistance profiling. PCR-based approaches may be more cost-effective than traditional test procedures [39].

Gene set analysis methods are selected to diagnose diseases because of the ease of collecting blood, sputum, saliva, serum, and other gene expression data. It is necessary to identify the best strategy and design for addressing a specific issue because gene analysis experiment needs significant time and financial investment. Technical difficulties such as sample preparation, array spotting, signal acquisition, dye intensity bias, normalization, and sample contamination can lead to inconsistencies or inaccurate results [7]. Even if no technological concerns exist, an inappropriate design might make array data analysis difficult.

Machine learning (ML) and deep learning (DL) artificial intelligence techniques can be utilized to make effective diagnoses of certain diseases. The fundamental mechanism, however, supports explainability in the decision-making process. However, [8] and [26] have pointed out that deep learning techniques' manifold transformation strategy does not perform effectively, even for large datasets with causal correlations.

In this study, we investigated how artificial intelligence algorithms that can reason under ambiguity could be used to diagnose Alzheimer's disease using gene expression data from blood samples. However, Knowledge-based systems such as Fuzzy Inference Systems , the Bayesian approach , Dempster-Shafer theory, and MYCIN are capable of reasoning under uncertainty [13]. We chose the disjunctive belief rule-based expert system (BRBES) technique because it can reason under different types of uncertainty, such as imprecision, ambiguity, vagueness, incompleteness, ignorance, unpredictability. According to our knowledge, BRBES has never been used in the diagnosis of Alzheimer's disease. Also, class imbalance is an essential problem in supervised classification of real world datasets. We tried to utilize BRBES' consequent utility parameters in a way that will address the class imbalance problem.

## 2   Related Work

Alzheimer's disease is gradually becoming a major global health and economic issue, prompting extensive scientific research into the underlying genetic risk factors and regulatory indicators [34]. Furthermore, clinical trials demonstrate that patients with Alzheimer's disease have a wide range of symptoms and responds to different treatments, implying that there are numerous biological origins for the disease [30]. This complicates the investigation of AD even further. Data acquired through high throughput gene expression profiling has provided new opportunities for a better understanding of complicated disease mechanisms and pathways at a molecular level in recent years [25].

Using cutting-edge computing technology like GPUs, deep learning models have performed a wide range of experiments for the diagnosis and prediction of Alzheimer's disease [36]. Using both high-throughput screening data and a deep learning-based prediction, this study [23] discovered gene mutations and unusual splicing of the PLC1 gene in AD. Another study applied the ensemble of random-forest and regularized regression model (LASSO) to AD-related microarray datasets from four brain regions to find novel genetic biomarkers using a machine learning-based feature-selection classification scheme [34]. However, a few studies have employed blood-based expression data to identify significant genes related to Alzheimer's disease or to predict early symptoms of a disease [4]. Blood samples are easy to acquire, less intrusive, and contain proteins, peptides, nucleic acids, lipids, and other metabolites [25]. Hampel et al. [10] investigated 19 blood-based biomarkers, demonstrating that blood-based biomarker synthesis and standardization are crucial in the identification of Alzheimer's disease. As a result, blood-based biomarkers will aid in interpreting the complexity and variety of Alzheimer's disease.

Deep learning, a branch of artificial intelligence (AI) inspired by the nervous system, has recently made complicated, high-dimensional, nonlinear systems more accessible to model and analyze [5]. Deep learning models require enormous amounts of data to be available. Health care, on the other hand, is a distinct field. In reality, the world's population (as of September 2016) is just 7.5 billion people, the majority of them lacking access to primary health care. Consequently, we won't be able to formulate a comprehensive deep learning model for many patients [29]. Despite the fact that deep learning models have shown to be effective in a wide range of applications, they are frequently regarded as black boxes. Indeed, model interpretability (i.e., determining which phenotypes drive the predictions) is crucial for convincing medical practitioners to adopt the predictive system's recommendations [29].

On the other hand, the diseases are highly diverse, and we still don't fully understand the causes and progress of the vast majority of them [29]. Data sparsity, redundancy, and missing values make it challenging to train a good deep learning model with diverse data sets [29]. Deep learning approaches disregard data uncertainty and are susceptible to problems like catastrophic forgetting. However, Raihan et al. investigated the idea of utilizing artificial intelligence systems that can reason with ambiguity to detect Parkinson's disease using many types of speech signal attributes [32]. They used the disjunctive belief rule-based expert system (BRBES) to handle uncertainties such as imprecision, ambiguity, vagueness, incompleteness, ignorance, and unpredictability. Furthermore, Raihan et al. employed a BRBES to detect COVID-19 in adult pneumonia patients based on hematological and CT scan data of lung tissue infection. BRBES-based adaptive Differential Evolution, a nature-inspired optimization algorithm, is used to optimize the system (BRBaDE) [33]. This study [1] proposes combining data and knowledge-driven methodologies into a unified framework to identify the chances of survival of a patient suffering from COVID-19. They trained Xception, InceptionResNetV2, and VGG Net are pre-trained neural network models using X-ray images to identify critical and non-criticalCOVID-19 patients. This study then assessed the prediction result and specified eight other major risk indicators linked with COVID-19 patients by a knowledge-driven belief rule-based expert system. Therefore, the article [37] aims to provide a novel optimal training approach that combines DE and BRBES. Because it can generate near-optimal values for both control parameters while maintaining balanced exploitation and exploration in the problem space, this method is called enhanced belief rule-based adaptive differential evolution algorithm. In addition, a novel optimization technique based on eBRBaDE is provided, which takes into account both BRBES variables and structure. In conclusion, disjunctive BRBES can deal with uncertainty in real-world data without becoming exponentially complex, and it can be optimized using gradient-free techniques. Therefore, we'll investigate how BRBES performs on diverse gene expression data from blood samples of Alzheimer's patients in the next section.

# 3  Methodology

Our research work is built on the insight gained in the research done in [9] and [38]. From these two researches, we learned about thirteen hub genes associated with AD. Hub genes are genes that have several connections with other genes, resulting in an influential role in gene regulation. The thirteen hub genes are RPS17, RPL26, RPS27A, COX7C, RPS24, RPL31, EEF1B2, RPS27, TOMM7, RPL23, GAPDH, RHOA, and RPS29. For our experiment, we collected series matrix data of our desired datasets from the Gene Expression Omnibus (GEO) [3] and conducted GEO2R (http://www.ncbi.nlm.nih.gov/geo/geo2r) analysis.

The adjusted p-value was selected as 0.05 and log 2-fold change (logFC) was selected to be $> 0.5$. The samples were divided into three groups based on disease status which are AD (Alzheimer's Disease), MCI (Mild Cognitive Impairment), and Control group represented respectively by the digits 2, 1 and 0. In gene expression profiling, multiple probe molecules may identify the same gene. Hence, after performing GEO2R, some of the gene symbols of the resulting table had more than one probe sequences mapped to them. This was the case for the thirteen hub genes we selected for our experiment too. For instance, gene RPS17's expression values in the series matrix file were recorded against four probe ids. But our research plan was to consider each hub gene as a feature for the final dataset, where the expression values will be data samples. There were two options available to us: 1) Using some filtering criteria, to select one from multiple probes associated with a gene and use the expression set available against it, 2) To consider each probe as a different sample of the gene, and hence forming the dataset by considering each combination of expression sets of the probes. The 2nd approach would also result in massive data augmentation. However, due to limitation of computational resources and time, it couldn't be implemented. The first approach on the other hand, was implementable within the available resources. Since low adjusted p-value represents more significance, lowest p-value was selected as the filtering criteria. We selected the probes with the lowest adjusted p-value to represent the expression of the gene. The final dataset was split for 5-fold cross validation and input into the BRBES. The BRBES was then optimized using a gradient free algorithm. The entire process is depicted in Fig. 1.

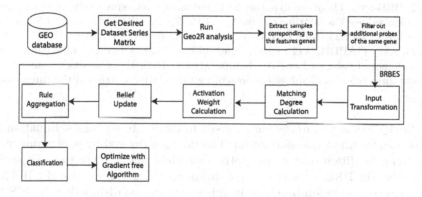

**Fig. 1.** The methodology of experiment.

## 3.1   BRBES

A belief rule base (BRB) is the knowledge base of a Belief Rule-Based Expert System (BRBES), while evidential reasoning is the inference engine (ER). While BRBES can represent ambiguous knowledge, evidential reasoning can acquire knowledge from ambiguous and diverse information. BRBES, unlike the conventional IF-THEN rule base, can deal with sophisticated non-linear causality in the presence of uncertainty. It is comprised of two major components: antecedent and consequent. Each antecedent attribute has certain referential values linked with it. The resulting attribute is given a distribution of belief degrees. In the conventional IF-THEN rule, antecedents and consequent attributes are associated with a linear causal relationship. However, this relationship is non-linear in the case of a belief rule. BRB can be formed utilizing both conjunction operator (AND). and disjunctive operator (OR). Evidential Reasoning (ER) can deal with a wide range of data uncertainty. As shown in Fig. 1 BRBES's evidential reasoning includes input transformation, matching degree computation, rule activation weight calculation, belief update, and rule aggregation. The input antecedent attribute value is distributed over the referential values of that antecedent attribute using input transformation.

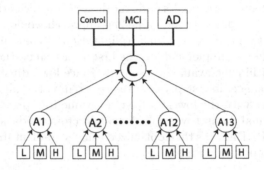

**Fig. 2.** BRB-tree. There are 13 antecedent attributes, each representing a specific gene's expression value. The attributes are A1 : RPS17, A2 : RPL26, A3 : RPS27A, A4 : COX7C, A5 : RPS24, A6 : RPL31, A7 : EEF1B2, A8 : RPS27, A9 : TOMM7, A10 : RPL23, A11 : GAPDH, A12 : RHOA, and A13 : RPS29. All antecdent attributes have three referential values - Low(L), Medium(M) and High(H). The single consequent C also has three referential values - representing the relative weights of the three classes

Matching degrees are the names given to these altered values. Equation 4 of [14] is used for input transformation. The rules are derived by performing multiplication or addition operations on the individual matching degrees, depending on whether the BRB is conjunctive or disjunctive. The conjunctive BRBES faces combinatorial explosion problem. In this study, we use disjunctive BRBES that can avoid exponential complexity, and address uncertainty in real-world data. When there are n attributes, disjunctive BRBES requires the same number of referential values $m_i$ for all attributes and always provides m rules. Each rule has the total matching degrees ($\alpha_i$ where i = 1,..., l and l means the rules) after the input transformation operation. Equation 4 of [41] is used to determine total matching degrees for disjunctive BRBES. Using Equation 4 of [17], the rule's activation weight ($w_i$) is determined using the total matching degrees ($\alpha_i$) and relative rule weights ($\theta_i$). The sum of a rule base's rule activation weights should be one, and if a rule isn't active, it should be zero. After that, the belief update operation generates an initial belief matrix from a random number of ranges [0,1]. The belief matrix will be a table with L columns and N rows if there are L rules and N referential values.

The summation of the values in each column in the matrix is less than or equal to 1. As a result, the sum of each rule's degrees of belief must be less than or equal to 1. Equation 7 is used to update belief degrees after the belief matrix has been generated. Because there may be insufficient data for any antecedent attributes due to ignorance, updating the degrees of confidence is critical. The *tau* variable and the matching degrees of each antecedent attribute are used in the belief update procedure. Thus it addresses the uncertainty caused by data incompleteness or ignorance. Finally, evidential reasoning combines all of the rules and uses Equation 5 of [20] to get the output for the input antecedent attributes. The output value will be dispersed over the subsequent referential values in a fuzzy form. Equation 12 of [42] as well as other approaches can then be used to generate a numerical or crisp value. We chose disjunctive BRBES in this study because disjunctive BRBES does not expand exponentially. There were three referential values for all antecedent and consequent attributes: Low (L), Medium (M), and High (H). The dataset was rescaled using the maximum and minimum values in the dataset to be in the range [0,1]. Then the utility values corresponding to low, medium and high were 0, 0.5 and 1 respectively. The details of implementing the BRBES are available in [21].

## 3.2 Dataset

In this research, datasets GSE63060 and GSE63061 [35] of the Gene Expression Omnibus (GEO) Database [3] were used for experimentation. Both datasets are subseries' of the superseries GSE63063 [35]. These are expression profile datasets which respectively contain samples from 329 and 388 patients. The platforms used by the creators of these datasets were respectively Illumina HumanHT-12 V3.0 expression beadchip and Illumina HumanHT-12 V4.0 expression beadchip. The data was available normalized in series matrix format. The normalization of both datasets was done using Robust Multiarray Averaging (RMA) method. Both datasets were first processed in the way shown in Fig. 1. Then the processed datasets were combined to generate the operational dataset. After combining the datasets, there were 714 samples (Control : 239. MCI : 192, AD: 284). The three classes Control, MCI and AD were labeled as 0, 1 and, 2 in the final dataset.

## 3.3 Model Training

During experimentation, 5-fold cross-validation was done to check on model over-fitting. The model was trained using BRBaDE [21], which is a variant of the gradient-free optimization algorithm called differential evolution (DE). BRBaDE provides a balanced implementation of exploration and exploitation by varying the crossover and mutation factors over iterations using an additional BRBES. The parameters chosen for being optimized were the non-terminal antecedent reference values, rule weights, belief degrees of the belief update matrix and the consequent referential utility values. Unlike previous works [21,32,33], mean square error was not used in our experiment as we did not sum up the consequent belief degrees. Since this is a classification problem, we utilized BRBES's unique ability to represent the consequent as a distribution of beliefs to represent the classes. The consequent referential values were identified as Control, MCI and AD. After multiplying with consequent referential utility values, the class having the highest value was determined as the final crisp output (i.e., 0, 1 or 2 in our case). Then, classification error was used as the function to minimize to optimize the BRBES through BRBaDE. The model was optimized for 5000 iterations with number of population being ten times the number of parameters. The training, test set prediction of BRBES was done using MATLAB while in case of the other machine learning models, python was used on the Google colaboratory (colab) platform. The peformance evaluation of all models and p-test was performed using colab as well.

## 4    Results and Discussion

We have used BRBES for our classification and prediction. The performance of the model is compared with other machine learning models such as Naive Bayes, K-Nearest Neighbors, and Random Forest. In a confusion matrix, the performance of classification models are displayed. Classification accuracy alone can be misleading if the classes are unbalanced or there are more than two classes in the dataset. An accurate understanding of a classification model's errors and successes can be obtained from a confusion matrix. With a balanced dataset, accuracy is a good measure of classification. Accuracy refers to the number of correctly classified instances versus the total number of instances. However, since our dataset has class imbalance, other metrics are needed for a fair evaluation. The measure of precision is the dispersion or closeness of measurements. Recall or sensitivity is known as the percentage of correct positive predictions compared to the total number of positive examples. In order to compare models, the F1-score combines precision and recall into a single metric. It is computed by taking their harmonic mean of precision and recall. F1-score is generally a good measurement for comparing model performances. Specificity is determined by the proportion of true negatives that are correctly predicted by the model. Since it is a multiclass classification, macro average of the class-wise metrics have been depicted. The evaluation in light of the above performance metrics are shown in Table 1. In this reseach, 5-fold cross validation was performed. Hence, the mean and standard deviation were chosen to represent the overall performance of the models across all the folds. Mean is a representative of central tendency of the results while standard deviation shows the dispersion in them. They are shown in Table 1. To evaluate the significance of BRBES models performance against, the other models, one tailed p-test with p = 0.05 was performed on the mean values of the metrics. The results of the p-test have been shown in Table 2. Also, the best confusion matrix among the five folds for each of the four models are shown in Fig. 3.

If we observe Table 1 and Fig. 3, we can see that BRBES clearly outperforms other models in terms of specificity, although other perform better in terms of

**Table 1.** Comparison of BRBES' performance with traditional machine learning algorithms using classification metrics Accuracy(Acc), Precision (Prec), Sensitivity/Recall (Sens), Specificity (Spec) and F1-score(F1). The models compared are BRBES, Naive Bayes (NB), Random Forest (RF) and K-nearest Neighor (KNN). The mean and standard deviation (SD) of the metrics across the five folds represent the central tendency and dispersion of the results.

| Algorithms | BRBES | | | | | NB | | | | | RF | | | | | KNN | | | | |
|---|---|---|---|---|---|---|---|---|---|---|---|---|---|---|---|---|---|---|---|---|
| Features | Acc | Prec | Sens | Spec | F1 | Acc | Prec | Sens | Spec | F1 | Acc | Prec | Sens | Spec | F1 | Acc | Prec | Sens | Spec | F1 |
| Fold-1 | 0.35 | 0.23 | 0.31 | **0.35** | 0.29 | 0.44 | 0.47 | 0.47 | 0.28 | 0.45 | 0.51 | 0.48 | 0.49 | 0.24 | 0.49 | 0.51 | 0.48 | 0.49 | 0.24 | 0.50 |
| Fold-2 | 0.42 | 0.41 | 0.39 | **0.30** | 0.39 | 0.42 | 0.43 | 0.42 | 0.26 | 0.43 | 0.50 | 0.49 | 0.47 | 0.26 | 0.48 | 0.41 | 0.38 | 0.39 | 0.30 | 0.40 |
| Fold-3 | 0.42 | 0.28 | 0.37 | **0.31** | 0.35 | 0.48 | 0.51 | 0.48 | 0.26 | 0.48 | 0.56 | 0.51 | 0.50 | 0.24 | 0.52 | 0.49 | 0.46 | 0.47 | 0.26 | 0.48 |
| Fold-4 | 0.41 | 0.42 | 0.36 | **0.34** | 0.35 | 0.48 | 0.49 | 0.49 | 0.26 | 0.48 | 0.50 | 0.48 | 0.48 | 0.25 | 0.50 | 0.49 | 0.48 | 0.48 | 0.25 | 0.49 |
| Fold-5 | 0.43 | 0.29 | 0.38 | **0.30** | 0.36 | 0.38 | 0.45 | 0.39 | 0.31 | 0.39 | 0.49 | 0.44 | 0.46 | 0.25 | 0.47 | 0.50 | 0.47 | 0.48 | 0.25 | 0.49 |
| Mean | 0.406 | 0.326 | 0.362 | **0.32** | 0.348 | 0.44 | 0.47 | 0.45 | 0.274 | 0.446 | 0.512 | 0.48 | 0.48 | 0.248 | 0.492 | 0.48 | 0.454 | 0.462 | 0.26 | 0.472 |
| SD | **0.032** | 0.084 | **0.0311** | 0.023 | **0.0363** | 0.0424 | 0.0316 | 0.043 | 0.0219 | 0.0378 | 0.0277 | 0.0254 | 0.0158 | 0.0083 | 0.0192 | 0.04 | 0.0421 | 0.0408 | 0.0234 | 0.0408 |

**Table 2.** One tailed P-test of the BRBES model's metrics averaged across the five fold. The inference D stands for "Difference between mean performance is probably real" and S stands for "Algorithms probably have the same performance". The p-value = 0.05 was used.

| Acc | | | Prec | | | Sens | | | Spec | | | F1 | | |
|---|---|---|---|---|---|---|---|---|---|---|---|---|---|---|
| Model | p-value | Inference | Model | p-value | Inference | Model | p-value | Inference | Model | p-value | Inference | Model | p-value | Inference |
| NB | 0.129038 | S | NB | 0.019381 | D | NB | 0.099165 | S | NB | 0.000766 | D | NB | 0.090321 | S |
| RF | 0.002467 | D | RF | 0.009419 | D | RF | 0.008212 | D | RF | 0.000124 | D | RF | 0.003749 | D |
| KNN | 0.025783 | D | KNN | 0.077684 | S | KNN | 0.053969 | S | KNN | 0.000194 | D | KNN | 0.035882 | D |

other metrics. On investigating the reason behind this phenomenon, we learned that BRBES was not being able to detect MCI classes well whereas other classes were. This indicates a requirement of further improvement in the optimization strategy of BRBES. However, mild cognitive impairment (MCI) is known to be caused by AD and is a precursor of AD in most cases [2,31]. Figure 3 shows the best confusion matrices among the five folds for each model. The criteria for best was how well were the control and AD classes classified, as the focus of this research is AD diagnosis. If two matrices had reciprocal superiority in respect of these two classes, we looked for two other indicators based on the fact that AD is a precursor of MCI. We looked at the false negative distribution of class 1 i.e., MCI. If a matrix had more MCI false negative assigned to AD and less assigned control, we considered it as the better matrix. Based on this criteria, fold-4s of BRBES and Naive Bayes, fold-3 of Random forest and fold-1 of KNN were selected for representing in this research. It can be observed that BRBES has a high true positive for AD compared to others. Also, if we observed in light of the principle of MCI false negatives, we will see that compared to others, BRBES has predicted the least number of MCI classes as control and most number of MCI classes (compared to the other models) to AD. Hence, although BRBES did not succeed well in exactly distinguishing MCI, the direction in which it predicted most MCI classes, is in line with the reality that MCI is caused by AD.

Though BRBES could not outperform the other models in metrics other than specificity, it's standard deviation of accuracy, sensitivity and F1-score is lesser than those of Naive Bayes and KNN. Standard deviation is a measure of

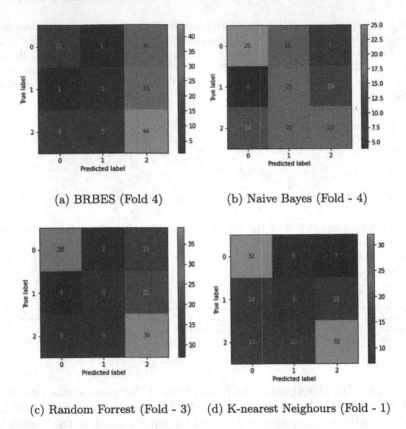

(a) BRBES (Fold 4)    (b) Naive Bayes (Fold - 4)

(c) Random Forrest (Fold - 3)    (d) K-nearest Neighours (Fold - 1)

**Fig. 3.** Confusion matrices of best folds

dispersion of data. The lesser it is, the lesser the data points fluctuate away from the central tendency. Therefore, in accuracy, sensitivity and F1-score, BRBES is more stable than Naive Bayes and KNN. Aside from this, Table 2 shows the significance test results. The metrics used in this research are such that the higher they are, the better the performance. Apart from specificity, the other metrics of BRBES are lower than Naive Bayes, Random Forest and KNN. However, if we observe the p-test results, we'll see that Naive Bayes's performance in accuracy, sensitivity and f1-score isn't significantly higher than those of BRBES. Similar can be said about KNN in respect of precision and sensitivity, where the performance is not significantly higher than BRBES. On the other hand, the metric at which BRBES outperformed all three models i.e., specificity, shows significant difference of performance. The high specificity denotes that BRBES is comparatively better at diagnosing healthy patients as negative, rather than diseased. If medication and treatment procedures of AD is applied on a healthy patient based on such misdiagnosis, then that may prove harmful to the patient.

Moreover, we have attempted to address the class imbalance problem in real world datasets using the uncertainty-handling features of BRBES. In a typical

BRBES, the output utilities are multiplied with the corresponding consequent beliefs in a sorted manner, as referential values need to be sequential. However, in our experiment, during training we obtained the class distribution information for each training fold. Then at the moment of using the consequent utilities, we multiplied in a way to adjust the class imbalance. That is, the highest occurring class was multiplied with the lowest utility values and the lowest occurring class with the highest utilities. Those in the middle were multiplied in a similar proportion i.e., the lower the class occurrence, the higher the multiplied output utility and vice versa. Hence utility values became class weights. During testing, we again collected the class ratios in the test folds and utilized the trained consequent utilities in the same fashion. One might ask, if the utilities require class ratio information, how can they be utilized in real time diagnosis of individual patients. In such cases, the demographic observations of distribution of AD, MCI and control can be used to represent class ratio.

Gene expression is the process by which information encoded in genes is used to create RNA molecules that code for proteins or noncoding RNA molecules that perform other activities. Simultaneous genome-wide analysis of gene expression and genetic variation allows the mapping of genetic factors underlying individual differences in quantitative expression levels. Interactions among different genes and the surrounding environment can result in many genetic and neurological diseases. So, a biological approach is implicit in finding the causes of such diseases. AD is a progressive neurodegenerative disease characterized by the presence of amyloid deposits and neurofibrillary tangles, in addition to the loss of cortical neurons and synapses. Many underlying protectives and disease-modifying factors may contribute to the core mechanism of AD. Though the earliest cognitive sign is known to be loss and deficit in episodic memory, it is not sufficient to detect AD. The damages done happens long before showing any clinical signs. The detection method needs to be sensitive to memory loss related to age, brain disorder, and depression. Early detection and intervention are key components in ensuring that a patient gets the care needed to lead a moderate life. Due to the uncertain nature of the underlying causes and its manifesting symptoms, we have proposed a Belief Rule-based Expert System (BRBES). BRBES uses a belief rule base (BRB) as a knowledge base and evidential reasoning(ER) as an inference engine [18]. It has been tested in multiple past studies to be able to handle a wide range of uncertainties, including vagueness, ambiguity, imprecision, incompleteness, ignorance, and randomness [16]. BRBES is also widely used in medical fields where several uncertainties are associated [14,15,22,40]. To our knowledge, using BRBES with gene expression for predicting Alzheimer's disease has never been done before. The novelty of our research lies in the analysis of gene expression using BRBES. It opens the frontier to new insights and topics for understanding AD and the various uncertainties associated with its underlying causes. Moreover, the parameters in a BRBES are structured and the model itself is rule based. This allows the development of an explainable AI model to be applied to whole blood gene expression based diagnosis.

One of the limitations of this research is that despite attempting to address the class imbalance, BRBES did not perform well in detecting the lowest occurring class 1, corresponding to MCI. It is indeed a fact to be acknowledged that BRBES requires further improvement, if it is to be applied in A.I. based diagnosis of AD from whole blood gene expression data. Islam et al. [37] obtained better results by applying joint optimization to optimize BRBES learning. In this type of optimization, both the structure and parameters of the BRBES are optimized. Hence applying joint optimization has a potential chance of improving the BRBES's performance in the current problem.

## 5    Conclusion

In this study, the prospect of a Belief Rule-based expert system optimized with the gradient-free algorithm BRBaDE for identifying Alzheimer's patients based on whole blood gene expression data was investigated systematically. The problem of class imbalance was attempted to be addressed by using BRBES consequent utilities as class weights. BRBES obtained higher specificity compared to other machine learning models such as Naive bayes, Random Forest, and KNN. But it did not perform quite well in other classification metrics compared to other models. Therefore in future works, we will explore how to overcome the performance limitations of BRBES. In [1], an enhanced form of BRBaDE optimization has been used alongside deep learning for reasoning with BRBES, which generated robust results. The joint optimization of structure and parameter can be combined with deep learning and enhanced BRBaDE (eBRBaDE) [37] to gain better results. Hence, we would apply the joint optimization technique combined with deep learning and eBRBaDE to make up for the limitations in decision-making of BRBES.

**Acknowledgement.** We thank M.S.H., R.U.I., and K.A. for their contributions to conception and methodology, as well as M.S.H. and R.U.I. for their insightful comments on the paper. M.A., S.M.S.R., and A.S., our fellow researchers, contributed valuable insight and knowledge that substantially assisted the research. We also want to thank Shagufta Mizan and Mahmud Shah Raihan for their helpful recommendations on technical and domain-specific challenges.

**Code Availability.** The code for this research is available at https://tinyurl.com/47fpybky.

## References

1. Ahmed, T.U., Jamil, M.N., Hossain, M.S., Islam, R.U., Andersson, K.: An integrated deep learning and belief rule base intelligent system to predict survival of COVID-19 patient under uncertainty. Cogn. Comput. **14**, 660–676 (2022). https://doi.org/10.1007/s12559-021-09978-8
2. Bachurin, S.O., Gavrilova, S.I., Samsonova, A., Barreto, G.E., Aliev, G.: Mild cognitive impairment due to Alzheimer disease: contemporary approaches to diagnostics and pharmacological intervention. Pharmacol. Res. **129**, 216–226 (2018)

3. Barrett, T., et al.: NCBI GEO: archive for functional genomics data sets-update. Nucleic Acids Res. **41**(D1), D991–D995 (2012)
4. Cooper, Y.A., Nachun, D., Dokuru, D., Yang, Z., Karydas, A.M., Serrero, G., Yue, B.: Progranulin levels in blood in Alzheimer's disease and mild cognitive impairment. Ann. Clin. Translat. Neurol. **5**(5), 616–629 (2018). https://doi.org/10.1002/acn3.560
5. Cortes-Briones, J.A., Tapia-Rivas, N.I., D'Souza, D.C., Estevez, P.A.: Going deep into schizophrenia with artificial intelligence. Schizophr. Res. (2021). https://doi.org/10.1016/j.schres.2021.05.018
6. Dubois, B., et al.: Research criteria for the diagnosis of Alzheimer's disease: revising the NINCDS-ADRDA criteria. Lancet Neurol. **6**(8), 734–746 (2007). https://doi.org/10.1016/S1474-4422(07)70178-3
7. Fournier, M.V., Carvalho, P.C., Magee, D.D., da Carvalho, M.G.C., Appasani, K.: Experimental design for gene expression analysis. In: Bioarrays, pp. 29–44. Humana Press, Totowa, NJ (2007). https://doi.org/10.1007/978-1-59745-328-8_3
8. Grossberg, S.: A path toward explainable AI and autonomous adaptive intelligence: deep learning, adaptive resonance, and models of perception, emotion, and action. Front. Neurorobot. **14** (2020)
9. Gui, H., Gong, Q., Jiang, J., Liu, M., Li, H.: Identification of hub genes in patients with Alzheimer disease and obstructive sleep apnea syndrome using integrated bioinformatics analysis. Comput. Math. Methods Med. **2021**, 9491–9502 (2021)
10. Hampel, H., et al.: Blood-based biomarkers for Alzheimer disease: mapping the road to the clinic. Nat. Rev. Neurol. **14**(11), 639–652 (2018). https://doi.org/10.1038/s41582-018-0079-7
11. Hao, S., Wang, R., Zhang, Y., Zhan, H.: Prediction of Alzheimer's disease-associated genes by integration of GWAS summary data and expression data. Front. Genet. **9** (2019). https://doi.org/10.3389/fgene.2018.00653
12. Harold, D., et al.: Genome-wide association study identifies variants at CLU and cr1 associated with Alzheimer's disease. Nat. Genet. **41**(10), 1088–1093 (2009). https://doi.org/10.1038/ng.440
13. Henkind, S.J., Harrison, M.C.: An analysis of four uncertainty calculi. IEEE Trans. Syst. Man Cybernet. **18**(5), 700–714 (1988)
14. Hossain, M.S., Ahmed, F., Andersson, K., et al.: A belief rule based expert system to assess tuberculosis under uncertainty. J. Med. Syst **41**(3), 43 (2017)
15. Hossain, M.S., Andersson, K., Naznin, S.: A belief rule based expert system to diagnose measles under uncertainty. In: World Congress in Computer Science, Computer Engineering, and Applied Computing (WORLDCOMP 2015): The 2015 International Conference on Health Informatics and Medical Systems 27 July 2015–30 July 2015, pp. 17–23. CSREA Press (2015)
16. Hossain, M.S., Habib, I.B., Andersson, K.: A belief rule based expert system to diagnose dengue fever under uncertainty. In: 2017 Computing Conference, pp. 179–186. IEEE (2017)
17. Hossain, M.S., Khalid, M.S., Akter, S., Dey, S.: A belief rule-based expert system to diagnose influenza. In: 2014 9Th International Forum on Strategic Technology (IFOST), pp. 113–116. IEEE (2014)
18. Hossain, M.S., Rahaman, S., Mustafa, R., Andersson, K.: A belief rule-based expert system to assess suspicion of acute coronary syndrome (ACS) under uncertainty. Soft Comput. **22**(22), 7571–7586 (2018)
19. Hosseinian, S., Arefian, E., Rakhsh-Khorshid, H., Scheltens, P.: A meta-analysis of gene expression data highlights synaptic dysfunction in the hippocampus of brains

with Alzheimer's disease. Sci. Rep. **10**, pp. 8384, 734–746 (2020). https://doi.org/10.1038/s41598-020-64452-z

20. Islam, R.U., Hossain, M.S., Andersson, K.: A deep learning inspired belief rule-based expert system. IEEE Access **8**, 190637–190651 (2020)
21. Islam, R.U., Ruci, X., Hossain, M.S., Andersson, K., Kor, A.L.: Capacity management of hyperscale data centers using predictive modelling. Energies **12**(18), 3438 (2019)
22. Karim, R., Andersson, K., Hossain, M.S., Uddin, M.J., Meah, M.P.: A belief rule based expert system to assess clinical bronchopneumonia suspicion. In: 2016 Future Technologies Conference (FTC), pp. 655–660. IEEE (2016)
23. Kim, S.H., et al.: Prediction of Alzheimer's disease-specific phospholipase c gamma-1 SNV by deep learning-based approach for high-throughput screening. Proc. Natl Acad. Sci. **118**(3), e2011250118 (2021). https://doi.org/10.1073/pnas.2011250118
24. Lambert, J.C., et al.: Meta-analysis of 74,046 individuals identifies 11 new susceptibility loci for Alzheimer's disease. Nat. Genet. **45**(12), 1452–1458 (2013). https://doi.org/10.1038/ng.2802
25. Lee, T., Lee, H.: Prediction of Alzheimer's disease using blood gene expression data. Sci. Rep. **10**(1), 1–13 (2020). https://doi.org/10.1038/s41598-020-60595-1
26. Mahmud, M., Kaiser, M.S., McGinnity, T.M., Hussain, A.: Deep learning in mining biological data. Cogn. Comput. **13**(1), 1–33 (2021)
27. Mahmud, M., Kaiser, M.S., Hussain, A., Vassanelli, S.: Applications of deep learning and reinforcement learning to biological data. IEEE Trans. Neural Netw. Learn. Syst. **29**(6), 2063–2079 (2018). https://doi.org/10.1109/TNNLS.2018.2790388
28. Noor, M.B.T., Zenia, N.Z., Kaiser, M.S., Mamun, S.A., Mahmud, M.: Application of deep learning in detecting neurological disorders from magnetic resonance images: a survey on the detection of Alzheimer's disease, Parkinson's disease and schizophrenia. Brain Inform. **7**(1), 1–21 (2020). https://doi.org/10.1186/s40708-020-00112-2
29. Miotto, R., Wang, F., Wang, S., Jiang, X., Dudley, J.T.: Deep learning for healthcare: review, opportunities and challenges. Brief. Bioinform. **196**, 1236–1246 (2018)
30. Oxford, A.E., Stewart, E.S., Rohn, T.T.: Clinical trials in Alzheimer's disease: a hurdle in the path of remedy. Int. J. Alzheimer's Dis. **2020** (2020)
31. Petersen, R.C., et al.: Mild cognitive impairment due to Alzheimer disease in the community. Ann. Neurol. **74**(2), 199–208 (2013)
32. Raihan, S., Zisad, S.N., Islam, R.U., Hossain, M.S., Andersson, K.: A Belief Rule base approach to support comparison of digital speech signal features for parkinson's disease diagnosis. In: Mahmud, M., Kaiser, M.S., Vassanelli, S., Dai, Q., Zhong, N. (eds.) BI 2021. LNCS (LNAI), vol. 12960, pp. 388–400. Springer, Cham (2021). https://doi.org/10.1007/978-3-030-86993-9_35
33. Shafkat Raihan, S.M., Islam, R.U., Hossain, M.S., Andersson, K.: A BRBES to support diagnosis of COVID-19 Using clinical and CT scan data. In: Arefin, M.S., Kaiser, M.S., Bandyopadhyay, A., Ahad, M.A.R., Ray, K. (eds.) Proceedings of the International Conference on Big Data, IoT, and Machine Learning. LNDECT, vol. 95, pp. 483–496. Springer, Singapore (2022). https://doi.org/10.1007/978-981-16-6636-0_37
34. Sharma, A., Dey., P.: A machine learning approach to unmask novel gene signatures and prediction of Alzheimer's disease within different brain regions. Genomics **113**(4), 1778–1789 (2021). https://doi.org/10.1016/j.ygeno.2021.04.028
35. Sood, S., et al.: A novel multi-tissue RNA diagnostic of healthy ageing relates to cognitive health status. Genome Biol. **16**(1), 1–17 (2015)

36. Tanveer, M., et al.: Machine learning techniques for the diagnosis of Alzheimer's disease: a review. ACM Trans. Multimedia Comput. Commun. Appl. **16**(1s) (2020). https://doi.org/10.1145/3344998
37. Ul Islam, R., Hossain, M.S., Andersson, K.: A learning mechanism for BRBES using enhanced belief rule-based adaptive differential evolution. In: 2020 Joint 9th International Conference on Informatics, Electronics Vision (ICIEV) and 2020 4th International Conference on Imaging, Vision Pattern Recognition (icIVPR), pp. 1–10 (2020). https://doi.org/10.1109/ICIEVicIVPR48672.2020.9306521
38. Xue, W., Li, J., Fu, K., Teng, W.: Differential expression of mRNAs in peripheral blood related to prodrome and progression of Alzheimer's disease. BioMed Res. Int. **2020** (2020)
39. Yang, S., Rothman, R.E.: PCR-based diagnostics for infectious diseases: uses, limitations, and future applications in acute-care settings. Lancet. Infect. Dis. **4**, 337–348 (2004). https://doi.org/10.1016/S1473-3099(04)01044-8
40. Zisad, S.N., Hossain, M.S., Andersson, K.: Speech emotion recognition in neurological disorders using convolutional neural network. In: Mahmud, M., Vassanelli, S., Kaiser, M.S., Zhong, N. (eds.) BI 2020. LNCS (LNAI), vol. 12241, pp. 287–296. Springer, Cham (2020). https://doi.org/10.1007/978-3-030-59277-6_26
41. Zisad, S.N., Chowdhury, E., Hossain, M.S., Islam, R.U., Andersson, K.: An integrated deep learning and belief rule-based expert system for visual sentiment analysis under uncertainty. Algorithms **14**(7), 213 (2021)
42. Zisad, S.N., Hossain, M.S., Hossain, M.S., Andersson, K.: An integrated neural network and SEIR model to predict Covid-19. Algorithms **14**(3) (2021). https://doi.org/10.3390/a14030094, https://www.mdpi.com/1999-4893/14/3/94

# Feature-Selected Graph Spatial Attention Network for Addictive Brain-Networks Identification

Changwei Gong, Changhong Jing, Junren Pan, Yishan Wang, and Shuqiang Wang[✉]

Shenzhen Institutes of Advanced Technology, Chinese Academy of Sciences, Shenzhen, China
{cw.gong,ch.jing,jr.pan,ys.wang,sq.wang}@siat.ac.cn

**Abstract.** Functional alterations in the relevant neural circuits occur from drug addiction over a certain period. And these significant alterations are also revealed by analyzing fMRI. However, because of fMRI's high dimensionality and poor signal-to-noise ratio, it is challenging to encode efficient and robust brain regional embeddings for both graph-level identification and region-level biomarkers detection tasks between nicotine addiction (NA) and healthy control (HC) groups. In this work, we represent the fMRI of the rat brain as a graph with biological attributes and propose a novel feature-selected graph spatial attention network (FGSAN) to extract the biomarkers of addiction and identify from these brain networks. Specially, a graph spatial attention encoder is employed to capture the features of spatiotemporal brain networks with spatial information. The method simultaneously adopts a Bayesian feature selection strategy to optimize the model and improve classification task by constraining features. Experiments on an addiction-related neural imaging dataset show that the proposed model can obtain superior performance and detect interpretable biomarkers associated with addiction-relevant neural circuits.

**Keywords:** Neural imaging computing · Brain networks · Graph attention · Generative deep learning

## 1 Introduction

Medical image computing is becoming increasingly significant in researching many diseases because it enables the extraction and use of quantitative picture characteristics from routine medical imaging at high throughput, hence improving diagnostic, prognostic, and predictive accuracy. Neuroimaging, a bridge field integrating medical imaging computers and neuroscience, has also grown in recent years. Neuroimaging is a powerful tool for studying neuroscience and interpreting the anatomical structure and activity of the brain through qualitative and quantitative analysis of images in two and three dimensions by using

© Springer Nature Switzerland AG 2022
M. Mahmud et al. (Eds.): BI 2022, LNAI 13406, pp. 316–326, 2022
https://doi.org/10.1007/978-3-031-15037-1_26

imaging methods, as well as for resolving unresolved issues in the field of neurosciences and diagnosing and treating brain diseases.

The development of MRI changed the study of neuroanatomy by making it feasible to conduct in vivo experiments with sufficient contrast to different brain regions for the first time. Researchers may estimate the microstructure inside a voxel using a computational method for MRI-based neuroanatomical investigations. The capacity to gather high-quality, comprehensive information from in vivo imaging has certainly shaped researchers' knowledge of neuroanatomical and structure-function interactions and provided new insights into various disease processes. The introduction of functional neuroimaging in the past three decades has raised much enthusiasm about its potential to revolutionize researchers' knowledge of the physical foundation of the brain and to offer valuable tools for clinical and research study. Functional magnetic resonance imaging (fMRI) and resting-state functional magnetic resonance imaging (rs-fMRI) [1] are the most powerful noninvasive functional imaging techniques available at the time. Functional connection [2] in brain networks is often generated through the observation of fMRI time series, and functional brain networks [3] describe statistical correlation patterns between neuronal regions. Significant progress has been made in functional brain network analysis using fMRI data over the last decade. The variation of functional connectivity between brain areas has been widely investigated in terms of brain diseases [4], as well as the association between cognitive impairments and degenerative neurological and psychiatric disorders [5].

Addiction is a disorder of the functioning brain characterized by abnormal behavior [6]. Addicts are driven by an overwhelming need to seek and consume drugs constantly. Although after prolonged withdrawal and awareness of the harmful health implications of drug use and the detrimental impact on family and society, addicts face the risk of relapse. Pioneering functional MRI studies have shown that nicotine activates various brain regions [7]. However, few neuroimaging computational approaches have used functional MRI to investigate the relationship between nicotine addiction and altered neuronal activity patterns throughout the brain and identify these patterns and detect regional neuroimaging biomarkers. Therefore, research into the neural mechanisms and supporting diagnoses associated with nicotine and other drug addiction has become increasingly critical.

**Related Work.** Machine learning technology has been widely used in the recognition of natural scenes [8–10]. In brain image computing, machine learning-based artificial intelligence technology has a broader scenario to make the analysis technology of brain images sink, effectively improving the efficiency and diagnostic accuracy of physicians' treatment [11]. Brain image analysis technology for brain disease research can explore the disease's mechanism and understand the brain's operation process [12]. Recent advances in machine learning, particularly in deep learning, are helping to identify, classify and quantify existing brain images [13]. At the heart of these advances is the ability to automatically generalize hierarchical features from data rather than manually discovering and designing features based on domain-specific knowledge, as was previously the case [14]. Deep learning is rapidly becoming state-of-the-art and replacing many original machine learning-based algorithms. Due to the development of deep learning, various neuroscience applications have simultaneously improved their performance significantly. Deep learning methods are a new approach for processing high-dimensional brain image data and extracting low-dimensional features [15–17]. For instance, convolutional neural network (CNN) methods [18] reduce the dimensionality of medical image data by convolution operator to allow the effective identification of patterns in neuroimaging. Generative adversarial strategies can simulate the real distribution of data to reduce the interference caused by noise and enhance the robustness of the model [19]. GAN(Generative Adversarial Network), which is based on variational methods [20,21], is widely used in medical image computing [22]. GAN is usually unsupervised in training, and the newly generated data have the same distribution as the real data, thus allowing robust and complex representation learning, making it a commonly used method in medical image computation. However, existing methods for processing network structured data to obtain interpretable and deterministic biological markers are still challenging, especially for high-dimensional and sparse network datasets.

To solve these issues, we developed a novel feature-selected graph spatial attention network(FGSAN) to identify the efficient patterns of addiction-relevant brain networks from fMRI data and detect discriminative biomarkers of addiction-relevant brain regions that are interpreted by neuroscientific addiction circuit mechanism. The designed feature selection is efficient for graph representation learning and obtaining more helpful brain network embeddings to extract more accurately addiction-relevant biomarkers.

## 2 Method

Our FGSAN is composed of three primary components: 1) an encoder consists of graph positional attention layer; 2) a feature selector with bayesian feature selection strategy; and 3) a classifier. The specific architecture are demonstrated in Fig. 1.

In the encoder($E$), self-attention mechanism is adopted to transform the time series of brain regions $X = \{x_n\}_{n=1}^{N} \in \mathbb{R}^{N \times D}$ and dynamic brain functional connectivity $\{A^t\}_{t=1}^{T}$ into the embeddings $Z = \{z_n\}_{n=1}^{N} \in \mathbb{R}^{N \times d}$. Moreover, in the feature selector, latent binary random vectors $B = \{b_n\}_{n=1}^{N}$ are introduced to infer the posterior probability distribution and select more efficient brain regional features. Therefore, the encoder is trained with double objectives: a bayesian feature selection loss considered as the feature sparsity penalty, and a classification loss for identifying nicotine addiction.

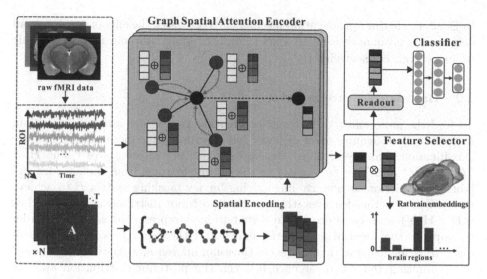

**Fig. 1.** Proposed feature-selected graph spatial attention network for identifying brain addiction.

## 2.1 Graph Spatial Attention Encoder

The graph spatial attention encoder aims to embed the regional brain imaging features aggregated with dynamic brain network attributes into a low-dimensional latent space. The proposed layer that composes the encoder is based on the graph attention networks(GAT) [23] with the addition of spatial encoding. It allows each regional brain node to focus adaptively on other nodes according to the spatial information of the graph-structure connectivities in the brain networks.

Therefore, the attention coefficient, which is combined a shared attentional mechanism and spatial encoding for brain connectivities, can be expressed as:

$$\alpha_n^l(i,j) = \frac{\exp\left(\tanh\left(\left[\mathbf{h}_n^l(i)\mathbf{W}^l \quad \mathbf{h}_n^l(j)\mathbf{W}^l\right] \cdot \mathbf{c}^l + s_{\psi(x_i,x_j)}\right)\right)}{\sum_{j\in\mathcal{N}(i)}\exp\left(\tanh\left(\left[\mathbf{h}_n^l(i)\mathbf{W}^l \quad \mathbf{h}_n^l(j)\mathbf{W}^l\right] \cdot \mathbf{c}^l + s_{\psi(x_i,x_j)}\right)\right)} \tag{1}$$

here $h_n^l(i)$ is a hidden representation for brain node $i$ at $l$th layer, $W^l \in \mathbb{R}^{d_l \times d_{l+1}}$ is a parameterized weight matrix considered as the graph convolutional filter,$c^l$ is a weight vector that can be learned in the train phase, and $S_{\psi(x_i,x_j)}$ is a scalar that can be learned and is indexed by $\psi(x_i,x_j)$ with positional information. It indicates the spatial encoding and is accessible throughout all layers.

Formally, let $\mathbf{h}_n^{l+1}(i)$ represent the output representation at $l$th layer, our graph spatial attention layer is given as follow:

$$\mathbf{h}_n^{l+1}(i) = \sigma\left(\sum_{j\in\mathcal{N}(i)} \alpha_n^l(i,j)\mathbf{h}_n^l(j)\mathbf{W}^l\right) \tag{2}$$

In Eq. 2, the feature propagation mechanism aggregates the effects across overall neighboring brain nodes and attaches spatial encoding information from dynamic brain network connectivity $\{A^t\}_{t=1}^{T}$.

## 2.2   Bayesian Feature Selector

To find the most effective features for identification from many regional brain features and to acquire a set of fewer but discriminative biomarkers to reduce classification error, we employ the bayesian feature selector. We define $\mathbf{H} = \{H_1^o, ..., H_n^o\}$ and $\mathbf{Y} = \{y_1, ..., y_n\}$ as the output features from the encoder and labels of addiction or not. By introducing binary masking matrix $B$ to achieve the goal of selecting features, the expected posterior distribution is denoted as $p(\mathbf{B} \mid \mathbf{H}, \mathbf{Y})$ and an approximate distribution is represented as $q(\cdot)$. In order to improve the identification performance and the accuracy of the model in discriminating features, in the view of Bayesian inference, we optimize the model by minimizing the KL divergence between the posterior distribution and the approximate distribution:

$$\underset{q(\cdot)}{\mathrm{argmin}} KL(q(\mathbf{B}) \| p(\mathbf{B} \mid \mathbf{H}, \mathbf{Y})) = -E_q \left[\log \left(p(\mathbf{B} \mid \mathbf{H}, \mathbf{Y})\right)\right] + KL\left(q\left(\mathbf{B}\right) \| p\left(\mathbf{B}\right)\right)$$
(3)

In Eq. 3, the first term corresponds to a binary cross entropy loss for identification task where the input features $\mathbf{H}$ are masked by $\mathbf{B}$, and the second term becomes a loss for learning the probability scores $\mathbf{z}$ which is used to compute the binary matrix $\mathbf{B}$ by Bernoulli sampling method:

$$\mathbf{b}_n = \sigma \left( \frac{\log (\mathbf{z}) - \log (1 - \mathbf{z}) + \log (\mathbf{u}_n) - \log (1 - \mathbf{u}_n)}{r} \right)$$
(4)

where $\mathbf{u}_n$ is sampled from a uniform distribution from 0 to 1, and $r$ is the relaxation parameter of Bernoulli sampling.

## 2.3   Classifier and Loss Function

To integrate the information of each node for the graph-level identification, we utilize a readout function to cluster node features together by simply averaging them:

$$\mathcal{R}(\mathbf{H}) = \sigma \left( \frac{1}{N} \sum_{i=1}^{N} \vec{h}_i \right)$$
(5)

where $\sigma$ is nonlinear activation function. The readout function is similar to the graph pooling operation. Other graph pooling methods can be used to replace it. The selected and readout features are delivered to a multi-layer perceptron(MLP) to derive the final identification of predicted labels $\hat{y}$.

The total loss function is the interpretation of Eq. 3:

$$\mathcal{L}(\mathbf{X}, \mathbf{A}) = -\sum_{n=1}^{N} (y_n \log(\hat{y}_n) + (1 - y_n) \log(1 - \hat{y}_n)) + KL(\text{Ber}(\mathbf{z}) \parallel \text{Ber}(\mathbf{s})) \tag{6}$$

The first term is used to guide the MLP in the classification of the selected features. Furthermore, the second term is applied for training the selector to learn the probability mapping to the feature mask. Here Ber($\mathbf{s}$) is a binary random vector that contains sparse elements for the purpose of complying with sparsity.

## 3    Experiments

**Dataset and Preparation.** The animal addiction experiment dataset contains two types of data with equal numbers: functional MRI images of nicotine non-addicted and nicotine addicted, each with 800 time series. By preprocessing long-term functional MRI scans of experimental rats, we were able to create the dynamic brain network dataset needed for the experiment. The Statistical Parametric Mapping 8 (SPM8) program was used to do the first preprocessing in MATLAB. Functional data were aligned and unwarped to account for head motion, and the mean motion-corrected picture was coregistered with the high-resolution anatomical T2 image. The functional data were then smoothed using an isotropic Gaussian kernel with a 3 mm full-width at half-maximum (FWHM). 150 functional network regions were identified using the Wister rat brain atlas. We assessed the spectral link between regional time series using magnitude-squared coherence, resulting in a $150 \times 150$ functional connection matrix for each time step, whose members represented the intensity of functional connectivity between all pairings of regions.

**Implementation Detail.** The PyTorch backend was used to implement FGSAN. One Nvidia GeForce RTX 2080 Ti was used to speed up the network's training. During training, the learning rate was set at 0.001, and the training epoch was set to 500. Adam was used as an optimizer with a weight decay of 0.01 to reduce overfitting. We construct the encoder with three graph spatial attention layers. All trials are repeated ten times, and the results are averaged. The regularization value was set to 0.5 for all datasets and techniques.

**Metrics.** Evaluation of binary classification performance is based on quantitative measures in four key metrics: 1) accuracy (ACC); 2) Precision (PREC); 3) Sensitive (SEN); and 4) Specificity(SPEC). Our proposed method is evaluated by 8-fold cross-validation.

### 3.1    Ablation Study

As indicated in Table 1, we conducted ablation research on identification to evaluate the effectiveness of our proposed encoder and bayesian feature selector, and two significant results were achieved: 1) In the comparison of the baseline encoder approach showed impressive performance on the binary addiction-related classification. This is due to the fact that the attachment of spatial encoding enables the attention mechanism to get more positional information and learn better graph representations; 2) The approach with feature selector is generally performed well. It represents that feature selection plays its role as an auxiliary to identifying the graph-structure patterns, and better embeddings are selected to make the model perform classification tasks well.

**Table 1.** Comparison of various classification indicators of ablation experiments.

| Method | Metrics | | | |
|---|---|---|---|---|
| | ACC | PREC | SEN | SPEC |
| GSAN | 70.42 | 79.87 | 74.38 | 62.50 |
| FGSAN (GAT-encoder) | 77.92 | 84.97 | 81.25 | 71.25 |
| FGSAN | **82.08** | **87.74** | **84.38** | **74.25** |

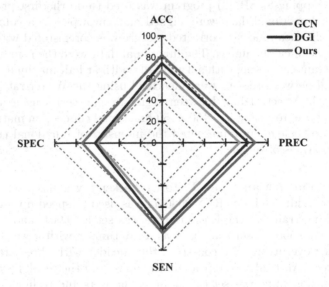

**Fig. 2.** The performance comparison of FGSAN with other models. The method proposed in this paper is compared with the existing methods for classification experiments. The red line represents the method proposed in this paper. (Color figure online)

**Table 2.** TOP five regional brain biomarkers extracted by the FGSAN model.

| No. | ROI name of biomarkers |
|-----|------------------------|
| 1   | Midbrain.R             |
| 2   | Diagonal domain.R      |
| 3   | Primary motor cortex.R |
| 4   | Hippocampal formation.L |
| 5   | Insular cortex.L       |

## 3.2 Identification Performance

This section conducts relevant comparative experiments to verify the superiority of FGSAN. The method proposed in this paper is compared with the existing GCN and DGI [24] methods. DGI learns node embeddings in an unsupervised manner. DGI can continuously optimize model results by maximizing the degree of correlation between two random variables. After multiple experimental verifications, it is found that our proposed FGSAN method is significantly better than existing methods in classification indicators. As shown in Fig. 2, the method proposed in this paper has noticeable performance improvement compared with DGI and GCN. FGSAN outperforms the other two methods in every index of the binary classification experiment. The binary classification performance is outstanding on SPEC metrics, and FGSAN significantly outperforms the other two methods.

## 3.3 Interpretable Brain Regional Biomarkers

The method presented here identified five brain regions with higher weights associated with nicotine addiction. As shown in Table 2, the five brain regions with higher weights are Midbrain.R [25], Diagonal domain.R [26], Primary motor cortex.R [27], Hippocampal formation.I [28], and Insular cortex.L [29]. These five brain regions have been proven to be associated with nicotine addiction in previous research work. The brain regions discovered by our model are recognized by experts in the relevant brain regions. We visualized the locations of these five brain regions. As shown in Fig. 3, the locations of the five addiction-related brain regions found by the model in the rat brain are shown in three different directions.

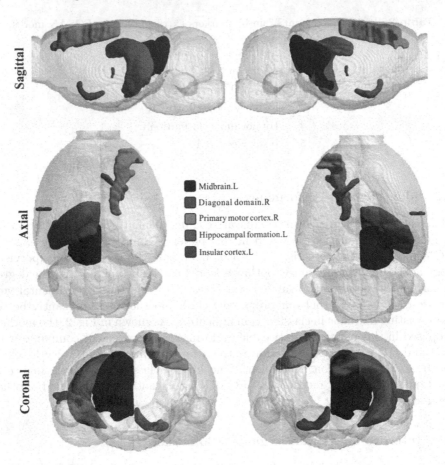

**Fig. 3.** Visualization of top-five addiction-related brain regions. These five brain regions are all brain regions with higher weights output by the model. Their relevance to nicotine addiction was separately validated in previous work.

## 4   Conclusion

In this research, we propose a new model called feature-selected graph spatial attention network (FGSAN) for exploiting effective and interpretable regional brain biomarkers and utilizing features of these biomarkers to identify the addiction-related brain network patterns. Detailed model discussions were conducted to examine the proposed FGSAN and the encoder's and feature selector's superiority, among other concerns. We obtained better results than the comparison method by using the selected graph representations for classification, indicating an advantage in graph feature extraction that may yield better graph embeddings in the latent space. And more significantly, these embeddings can be well explained in the neuroscience of addiction. Continuing our investigation into the brain processes of nicotine addiction in rats will focus on our future research.

**Acknowledgement.** This work was supported by the National Natural Science Foundations of China under Grants 62172403 and 81901834, the Distinguished Young Scholars Fund of Guangdong under Grant 2021B1515020019, Guangdong Basic and Applied Basic Research Fundation under Grant 2020A1515010654, the Excellent Young Scholars of Shenzhen under Grant RCYX20200714114641211 and Shenzhen Key Basic Research Projects under Grant JCYJ20200109115641762.

# References

1. Heeger, D.J., Ress, D.: What does fMRI tell us about neuronal activity? Nat. Rev. Neurosci. **3**(2), 142–151 (2002)
2. Allen, E.A., Damaraju, E., Plis, S.M., et al.: Tracking whole-brain connectivity dynamics in the resting state. Cereb. Cortex **24**(3), 663–676 (2014)
3. Petri, G., Expert, P., Turkheimer, F., et al.: Homological scaffolds of brain functional networks. J. R. Soc. Interface **11**(101), 20140873 (2014)
4. Thompson, G.J., Magnuson, M.E., Merritt, M.D., et al.: Short-time windows of correlation between large-scale functional brain networks predict vigilance intraindividually and interindividually. Hum. Brain Mapp. **34**(12), 3280–3298 (2013)
5. Wang, S., Wang, H., Cheung, A.C., Shen, Y., Gan, M.: Ensemble of 3D densely connected convolutional network for diagnosis of mild cognitive impairment and Alzheimer's disease. In: Wani, M.A., Kantardzic, M., Sayed-Mouchaweh, M. (eds.) Deep Learning Applications. AISC, vol. 1098, pp. 53–73. Springer, Singapore (2020). https://doi.org/10.1007/978-981-15-1816-4_4
6. Li, Z., DiFranza, J.R., Wellman, R.J., et al.: Imaging brain activation in nicotine-sensitized rats. Brain Res. **1199**, 91–99 (2008)
7. Bruijnzeel, A.W., Alexander, J.C., Perez, P.D., et al.: Acute nicotine administration increases BOLD fMRI signal in brain regions involved in reward signaling and compulsive drug intake in rats. Int. J. Neuropsychopharmacol. **18**(2) (2015)
8. Wang, S., Wang, X., Shen, Y., et al.: An ensemble-based densely-connected deep learning system for assessment of skeletal maturity. IEEE Trans. Syst. Man Cybern. Syst. **52**(1), 426–437 (2020)
9. Wang, S., Hu, Y., et al.: Classification of diffusion tensor metrics for the diagnosis of a myelopathic cord using machine learning. Int. J. Neural Syst. **28**(2), 1750036 (2018)
10. Wang, S., Shen, Y., et al.: Skeletal maturity recognition using a fully automated system with convolutional neural networks. IEEE Access **6**, 29979–29993 (2018)
11. Yu, S., et al.: Multi-scale enhanced graph convolutional network for early mild cognitive impairment detection. In: Martel, A.L., et al. (eds.) MICCAI 2020. LNCS, vol. 12267, pp. 228–237. Springer, Cham (2020). https://doi.org/10.1007/978-3-030-59728-3_23
12. You, S., Lei, B., et al.: Fine perceptive GANs for brain MR image super-resolution in wavelet domain. IEEE Trans. Neural Netw. Learn. Syst. (2022). https://doi.org/10.1109/TNNLS.2022.3153088
13. Yu, W., Lei, B., Ng, M.K., et al.: Tensorizing GAN with high-order pooling for Alzheimer's disease assessment. IEEE Trans. Neural Netw. Learn. Syst. (2021). https://doi.org/10.1109/TNNLS.2021.3063516
14. Hu, S., Shen, Y., Wang, S., Lei, B.: Brain MR to PET synthesis via bidirectional generative adversarial network. In: Martel, A.L., et al. (eds.) MICCAI 2020. LNCS, vol. 12262, pp. 698–707. Springer, Cham (2020). https://doi.org/10.1007/978-3-030-59713-9_67

15. Hu, S., Lei, B., et al.: Bidirectional mapping generative adversarial networks for brain MR to PET synthesis. IEEE Trans. Med. Imaging **41**(1), 145–157 (2021)
16. Hu, S., Yuan, J., et al.: Cross-modality synthesis from MRI to PET using adversarial U-net with different normalization. In: 2019 International Conference on Medical Imaging Physics and Engineering, pp. 1–5. IEEE (2019)
17. Hu, S., Yu, W., Chen, Z., et al.: Medical image reconstruction using generative adversarial network for Alzheimer disease assessment with class-imbalance problem. In: 2020 IEEE 6th International Conference on Computer and Communications (ICCC), pp. 1323–1327. IEEE (2020)
18. Wang, S., Shen, Y., Zeng, D., et al.: Bone age assessment using convolutional neural networks. In: 2018 International Conference on Artificial Intelligence and Big Data (ICAIBD), pp. 175–178. IEEE (2018)
19. Yu, W., Lei, B., et al.: Morphological feature visualization of Alzheimer's disease via multidirectional perception GAN. IEEE Trans. Neural Netw. Learn. Syst. (2022). https://doi.org/10.1109/TNNLS.2021.3118369
20. Wang, S.Q.: A variational approach to nonlinear two-point boundary value problems. Comput. Math. Appl. **58**(11–12), 2452–2455 (2009)
21. Mo, L.F., et al.: A variational approach to nonlinear two-point boundary value problems. Nonlinear Anal. Theory Methods Appl. **71**(12), e834–e838 (2009)
22. Wang, S., Wanng, X., et al.: Diabetic retinopathy diagnosis using multichannel generative adversarial network with semisupervision. IEEE Trans. Autom. Sci. Eng. **18**(2), 574–585 (2020)
23. Veličković, P., Cucurull, G., Casanova, A., et al.: Graph attention networks. arXiv preprint arXiv:1710.10903 (2017)
24. Velickovic, P., Fedus, W., Hamilton, W.L., et al.: Deep graph infomax. ICLR (Poster) **2**(3), 4 (2019)
25. Nguyen, C., Mondoloni, S., Le Borgne, T., et al.: Nicotine inhibits the VTA-to-amygdala dopamine pathway to promote anxiety. Neuron **109**(16), 2604–2615.e9 (2021)
26. Flannery, J.S., Riedel, M.C., Poudel, R., et al.: Habenular and striatal activity during performance feedback are differentially linked with state-like and trait-like aspects of tobacco use disorder. Sci. Adv. **5**(10), eaax2084 (2019)
27. Smolka, M.N., Bühler, M., Klein, S., et al.: Severity of nicotine dependence modulates cue-induced brain activity in regions involved in motor preparation and imagery. Psychopharmacology **184**(3), 577–588 (2006)
28. Ghasemzadeh, Z., Sardari, M., Javadi, P., et al.: Expression analysis of hippocampal and amygdala CREB-BDNF signaling pathway in nicotine-induced reward under stress in rats. Brain Res. **1741**, 146885 (2020)
29. Keeley, R.J., Hsu, L.M., Brynildsen, J.K., et al.: Intrinsic differences in insular circuits moderate the negative association between nicotine dependence and cingulate-striatal connectivity strength. Neuropsychopharmacology **45**(6), 1042–1049 (2020)

# Brain-Machine Intelligence
and Brain-Inspired Computing

# Biologically Inspired Neural Path Finding

Hang Li[1,3](✉), Qadeer Khan[2], Volker Tresp[1,3], and Daniel Cremers[2]

[1] Ludwig Maximilian University of Munich, Munich, Germany
[2] Technical University of Munich, Munich, Germany
[3] Siemens AG, Munich, Germany
hang.li@siemens.com

**Abstract.** The human brain can be considered to be a graphical structure comprising of tens of billions of biological neurons connected by synapses. It has the remarkable ability to automatically re-route information flow through alternate paths, in case some neurons are damaged. Moreover, the brain is capable of retaining information and applying it to similar but completely unseen scenarios. In this paper, we take inspiration from these attributes of the brain to develop a computational framework to find the optimal low cost path between a source node and a destination node in a generalized graph. We show that our framework is capable of handling unseen graphs at test time. Moreover, it can find alternate optimal paths, when nodes are arbitrarily added or removed during inference, while maintaining a fixed prediction time. Code accompanying this work can be found here: https://github.com/hangligit/pathfinding.

**Keywords:** Cognition · Path finding · Graphical Neural Networks

## 1 Introduction

We are inundated with graphical structures of various forms in this contemporary era of digitization. This includes, for e.g., social networks [15], wherein the nodes represent individuals and the edges characterize the social connections between the individuals. Another popular form of network includes recommender systems [25] that can be represented as bipartite graphs. The users/products represent the nodes, while the edges depict the rating of likes/dislikes of a user for a certain product. Other graphs include citation networks [24], molecular structures used in drug discovery [10].

Although concurrent implementation of these graphical structures are computationally powerful in number-crunching, they lack the cognitive understanding to draw meaningful conclusions that can readily be interpreted. On the other hand, one of the most sophisticated and yet least understood graphical networks is the human brain [20]. Rather than consisting of computational nodes, it is comprised of tens of billions of biological neurons both sending and receiving information to the neighbouring neurons through the connecting synapses [2,3]. One amazing attribute of the human brain is its ability to learn to automatically adapt and efficiently reroute information through alternate neural

---

H. Li and Q. Khan—Contributed equally.

M. Mahmud et al. (Eds.): BI 2022, LNAI 13406, pp. 329–342, 2022
https://doi.org/10.1007/978-3-031-15037-1_27

paths, in case of certain damaged neurons [26]. Another important attribute is the capability to interpret distinguishing patterns in data and retain this information to be applied in similar circumstances in the future [16]. For e.g., a child touching a hot cup of coffee once or twice would feel a sensation of pain. The child's brain will retain this experience to avoid touching hot cups in the future even if the cups are of different size/colour/shape etc. However, unlike computers whose computation power has been exponentially rising over the past 4 decades, the capacity of the human brain to process information is limited by biological constraints. Therefore, is it possible to combine the benign attributes of the human brain with the processing power of computational resources? In this work, we explore this possibility in the context of path optimization.

The ability to navigate through a network from a source to a destination node while optimizing for the lowest cost is an important problem. It has a tremendous number of diverse applications, for e.g., the ubiquitous vehicle/robot navigation. The cost could involve minimizing either the distance travelled, time taken, or even the traffic congestion encountered. Other less frequent, but critical, use cases are search and rescue operations involving unmanned aerial vehicles. Here, minimizing the battery usage and the data transmission are important factors to be optimized for. Traditionally, these problems can either be solved heuristically using approaches such as A-star or by deploying *"shortest path"* algorithms such as Depth First Search (DFS), Breadth-First Search (BFS), Djikstra, etc. These approaches tend to start with the source node and progressively traverse the graph through the neighbouring nodes, then neighbours of the neighbours until the destination node is found. Although accurate, computational complexity rises with the number of hops between the source and destination nodes. On the other hand, given a visual map drawn to scale, humans are fairly good at quickly determining the approximate optimal path [4], irrespective of the number of hops between the nodes. Is it also possible to additionally emulate this one-shot prediction capability in a computational setting? In this regard, we propose using Graphical Neural Networks (GNNs) to find the path with the lowest cost. Our framework has the following attributes:

1. If a node(s) or edge(s) is arbitrarily removed from the graph structure, the optimal path is automatically rerouted through the remaining nodes/edges to find the next best solution.
2. The framework can generalize to find the optimal path even on unseen graphs.
3. The time taken to find the lowest cost path between the source and destination node remains constant irrespective of the number of hops between them.

## 2 Related Work

### 2.1 Artificial Neural Networks, ANNs

Over the last decade, the advent of data-driven, learning-based methods for training artificial neural networks has made tremendous strides in achieving unprecedented levels of performance on various tasks such as natural language processing [21], computer vision [14], medical diagnosis [19], etc. Such networks have the capability to extract meaningful information from the training data and extrapolate this to completely unseen test data. In fact, they have achieved on par human performance [7] on tasks such as classification, disease diagnosis, etc. We also deploy ANNs to achieve generalization on unseen data (graphs).

## 2.2 Graph Representation

Among the various ANN paradigms, feed-forward architectures such as Convolutional Neural Networks (CNNs), Multi-Layer Perceptrons (MLPs) are ubiquitous. However, on tasks such as path optimization, there is ambiguity on how the graph structure should be represented when input through such architectures. One approach is to input the graph as an adjacency matrix. [5] use the connectome [1] as input to a CNN to predict autism in patients. The connectome is an adjacency matrix, encoding brain connectivity as graphs between certain pre-selected regions in the brain. [13] used a pre-determined number of regions in the connectome to train BrainNetCNN for predicting neurodevelopment. However, one major limitation of using adjacency matrices is that the number of nodes forming the input to the network cannot change at inference time. Otherwise, the network needs to be trained from scratch if the number of nodes is increased. Our framework does not suffer from this limitation and the number of nodes forming the input to the network can be changed without retraining the network. In fact, we show in the experiments that our method is capable of automatically rerouting to an alternate path, if some nodes/edges are removed at test time.

## 2.3 Reinforcement Learning, RL

RL is an alternate strategy for determining the optimal path in a map/graph. Taking inspiration from human psychology [17], a reward function is defined. The agent explores the environment in a hit-and-trial manner incurring rewards along the way [22]. If the training parameters are carefully chosen, the agent converges to an optimal policy. [18] demonstrated path planning on small unseen maps. Instead of the adjacency matrix, they directly used the map represented as a grid. While this can handle maps with arbitrary structure and nodes, it is constrained to only planar graphs. In contrast, our framework can additionally handle graphs with non-planar structure.

## 2.4 Shortest Path Algorithms

Shortest path algorithms such as DFS, BFS, Djikstra & their modifications have been used in a wide array of applications. These range from marine navigation [6], software defined networking [12], maze solving [11] to even optimal planning of sales persons [27]. The limitation of these methods is that the time to find the optimal path is not constant. Rather it depends on the number of nodes & edges in the graph. For dense graphs, the computational complexity can be of polynomial order of the number of nodes. On the other hand, the computational complexity of our method is constant. Irrespective of the number of hops between the source and destination nodes, our framework takes the same time to find the optimal path.

## 3 Framework

The task tackled here is to find the lowest cost path between a source and a destination node for an undirected graphical structure, $G$. The nodes are connected through edges having arbitrary costs. The edge $e_{i,j} \in E$ connects node $i$ ($v_i \in V$) to node $j$ ($v_j \in V$). Here $V$ and $E$ are the sets containing all nodes and edges respectively.

Traditionally these tasks are handled by graph traversal algorithms. One example is Djikstra's algorithm. The algorithm starts with the source node and gradually traverses the graph, hopping from neighbouring nodes to eventually reach the destination in the lowest cost. Algorithm 1 shows the pseudo-code of optimal path finding in the graph. As can be seen in line 10, the algorithm loops through all neighbours of node $v$. An edge indicates the presence of neighbours. Now, if either an edge or a node were to be removed during the course of graph traversal, then all downstream computations would need to be performed again to determine the next optimal path. This could be because, the edge in the optimal path now no longer exists.

---

**Algorithm 1: Dijkstra's Algorithm for the Shortest Path**

**Input:** $G = (V, E)$, $v_{source}$, $v_{destination}$
**Output:** Shortest path $l$ and distance $d$ for the path

1  $Q \leftarrow []$                                                    ▷ Initialize an empty list
2  $\forall v_i \in V : cost[v_i] \leftarrow \text{Inf}, path[v_i] \leftarrow \text{Null}, Q.add(v_i)$    ▷ *cost* stores the minimal distance
   from the source node to each node, *path* is used to trace parent node once the low cost
   path is found.
3  $cost[v_{source}] = 0$
4  **while** $Q$ *is not empty* **do**
5      $v_i \leftarrow \arg\min cost[v_k], \forall v_k \in Q$          ▷ Return node in $Q$ with the lowest cost
6      $Q.remove(v_i)$
7      **if** $v_i = v_{destination}$ **then**
8          **break**
9      **end**
10     **for** $v_j \in neighbors(v_i)$ *and* $v_j \in Q$ **do**
11         $dist \leftarrow cost[v_i] + e_{ij}$
12         **if** $dist < cost[v_j]$ **then**
13             $cost[v_j] \leftarrow dist$                      ▷ Update the lowest cost
14             $path[v_j] \leftarrow v_i$
15         **end**
16     **end**
17 **end**
18 $l \leftarrow path[v_{destination}]$                      ▷ Iteratively trace the parent node till the source node
19 $d \leftarrow cost[v_{destination}]$
20 **return** $l, d$

---

In our framework, we use ANNs, as they are capable of learning patterns in the data and robustly applying them to unseen data. However, in the context of optimal path finding on graphs, we would like our framework to possess two additional properties:

1. It should be invariant to the permutations/ordering of the nodes.
2. Addition/removal of nodes should not render the training of the ANN useless. Rather it should be capable of being trained & tested on any number of nodes.

Traditional feedforward networks such as MLPs do not possess these two important attributes. They are susceptible to node ordering and cannot easily handle addition of new nodes. Figure 1 depicts the implications on the adjacency matrix, when the node order is changed and when a new node is added. In the node re-ordering/permutation case, the adjacency matrix is completely different, despite the graphs being isomorphic. In the scenario of node addition, the adjacency matrix is extended. To accommodate this extension, the architecture of the MLP would also need to be changed; thereby requiring re-training.

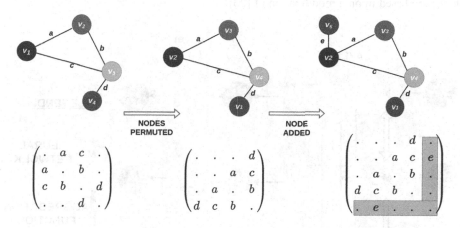

**Fig. 1.** Shows the implications of permuting the node order and adding an additional node on the adjacency matrix of a graph.

To circumvent these issues, we also use MLPs, but in the paradigm of a Graphical Neural Network. Let the input features for a node $i$ be represented by $z_i^{(0)}$. These input features for each node are passed through a series of graphical layers to produce latent embeddings ($z_i^{(l)}$, for node $i$ at layer $l$). Figure 2 depicts a high level overview of the constituents of layer $l$. For simplicity, we demonstrate the information flow for the first graph shown in Fig. 1. Note that the layer $l$ takes the embeddings ($z^{(l-1)}$) for each node from the previous layer $l-1$ as input to produce corresponding embeddings $z^{(l)}$ as output. The inputs are first passed through a neural network ($M$) comprised of fully connected layer(s) followed by a non-linearity. An important characteristic of this neural network is that the weights are shared between all nodes. Hence, nodes can conveniently be added or removed from a graph without re-training the network. This is because the added node can simply use the same weights as those of the other nodes. The output of the neural network is then passed through an aggregation function. For each node, the input to the aggregation function depends on which are its neighbours. For e.g., the neighbours of $v_1$ are $v_2$ and $v_3$. Hence, information from $M(z_2^{(l-1)})$ and

$M(z_3^{(l-1)})$ is aggregated to produce $z_1^{(l)}$. The aggregation function is chosen so that its output is invariant to the order of the input. Hence, even if the ordering of nodes in a graph is changed, the output remains the same. Some examples of order invariant aggregation functions include summation, mean, taking the maximum/minimum etc. for each scalar value of the input vectors. Note that in the first layer, each node would incorporate information from its immediate neighbours, the next layer will implicitly draw information from the neighbours of its neighbours. The deeper we go into the network, each node will retrieve information from nodes farther away from it in the graph.

The output embedding of the last graph layer is then passed through to a classifier which predicts whether or not the corresponding node falls within the optimal path. Next, we describe the mathematical details of the graph layers, the input node features, the loss function to train the weights and how the edge weights are incorporated into the graph based upon a modification of [23].

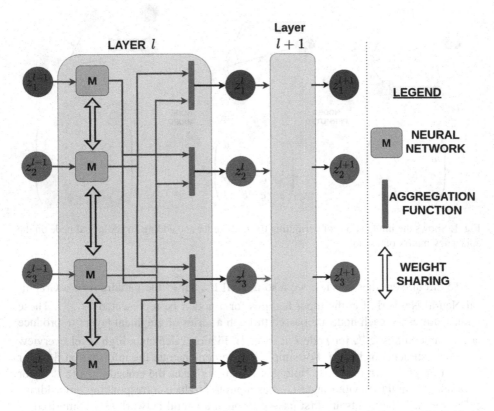

**Fig. 2.** Gives the high-level overview of graphical layer $l$, for the first graph shown in Fig. 1. Node embeddings $(z^{(l-1)})$ from the previous $l-1$ layer are taken as input to produce node embeddings $z^{(l)}$ which can then be fed to the next $l+1$ layer to produce embedding $z^{(l+1)}$ and so on.

The embedding $z_i^{(l)} \in \mathbb{R}^{d_l}$ of a node $i$ at the $l$-th layer is updated as:

$$z_i^{(l)} = D(\sigma(\hat{z}_i^{(l)})). \tag{1}$$

Here, $\sigma$ is the non-linearity (we use LeakyReLU). $D$ is the dropout layer. Note that $\hat{z}$ is obtained from the input node features of the previous layer, i.e., $z_i^{(l-1)} (\in \mathbb{R}^{d_{l-1}})$ in the following manner:

$$\hat{z}_i^{(l)} = \sum_{j \in \mathcal{N}(i) \cup \{i\}} \alpha_{ij} \left( \mathbf{W}^{(l)} z_j^{(l-1)} \right) \tag{2}$$

where $W^{(l)} \in \mathbb{R}^{d_{(l)} \times d_{(l-1)}}$ are the trainable parameters of the neural network. Meanwhile, $\mathcal{N}(i) \in V$ is the set of neighboring nodes of $i$ across which aggregation is done through summation. The scalar weights $\alpha_{ij}$ incorporate the edge cost between nodes $i$ and $j$ by way of this equation:

$$\alpha_{ij} = \frac{\exp(\mathbf{a}^\top \sigma([\mathbf{W}^{(l)} z_i || \mathbf{W}^{(l)} z_j || \mathbf{W}^{\mathbf{e}} e_{ij}]))}{\sum_{j' \in \mathcal{N}(i) \cup \{i\}} \exp(\mathbf{a}^\top \sigma(\mathbf{W}^{(l)} z_i || \mathbf{W}^{(l)} z_{j'} || \mathbf{W}^{\mathbf{e}} e_{ij'}))}. \tag{3}$$

The edge weights $e_{ij}$ are first mapped to a $d_{(l)}$ dimensional hidden feature representation $h_{ij} = \mathbf{W}^{\mathbf{e}} e_{ij}$ where $\mathbf{W}^{\mathbf{e}} \in \mathbb{R}^{d_{(l)}}$. The $||$ symbol represents a concatenation of vectors. $\mathbf{a} \in \mathbb{R}^{3d_{(l)}}$ and $\mathbf{W}^{\mathbf{e}}$ are trainable parameters.

Note $z_i^{(0)} \in \mathbb{R}^3$ are the one-hot encoded input features representing whether a node in the graph is either the source, the destination or otherwise.

The output from the final graph layer $L$ is the node embedding $z_i^{(L)}$. In the final layer, we also determine the edge embedding $(u_{ij})$ for each edge. It is the element-wise sum of embeddings of nodes that it connects to, i.e., $u_{ij} = z_i^{(L)} + z_j^{(L)}$

These edge embeddings and final layer node embeddings are passed through their respective MLP classification layers. It predicts the probabilities of them being in the optimal path. This probability for the node $i$ and edge $ij$ are respectively given by the following equations:

$$\hat{p}_i = \sigma_2(\mathbf{W}_2^n(\sigma(\mathbf{W}_1^n z_i^{(L)} + \mathbf{b}_1^n) + \mathbf{b}_2^n)) \tag{4}$$

$$\hat{p}_{ij} = \sigma_2(\mathbf{W}_2^e(\sigma(\mathbf{W}_1^e u_{ij} + \mathbf{b}_1^e) + \mathbf{b}_2^e)). \tag{5}$$

$\mathbf{W}_1^n, \mathbf{W}_1^e (\in \mathbb{R}^{m \times d_{(L)}})$, $\mathbf{W}_2^n, \mathbf{W}_2^e (\in \mathbb{R}^{1 \times m})$, $\mathbf{b}_1^e, \mathbf{b}_1^n (\in \mathbb{R}^m)$, $\mathbf{b}_2^e, \mathbf{b}_2^n (\in \mathbb{R})$ are also the trainable parameters of the model. $m$ is a hyper-parameter. $\sigma_2$ is the sigmoid non-linearity. One may ask why we need separate weights for the node & edge classifications. Or even why is the edge classification needed at all? This is because two nodes being in the optimal path does not imply that the edge connecting them will necessarily be in the optimal path. Figure 4 describes a simple example demonstrating the importance of additionally predicting the probability of the edge being in the optimal path. Although after edge removal, nodes 3 & 4 are in the optimal path, but the edge connecting them ($cost = 8$) is not. We also empirically found that predicting the probability for both edges & nodes is better than predicting for only the nodes or only the edges.

The loss function is the binary cross entropy between the predicted probability and the ground truth over all training samples

$$\min_{\mathbf{W},\mathbf{b},\mathbf{a}} \mathbb{E}_{G, y \sim \text{Data}} - [y \log \hat{p} + (1-y) \log(1-\hat{p})].$$

The ground truth can be obtained directly while constructing a random graph structure of larger cost around the optimal path. Or using shortest-path algorithms on known graphs.

## 4   Experiments

Our model is trained with a learning rate of 1e–4 with the Adam optimizer used for updating the weights. The data comprises of a total 10000 different arbitrarily created graphical structures with up to 30 nodes. The training, validation and test split is as per the ratio – 0.70:0.15:0.15. The test set is comprised of graphs with an arbitrary number of nodes. This serves to analyze if the model can handle different number of nodes in the inference graph. The test set also contains graph samples wherein some nodes/edges have been arbitrarily removed. This is to see if the model can determine alternate paths in case of such removal. Also, note that each of the 10000 structures is comprised of 10 different edge weight combinations for a total of 100000 samples. The ground truth labels for the loss function are obtained using [8]. The metric we use for quantitative evaluation is the *Path Accuracy*. It is the ratio of the number of graph samples in the unseen test set, wherein the class of every node/edge in the graph is correctly predicted. Hence, not only every node/edge in the optimal path must be classified as such but the nodes/edges not in the optimal path should also be correctly classified as not belonging to the optimal trajectory. Table 1 reports the *Path Accuracy* metric on both the training and unseen test set for our method and its variations which we elaborate in the following subsections.

**Table 1.** Reports the *Path Accuracy* metric for our method and its variations for both the training and test set. (Higher is better)

|  | Ours | Fixed structure | Fixed nodes | Nodes only | Edge only |
|---|---|---|---|---|---|
| Training data | 98.01 | 99.26 | 99.41 | 97.75 | 97.43 |
| Test data (Unseen) | **98.02** | 68.41 | 72.18 | 97.62 | 97.41 |

### 4.1   Unseen Test Data

From Table 1 it can be seen that our model is capable of maintaining good *Path Accuracy* performance even on unseen test data. Note that the test data comprises of graph samples with an arbitrary number of nodes between 3 and 50. In addition, it also contains graph samples wherein the edges/nodes are arbitrarily removed. Our model is capable of robustly handling both scenarios. Figure 3 shows a plot of the accuracy as the number of nodes is changed. Note that as the number of nodes in the graph is changed, the accuracy as depicted by the green curve remains fairly consistent. This is because our model is trained to handle such instance with variable number of nodes in the graph.

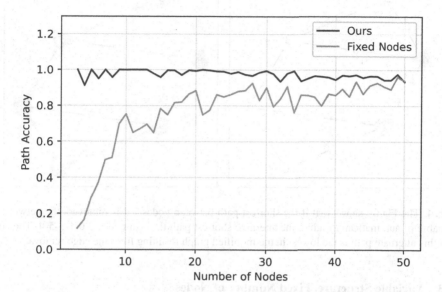

**Fig. 3.** The plot shows that, as the number of nodes is changed, the path accuracy metric of our model (in green) remains constant. It is interesting to note that even though the model was trained with up to a maximum of 30 nodes, it still maintains good performance beyond this number. The red curve on the plot shows the performance for a model trained with a fixed number of nodes. Its performance deteriorates when evaluated on a smaller number of nodes.

Meanwhile, Fig. 4 demonstrates a simple example of finding an optimal alternate path in the case of a removed edge. Note that initially in the original graph, the optimal path between nodes 2 and 4 is the direct edge connecting the two nodes having a cost of 1. However, when this edge is removed the alternate lowest cost path between the nodes is 2-0-1-3-5-4. This alternate path has a cost of 7 which is the lowest in the graph after the edge removal.

## 4.2  Fixed Structure, Fixed Number of Nodes

Note that in our framework not only the number of nodes can change, but also the structure of the graph constituted by the same nodes can vary. To demonstrate this, we train another model wherein both the structure and the number of nodes (30) are kept constant. Only the edge weights are changed. Consider the $2^{nd}$ column of Table 1 for the results. While the model performs well on the training samples containing graphs of the same structure & nodes, its performance on the unseen test data drops dramatically. This is because when training the model, it is not accustomed to handling variable nodes & structures of the test data.

**EDGE 2-4 removed**

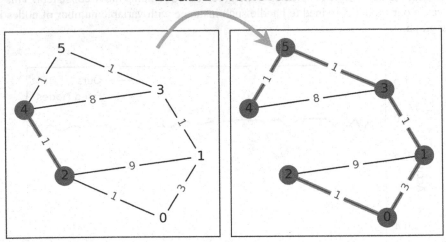

**Fig. 4.** The Figure shows that if the shortest path between nodes 2-4 is removed, the network is capable of automatically finding the alternate shortest path through nodes 2-0-1-3-5-4. The cost via this alternate path is the lowest in the modified graph resulting from the edge removal

### 4.3    Variable Structure, Fixed Number of Nodes

Here, we train yet another model with the same number of nodes, but for which the structure of the graph can change. Note that the performance of this model is better than the previous model, as it is capable of handling arbitrary structures. However, its test accuracy is still not better than our approach. The reason can be inferred from the red curve in Fig. 3, wherein the performance is only good around the number of nodes it is trained on, but deteriorates drastically on lesser number of nodes.

### 4.4    Loss Functions

In addition to classifying the nodes in the optimal path, our loss function also incorporates classifying the edges connecting the nodes in the path. The last 2 columns in Table 1 shows the implications of training with the binary cross entropy function only for the nodes and only for the edges. As can be seen, the performance of our model, which combines both loss functions, is superior to the models trained with only the individual loss functions.

### 4.5    Comparision with BrainNetCNN Approach

Note that the BrainNetCNN approach uses adjacency matrices, which requires filter sizes in the CNN to be fixed. Hence, graphs with an arbitrary number of nodes cannot readily be handled. The original BrainNetCNN was meant for classifying neurodevelopment in patients. Therefore, we slightly modify the deeper layers to classify nodes/edges in the optimal path instead. We trained that model on graphs with both fixed structure and variable structure, each with a fixed number of nodes. As the convolutional layer cannot deal with node permutation, we introduce another set of graphs where the nodes are randomly permutated, resulting in a transformed adjacency matrix. As we can see from Table 2, the performance of this model on the test set increases when we consider random permutation during training. However, neither permutation nor training with variable structures can enable the model to work on an arbitrarily greater number of nodes.

**Table 2.** Reports the *Path Accuracy* metric for BrainNetCNN method and its variations for both the training and test set. (Higher is better)

|  | Fixed structure | Node permutation | Variable structure |
|---|---|---|---|
| Training data | 99.99 | 98.53 | 99.91 |
| Test data (Unseen) | 40.06 | 93.10 | **97.09** |

## 4.6 Relative Prediction Time

Figure 5 reports the relative time to find the optimal path as the number of hops between the source and destination nodes is increased. It is normalized by the time taken to find the optimal path between nodes one hop away. As can be seen, this number remains stable for our approach. Hence, irrespective of the number of hops we have in the graph, the prediction time remains the same. One explanation is that a forward pass of our model always involves the same number of graph Convolutional layers. Compare this with Djikstra's algorithm wherein the relative time increases with the number of hops.

## 4.7 Evaluation on a Real World Dataset

We also evaluated our approach of optimal path finding on maps from the real-world KITTI [9] dataset and found that it achieved a perfect score on the *Path Accuracy* metric. One plausible explanation for this is that the maps of the road structure in KITTI are on a plane. Our model, in contrast, was trained with non-planar graphs which tend to be more challenging to handle and hence do not achieve a perfect score when evaluated on a test set comprising non-planar graphs. Figure 6 shows predicted paths on a KITTI map returned by our model under three different scenarios. We see that our model can flexibly re-route the path to reach the destination when roads are inaccessible.

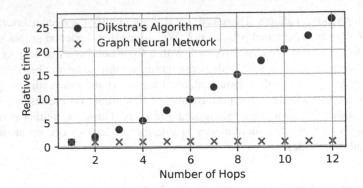

**Fig. 5.** The plot shows the relative prediction time as a function of the number of hops between the source and destination nodes.

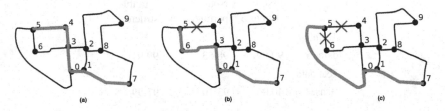

**Fig. 6.** The Figure shows a map from the KITTI dataset, where locations of interest are modeled as nodes in the graph. The numbers represent node ids and the green path is the shortest path from location 5 to location 7 predicted by our model. We show the predictions when (a) all roads are reachable, (b) one road (4–5) is blocked (marked as a red cross), (c) two roads (4–5, 5–6) are blocked. (Color figure online)

## 5  Conclusion

In this paper we demonstrated how our biologically inspired computational framework is capable of optimal path finding. It mimics the behaviour of the brain to find alternate shortest paths on unseen data even when nodes/edges are removed. This is unlike adjacency-matrix based conventional feedforward approaches which cannot easily be trained with varying numbers of nodes. As we developed our framework for generalized graph structures, it can be extended to various applications.

**Acknowledgement.** This work was supported by the Munich Center for Machine Learning and the BMBF-project MLWin.

## References

1. Fornito, A., Zalesky, A., Bullmore, E.: Connectivity matrices and brain graphs. In: Fundamentals of Brain Network Analysis, pp. 89–113. Academic Press, San Diego (2016)

2. Azevedo, F.A., et al.: Equal numbers of neuronal and nonneuronal cells make the human brain an isometrically scaled-up primate brain. J. Compar. Neurol. **513**(5), 532–541 (2009)
3. Bastos, A.M., et al.: Canonical microcircuits for predictive coding. Neuron **76**(4), 695–711 (2012)
4. Bongiorno, C., et al.: Vector-based pedestrian navigation in cities. Nat. Comput. Sci. **1**(10), 678–685 (2021)
5. Brown, C.J., et al.: Connectome priors in deep neural networks to predict autism. In: 2018 IEEE 15th International Symposium on Biomedical Imaging, pp. 110–113 (2018)
6. Cheng, Z., et al.: The method based on Dijkstra of multi-directional ship's path planning. In: 2020 Chinese Control and Decision Conference (CCDC), pp. 5142–5146 (2020)
7. Cireşan, D., et al.: Multi-column deep neural network for traffic sign classification. Neural Netw. **32**, 333–338 (2012), selected Papers from IJCNN 2011
8. Dijkstra, E.W.: A note on two problems in connexion with graphs. Num. Math. **1**(1), 269–271 (1959)
9. Geiger, A., et al.: Are we ready for autonomous driving? The KITTI vision benchmark suite. In: Conference on Computer Vision and Pattern Recognition (CVPR) (2012)
10. Gilmer, J., et al.: Neural message passing for quantum chemistry. In: International Conference on Machine Learning, pp. 1263–1272. PMLR (2017)
11. Hidayatullah, A.S., et al.: Realization of depth first search algorithm on line maze solver robot. In: 2017 International Conference on Control, Electronics, Renewable Energy and Communications (ICCREC), pp. 247–251 (2017)
12. Jiang, J.R., et al.: Extending Dijkstra's shortest path algorithm for software defined networking. In: The 16th Asia-Pacific Network Operations & Management Symposium (2014)
13. Kawahara, J., et al.: Brainnetcnn: convolutional neural networks for brain networks; towards predicting neurodevelopment. NeuroImage **146**, 1038–1049 (2017)
14. Krizhevsky, et al.: ImageNet classification with deep convolutional neural networks. In: Advances in Neural Information Processing Systems, vol. 25. Curran Associates, Inc. (2012)
15. Leskovec, J., Rajaraman, A., Ullman, J.D.: Mining Social-Network Graphs, 2 edn. p. 325–383. Cambridge University Press, London (2014)
16. Mattson, M.P.: Superior pattern processing is the essence of the evolved human brain. Front. Neurosci. **8**, 265 (2014)
17. Niv, Y.: Reinforcement learning in the brain. Special Issue: Dynamic Decision Making. J. Math. Psychol. **53**(3), 139–154 (2009)
18. Panov, A.I., et al.: Grid path planning with deep reinforcement learning: preliminary results. Procedia Comput. Sci. **123**, 347–353 (2018)
19. Pasa, F., et al.: Efficient deep network architectures for fast chest X-ray tuberculosis screening and visualization. Sci. Rep. **9** (2019)
20. Peer, M., Brunec, I.K., Newcombe, N.S., Epstein, R.A.: Structuring knowledge with cognitive maps and cognitive graphs. Trends Cogn. Sci. **25**(1), 37–54 (2021)
21. Radford, A., Wu, J., Child, R., Luan, D., Amodei, D., Sutskever, I., et al.: Language models are unsupervised multitask learners. OpenAI Blog **1**(8), 9 (2019)
22. Sutton, R.S., Barto, A.G.: Reinforcement Learning: An Introduction. MIT Press, London (2018)
23. Velickovic, P., Cucurull, G., Casanova, A., Romero, A., Lio, P., Bengio, Y.: Graph attention networks. stat **1050**, 20 (2017)
24. Yang, Z., Cohen, W., Salakhudinov, R.: Revisiting semi-supervised learning with graph embeddings. In: Balcan, M.F., Weinberger, K.Q. (eds.) Proceedings of the 33rd International Conference on Machine Learning Research, vol. 48, pp. 40–48. PMLR, New York, USA, 20–22 June 2016. https://proceedings.mlr.press/v48/yanga16.html

25. Ying, R., et al.: Graph convolutional neural networks for web-scale recommender systems. In: Proceedings of the 24th ACM SIGKDD International Conference on Knowledge Discovery & Data Mining, pp. 974–983 (2018)
26. Zelikowsky, M., et al.: Prefrontal microcircuit underlies contextual learning after hippocampal loss. Proc. Natl. Acad. Sci. **110**(24), 9938–9943 (2013)
27. Žunić, E., et al.: Software solution for optimal planning of sales persons work based on depth-first search and breadth-first search algorithms. In: 39th International Convention on Information and Communication Technology, Electronics and Microelectronics (MIPRO) (2016)

# A Second-Order Adaptive Social-Behavioural Model for Individual and Duo Motor Learning

Ege de Bruin, Matthijs Weier, and Jan Treur[✉]

Faculty of Science, Athena Institute and Social AI Group, Vrije Universiteit Amsterdam,
Amsterdam, The Netherlands
j.treur@vu.nl

**Abstract.** This paper addresses computational analysis by psychological knowledge in motor learning of how people with certain personalities, alone and in pairs, are being influenced by several factors during their motor learning processes. To this end a second-order adaptive network model was designed for the social and behavioural processes involved. Example simulations show how the model fits to different situations. Mathematical analysis was performed for verification and parameter tuning for validation.

## 1 Introduction

Motor learning can be regarded as a broad concept that involves many different phenomena, disciplines, and applications. The concept, for example, encompasses great theoretical and experimental interest among neuroscientists, psychologists, and physiologists (Krakauer et al. 2019). It enables humans and animals to gain new skills or it improves the accuracy and smoothness of a physical action (Wolpert and Flanagan 2010). Therefore, motor learning has tremendous practical relevance among babies, injured people who rehabilitate, dancers, musicians, drivers, sporters, or coaches and teachers (Krakauer et al. 2019).

Cano-De-La-Cuerda et al. (2015) propose several factors affecting motor learning. Among others, they mention the relevance of practice and motivation. Implying that the more someone practises or wants to learn something, the better someone gets good at something. These two factors imply a behavioural or psychological and personal influence and that is where the focus will be on in this paper. To build on that, other scientists have proposed related factors that may play a role in the behaviour of people in motor learning as well. Motivation, for example, can be divided into intrinsic and extrinsic motivation, each using different dynamics to influence the performance in the process of motor learning (Benabou and Tirole 2003). Additionally, personal dynamics such as self-confidence or the belief to acquire a certain skill appear to be relevant for motivation levels as well (Benabou and Tirole 2003; Wattie and Baker 2017). Lastly, particularly relevant in sports, different types of learning exist, such as auditory instructions, mental visualisation, or kinesthetically, which imply different behaviours in motor learning as well (Predoiu et al. 2020; Effenberg et al. 2007; Guillot and Collet 2008).

The aim of this research is to contribute to the psychological knowledge in motor learning by helping to understand how people with certain personalities, individually and

© Springer Nature Switzerland AG 2022
M. Mahmud et al. (Eds.): BI 2022, LNAI 13406, pp. 343–358, 2022
https://doi.org/10.1007/978-3-031-15037-1_28

in pairs, are being influenced by several factors during their motor learning process. Two research questions that adhere to this configurative approach are formulated as follows:

1. How do different individual dynamics influence the performance in motor learning of an individual?
2. How do duo dynamics influence the performance in motor learning of an individual?

To answer these research questions, a second-order adaptive mental model is designed. The model contains two persons each having their own mental model. Links between the two models are included to analyse duo dynamics. By means of this model, several scenarios are expounded based on a sports context through which three simulations are proposed that indicate the impact of individual dynamics on the performance in motor learning of an individual, and 2) three simulations are proposed that provide implications on how duo dynamics influence the performance in motor learning of an individual.

In this paper, after the current section, the second section provides a background of relevant literature regarding the main concepts. In the third section, the design of the network model is proposed which constitutes the base model in this paper. In the fourth section, the upper described simulations are presented as results. After that, in section five, verification and validation of the model are discussed. In the final section, a discussion is proposed in which the main findings are discussed, the research question is answered, the strengths and limitations of the paper are addressed and lastly, the implications for further research are provided.

## 2  Background Literature

This section discusses relevant concepts important in the dynamics of motor learning and provides an explanation and justification on why certain factors are incorporated in the design of the model this research applies.

As Wolpert and Flanagan (2010) imply in their paper, motor learning is about gaining new skills or improving the accuracy or smoothness of a movement. This encapsulation provides a rather simplistic description of what motor learning is about. To deepen the understanding around the concept, some formal definitions will be discussed and compared. Krakauer (2006) and Umphred and Lazaro (2012) both discuss the essentiality of practice. And second, "permanent changes' used by Krakauer (2006) compared to 'makes automatic the desired movement' used by Umphred and Lazaro (2012) both address a similarly long-lasting resolution of the process.

To elaborate on the concept of practice in light of this paper, one type of learning related to this research is used. Reviewed comprehensively by Ridderinkhof and Brass (2015) is Kinesthetic Motor Imaginary (KMI). This is a widely used technique among professional athletes to improve motor performance without overt motor output. This visual type of learning thus "enables one to practice movements without needing to physically perform them" (Ridderinkhof et al. 2002, p. 54).

As is described by Cano-De-La-Cuerda et al. (2015), motivation also plays a significant role in motor learning. Motivation is an explanation of why people perform certain behaviour. It provides reason, for example, to initiate, continue or terminate an action (Wasserman and Wasserman 2020). Benabou and Tirole (2003) discussed the distinction and interrelation between intrinsic and extrinsic motivation. Extrinsic motivation is described as motivation initiated by external rewards (Wasserman and Wasserman 2020; Benabou and Tirole 2003). Comparably, intrinsic motivation is "the individual's desire to perform the task for its own sake" (Benabou and Tirole 2003, p. 490). On top of that, they describe the phenomenon called the 'undermining effect'. This effect means that rewards are often counterproductive because they undermine "intrinsic motivation".

As described by Benabou and Tirole (2003), a concept closely related to intrinsic motivation, and therefore interesting to integrate into this research, is confidence. They describe the relationship as that when people have higher self-esteem they are more motivated to start, continue or terminate certain behaviour. What is interesting, however, is that in the case that confidence reaches too high, this would negatively affect the intrinsic motivation of someone (Benabou and Tirole 2003).

A final compounding factor influencing the dynamics between intrinsic motivation and practice, in order to improve performance in motor learning, is based on the belief that skills are predominantly acquirable and attributes poor performance to a lack of effort or insufficient preparation. This contrasts with the belief of 'inherent ability', which encapsulates that skills are predominantly unchangeable (Wattie and Baker 2017). As we believe skills are acquirable, the model described in the following section incorporates the acquirable skill belief as an influencing factor in motor learning.

**Research questions.** Based on this background, several sub-questions are formulated which contribute to answering the two research questions proposed in the introduction:

1. How do different individual dynamics influence the performance in motor learning of an individual?

   - To what extent do acquirable skill beliefs influence intrinsic motivation, and what does that imply for the performance in motor learning?
   - How does visualising influence confidence, and what does that imply for the performance in motor learning?
   - To what extent does overconfidence influence the performance in motor learning of an individual?
   - How do intrinsic and extrinsic motivation each influence the performance in motor learning?

2. How do duo dynamics influence the performance in motor learning of an individual?

   - How do different motivation levels in duo-learning influence the performance in motor learning?
   - How does competitiveness influence the performance in motor learning?

## 3   Method Used

In this section, we will elaborate on our model. We will explain how we have built the model, which decisions we made based on the previous sections, and eventually show the resulting model which we will use for analysis. In the first part of this section, the network-oriented modeling approach used is briefly explained. Next, a one-person model will be explained, and in the last part we will add a second person to this model and we will explain how the persons work together.

The conceptual representation of the causal network model consists of states and connections between the states. These connections can represent a causal impact. It is assumed that the states have activation levels that vary over time. Adaptation of causal relations and other network characteristics are incorporated in the approach too (Treur 2020). The network structure characteristics used are as follows:

**Connectivity of the network** Connection weights $\omega_{X,Y}$ for each connection from a state (or node) $X$ to a state $Y$.
**Aggregation of multiple impacts** A combination function $\mathbf{c}_Y(..)$ for each state $Y$ to determine the aggregation of incoming causal impacts.
**Timing in the network** A speed factor $\eta_Y$ for each state.

In Table 1 the combination functions used are explained. The way in which these network characteristics define the dynamics of a network model is explained as follows.

$$\mathbf{impact}_{X_i,Y}(t) = \omega_{X_i,Y}X(t) \tag{1}$$
$$\mathbf{aggimpact}_Y(t) = \mathbf{c}_Y(\mathbf{impact}_{X_1,Y}(t),..., \mathbf{impact}_{X_k,Y}(t))$$

Here $X_1,.., X_k$ are the states from which state $Y$ gets incoming connections. This is assembled in the following canonical differential equation used for all states:

$$dY(t)/dt = \eta_Y [\mathbf{aggimpact}_Y(t) - Y(t)] \tag{2}$$

This differential equation can be rewritten into difference equation format to determine the state values with regard to the change in time $\Delta t$:

$$Y(t + \Delta t) = Y(t) + \eta_Y [\mathbf{aggimpact}_Y(t) - Y(t)]\Delta t \tag{3}$$
$$= Y(t) + \eta_Y [\mathbf{c}_Y(\omega_{X_1,Y}X(t), ...., \omega_{X_k,Y}X(t)) - Y(t)]\Delta t$$

Moreover, self-model states (also called reification states) were added to the network to make some of the network characteristics adaptive. For this model, these self-model states are of type $\mathbf{W}_{X,Y}$ and $\mathbf{H}_{X,Y}$. The W-states $\mathbf{W}_{X,Y}$ are first-order self-model states; they represent their corresponding connection weight $\omega_{X,Y}$. These states are used for plasticity by Hebbian learning (Hebb 1949; Shatz 1992). Additionally, in this model there are five second-order self-model states $\mathbf{H}_{\mathbf{w}_{X,Y}}$ representing the timing (speed factor) characteristic $\eta_{\mathbf{w}_{X,Y}}$ for the mentioned first-order self model states $\mathbf{W}_{X,Y}$. Adding these speed factors allowed for determining the moment when each of the learning activities would take place. In this way, metaplasticity (Abraham and Bear 1996) of the model was ensured.

**Table 1.** Combination functions used

| Name | Description | Formula | Parameters | Used for |
|---|---|---|---|---|
| $id(V_1, \ldots, V_k)$ | Identity function | $V_1$ | - | $X_6, X_{14}, X_{18}$ |
| $comp\text{-}id(V_1, \ldots, V_k)$ | Complementary identity function | $1 - V_1$ | - | $X_7, X_{11},$ $X_{19}, X_{23}$ |
| $ssum_\lambda(V_1, \ldots, V_k)$ | Scaled sum | $(V_1 + \cdots + V_k)/\lambda$ | Scaling factor $\lambda$ | $X_1, X_2, X_4, X_5,$ $X_{13}, X_{16}, X_{17}$ |
| $alogistic_{\sigma,\tau}(V_1, \ldots, V_k)$ | Advanced logistic sum | $[\dfrac{1}{1 + e^{-\sigma(V_1 + \cdots + V_k - \tau)}}$ $- \dfrac{1}{1+e^{\sigma\tau}}](1+e^{-\sigma\tau})$ | Steepness $\sigma$ Threshold $\tau$ | $X_3, X_9,$ $X_{15}, X_{21}$ |
| $hebb_\mu(V_1, V_2, W)$ | Hebbian learning: positive weights | $V_1 V_2 (1-W) + \mu W$ $V_1, V_2$ activation levels of connected states; $W$ activation level of **W**-state | Persistence factor $\mu$ | **W**-states $X_{12}, X_{24}$ |
| $hebbneg_\mu(V_1, V_2, W)$ | Hebbian learning: negative weights | $-V_1(1-V_2)(1+W) + \mu W$ $V_1, V_2$ activation levels of connected states; $W$ activation level of **W**-state | Persistence factor $\mu$ | **W**-states $X_{10}, X_{22}$ |
| $stepmod_{\rho,\delta}(\ldots)$ | Repeated activation | $1$ if $t \bmod \rho \geq \delta$, else $0$ (time $t$) | Repetition $\rho$ Duration $\delta$ | $X_8, X_{20}$ |

A total of 12 states are used in the second-order model for one person, thereby using seven different combination functions for them as shown in Table 1, last column. The full specification of the connections, weights, speed factors, and combination functions can be found in the tables in the Appendix available as Linked Data at URL https://www.researchgate.net/publication/357648578.

The central aspect in our model is the performance ($X_6$) in motor learning of the person. As mentioned before, the amount of practice is important for performance. Therefore, a state is added which represents the practice ($X_5$). This state has a connection to the performance and an incoming connection from motivation ($X_4$). This is the state which represents the general amount of motivation a person has in this particular skill, and it is dependent on two different types of motivation.

At first, there is extrinsic motivation ($X_2$), which is motivation coming from external rewards. Secondly, there is intrinsic motivation ($X_3$), which is the direct satisfaction this particular skill brings to the person. Both of these motivations connect to motivation, and there is a connection from extrinsic to intrinsic motivation as well. This is the previously mentioned undermining effect, therefore this connection has a negative weight. Extrinsic motivation has a direct incoming connection from performance, the higher the performance the more extrinsic motivation there is. Intrinsic motivation has an incoming connection from confidence ($X_1$), which in turn has an incoming connection from performance. There are three other states to be mentioned. At first, there is acquirable skill belief ($X_7$). This state has an incoming connection from performance, but it is inversely proportional to it. The worse the performance is, the more there is to gain in this particular skill. And when the performance is at its highest, there is no skill to be acquired anymore. This acquirable skill belief has a direct connection to intrinsic motivation. There is also a state representing visualising ($X_8$). This is a context state which can be either turned on or off, and it influences both confidence and practice directly. Lastly, there is a state representing overconfidence ($X_9$), which only activates when confidence becomes too low. It represents the general idea of overconfidence, where too much confidence can cause the person to be lazy and therefore less motivated.

Lastly, there are a few self-model states of first- and second-order. There is a first-order self-model **W**-state ($X_{10}$) which represents a Hebbian learning process for the negative connection from extrinsic motivation to intrinsic motivation. It uses the negative Hebbian function **hebbneg**, which makes that the weight becomes stronger negative over time when extrinsic motivation is high while intrinsic motivation is low. A higher-order self-model **H$_W$**-state ($X_{12}$) manages the speed of this **W**-state. The more performance someone has at a particular motor learning skill, the harder it becomes to improve upon this skill. Therefore, a first-order self-model **H**-state $X_{11}$ was added which is the inverse of the performance and controls the speed factor of performance.

All states with only one incoming connection use an id function. Confidence, motivation and practice use a scaled sum function, while intrinsic motivation and overconfidence use an alogistic function. Overconfidence has a high steepness and threshold value, it should not increase immediately but it should increase fast. Table 2 contains an overview of the states for the one-person model with their explanations.

**Table 2.** States of the single person model with their explanation.

| State | State name | State explanation |
|-------|-----------|-------------------|
| $X_1$ | C1 | Confidence of the person |
| $X_2$ | EM1 | Extrinsic motivation of the person |
| $X_3$ | IM1 | Intrinsic motivation of the person |
| $X_4$ | M1 | Weighted average of the motivation |
| $X_5$ | Pr1 | (Amount and type of) Practice of the person |
| $X_6$ | Pe1 | Performance of the person |
| $X_7$ | Asb1 | Acquirable skill belief of the person |
| $X_8$ | V1 | Visualizing |
| $X_9$ | O1 | Overconfidence of the person |
| $X_{10}$ | $\mathbf{W}_{EM1,IM1}$ | First-order self-model state for the weight of the connection from $X_2$ (EM1) to $X_3$ (IM1) |
| $X_{11}$ | $\mathbf{H}_{Pe1}$ | First-order self-model state for the speed factor of $X_6$ (Pe1) |
| $X_{12}$ | $\mathbf{H}_{\mathbf{W}EM1,IM1}$ | Second-order self-model state for the speed factor of $X_{10}$ ($\mathbf{W}_{EM1,IM1}$) |

For the two-person model, context states will be used for the second person. The two context states represent the second person's intrinsic motivation and performance. The second person's intrinsic motivation influences the intrinsic motivation of the first person, and the second person's performance influences both the intrinsic and extrinsic motivation of the first person.

A total of 14 states are used in the second-order model, and seven combination functions are used. A full overview of the model can be seen in Fig. 1, and the values used for the connections, weights, speed factors and combination functions can be seen in the tables in the Appendix (Linked Data) at https://www.researchgate.net/publication/357648578. The speed factors and combination function variables remain the same compared to the single-person model.

In next section, we will investigate this model, show the base result and answer the research questions.

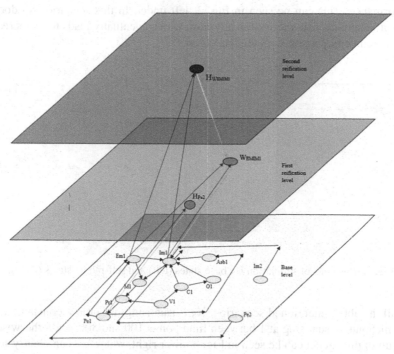

**Fig. 1.** 3D figure of the connectivity of the full two-person model.

## 4  Simulation Results

In Fig. 2 the base of the single-person model is shown; in such graphs, time $t$ from formulaa (1), (2), (3) is on the horizontal axis and activation level $Y(t)$ on the vertical axis. This is the result of running the model with the parameters shown in the tables in the Appendix available as Linked Data at https://www.researchgate.net/publication/357648578. All values are initially 0.5, except for $X_9$ (overconfidence) and all higher-order states, which are all initially 0. The state for performance, $X_6$, initially increases to around 0.9, and after a few timesteps, it converges to a value of around 0.85.

That the value is going up and down for a while is due to some factors. At some point, it is going down because $X_9$ (overconfidence) increases. Moreover, $X_3$ (intrinsic motivation) decreases because the strength of the connection between $X_2$ (extrinsic motivation) and $X_3$ increases due to Hebbian learning, and $X_2$ itself is also increasing.

Performance still converges at a high value due to an increase of intrinsic motivation, which is caused by a stabilising $X_7$ (acquirable skill belief). This effect of acquirable skill belief can be seen in Fig. 3, upper graphs. Two graphs are shown wherein the graph on the left everything is initially set to 0, and in the graph on the right, there is no effect of acquirable skill belief. This means that $X_7$ does not have an effect on intrinsic motivation. The connection weight value from $X_7$ to $X_3$ is put to 0, and a decrease in performance can be noticed in the graph. On the other hand, overconfidence has a negative effect on performance. This can be seen in Fig. 3, left under. In this scenario, $X_9$ does not have an effect on intrinsic motivation anymore which eventually leads to an increase of performance in comparison with the base model.

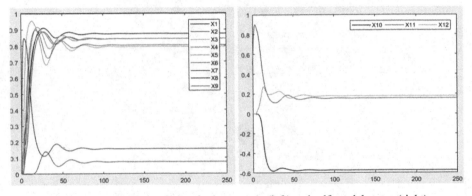

**Fig. 2.** Base model simulation for base states (left) and self-model states (right).

In all the above-mentioned scenarios, $X_8$ (visualising) is set at a constant value of 1. To which puts visualising at 1 between time points 100 and 300, and otherwise at 0. The result of this model can be seen in Fig. 3 lower right, where we can clearly see that visualising has a positive effect on performance.

Motivation, both intrinsic and extrinsic, have an important influence on the model. Different ratios of intrinsic and extrinsic motivation do influence the model. In the base model, motivation has a ratio of 80% intrinsic and 20% extrinsic motivation, as we assumed this person values intrinsic motivation more than extrinsic motivation. In Fig. 3 we experimented with two other ratios. In the first figure, motivation is 100% intrinsic motivation, and in the third figure motivation is 100% extrinsic motivation. From the figures, we can see that the performance is better when extrinsic motivation has a higher share. This is due to the fact that extrinsic motivation has a negative effect on intrinsic motivation. Therefore, when performance is at its highest, extrinsic motivation will also be high, causing intrinsic motivation to decrease. There is no negative influence on extrinsic motivation, so when motivation only consists of extrinsic motivation, both performance and extrinsic motivation will eventually rise to a value of 1.

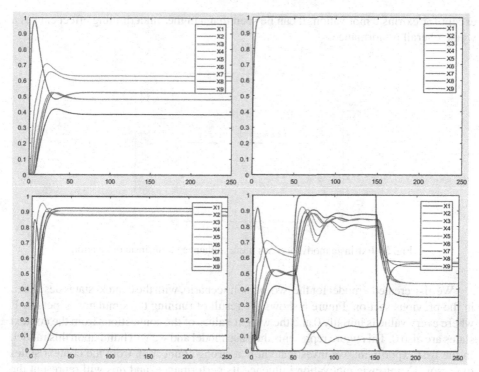

**Fig. 3.** Upper graphs: effect for removing acquirable skill belief when everything is initially 0. Lower left: without the effect of overconfidence. Lower right: effect of visualising

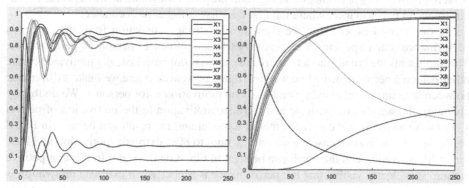

**Fig. 4.** Left: Motivation = 100% intrinsic motivation. Right: Motivation = 100% extrinsic motivation

That extrinsic motivation has a negative effect on intrinsic motivation is due to the previously mentioned undermining effect. The strength of this effect can be seen in Fig. 5. Here extrinsic motivation has more influence on intrinsic motivation. To be precise, in the model we lowered the weights of all incoming connections of intrinsic motivation, except for extrinsic motivation. It can be seen that a higher undermining effect causes a worse overall performance.

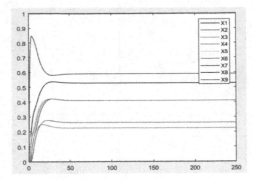

**Fig. 5.** Extrinsic motivation has more influence on intrinsic motivation

We also created a model for the two-person scenario, with the context states described in the previous section. Figure 6 shows the result of running the simulator of person 1, where every value is initially 0 and the weight values of the connections from the context states are also 0. This figure represents the base model and we will build upon this model. In the first experiment, we investigate how a strong connection from the context states to person 1's intrinsic motivation influence its performance, and this will represent the "friend" model. In Fig. 7 on the left, we see what happens in that case if both context states, performance and intrinsic motivation, are high, and in Fig. 7 on the right, we see what happens if only performance is high and intrinsic motivation is low. There is a clear difference in performance, where the first case has a higher performance.

In our second experiment, we show how a strong connection from the context's performance state to person 1's extrinsic motivation influences person 1's performance. This represents the "rival" model, where the person is only extrinsically motivated by the other person's performance. Here we investigate two cases where we make a difference between how important extrinsic and intrinsic motivation is for person 1. We do this by changing the weights of extrinsic and intrinsic motivation to the motivation of person 1. In the first case it is the same as the base model and the result can be seen in Fig. 8 on the left, in the second case we switch the ratio to 80% extrinsic motivation and 20% intrinsic motivation and the result can be seen in Fig. 8 on the right. In this competitive setting, it is clearly visible that the performance is higher when extrinsic motivation is more important.

Finally, we look into what a balance in connections can do for a person's learning. All the connections from the context states are now activated and both context states are set to 1. Moreover, motivation now is 50% extrinsic and 50% intrinsic motivation and the result of this model can be seen in Fig. 9. In comparison with all other models of the simplified 2 person model, this one scores the best.

The models, for both the single and two-person models, show interesting results which give an insight into how different aspects influence a person's motoric learning ability. In the next section, we will use these results to answer our research questions.

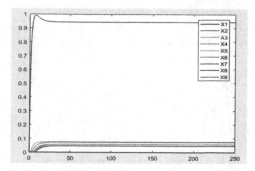

**Fig. 6.** Base result simplified two-person model

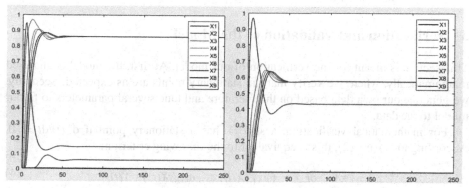

**Fig. 7.** Friend model, Left: second person high intrinsic motivation, Right: second person low intrinsic motivation.

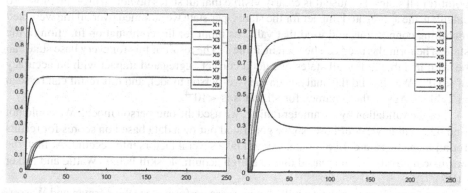

**Fig. 8.** Competitive model, Left: Intrinsic motivation is more important to person 1, Right: Extrinsic motivation is more important to person 1.

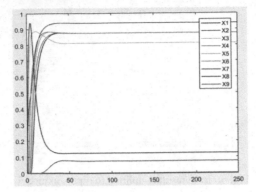

**Fig. 9.** Competition and cooperation are both important for person 1.

# 5   Verification and Validation of the Model

This section is meant for the verification of our model. At first, the model is analysed mathematically, where we verify that the stationary points are as expected. Secondly, we generate our own data based on the literature and tune several parameters to fit our model to the data.

For mathematical verification, a state $Y$ has a stationary point if $dY(t)/dt = 0$. According to (1) and (2), this is equivalent to the following criterion:

$$\eta_Y = 0 \quad \text{or} \quad \mathbf{c}_Y(\omega_{X_1,Y}X(t), ...., \omega_{X_k,Y}X(t)) = Y(t) \tag{4}$$

For the mathematical analysis, we looked at the one-person model and see whether the resulting model is accurate. We took the final time point, namely 400, as the stationary point for all states, because it is clearly visible that all states do not change anymore. To calculate the aggregated impact for the states, per state we summed over all the weighted incoming connections and used that value as input for the combination function of the state. The formulas used can be seen in Table 1. The result of this for every base state can be seen in Table 2. For all states, we get a correct aggregated impact with an accuracy of $<10^{-4}$. We also did the analysis on the two-person model, and this result can be seen in Table 3. Again, the accuracy for all states is $<10^{-4}$.

For the validation by parameter tuning, we used the one-person model. We could not find data online we could use, so we generated our own data based on scores for results found in the literature. In our data, we will take several factors into account. At first, the intrinsic motivation is increased due to a high acquirable skill belief (Wattie and Baker 2017).

This increase in motivation will also increase performance (Wasserman and Wasserman 2020), though it will increase slower. With the performance increasing, two things will happen. Firstly, due to the performance increase, extrinsic motivation will also increase. This will cause an undermining effect, which will decrease intrinsic motivation (Benabou and Tirole 2003, p. 490). Moreover, the confidence will increase at such a level that its effect on intrinsic motivation will be less, or even make it decrease (Benabou and Tirole 2003). But eventually, the model will find a stationary point where the

**Table 3.** Aggregated impact for all base states in the single person model, with their accuracy.

| State $X_i$ | $X_1$ | $X_2$ | $X_3$ | $X_4$ | $X_5$ | $X_6$ | $X_7$ | $X_8$ | $X_9$ |
|---|---|---|---|---|---|---|---|---|---|
| Time point t | 400 | 400 | 400 | 400 | 400 | 400 | 400 | 400 | 400 |
| $X_i(t)$ | 0.8747 | 0.8434 | 0.7945 | 0.8043 | 0.8434 | 0.8434 | 0.1566 | 1 | 0.0755 |
| aggimpact$_{Xi}(t)$ | 0.8747 | 0.8434 | 0.7945 | 0.8043 | 0.8434 | 0.8434 | 0.1566 | 1 | 0.0755 |
| deviation | $<10^{-4}$ | $<10^{-4}$ | $<10^{-4}$ | $<10^{-4}$ | $<10^{-4}$ | $<10^{-4}$ | $<10^{-4}$ | $<10^{-4}$ | $< 10^{-4}$ |

performance will still have increased. The resulting data can be found in the mentioned Appendix.

The parameters which were tuned are all (non-adaptive) speed factors, the weights of the incoming connections of intrinsic motivation, the combination function parameters of intrinsic motivation, and the Hebbian function parameter. All initial values are set to 0 and visualising has no effect on confidence and practice. We ran the simulated annealing algorithm, and after 7000 iterations the best RMSE was 0.08793. An overview of the parameters with their values can be seen in the Appendix, and the resulting model can be seen in Fig. 10.

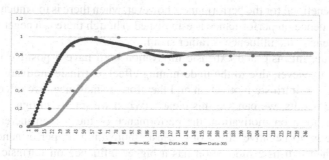

**Fig. 10.** Simulation of the model with the tuned parameters.

The fit is decent, but it is not as curvy as was expected in the data. The differences between the chosen values for the parameters and the values we used in the previous sections are mostly visible in the speed factors and alogistic parameters. Firstly, almost all speed factors are much lower, except for confidence and the second-order state for the Hebbian weight between extrinsic motivation and intrinsic motivation. Secondly, the values for the alogistic parameters of intrinsic motivation are completely different, the steepness almost doubled and the threshold is much lower. This has also caused the incoming connection weight values for intrinsic motivation to be lower than our original model. Finally, there is a difference in the Hebbian parameter. It has increased causing the weight of the connection from extrinsic to intrinsic motivation to be higher.

# 6  Discussion

The aim of this research was to contribute to the psychological knowledge in motor learning by helping to understand how people with certain personalities, alone and in pairs, are being influenced by several factors during their motor learning process. This was done by addressing several research questions. In this section, these questions are addressed and answered by means of a discussion based on our results. Subsequently, we reflect on our choices and results and give several options for future research.

First of all, with regard to individual motor learning, we did observe a difference in performance when acquirable skill belief is mitigated, namely the performance will decrease. However, the biggest difference can be seen when every other value is initially set to 0. Then we can really see the effect of acquirable skill belief, which makes a lot of sense. When everything is initially low, there is a lot of skill to be acquired. And when the person believes in this acquirable skill, it will motivate him or her to practice.

In addition, visualising appears to have a positive effect on confidence. Moreover, it also positively affects practice, and both these effects cause an increase in performance. In our results, we however do not observe a long-term influence of visualising. When visualising increases we see a clear increase in performance, but when visualising decreases again the performance decreases to its previous value.

Regarding overconfidence, this has a negative effect on performance. Confidence definitely is beneficial for the performance, however, when there is too much confidence, a negative influence on performance is established. Though there is a negative influence of overconfidence, this influence is rather small.

To continue, intrinsic and extrinsic motivation both have a positive influence on performance. However, due to the undermining effect, extrinsic motivation also has a negative effect on intrinsic motivation and therefore a small negative effect on performance. In the results, we can see this clearly. When we totally mitigate the effect of intrinsic motivation on motivation, the performance of the person increases. This is because there is no negative effect of extrinsic motivation on performance anymore. Moreover, when extrinsic motivation has a bigger influence on intrinsic motivation, making the undermining effect more prominent, this clearly has a negative effect on the performance.

Regarding the influence of duo learning on the performance of an individual; the best motivation level of a person in duo learning depends on the setting. In a teamwork setting, the person performs best when the other person is not only performing well but motivated as well. This is a nice representation of how empathy works, where a person performs well when it feels that the other is intrinsically motivated. In a competitive setting, where the person is solely motivated by performing better than the opponent, the best mindset is also a competitive mindset. There is no intrinsic motivation to be gained by the other person performing well, and getting the motivation only from extrinsic motivation will then increase the performance.

From the results, we can also conclude that a person thrives when there is a balance of competitiveness and cooperation. As previously mentioned, in a competitive setting a competitive mindset does perform better than a non-competitive mindset. But the performance is still worse than when the people are cooperating well. The best performance can be achieved when there is cooperation, but also including some competitiveness. This competitiveness is needed to keep the person on edge to perform better.

Altogether, the performance in motor learning on an individual is influenced by several individual dynamics. The acquirable skill belief appears to have influence when everything is initially zero, as when the person believes in this acquirable skill, it will motivate him or her to practice and therefore increase the performance in motor learning. Regarding visual learning, it appears to have an influence on confidence and practice and therefore increases the performance in motor learning. However, no long-term influence was indicated. To continue, too much confidence seems to have a small negative effect on the performance in motor learning. Lastly, both intrinsic and extrinsic motivation have a positive influence on performance. However, due to the undermining effect, extrinsic motivation also has a negative effect on intrinsic motivation and therefore a small negative effect on performance. On top of that, the performance in motor learning of an individual is also influenced by several duo dynamics. In a teamwork setting, the individual performs best in motor learning when the other person is not only performing well but also motivated. In a competitive setting, where the person is solely motivated by performing better than the opponent, the best mindset to reach the highest performance in motor learning is a competitive mindset. Lastly, someone's performance in motor learning thrives when there is a balance between competitiveness and cooperation.

To briefly reflect on this research, a non-adaptive state is used to incorporate the influence of the acquirable skill belief on the performance in motor learning. However, by doing this, the state of acquirable skill belief increases immediately without any performance, because this is modelled as such. By making the state adaptive, the acquirable skill belief remains zero at the beginning of the simulation, resulting in a more realistic representation. Future research could explore this line of thought.

In addition, this research incorporated several factors of influence regarding the performance in motor learning. However, many other factors of influence exist. To name a few social factors, the way someone gets instructed or how someone receives feedback might be important. But also the memory of someone or the possibility of errors with regard to the motoric activity are valuable for consideration (Cano-De-La-Cuerda et al. (2015). Further research could focus on enhancing the breadth of this model by incorporating those factors of influence as well. Moreover, further research could also centre its attention towards a deeper understanding of the factors which are incorporated. Extrinsic motivation, for example, is not just influenced by the performance of him or herself, or of someone else. The extrinsic motivation assumingly is, for example, also influenced by the type of reward someone gets offered. Lastly, this research indicated that it is quite difficult to compare the single-person model with the two-person model, as both models are distinguishable. Further research may also focus on designing an integrated model which enables a comparison of both.

# References

Abraham, W.C., Bear, M.F.: Metaplasticity: the plasticity of synaptic plasticity. Trends Neurosci. **19**(4), 126–130 (1996)

Benabou, R., Tirole, J.: Intrinsic and extrinsic motivation. Rev. Econ. Stud. **70**(3), 489–520 (2003)

Cano-De-La-Cuerda, R., et al.: Theories and control models and motor learning: clinical applications in neurorehabilitation. Neurología (English Edition) **30**(1), 32–41 (2015)

Effenberg, A.O., Weber, A., Mattes, K., Fehse, U., Mechling, H.: Motor learning and auditory information: Is movement sonification efficient?. J. Sport Exerc. Psychol. **29** (2007)

Guillot, A., Collet, C.: Construction of the motor imagery integrative model in sport: a review and theoretical investigation of motor imagery use. Int. Rev. Sport Exerc. Psychol. **1**(1), 31–44 (2008)

Hebb, D.O.: The Organization of Behavior: A Neuropsychological Theory. John Wiley and Sons, New York (1949)

Krakauer, J.W.: Motor learning: its relevance to stroke recovery and neurorehabilitation. Curr. Opin. Neurol. **19**(1), 84–90 (2006)

Krakauer, J.W., Hadjiosif, A.M., Xu, J., Wong, A.L., Haith, A.M.: Motor learning. Compr. Physiol. **9**(2), 613–663 (2019)

Predoiu, R., et al.: Visualisation techniques in sport–the mental road map for success. Phys. Educ. Sport Kinetotherapy J. **59**(3), 245–256 (2020)

Ridderinkhof, K.R., et al.: Alcohol consumption impairs detection of performance errors in mediofrontal cortex. Science (2002). (New York, N.Y.)

Shatz, C.J.: The developing brain. Sci. Am. **267**, 60–67 (1992)

Treur, J.: Network-Oriented Modeling for Adaptive Networks: Designing Higher-Order Adaptive Biological, Mental and Social Network Models. Springer, Cham (2020). https://doi.org/10.1007/978-3-030-31445-3

Umphred, D.A., Lazaro, R.T.: Neurological Rehabilitation. Elsevier Health Sciences, St. Louis (2012)

Wasserman, T., Wasserman, L.: Motivation: state, trait, or both. In: Motivation, Effort, and the Neural Network Model. NNMAI, pp. 93–101. Springer, Cham (2020). https://doi.org/10.1007/978-3-030-58724-6_8

Wattie, N., Baker, J.: Why conceptualizations of talent matter: implications for skill acquisition and talent identification and development. In Routledge Handbook of Talent Identification and Development in Sport, pp. 69–79. Routledge (2017)

Wolpert, D.M., Flanagan, J.R.: Motor learning. Curr. Biol. **20**(11), R467–R472 (2010)

# EEG Signal Classification Using Shallow FBCSP ConvNet with a New Cropping Strategy

Yifeng Sun[1,2], Hao Lan Zhang[2,3(✉)] (iD), Yifan Lu[2], and Yun Xue[4]

[1] Zhejiang University, Hangzhou, Zhejiang, China
[2] SCDM Center, NIT, Zhejiang University, Ningbo, China
[3] Guangdong University of Technology, Guangdong, China
haolan.zhang@nit.zju.edu.cn
[4] South China Normal University, Guangdong, China

**Abstract.** Raw EEG signal is dynamically collected from electrode channels distributing on the scalp surface and stored in computers as a 2D array of electrode channel (space) and time. In the past, most experiments were based on pure 2D EEG signal array of space and time. Shallow FBCSP ConvNet [5] is one of the successful models in handling 2D EEG signal array, which comes from FBCSP algorithm [4], a widely used algorithm in EEG decoding. With an original cropping strategy, Shallow FBCSP ConvNet reaches a high accuracy in EEG signal classification. In this paper, we propose a new cropping strategy to generate 3D EEG signal array of space, time and cropped piece. With redesigning the existing 2D Shallow FBCSP ConvNet model to become a 3D model, we obtained a good experimental result.

**Keywords:** 2D EEG signal · Shallow FBCSP ConvNet · Cropping strategy · 3D array

## 1 Introduction

Brain computer interface (BCI) is a technology that establishes a direct connection path between human or animal brain and external equipment. BCI technology based on electroencephalography (EEG) is an effective and successful technology so far, which benefits from the non-invasive and easy acquisition of EEG signal and good time resolution.

BCI technology based on EEG has been widely used in many fields, such as motor imagery [1], sleep stage analysis [2], emotion recognition [3] and so on. In the field of motor imagery, this technology can help people with physical disabilities achieve brain manipulation of wheelchairs and other equipment to achieve limb movement; In the field of sleep state analysis, this technology can help doctors analyze patients' sleep state to monitor and diagnosing the disease.

Nowadays, the implementation of BCI technology based on EEG is roughly divided into two steps: 1) EEG raw signal processing including data preprocessing, such as filtering, artifact removal, and key feature extraction techniques. 2)

© Springer Nature Switzerland AG 2022
M. Mahmud et al. (Eds.): BI 2022, LNAI 13406, pp. 359–368, 2022
https://doi.org/10.1007/978-3-031-15037-1_29

Pattern recognition of the processed signal usually using machine learning technology to classify the input features. In this paper, after simple preprocessing of EEG raw data, data cropping is carried out to generate 3D array, then convolution is used to extract the three dimensional features respectively to generate feature vectors, and finally the feature vectors are classified.

## 2   Related Work

### 2.1   FBCSP - Filter Bank Common Spatial Pattern

FBCSP [4], a method that is widely used in EEG decoding and has won several EEG decoding competitions on BCI competition IV 2a and 2b, is the model source of Shallow FBCSP ConvNet which is used in our experiment. The pipeline of FBCSP is shown as follows (see Fig. 1):

*1. Band-Pass Filtering:* The first stage employs a filter bank that decomposes the EEG into multiple frequency pass bands ranging from 4–8 Hz, 8–12 Hz,..., 36–40 Hz, which cover 4–40 Hz (the frequency range depends on the experimental requirements).

*2. Spatial Filtering:* In second stage, per frequency band, the common spatial patterns (CSP) algorithm is applied to extract spatial filters. CSP aims to extract spatial filters that make the trials discriminable by the power of the spatially filtered trial signal. The spatial filters correspond to the learned parameters $\theta_\phi$ in FBCSP then are applied to the EEG signal.

*3. Feature Selection:* The third stage employs a feature selection algorithm to select discriminative CSP features from $V(x_i, \theta_\phi)$, where $x_i$ denotes raw EEG signal and $\theta_\phi$ denotes the parameters in stage 2. Specifically, feature vectors are the log-variance of the spatially filtered trial signal for each frequency band and for each spatial filter.

*4. Classifier:* The forth stage employs a trained classifier to predict pretrial labels based on the feature vectors.

### 2.2   Shallow FBCSP ConvNet

In [5], three convolution models have been proposed, among which the best one is Shallow FBCSP ConvNet. The Shallow FBCSP ConvNet is designed according to FBCSP algorithm and uses two convolutions which respectively applied on spatial dimension and time dimension to extract features. Then follows a mean pooling layer to downsize and a linear classification module(a full connection layer + softmax) to classify. Figure 2 illustrates the process of the Shallow FBCSP ConvNet.

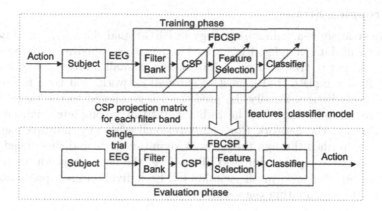

**Fig. 1.** [4] Architecture of the filter bank common spatial pattern (FBCSP) algorithm for the training and evaluation phases.

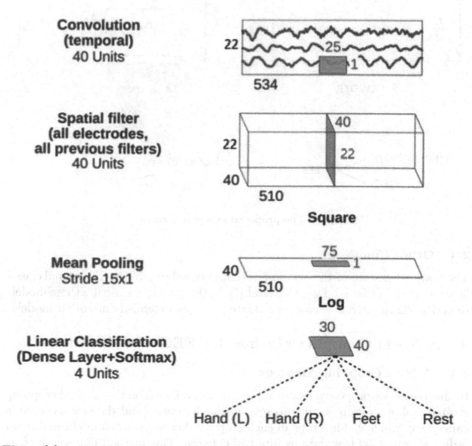

**Fig. 2.** [5] Architecture of the Shallow FBCSP ConvNet where 22 electrode channels constitute spatial dimension and 534 time points constitute time dimension.

## 2.3  Cropping Strategy

Cropping strategy is a common strategy in EEG signal classification to increase the number of data samples. EEG signal is usually cropped in the time dimension, and an entire trial is divided into multiple small crops. As Fig. 3 shows, on the left, a complete trial is pushed through network, and then the network produces a prediction. Finally the prediction is compared to the target (label) for that to compute loss; On the right, instead of a complete trial, crops are pushed through the network (for computational efficiency, multiple neighboring crops are pushed through the network simultaneously and these neighboring crops are called compute windows). Therefore, the network produces multiple predictions(one per crop in the window). The individual crop predictions are averaged before computing the loss function.

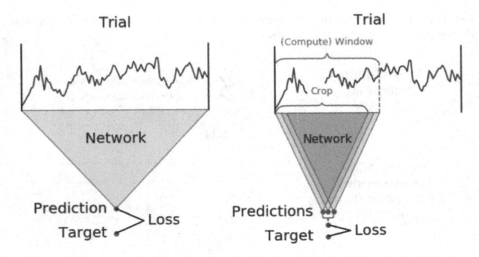

**Fig. 3.** The proposed cropping strategy.

## 2.4  Other ConvNets

There are other state-of-the-art models that also perform well in EEG signal classification like EEGNet [8], DeepConvNet [5]. In this paper, we also use these models to verify whether the new cropping strategy can be extended onto other models.

## 3  A Novel Cropping Method for EEG Classification

### 3.1  A New Cropping Strategy

In this paper, we propose a new cropping strategy. Based on the original cropping strategy [5], each crop is cut into several smaller crops, and the original crop is called crop window. The crops in each crop window are stacked in chronological order to form a 3D new data as input of network. This method not only retains the data enhancement of the original cropping strategy, but also makes each crop window have a internal chronological order. This is also in line with the practical significance of EEG motor imagery (for example, a hand raising action can be disassembled into three sequential sub actions: lifting, holding and lowering).

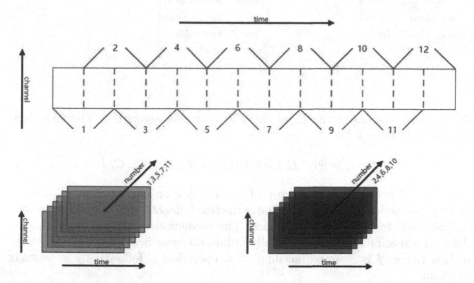

**Fig. 4.** New cropping strategy: a trial produces two crop windows which have overlapping parts. Each crop window produces several crops and crops are stacked in chronological order to form a 3D data.

### 3.2  Model Construction and Work Flow

The original Shallow FBCSP ConvNet is a two-dimensional convolution neural network, which only respectively convolutes the time dimension and space dimension of EEG signal. After being processed by new cop strategy, the data has the third dimension, crop number (in chronological order). Thus after convoluting the time dimension and space dimension, we also need to convolute the crop number dimension (see the left picture in Table 1). This is a bit similar to the convolution of 2D data in the time dimension after the pooling layer(see the right picture in Table 1). But in fact, it reduces the number of convolution operations, reduces over fitting, and is more in line with the actual practical meaning mentioned in Sect. 3.1.

After passing the 3D data through the 3D convolution neural network, each crop window will get an n-dimensional prediction vector P (n is the number of motor imagery types): In the training phase: define a loss function Ψ. The parameter is the prediction vector P and the actual label corresponding to the vector, and then the loss vector Loss is calculated, which is used to calculate

**Table 1.** The difference between 3D and normal 2D convolutional neural models

| Convoluting in crop number dimension | Convoluting in time dimension after pooling layer |
|---|---|
| *(conv_time): Conv3d* | *(conv_time): Conv2d* |
| *(conv_spat): Conv3d* | *(conv_spat): Conv2d* |
| *(pool): AvgPool3d* | *(pool): AvgPool3d* |
| *(conv_crop): Conv3d* | *(conv_time): Conv2d* |
| *(conv_classifier): Conv3d* | *(conv_classifier): Conv2d* |

the gradient descent of the Error Back Propagation algorithm. The formula is expressed as follows:

$$Loss_i = \Psi(h(D_i), label_i), Di = [C_{i1}, C_{i2}, ..., C_{ij}] \tag{1}$$

where $C_{ij}$ denotes the $j-th$ crop of the $i-th$ crop window and $D_i$ denotes $i-th$ crop window in 3D data format. Function h denotes the operation through the network. In the evaluation phase: The prediction vectors $p_i$ from $D_i$ pass through a specific function f to finally obtain the classification type of the trial. In this paper, $f$ is a simple accumulation operation $\Sigma$ followed by an argmax function.

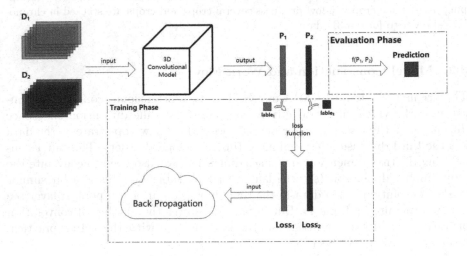

**Fig. 5.** The work flow of the proposed method.

# 4    Experimental Analysis

## 4.1    Data and Preprocessing

The data set selected in this paper is BCI_IV_2a. The sampling frequency of data is 250 Hz and there are 25 electrode channels (22 EEG channels and 3 EOG channels). There are nine subjects in this data set, each subject conducted two sessions on different days (as training set session and test set session respectively), each session is composed of 6 runs, and each run is composed of 48 trials. Figure 6 illustrates a trial. In the preprocessing stage, The experimental data are filtered in the frequency band of 4–38 Hz to eliminate interference caused by eye movement [6]. Afterwards, we applied electrode-wise exponential moving standardization to compute exponential moving means and variances for each channel and used these to standardize the continuous data [7]. At last, we extracted each trial according to –0.5 s 4 s when cue occurs. As the sampling frequency is 250 Hz and we removed the EOG channels to eliminate interference of eye movement, each trial is represented by a 22 * 1126(4.5 * 250 + 1, we didn't drop the last time points) array.

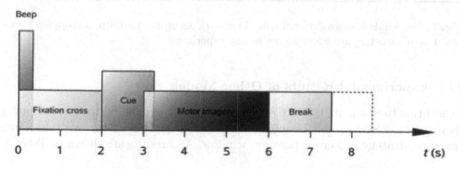

**Fig. 6.** In each trial, the cross appears between 0–2 s, followed by the left, right, lower and upper arrow prompts of 1.25 s. The imaginary categories are left hand, right hand, feet and tongue respectively. Between 3 and 6 s, it is motor imagery. After 6 s, the cross disappears and the subject begins to rest briefly.

## 4.2    Experimental Results of Shallow FBCSP ConvNet

The comparative experiment of this paper is carried out between new cropping strategy +3D neural network and original cropping strategy +2D neural network which were both based on the Shallow FBCSP ConvNet. The data processed by the two kinds of crop strategies go through the two models in Fig. 7 respectively, and results are shown in Table 2 and 3. For both tables, crop window is always 1001 (4 s * 250 Hz + 1, We didn't drop the last time points, neither), and the difference is the number of crop windows. For new cropping strategy, we divided each crop window into 3 and 6 crops respectively. 3 crops in each crop window pratically corresponded to three sub actions: lifting, holding and lowering. 6 crops in each crop windows was just to obtain smaller granularity while maintaining a multiple of 3. Note that subject 4 has data problem so we didn't experiment on it.

```
(conv_time): Conv3d(1, 40, kernel_size=(1, 25, 1), stride=(1, 1, 1))
(conv_spat): Conv3d(40, 40, kernel_size=(1, 1, 22), stride=(1, 1, 1), bias=False)
(bnorm): BatchNorm3d(40, eps=1e-05, momentum=0.1, affine=True, track_running_stats=True)
(conv_nonlin_exp): Expression(expression=square)
(pool): AvgPool3d(kernel_size=(1, 75, 1), stride=(1, 1, 1), padding=0)
(pool_nonlin_exp): Expression(expression=safe_log)
(drop): Dropout(p=0.5, inplace=False)
(conv_crop): Conv3d(40, 40, kernel_size=(6, 1, 1), stride=(1, 1, 1), dilation=[1, 1, 1], bias=False)
(conv_classifier): Conv3d(40, 4, kernel_size=(1, 27, 1), stride=(1, 1, 1), dilation=(1, 15, 1))
(softmax): LogSoftmax(dim=1)
(squeeze): Expression(expression=squeeze_final_output)
```

```
(conv_time): Conv2d(1, 40, kernel_size=(25, 1), stride=(1, 1))
(conv_spat): Conv2d(40, 40, kernel_size=(1, 22), stride=(1, 1), bias=False)
(bnorm): BatchNorm2d(40, eps=1e-05, momentum=0.1, affine=True, track_running_stats=True)
(conv_nonlin_exp): Expression(expression=square)
(pool): AvgPool2d(kernel_size=(75, 1), stride=(1, 1), padding=0)
(pool_nonlin_exp): Expression(expression=safe_log)
(drop): Dropout(p=0.5, inplace=False)
(conv_classifier): Conv2d(40, 4, kernel_size=(61, 1), stride=(1, 1), dilation=(15, 1))
(softmax): LogSoftmax(dim=1)
(squeeze): Expression(expression=squeeze_final_output)
```

**Fig. 7.** Two kinds of convolutional neural network according to diffirent cropping strategy. The parameters are what we set in out experiment.

## 4.3   Experimental Results of Other Models

In addition to Shallow FBCSP ConvNet, we also experimented the new cropping strategy on EEGNet and DeepConvNet. For both models, we used the same cropping strategy of 3 crops per crop window. And results are shown in Table 4.

**Table 2.** Original cropping strategy divided each trial (time dimensional length is 1126) into 2 crop windows whose index range from 0–999 and 126–1125. New cropping strategy divided each trial into also 2 crop windows whose index range from 1). {0–499, 250–749, 500–999} and {126–625, 376–875, 626–1125}, each crop window has 3 crops. 2). {0–499, 100–599, 200–699, 300–799, 400–899, 500–999} and {126–625, 226–725, 326–825, 426–925, 526–1025, 626–1125}, each crop window has 6 crops.

| Strategy | Subject ID | | | | | | | |
|---|---|---|---|---|---|---|---|---|
|  | 1 | 2 | 3 | 5 | 6 | 7 | 8 | 9 |
| Original cropping strategy + 2D neural network | 62.5% | 33.0% | 66.7% | 32.6% | 41.0% | 53.1% | 62.5% | 70.8% |
| New cropping strategy + 3D neural network + 3 crops per crop window | 67.4% | 37.5% | 73.6% | 35.1% | 43.1% | 56.6% | 69.8% | 70.1% |
| New cropping strategy + 3D neural network + 6 crops per crop window | 62.5% | 35.1% | 68.4% | 37.5% | 39.2% | 54.9% | 71.2% | 69.8% |

**Table 3.** Original cropping strategy divided each trial (time dimensional length is 1126) into 3 crop windows whose index range from 0–999, 63–1035, 126–1125. New cropping strategy divided each trial into also 3 crop windows whose index range from 1). {0–499, 250–749, 500–999}, {63–562, 313–812, 563–1062} and {126–625, 376–875, 626–1125}, each crop window has 3 crops. 2). {0–499, 100–599, 200–699, 300–799, 400–899, 500–999}, {63–562, 163–662, 263–762, 363–862, 463–962, 563–1062} and {126–625, 226–725, 326–825, 426–925, 526–1025, 626–1125}, each crop window has 6 crops.

| Strategy | Subject ID | | | | | | | |
|---|---|---|---|---|---|---|---|---|
| | 1 | 2 | 3 | 5 | 6 | 7 | 8 | 9 |
| Original cropping strategy + 2D neural network | 67.4% | 39.6% | 71.2% | 34.7% | 44.4% | 56.6% | 71.2% | 71.5% |
| New cropping strategy + 3D neural network + 3 crops per crop window | 71.69% | 39.9% | 75.7% | 38.5% | 45.8% | 69.8% | 76.4% | 72.2% |
| New cropping strategy + 3D neural network + 6 crops per crop window | 68.8% | 39.6% | 76.7% | 35.4% | 44.4% | 58.3% | 75.7% | 74.0% |

**Table 4.** For both models, the top line is the result of original cropping strategy with 2D neural network and the bottom line is the result of new cropping strategy of 3 crops per crop window with 3D neural network. The results show that the effect of the new strategy on EEGNet and DeepConvNet was not as good as that on shallow FBCSP ConvNet.

| Model | Subject ID | | | | | | | |
|---|---|---|---|---|---|---|---|---|
| | 1 | 2 | 3 | 5 | 6 | 7 | 8 | 9 |
| EEGNet | 56.9% | 29.9% | 64.6% | 33.7% | 36.6% | 41.0% | 67.7% | 68.4% |
| | 63.2% | 28.8% | 66.7% | 33.0% | 36.8% | 45.5% | 67.7% | 67.7% |
| DeepConvNet | 53.8% | 29.2% | 60.1% | 34.0% | 39.2% | 49.3% | 63.9% | 70.1% |
| | 61.8% | 34.0% | 59.7% | 33.3% | 41.7% | 51.4% | 62.5% | 72.9% |

## 5  Conclusion and Future work

Experiments show that for time series such as EEG signal, on the original commonly used cropping strategy, which plays the role of data enhancement, the appropriate internal time slice of each crop window and the design of the corresponding convolution model can improve the accuracy of classification, especially for Shallow FBCSP ConvNet.

In the future, for the time series data of motor imagery with some sub actions, the whole motor imagery sequence can be cropped according to sub actions and one sub action corresponds to one crop which makes the whole process of training model more practical. In this paper, every crop in each crop window shares the convolution of time and space dimensions (conv_time and conv_spat). Future work will try to use the way of incomplete-sharing convolution template (meaning that crops in each crop window will use convolutions of different weights because there are some differences between sub actions) to design the model according to the characteristics of the data set.

**Acknowledgements.** This work is partially supported by Humanity and Social Science Foundation of the Ministry of Education of China (21A13022003), Zhejiang Provincial Natural Science Fund (LY19F030010), Zhejiang Provincial Social Science Fund (20NDJC216YB), Zhejiang Provincial Educational Science Scheme 2021 (GH2021642) and National Natural Science Foundation of China Grant (No. 72071049), Ningbo public welfare science and technology plan Grant No. 2021S093.

# References

1. Huang, C., et al.: Predicting Human Intention-Behavior Through EEG Signal Analysis Using Multi-Scale CNN. IEEE/ACM Trans. Comput. Biol. Bioinform. **18**(5), 1722–1729 (2021)
2. Koolen, N.: Automated classification of neonatal sleep states using EEG. Clin. Neurophysiol. **1286**, 1100–1108 (2017), ISSN: 1388-2457
3. Qing, C., Qiao, R., Xu, X., Cheng, Y.: Interpretable Emotor recognition using EEG signals. IEEE Access **7**, 94160–94170 (2019). https://doi.org/10.1109/ACCESS. 2019.2928691
4. Ang, K.K., Chin, Z.Y., Zhang, H., Guan, C.: Filter bank common spatial pattern (FBCSP) in brain-computer interface. In IEEE International Joint Conference on Neural Networks, 2008. IJCNN 2008. (IEEE World Congress on Computational Intelligence), pp 2390–2397 (2008)
5. Schirrmeister, R.T., et al.: Deep learning with convolutional neural networks for EEG decoding and visualization. Hum. Brain Mapp. **38**(11), 5391–5420. Epub 2017 Aug 7. PMID: 28782865; PMCID: PMC5655781 https://doi.org/10.1002/hbm. 23730
6. Gratton, G.: Dealing with artifacts: the EOG contamination of the event-related brain potential. Behav. Res. Methods. Instrum. Comput. **30**(1), 44–53 (1998)
7. Schirrmeister, R.T., et al.: Deep learning with convolutional neural networks for EEG decoding and visualization. arXiv:1703.05051v1 [cs.LG]
8. Lawhern, V.J., Solon, A.J., Waytowich, N.R., Gordon, S.M., Hung, C.P., Lance, B.J.: EEGNet: a compact convolutional network for EEGbased brain-computer interfaces. J. Neural Eng. (2016). https://doi.org/10.1088/1741-2552/aace8c

# Becoming Attuned to Each Other Over Time: A Computational Neural Agent Model for the Role of Time Lags in Subjective Synchrony Detection and Related Behavioral Adaptivity

Sophie C. F. Hendrikse[1,2(✉)], Jan Treur[3], Tom F. Wilderjans[1,2,4], Suzanne Dikker[1,5], and Sander L. Koole[1]

[1] Amsterdam Emotion Regulation Lab, Department of Clinical Psychology, Vrije Universiteit Amsterdam, Amsterdam, The Netherlands
{s.c.f.hendrikse,s.l.koole}@vu.nl
[2] Methodology and Statistics Research Unit, Faculty of Social and Behavioral Sciences, Institute of Psychology, Leiden University, Leiden, The Netherlands
t.f.wilderjans@fsw.leidenuniv.nl
[3] Social AI Group, Department of Computer Science, Vrije Universiteit Amsterdam, Amsterdam, The Netherlands
j.treur@vu.nl
[4] Research Group of Quantitative Psychology and Individual Differences, Faculty of Psychology and Educational Sciences, Katholieke Universiteit (KU) Leuven, Leuven, Belgium
[5] NYU – Max Planck Center for Language, Music and Emotion, New York University, New York, USA

**Abstract.** Interpersonal synchrony usually means that people mutually adapt their behavior to each other over time. Such behavioral adaptivity is assumed to be driven by some form of subjective internal synchrony detection. In contrast to objective synchrony detection by an external (third-party) observer, subjective synchrony detection relies solely on information that is perceived by each of the synchronizing persons. Simultaneous actions of the two persons in principle cannot be sensed instantaneously by one of the two persons, but will involve time lags. These time lags reflect the time differences between a person's own actions and the sensing of the actions of the other person. In the computational agent model described in this paper, we explore the role of time lags in different types of subjective synchrony detection and its involvement in behavioral adaptivity. Multiple simulation experiments show expected types of patterns of subjective time-lagged synchrony detection and related behavioral adaptivity.

## 1 Introduction

When two persons become synchronized in their behavior, they tend to experience a number of relation benefits such as more closeness, concentration, coordination, cooperation, affiliation, alliance, connection, and bonding (Accetto et al. 2018; Hove and Risen

© Springer Nature Switzerland AG 2022
M. Mahmud et al. (Eds.): BI 2022, LNAI 13406, pp. 369–383, 2022
https://doi.org/10.1007/978-3-031-15037-1_30

2009; Hu, Cheng, Pan, Hu, 2022; Kirschner and Tomasello 2010; Koole and Tschacher 2016; Palumbo et al. 2017; Prince and Brown 2022; Ramseyer and Tschacher 2011; Sharpley at al. 2001; Tarr et al. 2016; Valdesolo et al. 2010; Valdesolo and DeSteno, 2011; Wiltermuth and Heath 2009). In order for these relational benefits to emerge, it stands to reason that people are capable of detecting synchrony based on the (subjective) information; e.g., (Dhamala, Assisi, Jirsa, Steinberg, Kelso, 2007) that is available via sensing of their own actions and sensing the other person's actions. The pathways for sensing own actions are based on internal mechanisms whereas the pathways for sensing actions of the other person partly involve mechanisms used in the external world and for sensing. Therefore, it has to be taken into account that simultaneous actions of the two persons in principle cannot be sensed instantaneously, but will involve time lags. Any mechanism for subjective synchrony detection therefore has to incorporate this time lag.

The computational adaptive neural agent model described in the current paper introduces two computational mechanisms for subjective synchrony detection using time lags and in addition covers how these different types of synchrony detection lead to behavioral adaptivity concerning the interaction with the other person. The model addresses intrapersonal synchrony and interpersonal synchrony for three different modalities: movement, affective and verbal responses. Simulation experiments were based on an experimental scenario, in which different stimuli for each of the two agents alternate over time independently and the same holds for periods in which communication is allowed. This work extends our previous work (Hendrikse et al. 2022c) where time differences in the pathways toward the detector states from the own actions and sensing the actions of the other were assumed to be non-existent. In the current paper, we describe simulation experiments in which we varied the computations and sizes of these time lags.

The design of the adaptive neural agent model was based on the self-modeling network modeling approach introduced in Treur (2020a, b); this is briefly described in Sect. 3. The simulation experiments were conducted using the available dedicated software environment; some are described in Sect. 5. In Sect. 2 background literature is discussed and in Sect. 4 the designed adaptive neural agent model is described in more detail. Finally, Sect. 6 contains a discussion and conclusion.

## 2  Background Perspectives

There is an extensive literature in the behavioral sciences describing how synchronies between two persons can be detected from an objective external third-person (observer) point of view; e.g., (Altmann 2011; Behrens et al. 2020; Schoenherr et al. 2019a, b). A basic assumption here is that an external observer has objective information available on the (movement, affective, verbal) actions of the two persons. For the sake of brevity, this can be termed objective synchrony detection. In contrast, subjective synchrony detection occurs when synchrony is detected by each of the two persons in the considered dyad. These persons usually do not have access to objective information about their joint actions. Subjective synchrony detection has a distinct profile of characteristics. The following characteristics have been addressed in the model:

**Asynchrony of Pathways: Fast Sensing of Self, Slow Sensing of Other.** For someone to notice or experience synchrony for themselves, several dedicated mechanisms and pathways have to be used. More specifically, this subjective form of synchrony detection essentially depends on subjective information acquired by a person on actions (e.g., movements, affective reactions, verbal responses) by the self and actions by the other. Therefore, it is crucial to consider the pathways that enable a person to sense own and other's actions. Roughly speaking, the pathways leading to subjective synchrony detection within a person may be sketched as follows:

mutual interaction →
patterns of own actions            and  patterns of actions of the other →
internal sensing                   and  external sensing →
patterns of sensed own actions     and  patterns of sensed actions of the other →
patterns of synchrony for sensed own actions and sensed actions of the other →
subjective synchrony detector states

Even in this simplified sequence of events, it should be noted that the internal and external sensing processes occur in parallel, but differ in timing: Generally, sensing self is faster than sensing the other; see also, e.g., (Rayner et al. 2009; Shelton and Kumar 2010; Thompson et al. 2014). This makes that the generated subjective information from both sides does not refer to the same time point; due to the differently paced parallel pathways, a time lag is created between when the two types of information become available for processing in the brain. In the literature addressing objective synchrony detection from an external observer viewpoint, a number of approaches have been developed to handle time lags; e.g., (Schoenherr et al. 2019a, b). These methods have been used as inspiration for the way in which, for the subjective synchrony detection introduced here, time lags have been handled based on sliding (rolling) time windows.

**Asymmetry of Time: Only Past, No Future.** Subjective synchrony detection is also different from objective synchrony detection in a second way. In subjective synchrony detection, people only have information from the past available. People do not have information available from the future, given that sensing does not address future states. In contrast, researchers who analyze objective synchrony detection within already completed time series, in many cases future time points are freely used as well, for example, to determine a global mean level of a signal over time. Regarding subjective synchrony detection, this can only be done for the past. Even if these computations are only done locally by considering some type of sliding (or rolling) window, for the subjective case such a window will necessarily have a focus only on values from the past, as values from the future are simply not available yet.

**Anormality of Signals: Non-normalized Levels.** A third issue that distinguishes subjective synchrony detection from objective synchrony detection is that it is plausible, at least for humans, that the level of detected synchrony depends both on timing and strength of the signals. This is in contrast to some approaches for objective synchrony detection where the absolute strength of signals is changed to a more relative strength by applying a normalizing factor to the signals during the detection process.

**From Subjective Synchrony Detection to Behavioral Adaptivity.** After subjective synchrony detection occurs, a subsequent issue is how this affects the interaction. For example, Prince and Brown (2022) suggested that synchrony induces what they call partnered interaction, which is: '...real-time behavioral adaptivity between the partners, as studied in a large literature devoted to joint action and joint agency (e.g., Accetto et al. 2018; Fairhurst et al. 2013; Izawa et al. 2008; Keller et al. 2014; Pacherie 2012)'. This perspective is also adopted here. Two types of behavioral adaptivity are addressed:

- short term affiliation, modeled based on changed thresholds for intrinsic excitabilities of states (nonsynaptic plasticity)
- long-term bonding, modeled based on the changed strengths of connections (synaptic plasticity)

In the neuroscientific literature, such as (Chandra and Barkai 2016), the distinction between synaptic and nonsynaptic (intrinsic) adaptation is discussed in some detail. A classical notion of synaptic plasticity is Hebbian learning; e.g., (Hebb 1949; Shatz 1992). Nonsynaptic adaptation of intrinsic excitability of (neural) states has been addressed in more detail recently; e.g., (Chandra and Barkai 2016; Debanne et al. 2019; Zhang et al. 2021). The latter form of adaptation has been related, for example, to how deviant dopamine levels during sleep can result in dreams that might use more associations due to easier excitable neurons; e.g., (Boot et al. 2017). A difference in pace is assumed here as well between the two adaptation processes that happen in parallel. The adaptation of connections is assumed to take place at a slow pace and the adaptation of intrinsic excitabilities at a fast pace. Finally, plasticity is often highly context-dependent according to what is called metaplasticity; e.g., (Abraham and Bear 1996; Robinson et al. 2016). To enable context-sensitive control of plasticity, second-order adaptation has been included, which makes the model more realistic.

## 3   The Self-modeling Network Modeling Approach Used

In this section, the network-oriented modeling approach used as described in Treur (2020a, b) is briefly introduced. This modeling approach allows to model in a network-oriented manner any adaptive dynamical systems model, as shown in Treur (2021). As discussed above, in this case the challenge is to model an interplay of a number of dynamic and adaptive processes, which typically requires a complex adaptive dynamical system.

Following Treur (2020a, b), a temporal-causal network model is characterized by (here $X$ and $Y$ denote nodes of the network, also called states):

- **Connectivity characteristics.** Connections from a state $X$ to a state $Y$ and their weights $\omega_{X,Y}$
- **Aggregation characteristics.** For any state $Y$, some combination function $c_Y(..)$ defines the aggregation that is applied to the impacts $\omega_{X,Y}X(t)$ on $Y$ from its incoming connections from states $X$
- **Timing characteristics.** Each state $Y$ has a speed factor $\eta_Y$ defining how fast it changes for a given causal impact

The following difference equations that are used for simulation, incorporate these network characteristics $\omega_{X,Y}$, $c_Y(..)$ and $\eta_Y$ in a standard, canonical numerical format:

$$Y(t + \Delta t) = Y(t) + \eta_Y[c_Y(\omega_{X_1,Y}X_1(t), \ldots, \omega_{X_k,Y}X_k(t)) - Y(t)]\Delta t \qquad (1)$$

for any state $Y$ and where $X_1$ to $X_k$ are the states from which $Y$ receives its incoming connections. Within the software environment described in Treur (2020a, Ch. 9), a large number of currently around 60 useful basic combination functions are included in a combination function library. The combination functions that are applied in the model introduced here can be found in Table 1. Here the $W$ indicates a sliding window; for further explanation, see Sect. 4.

**Table 1.** The combination functions used in the introduced neural agent model.

| Function | Notation | Formula | Parameters | Used for |
|---|---|---|---|---|
| Advanced logistic sum | $\text{alogistic}_{\sigma,\tau}(V_1, \ldots, V_k)$ | $\left[\dfrac{1}{1+e^{-\sigma(V_1+\cdots+V_k-\tau)}} - \dfrac{1}{1+e^{\sigma\tau}}\right](1+e^{-\sigma\tau})$ | Steepness $\sigma$ Excitability threshold $\tau$ | $X_4$-$X_5$, $X_{10}$-$X_{16}$, $X_{24}$-$X_{26}$, $X_{31}$-$X_{38}$, $X_{45}$-$X_{47}$, $X_{54}$-$X_{59}$, $X_{63}$-$X_{71}$, $X_{75}$-$X_{93}$ |
| Complemental lagged difference | $\text{compdifflag}_{\iota,\delta,\lambda}(W_1, W_2)$ | $0$ if $W_1(\iota,\delta,\lambda) = W_2(\iota,\delta,1) = 0$ $1 - \dfrac{|W_2(\iota,\delta,1)-W_1(\iota,\delta,\lambda)|}{\max(W_1(\iota,\delta,\lambda)W_2(\iota,\delta,1))}$ else | $\iota,\delta$ state identifier $\lambda$ time lag | $X_{18}$-$X_{23}$, $X_{39}$-$X_{44}$ (synchrony detectors) |
| Complemental one-sided lagged average difference | $\text{compdifflag1av}_{\iota,\delta,\lambda}(W_1, W_2)$ | $1-\text{av}\left(\dfrac{|W_2(\iota,\delta,1)-W_1(\iota,\delta,v)|}{\max(W_1(\iota,\delta,v)W_2(\iota,\delta,1))}\right)$ for $1\leq v\leq\lambda$ (average) | $\iota,\delta$ state identifier $\lambda$ max time lag | $X_{18}$-$X_{23}$, $X_{39}$-$X_{44}$ (synchrony detectors) |
| Stepmod | $\text{stepmod}_{\rho,\delta}(V)$ | $0$ if $0 \leq$ time $t$ mod $\rho \leq \delta$ $1$ else | Repetition $\rho$ Step time $\delta$ | $X_2$ (stimulus person A) $X_{60}$-$X_{62}$, $X_{72}$-$X_{74}$ (communication channels) |
| Stepmodopp | $\text{stepmodopp}_{\rho,\delta}(V)$ | $0$ if $\delta \leq$ time $t$ mod $\rho \leq \rho$ $1$ else | Repetition $\rho$ Step time $\delta$ | $X_1$ (stimulus person B) |
| Euclidean | $\text{eucl}_{n,\lambda}(V_1, \ldots, V_k)$ | $\sqrt[n]{\dfrac{V_1^n + \cdots + V_k^n}{\lambda}}$ | Order $n$ Scaling factor $\lambda$ | $X_6$-$X_9$, $X_{27}$-$X_{30}$ (sensing) $X_{48}$-$X_{53}$ (communication) |

The two combination functions in the second and third row address different approaches for synchrony detection based on sliding windows for time lags; they were specifically developed and included in the library for the research reported here. They will be explained in Sect. 4.

By using a *self-modeling network* (also called a *reified* network), a similar network-oriented conceptualization can also be applied to *adaptive* networks; see Treur (2020a, b). This works through the addition of new states to the network (called *self-model states*) which represent (adaptive) network characteristics. In the graphical 3D-format as shown in Sect. 4, such additional states are depicted at a next (higher) level (called *self-model level* or *reification level*), where the original network is at the *base level*.

As an example, the weight $\omega_{X,Y}$ of a connection from state $X$ to state $Y$ can be represented (at a next/higher self-model level) by a self-model state named $\mathbf{W}_{X,Y}$. Similarly, all other network characteristics from $\omega_{X,Y}$, $c_Y(..)$ and $\eta_Y$ can be made adaptive by including self-model states for them. As another example, an adaptive excitability threshold $\tau_Y$ (as parameter for a logistic combination function) for state $Y$ can be represented by a self-model state named $\mathbf{T}_Y$ and an adaptive speed factor $\eta_Y$ can be represented by a self-model state named $\mathbf{H}_Y$. As the outcome of self-modeling is also a temporal-causal network model itself, as has been shown in Treur (2020a, Ch. 10), this self-modeling network construction can easily be applied iteratively to obtain multiple orders of self-models (first-order, second-order, …). The second-order self-model level can be used to make the adaptation speed context-sensitive as addressed by metaplasticity literature such as Abraham and Bear (1996); Robinson et al. (2016). For instance, the metaplasticity principle 'Adaptation accelerates with increasing stimulus exposure' formulated by Robinson et al. (2016) has been modeled by using second-order self-model states for the introduced model, as will be discussed in Sect. 4. Such a second-order self-model may include a second-order self-model state $\mathbf{H}_{\mathbf{W}_{X,Y}}$ representing the speed factor $\eta_{\mathbf{W}_{X,Y}}$ for the dynamics of first-order self-model state $\mathbf{W}_{X,Y}$, which in turn represents the adaptation of connection weight $\omega_{X,Y}$. Similarly, a second-order self-model may include a second-order self-model state $\mathbf{H}_{\mathbf{T}_Y}$ representing the speed factor $\eta_{\mathbf{T}_Y}$ for the dynamics of first-order self-model state $\mathbf{T}_Y$, which in turn represents the adaptation of excitability threshold $\tau_Y$ for $Y$.

## 4    The Adaptive Neural Agent Model

In this section, the introduced adaptive neural agent model is explained in some detail. The controlled adaptive agent design uses a self-modeling network architecture of three levels as discussed in Sect. 3: a base level, a first-order self-model level, and a second-order self-model level. Here the (middle) first-order self-model level models how connections of the base level are adapted over time, and the (upper) second-order self-model level models the control over the adaptation. In the Appendix available as Linked Data at URL https://www.researchgate.net/publication/359993066 detailed explanations of all states and a complete specification of the model by role matrices can be found. Figure 1 shows a graphical overview of the base level of the agent model (agents are indicated by the big boxes).

**Sensing, Sensory Processing, Conscious Emotions, Preparing and Acting.** In Fig. 1, the boxes indicate agents, where states involved in sensing can be found on the left-hand side, and states involved in execution or expression of actions (move, exp_affect, talk) on the right-hand side. Within a box the agent's internal mental states are depicted: sensory representation states (rep), preparation states (prep) for each of the three modalities (movement $m$, expression of affect $b$, and verbal action $v$), and a conscious emotion state. The representation states for the modalities have outgoing connections to the corresponding preparation states and incoming (prediction) connections back to model internal mental simulation (Damasio 1999; Hesslow 2002). World states are modeled for dynamic stimuli sensed by the agents and the world situation's suitability for enabling interaction is modeled similarly. Finally, two context states model the (default) conditions to maintain excitability thresholds.

**The Synchrony Detector States and Their Incoming Pathways.** Six synchrony detector states (depicted in Fig. 1 by the darker pink diamond shapes) are introduced, three *intrapersonal synchrony detector states* for the three pairs of the three modalities: movement - emotion ($m$-$b$), movement - verbal ($m$-$v$), emotion - verbal ($b$-$v$). These synchrony detector states have incoming connections from the two execution states for the modalities they address. Following Grandjean et al. (2008), the conscious emotion state is triggered by incoming connections from the preparation state for affective response $b$ together with the three intrapersonal synchrony detector states. In addition, the conscious emotion state has an incoming connection from the verbal action execution state (for noticing the emotion in the verbal utterance) and an outgoing connection to the preparation of the verbal action (for emotion integration in the verbal action preparation).

In addition, three *interpersonal synchrony detector states* are included for the three modalities $m$, $b$, and $v$. Each of them has two incoming connections: from the sensing state (used for representing the action of the other person) and the execution state (representing the own action) of the modality addressed.

As discussed conceptually in Sect. 2, acquiring information about the actions from the other person follows a longer and therefore slower pathway (via the external world and sensors) than for the own actions. In Figs. 1 and 2 it can be seen that the pathways for sensing the own actions and for sensing the actions of the other person are indeed of different lengths.

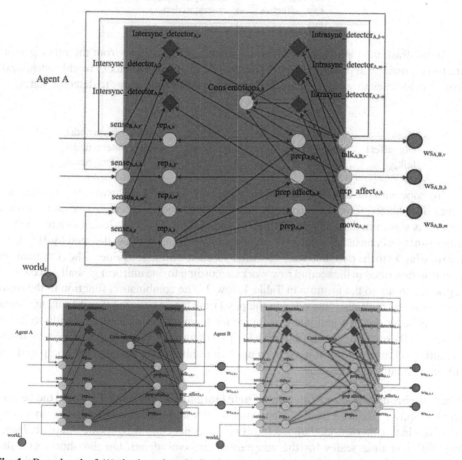

**Fig. 1.** Base level of (1) the introduced adaptive neural agent model (upper picture) with three modalities and (in dark pink) six synchrony detector states for intrapersonal synchrony and interpersonal synchrony and (2) how the agents interact (lower picture) according to the three modalities. (Color figure online)

The pathways for sensing own actions are the one-connection pathways from execution states directly to detector states: the upward arrows from states move, exp_affect and talk in Fig. 1. More specifically, for internal sensing for intrapersonal synchrony detectors within an agent $A$ just the following one-step internal pathways are used

| | | | | | |
|---|---|---|---|---|---|
| $move_{m,A}$ | $\rightarrow$ | $intrasyncdet_{A,b\text{-}m}$ | $move_{m,A}$ | $\rightarrow$ | $intrasyncdet_{A,m\text{-}v}$ |
| $exp\_affect_{b,A}$ | $\rightarrow$ | $intrasyncdet_{A,b\text{-}v}$ | $exp\_affect_{b,A}$ | $\rightarrow$ | $intrasyncdet_{A,b\text{-}m}$ |
| $talk_{A,B,v}$ | $\rightarrow$ | $intrasyncdet_{A,m\text{-}v}$ | $talk_{A,B,v}$ | $\rightarrow$ | $intrasyncdet_{A,b\text{-}v}$ |

Moreover, for internal sensing for interpersonal synchrony detectors the following one-step internal pathways are used

| | | |
|---|---|---|
| $move_{m,A}$ | $\rightarrow$ | $intersyncdet_{B,A,m}$ |
| $exp\_affect_{b,A}$ | $\rightarrow$ | $intersyncdet_{B,A,b}$ |
| $talk_{A,B,v}$ | $\rightarrow$ | $intersyncdet_{B,A,v}$ |

In contrast, the pathways for external sensing of the actions from the other person are three-connection pathways, first from move, exp_affect and talk to world states, next from world states to sensing states, and finally from sensing states to detector states.

| | | | | | | | |
|---|---|---|---|---|---|---|---|
| $move_{m,B}$ | $\rightarrow$ | $WS_{m,B,A}$ | $\rightarrow$ | $sense_{B,m,A}$ | $\rightarrow$ | $intersyncdet_{B,A,m}$ |
| $exp\_affect_{b,B}$ | $\rightarrow$ | $WS_{b,B,A}$ | $\rightarrow$ | $sense_{B,b,A}$ | $\rightarrow$ | $intersyncdet_{B,A,b}$ |
| $talk_{B,A,v}$ | $\rightarrow$ | $WS_{v,B,A}$ | $\rightarrow$ | $sense_{B,v,A}$ | $\rightarrow$ | $intersyncdet_{B,A,v}$ |

To cope with the time lags caused by these differences in pathways, for the detector states time-lagged forms of synchrony detection are used based on the two combination functions shown in the second and third row in Table 1. For each detector state, each of these functions consist of a detector-state-specific sliding window denoted by $W(\iota\delta, \lambda)$ for time lag $\lambda$ (to the past) and state identifier $\iota\delta$, each with $\lambda + 1$ values. The combination function described in the second row works according to one uniform globally fixed time lag $\lambda$ according to the formula in Table 1, row 2. The combination function in the third row considers multiple (one-sided to the past) time lags $v$ between 0 and some maximal time lag $\lambda$ for the past and takes averages for them according to the formula in Table 1, row 3. These combination functions for two (heuristic) methods for subjective time-lagged synchrony detection have been applied as alternative options and compared for different simulation scenarios.

**The Synchrony Detector States and Their Outgoing Pathways.** To model the behavioral adaptivity induced by the synchrony detection, for some states and connections involved in the interaction, their excitability and connection weights are adaptive. Here, two different time scales for the adaptations are considered. On the short-term, the excitability of such states is enhanced, so that these states become more responsive or sensitive. On the long-term, the weights of such connections are made stronger so that propagation between states is strengthened (a form of a more endurable bonding). The

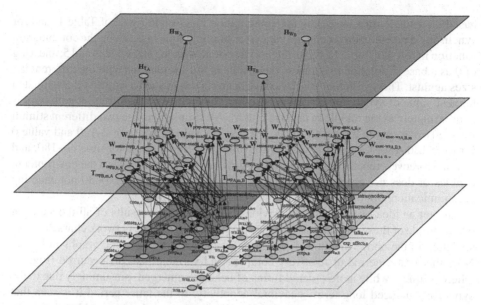

**Fig. 2.** Overview of the overall second-order adaptive network model.

more synchrony is detected, the lower the excitability thresholds will become (short-term adaptation) and weights for these connections will slowly become stronger (long-term adaptation); each type of all these adaptations contributes in its own way (and time scale). This makes the sensed signals more accessible to the brain and expressions of modalities to the other agent stronger. These forms of adaptivity were modeled using the notion of self-modeling of the network model:

- first-order self-model **T**-states $\mathbf{T}_Y$ for short-term adaptation of the adaptive base excitability thresholds $\tau_Y$, for the internal representation states and execution states $Y$ for the three considered modalities (movement, affective response and verbal action)
- first-order self-model **W**-states $\mathbf{W}_{X,Y}$ for adaptation of the adaptive connection weights $\omega_{X,Y}$ for internal connections from sense states to representation states and from preparation states to execution states
- second-order self-model $\mathbf{H_T}$-states to control the adaptation of the adaptive excitability thresholds $\tau_Y$ and second-order self-model $\mathbf{H_W}$-states to control the adaptation of the adaptive base connection weights $\omega_{X,Y}$; this follows the second-order adaptation (or metaplasticity) principle 'Adaptation accelerates with stimulus exposure' (Robinson et al. 2016)

## 5   Simulation Results

To investigate the effect of time lags on the synchrony detection and consequently on the induced behavioral adaptivity, several simulation experiments during 1440 time units (2880 iterations) have been conducted for a variety of lags, both for synchrony detection based on a single time lag (using the combination function in row 2 of Table 1) and for synchrony detection based on an average over multiple time lags (using the combination function in row 3 of Table 1). Experiments were done with lag sizes of 2, 3 and 5, and a lag of 0 as a base simulation to compare the results of the simulations with the different lag sizes against. These different lag sizes have been chosen in such a way that the estimated highest value of synchrony detection based on the lengths of the different pathways is approximately in the middle (a lag size of 2.5). All simulations use two different stimuli for the two agents in a repetitive way: for agent A value 1 for time 0–120 and value 0 for time 120–180, for agent B value 0 for time 0–60 and value 1 for time 60–180, and so on. Moreover, repetitive intervals of 30 time units were used where the environment enables or does not enable (verbal and nonverbal) communication: 0–30 not enabling communication, 30–60 enabling communication, and so on.

To get an idea of the general behavior of the agents, the results of all the states of one example of these simulations (for the specific settings of the network characteristics specified in the above-mentioned Appendix) is depicted by the three graphs in Fig. 3. Note that first a period of relatively complex and variable patterns occurred (Fig. 3), whereas after a while more ordered forms of behavior emerged, presumingly due to the synchrony-induced long-term behavioral adaptivity. In the latter period it is seen that interpersonal synchrony is systematically high in the communication enabling intervals. The two forms of (short-term and long-term) synchrony-induced behavioral adaptivity are illustrated in the lower graph of Fig. 3: the W-states (representing connection weights) for long-term adaptivity start at 0.4 and meander upward to around 0.8 and the T-states (representing excitability thresholds) for short-term adaptivity start at 0.7 and fluctuate with the communication enabling periods: low, down to 0.2, when communication is enabled (and therefore high interpersonal synchrony is detected), and higher, around 0.4, when communication is not enabled. The same patterns of results, including the apparently two kinds of episodes (more chaotic patterns followed by ordered patterns), were obtained in all simulation patterns. Therefore, the simulation results are evaluated over the first and second half of the time interval within a simulation.

An overview of the outcomes of the simulation experiments is shown in Tables 2 (averages over time period 0–720) and 3 (averages over time period 721–1440). In each of these tables the upper part summarizes the results for the single lag detection and the lower part for the averages over multiple lags in the past. As can be seen, these averages do differ for different lags but the differences are not dramatic. The yellow highlighted numbers indicate the highest values per category. As an example, in Table 2, in the first column of agent B for movement the base number for lag 0 is 0.522 whereas for multiple lags up to 2 (or up to 5) the number is 0.565. The difference between these numbers is 0.043, which makes a relative difference (with respect to the base number 0.522) of 8%. The other differences vary but in general are smaller. Roughly, it can be seen that especially for the first phase most of these highest numbers occur for lags of 2 or 3 time units.

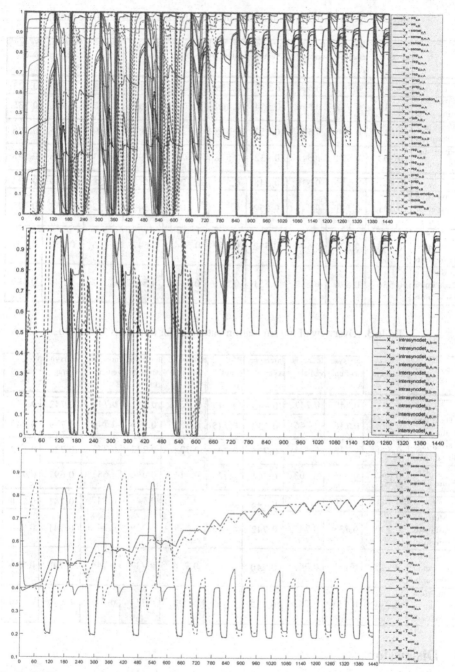

**Fig. 3.** Different views at one example simulation for averaged multiple time lags up to 2 time units. Upper graph: base states except the synchrony detectors. Middle graph: time-lagged synchrony detectors. Lower graph: the behavioral adaptivity **T**-states (short term adaptation) and **W**-states (long-term adaptation).

**Table 2.** Overview of the simulation outcomes for the first 0–720 time units.

|  | Intersync movement A | Intersync emotion A | Intersync verbal A | Intersync Average A | W-states A | Intersync movement B | Intersync emotion B | Intersync verbal B | Intersync Average B | W-states B |
|---|---|---|---|---|---|---|---|---|---|---|
| Lag 0 | 0.541 | 0.565 | 0.538 | 0.548 | 0.539 | 0.522 | 0.511 | 0.528 | 0.520 | 0.523 |
| Fixed lag: 2 time units | 0.539 | 0.577 | 0.546 | 0.554 | 0.569 | 0.526 | 0.507 | 0.530 | 0.521 | 0.535 |
| Fixed lag: 3 time units | 0.535 | 0.580 | 0.544 | 0.553 | 0.578 | 0.528 | 0.506 | 0.480 | 0.505 | 0.548 |
| Fixed lag: 5 time units | 0.503 | 0.574 | 0.518 | 0.532 | 0.578 | 0.526 | 0.498 | 0.493 | 0.506 | 0.548 |
| Lag 0 | 0.541 | 0.565 | 0.538 | 0.548 | 0.539 | 0.522 | 0.511 | 0.528 | 0.520 | 0.523 |
| Multiple lags: up to 2 time units | 0.541 | 0.571 | 0.543 | 0.552 | 0.551 | 0.565 | 0.549 | 0.552 | 0.555 | 0.527 |
| Multiple lags: up to 3 time units | 0.540 | 0.573 | 0.544 | 0.552 | 0.559 | 0.564 | 0.547 | 0.506 | 0.539 | 0.531 |
| Multiple lags: up to 5 time units | 0.536 | 0.576 | 0.542 | 0.551 | 0.570 | 0.565 | 0.545 | 0.537 | 0.549 | 0.539 |

**Table 3.** Overview of the simulation outcomes for time units 721–1440

|  | Intersync movement A | Intersync emotion A | Intersync verbal A | Intersync Average A | W-states A | Intersync movement B | Intersync emotion B | Intersync verbal B | Intersync Average B | W-states B |
|---|---|---|---|---|---|---|---|---|---|---|
| Lag 0 | 0.741 | 0.740 | 0.747 | 0.743 | 0.743 | 0.738 | 0.741 | 0.747 | 0.742 | 0.740 |
| Fixed lag: 2 time units | 0.736 | 0.736 | 0.746 | 0.739 | 0.745 | 0.735 | 0.736 | 0.746 | 0.739 | 0.740 |
| Fixed lag: 3 time units | 0.731 | 0.733 | 0.743 | 0.736 | 0.745 | 0.732 | 0.733 | 0.743 | 0.736 | 0.742 |
| Fixed lag: 5 time units | 0.694 | 0.705 | 0.703 | 0.701 | 0.723 | 0.711 | 0.696 | 0.683 | 0.697 | 0.712 |
| Lag 0 | 0.741 | 0.740 | 0.747 | 0.743 | 0.743 | 0.738 | 0.741 | 0.747 | 0.742 | 0.740 |
| Multiple lags: up to 2 time units | 0.739 | 0.738 | 0.747 | 0.742 | 0.743 | 0.737 | 0.739 | 0.747 | 0.741 | 0.738 |
| Multiple lags: up to 3 time units | 0.737 | 0.737 | 0.746 | 0.740 | 0.743 | 0.736 | 0.737 | 0.746 | 0.740 | 0.739 |
| Multiple lags: up to 5 time units | 0.733 | 0.734 | 0.743 | 0.737 | 0.744 | 0.733 | 0.734 | 0.743 | 0.737 | 0.739 |

# 6   Discussion

Interpersonal synchrony relates to behavioral adaptivity in the interaction and relationship between the synchronized persons; e.g., (Accetto et al. 2018; Hove and Risen 2009; Kirschner and Tomasello 2010; Koole and Tschacher 2016; Palumbo et al. 2017; Prince and Brown 2022; Tarr et al. 2016; Valdesolo et al. 2010; Wiltermuth and Heath 2009).

To explain the relation between synchrony and behavioral adaptivity, in Hendrikse et al. (2022c) subjective synchrony detector states were introduced and the pathways from these detector states to the behavioral adaptivity were explored in more detail. However, the pathways toward the detector states from the own actions and sensing the actions of the other were assumed to be simple. As discussed in the current paper, acquiring information about the actions from the other person follows slower pathways (via the external world and sensors) than for the own actions. Therefore, two combination functions for two (heuristic) methods for subjective synchrony detection with time lags have been applied as alternative options and compared for different simulation scenarios. The first function works according to a uniform globally fixed time lag. The other combination function calculates the averages over different time lags. Simulation results, as depicted in Tables 2 and 3, do show differences for synchrony detection (and the induced behavioral adaptivity) over different time lags applied but these differences are relatively modest.

Computational modeling of synchrony between agents was already investigated in earlier work such as Hendrikse et al. (2022a, b). However, in the models described there, no internal detection of synchrony is incorporated. Moreover, in Hendrikse et al. (2022b) no behavioral adaptivity was covered, whereas in Hendrikse et al. (2022a) another type of adaptivity was modeled, namely of internal connections from representations to preparations. As already mentioned above, in Hendrikse et al. (2022c) also internal synchrony detector states were used, in that case with the focus on the induced behavioral adaptivity, thereby neglecting the differences in timing of the incoming signals to these detector states by implicitly assuming the sensing processes being synchronous. In contrast, the current paper explored different ways in which asynchronous sensing processes for subjective synchrony detection can be addressed computationally by considering time lags. Thus, a more realistic human-like adaptive agent model was obtained for subjectively detected synchrony. The model can provide a basis to develop adaptive virtual agents that are able to concentrate and bond with each other and in the further future with humans by behavioral adaptivity. Furthermore, future research could consider the notion of social presence (Tschacher et al. 2018) by dynamically detecting the time differences between the actions of an agent itself and another agent. Our model implies that time differences might slightly affect the simultaneously experienced presence of the two agents, because higher interpersonal synchrony scores have been reached when a time lag was taken into account.

# References

Abraham, W.C., Bear, M.F.: Metaplasticity: the plasticity of synaptic plasticity. Trends Neurosci. **19**(4), 126–130 (1996)

Accetto, M., Treur, J., Villa, V.: An adaptive cognitive-social model for mirroring and social bonding during synchronous joint action. Proc. BICA 2018. Procedia Computer Science, vol. 145, pp. 3–12 (2018)

Altmann, U.: Investigation of movement synchrony using windowed cross-lagged regression. In: Esposito, A., Vinciarelli, A., Vicsi, K., Pelachaud, C., Nijholt, A. (eds.) Analysis of verbal and nonverbal communication and enactment. The processing issues. LNCS, vol. 6800, pp. 335–345. Springer, Heidelberg (2011). https://doi.org/10.1007/978-3-642-25775-9_31

Behrens, F., Moulder, R.G., Boker, S.M., Kret, M.E.: Quantifying physiological synchrony through windowed cross-correlation analysis: Statistical and theoretical considerations. BioRxiv (2020)

Boot, N., Baas, M., Van Gaal, S., Cools, R., De Dreu, C.K.W.: Creative cognition and dopaminergic modulation of fronto-striatal networks: Integrative review and research agenda. Neurosci. Biobehav. Rev. **78**, 13–23 (2017)

Chandra, N., Barkai, E.: A non-synaptic mechanism of complex learning: modulation of intrinsic neuronal excitability. Neurobiol. Learn. Mem. **154**, 30–36 (2018)

Damasio, A.R.: The feeling of what happens: Body and emotion in the making of consciousness. Houghton Mifflin Harcourt (1999)

Debanne, D., Inglebert, Y., Russier, M.: Plasticity of intrinsic neuronal excitability. Curr. Opin. Neurobiol. **54**, 73–82 (2019)

Dhamala, M., Assisi, C.G., Jirsa, V.K., Steinberg, F.L., Kelso, J.A.S.: Multisensory integration for timing engages different brain networks. NeuroImage **34**, 764–773 (2007)

Fairhurst, M.T., Janata, P., Keller, P.E.: Being and feeling in sync with an adaptive virtual partner: Brain mechanisms underlying dynamic cooperativity. Cereb. Cortex **23**(11), 2592–2600 (2013). https://doi.org/10.1093/cercor/bhs243

Grandjean, D., Sander, D., Scherer, K.R.: Conscious emotional experience emerges as a function of multilevel, appraisal-driven response synchronization. Conscious. Cogn. **17**(2), 484–495 (2008)

Hebb, D.O.: The organization of behavior: A neuropsychological theory. John Wiley and Sons, New York (1949)

Hendrikse, S.C.F., Kluiver, S., Treur, J., Wilderjans, T.F., Dikker, S., Koole, S.L.: How virtual agents can learn to synchronize: an adaptive joint decision-making model of psychotherapy. Proceedings of BICA 2021 (2022a, to appear)

Hendrikse, S.C.F., Treur, J., Wilderjans, T.F., Dikker, S., Koole, S.L.: On the same wavelengths: emergence of multiple synchronies among multiple agents. In: Van Dam, K.H., Verstaevel, N. (eds.) MABS 2021. LNCS (LNAI), vol. 13128, pp. 57–71. Springer, Cham (2022b). https://doi.org/10.1007/978-3-030-94548-0_5

Hendrikse, S.C.F., Treur, J., Wilderjans, T.F., Dikker, S., Koole, S.L.: A second-order multi-adaptive neural agent model for synchrony-related short- and long-term affiliation. In: Proceedings of the 18th International Conference on Artificial Intelligence Applications and Innovations, AIAI 2022. Advances in Information and Communication Technology, Springer Nature (2022c, in press)

Hesslow, G.: Conscious thought as simulation of behaviour and perception. Trends Cogn. Sci. **6**, 242–247 (2002)

Hove, M.J., Risen, J.L.: It's all in the timing: interpersonal synchrony increases affiliation. Soc. Cogn. **27**(6), 949–960 (2009)

Hu, Yin., Cheng, X., Pan,Y., Hu, Yi.: The intrapersonal and interpersonal consequences of interpersonal synchrony. Acta Psychol. **224**, e103513 (2022)

Izawa, J., Rane, T., Donchin, O., Shadmehr, R.: Motor adaptation as a process of reoptimization. J. Neurosci.: Offic. J. Soc. Neurosci. **28**(11), 2883–2891 (2008). https://doi.org/10.1523/JNEUROSCI.5359-07.2008

Keller, P.E., Novembre, G., Hove, M.J.: Rhythm in joint action: psychological and neurophysiological mechanisms for real-time interpersonal coordination. Philosoph. Trans. Roy. Soc. London, Ser. B. Biol. Sci. **369**(1658), Article 20130394 (2014)

Kirschner, S., Tomasello, M.: Joint music making promotes prosocial behavior in 4-year-old children. Evol. Hum. Behav. **31**, 354–364 (2010)

Koole, S.L., Tschacher, W.: Synchrony in psychotherapy: a review and an integrative framework for the therapeutic alliance. Front. Psychol. **7**, 862 (2016)

Koole, S.L., Tschacher, W., Butler, E., Dikker, S., Wilderjans, T.F.: In sync with your shrink. In: Forgas, J.P., Crano, W.D., Fiedler, K. (eds.) Applications of Social Psychology, pp. 161–184. Taylor and Francis, Milton Park (2020)

Pacherie, E.: The phenomenology of joint action: self-agency vs. joint-agency. In: A. Seeman (ed.), Joint Attention: New Developments, pp. 343–389. MIT Press (2012)

Palumbo, R.V., et al.: Interpersonal autonomic physiology: a systematic review of the literature. Pers. Soc. Psychol. Rev. **21**(2), 99–141 (2017)

Prince, K., Brown, S.: Neural correlates of partnered interaction as revealed by cross-domain ALE meta-analysis. Psychol. Neurosci. **15**(1), 1–13 (2022)

Ramseyer, F., Tschacher, W.: Nonverbal synchrony in psychotherapy: coordinated body movement reflects relationship quality and outcome. J. Consult. Clin. Psychol. **79**, 284–295 (2011)

Rayner, K., Smith, T.J., Malcolm, G.L., Henderson, J.M.: Eye movements and visual encoding during scene perception. Psychol. Sci. **20**(1), 6–10 (2009)

Robinson, B.L., Harper, N.S., McAlpine, D.: Meta-adaptation in the auditory midbrain under cortical influence. Nat. Commun. **7**, e13442 (2016)

Schoenherr, D., et al.: Identification of movement synchrony: validation of windowed cross-lagged correlation and -regression with peak-picking algorithm. PLoS ONE **14**(2), e0211494 (2019). https://doi.org/10.1371/journal.pone.0211494

Schoenherr, D., et al.: Quantification of nonverbal synchrony using linear time series analysis methods: lack of convergent validity and evidence for facets of synchrony. Behav. Res. Methods **51**(1), 361–383 (2018). https://doi.org/10.3758/s13428-018-1139-z

Sharpley, C.F., Halat, J., Rabinowicz, T., Weiland, B., Stafford, J.: Standard posture, postural mirroring and client-perceived rapport. Couns. Psychol. Q. **14**, 267–280 (2001). https://doi.org/10.1080/09515070110088843

Shatz, C.J.: The developing brain. Sci. Am. **267**, 60–67 (1992)

Shelton, J., Kumar, G.: Comparison between auditory and visual simple reaction times. Neurosci. Med. **1**(1), 30–32 (2010)

Tarr, B., Launay, J., Dunbar, R.I.M.: Silent disco: dancing in synchrony leads to elevated pain thresholds and social closeness. Evol. Hum. Beh. **37**(5), 343–349 (2016)

Thompson, J.J., Blair, M.R., Henrey, A.J.: Over the hill at 24: persistent age-related cognitive-motor decline in reaction times in an ecologically valid video game task begins in early adulthood. PLoS ONE **9**(4), e94215 (2014)

Treur, J.: Network-oriented modeling for adaptive networks: designing higher-order adaptive biological, mental and social network models. SSDC, vol. 251. Springer, Cham (2020a). https://doi.org/10.1007/978-3-030-31445-3

Treur, J.: Modeling multi-order adaptive processes by self-modeling networks (Keynote Speech). In: Tallón-Ballesteros, A.J., Chen, C.-H. (eds.) Proceedings of the 2nd International Conference on Machine Learning and Intelligent Systems, MLIS 2020. Frontiers in Artificial Intelligence and Applications, vol. 332, p. 206–217. IOS Press (2020b)

Treur, J.: On the dynamics and adaptivity of mental processes: relating adaptive dynamical systems and self-modeling network models by mathematical analysis. Cogn. Syst. Res. **70**, 93–100 (2021)

Tschacher, W., Ramseyer, F., Koole, S.L.: Sharing the now in the social present: Duration of nonverbal synchrony is linked with personality. J. Pers. **86**(2), 129–138 (2018)

Valdesolo, P., DeSteno, D.: Synchrony and the social tuning of compassion. Emotion **11**, 262 (2011). https://doi.org/10.1037/a0021302

Valdesolo, P., Ouyang, J., DeSteno, D.: The rhythm of joint action: Synchrony promotes cooperative ability. J. Exp. Soc. Psychol. **46**(4), 693–695 (2010)

Wiltermuth, S.S., Heath, C.: Synchrony and cooperation. Psychol. Sci. **20**(1), 1–5 (2009)

Zhang, A., Li, X., Gao, Y., Niu, Y.: Event-Driven Intrinsic Plasticity for Spiking Convolutional Neural Networks.IEEE Trans. Neural Netw. Learn. Syst. (2021). https://doi.org/10.1109/tnnls.2021.3084955

# Author Index

Printed in the United States
by Baker & Taylor Publisher Services

Printed in the United States
by Baker & Taylor Publisher Services